T0316771

The Anthem Other Canon Series

The **Anthem Other Canon Series** is a collaborative
series between Anthem Press and The Other Canon Foundation.
The Other Canon – also described as 'reality economics' – studies
the economy as a real object rather than as the behaviour
of a model economy based on core axioms, assumptions
and techniques. The series publishes classical and contemporary
works in this tradition, spanning evolutionary, institutional,
and Post-Keynesian economics, the history of economic thought
and economic policy, economic sociology and technology
governance, and works on the theory of uneven development
and in the tradition of the German historical school.

Other Titles in the Series

Techno-Economic Paradigms

Techno-Economic Paradigms:

Essays in Honour of Carlota Perez

Edited by
WOLFGANG DRECHSLER,
RAINER KATTEL AND
ERIK S. REINERT

ANTHEM PRESS
LONDON · NEW YORK · DELHI

Anthem Press
An imprint of Wimbledon Publishing Company
www.anthempress.com

This edition first published in UK and USA 2009
by ANTHEM PRESS
75 – 76 Blackfriars Road, London SE1 8HA, UK
or PO Box 9779, London SW19 7ZG, UK
and
244 Madison Ave. #116, New York, NY 10016, USA

British Library Cataloguing in Publication Data
A catalogue record for this book is available from the British Library.

Library of Congress Cataloging in Publication Data
A catalog record for this book has been requested.

ISBN-13: 978 1 84331 785 2 (Hbk)
ISBN-10: 1 84331 785 0 (Hbk)

1 3 5 7 9 10 8 6 4 2

TABLE OF CONTENTS

PREFACE

The year 2009 marks a round and significant birthday for Carlota Perez thus presents us with a welcome occasion to celebrate her work. There could not be a better time to do this, because the events, as this book goes to press, have impressively proven its relevance and accuracy. By now, this has been widely noticed in scholarship and media, by large corporations, governments and supranational organizations, and NGOs alike, and Carlota has attracted what could almost be called a cult following. Well beyond her home base of Evolutionary Economics, we see the economic world, as it is really unfolding, with other eyes because of her theory of Techno-Economic Paradigms (TEPs) – and there are few economists today about whom this can be said. For us, her friends and colleagues at Tallinn University of Technology's Technology Governance graduate program – which has served as the academic-institutional center both for Carlota and for the reflection of her work in recent years – who have worked closely with her over many years, the idea of a *Festschrift* seemed obvious.

However, as many references as there are to her work (and as many unacknowledged takeovers of her theory!), a detailed and somewhat comprehensive account of the work is still missing. We had discussed and tentatively planned such a book, or special journal issue, for quite a while, and so it seemed obvious to combine this project with the current celebration. Therefore, we decided not to have an 'open' *Festschrift* where every invited author could freely choose her or his topic, but rather to organize a book with contributions by scholars who have all personally worked with Carlota on the specific subject of Techno-Economic Paradigms. The result, we think, shows that this was the right approach, because what has emerged is indeed a quite cohesive array of perspectives, and aspects, of TEPs.

The contributions can be grouped as follows: the idea of cycles and stages in economic development, one of the key elements in the Perez framework, is dealt with by Freeman and Reinert. Freeman looks at the discussion of Schumpeter and business cycles in the Perezian context of great surges of development, and Reinert discusses her work in the light of previous stage theories in economics. Another key feature of Carlota's thought – financial capital and its impact on the economy – is the main focus of three contributors: Janeway, Kregel, and Palma. Janeway explores the role of the venture capitalist in the economy, while Palma describes the impact of 'financialization' on the United States economy in the recent decades. Kregel's contribution deals with various layers of financial innovations and how they feed into and upon technological revolutions.

By far the largest number of contributors deal with TEPs and their impact on development. While Nelson's and Bessant and Rush's papers tackle general issues of innovation and development, Cassiolato et al., Dutrénit and Vera-Cruz, Hobday, and Nurse deal directly with developing-country challenges. These papers, on the one hand, seek to exemplify how TEPs influence developing countries and, on the other, show how successful catching-up strategies can and have been formed following the logic inherent in great surges of development. Kattel looks at how innovation in small states is influenced by TEPs.

The impact of the ICT revolution, being the carrier of the current TEP and thus an obvious focus of attention, is discussed at length by Lundvall and Burgelman. One of the key issues for future research is the impact of paradigms on governance structures and vice versa. Drechsler's and Rochet's contributions look into these issues. Mjøset's paper dives deeply into methodological issues of Perez' work; Dosi et al.'s contribution is equally involved in the discussion of the nature of the current paradigm from a statistical viewpoint and seeks to show how the data bear out ideas developed by Perez.

Two key contributions to the *Festschrift* are to be found at the end: the first biographical sketch and the first bibliography of Carlota Perez, upon which further research will have to be built. The biography is written by Reinert and Sagalovsky. The bibliography, based on information by Carlota for other purposes, was mainly structured and edited by Drechsler; he was ably helped by Carlota's Tallinn assistant, Caetano Penna, by Thomas Duve, and by Ingbert Edenhofer, who also helped with language and formatting of several of the texts and who sacrificed several summer days on very short notice on galley proofing. All references in the individual contributions are cross-referenced to the bibliography as well, with the respective number given in brackets []. All websites were valid as of July 2009.

The editors would like to thank the Estonian Science Foundation (Grant no.s 6703 and 7577) for supporting this endeavor.

Wolfgang Drechsler, Rainer Kattel and Erik S. Reinert

Techno-Economic Paradigms

Chapter One:

INTRODUCTION: CARLOTA PEREZ AND EVOLUTIONARY ECONOMICS

Rainer Kattel
with Wolfgang Drechsler and Erik S. Reinert

Any reader of Carlota Perez' work who has been following the global financial meltdown beginning to unfold in the Fall of 2008 must pinch herself as 'it' is indeed happening again. 'It' is not only a financial crisis of enormous proportions, but in fact, what Perez calls a turning point in the middle of the diffusion of a techno-economic paradigm. Such turning points have taken place rather regularly since the Industrial Revolution with roughly half-century intervals between them, and they consists essentially of two aspects: huge financial meltdown (think of the canal panic of 1793, the railway panic of 1847, or the great depression following 1929 stock market crash) followed by an institutional renewal of historic dimensions (think of the Victorian boom preceded by the repeal of the Corn Laws and introducing legislation to improve factory conditions and urban sanitation, professionalization of the civil service, etc., or the welfare state reforms and the Keynesian policies and institutions facilitating the post-World War II Golden Age). Accordingly, the Perez framework predicted that the turning point for the current ICT-led techno-economic paradigm should have taken place during the first years of twenty-first century. What started as a bursting of the dot-com bubble in 2000 ended in 2008 as a full-blown global financial crisis. This is, then, the turning point and thus, we are confronting the need for sweeping institutional changes to bring forth a golden age based on the global spread of the growth potential of the current paradigm based on information technology. Indeed, while successive technological revolutions and their techno-economic paradigms are, as Perez shows, the fundamental feature of capitalism after the industrial revolution, the turning points in the middle of these paradigms are historic occasions when capitalism is reconfigured to save itself from itself.

The fact alone that Perez' framework is proven to be accurate before our own eyes should give sufficient justification why we celebrate her 2009 round birthday with a scholarly homage – with a discussion of her work. However, in this brief introduction, rather than attempting a *Gesamtschau* of her work, let alone of its reception so far, we merely want show that her work, in particular her seminal 2002 book *Technological Revolutions and Financial Capital: The Dynamics of Bubbles and Golden Ages*, has made significant and lasting contributions in three specific areas connected to Evolutionary Economics, and to show how she has contributed, and has the potential to contribute even more significantly, to the development of that school of thought. In doing so, we interpret Perez' work, inevitably, from our perspective and not from hers, so that it may very well be that she herself might be the most surprised by what we argue her work to mean, and to imply.

According to our perspective, then, Perez' framework helps to explain, first, socioeconomic history since the industrial revolution on a technological basis without being deterministic; second, it creates a systematic theoretical framework to complement evolutionary economics with long-term macro-dynamics; and third, it shows how a viable methodological alternative to mainstream neoclassical modelling can be founded. In what follows, we will discuss, albeit briefly, her contribution to each of these areas and conclude with some perspectives her framework opens up for new significant research.

The Framework

We begin our discussion of Carlota's work with a brief summary of the concept of techno-economic paradigms. This is how Perez sums up the ideas of great surges and paradigms:

> There has been a technological revolution every 40 to 60 years, beginning with the Industrial Revolution in England at the end of the 18th Century; each has generated a great surge of development, diffusing unevenly across the world from an initial core country. … The great wealth creating potential provided by each of them stems from the combination of the new technologies, industries and infrastructures with a set of generic technologies and organisational principles capable of modernising the rest of the economy. The resulting best practice frontier is superior to the previous one and becomes the new common sense for efficiency – a new techno-economic paradigm – that defines the guidelines for innovation and competitiveness. … The propagation is highly uneven in coverage and timing, by sectors and by regions, in each country and across the world. (Perez 2006)

The paradigms describe the direction in which technological change and innovation are most likely to take place (and are most profitable) in a given period: which organizational forms and finance are conducive to innovations, which technological capabilities and skills are needed or should be developed, and so forth. Table 1.1 summarizes these paradigms since the Industrial Revolution.

However, the surges consist of two halves, in which the paradigm develops and diffuses under very different conditions as shown in Figure 1.1.

The framework thus shows how a competitive free market economy is, first, necessarily driven by clusters of innovations and, second, how innovations in turn thrust economies into long surges of leaping productivity that enables the creation of new industries, jobs, products and services accompanied by the destruction of the old ones. Perez shows how this process of what Schumpeter called creative destruction repeats itself periodically in form but never in substance (there will not be another dot-com bubble, but there will be similar technology-driven bubbles) and how this repetitive character of the free market economy leads to periodic institutional renewal.

The framework is indeed so ambitious that it tries to explain the entirety of post-industrial revolution capitalism and to show why specific technologies, innovations and regions thrived at given points in time. It is, however, important to note that the framework is not deterministic; it does not, for instance, tell what will be at the core of the next technological revolution. The framework simply indicates that there will be another surge starting when the current paradigm reaches maturity, probably in 20–30 years time, followed in another quarter century or so by similarly upsetting financial troubles as the ones we are currently experiencing. In fact, what she suggests is that this repetitiveness is the very logic of capitalism (2002, 166).

The Perez framework fuses two very different schools of economic thought into something truly original. One the one hand, her framework builds on nineteenth-century cycle and crises theories that culminate in Kondratiev's work on long waves of economic development, and that at the same time paved the way for Keynes' thought.[1] On the other hand, it is strongly rooted in (neo-) Schumpeterian or evolutionary research on innovation, technological trajectories and creative destruction associated with the names of Richard Nelson, Bengt-Åke Lundvall, Giovanni Dosi and in particular, Chris Freeman, with whom she has sustained a long-term collaboration – all of them contributors to the present *Festschrift*. The former scholars offered the questions and the historical long-term framework and the neo-Schumpeterians explained how innovations, working through individual companies and industrial sectors, end up changing whole economies.

In the neo-Schumpeterian camp, Chris Freeman is almost the only one to have tackled long-term structural change and macroeconomic issues. In his *Economics of Industrial Innovation* (1974) he discussed the development of

Table 1.1. Techno-Economic Paradigms

Technological Revolution Core Country	New Technologies and New or Redefined Industries	New or Redefined Infrastructures	Techno-Economic Paradigm 'Common-Sense' Innovation Principles
FIRST: From 1771 *The 'Industrial Revolution'* Britain	Mechanized cotton industry Wrought iron Machinery	Canals and waterways Turnpike roads Water power (highly improved water wheels)	Factory production Mechanization Productivity/time keeping and time saving Fluidity of movement (as ideal for machines with water-power and for transport through canals and other waterways) Local networks
SECOND: From 1829 *Age of Steam and Railways* In Britain and spreading to Continent and USA	Steam engines and machinery (made in iron; fuelled by coal) Iron and coal mining (now playing a central role in growth) Railway construction Rolling stock production Steam power for many industries (including textiles)	Railways (use of steam engine) Universal postal service Telegraph (mainly nationally along railway lines) Great ports, great depots and worldwide sailing ships City gas	Economies of agglomeration/industrial cities/national markets Power centres with national networks Scale as progress Standard parts/machine-made machines Energy where needed (steam) Interdependent movement (of machines and of means of transport)
THIRD: From 1875 *Age of Steel, Electricity and Heavy Engineering* USA and Germany overtaking Britain	Cheap steel (especially Bessemer) Full development of steam engine for steel ships Heavy chemistry and civil engineering Electrical equipment industry Copper and cables Canned and bottled food Paper and packaging	Worldwide shipping in rapid steel steamships (use of Suez Canal) Worldwide railways (use of cheap steel rails and bolts in standard sizes). Great bridges and tunnels Worldwide telegraph Telephone (mainly nationally) Electrical networks (for illumination and industrial use)	Giant structures (steel) Economies of scale of plant/vertical integration Distributed power for industry (electricity) Science as a productive force Worldwide networks and empires (including cartels) Universal standardization Cost accounting for control and efficiency Great scale for world market power/'small' is successful, if local

FOURTH: From 1908 *Age of Oil, the Automobile and Mass Production* In USA and spreading to Europe	Mass-produced automobiles Cheap oil and oil fuels Petrochemicals (synthetics) Internal combustion engine for automobiles, transport, tractors, airplanes, war tanks and electricity Home electrical appliances Refrigerated and frozen foods	Networks of roads, highways, ports and airports Networks of oil ducts Universal electricity (industry and homes) Worldwide analog telecommunications (telephone, telex and cablegram) wire and wireless	Mass production/mass markets Economies of scale (product and market volume)/horizontal integration Standardization of products Energy intensity (oil based) Synthetic materials Functional specialization/hierarchical pyramids Centralization/metropolitan centres – suburbanization National powers, world agreements and confrontations
FIFTH: From 1971 *Age of Information and Telecommunications* In USA, spreading to Europe and Asia	The information revolution: Cheap microelectronics. Computers, software Telecommunications Control instruments Computer-aided biotechnology and new materials	World digital telecommunications (cable, fibre optics, radio and satellite) Internet/electronic mail and other e-services Multiple source, flexible use, electricity networks High-speed physical transport links (by land, air and water)	Information-intensity (microelectronics-based ICT) Decentralized integration/network structures Knowledge as capital/intangible value added Heterogeneity, diversity, adaptability Segmentation of markets/proliferation of niches Economies of scope and specialization combined with scale Globalization/interaction between the global and the local Inward and outward cooperation/clusters Instant contact and action/instant global communications

Source: Perez 2006.

Figure 1.1. Two Halves of Techno-Economic Paradigm Diffusion

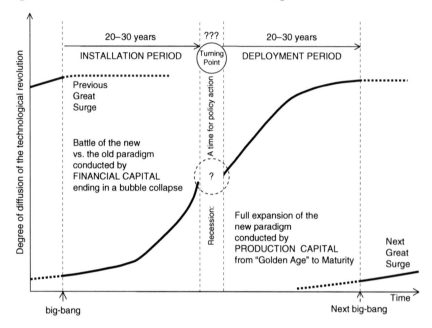

Source: based on Perez 2002, 37.

New Technology Systems and in *Technology Policy and Economic Performance: Lessons from Japan* (1987) he introduced the concept of National Systems of Innovation looking at the interconnections between technology, economics and institutions. He also developed the notion of long waves, following on from Kondratiev and Schumpeter, using a historical approach (see 1982 with Clark and Soete, 1988 with Perez and 2001 with Louçã). He is rightly considered a leader in this field.

Full versions of Kondratiev's writings on long waves are available in English only since 1998. The 1935 publication in the *Review of Economic Statistics* was a heavily abridged version of the original and left the impression that Kondratiev did not explain why long waves of development actually take place (see also Perez 1983). However, in the original 1926 publication Kondratiev delves at length into the question of the causes of long waves (1998, 53–60). He explains that 'It is clear … that the rising wave of a long cycle is associated with a renewal and extension of the main capital items, with radical changes and regrouping of the main productive forces of society' (1998, 57).

Yet, the dating of Perez differs from Kondratiev's by about 20 years, i.e., Perez surges or paradigms start about two decades earlier than Kondratiev waves (Kondratiev 1998, 36). While Kondratiev argued that before every rising wave significant technological revolutions are taking place, he dated the waves according to a few key aggregate economic data such as interest rates, trade volume, etc. According to him, during the rising half of the wave, all such aggregate indicators rise, and during the second half, they are respectively falling. Thus, Kondratiev's rising halves of waves represent, in fact, the deployment and maturity periods in Perez' paradigms (the decades after the turning point) when the potential of a technological revolution is being fully realized. However, this also (partially) explains why Perez does not use in her later writings the term 'Kondratiev waves' but rather great surges of development. What she means is substantially different from Kondratiev. The difference is the neo-Schumpeterian core of her thinking. She follows the whole trajectory of each technological revolution from its irruption as a promise in a basically mature industrial landscape to its full diffusion and final maturity, when it is in turn replaced. What she singles out is the sequence in the process of assimilation by the economy and society.

Around the same time of Perez' first publications on surges and paradigms (1983; referring to them as Kondratievs and 'styles'), Dosi (1982) had published his highly influential article on technical paradigms. That was the same year that Nelson and Winter (1982) published their seminal *Evolutionary Theory of Economic Change* where they referred to routines and technological regimes and when Freeman, Clark and Soete (1982) brought out *Unemployment and Technical Innovation: A Study of Long Waves in Economic Development*. The impact of the information revolution had obviously generated a fruitful academic ferment in the neo-Schumpeterian community.

Although Dosi's analysis focuses on individual technologies, it fully develops the notion of a directionality in technical change (see further Tunzelman et al. 2008). As later expressed by Dosi and Luc Soete (1988, 418): 'Technology ... cannot be reduced to freely available information or to a set of "blueprints": on the contrary, each "technological paradigm" with its forms of specific knowledge yields relatively ordered cumulative and irreversible patterns of technical change.' This will allow Perez to refer to her concept as a meta-paradigm, serving as an umbrella for the various individual trajectories.

Similarly, Nelson and Winter's (1982, 258–259) technological trajectories and regimes refer to sets of skills and technological solutions that in competitive environments obtain specific path-dependent characteristics and thus give rise to paradigmatic changes in specific companies and/or industries.

Freeman et al. (1982) go much further into the macro-level by analyzing new technology systems and focusing on massive processes of technological diffusion rather than on individual innovations or even single industries.

These concepts are highly valuable because they are developed bottom-up from individual skills and company-level behaviour towards a higher level of complexity and help to explain how Schumpeterian creative destruction shapes economies and competitive environments. They represent great advances in understanding how economies work, and they form the core of evolutionary theory today. Yet, in our view, evolutionary theory, despite its indubitable merits, has avoided certain questions. First, although it analyses radical innovations and their life cycle and even their clustering, it does not discuss the issue of why certain technologies and institutions emerge and prevail at specific points in history. Second, evolutionary theory has largely remained a microeconomic theory with ramifications towards the meso-level of industries, sectors and regional clusters. The most developed aspect at the macro-level has been the notion of 'National Systems of Innovation'. That concept has allowed the study of the interactions between firms, academia and the institutional context in the processes of innovation and its implications for growth and the dynamics of national economies. It has not systematically tackled the classical area covered by macroeconomics, neglecting in particular the connections with finance. Third, we would argue that there has not been a determined effort to develop a methodology for macroeconomics that is adequate to an evolutionary perspective. Instead, they have persisted in trying to put evolutionary thinking into mathematical models. This may have been inherited from Schumpeter himself, although not his interest in finance. Below we attempt to show that the framework developed by Perez is an important complement to evolutionary theory, which sheds light on how these shortcomings could be overcome.

Explaining History

Evolutionary theory, in particular the Schumpeterian kind, is often at its best explaining why and how a certain institution (for instance, patents) or a product (for instance, VCRs) came about and why it was successful in the given particular context – or the opposite (see also Janeway's contribution in this volume). Evolutionary theory is equally helpful, especially in its institutionalist version á la Thorstein Veblen or John Kenneth Galbraith, in bringing forth grand narratives about a particular age (further on institutionalism, see Hodgson 2004). What evolutionary theory lacks is the connecting theoretical edifice explaining how and why a particular product or institution is not simply an outgrowth of an isolated context but rather part of an interrelated process that can partly explain why it happened then and there. The lack of such an edifice is one of the shortcomings for economic policymaking based on evolutionary ideas: every successful case (company, region, country) seems highly idiosyncratic and unique. The Perez framework provides precisely such an edifice. We illustrate this by one brief example.

Paul Krugman won the 2008 Nobel Prize in economics in part for his work on 'new economic geography', which, to put it simply, showed how increasing returns to scale lead to urban agglomerations. His 1991 essay on the topic sought to answer 'how far ... the tendency toward geographical concentration [will] proceed, and where ... manufacturing production [will] actually end up' (1991, 468). Krugman's primary example is the industrialization and urbanization of the American East Coast in the middle of the nineteenth century (see also Krugman 2008). The early nineteenth-century United States satisfied, as he explains, the criteria for agglomeration effects *not* to emerge: 'the bulk of the population would have been engaged in agriculture, the small manufacturing and commercial sector would not have been marked by very substantial economies of scale, and the costs of transportation would have ensured that most of the needs that could not be satisfied by rural production would be satisfied by small towns serving local market areas' (1991, 468). However, 'let the society spend a higher fraction of income on non-agricultural goods and services; let the factory system and eventually mass production emerge, and with them economies of large scale production; and let the canals, railroads, and finally automobiles lower transportation costs' (1991, 487). This, of course, is more or less what happened with the East Coast during the subsequent century.

For Krugman, this shows that 'the role of history and accident in determining the location of industry' is pivotal (Krugman 1994a, 224; see also 225–226). A typical evolutionary economist would argue that there was nothing accidental in the rise of the East Coast manufacturing. Technological learning and accumulation do not only account for the most important endowments – and thus, do explain differences between countries' levels of development (Dosi and Soete 1988), but, more importantly, technology is not freely available but rather is in its development always dependent on the policy framework and the conditions created by the latter. In other words, United States nineteenth century development has to be seen in the light of industrial policies pursued since Hamilton's 1791 *Report on Manufactures* (see Reinert 2007).

However, if we look at this particular issue from the perspective of Perez' framework, it becomes clear why certain historically highly important 'accidents' took place and why Hamiltonian policies succeeded in the middle of the nineteenth century at the United States East Coast. This time is the height of the second paradigm or great surge of development, the *Age of Steam and Railways*. Indeed, seen in the light of paradigms, the East Coast experience makes eminent sense, as it offered an almost perfect window of opportunity for that particular paradigm to fully expand. And the key to this expansion (why it happened at that time and at that place) is the unique nature of American industrialization and trade in the nineteenth century. As Keynes (1933) and Nurkse (1961) have argued, the 'new countries' within and without the British Empire – but the United States first and foremost – were 'high-income countries from the start: effective markets as well as efficient producers' (Nurkse 1961, 243). America was highly resource-rich, but at the same time populated by a workforce essentially on the same skill level as that of Britain (1961, 143). And as Perez has shown, scale and agglomeration were the second paradigm's 'common sense practices' (see Table 1.1 above). The East Coast was therefore ideally suited for the expansion phase of the second paradigm and, given the technologies diffusing at the time, this expansion was bound to take place as fast-paced agglomeration with rail links for market expansion and supplies. It is not a historical accident nor is it explained just by policy-induced industrialization. It was 'getting the paradigm right' through a policy mix favouring increasing returns activities and retaining competitive pressures at the same time.[2]

Thus, the Perez framework can make sense of the interconnection between technology, industrial geography and policy in the specific historical context of East Coast industrialization and urbanization. And going further, it can allow a more thorough analysis of the processes of catching up and forging ahead that characterized US development from the mid-nineteenth century, when it protected its industry and copied British Technology, through the development of steel-based heavy industry and infrastructures, favouring oligopolies, until its emergence as hegemonic power after World War II, with the diffusion of the mass production revolution, initiated by Henry Ford's Model T.

Evolutionary theorists are right to assume a key role for policy in industrialization; yet, placing policy into a larger framework such as the one suggested by Perez prevents policy, too, from looking like a mere accident tied to specific persons or political upheavals – although either may play a crucial role.

During the winter of 2008–2009, for instance, there have been many voices calling for a new Bretton Woods and many others comparing the post-meltdown recession to the 1930s. That is indeed exactly right, and that is what the Perezian perspective indicates. The question is whether this understanding leads to clear policy recommendations. For some purposes, a thorough analysis of the consequences of the policies in the 1930s can be very useful, but in terms of guiding a recovery and constructing effective policies, it is much more fruitful to understand that the crash marks the turning point of the information technology surge; that a golden age can be ahead; that policies have to not only regulate finance and to do so at a global level too, but they also have to tilt the playing field in favour of the real production economy and of sustainability; that the ICT paradigm can bring as much global welfare with the adequate policies, as the Welfare State boom after World War II brought to the advanced countries. Switching the power over investment from finance to production is the goal; how it is attained is the task of imaginative government policy.

Indeed, because of Perez' framework, history is not just vitally important for economics (again), but perhaps even more importantly, economics can become genuinely important for the social sciences in helping to understand and explain pivotal events during the past two hundred years and help policymaking in ways impossible before.

Systematic Evolutionary Theory

The premises of evolutionary theory are at fundamental difference with the prevailing neoclassical theory. As Nelson and Winter (1982, viii) argued, the key discrepancy lies in understanding the role of technology in economic growth that leads to substantial differences in how the behaviour of firms and industrial dynamics are understood. The neoclassical model assumes that firm behaviour is fundamentally explained by the idea of profit maximization and that the macroeconomic world is best understood by its tendencies towards equilibrium (1982, 12–13). Both assumptions, first, facilitate the use of mathematical modelling in economics and, second, are decidedly not shared by evolutionary economists.

In the eyes of evolutionary economists, firm behaviour is much better explained through concepts like skills, routines, path dependencies within firms and industries and imperfect competition that to a large extent are determined by technological change. The macroeconomic world, on the other hand, is better explained through incessant change driven by the changes on the firm level leading up to the process of creative destruction. Both these processes also explain, in their view, the difference between countries and regions (see, e.g., Dosi and Soete 1988). Table 1.2 summarizes the differences between neoclassical and evolutionary approaches.

However, despite an elaborate and highly promising set of (counter-) assumptions by the evolutionary theorists, while developing original theory and research about firm-level behaviour, evolutionary theory has not fully rejected the neoclassical approach on the level of macroeconomic issues. Indeed, it seems as if the field believed Krugman's opinion that the pioneers of development thinking – many of whom were, if not directly students of Schumpeter, then at least clearly sympathetic to his thought – were lost to the dustbin of history because of their lack of modelling rigor (Krugman 1994b).

However, mathematical modelling is not a value-free methodological tool but rather forms an essential part of the neoclassical approach (see Drechsler 2000a and 2004). Essentially, this means that attempting to model evolutionary theories is bound to fail; the mathematical modelling tools are bound to stay mostly self-referential, descriptive and, to say it with Wittgenstein, mean nothing (quoted in Heath 1974, 25 note 5 [as 'the remark attributed to Wittgenstein']). Indeed, such an approach to social and economic reality is based on a profoundly simplified understanding of the same reality. As Isaiah Berlin (1996, 53)

Table 1.2. Neo-Classical and Evolutionary Approach Compared

Neo-Classical Theory	Evolutionary Theory
Use of physical metaphors	Use of biological metaphors
'Equilibrium' as a central	Emphasis on factors causing disequilibrium
Static/comparative statics	Dynamic
High degree of precision	Less precise, open to non-quantifiable factors
Assumes perfect information	Operates under uncertainty
Time not an issue	'History matters'
Entrepreneurship unimportant	Entrepreneurship central factor
'All economic activities are equal' (potato chips, wood chips, computer chips)	Economic activities are different because there are innovation 'focuses' at any point in time
The 'representative firm'	The 'representative firm' does not exist
The market as price setter	The market also as selection mechanism among firms
Technology as a free good	Technology as an important factor in wealth creation and distribution

Source: Based on Reinert and Riiser 1994.

put it, 'To demand or preach mechanical precision, even in principle, in a field incapable of it is to be blind and mislead others.'

With the use of mathematical modelling, evolutionary theory imports precisely the weaknesses of the neoclassical approach so vehemently rejected by the fundamental evolutionary assumptions (see Table 1.2 above). The universality of the postulates of classical macroeconomics demands that the essential components of the evolutionary approach – history, technology, differentiation and institutions – be left out of the picture. But most of all, their models cannot handle the real-world complexity that evolutionary theory captures and explains. Therefore, mathematical modelling is truly a Trojan horse for evolutionary theory and risks leaving it with little if any policy relevance.

Evolutionary theory is still to develop its own original macroeconomic approach that complements its accomplishments in the micro- and meso-economic spheres. In order to do this, evolutionary theory should be able to add finance into its theoretical base and framework. While there are already a few – excellent – attempts to do so (see, e.g., Kregel and Burlamaqui 2005 and 2006), we argue that the framework developed by Perez could serve as the basis for such a theory.

Perez, basing herself on core evolutionary ideas, shows how individual behaviour and company-level development, skills and routines that are spurred by technological development and lead to innovations, are related to institutions and institutional change. However, she goes further than that: in fact, she shows how the financial infrastructure interplays with innovations and economic activities. Thus, she is able to relate microeconomic innovations with macroeconomic policies and activities without falling back on mathematical models but rather through marrying the historical account (which grows out of Schumpeterian analysis) with institutional change and macroeconomic (e.g., labour market) and financial issues (e.g., role of financing in technology).

It must be conceded that creating such a systematic embedding for evolutionary theory is not the direct aim of Perez' writings and thus how to utilize her framework for developing evolutionary macroeconomic theory is one of the key challenges for future research. The role of financial scaffolding in the economy as well is something that could be analyzed in much greater detail in Perez' framework. This, again, is one of the key tasks for further research in evolutionary macroeconomic theory building.

However, such a macroeconomic theory needs to be articulated not in mathematical models, but rather by means of a viable and original methodological alternative that does not assume history and reality away but rather delivers tools to understand them. Indeed, this is what Nelson and Winter (1982, 382) already attempted. We would say that Perez provides elements to widen and enrich such an alternative. Unpopular as this might be with the current mainstream, it could gain the high ground as a valid alternative, as the whole 'free market' certainties of the neoclassics fall in disrepute among the ruins of the global meltdown.

A Viable Methodological Alternative

The key methodological problem with neoclassical economics and with the mathematical modelling it uses is the issue that the real economy does not deal simply with facts, but also with intentions and expectations. However, as was noted by Keynes, expectations about future earnings fundamentally shape producers' economic behaviour today, that is, current intentions (Keynes 1997, 46–50). What we see here is a loop or a circle that feeds upon itself to keep in motion. In essence, the loop works on how its participants interpret the future while knowing that the very interpretations (changing intentions) are changing the expectations and thus, the future.

In philosophical terms, we can call this a hermeneutical problem: in order to understand a sentence in a poem or in a book, the reader would need to know the entire poem or book. However, this is not how we operate. What happens is that while reading, we in fact constantly reinterpret the whole text. This means, of course, that our reading changes the meaning of the text – for us.[3]

But is there a meaning of a text outside of our reading? Hans-Georg Gadamer, the most important hermeneutical philosopher of the twentieth century, called the act of meaning arising from the reading the 'fusion of horizons' (Gadamer 1990).[4] Understanding and interpretation is always a result of fusion of differing and diverse horizons and the process is incessant and fundamental – we cannot step out of it and only observe it. This means, in addition, that next to understanding and interpretation, misunderstanding and misinterpretation is rampant and, in fact, normal.

At this point, the connection to economics becomes important and visible as shown by Keynesian analysis and in particular by Hyman Minsky's ideas about financial instability. According to Minsky (2008), the stability that free market economies experience from time to time is itself destabilizing as it lowers the standards for 'cushions of safety' and thus paves the way for riskier investments that are not recognized as such at the time.[5] This is fundamentally a hermeneutical problem and, as Minsky shows, capitalism has not found an answer, probably because it is part of human nature not to be able to step out of the hermeneutical circle either in communication or in economics.

However, if we look at the microeconomic foundations of evolutionary economics, then the hermeneutical character of the key ideas is equally evident and important. As we argued above, the core ideas about individual and firm behaviour in evolutionary thinking are skills and routines that are both related to a changing technological basis and result from constant learning and feedback within and without the organization (the latter being the market). Skills as 'tacit knowledge', routines as 'organizational memory', 'remembering by doing' and other similar concepts at the core of evolutionary thinking (Nelson and Winter 1982, 72–76, 88–89, 98–99) are obviously carried by the same idea of the hermeneutical circle. Indeed, concepts like path dependency, technological trajectories, forward and backward feedback linkages are based on the same idea that understanding is based on loop-like processes of constant learning.

This approach, clearly evident in their fundamental ideas of both Keynesian and evolutionary thinking, has however not found any methodological development. The key challenge such a hermeneutical understanding of economic life throws up is related to values, ethics or political economy in most general terms. This challenge, in turn, can be split into two specific sub-questions: first, what role do values play in economics; and second, how does the hermeneutical circle express itself in policy questions.

Robert Frank (1997) has shown how our perception about what we consider good or bad in the socioeconomic realm is dependent upon what he calls our 'frame of reference'. In other words, we judge our own well-being according to how well we think we are doing in comparison to others around us. However, and this is the catch, the frame of reference in turn – how well others are doing – is largely determined by our collective decisions about taxes, city planning, etc. Thus, if we decide to invest in better public transport and pay higher taxes for that, we gain, so Frank's argument goes, more time to spend with our friends, which in turn enhances the chances that we take in future such decisions that create a better frame of reference for all of us. This also works in reverse.

In other words, Frank has shown (without using such terms) that value creation is largely a result of socioeconomic decision-making that is a cumulative and circular process. This was already expressed by Gustav von Schmoller, a key thinker of the German Historical School and the head of its 'Younger' period,[6] in his *The Idea of Justice in Political Economy*: 'Every larger undertaking, whenever it unites continuously a certain number of men for a common economic purpose, reveals itself as a moral community' (Schmoller 1881). It is important to realize that in terms of policy development, this means that there are no longer-lasting Pareto-optimal solutions, as the optimality itself changes; indeed, such a notion of optimality is flawed from the beginning in this framework (unless it is used as a heuristic utopia).

However, in evolutionary thinking and especially in Perez' framework, learning and more importantly, technology, become vitally important factors shaping the very frame of reference. Indeed, it can be argued that what Perez calls a techno-economic paradigm, with its shifts between finance- and production-led capitalism and its cumulative processes of learning and then 'unlearning', is one of the key determinants of the changing of the frame of reference (values). Perez helps us to realize, first, how hermeneutically defined processes are defining much of economic life, and second, how these processes are fundamentally shaping our values and thus the evolvement of policy.

The Perez framework can aid us in realizing the hermeneutical character of the economy and the nature of dynamic structural change. To develop this into a full methodological framework is, of course, one of the more difficult tasks for future research.

New Research Directions

We have argued above that Perez' work provides important elements for facing the next challenges facing evolutionary theory. However, as we have shown, there are key issues for further research. We would like to highlight here the three most important areas:

First, how do changes in the governance structure interplay with technological development in long-term evolutionary processes? This question will become one of the fundamental issues for shaping the next deployment and even more, the following techno-economic paradigm. Is it possible to steer the development of technology into ethically more desirable directions, i.e., change the frame of reference proactively (e.g., environment, genetic research, nanotechnology)? What kind of governance structures are needed for such policy developments? (See the contributions by Drechsler and Rochet to this volume.)

Second, how to develop original evolutionary macroeconomic theory without reverting back to neoclassical modelling fallacies?[7] This is a crucial question for the next decade or so as, following the meltdown of 2008, there are bound to be significant changes in global macroeconomic policies and evolutionary theory needs to bring the innovation-based approach to the debates, and to do so by developing original solutions.

Third, mathematical modelling in economics misses most of the economic reality; it has also decoupled economics from policy decision-making (apart from the mere legitimization of already-arrived-at decisions) and, in turn, from the impact values have on the economy and vice versa. This needs an entirely new hermeneutical approach to economics.

In all three areas, Carlota Perez' work gives a potentially trailblazing contribution. Having evolved from and in parallel with most key evolutionary thinkers, most notably Chris Freeman, her work is, in sum, one of the most fruitful outgrowths of Evolutionary Economics in the last half century. With this brief introduction, we hope to have shown how her work could and indeed should be utilized by future research in order to make the impact and influence of Evolutionary Economics – and of course economics and indeed the genuinely social sciences generally – even greater than it already is.

References

Allen, P. 1988. 'Evolution, Innovation and Economics.' In G. Dosi et al. (eds). *Technical Change and Economic Theory*. London: Pinter, 95–120.

Berlin, I. 1996. *The Sense of Reality: Studies in Ideas and Their History*. London: Chatto and Windus.

Dosi, G. 1982. 'Technological Paradigms and Technological Trajectories.' *Research Policy* 11, 147–162.

Dosi, G. and L. Soete. 1988. 'Technical Change and International Trade.' In G. Dosi et al. (eds). *Technical Change and Economic Theory*. London: Pinter, 401–431.

Dosi, G. et al. (eds). 1988. *Technical Change and Economic Theory*. London: Pinter.

Drechsler, W. 2000a. 'On the Possibility of Quantitative-Mathematical Social Science, Chiefly Economics: Some Preliminary Considerations.' *Journal of Economic Studies* 27, 246–259.

_____. 2000b. 'Zu Werner Sombarts Theorie der Soziologie und zu seiner Biographie.' In J. G. Backhaus (ed.). *Werner Sombart: Klassiker der Sozialwissenschaft. Eine kritische Bestandsaufnahme*. Marburg: Metropolis, 83–100.

_____. 2004. 'Natural vs. Social Sciences: On Understanding in Economics.' In E. S. Reinert (ed.). *Globalization, Economic Development and Inequality: An Alternative Perspective*. Cheltenham: Elgar, 71–87.

Frank, R. H. 1997. 'The Frame of Reference as a Public Good.' *The Economic Journal* 107, 1832–1847.

Freeman, C. 1974. *The Economics of Industrial Innovation*. London: Routledge.

————. 1987. *Technology Policy and Economic Performance: Lessons from Japan*. London: Pinter.

Freeman, C., J. Clark and L. Soete. 1982. *Unemployment and Technical Innovation: A Study of Long Waves and Economic Development*. London: Greenwood.

Freeman, C. and F. Louçã. 2001. *As Times Goes By: From the Industrial Revolutions to the Information Revolution*. Oxford: Oxford University Press.

Gadamer, H.-G. 1990. *Wahrheit und Methode. Grundzüge einer philosophischen Hermeneutik. Gesammelte Werke* 1, Tübingen: Mohr/Siebeck.

Hastorf, A. H. and H. Cantril. 1954. 'They Saw a Game: A Case Study.' *Journal of Abnormal and Social Psychology* 49, 129–134.

Heath, P. 1974. *Philosopher's Alice*. New York: St Martin's Press.

Hodgson, G. M. 2004. *The Evolution of Institutional Economics*. London: Routledge.

Keynes, J. M. 1933. 'National Self-Sufficiency.' *The Yale Review* 22, 755–769.

————. 1997. *The General Theory of Employment, Interest, and Money*. Amherst, NY: Prometheus Books.

Kondratiev, N. 1935. 'The Long Waves in Economic Life.' *Review of Economic Statistics* 37, 105–115.

————. 1998. *The Works of Nikolai D. Kondratiev*. N. Makasheva, W. J. Samuels and V. Barnett (eds). Vol. 1. London: Pickering and Chatto.

Kregel, J. and L. Burlamaqui. 2005. 'Innovation, Competition and Financial Vulnerability in Economic Development.' *Revista de Economia Política* 25, 5–22.

————. 2006. 'Finance, Competition, Instability, and Development Microfoundations and Financial Scaffolding of the Economy.' *The Other Canon Foundation and Tallinn University of Technology Working Papers in Technology Governance and Economic Dynamics* 4.

Krugman, P. 1991. 'Increasing Returns and Economic Geography.' *Journal of Political Economy* 99, 483–499.

————. 1994a. *Peddling Prosperity. Economic Sense and Nonsense in the Age of Diminished Expectations*. New York and London: W. W. Norton.

————. 1994b. 'The Fall and Rise of Development Economics.' Available at http://web.mit.edu/krugman/www/dishpan.html.

————. 2008. The Sveriges Riksbank Prize in Economic Sciences in Memory of Alfred Nobel 2008: lecture and slides. Available at http://nobelprize.org/nobel_prizes/economics/laureates/2008/krugman-lecture.html.

Lawn, C. 2006. *Gadamer: A Guide for the Perplexed*. London and New York: Continuum.

Minsky, H. P. 2008. *Stabilizing an Unstable Economy*. New York: Yale University Press.

Nelson, R. and S. Winter. 1982. *An Evolutionary Theory of Economic Change*. Cambridge, MA: Harvard University Press.

Nurkse, R. 1961. *Equilibrium and Growth in the World Economy*. G. Haberler and R. M. Stern (eds). Harvard Economic Studies CXVIII. Cambridge, MA: Harvard University Press.

Perez, C. 1983. 'Structural Change and Assimilation of New Technologies in the Economic and Social Systems.' *Futures* 15, 357–375. [3.1]

————. 2002. *Technological Revolutions and Financial Capital: The Dynamics of Bubbles and Golden Ages*. Cheltenham: Edward Elgar. [74.1]

————. 2006. 'Respecialisation and the Deployment of the ICT Paradigm: An Essay on the Present Challenges of Globalization.' In R. Compañó et al. (eds). *The Future of the Information Society in Europe: Contributions to the Debate*. Seville, Spain: European Commission, Directorate General Joint Research Centre. [77.2]

Perez, C. and C. Freeman. 1988. 'Structural Crises of Adjustment, Business Cycles and Investment Behaviour.' In G. Dosi et al. (eds). *Technical Change and Economic Theory*. London: Pinter, 38–66. [20.1]

Reinert, E. S. 2007. *How Rich Countries Got Rich … and Why Poor Countries Stay Poor*. London: Constable & Robinson.

Reinert, E. S. and V. Riiser. 1994. 'Recent Trends in Economic Theory: Implications for Development Geography.' STEP report 12. Oslo: STEP.

v. Schmoller, G. 1881. 'The Idea of Justice in Political Economy.' *Annals of the American Academy of Political and Social Science* 4, 697–737.

Sombart, W. 1904. 'Versuch einer Systematik der Wirtschaftskrisen.' *Archiv für Socialwissenschaft und Socialpolitik* 1, Neue Folge, 1–21.

————. 1956 [1936]. 'Soziologie: Was sie ist und was sie sein sollte.' In W. Sombart. In *Noo-Soziologie*. Berlin: Duncker & Humblot, 95–123.

Soros, G. 2008. *The New Paradigm for Financial Markets: The Credit Crisis of 2008 and What it Means*. New York: Public Affairs.

v. Tunzelmann, N. et al. 2008. 'Technological Paradigms: Past, Present and Future.' *Industrial and Corporate Change* 17, 467–484.

Chapter Two:

DEVELOPING INNOVATION CAPABILITY: MEETING THE POLICY CHALLENGE

John Bessant
Imperial College Business School, London
and
Howard Rush
University of Brighton

Introduction

The challenge of innovation is clear – if businesses fail to change what they offer or the ways in which they create and deliver those offerings (product and process innovation), they risk being outpaced in an increasingly competitive global environment. Even those with the capacity to innovate their products and processes risk challenge from others with alternative business models or marketing propositions. So innovation is important – but the key issue is not in the innovation itself, but rather the *capability* within the organization to repeat the trick, to produce a continuing stream of innovation in a dynamic and shifting environment.

We have a growing understanding of the elements that make up such 'innovation capability' (IC) derived from extensive research on the innovation process. From a comparatively early stage interest grew in looking at innovation not simply in terms of its nature (i.e., radical or incremental) or the sources (i.e., knowledge push or demand pull), but rather how the process was organized and managed (Tidd et al. 2005). A variety of studies began to draw attention to the range of managerial and organizational factors that affected whether and how a firm innovated (Carter and Williams 1957; Langrish et al. 1972; Rothwell 1977; Cooper 2001).

Other strands of research have also contributed to our understanding; for example, development studies focused extensively on issues of learning and of technology transfer and helped us understand the nature of the capabilities needed to move from a position of technological dependence to one of strength (Lall 1992; Bell and Pavitt 1993; Figuereido 2001). Studies of learning behaviour suggest that a firm's learning repertoire – its ability to construct learning experiences (by doing, by experimenting (R&D), by collaborating, by exporting, etc.) – led to some accumulation of capability that placed the firm in a stronger position for future innovative activity (Arrow 1962; Bell and Scott-Kemmis 1990; Hobday 1995).

One of the most influential recent contributions has been under the label of 'absorptive capacity' – how capable is a firm of acquiring and using knowledge to create new products, processes, services and thus to grow? Originally, the term was coined by Cohen and Levinthal (1990) who described it as 'the ability of a firm to recognize the value of new, external information, assimilate it, and apply it to commercial ends' (Cohen and Levinthal 1990). They saw it as 'largely a function of the firm's level of prior related knowledge'. Zahra and George (2002) reviewed and extended the absorptive capacity (AC) construct, suggesting that several different processes were involved – rather than a simple absorption of new knowledge, there were discrete activities linked to search, acquisition, assimilation and exploitation. What they termed 'potential AC' relates to how a firm may value and acquire knowledge, although not necessarily exploit it. The firm's ability to transform and exploit the knowledge is captured by what they termed 'realized AC'. By distinguishing between potential and realized absorptive capacity, they highlight the point that some firms may be aware of and even able to access new external knowledge but are unable to leverage and exploit it.

Their work spawned extensive discussion and application. However, the resulting proliferation of use of the term led to problems highlighted by Lane et al. (2006), who tried to evaluate how much divergence there has been in the field. In an extensive literature survey (289 articles) they identified only six papers that extended the understanding of absorptive capacity in any meaningful way (Lane, Koka et al. 2006).

The emerging picture is of a complex, multi-attribute capability rather than a single organizational skill (Todorova and Durisin 2007). Acquiring and using new knowledge involves multiple and different activities around search, acquisition, assimilation and implementation, and connectivity between these is important. AC is associated with various kinds of search and subsequent activities, not just formal R&D as might be carried out in large firms. Mechanisms whereby small- and medium-size enterprises (SMEs) explore and develop process innovations, for example, are also relevant and can be mapped onto a model of AC (Hoffman, Parejo et al. 1997).

AC is about accumulated learning and embedding of capabilities – search, acquire, assimilate, etc. – in the form of routines (structures, processes, policies and procedures) that allow them to repeat the innovation trick. We suggest that the concept of absorptive capacity represents another label for the idea of 'innovation capability' and helps extend our understanding of what organizational and managerial skills are needed to sustain innovation. Importantly, this is not simply an analytical construct – it might also offer insights that can be used to guide policy interventions to help support firms in the innovation process.

In fact, while much of the argument made above (and further developed in the main section of this chapter) is well known in the academic literature, of less visibility and credit for the deepening of our understanding of the role of innovation capabilities and absorptive capacity has been the role played by policymakers and practitioners. From the 1970s onward, a deepening appreciation of the need to strengthen such capability (more usually referred to as 'technological capability' in those days) led the introduction of new programmes and policies throughout the OECD countries (in particular within northern Europe). These were in response to the perceived importance of introducing new micro-electronically based technologies (e.g., computer-aided design, computer-aided manufacture, flexible manufacturing systems) as a means of improving competitive performance. An overriding concern of policymakers at the time was the need to build the technological capabilities required in the design, development and implementation of what were generally referred to as 'new technologies' – capabilities that were in short supply at the time (e.g., see Vickery and Blau 1989; Northcott et al. 1985, 1986).

A small number of policymakers in Latin America were also concerned with experimenting with and introducing some of these ideas into practice. Carlota Perez was one of the first. It was as a practicing policy agent, having become a consultant to the Venezuelan Ministerio de Formento in the mid-1980s (having been the Director of Technology at the Ministry between 1980 and 1983) that we first worked with Carlota Perez in the development of PAI (Projecto de Actualizacion), a UNIDO-funded initiative aimed at building innovation capabilities for Venezuelan industry. Carlota, although already pursuing the development of her theoretical thinking on technological paradigms and waves of innovation, for which she is justifiably recognized today (Perez 1983, 1985, and 1988), put together a team of twelve young and energetic engineers and social scientists from various government agencies and NGOs to construct and introduce the first practical innovation policy in the region, the cornerstone of which was the training and development of a cadre of 'innovation consultants' as a mechanism for the diffusion of new thinking into Venezuelan industry. Between 1985 and 1987 an intense period of collaboration ensued between

CENTRIM (the Centre for Research in Innovation Management at the University of Brighton[1]) and the PAI team. During this period, a policy approach, appropriate to the local conditions and environment, was elaborated, a consultant's toolkit created, awareness-raising materials (including videos) created, conferences and seminars held and courses conducted, aimed at a variety of audiences including industrialists, consultants, administrators, etc., as a means of transferring the tools and techniques to agencies and firms in Venezuela. We shall return to this story in the final section of the chapter. However, it is clear that the interplay between academic researchers and policymakers in closing the loop between theory and practice has, to our minds, contributed greatly to our understanding of the importance of and means of developing absorptive capacity.

Developing Absorptive Capacity

Absorptive capacity is clearly not evenly distributed across a population. For the reasons outlined above, firms may find difficulties in growing through acquiring and using new knowledge. Some may simply be unaware of the need to change, never mind having the capability to manage such change. Such firms – a classic problem of SME growth for example – differ from those that recognize in some strategic way the need to change, to acquire and use new knowledge but lack the capability to target their search or to assimilate and make effective use of new knowledge once identified. Others may be clear about what they need, but lack capability in finding and acquiring it. And others may have well-developed routines for dealing with all of these issues and represent resources on which less-experienced firms might draw – as is the case with some major supply chains focused around a core central player (Hobday, Rush and Bessant 2004).

Figure 2.1 indicates a crude typology, ranging from firms that are 'unconsciously ignorant' (they don't know that they don't know) through to high-performing, knowledge-based enterprises (based upon a typology used by Arnold and Thuriaux 1998). The distinguishing feature is their capability to organize and manage the innovation process in its entirety, from search through selection to effective implementation of new knowledge. Such capability – absorptive capacity – is not a matter of getting lucky once, but of having an embedded high-order set of learning routines.

With this grouping, we can identify simple archetypes that highlight differences in absorptive capacity.[2] Type A firms (unaware/passive) can be characterized as being 'unconscious' or unaware about the need for technological improvement. They do not realize or recognize the need for technological change in what may be a hostile environment and where

Figure 2.1. Groups of Firms According to Absorptive Capacity

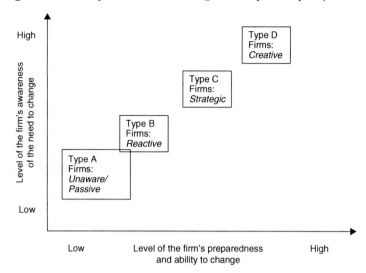

technological know-how and ability may be vital to survival. They do not know where or what they might improve, or how to go about the process of technology upgrading. As such, they are highly vulnerable to competitive forces. For example, if low-cost competitors enter – or the market demands faster delivery or higher quality – they are often not able to pick up the relevant signals or respond quickly. Even if they do, they may waste scarce resources by targeting the wrong kinds of improvement.

These companies are weak and ill prepared in all major areas of technology acquisition, use, development, strategy, and so on. A thoroughgoing basic improvement programme is probably urgently needed. Help is needed in: enabling these firms in recognizing the need for change (the 'wake-up call'); developing a strategic framework for manufacturing and other activities; identifying relevant and appropriate changes; and acquiring and implementing necessary technologies. They may also require assistance in sustaining this process of change over the long term.

Type B firms (reactive) recognize the challenge of change and the need for continuous improvements in technological capabilities. However, they are unclear about how to go about the process in the most effective fashion. Because their internal resources are limited – they often lack key skills and experience in technology – they tend to react to technological threats and possibilities, but are unable to shape and exploit events to their advantage. Their external networks are usually poorly developed. Most technological know-how comes from their suppliers and from observing the behaviour of other firms in their sector. They may well be 'keeping up' with other firms that may have similar weaknesses and limitations in technological capability. Typically, this group treats symptoms rather than root causes of problems – for example, dealing with bottleneck operations by replacing machinery only to find that the problem gets worse because the root cause is, in fact, in production scheduling.

The needs of this group centre first on the development of a strategic framework for technological change, so that key priority areas can be addressed. Allied to this, are needs in searching wider for solutions, in exploring new concepts (for example changing production layout rather than simply acquiring new machinery), and in acquiring and implementing new product and process capabilities. In the longer term, such firms could be expected to develop an internal capability for strategic upgrading and require less and less support.

Type C (strategic) firms have a well-developed sense of the need for technological change. They are highly capable in implementing new projects and take a strategic approach to the process of continuous innovation. They have a clear idea of priorities as to what has to be done, when and by whom, and also have strong internal capabilities in both technical and managerial areas and can implement changes with skill and speed. These firms benefit from a consciously developed strategic framework in terms of search, acquisition, implementation and improvement of technology. However, they tend to lack the capabilities to redefine markets through new technology, or to create new market opportunities. They tend to compete within the boundaries of an existing industry and may become 'trapped' in a mature or slow-growth sector, despite having exploited technology efficiently within the boundaries of the industry. Sometimes, they are limited in knowing where and how to acquire new technologies beyond the boundaries of their traditional business.

Overall these companies have strong in-house capabilities and think strategically about technology in the medium and long term. In some areas, these firms may be behind the international technology frontier, but they have many important strengths upon which to build.

The needs of this group are essentially around providing complementary support to internal capabilities and challenging existing business models. Improving access to specialist technical and marketing expertise, enabling access to new networks of technology providers (for example, overseas sources) can assist these firms to think 'outside' of the industrial box they find themselves in, should the need arise. Such firms may also benefit from occasional, project-based support from consultancy companies or from specialist research and technology organizations, locally or internationally. These firms may benefit from improved access to graduates and from linking up with universities that offer new ideas, access to advanced technology and new skills.

Type D firms (creative) have fully developed sets of technological capabilities and are able to help define the international technology frontier. In many areas, they take a creative and proactive approach to exploiting technology for competitive advantage. They are at ease with modern strategic frameworks for innovation and take it upon themselves to 'rewrite' the rules of the competitive game with respect to technology, markets and organization. Strong internal resources are coupled with a high degree of absorptive capacity that can enable diversification into other sectors, where their own skills and capabilities bring new advantages and redefine the ways in which firms traditionally compete, or wish to compete. Their technology and market networks are extensive so that they are kept informed about new technological opportunities and remain in touch with suppliers of equipment and ideas.

There are only a few firms in this category and they are generally seen as 'risk takers' although, like most businesses, they tend to avoid unnecessary or uncalculated risks. Some creative firms emerge from traditional and mature sectors to challenge the way business is conducted. For example, Nokia, the Finnish company, moved from pulp-and-paper into electronics and eventually became a world leader in mobile telecommunications, showing that it was possible to make very high margins in the production of handsets within the developed countries, when most competitors believed its was impossible to achieve this goal (e.g., Ericsson and Motorola viewed handsets as low-margin commodity products). Another example is IBM, which transformed itself from being a 'dinosaur' of the computer industry, to one of the fastest growing, most highly profitable information technology companies in the world, capable of leading the advance of 'e-commerce' technology in the late 1990s.

The needs of this group are mainly around complementing existing internal capabilities with outside sources, assessing risks and uncertainties and sustaining their position as a 'rule breaker'. They tend to be open companies that collaborate and learn from partners in the external environment and invest in developing new technologies and resources, for example in leading universities around the world. From time to time projects emerge that threaten to disrupt their existing businesses and they are often in a strong position to convert such threats into new market opportunities. Such firms may need to develop new contacts with specialist groups (domestic and overseas) in order to resolve complex technical problems and generate new opportunities.

Learning to Innovate

How do firms progress along the two axes in Figure 2.1? How do they build absorptive capacity/innovation capability? These are key questions not just for the enterprises themselves but also for a variety of policy actors with a stake in their long-term performance and growth. These might include regional development agencies, sectoral trade associations or major supply chain 'owners' dependent on tiers of smaller and weaker firms in their networks.

Reviewing the literature on why and when firms take in external knowledge suggests that this is not – as is sometimes assumed – a function of firm size or age. It appears instead, that the process is more one of transitions via crisis – turning points (Phelps et al. 2007). Some firms do not make the transition; others learn up to a limited level. Research at Durham University in the UK identified a series of 'myths' that small firms advance as reasons for deliberately not growing – for example, because of the assumption that growth will increase unnecessary bureaucracy and strangle the business (Allinson et al. 2006). Equally, the ability to move forwards depends on the past – a point made forcibly by Cohen and Levinthal in their original studies.

Difference in level of AC – see Figure 2.1 – places emphasis on how firms develop and reinforce key innovation management routines – in other words their ability to *learn*. We suggest that the process involves two complementary kinds of learning. Type 1 – adaptive learning – is about reinforcing and establishing relevant routines for dealing with a particular level of environmental complexity, and type 2 – generative learning – for taking on new levels of complexity (Argyris and Schon 1970; Senge 1990).[3]

The analogy with human organisms is helpful here – as firms develop maturity they become capable of managing an increasingly sophisticated set of external challenges. It raises the key question for policy agents of how development of innovation capability might be facilitated – how can they help firms learn to learn? The question of whether to intervene is, of course, a political one but on the assumption that *laissez faire* is not an acceptable option – that the market fails in some way and there is a case that can be made for support. The question then becomes when and how could that be delivered?

Helping Firms Develop Innovation Capability

Attempts on the part of policy agents to support, enable or facilitate the innovation process have been a feature of the policy landscape and literature for some time and there has been considerable evolution in the approaches used (Dodgson and Bessant 1996). In particular there has been a shift away from financial and broad-based incentives towards more targeted mechanisms aimed, for example, at specific types of firms, of different regions or in support of adoption of particular technologies (Bessant and Rush 1993). Underpinning this evolution was a recognition that firms differ in their needs and abilities to take on board new knowledge and policy aimed at helping the weaker, less experienced firm would help deal with perceived market failures. In other words there was growing recognition of the absorptive capacity issue highlighted above and an expansion of schemes that worked to compensate for gaps and weaknesses. For example many schemes have involved the use of intermediaries – innovation consultants – to help not only with the short-term problem of developing a technology strategy or adopting a particular innovation but in building long-term internal capability for firms to undertake this on their own in the future (Bessant and Rush 1995). Whilst there are relatively few longitudinal evaluations of policy support there does seem to be evidence that not only do such schemes promote the targeted behaviour (for example adoption of a specific technology) but they also develop internal capability – i.e., they enable progress up the absorptive capacity curve in Figure 2.1 (Rush, Bessant et al. 2004).

If we take this perspective – of how policy measures might enhance and develop absorptive capacity – then it is possible to review a number of approaches that have emerged over the past fifty years. In particular, we can characterize them into an emergent typology (see Table 2.1) that moves along a continuum from *laissez faire* – i.e., leave it to the market and do not intervene – through to different modes of intervention. They provide useful illustrations of the ways in which long-term firm capability can be developed, and of the barriers to doing so, and we discuss them in more detail in the following section.

Broadcast Mode

Whilst early industrial policy focused on financial support for investment, later development saw a shift towards other mechanisms (Bessant and Rush 1992).[4] 'Broadcast' mode refers to providing information in various forms to help improve awareness of firms about the need to change and to facilitate more effective search. Whilst information may be made available in 'passive' form – where the policy agent acts as a 'signpost' or 'library', there is often a deliberate promotional aspect – for example, various forms of awareness campaigns that are designed to challenge the firms and cause them to question whether they need to take new knowledge on board.

For example, early UK government policies designed to promote innovation were often simply letters and circulars from the relevant ministries but there has been a massive increase in the range and sophistication of such mechanisms during the past 25 years.[5] The 'Managing in the 90s' programme and its successor 'Fit for the Future', operated by the DTI and the Confederation of British Industries (CBI), made use of public presentations, road shows, breakfast briefings, television, radio, videos, CDs, DVDs and extensive web presence to promote innovation to a manufacturing audience. Much of this was targeted, both in terms of the technologies/techniques being promoted and in the sectors or firm types being addressed.

Table 2.1. **Outline Typology of Intervention Modes to Develop Absorptive Capacity**

Mode	Deployment Options Within Mode	Policy Examples	Comments
Laissez-faire Leave it to the market (no intervention)	—	—	Evidence of 'market failure' – some firms are persistent non-adopters of external knowledge proven to be of value. For example, despite 'world-class manufacturing' techniques being available for 25 years, there is still a long tail of non-adopters (Adams and Bessant 2008, forthcoming)
Broadcast mode Raise level of awareness by different ways of letting target population know	Non-specific – general broadcast awareness campaign	'Manufacturing into the 90s', and 'Fit for the future' campaigns operated by UK Department of Trade and Industry and Confederation of British Industry	Helps with 'awareness' and 'search' elements of AC development but may not be sufficient because it does not address assimilation and exploitation aspects. Evidence suggests this raises general level of awareness but does not deal with specific concerns of individual firms nor does it help with configuration and adaptation issues (Rush et al. 2004)
Peer-assisted mode Use agents to engage with the adopter to help frame and explore the promising practice	'Missionary' work to take the message to isolated potential adopters Consultancy support for: articulation of need; exploration of options, and; configuration and implementation	Innovation counsellors model – Business Links (UK), IRAP (Canada), TEKES (Finland) etc… Support for professional consultants to undertake this under broad regulatory framework offered by policy agent, e.g. Enterprise initiative, Inside UK Enterprise	Evidence suggests such assistance can help deal with changing perceptions of key innovation attributes (Northcott et al. 1986; Rush et al. 1994)

| **Peer-assisted mode** Use approaches that encourage learning from and with others | Vicarious experience sharing via learning by visiting and questioning 'people-like-us' Sectoral firm-to-firm programmes incorporating, for e.g., 'Master class' models or peer-to-peer learning Regional programmes (clusters and best practice clubs) Topic clubs, e.g., CIRCA, JIT clubs Supply chain learning | Industry Forum set up by UK Society of Motor Manufacturers and Traders with support from the (UK) Dept of Trade and Industry, and other fora established in aerospace, textiles, oil and gas, etc Supply chain learning initiatives | Evidence suggests peer-assisted learning can enhance several aspects of learning including awareness, experimentation, risk-sharing, etc. (Dyer and Nobeoka 2000; Bessant et al. 2003) |

In terms of diffusion theory we can see the potential contribution of such approaches at an early stage on the diffusion curve (Rogers 1995). Economic rationality is a strong force at this point and different mechanisms within the broadcast mode have the effect of taking this message out to potential adopters who can then see the relative advantage and adopt. Whilst such a model works well for innovations that are easily 'packaged' (like industrial robots) it may be less successful when a high degree of configuration and adaptation is required.

Broadcast mechanisms have evolved to include not only information but an increasing component of telling the story in context and often in the words and experience of early users. For example one of the more successful schemes within the 'Fit for the Future' panoply was 'Inside UK Enterprise' – a scheme of factory visits that allowed potential adopters to visit and see for themselves a wide range of innovations actually working in a range of different size and sectoral contexts. Similarly many of the road shows increasingly featured presentations from early adopters and there was a growing library of such case studies on the website.

Agent-Assisted Mode

'Agent-assisted' modes of intervention are designed to deal with the gap between awareness and search – and the subsequent assimilation and exploitation aspects of absorptive capacity development. As a result of effective broadcast mechanisms, firms may have a general awareness of the potential of the innovation on offer, but do not see its relevance or applicability to them. Mapped on to the absorptive capacity model, the problem lies in assimilation and exploitation rather than awareness. Under such conditions there may be a role for some form of intervention based on individuals helping potential adopters explore and experiment before committing themselves to a decision (Bessant and Rush, 1995). Consultants, 'innovation counsellors' and others act as intermediaries, helping decision-makers within the firm explore, articulate and make their adoption decisions. The effectiveness of these approaches depends to some extent on social system variables such as the perception of the 'agent' as someone who is credible, understands the context and can offer challenging and reliable input to the decision process. 'People like us' are preferred to those from government, academe or large, high-technology businesses who may be perceived as coming from different contexts.

Innovation agents of this kind can also help firms position the potential innovation in a wider strategic context (in the process articulating the economic rationality argument) – this was the philosophy behind UK schemes like 'Making IT Fit' that helped less experienced firms develop a manufacturing strategy within which they could see the relevance of innovations and the arguments for their deployment. They can provide a window on the experience of others in similar circumstances – a focused set of case studies and experiences that – viewed through a diffusion theory lens – help deal with observability and compatibility concerns and that generate a degree of isomorphic pressure. And they can help facilitate a degree of 'safe' experimentation and configuration around a generic idea. Much of the work of the UK's Manufacturing Advisory Service operates on this basis with trained consultants offering a 'hand-holding' introduction into implementing new manufacturing techniques.

Agent-assist mechanisms have become an increasingly important element in many national and regional innovation policy frameworks and have had demonstrable influence in capability development and in accelerating take-up of new techniques. For example, the long-established Knowledge Transfer Partnership model in the UK is based on placing graduates in SMEs to act as a bridge to universities, in the process enhancing the absorptive capacity of the firm over a sustained two- to three-year period. Many small firms support schemes within the Business Link and other regional development frameworks, making use of counsellors and consultants in fields like innovation, design and marketing. The UK Trade and Investment organization provides help with brokers and other agents to help UK firms learn to export. Nor is this confined to public policy. Within several of the Industry Forum models, the idea of 'guest engineers' being placed in SMEs to help facilitate learning of new approaches to manufacturing and operations has been pioneered.

Peer-Assisted Mode

Understanding the potential value in working within the social system underpins a third approach, which we term 'peer-assisted', where emphasis is placed on firms learning from and with each other. This aspect of learning has something in common with the principles of learning within groups instead of at the individual level. In particular the active participation of others in the process of challenge and support is recognized as a powerful enabling resource and was developed into a widely used approach termed 'action learning' (McGill and Warner Weil 1989). This concept stresses the value of experiential learning and the benefits that can come from gaining different forms of support from others in moving around the learning cycle. Part of the vision of Revans, one of the pioneers of the concept, involved the idea of 'comrades in adversity' working together to tackle complex and open-ended problems. (Pedler 1983; Revans 1983)

The potential benefits of shared learning include the following:

- shared learning has the potential for challenge and structured critical reflection from different perspectives
- different perspectives can bring in new concepts (or old concepts that are new to the learner)
- shared experimentation can reduce perceived and actual costs risks in trying new things
- shared experiences can provide support and open new lines of inquiry or exploration
- shared learning helps explicate the systems principles, seeing the patterns – separating 'the wood from the trees'
- shared learning provides an environment for surfacing assumptions and exploring mental models outside of the normal experience of individual organizations – helps prevent 'not invented here' and other effects

Arguably, this approach has much to offer inter-organizational learning, and the experience of regional clusters of small firms provides one important piece of evidence in support of this (Piore and Sabel 1982; Best 2001).

Such mechanisms are based on the principle that adoption of new ideas can be accelerated by the engagement of 'people like us' alongside potential adopters. This embraces Roger's notion of 'homophily', in which the communication of innovation is enhanced by its being carried out by people who are perceived as similar along key dimensions such as social status, experience, education, etc. Applied at the firm level, it suggests that potential adopters will be persuaded by both broadcast messages and agent-led intervention if this comes from people and organizations perceived as coming from a similar context.

Peer-assist mechanisms typically make use of firm-to-firm interactions to accelerate diffusion. One example is in the field of 'supply chain learning' (SCL) in which key players in an extended supply chain or network organize a process of innovation across the system, deploying various peer-assist mechanisms (DTI/CBI 2001). Such efforts are usually focused on upgrading key performance dimensions – such as quality, cost and delivery – that are susceptible to improvement through the adoption and implementation of 'world-class manufacturing' (WCM). Studies of facilitated learning/capability development behaviour in supply chains suggest considerable potential – one of the most notable examples being the case of the *kyoryokukai* (supplier associations) of Japanese manufacturers in the second half of the twentieth century (Cusumano 1985; Hines 1994; Dyer and Nobeoka 2000). Hines reports on other examples of supplier associations (including those in the UK) that have contributed to sustainable growth and development in a number of sectors particularly engineering and automotive (Hines, Cousins et al. 1999). Lamming (Lamming 1993) identifies such learning as a key feature of 'lean supply'. Marsh and Shaw describe collaborative learning experiences in the wine industry including elements of SCL, whilst the AFFA study reports on other experiences in the agricultural and food sector in Australia (AFFA 1998; Marsh and Shaw 2000). Case studies of SCL in the Dutch and UK food industries, the construction sector and aerospace provide further examples of different modes of SCL organization (AFFA 2000; Dent 2001). Humhprey et al. (1998) describe their emergence in a developing country context (India). Importantly these are not simply the by-products of network or supply chain activities; as one report comments, 'learning is not a natural feature of business networks. It is unlikely to thrive unless it is part of the emergent new models for inter-company collaboration that stress trust, cooperation and mutual dependence' (DTI 2000; DTI and Cabinet Office 2000).

A major sectoral initiative along these lines has been the UK's 'Industry Forum' (IF) approach, which originated as a sector-level activity in the automotive components field. Co-ordinated by the Society of Motor manufacturers and Traders (SMMT) and backed by the UK Department of Trade and Industry, IF developed an approach to facilitating learning about and adoption of WCM involving core metrics of performance (cost, quality and delivery) and multiple approaches to facilitating learning about and experimentation with the new practices. Its success in the automotive sector led to more widespread promotion as a policy option and in the 2000 White Paper on Competitiveness, provision was made to launch up to 13 other programmes in different sectors (aerospace, ceramics, construction and construction equipment, metals industries, oil and gas, printing industries, process and chemicals, red meat industry, shipbuilding, textiles and tourism and hospitality) (Chambers 1996; Bateman and David 2002).

IF and its derivatives operate on the basis of multiple mechanisms to engage and enable adoption of new ideas. Typically, there is a core framework that involves some form of 'benchmarking' that creates a motivation for change in order to close performance gaps in key areas like cost, quality and delivery. Although such data is widely available outside of peer-assist schemes, we would argue that it is the exposure to such benchmarking in the company of peers that creates a strong isomorphic pressure for change that underpins the adoption decision. Enabling learning and configuration involves demonstrations and exposure to other experience together with a phase of facilitated learning-by-doing that enables local configuration to suit particular contexts and that deals with many of the perceived compatibility questions raised by WCM. These mechanisms include a high level of people-based support, for example, through the loan of engineers and other experienced personnel as transfer agents.

There is growing evidence to support the use of peer-assist modes of intervention. For example, in South Africa the domestic automotive components sector faced significant performance gaps as it moved into the post-apartheid era. Catching up to the 'world class' frontier became an urgent priority and central to it was the need to adopt WCM rapidly and widely. One approach was the formation of a series of 'benchmarking clubs' in key regions where the sector was a significant element in the local economy – around Durban, along the Eastern Cape seaboard and in the areas between Pretoria and Johannesburg. These clubs operated in similar fashion to IF, using a mixture of benchmarking to develop shared motivation for change allied to extensive inter-firm support for experimenting with and learning about WCM and particularly, how it could be adapted and configured to suit very different educational, social and cultural conditions (Morris et al. 2006).

The model has been applied in a number of other contexts – for example, within 'communities of practice' across and between organizations (Wenger 1999), in regional development (Best 2001), in developing cross-sectoral search capabilities (Bessant and Von Stamm 2007) and in supporting micro-scale entrepreneurial businesses (Bessant 2008). 'Profitnet' is an ambitious programme in the south of the UK that has been establishing a variety of such learning networks across 500 enterprises, and initial results suggests considerable enhancement of their absorptive capacity, as measured by their propensity to seek out and use new sources of knowledge and to extend their linkages.

Conclusions/Reflections

Innovation Capability is an important concept because it explains the differences in firm capability to innovate across sectors, and also the challenge to policy agents to help firms learn to learn, not merely to deal with specific technological issues. It can highlight where, when and how intervention can take place without being distorting or featherbedding.[6] We can use the absorptive capacity/innovation capability lens outlined above to review industrial policy options. Given the preceding discussion, policy agents might do two things:

- First, identify and understand where a firm currently is in terms of the Figure 2.1 map – via assessment of their IC. This helps identify where they have specific development needs and might point to where those needs could be best met – e.g., signposting, or KTP (Knowledge Transfer Partnership) to provide internal skills that are missing, or training in project management, or business planning, etc. CENTRIM, for example, has gone down this route, participating in over 20 knowledge partner transfer schemes during the past ten years and in their development of a series of audit tools that locate the firm on the IC trajectory and identify the strengths and weaknesses of the organization.

- Second, intervene in ways that enhance – preferably in targeted fashion – the IC of the target firms. How they can do this raises a number of options, and as Table 2.1 indicates, these can take the form of broadcast, agent, peer assist or some combination. This was the direction largely taken by the Venezuelan PAI referred to in the introduction. Once the policy mechanisms were designed and piloted, the programme was located in the NGO Fin Productividad where, by the early 1990s, over sixty people had been trained as innovation consultants. The programme of development and diffusion continued through the Corporation Andina de Formento (CAF) where the ideas also diffuse to the other countries within the Andean Pact group through programmes such as PAC (Program of Support for Competitiveness).[7] In addition to Venezuela, innovation consultants have now been trained and are operating in Bolivia, Ecuador, Colombia and Peru.

While Carlota Perez may be better known for her important contributions to the theoretical understanding of long waves, for us, she has also been an inspiration of engagement between the theory and practice communities. Implicitly, she understood the absorptive capacity issue – that firms weren't just going to take on the new technology, but would need help – in raising awareness and also in learning to exploit the potential in their specific enterprises. She also saw the need to develop absorptive capacity, not just within firms, but also in policymaking- or promoting organizations (e.g., Ministerio de Formento and Fin Productividade) and set about hiring a cadre of engineers and social scientists who understood the technology – and in training them up as innovation agents. Her commitment to the link between theory and practice continues to this day, as does her relationship with CENTRIM and to the region – via for, example, her promotion of CENTRIM's Innovation Management course (which facilitates the development of innovation capabilities) in Venezuela.

References

Adams, R. and J. Bessant. 2008. 'Policy Mechanisms to Accelerate Innovation Adoption.' In J. Bessant and T. Venables (eds). *Creating Wealth from Knowledge: Meeting the Innovation Challenge*. Cheltenham: Edward Elgar.

AFFA. 1998. *Chains of Success*. Canberra, Department of Agriculture, Fisheries and Forestry, Australia.

———. 2000. *Supply Chain Learning: Chain Reversal and Shared Learning for Global Competitiveness*. Canberra: Department of Agriculture, Fisheries and Forestry, Australia.

Allinson, G. et al. 2006. *Myths Surrounding Growing a Business.* London: Small Business Service, DBERR.

Argyris, C. and D. Schon. 1970. *Organizational Learning.* Reading, MA: Addison Wesley.

Arnold, E. and B. Thuriaux. 1998. 'Developing Firms' Technological Capabilities.' Working paper. Technopolis, Brighton.

Arrow, K. 1962. 'The Economic Implications of Learning by Doing.' *Review of Economic Studies* 29, 155–173.

Bell, M. and K. Pavitt. 1993. 'Technological Accumulation and Industrial Growth.' *Industrial and Corporate Change* 2, 157–211.

Bell, R. M. and D. Scott-Kemmis. 1990. 'The Mythology of Learning-by-Doing in World War II Airframe and Ship Production.' Science Policy Research Unit, University of Sussex.

Bessant, J. 2008. *Using Learning Networks as an Aid to Innovation. Inside the Innovation Matrix.* Sydney: Australian Business Foundation.

Bessant, J. and H. Rush. 1992. 'Revolution in Three-Quarter Time: Lessons from the Diffusion of Advanced Manufacturing Technologies.' *Technology Analysis and Strategic Management* 4, 3–20.

———. 1993. 'Government Support of Manufacturing Innovations: Two Country-Level Case Studies.' *IEEE Transactions on Engineering Management* 40, 79–90.

———. 1995. 'Building Bridges for Innovation; The Role of Consultants in Technology Transfer.' *Research Policy* 24, 97–114.

Bessant, J. and B. v. Stamm. 2007. *Twelve Search Strategies Which Might Save Your Organization.* London: AIM Executive Briefing.

Bessant, J. et al. 2003. 'Putting Supply Chain Learning Into Practice.' *International Journal of Operations and Production Management* 23, 167–184.

Best, M. 2001. *The New Competitive Advantage.* Oxford: Oxford University Press.

Bateman, N. and A. David. 2002. 'Process Improvement Programmes: A Model for Assessing Sustainability.' *International Journal of Operations and Production Management* 22, 515–526.

Carter, C. and B. Williams. 1957. *Industry and Technical Progress.* Oxford: Oxford University Press.

Chambers, N. 1996. The Future of the Offshore Oil and Gas Industry. CRINE Conference – Learning to Survive, London, CRINE/DTI.

Cohen, W. and D. Levinthal. 1990. 'Absorptive Capacity: A New Perspective on Learning and Innovation.' *Administrative Science Quarterly* 35, 128–152.

Cooper, R. 2001. *Winning at New Products.* 3rd edn. London: Kegan Page.

Cusumano, M. 1985. *The Japanese Automobile Industry: Technology and Management at Nissan and Toyota.* Cambridge, MA: Harvard University Press.

Dent, R. 2001. *Collective Knowledge Development, Organisational Learning and Learning Networks: An Integrated Framework.* Swindon: Economic and Social Research Council.

Dodgson, M. and J. Bessant. 1996. *Effective Innovation Policy.* London: International Thomson Business Press.

DTI. 2000. *Learning Across Business Networks.* London: Department of Trade and Industry.

DTI and Cabinet Office. 2000. *Learning Across Business Networks.* London: Department of Trade and Industry.

DTI/CBI. 2001. *Supply Chain Learning: A Resource for Management.* London: DTI/CBI 'Fit for the Future.'

Dyer, J. and K. Nobeoka. 2000. 'Creating and Managing a High-Performance Knowledge-Sharing Network: The Toyota Case.' *Strategic Management Journal* 21, 345–367.

Dyer, J. H. and H. Singh. 1998. 'The Relational View: Cooperative Strategy and Sources of Interorganisational Competitive Advantage.' *The Academy of Management Review* 23, 660–679.

Figuereido, P. 2001. *Technological Learning and Competitive Performance*. Cheltenham: Edward Elgar.

Griliches, Z. 1957. 'Hybrid Corn: An Exploration in the Economics of Technological Change.' *Econometrica* 25, 501–522.

Hines, P. 1994. *Creating World Class Suppliers: Unlocking Mutual Competitive Advantage*. London: Pitman.

Hines, P., P. Cousins et al. 1999. *Value Stream Management: The Development of Lean Supply Chains*. London: Financial Times Management.

Hobday, M. 1995. *Innovation in East Asia: The Challenge to Japan*. London: Edward Elgar.

Hobday, M., H. Rush and J. Bessant. 2001. 'Firm-Level Innovation in the Korean Economy.' Report to the World Bank. Washington, DC: The World Bank.

———. 2004. 'Approaching the Innovation Frontier in Korea: The Transition Phase to Leadership.' *Research Policy* 33, 1433–1457.

Hoffman, K., M. Parejo et al. 1997. 'Small Firms, R&D, Technology and Innovation in the UK.' *Technovation* 18, 39–55.

Humphrey, J., R. Kaplinsky et al. 1998. *Corporate Restructuring: Crompton Greaves and the Challenge of Globalisation*. New Delhi: Sage.

Lall, S. 1992. 'Technological Capabilities and Industrialisation.' *World Development* 20, 165–186.

Lamming, R. 1993. *Beyond Partnership*. London: Prentice-Hall.

Lane, P. et al. 2006. 'The Reification of Absorptive Capacity: A Critical Review and Rejuvenation of the Construct.' *Academy of Management Review* 31, 833–863.

Langrish, J. et al. 1972. *Wealth from Knowledge*. London: Macmillan.

Marsh, I. and B. Shaw. 2000. 'Australia's Wine Industry. Collaboration and Learning as Causes of Competitive Success.' Working paper, Melbourne: Australian Graduate School of Management.

McGill, I. and S. Warner Weil. 1989. *Making Sense of Experiential Learning*. London: Open University Press.

Morris, M. et al. 2006. 'Using Learning Networks to Enable Industrial Development: Case Studies from South Africa.' *International Journal of Operations and Production Management* 26, 557–568.

Mowery, D. C., J. E. Oxley and B. S. Silverman. 1996. 'Strategic Alliances and Interfirm Knowledge Transfer.' *Strategic Management Journal* 17, 77–91.

Northcott, J. et al. 1985. *Promoting Innovation: Microelectricals Applications Programme*. London: Policy Studies Institute.

———. 1986. *Promoting Innovation 2: Microelectricals Consultancy Support*. London: London Policy Studies Institute.

Pedler, M. (ed.) 1983. *Action Learning in Practice*. London: Gower.

Perez, C. 1983. 'Structural Change and Assimilation of New Technologies in the Economic and Social Systems.' *Futures* 15, 357–375 [3.1]

———. 1985. 'Microelectronics, Long Waves and World Structural Change: New Perspectives for Developing Countries.' *World Development* 13, 441–463. [9.1]

———. 1988. 'New Technologies and Development.' In C. Freeman and B.-Å. Lundvall (eds). *Small Countries facing the Technological Revolution*. London: Pinter, 85–97 [21.1]

Phelps, R. 2007. 'Models of Organizational Growth: A Review with Implications for Knowledge and Learning.' *International Journal of Management Reviews* 9, 53–80.

Piore, M. and C. Sabel. 1982. *The Second Industrial Divide*. New York: Basic Books.

Revans, R. 1983. *Action Learning 2*. Buckingham: G. Wills + IMCB.

Rogers, E. 1995. *Diffusion of Innovations*. New York: Free Press.

Rothwell, R. 1977. 'The Characteristics of Successful Innovators and Technically Progressive Firms.' *R&D Management* 7, 191–206.

Rush, H., J. Bessant, and S. Lee. 2004. 'Assessing the Effectiveness of Technology Policy: A Long-Term View.' *Technology Analysis and Strategic Management* 16, 327–342.

Ryan, B and N. C. Gross. 1943. 'The Diffusion of Hybrid Seed Corn in Two Iowa Communities.' *Rural Sociology* 8, 16–24.

Senge, P. 1990. *The Fifth Discipline*. New York: Doubleday.

Szulanski, G. 2006. *Sticky Knowledge: Barriers to Knowing in the Firm*. London: Sage.

Tidd, J. et al. 2005. *Managing Innovation: Integrating Technological, Market and Organizational Change*. 3rd edn. Chichester: John Wiley.

Todorova, G. and B. Durisin. 2007. 'Absorptive Capacity: Valuing a Reconceptualisation.' *Academy of Management Review* 32, 774–796.

Wenger, E. 1999. *Communities of Practice: Learning, Meaning, and Identity*. Cambridge: Cambridge University Press.

Zahra, S. A. and G. George. 2002. 'Absorptive Capacity: A Review, Reconceptualization and Extension.' *Academy of Management Review* 27, 185–194.

Chapter Three:

SLOW FOOD, SLOW GROWTH ... SLOW ICT: THE VISION OF AMBIENT INTELLIGENCE

Jean-Claude Burgelman
Advisor DG Research, European Commission

More or less a decade ago, I started cooperating on a project that was to turn into one of the biggest thrills of my professional life.[1] At the Institute for Prospective Technological Studies (IPTS), we were tasked by the ISTAG to chart the future of Europe's information society.[2] European policy makers needed an independent vision that went beyond the infrastructure one being propagated mainly by the United States.[3] The result was a comprehensive concept called Ambient Intelligence (ISTAG 2001).[4] We produced a European project for 2010 and beyond based on several visions of the future and what they implied for research and development in information and communication technologies. Our focal point was that within a not-too-distant future, our real environment would be filled to the hilt with intelligent hardware and software. It would allow us to envisage what we would be able to do as employee, citizen, student, human being – you name it. That is why Ambient Intelligence is more than 'ubiquitous computing', one of the futuristic visions that was then especially popular in the United States.

Let me back up this vision with some excerpts:

Ambient Intelligence (AmI) stems from the convergence of three key technologies: Ubiquitous Computing, Ubiquitous Communication, and Intelligent User-Friendly Interfaces. In the AmI vision, humans will be surrounded by intelligent interfaces supported by computing and networking technology which is everywhere, embedded in everyday objects such as furniture, clothes, vehicles, roads and smart materials, even particles of decorative substances like paint. AmI implies a seamless environment of

computing, advanced networking technology and specific interfaces. It is
aware of the specific characteristics of human presence and personalities,
takes care of needs and is capable of responding intelligently to spoken or
gestured indications of desire, and even can engage in intelligent dialogue.
'Ambient Intelligence' should also be unobtrusive, often invisible: everywhere
and yet in our consciousness – nowhere unless we need it. Interaction should
be relaxing and enjoyable for the citizen, and not involve a steep learning
curve. Ambient Intelligence is therefore more than an enhanced Internet.
The idea of Ambient Intelligence is that if, as seems inevitable, we are going
to be increasingly surrounded by such devices, then for the health, comfort
and sanity of human society, we had better develop intelligent intuitive
interfaces capable of recognizing and responding to human needs of
individuals in a seamless, unobtrusive and often invisible way. That is why we
worked with the abbreviation of Ambient Intelligence as AmI – it should
signal a move beyond concepts such as 'user-friendliness', which tends to
objectify the relationship between people and technologies (as 'users'). AmI
should be based on a more seamless and humanistic notion such as a people
friendly information society. (Ducatel et al. 2005)

The last statement explains why the group of experts also enjoyed the French
jeu de mot, or pun, involving the AmI acronym: 'Ambient Intelligence: *mon meilleur
AmI.*' It went to the core of the issue: Technology in general and ICT specifically
had to be at the service of mankind.

The fact that such a statement and message was propagated by a group of
prominent representatives of industry and research carried special weight. Few
had expected this from a group of people traditionally considered to be nerdy.
And even fewer had expected this from a Directorate General of the European
Commission often reproached for being too technocratic and technology-driven.

Because of this message and the authority of ISTAG, this vision had quite an
immediate impact. Probably the first to take it on board was industry itself,
and Philips quickly embraced AmI. It later reached ICT policy circles at large
and only much later did it spread to academia. Even now, the ISTAG report is
still extensively quoted and remains one of IPTS' most downloaded reports. The
reason might well be that it is one of the few documents that so clearly set out an
ambitious European vision: technology-driven for sure, but technology at the
service of our societal ambitions.

When we assess now what was said about the future at the time, we have to
acknowledge that reality falls short of the vision we had in mind. After all, we still
don't live in intelligent environments that proactively help us out. Still, we have
to say that a great many elements of our vision have become commonplace.

The technological drive has taken us to the point that we are now in the midst of the development of the so-called ubiquitous networks, considered one of the most important building blocks of AmI. On top of that, every ICT company is committed to user-friendly innovation, which was one of ISTAG's key recommendations. It allows for the development of Radio Frequency Identification (RFID) devices and meshed networks that, in turn, foster proactive intervention. And the list goes on.

In fact, only two bottlenecks we listed in the report are still relevant.[5] The question remains of how we have to store and provide power to all the end-use equipment. AmI counted on powerful batteries that would stay alive well beyond a single day and preferably would be able to reenergize themselves. A second bottleneck in this intelligent environment centres on the need for proactive software that is able to anticipate or efficiently support all human behaviour.

I am not competent to judge the battery problem. But it does not seem impossible to me that the massive investment into developing alternative energy will produce a by-product that will solve the issue. In practice, the first laptop cases with fitted solar panels are already up for sale.

It leaves the lack of intelligent software as the most essential bottleneck on the road to a fully functioning intelligent environment. But the Web 2.0 developments give us hope. If this movement is seen as a comprehensive search for bottom-up knowledge creation and management, it does not seem too far-fetched to me to assume that this bottleneck will be fixed soon. Much is already there for all to see. Now, you can travel through New York, smartphone in hand, and your user profile will immediately show you which restaurant is most to your liking. You will be able to check the upcoming live sessions at a nearby jazz club and book a prime seat. If you like that handsome diner at the other table, check out whether the Facebook profile dovetails with yours. Or, buy-crimefree-guaranteed.com can not only provide you safe lodging but send you a simulation of your flat at the same time. All in real time, of course.

Examples are rife to show that when it comes to software based proactive knowledge, we have moved well beyond the expectations of 2000.

The Most Important Technological Trend
of the Last Decade

'Beam me up, Scotty!' Well, it still doesn't work. Scotty's transporter remains a figment of Star Trek fiction. Not that AmI scripts ever predicted differently. ISTAG always considered AmI as a sort of 'Reality ++', a significantly improved and more pleasant reality that viewed AmI as an upgraded version of the real world.

However, in retrospect, it is fair to say that the technological AmI vision and scenarios were on the mark. Even better, it seems to me that we are getting ever closer to turning it into reality. Though obviously, the target date of 2010 will be missed and not all expectations will be met.

A decade ago, no one had, for example, even heard of Web 2.0. So it comes as no surprise that ISTAG saw the future of knowledge-friendly software primarily as a massive increase of databases that, distributed on the old pre peer-to-peer paradigm, would first be stored in one place to be applied somewhere else later. Since it was the predominant reasoning around the turn of the millennium, it explains why the ISTAG experts, perhaps against better knowledge, considered it the future of smart software. With Web 2.0 that old dream of 'adaptable software' and 'content on the fly' became a reality. Technologically, I consider the impact of Web 2.0 therefore to be the most important development of ICT in the last decade. Specifically because the whole Web 2.0 movement, which goes well beyond YouTube and Facebook, turned the old communication paradigm on its head: the end user (whoever that may be) also becomes a content provider (YouTube, LinkedIn), a capacity provider (peer-to-peer) and an interface provider (open software).

The most fundamental criticism that the AmI movement could face centres on the fact that the vision was excessively based on an individualist conception of the future of services, including software. But next to no one would have anticipated a decade ago that the social dynamic of Web 2.0 would have had such a thorough impact on industrial logic. It turns Web 2.0 into a relevant correction to an AmI vision that proved too blinkered.

Such a change of paradigm, during which three components of a whole communication system (networks, interfaces and services/content) are simultaneously changed, is extremely rare.

It is the reason why I consider it the biggest leap forward in the history of the whole ICT revolution since the introduction of the PC. Only diehard technophobes will claim that Web 2.0 is just a passing phenomenon. Just consider how different things were less than five years ago. When in those days someone sought to sway European policymakers in both the private and public sector, it was still considered fashionable to call the ICT revolution dead, since everyone had a laptop and a PC.[6]

So, I not only consider Web 2.0 to be the most important breakthrough of the last twenty years, but also the most important stepping stone toward AmI. To put it differently: Because of the intertwining innovations in the areas of networking, interfacing and knowledge creation through Web 2.0, there no longer is any reason to assume that the technological evolution toward more AmI will not materialize. All the more so because the whole dynamic boosting Web 2.0 creates a more bottom-up, socially driven vision of the future and pushes aside the ICT's top-down individualistic view. Anyone now assessing the future of media has to take the success of YouTube, and its message that each viewer also wants to be a broadcaster, into full account. Anybody seriously involved in 'traffic management' now has a bigger job analysing how location-based services can be improved, rather than wondering whether the Internet highway needs any more lanes. When it comes to knowledge enhancement, the point no longer is to produce that knowledge yourself, but rather to integrate the elements of the Wikipedia dynamic.

All this has crystallized my vision of our technological future. Over the coming years, we will only have more shared and distributed networks, more intuitive and more end-user-driven content and knowledge creation. So, over the next decade, the real question is not what might happen to technology, since that, in principle, has few limits. Time and again, we have been wrong about what the limit of that 'sky' could be. Now, everything indicates that technology is not the highest hurdle. Moore's Law has risen from the grave as many times as it has been buried.

Now That More and More AmI Type of Technological Progress is a Given: What Will We Do With It?

It is a lot tougher to predict what kind of AmI will emerge in the future. A decade ago, the assumption among experts was that it would inevitably lead to 'More and faster': more supply, more channels, faster services, more interconnection, more 'any content, any service, anywhere, anytime', to quote the ad of a major European Telecom company. Based on such assumptions, it would have to lead to a 'hyper-efficient' society, backed by hyper-efficient citizens with a hyper-efficient education who are hyper-efficient in dealing with technology and so forth.

Unbridled economic growth and hyper-capitalism were without any question its socioeconomic cornerstones. It was even taken beyond the point of absurdity. At the height of the first Internet wave, some companies came onto the market offering to pay consumers if they used their services. Call it ultimate capitalism in which Adam Smith's invisible hand pays back what it should have taken.

In the end, it didn't really come to all that. 'Of course', we now say. The nonmaterial economy was not achieved. The daily rush-hour traffic jams are living testimony to that. The suspension of time and space through ICT – the end of distance – never became reality. Just look at the ever-increasing workload and job pressure, the relentless rise in business travel and the fact that the success of Silicon Valley could not be replicated any place else. Wherever the world truly turned smaller (for example, through a better use of logistical management) we only created different problems (like global competition and dependence).

However, we should not turn ourselves into Monday-morning quarterbacks and reassess this utopianism with belittling pity. The Parisian students of the May 1968 revolt had a vision of '*sous les pavees, la plage!* – beneath the cobblestones, the beach!' And even though they could not create their ideal society, one has to say that, clearly, the post-1968 world is different from the one that preceded it. And it does carry the seeds of May 1968 Utopia. And just like the May 68 hype, the first Internet bubble might have been a necessary phase. Following the analytical framework of Carlota Perez, it can be argued that during times of technological paradigm change, creativity should be given free rein (Perez 2002), let alone to change existing technological concepts. Indeed, to come up with peer-to-peer in a Unix world does take a radical leap of faith.

And in a sense, some of those wild, wacky ideas of yore did survive and make it to today. All right, sites that paid us to log on, as was predicted before the dot-com bubble burst, they never materialized. But look at the Google model, where everything is free because technology has turned targeted, tailored advertising into reality. So, in a sense, it can be seen as a derivative of this initial 'everything-must-go' vision. And nobody had anticipated that the concept of open software would turn the existing models in digital distribution upside down. At first it was illegal, like Napster, before they turned legit with initiatives like iTunes. And all that in turn helped lead to a creative commons with tens of thousands of licenses, yet another development no one had expected and one that would give a very strong boost to make main stream the movement of open innovation (OECD 2008).

In short, all the unlikely conjecture of the first Internet hype may have sounded crazy enough, but in a sense, a lot of it stuck. So, to assess the future of AmI, we should not only extrapolate based on technical know-how, but also look at the way technological trends are embedded in societal reality and vice versa.

AmI and Europe's Challenges

Here too, the case is pretty straightforward. If we look at the major challenges facing Europe and probably the rest of the world, too, over the coming decades, we can discern an emerging consensus on three of them. They are interrelated and they are big.

1. Economic growth in a global world has to be guaranteed; because growth allows for job creation, the funding of our welfare society and much more.

It has been almost unanimously agreed that this European growth must be based on the knowledge economy. What else is Europe left to compete with in this globalized world, given the fact that we do not want to see our standard of living slide into a drastic decline.

2. A second gigantic challenge is Europe's demographic evolution. How does the continent manage the greying of society and more immigration. Slowly, Europe's population pyramid is turned onto its head, and it shows in an increasingly negative dependency ratio (fewer workers to take care of more elders). Immigration is only part of the solution and engenders a different problem – integration.

3. The third challenge is green – how can we produce and consume enough energy while maintaining the ecological balance.

It is clear that in all three challenges, ICT, as an enabling technology and paradigm, has enormous contributions to make. It is evident that if we consider AmI a 'knowledge-based environment', future AmI applications will be needed to boost our creativity on the global stage (the first challenge). Such applications will be needed to develop Ambient Assisted Living services to contain the cost of health care (the second challenge). And ICT will be needed to create virtual working environments that are CO_2-free (third challenge). In other words, it is to be expected that the future developments will become part of these major challenges. It raises the question of what these services and applications will look like. Again, I think the sky is the limit. But it is beyond question that there will be enormous demand.

To some extent, the high level of risk-capital investment and the management of these projects by people who also boosted the Internet boom and the Web 2.0 breakthrough underscore this analysis.

It looks like the future is bright for ICT and that we can again look forward to 10 years of plenty with the ICT world, if they are developed as part of the solution of the globe's major problems. Yet, it doesn't mean that there is no dark side attached to these visions and scenarios. And they have to be taken seriously, lest they overshadow the bright side.

The Dark Side

ISTAG already warned, in its original version, that AmI carried a load beyond the positive message. Specifically, there were warnings about the invasion of privacy and because of this, it was stressed that AmI had to be controllable or 'on demand'. Some 'dark scenarios' spun a dreaded vision of a threatening technology that could, potentially, turn Orwellian (Wright et al. 2008). If our desire for a safe, protected world becomes too obsessive, it can push AmI, as such dark scenarios rightly predicted, down the slope toward total control and total loss of privacy.

But an Orwellian collapse because of our increasing need for security and control is only one aspect of what could possibly offset the positive development of AmI. A second scenario emerges from the darkness when we link the evolution toward AmI with the convergence debate: the dovetailing of ICT, biotechnology, robotics and nanotechnology. Bill Joy (2004), one of the former top brains of Sun Microsystems first warned us about this in a by now infamous article in Wired. It was infamous because a technophile like Joy called for a thorough assessment of where the sector was heading. He was the first to state that the ICT evolution toward nanorobots and enhanced humanity could lead to a sort of *Minority Report* society. And he added that because of the irreversibility of such trends, there needed to be careful consideration of the consequences.

The impact of all this is such that for the first time in human history, science will make it possible that people and their environment will be modelled at will, affecting both the deepest core of mankind and nature alike. It has always been one of mankind's deepest ambitions to control the world and extend human life, but the convergence of biogenetics, robotics and nanotechnology will allow for a giant leap forward in this process. Especially, the combination of these three disciplines will allow for applications to make your head spin. What about independent mini-drones that will be able to travel through your body and perform medical chores where necessary.

The fear raised by Joy's article is that the process will be irreversible. Much like Genetically Modified Organisms, once they are massively released in nature there is no way to retrieve them. Joy also said that a critical assessment has become impossible because, among other things, military applications appear to be too good to be true. The concept of a 'smart soldier' has been touted – a sort of *Blade Runner* character who is completely wired up and full of nanotechnology – so he can see at night through infrared lenses, needs almost no rest because of perfect diet and implant-based sleep management, can continue to fight despite a shattered knee since nanorobotics will instantly regenerate it. And he will probably be directed by a laptop from 20,000 kilometres away because, after all, he is only a tiny node within a whole network.

It is not even the issue whether this convergence will materialize – which, by the way, it will. First and foremost, I have a strong belief that the natural resistance of the ordinary citizen will be close to nonexistent. Most people would probably be committed proponents of early genetic intervention if it is clear that their unborn child would suffer from leukaemia. Ethically, that is an easy one – who would want a child to have leukaemia? So lets make it a bit more complicated. Would we also back such an intervention if the embryo would develop a harelip, heavy asthma, if it would become autistic, or if it would have an intelligence deficiency that would make it dependent on parental care throughout life? I think that even in the latter cases, many people would back genetic brinkmanship. It reinforces my conviction that we have only seen the beginning of genetic manipulation. It does not take a flight of fancy to realize that people would gladly become 200 years old. If it takes being fully wired with technology, I have no doubt they would be lining up, too. And, just to return to that smart military technology we were discussing, would it not be great it would allow us to let our leg grow back after it was smashed in a car crash?

On top of that, this convergence and evolution of AmI perfectly dovetails with something no one could have predicted a decade ago: the security neurosis following the terrorist attacks in the United States and Europe. It fits into the dark scenarios, since the attacks can be used as an all-purpose solution to start registering each and everyone – and everything. The potential of ICT is phenomenal. If all of our phone calls are registered, all of our data traffic scanned, all of our payments and purchases monitored through bar codes or RFID, if we have to biometrically check wherever we go, and if all this data is constantly linked, then any interested party, will know about 90 per cent of what we do during the day. If all of this is linked to our real-time monitored physical movements, we are getting pretty close to a *Minority Report* scenario.

And again, the citizen will have no doubt when faced with the question, you want security or privacy? Here is why it is not as simple as it seems: ICT's enormous archiving and tracing techniques did allow us to catch the Madrid terrorists within a week. Their phone traffic was archived; it was quickly known where they bought the mobiles that set off the bombs. By linking intelligent software, investigators knew within 48 hours where to look. And find they did.

In short, we need a far broader debate about the future of technology and mankind. We need to know where AmI is heading and how it can contribute to the three challenges the ICT world is facing – economic growth, sustainability and aging. And this is all the more so because the imminent scientific and technological developments are increasingly hard to fathom for our 'human' brains.

Take Iraq. It is now evident that the decision to go to war was not based on too many rational grounds (and this even apart from the debate whether it was justified). Yet at the same time, it put a process in motion that could not be stopped. Compare this to a tribal conflict 2,000 years ago when perhaps a few people died before bloody battle was ceased because one of the sides was simply exhausted. Add high-tech weapons to today's conflicts and we get the most brutal slaughter imaginable.

We see the same lack of 'natural' restraint when it comes to genetic manipulation and the monitoring of e-mail traffic. It takes precious little effort to get the ball rolling, but once it catches some momentum it becomes almost impossible to stop it. There still is a 'fix' possible for nuclear energy, but it will be as good as impossible to retrieve all genetically manipulated wheat from our food chain if it becomes obvious in twenty years time that it is harmful to half the world population.

In summary: the whole evolution toward AmI and convergence doesn't allow for much of a test and trial run and implies that we will have to carefully think through everything beforehand. And because the technological question has an easy answer – technologically, nearly everything is possible – it is clear to me that the most important debate about the future of ICT has to centre first and foremost on the ethical aspects. To put it differently, what kind of an Ambient Intelligence do we really want?

We will be able to learn from the errors we made a decade ago when we first set up the scenarios. Despite the rhetorical emphasis on consumer/mankind, AmI was a vision where technology drove the application and thus disregarded developments on the consumer side. On top of that, AmI saw mankind as strongly individualistic and underestimated the power of social interaction. If those scenarios had to be re-scripted today, Web 2.0 would have a strong impact.

Learning lessons from this, we have to ask how can we embed the AmI trends into the major challenges our world is facing while leaving the dark scenarios behind.

Food and the Future of AmI

The length limitations on this article only allow for a broad indication of a number of policy objectives. As a Belgian, I want to use an analogy relating to something that is dear to my heart (and stomach) – the slow food movement.[7] In itself, it is nothing more than a call to return our food culture to its essentials. Honest, seasonal products prepared, and tasted, at ease. We will happily chuck out those year-round fresh tomatoes that have either been grown in greenhouses or hauled from halfway across the globe at a staggering ecological cost. Instead, we want products from that magical Francophone place called '*terroir*' – that mix of time, space, soil and soul – for which we will pay fair prices. Slow food is the obvious alternative to fast food and its global monoculture. Good food, no doubt about it, but also based on quality when it comes to both the ingredients and the whole farm-to-fork process.

If we take this analogy further, we can say that the first AmI scenarios were the result of the fast-food ideology. How can we use ICT to produce faster, produce and consume more, live longer and stronger? It comes as no surprise that one of the most quoted AmI scenarios involved 'Maria' as a sort of super businesswoman who was flying around the world, managing her company up in the air, yet woman enough to find the time, largely because of AmI, to be a mom raising kids (even though mainly by smartphone). Maria was thus the typical exponent of 'fast growth'.

We increasingly see that the major challenges we will face, and that already have found a voice in the Global Justice Movement and the slow food movement itself, will increasingly push the debate toward what I would call 'slow growth'. A metaphor for having a good life, obviously, but not at the cost of the environment or the quality of life.

A slow-growth approach of AmI will stress the improvement of the quality of life through ICT and convergence instead of the improvement of human performance (see, e.g., Burgelman et al. 2006). Slow growth will use AmI to grow old with dignity instead of using AmI to work three additional hours a day. Such a vision of AmI stresses the development of services that will explore our collective knowledge to promote efficiency instead of services that target improved controls or additional machine-based intelligence.

Now, if our assessment of the societal trend toward slow growth is correct, it means that the dominant paradigm for the further development of AmI must, logically, be 'slow' too. What is more, AmI will have an essential role in any slow scenario of our future, because such a slow scenario is only attainable if we know how to use our collective knowledge to the fullest. This is exactly the potential of AmI 2.0.

References

Burgelman, J.-C. 1996a. 'Issues and Assumptions in Communications Policy and Research in Western Europe: A Critical Analysis.' In P. Schlesinger, R. Silverstone and J. Corner (eds). *International Media Research: A Critical Survey*. London and New York: Routledge, 123–153.

――――――. 1996b. 'Policy Challenges to the Creation of a European Info Society.' In J. Servaes (ed.). *The European Info Society: A Reality Check*. Bristol: Intellect, 59–86.

Burgelman, J.-C., R. Compano, N. Malinovski, O. Da Costa, I. Mattson, A. K. Bock and M. Cabrera. 2006. 'Converging Applications for Active Ageing Policy.' *Foresight* 8, 2, 30–42.

Burgelman, J.-C. and Y. Punie. 2006. 'Information, Society and Technology.' In E. Aerts and J. L. Encarnacao (eds). *True Visions. The Emergence of Ambient Intelligence*. Heidelberg: Springer, 17–34.

Ducatel, K., M. Bogdanowicz, F. Scapolo, J. Leijten and J.-C. Burgelman. 2005. 'That's What Friends Are For: AmI and the Information Society in 2010.' *e-Merging Media*. Munich: Springer, 181–200.

ISTAG. 2001. *Scenarios for Ambient Intelligence in 2010*. Available at ftp://ftp.cordis.lu/pub/ist/docs/istagscenarios2010.pdf.

Joy, B. 2004. 'Why the Future Doesn't Need us.' *Wired*. Available at http://www.wired.com/wired/archive/8.04/joy.html

OECD. 2008. 'Business Symposium on Open Innovation in Global Networks.' Policy Issues Paper. Available at http://www.oecd.org/dataoecd/28/48/40199686.pdf

Pascu, C., D. Osimo, M. Ulbrich, G. Turlea and J.-C. Burgelman. 2006. 'The Potential Disruptive Impact of Internet 2-Based Technologies.' *First Monday* 12. Available at http://www.firstmonday.org/issues/issue12_3/pascu/

Perez, C. 2002. *Technological Revolutions and Financial Capital: The Dynamics of Bubbles and Golden Ages.* Cheltenham: Edward Elgar. [74.1]

Wright, D., S. Gutwirth, M. Firedewald, E. Vildjiounaite and Y. Punie (eds). 2008. *Safeguards in a World of Ambient Intelligence.* Heidelberg: Springer.

Chapter Four:

TECHNICAL CHANGE AND STRUCTURAL INEQUALITIES: CONVERGING APPROACHES TO PROBLEMS OF UNDERDEVELOPMENT

José Eduardo Cassiolato
Federal University of Rio de Janeiro
Carlos Bianchi Pagola
Federal University of Rio de Janeiro
Helena Maria Martins Lastres
Brazilian Economic and Social Development Bank
and
Brazilian Ministry for Science and Technology

Introduction

One of the central preoccupations of the international research and policy agenda after the end of the Second World War was to come to terms with underdevelopment. Arguably, one of the most influential schools of thought on development during this period was the Latin American Structuralist Approach (LASA). Development theory and policy was shaped mostly by the analysis of the economic and social processes of production and knowledge creation. It followed a long-standing tradition that advocated that wealth originates from immaterial forces (creativity and knowledge) and that the accumulation of assets occurs through the incorporation of new technologies and innovation (Reinert and Daastøl 2004). Structural change and the connection between technical change and structural change were central to such developmental lines of argument.

There were two central arguments of LASA. First, the ideas that technical change plays a significant role in explaining development and underdevelopment and that specific knowledge and policies towards structural change were necessary to overcome backwardness. Technical change is a crucial component of an explanation of capitalism's evolution and in the determination of historical processes through which hierarchies of regions and countries are formed.[1]

Second, the proposition that underdeveloped countries were significantly different from industrial advanced ones. Hence, they could not follow the same paths towards development and that the catching-up idea had to be reconsidered. In the words of one of the leading Latin American structuralist economists, 'underdevelopment is ... an autonomous historical process, and not stages that economies that already achieved a superior degree of development had necessarily to go through' (Furtado 1961, 180).

At the end of the 1970s, the previous structuralism consensus was broken and a radical neoliberal program stating that long-run growth should be maximized through the pursuit of short-run allocative efficiency as determined by market forces gradually dominated the international agenda on development. In fact, 'development practically disappears as a specific question (remaining) only as the welfare achieved by the elimination of obstacles to market functioning' (Arocena and Sutz 2005, 16).

Around the same time, in advanced countries, a very fruitful thinking – associated with Schumpeter's idea – emphasizing the role of innovation as an engine of economic growth and the long-run cyclical character of technical change, was unfolding.[2] It is very well established that this line of reasoning was articulated in Christopher Freeman's paper of 1982, which pointed out the importance that several classical economists attached to innovation, accentuated its systemic and national character and stressed the crucial role of government policies to cope with the uncertainties associated with the upsurge of a new techno-economic paradigm.

The ability to master, combine and further elaborate these neo-Schumpeterian contributions and LASA's vision on innovation and development is the central piece of Carlota Perez' systematic effort of more than twenty-five years. Since her early works in the 1980s, she has developed an extensive production emphasizing the relevance of technical change processes to understanding the historical transformation of the capitalist system, the complex relationship between these processes and the socio-institutional change, as well as appropriated policies to cope with change.

Arguably, her better-known contributions are insights about capitalist crises related to the emergence of a new techno-economic paradigm and the role of policies to orient development. As far as underdeveloped countries' problems are concerned, these works generated the widespread idea of windows of opportunity. These ideas have been disseminated not only in academic circles, but also in national and international agencies devoted to science, technology and development policies. Their influence spread all over the world and particularly in Latin America. One example can be found in the setting up and in inspiring the research agenda of RedeSist, the Research Network on Local Productive and Innovative Systems, based at the Economics Institute of the Federal University of Rio de Janeiro, Brazil.

This paper aims at analysing the key aspects of Carlota's work that integrate LASA and the neo-Schumpeterian work on innovation and technical change. In this sense, in the following item we will attempt to show her main concern of building up a referential framework to the understanding of innovation and development problems. Some concepts introduced by Perez are also analysed: pervasiveness of new knowledge, and technologies and capacities needed for acquiring and using them. We also discuss how these topics influence the policymaking process, underscoring the relevance of public policies in Perez' work.

Connecting LASA with the Neo-Schumpeterian Work on Innovation: Perez' Contribution

In other works (Cassiolato et al. 2005 and Cassiolato and Lastres 2008) we addressed the relation between LASA and the neo-Schumpeterian school, particularly the emphasis on the systemic character of innovation, and proposed that there are five converging points between these schools. These connecting lines of reasoning are: (1) the relevance of technical progress to development process; (2) the preeminence of non-economic factors; (3) asymmetries in (and the dual character of) the process of development; (4) learning asymmetries; and (5) the specific importance of policy for structural change. In this paper we point out that Perez' work contributed to all of them, but added a sixth, the financial dimension. The six themes are covered next.

The Relevance of Technical Progress to the Development Process and the Pre-eminence of Non-Economic Factors

Within the analytical framework proposed by Carlota Perez, the development discussion is related to technological change. From her work of the early 1980s up to the more recent ones, there is the idea that a new developmental mode is triggered by innovations that have the capacity to change the way social life and production are organized. According to her analytical scheme, it is necessary to recognize the occurrence of certain key transformations in

organizational and technological capabilities to understand the transformations
that follow in the social, economic and political spheres:

> [W]hat provides the direction and shape of the movement are successive
> technological styles…based on a constellation of interrelated innovations
> both strictly technical and organizational, the diffusion of which is
> propelled by the profit motive. So for us the long waves represent distinct
> successive modes of development, responding to distinct successive
> technological styles. (Perez 1983, 358)

She introduces, in her 1983 paper, one of the main pillars of her work: the
idea that in order to understand development processes it is necessary to
have a comprehension of the dynamics of radical innovations in the
capitalist system. In fact, it is requires not only figuring out the economic and
technological processes by which a new technical solution arrives and
transforms the production system, but more than that, it is indispensable to
understand how change spreads through the production system and how the
existing institutional formats that regulate it resist change (Perez 1983, 1986,
1998 and 2002).

Throughout her work she gives a special role to radical innovations,
those that transform the old paradigm; they are responsible for setting off the
whole process of change of cycle.[3] Here, a key concept for her is the new
technological style that defines a whole set of technically possible alternative
solutions (Perez 1983, 360). Technological change, motivated by expectations of
economic benefits, activates and is the cause of the specific changes that
question the current developmental mode and the validity of socio-institutional
formats in place.

It is necessary to point out that her notion of technical change is in line with
some contributions of major LASA scholars, such as Furtado (1974 and 1983),
who emphasized the importance of understanding technological change from
a broader and systemic perspective.[4] As he pointed out (Furtado 1983), 'most of
the more significant manifestations of technical change can only be totally
captured through a global vision of the national system that includes the
perception of the relations of this system with the environment that controls
and influences it,'[5] and 'behind technical progress complex social modifications
are aligned, the logics of which should be understood as a previous step in any
development study.'[6] As the behaviour of economic variables rely on those
parameters – that are defined and evolve into a specific historical context – it is
quite difficult to isolate the study of economic phenomena from its historical
frame of reference (Furtado 1992). This assertion is more significant when
analyzing economic, social and technological systems that are significantly

heterogeneous, different from each other, as found within underdeveloped economies.

Perez' vision of technical change builds as well on the neo-Schumpeterian work of Chris Freeman (1995) who also considers development a systemic phenomenon, generated and sustained not only by inter-firm relations, but most significantly by complex inter-institutional and social network relations. Therefore, development – resulting from the introduction and diffusion of new technologies – may be considered as the outcome of cumulative trajectories historically built up according to institutional specificities and specialization patterns inherent to a determined country, region or sector.

In Perez' analysis of developmental modes, it is explicitly stated that they are not strictly economic phenomena. They are occurrences that are manifested in their impacts and subsequent transformation of all economic and socio-institutional fabric, both at national and international level.

Asymmetries in the Process of Development and Its Dual Character

Perez' work recollects one of the central tenets of the LASA's analysis: the comprehension of (under)development problems requires a broader, integrated approach that includes a whole set of interconnected components (Prebisch 1949). In this way, it is possible to interpret Perez' ideas, according to Celso Furtado's (1961) notion of underdevelopment: that a partial incorporation of a particular developmental mode, due to a limited and partial absorption of a new techno-economic paradigm, results in a particular form of development – underdevelopment. Such specific constitution does not mean any path towards development, but just a consequence of a vicious circle in which, according to the departure conditions, certain societies reproduce a path that does not allow for the full satisfaction of their needs, nor for the expansion of their capacities.

In this perspective, it is necessary to take into consideration the behaviour of social agents as well as trajectories of institutions. On these two pillars rest the essential fundamentals of the theoretical construction of structuralism's comparative historical analysis; peripheral Latin American underdeveloped structures conduct – more than determine – specific trajectories, which are a priori unknown. Development processes under peripheral conditions are dissimilar due to historical movements that are singular to the specific experiences of underdeveloped countries. In this context, underdevelopment may not, and should not, be considered as an anomaly or simply a backward state. Underdevelopment may be identified as a functioning pattern and specific evolution of some economies and societies. Social and economical peripheral structures determine a specific manner under which structural change occurs (industrialization during the 1950s and 1960s in Latin America, for example) and technical progress is introduced. Hence, different outcomes from those that happen in developed countries are to be expected (Furtado 1961; Rodriguez 2001).

Regarding the relationship between developed and underdeveloped countries, Perez' works bring at least two substantial (and connected) issues. First, it is essential to explore the difference between development and catching-up in Perez' perspective. Second, it is necessary to bring in a discussion about how power relations between countries operate, as it is an undeniably important dimension in the development process, for her and for the LASA approach.

Development implies a qualitative transformation and should not be conceived as merely following and catching-up with the leading countries, even if this was possible. Each country's historical experience is a unique process and differs from any other. This is a conception of development largely discussed in LASA writings, especially in Furtado's and Fajnzylber's studies.

In Perez' vision, technical change is a requisite for development, and technical upgrading is part of the developmental strategy. Taking advantage of the windows of opportunity requires searching and following a specific developmental path. Perez built these insights for analyses of the strategy of Southern Asian countries during the microelectronics revolution. In this regard, Perez stresses that those countries followed specific technological paths by developing appropriate industrial and technological policies (Perez 1996 and 2001).

Power relations play a significant role in development, too. For Furtado (1983) the concentration of economic power is associated with processes of accumulation and diffusion of technology in the history of capitalism. Power asymmetries take a central stage in the analytical framework of LASA as it points out that the relationship established between the underdeveloped countries and the developed centres is one of the main features of underdevelopment conditions (Prebisch 1949, Pinto 2000). The vision stressing the unequal character of capitalism and its hierarchic world system is one of the most significant contributions of LASA.[7]

Perez gives equal importance to the role of international relations for developmental strategies. Indeed, when she mentions that the developmental strategy is the pursuing of a mobile target, she dialogues with LASA's ideas by noting that 'developing countries are thus pursuing a moving target which not only advances all the time but also changes direction approximately every half century. If autarky is dismissed as an option, then development is a question of learning to play this game of constant shifts and variations, which is also a power game' (Perez 2001, 118). Considering developmental problems as those related to the unequal relationship between developed and underdeveloped countries, she points out that techno-economic change processes generate winners and losers.

Her ideas involve a notion of North-South and centre-periphery complementarities, yet at the same time offer the possibility of breaking the vicious circle of underdevelopment by adopting suitable policies (Perez 2001, 119). But this is certainly not another version of a dependency theory.[8] As mentioned above, she recognizes both the peripheral condition as an integral part of the world system, but builds on it as she discards the dichotomy between centre and periphery associated only with the differences between productivity of raw materials and industrial goods (Perez 1996 and 2008).

Learning Asymmetries: Failures in Knowledge Generation, Acquisition and Use as Underdevelopment Problems

How could underdeveloped countries achieve this moving target? The idea that national capacities to generate, acquire and use knowledge and new technologies are fundamental elements of the development process is present in Perez' contributions. Indeed, she notes the importance of knowledge accumulation by stressing the relevance that agents already possess to undertake innovation, as 'previous capital is needed to produce new capital, previous knowledge is needed to absorb new knowledge, skills must be available to acquire new skills, and a certain level of development is required to create the infrastructure and the agglomeration economies that make development possible' (Perez and Soete 1988, 459).

In her framework, these capacities are necessary requirements for the implementation of the new techno-economic paradigm. Also her notion of capabilities to cope with changes is much more appropriate than the more narrow idea of *absorptive capacities* (Cohen and Levinthal 1989) that has been widely used in the neo-Schumpeterian work on innovation and that is restricted to 'the ability to learn and implement the technologies and associated practices of already developed countries' (Dahlman and Nelson 1995, quoted by Criscuolo and Narula 2002, 2).

It is notable that such a notion explicitly assumes the belief that there are supposedly superior technologies of advanced countries that should be learnt by less developed ones. Both the early LASA work[9], and Perez' own efforts on (national) capacities did not endorse the implicit suggestion of a superiority of knowledge produced in advanced countries vis-à-vis knowledge generated in less-developed countries.

Perez' conception of capabilities is certainly rooted in older Latin American works of the 1970s. For example, one will find the importance of local capacity to generate, acquire and use knowledge in the work of Sábato and Botana (1975). This and other Latin American works on S&T and development also emphasized the need to extend the application of scientific technological capabilities to indigenous production problems and to link then to local knowledge and capabilities.

As seen above, there are different requirements for new technologies to spread throughout the economy. It is essential that the productive sector, government and society as a whole accept and are capable of using and diffusing the new techno-economic knowledge and practices (Freeman and Perez 1988; Perez 1986). Then, (2) the pervading capacity of the technology differs according to the country's capacity; (2) previous knowledge is essential for absorbing new knowledge; (3) the diffusion process of the new paradigm requires the generation of indigenous knowledge. In other terms, it is not possible to build the necessary absorptive capacity without a capacity to generate, acquire and use knowledge.

The emphasis on knowledge generation is based on today's well-known idea that innovation and diffusion are not separate stages, but are systemic processes simultaneously defined. In fact, these processes are mutually interrelated, and in order to get most of novel technologies, societies need to have capabilities to acquire, generate and use knowledge.

Summing up, capacities to use and diffuse new technologies and their pervasiveness are complementary to each other. The latter is not possible without the former. In this context, how can we explain diffusion failures? Why are these failures specific problems for underdeveloped countries?

For Perez, technological and economic efficiencies boost the diffusion of a techno-economic paradigm as they bring about changes in practical common sense (Perez 1983, 1986 and 2002). But she argues that problems in the acquisition and dissemination of new knowledge are a consequence of the socio-institutional resistance to change (Perez 1992, 2001 and 2008).

There are other relevant explanations for the failures in the adoption of new techno-economics practices. LASA's contributions to the understanding of problems of technological diffusion in Latin America take into account the high degree of structural heterogeneity within national economies and society. The analysis of how structural asymmetries restrain development processes, found in several LASA works, is one of the main features of the peripheral conditions according to the structuralist approach (Rodriguez 1981).[10]

In fact, the evolution of LASA shows a gradual change in emphasis from the concept of the dual economy to a perspective stressing structural heterogeneity. Such heterogeneity is a central feature of the Latin American economy and society, which is rooted on its structural organization. For LASA, the presence of significant structural inequalities hampers the diffusion of appropriate knowledge within society, reinforcing, as a consequence, the underdevelopment process.

Carlota Perez (1983) stresses the importance of this issue as she recognizes the distinctive development level and technological requirements of diverse economic sectors and actors of the society. Indeed, she emphasizes that the diffusion of the new techno-economic paradigm is neither equally distributed across all sectors and actors at the same moment nor with the same intensity (Perez 1983 and 2001). In this sense, the author argues that practices related to different paradigms do actually coexist as a result of different technological requirements and different socio-institutional arrangements.

The Role of the Financial Dimension

Perez' study of the influence of financial capital on development processes – in general and in periods of changes in techno-economic paradigms – is a particularly relevant contribution since this is a topic that has not been deeply analysed by the Latin-American structuralist and the neo-Schumpeterian approaches (Perez 2002).[11] In fact, Schumpeter (1934) recognized that for entrepreneurs to become the driving force in a process of innovation, they should be able to convince banks to provide the credit to finance innovation. Building on his ideas, Perez assigns to the financial dimension a key role for production and innovation and for development policies, stressing that any discussion about technical change and innovation systems has to include the financial dimension.

Her contribution is even more relevant, since in the last three decades, the increasing financialization of the world economic system has negatively affected the conditions under which key participants in systems of innovation command the necessary finance allowing them to undertake long-term innovation-related investment. This financialization is responsible for the relatively low priority given by firms to long-run concerns, neglecting those activities that have a longer payback period such as expenditure in human resources, R&D and innovation.[12]

Considering the destructive and dangerous character of this financialization, she argues that a certain degree of decoupling between financial and production capital is necessary to foster the emergence of a new paradigm. But she also warns that a recouping phase, when finance is adjusted to the needs of production again, is indispensable to the diffusion of the new technologies across the whole economy and society. This whole process is not smooth, but marked by disruptions and different impacts on all activities. In this context, the path of each country or region will depend on its capabilities to define and implement adequate policies. What policies are these? Who is the responsible for adopting and undertaking these policies? For Perez, the characteristics of a developmental mode will depend on how the socio-institutional milieu adopts the new paradigm. With such a view, she opens a wide scope for policy action.

The Importance of Policy for Structural Change: The Role of the State and Public Policy

For Perez, the idea that the generation and diffusion of knowledge are key factors to grasp the problems of underdevelopment has an important policy dimension. In fact, these processes do not occur under a natural umbrella of market forces, but require and depend upon the active role of the state, through policy.

The need to search for new models that orient policy – in conceptual and normative ways – is probably one of the main converging points of Latin American authors who concentrate their academic efforts on the study of innovation and development. Perez contributed to this debate in several ways, in particular with her notion of *suitable policies*, those that encapsulate the learning about past experiences and the specificities and complexities of present problems. They should aim primarily at constructing new forms of social and productive relations.

Policies towards better forms of social and economic relations are policies oriented towards the construction of a more harmonious and just society (Perez 1998, 18–23). Such normative definition is clearly aligned with work of LASA scholars such as Prebisch (1949), Furtado (1961) and Pinto (1976). And it goes further, in line with the new ECLAC scholars such as Fajnzylber (1983), who concentrated on tackling the problems of equity and on suggesting the opportunities of a productive transformation for a change towards a development mode that integrates efficiency and solidarity (ECLAC 1992).

The space for policy action depends upon a number of factors ranging from power relations to the possible options established by each new techno-economic paradigm.[13] Even if a central point about the new techno-economic paradigm is that it brings a new more efficient option for doing things, the policy implication is not the notion that there is only one way of doing things, but rather that the policy space consists of the construction of a manner for participating in the new historical moment.

As pointed out by her (Perez 2001 and 2008), the experience of Latin America and other regions shows that it is necessary to build a model that breaks with the sterile opposition between state and market. In this way, the systems of innovation approach offers a framework capable of overcoming this dichotomy as it permits situating the policy challenges in their specific context.[14]

Policies could only be adequate for a specific historical and geographical context.

As noted by Perez, the possibility of defining adequate policies is linked to the capacity to *read* the external and internal conditions. Regarding external conditions, Perez suggests that the import-substitution industrialization model (ISI) was an adequate policy solution to Latin America for a given period and an intelligent way of shaping a new form of interaction with the world economy. This strategy made possible the construction of an industrial infrastructure in the countries of the region, at the same time that mature industries of developed countries could expand their markets and extend the life cycle of their products (Perez 2001, 110).

Even though the policy was efficient for some time, it was not translated into a sustainable model and, even worse, did not allow for the setting up of a strategy oriented towards a prospective vision that could anticipate the change of paradigm. However, the eruption of the new techno-economic paradigm in the 1980s has coincided with another paradigm change, that of development policies. Policies of structural adjustment and institutional renovation had as one of their suppositions an acceleration of political–institutional change. It marked a process of creative destruction on which the political-institutional sphere and the productive and organizational formats of local firms (Katz 2000) suffered a strong process of destruction of old practices, but hardly any construction of alternatives.[15]

The construction of these creative formats is one of the central principles of any policy proposal. As Perez pointed out, 'most of the old models that explain reality and orient policy have fallen; the new ones do not show their effectiveness in terms of growth with equity. These are, then, times for experimentation, discussion and openness to alternative approaches' (Perez 1998, 1).

The likelihood of establishing such unconventional approaches – and of them being accepted – depends on the capacity of understanding the transformations of the techno-economic paradigm, and in particular, in what phase the paradigm is at any particular time. In this sense the policy consists of favouring actions that could take advantage of the opportunities opened in each moment of the cycle.

According to Perez, one can distinguish two key aspects in order to understand the main challenges for defining policies to get hold of the opportunity windows opened in each phase of the paradigm. First, it has to be recognized that this is a dynamic process that requires learning and experimentation, as pointed out above. It is needed to forecast changes in the prevailing paradigm and the possible rupture points. For policies to fulfil such role, it is necessary that they strengthen the aspects mentioned in the previous session; the endogenous creation of knowledge is a requisite and support diffusion processes (pervasiveness capability) as a way to integrate the society in the new development mode.

The second aspect is that the set of necessary policies does not contemplate only policies explicitly directed to R&D and innovation. As Perez (2008, 8) pointed out Asian countries that were able to advance significantly in their active S&T&I policies have associated them with a diffusion of collective visions of a developmental mode. In this sense, Perez follows a tradition initiated more than 30 years ago in Latin America by Amilcar Herrera (1975) that points out the scarce utility of specific policies towards S&T isolated from the remaining policies (industrial, trade, monetary, etc.). That is why traditional macro-economic policies have been called implicit industrial and technology policies in Latin America (Herrera 1975).

In fact, the discussion about S&T policies since the 1970s in Latin America went further, as it has been recognized that malignant macro-economic contexts and policies jeopardize long-run investments in real and intellectual capital and have larger negative implications to the industrial and technological development (Coutinho 2003). Problems such as hyper-inflation, high external debt and high interest rates are common significant constraints to technological and productive development in these countries.[16] Ignoring this perspective has led to the design of completely inoperative technology policies in the last 30 years, both in Latin America and in other underdeveloped countries.

Since her early papers of the 1980s where she started to develop her well-known approach on techno-economic paradigms, till the more recent ones where she analyses the relation of these cycles with finance and reflects on policy and development alternatives, she successfully integrated LASA and the neo-Schumpeterian approach to the study of the problems of development. The relation of these problems to processes of technical change, particularly innovation diffusion, power relations and structural problems of inequality, were examined before. Next, a wrapping up will be presented, pointing out the main questions that arise from Perez' work for a continuation of a research program that integrates both the neo-Schumpeterian perspective and LASA contributions.

Concluding Remarks: Opening and Illuminating Pathways

The work of Carlota Perez has been devoted to understanding technical change in a historical and territorial perspective, emphasizing diversity and, above all, that both theory and policy recommendations are highly context-dependent. The main argument of the paper is that Carlota Perez contributed significantly to the understanding of innovation and development problems, further elaborating LASA and the neo-Schumpeterian approaches.

We tried to point out her main contributions about some converging ideas between these two approaches:

- the relevance of technical progress to development process and the preeminence of non-economic factors
- the systemic and context-specific nature of knowledge and innovation processes
- the dual character and asymmetries of development and learning
- the role of financial capital in development and innovation analysis
- the relationship between innovation and development at different analytical – macro, micro – and normative levels
- the particular importance of policies to orient development in times of radical changes and crises

Along these lines, she opened and illuminated pathways leading to research programs and policy recommendations. One example is the research program of RedeSist, which was set up with the aim of investigating and understanding local processes of learning and capability accumulation in Brazil and other Latin American countries, as well as putting forward propositions for their mobilization. In order to achieve this, as part of an effort to create categories appropriate to the study of local specificities that affect production, innovation and development in different regions, we simultaneously drew on the systems of innovation and LASA frameworks (Cassiolato and Lastres 1999 and 2003).

Our first step was to try to derive from the *national system of innovation approach* an operational tool. This effort led to the development of the concept of *local productive and innovative systems and arrangements* (LIPS).[17] The basic argument is that to better understand the dynamics of a given system – and propose ways to promote it – it is necessary, not only to understand its particularities in depth, but also its weight and role inside knowledge and production chains and sectors that they are part of at the national and international levels. Specific contexts, cognitive and regulatory systems, as well as forms of interaction and learning are recognized as fundamental for generating and diffusing knowledge.

Drawing on Perez' work, the LIPS approach was conceived as a focusing device, which is complementary, not alternative to others, such as sector, production chain or individual organizations. Specific contexts, cognitive and regulatory systems, as well as forms of interaction and learning are recognized as fundamental for generating and diffusing knowledge. It is also clear that a particular system functions differently and requires different types of support if located in different parts of the world and within different countries.

The study of the local production and innovation processes is complemented by the analyses of the global relationships that envelope these processes. In this sense, the contribution of Carlota Perez, devoted to the study of the historical macro-level perspective and how it affects economic and technological change, is a key reference for building a theoretical framework that includes innovation problems within the (under)development concept of the LASA scholars.

More than opening and illuminating pathways, Carlota Perez has also contributed with some visionary insights of paramount importance. One example is her remark, twenty years ago, that 'the difficulties experienced by the world economy for the past two decades have a techno-economic origin and a socio-institutional solution' (Perez 1988, 2). The analysis of the crisis and related problems experienced in the end of the first decade of the millennium by the world economy confirms Perez' foresight, as powerful structures that benefit from the mass production, energy and material-intensive paradigm still resist change. It remains to be confirmed if the political, social and economic changes signalled in the leading world economy at the moment we finish this chapter (January 2009) constitute the solution referred to by Perez above.

References

Arocena, R. and J. Sutz. 2003. *Subdesarrollo e Innovación. Navegando contra el viento.* Organización de Estados Iberoamericanos. Madrid: Cambridge University Press.

———. 2005. 'Innovation Systems and Developing Countries.' DRUID Working Paper 2–5.

Cardoso, F. H. and E. Faletto. 1981. *Dependência e Desenvolvimento na América Latina: Ensaio de Interpretação e Sociologia.* 7th edn. Rio de Janeiro: Zahar.

Cassiolato, J. E. 1980. 'Notas sobre tecnologia na indústria de equipamentos para a produção de açúcar e álcool.' Paper presented at the V Annual Meeting of ANPEC, Nova Friburgo, Brazil.

Cassiolato, J. E., V. Guimarães, F. Peixoto and H. M. M. Lastres. 2005. Innovation Systems and Development: What Can We Learn from the Latin American Experience? Paper Presented at the 3rd Globelics Conference, Pretoria, South Africa.

Cassiolato, J. E. and H. M. M. Lastres. 2008. 'Discussing Innovation and Development: Converging Points Between the Latin American School and the Innovation Systems Perspective?' Globelics Working Paper 08–02.

Cassiolato, J. E. and H. M. M. Lastres (eds). 1999. *Globalização e Inovação Localizada: Experiências de Sistemas Locais no Mercosul.* Brasília: IBICT/MCT.

Cassiolato, J. E., H. M. M. Lastres and M. L. Maciel (eds). 2003. *Systems of Innovation and Development: Evidence from Brazil.* Cheltenham: Edward Elgar.

Chang, H.-J. 2002. *Kicking Away the Ladder: Development Strategy in Historical Perspective.* London: Anthem.

Cimoli, M., G. Porcile, A. Primi and S. Vergara. 2005. 'Cambio estructural, heterogeneidad productiva y tecnología en América Latina.' In M. Cimoli (ed.). *Heterogeneidad estructural, asimetrías tecnológicas y crecimiento en América Latina.* Santiago de Chile: CEPAL-BID.

Cohen, W. and D. Levinthal. 1989. 'Innovation and Learning: The Two Faces of R&D.' *Economic Journal, Royal Economic Society* 99 (397), 569–96.

————. 1990. 'Absorptive Capacity: A New Perspective on Learning and Innovation.' *Administrative Science Quarterly* 35, 128–158.

Coutinho, L. 2003. 'Macroeconomic Regimes and Business Strategies: An Alternative Industrial Policy for Brazil in the Wake of the XXIst Century.' In J. E. Cassiolato, H. M. M. Lastres and M. L. Maciel (eds). 2003. *Systems of Innovation and Development: Evidence from Brazil.* Cheltenham: Edward Elgar.

Criscuolo, P. and R. Narula. 2002. 'A Novel Approach to National Technological Accumulation and Absorptive Capacity: Aggregating Cohen and Levinthal.' Paper, DRUID Summer Conference, Copenhagen / Elsinore, 6–8 June.

Dahlman, C. and R. Nelson. 1995. 'Social Absorption Capability, National Innovation Systems and Economic Development'. In D. Perkins and B. Ho Koo (eds). *Social Capability and Long-Term Growth.* Basingstoke: Macmillan.

ECLAC (Economic Comisión for Latin America and the Caribbean). 1992. *Equidad y transformación productiva: un enfoque integrado.* Santiago de Chile: CEPAL.

Fajnzylber, F. 1983. *La Industrialización Trunca de América Latina.* México: Nueva Imagen.

————. 1989. 'Industrialización en América Latina: De la "caja negra" al "casillero vacío".' *Cuadernos de CEPAL* 60. Santiago de Chile: CEPAL.

Fiori, J. L. 2001. 'Sistema mundial: Império e pauperização para retomar o pensamento crítico latino-americano.' In J. L. Fiori and C. Medeiros (eds). *Polarização Mundial e Crescimento.* Petrópolis: Vozes.

Freeman, C. 1987. *Technology Policy and Economic Performance: Lessons from Japan.* London: Pinter.

————. 1995. 'The National System of Innovation in a Historical Perspective.' *Cambridge Journal of Economics* 19, 5–24.

————. 2003. 'A Hard Landing for the "New Economy"? Information Technology and the United States National System of Innovation.' In J. E. Cassiolato, H. M. M. Lastres and M. L. Maciel (eds). 2003. *Systems of Innovation and Development: Evidence from Brazil.* Cheltenham: Edward Elgar.

Freeman, C. and C. Perez. 1988. 'Structural Crisis of Adjustment, Business Cycles and Investment Behaviour'. In G. Dosi et al. (eds). *Technical Change and Economic Theory.* London: Pinter, 38–66. [20.1]

Furtado, C. 1961. *Desenvolvimento e Subdesenvolvimento.* Rio de Janeiro: Fundo de Cultura.

————. 1974. *O Mito do Desenvolvimento Econômico.* Rio de Janeiro: Paz e Terra.

————. 1983. *El subdesarrollo Latinoamericano. Ensayos de Celso Furtado.* México: Fondo de Cultura Económica.

————. 1992. 'O Subdesenvolvimento Revisitado.' *Economia e Sociedade* 1, 5–20.

Girvan, N. 1997a. *Poverty, Empowerment and Social Development in the Caribbean.* Kingston: UWI Canoe Press.

————. 1997b. 'Societies at Risk? The Caribbean and Global Change.' Paris: UNESCO, Management of Social Transformation (MOST), Discussion Paper No. 17.

Herrera, A. 1975. 'Los determinantes sociales de la política científica en América Latina: Política científica explícita y política científica implícita.' In J. Sábato (ed.). *El pensamiento latinoamericano en la problemática ciencia-tecnología-desarrollo-dependencia.* Buenos Aires: Paidos.

Hirschman, A. 1958. *The Strategy of Economic Development.* New Haven: Yale University Press.

Jameson, K. 1986. 'Latin American Structuralism: A Methodological Perspective.' *World Development* 14, 223–232.

Katz, J. 2000. 'Pasado y presente del comportamiento tecnológico de América Latina.' *Serie Desarrollo Productivo* 75. Santiago de Chile: CEPAL.

Katz, J. and M. Cimoli. 2001. 'Structural Reforms, Technological Gaps and Economic Development: A Latin American Perspective.' Paper, DRUID Nelson and Winter conference, Aalborg, Denmark.

Lastres, H. M. M. and J. E. Cassiolato. 2005. 'Innovation Systems and Local Productive Arrangements: New Strategies to Promote the Generation, Acquisition and Diffusion of Knowledge.' *Innovation: Management, Policy & Practice* 7/2.

Lastres, H. M. M., J. E. Cassiolato and M. L. Maciel. 2003 'Systems of Innovation for Development in the Knowledge Era.' In J. E. Cassiolato, H. M. M. Lastres and M. L. Maciel (eds). 2003. *Systems of Innovation and Development: Evidence from Brazil.* Cheltenham: Edward Elgar.

Myrdal, G. 1968. *Asian Drama. An Inquiry into the Poverty of Nations.* New York: Penguin.

Perez, C. 1983. 'Structural Change and Assimilation of New Technologies in the Economic and Social Systems.' *Futures* 15, 357–375. [3.1]

———. 1985. 'Microelectronics, Long Waves and World Structural Change: New Perspectives for Developing Countries.' *World Development* 13, 441–463. [9.1]

———. 1986. 'Las Nuevas Tecnologías: Una Visión de Conjunto.' In C. Ominami (ed.). *La Tercera Revolución Industrial: Impactos Internacionales del Actual Viraje Tecnológico.* Buenos Aires: Grupo Editor Latinoamericano, 43–90. [12.1]

———. 1988. 'The Institutional Implications of the Present Wave of Technical Change for Developing Countries.' Mimeo of a paper for the Seminar on *Technology and Long-Term Economic Growth Prospects.* Washington, D.C.: The World Bank. [19]

———. 1992. 'Cambio técnico, reestructuración competitiva y reforma institucional en los países en desarrollo.' *El Trimestre Económico* 59 (233), 23–64. [27.2]

———. 1996. 'La modernización industrial en América Latina y la herencia de la sustitución de importaciones.' *Comercio Exterior* 46, 347–363. [52]

———. 1998. 'Desafíos sociales y políticos del cambio de paradigma tecnológico.' In M. Pulido (ed.). *Venezuela: Desafíos y Propuestas.* Caracas: Editorial UCAB-SIC. [58.1]

———. 2001. 'Technological Change and Opportunities for Development as a Moving Target.' *Cepal Review* 75, 109–130. [72.2.1]

———. 2002. *Technological Revolutions and Financial Capital: The Dynamics of Bubbles and Golden Ages.* Cheltenham: Edward Elgar. [74.1]

———. 2008 'A Vision for Latin America: a Resource-Based Strategy for Technological Dynamism and Social Inclusion.' Paper, ECLAC Program in Technology Policy and Development in Latin America. [84.1.1]

Perez, C. and L. Soete. 1988. 'Catching up in Technology: Entry Barriers and Windows of Opportunity.' In G. Dosi et al. (eds). *Technical Change and Economic Theory.* London: Pinter. [23]

Pinto, A. 1976. 'Notas sobre a Distribuição da Renda e a Estratégia da Distribuição.' In *Distribuição de Renda na América Latina e Desenvolvimento.* São Paulo: Zahar.

———. 2000. 'Natureza e Implicações da Heterogeneidade Estrutural.' In *Cinqüenta anos de pensamento na CEPAL.* Rio de Janeiro: Record/CEPAL.

Porcile, G. and M. Holland. 2005. 'Brecha tecnológica y crecimiento en América Latina.' In M. Cimoli (ed.). *Heterogeneidad estructural, asimetrías tecnológicas y crecimiento en América Latina.* Santiago: CEPAL-BID.

Prebisch, R. 1949. *El Desarrollo Económico de América Latina y Algunos de sus Principales Problemas.* Santiago: CEPAL.

Reinert, E. S. and A. Daastøl. 2004. 'The Other Canon: The History of Renaissance Economics. Its Role as an Immaterial and Production-Based Canon in the History of

Economic Thought and in the History of Economic Policy.' In E. S. Reinert (ed.). *Globalization, Economic, Development and Inequality: An Alternative Perspective*. Cheltenham: Edward Elgar.

Rodríguez, O. 1981. *Teoria do subdesenvolvimento da Cepal*. Rio de Janeiro: Forense-Universitária.

———. 2001. 'Prebisch: Actualidad de sus ideas básicas.' *Revista de la CEPAL* 75, 41–52.

Sábato, J. and N. Botana. 1975. 'La ciencia y la tecnología en desarrollo futuro de América Latina.' In J. Sábato (ed.). *El pensamiento latinoamericano en la problemática ciencia-tecnología-desarrollo-dependencia*. Buenos Aires: Paidos.

Schumpeter, J. A. 1934. *Theory of Economic Development*. Cambridge: Harvard University Press.

Singer, H. et al. 1950. 'The Distribution of Gains between Investing and Borrowing Countries.' *American Economic Review* 15, 473–485.

Singer, H. et al. 1970. *The Sussex Manifesto: Science and Technology for Developing Countries during the Second Development Decade*. IDS Reprints No. 101. Brighton: Institute of Development Studies.

Chapter Five:

THE NEW TECHNO-ECONOMIC PARADIGM AND ITS IMPACT ON INDUSTRIAL STRUCTURE

Giovanni Dosi
LEM, Scuola Superiore Sant'Anna, Pisa
and
University of Manchester
Alfonso Gambardella
Bocconi University, Milan
Marco Grazzi
LEM, Scuola Superiore Sant'Anna, Pisa
Luigi Orsenigo
University of Brescia

Introduction

There is little doubt that over the last three decades, the world economy has witnessed the emergence of a cluster of new technologies – that is, a new broad techno-economic paradigm in the sense of Freeman and Perez (1988) – centred on electronic-based information and communication technologies. Such ICT technologies not only gave rise to new industries but, equally important, deeply transformed incumbent industries (and for that matter, also service activities), their organizational patterns and their drivers of competitive success.

Granted such 'revolutionary' features of the emerging ICT-based (and possibly life science-based) technologies in manufacturing and services, what has been their impact upon the vertical and horizontal boundaries of the firms? What is the evidence supporting the view according to which the new techno-economic paradigm is conducive to a progressive fading away of the

Chandlerian multidivisional corporation, which was at the centre of the previous techno-economic paradigm, in favour of more specialized, less vertically integrated structures? Is it true that large firms are generally losing their advantage in favour of smaller ones? And more generally, how robust is the evidence, if any, of a 'vanishing visible hand' (Langlois, 2003) in favour of a more market-centred organization of economic activities?

In this work we address these issues, drawing both on several pieces of circumstantial evidence and on firm-level statistical data. In fact, if the sources of competitive advantage conditional on firm size had significantly changed, this should reflect also on changes in the size distribution of firms, on their growth profiles and on the degrees of concentration of industries. These are the variables we analyze in the section on Structure and Dynamics, together with some evidence on the relationship between size and innovation, on entry and exit, and on job creation in different size classes. Since, plausibly, the mark of a hypothetical 'revolution' in the forms of economic organization should be found quite universally, when possible we try to disentangle those properties that are country- and industry-specific and others that robustly apply across national boarders and at different levels of aggregation.

In a nutshell, the evidence that we analyse does not support any notion of revolution; rather, it hints at detectable, but rather incremental changes in the size distribution in favour of smaller size classes, which might, however, have already stopped in some countries. Size distributions are, of course, a very rough indicator of underlying patterns of competitive advantage and of inter-organizational division of labour.

Building on the foregoing statistical evidence and on an evolutionary conceptual framework on size dynamics, our qualitative appreciation of the changes in the organization of industries associated with the new techno-economic paradigm suggests that it certainly has significantly influenced both firm boundaries and patterns of inter-organizational division of labour. However, there is hardly any sign of a 'third Industrial Revolution', at least if by the latter, one means a revolution in the role of the 'visible hand' of organizations (as distinct from market exchanges) and in the relative competitive advantages of size such as compared to previous phases of capitalist development.

Structure and Dynamics of Industries: Some "Stylized Facts" and Long-Term Trends

Let us begin by focusing on the invariances and changes in the structure of industries and growth processes,[1] trying to distinguish, from the very beginning, between those regularities that are common to all industrial sectors and those that reveal a high degree of sectoral or national specificities.

Size Distributions

The skewness of size distributions, over an impressively wide support, is probably the most known 'stylized facts' concerning industrial structures. Such regularity holds true independently of the unit of observation (might it be the firm or the establishment) and of the chosen proxy for size (might it be sales, value added, or number of employees). In fact, at a first approximation and at the *aggregate* manufacturing level, the distribution of firm size is well described by a Pareto distribution.[2]

The (cumulative) probability density function, of a Pareto distribution of discrete random variables is

$$Pr[s \geq s_i] = \left(\frac{s_0}{s_i}\right)^{\alpha} \tag{1}$$

where s_0 is the smallest firm size and $s_i \geq s_0$ is the size of the i-th firm, as increasingly ranked. In the following, one of the statistics that we will show is the right-cumulated function

$$F(s) = (as)^{-\alpha} \tag{2}$$

These statistics are a first way to characterize the density in populations of different size classes. Pareto law (Eq. 1) under the restriction that $\alpha = 1$, reduces to so-called Zipf law,[3] linking the log of the rank and log of the variable being analyzed

$$sr^{\beta} = A \tag{3}$$

where r is the rank and s, in our case, is a proxy for size (choosing sales, value added, or employees does not significantly affect the analysis: cf. Bottazzi et al. (2007)).

The largest firm is assigned rank 1. β and A are parameters, the former being an indicator of the degree of concentration of whatever measure in the population. Zipf plots are the other statistics that we shall use to characterize firm size distribution.

Figures 5.1 and 5.2 display the kernel estimate of the density of firm size for the world medium-large publicly quoted companies and for France and Italy.[4] The reader should not pay too much attention to the smaller-size densities that are affected by the truncation of the observations at a given threshold, in these samples of 20 employees.[5]

The evidence shows that the skewness in the distribution is very robust and quite invariant over time. Also note that skewness and the width of the support are not results of an ad hoc choice of the proxy for size (recall, for example, that Figure 5.1 is based on sales measures and Figure 5.2 on employment).[6]

Figure 5.1. (Left) Size Distribution of World's Largest Firms (in Terms of Sales). (Right) Right Cumulated Distribution. All Publicly Quoted Firms with More Than 500 Employees from the Bureau Van Dijk (2005) Databank. Observations are in Log and Normalized with the Mean

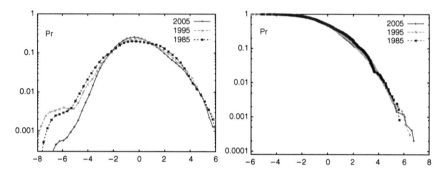

Figure 5.2. Size Distribution (Employment Measures) of Firms with More Than 20 Employees (Logscale). France (Left) and Italy (Right)

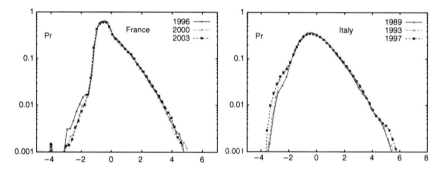

The relative stability of the (nearly) Pareto upper tail of the distribution is confirmed by the evidence on Fortune 500 data since 1955, over which we estimate both the linear and quadratic form of Eq. 3, which are, respectively

$$\log s_i = \alpha - \beta \log r_i + \varepsilon_i \tag{4}$$

and

$$\log s_i = \alpha - \gamma (\log r_i)^2 + \varepsilon_i \tag{5}$$

where $\alpha = \log A$. The estimates (see Figure 5.3 and Table 5.1) while highlighting the (rough) fit of the Zipf relation in its canonic (linear) form, also reveal that if anything has changed in the size distribution of the top firms, this has been far from dramatic: consider the coefficients β in the linear estimation.

To repeat, although the approximation of the distribution with Pareto (Zipf) ones are highly imperfect ones, as discussed at greater length in

Figure 5.3. Zipf Fit of Sales Distribution for Fortune 500 Firms, Various Years

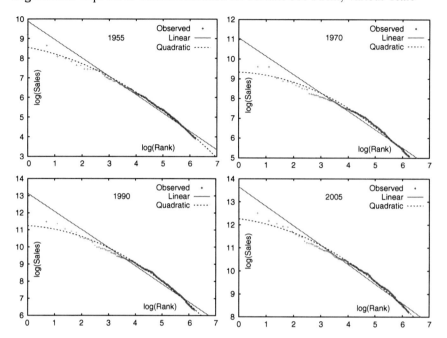

Dosi et al. (1995), the skewness property is extremely robust. Further, the coefficients of the Pareto (Zipf) estimates slightly differ across countries but the fit is quite robust at the level of broadly defined manufacturing aggregates.

Sectoral Specificities

As conjectured on the ground of an evolutionary model in Dosi et al. (1995) and empirically shown in Bottazzi et al. (2007) on Italian data, disaggregated size distributions continue to display skewness and a wide support. That is, coexistence of firms with very different sizes is the norm, but the departures from a Pareto-shape are often very wide (sometimes the distributions are even bimodal or trimodal).

The structure of each industry, in turn, is the outcome of its evolutionary history, driven by the underlying patterns of technological and organizational learning and the competitive interactions. In particular, industries differ in term of (1) intensity of innovative efforts and even more so in the modes through which they undertake them (e.g., through formal R&D, learning by doing, learning by using, etc.); (2) their revealed rates of innovation; (3) the rates of productivity growth; and (4) the patterns of inter-organizational division of

Table 5.1. **Fortune 500; Zipf Fit. Linear and Quadratic Models**

Year	Linear Mode		QuadraticModel		
	α	β	α	β	γ
1955	**9.871**	**−0.931**	**8.548**	−0.263	**−0.077**
	(0.083)	(0.015)	(0.204)	(0.089)	(0.009)
1970	**11.069**	**−0.928**	**9.342**	−0.056	**−0.100**
	(0.103)	(0.019)	(0.249)	(0.124)	(0.011)
1980	**12.506**	**−0.997**	**10.704**	−0.087	**−0.104**
	(0.106)	(0.019)	(0.499)	(0.149)	(0.010)
1990	**13.143**	**−1.059**	**11.254**	−0.105	**−0.109**
	(0.119)	(0.118)	(0.181)	(0.077)	(0.008)
2000	**13.254**	**−0.809**	**11.727**	−0.038	**−0.088**
	(0.096)	(0.017)	(0.185)	(0.078)	(0.008)
2005	**13.649**	**−0.843**	**12.264**	**−0.143**	**−0.080**
	(0.087)	(0.016)	(0.130)	(0.056)	(0.005)

5 % statistically significant coefficients are in bold; standard errors in brackets.

labour.[7] Plausibly, such differences might also entail size-biased capabilities to innovate. Together, they certainly yield different potentials to grow, conditional on the specific 'regimes' of technological learning. One of the aims of the well-known taxonomy by Keith Pavitt (1984) is precisely to capture such relations and also try to map 'industry types' (defined according to their learning modes) and firm size. To recall, Pavitt taxonomy comprises four groups of sectors, namely:

(1) 'supplier dominated' sectors, whose innovative opportunities mostly come through the acquisition of new pieces of machinery and new intermediate inputs (textile, clothing, metal products belong to this category)
(2) 'specialized suppliers', including producers of industrial machinery and equipments
(3) 'scale intensive' sectors, where in the sheer scale of production influences the ability to exploit innovative opportunities partly endogenously generated and partly stemming from science-based inputs (see below)[8]
(4) 'science-based' industries, whose innovative opportunities co-evolve, especially in the early stage of their life with advances in pure and applied sciences (microelectronics, informatics, drugs and bioengineering in particular are good examples)

Pavitt's evidence was drawing upon the characteristics of a sample of British innovators. Do different families of industries display diverse size distribution profiles also over greater samples,[9] including, of course, innovating and non-innovating firms?

Figures 5.4 and 5.5 and Table 5.2 presents Zipf estimates on Italian and French manufacturing sectors.[10]

The results do indeed vindicate the notion that technology-specific facts exert a significant influence on industry structures.[11] Consider again (in particular) the linear Zipf model (with all the foregoing *caveats* in mind) and recall that, roughly speaking, a higher absolute value of the β coefficient means a higher size advantage of the biggest firms. In fact, size advantages are relatively more important in scale intensive sectors (not surprising as such, but corroborating the soundness of the taxonomy) and in science-based ones, while they are least important in 'supplier dominated' sectors.

A first account of the Italian and French cases interestingly lends support to the hypothesis of a significant role played by the specific technological regime in shaping the industry structure of different sectors that holds across countries. This is apparent comparing the coefficients for France and Italy in Table 5.2. Estimated β belonging to the same groups are, indeed, very similar for both France and Italy.

Figure 5.4. Zipf Fit of Sectors Grouped According to Pavitt Taxonomy, Italian and French Manufacturing Industry

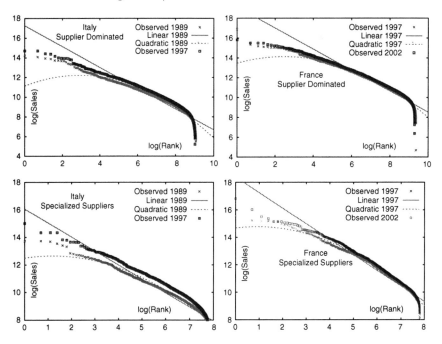

Figure 5.5. Zipf Fit of Sectors Grouped according to Pavitt Taxonomy, Italian and French Manufacturing Industry

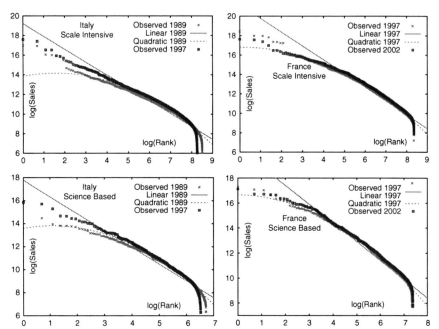

Note also that from the '80s to the '90s there is no evidence, so to speak, of a 'shrinking top'. On the contrary, even in a country like Italy, notoriously characterized by a small-firm bias, the β coefficient remains constant or slightly increases.

In fact, in order to study more generally the possible changes in industrial structures from the 'Fordist golden age' of the '50s and '60s to the current period, one would ideally require size distributions for the major OECD countries over the whole population of firms (at least above some threshold) going back over time. Unfortunately, they are not available. Hence, in order to get some further hints of the dynamics of industrial structures let us look at the dynamics of the number of firms and of employment by broad size cohort and at the degree of industrial concentration.

Number of Firms and Employment by Size Classes

Tables 5.3 and 5.4 report the distribution of the number of firms and of employment by size cohorts. The length of the footnotes to the tables, flagging differences in sources, coverage and cohort breakdown should warn the reader about making too strong inferences from such data. With that in mind, the data

Table 5.2. **Zipf Fit. Linear and Quadratic Models. Our Elaboration on Micro.1 and EAE Databank**

Sector	Year	Linear Model		Quadratic Model		
		α	β	α	β	γ
ITA – Supplier Dominated	1989	**17.263**	**−1.058**	**11.131**	**0.743**	**−0.127**
		(0.065)	(0.008)	(0.399)	(0.110)	(0.007)
ITA – Supplier Dominated	1997	**18.028**	**−1.122**	**11.264**	**0.878**	**−0.142**
		(0.074)	(0.009)	(0.447)	(0.124)	(0.008)
FRA – Supplier Dominated	1997	**19.134**	**−1.061**	**13.477**	**0.531**	**−0.108**
		(0.022)	(0.002)	(0.053)	(0.014)	(0.001)
FRA – Supplier Dominated	2002	**19.297**	**−1.064**	**13.714**	**0.524**	**−0.108**
		(0.023)	(0.003)	(0.053)	(0.014)	(0.001)
ITA – Scale Intensive	1989	**19.223**	**−1.310**	**13.833**	**0.418**	**−0.132**
		(0.080)	(0.010)	(0.499)	(0.149)	(0.010)
ITA – Scale Intensive	1997	**19.861**	**−1.370**	**14.313**	**0.479**	**−0.146**
		(0.092)	(0.012)	(0.551)	(0.170)	(0.012)
FRA – Scale Intensive	1997	**21.201**	**−1.418**	**16.807**	0.026	**−0.113**
		(0.027)	(0.003)	(0.040)	(0.012)	(0.001)
FRA – Scale Intensive	2002	**21.273**	**−1.402**	**16.234**	**0.252**	**−0.129**
		(0.030)	(0.004)	(0.039)	(0.012)	(0.001)
ITA – Specialized Suppliers	1989	**16.068**	**−1.017**	**12.505**	**0.254**	**−0.107**
		(0.081)	(0.011)	(0.271)	(0.088)	(0.007)
ITA – Specialized Suppliers	1997	**17.137**	**−1.120**	**13.048**	**0.353**	**−0.125**
		(0.095)	(0.013)	(0.364)	(0.121)	(0.009)
FRA – Specialized Suppliers	1997	**18.381**	**−1.133**	**14.673**	**0.207**	**−0.114**
		(0.033)	(0.004)	(0.045)	(0.015)	(0.001)
FRA – Specialized Suppliers	2002	**18.821**	**−1.177**	**15.376**	**0.071**	**−0.107**
		(0.031)	(0.004)	(0.042)	(0.014)	(0.001)
ITA – Science Based	1989	**17.777**	**−1.458**	**13.578**	0.428	**−0.195**
		(0.195)	(0.033)	(0.549)	(0.220)	(0.021)
ITA – Science Based	1997	**18.405**	**−1.547**	**14.745**	0.171	**−0.185**
		(0.195)	(0.035)	(0.360)	(0.151)	(0.015)
FRA – Science Based	1997	**20.406**	**−1.500**	**16.661**	−0.024	**−0.136**
		(0.046)	(0.007)	(0.059)	(0.021)	(0.002)
FRA – Science Based	2002	**20.500**	**−1.489**	**16.774**	−0.031	**−0.134**
		(0.047)	(0.007)	(0.070)	(0.026)	(0.002)
ITA – All Manufacturing	1989	**19.430**	**−1.188**	**12.683**	**0.604**	**−0.115**
		(0.047)	(0.005)	(0.393)	(0.099)	(0.006)
ITA – All Manufacturing	1997	**20.305**	**−1.267**	**12.915**	**0.732**	**−0.131**
		(0.054)	(0.006)	(0.444)	(0.114)	(0.007)
FRA – All Manufacturing	1997	**21.354**	**−1.219**	**15.788**	**0.232**	**−0.091**
		(0.015)	(0.002)	(0.040)	(0.010)	(0.001)
FRA – All Manufacturing	2007	**21.536**	**−1.222**	**15.718**	**0.299**	**−0.096**
		(0.018)	(0.002)	(0.039)	(0.010)	(0.006)

5% statistically significant coefficients are in bold; standard errors in brackets.

Table 5.3. Distribution of Firms Per Size, Percentages

Country	Year	0–9	10–19	20–49	50–99	50–250	100–499	250+	500+
	1962[a]	...	36.9[1]	34.1	13.6	...	12.8	...	2.7
	1977[a]	...	28.4[1]	38.3	14.6	...	15.1	...	3.6
	1990[a]	...	34.9[1]	37.8	13.4	...	11.5	...	2.5
France	1996[b]	82.7	7.2	6.0	2.0	...	1.8	...	0.3
	1997[b]	82.4	7.3	6.2	2.0	...	1.8	...	0.3
	2000[b]	82.1	7.3	6.4	1.9	...	1.9	...	0.4
	2001[b]	81.8	7.5	6.4	2.0	...	1.9	...	0.4
	2003[b]	82.8	7.2	6.0	...	3.2	...	0.8	...
	1967[a]	58.9[2]	...	17.9[3]	9.8	...	11.0	...	2.5
	1977[a]	56.6[2]	...	20.2[3]	10.2	...	10.3	...	2.6
	1990[a]	60.3[2]	...	17.7[3]	9.6	...	10.0	...	2.4
Germany	2000[b]	67.3	16.3	7.4	4.1	...	4.1	...	0.8
	2001[b]	64.0	18.8	7.7	4.3	...	4.3	...	0.9
	2002[b]	62.1	18.4	8.9	...	8.4	...	2.2	...
	2004[b]	59.9	21.4	8.4	...	8.2	...	2.1	...
	1968[a]	62.5[2]	...	10.3[3]	10.4	...	13.4	...	3.4
	1977[a]	54.3	15.0	13.6	6.8	...	8.1	...	2.3
	1990[a]	66.2	13.3	10.2	4.5	...	4.8	...	1.0
	1996[b]	71.5	12.1	8.8	3.4	...	3.5	...	0.7
UK	1997[b]	72.0	12.1	8.4	3.3	...	3.5	...	0.7
	2000[b]	70.7	13.4	8.3	3.6	...	3.4	...	0.6
	2001[b]	71.7	12.2	8.8	3.5	...	3.2	...	0.6
	2002[b]	71.2	12.5	9.0	...	5.9	...	1.4	...
	2003[b]	72.9	11.8	8.5	...	5.5	...	1.3	...
	1971[a]	...	48.0[1]	31.4	11.2	...	8.2	...	1.3
	1981[a]	...	57.3[1]	27.4	8.4	...	6.2	...	0.9
	1991[a]	...	59.0[1]	28.5	7.0	...	4.8	...	0.7
	1996[b]	83.7	9.5	4.8	1.1	...	0.8	...	0.1
Italy	1997[b]	83.1	9.7	5.1	1.2	...	0.8	...	0.1
	1998[b]	83.5	9.6	4.8	1.2	...	0.8	...	0.1
	1999[b]	83.5	9.6	4.8	1.1	...	0.8	...	0.1
	2000[b]	83.5	9.6	4.7	1.2	...	0.8	...	0.1
	2001[b]	83.3	9.8	4.8	1.2	...	0.8	...	0.1
	2002[b]	83.4	9.7	4.7	...	1.9	...	0.3	...
	2004[b]	82.8	10.1	4.8	...	2.0	...	0.3	...
	1967[a]	72.7	13.9	8.1	2.9	...	2.0	...	0.3
	1975[a]	76.2	12.3	7.0	2.5	...	1.7	...	0.3
Japan	1990[a]	73.7	11.9	9.4	2.9	...	2.0	...	0.3
	1999[c]	71.6	13.5	9.2	3.0	...	2.5[8]	...	0.2[9]
	2001[c]	71.6	13.5	9.2	3.0	...	2.5[8]	...	0.2[9]
	2004[c]	72.1	13.2	9.0	3.0	...	2.5[8]	...	0.2[9]
	1972[d]	88.8	5.9	4.6[5]	...	...	0.6	...	0.1
	1977[d]	89.4	5.6	4.3[5]	...	...	0.6	...	0.1
	1982[d]	80.9	10.4	7.5[5]	...	...	1.0	...	0.2
USA	1988[e]	78.8	10.9	8.7[5]	...	...	1.3	...	0.3
	1992[e]	78.9	10.8	8.6[5]	...	...	1.4	...	0.3
	1997[e]	78.8	10.7	8.8[5]	...	...	1.4	...	0.3
	1999[e]	78.5	10.8	8.9[5]	...	...	1.5	...	0.3
	2000[e]	78.2	10.9	9.1[5]	...	...	1.5	...	0.3
	2003[e]	78.6	10.8	8.9[5]	...	...	1.5	...	0.3

(a) OECD (1995).
(b) EUROSTAT (2006).
(c) Japan Statistical Bureau (2006); Only Inc.
(d) U. S. Bureau of the Census (1976, 1981, 1986).
(e) U. S. Bureau of the Census (2006); Only Inc.

(0) OECD (2006); Manufact.only.
(1) Bigger than 10 employees.
(2) The smallest cohort is 0–24.
(3) Cohort of range 25–49.
(4) Plants, rather than firms.

(5) 20–99.
(6) 100–249.
(7) 250–499.
(8) 100–999.
(9) 1000+.

Table 5.4. **Employment Share Per Size Cohort, Percentages**

Country	Year	0–9	10–19	20–49	50–99	50–250	100–499	250+	500+
	1962[a]	...	4.7[1]	10.0	8.8	...	24.5	...	51.9
	1977[a]	...	3.1[1]	9.3	7.9	...	24.4	...	55.3
	1990[a]	...	5.7[1]	13.4	10.4	...	25.7	...	44.7
France	1996[b]	13.0	6.3	13.1	8.4	...	23.5	...	35.7
	1997[b]	13.1	6.2	13.4	8.4	...	23.7	...	35.2
	2000[b]	12.2	6.2	12.9	8.5	...	24.3	...	35.9
	2001[b]	11.8	6.3	12.7	8.5	...	24.5	...	36.2
	2003	12.1	6.5	12.5	...	22.1	...	46.9	...
	1967[a]	3.9[2]	...	6.2[3]	7.5	...	25.2	...	57.2
	1977[a]	3.9[2]	...	6.9[3]	7.7	...	23.5	...	58.0
	1990[a]	4.7[2]	...	6.8[3]	7.8	...	24.1	...	56.6
Germany	2000[b]	7.2	7.1	7.5	8.8	...	25.8	...	43.6
	2001[b]	7.0	7.7	7.4	8.7	...	25.8	...	43.4
	2002[b]	6.7	6.7	7.8	...	23.7	...	55.1	...
	2004[b]	6.6	8.5	7.7	...	23.6	...	53.6	...
	1968[a]	6.8[2]	...	4.2[3]	8.0	...	31.6	...	49.5
	1977[a]	3.8	3.2	6.2	7.1	...	25.6	...	54.3
	1990[a]	5.8	4.4	9.6	9.3	...	30.0	...	40.9
UK	1996[b]	11.4	6.8	11.2	9.7	...	28.1	...	32.8
	1997[b]	9.4	7.1	10.9	9.5	...	29.5	...	33.6
	2000[b]	10.0	7.6	10.5	10.0	...	28.3	...	33.6
	2001[b]	10.1	7.2	11.7	10.4	...	28.0	...	32.6
	2002[b]	10.5	7.5	12.1	...	26.0	...	43.9	...
	2003[b]	10.9	7.4	12.0	...	25.4	...	44.3	...
	1971[a]	...	9.8[1]	14.6	11.8		24.1	...	39.7
	1981[a]	...	15.1[1]	16.2	11.6		23.8	...	33.4
	1991[a]	...	19.5[1]	20.2	11.8		22.3	...	26.2
	1995[a]	24.1	14.7	25.5[5]	...	10.0[6]	6.2[7]	...	19.4
	1996[b]	24.7	15.1	16.3	9.2	...	16.8	...	17.9
Italy	1997[b]	24.4	15.1	16.6	9.7	...	17.1	...	17.1
	1999[b]	25.3	15.1	16.6	9.5	...	17.1	...	16.4
	2000[b]	25.1	15.1	16.2	9.6	...	17.5	...	16.5
	2001[b]	25.1	15.2	16.0	9.9	...	17.4	...	16.4
	2002[b]	25.5	15.1	15.9	...	20.7	...	22.8	16.4
	2004[b]	25.5	15.3	16.1	...	21.0	...	22.1	...
	1967[a]	16.4	11.2	14.3	11.3	...	22.1	...	24.8
	1975[a]	19.1	11.3	14.1	11.1	...	21.2	...	23.1
Japan	1990[a]	17.6	10.1	17.0	12.2	...	23.1	...	20.0
	1999[c]	10.6	8.6	13.2	9.8	...	28.4[8]	...	29.5[9]
	2001[c]	10.8	8.7	13.1	9.7	...	28.3[8]	...	29.4[9]
	2004[c]	11.0	8.6	13.0	9.9	...	29.3[8]	...	28.2[9]
	1972[d]	13.4	8.6	19.3[5]	...	...	12.2	...	46.5
	1977[d]	13.2	8.4	18.5[5]	...	...	12.4	...	47.5
	1982[d]	16.5	9.5	19.8[5]	...	...	13.0	...	41.3
	1988[e]	12.6	8.3	19.2[5]	...	...	14.5	...	45.5
	1992[e]	12.3	8.0	18.4[5]	...	...	14.3	...	47.0
USA	1997[e]	11.6	7.6	18.1[5]	...	...	14.5	...	48.2
	1999[e]	11.1	7.3	17.8[5]	...	...	14.1	...	49.7
	2000[e]	10.8	7.3	17.8[5]	...	...	14.3	...	49.9
	2003[e]	11.0	7.3	17.8[5]	...	...	14.5	...	49.3

(a) OECD (1995).
(b) EUROSTAT (2006).
(c) Japan Statistical Bureau (2006); Only Inc.
(d) U. S. Bureau of the Census (1976, 1981, 1986).
(e) U. S. Bureau of the Census (2006); Only Inc.

(0) OECD (2006); Manufact. only.
(1) Bigger than 10 employees.
(2) The smallest cohort is 0–24.
(3) Cohort of range 25–49.
(4) Plants, rather than firms.

(5) 20–99.
(6) 100–249.
(7) 250–499.
(8) 100–999.
(9) 1000+.

do not seem to reveal anything reminding a revolution either with respect to the percentage distribution of firms or their employment share. At a first look, Germany, France, the US and the UK (in terms of employment share only) do appear to conform to the story of a growing hegemony of bigger firms up to the '70s with a turning point thereafter. However, in some countries like the UK, Germany and Italy, the share of employment in the bigger size cohort continue to fall since (and less so in Japan, too, with a corresponding growth in the medium-large share.)[12] Conversely, the US evidence appears to suggest a *reversal* of such a trend with a growing share in the number of big firms in manufacturing and a growing share in big-size employment in both manufacturing and overall economy.

Industrial Concentration

Next, let us consider, in turn, proxies for industrial and geographical concentration. Let us start from the former on the grounds of the Osiris databank (Bureau Van Dijk, 2005), which covers publicly quoted companies, in principle all over the world. Ideally, the measure ought to be calculated on the universe of firms in a given sector. Short of that, and given the biases associated with the lower size bound in the databank,[13] we feel safer to consider concentration in the *upper tail* of the distribution.

$$D_{20}^4(t) = \frac{C_4}{C_{20}} \qquad t = 1982, \ldots, 2005 \qquad (6)$$

where C_4 and C_{20} are the sums of the market shares of the top 4 and top 20 firms in each sector, respectively. If a sector is highly concentrated, D_{20}^4 would be near to 1, while it would be $1/5$ if all firms were identical.

Figure 5.6 displays the densities of the concentration measure over the last two decades for all three digit sectors with more than 45 observations. Interestingly, the *shapes* of the distributions change a good deal, while the *means* of the distributions vary much less. The modal value of the concentration rates falls from the mid-'80s to the mid-'90s, remaining roughly stable thereafter. At the same time the upper tail gets fatter. An increasing number of sectors displays $D_{20}^4(t)$ statistics above 0.7, meaning that the first four firms in the 'world', as defined in the Osiris dataset, in a particular sector, account for more than 70 per cent of the top 20 firms in the same sectoral data record.

Note also that the lower tail seems to be remarkably stable over the last two decades. This body of evidence, in principle, is not at all in conflict with the evidence put forward by Ghemawat and Ghadar (2006) suggesting that market globalization *has not, in general,* carried along an increasing industrial concentration (under all the ambiguities of measurement of corporate sales as distinct from the actual production, etc.). Our somewhat symmetric point is

Figure 5.6. Probability Densities of the Sectoral Concentration Index D_{20}^4 in terms of Total Sales, Different Years (Kernel Estimates). The Support of these Densities is [0.3 0.95]. World's Largest Firms Bureau Van Dijk (2005) Database

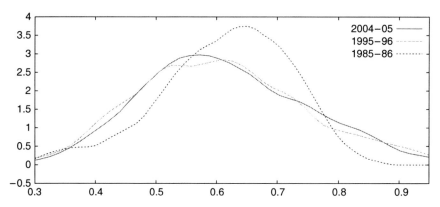

that the new techno-economic paradigm has neither brought along flattening and shrinking size distributions or a generalized fall in the measures of industrial concentration across sectors and across countries.

A quite distinct issue concerns the geographical concentration of industrial activities across countries or regions. Of course, the original legal location of any one firm is a very noisy indication for the location of the overall activities of each large firm (most likely MNCs). Still the national origin of world top-size firms is informative in its own right. Moreover, it continues to hold true that core activities such as strategic management and R&D are mostly performed in country of origin (Cantwell and Iammarino, 2001).

At this level of analysis, *first*, the evidence from the Fortune 500 upper tail of the size distribution displays a persistent dominance of US-based firms: see Table 5.5. However, *second*, the relative balance amongst big firms[14] has shifted from the '80s to the '90s in favour of non-US firms (cf. Figure 5.7). It is a decline that operated mostly in favour of Japan and to a less extent, of European firms in the last part of the twentieth century. It arrested over the latest period, statistically highlighting a European and Japanese slowdown vis-à-vis non-OECD countries, together with the emergence of newer players (e.g., Korean and Chinese oligopolists).

The Dynamics of Corporate Growth

Clearly, the observed industrial structures – including size distributions and degrees of concentration – are the outcome of the underlying processes of growth of incumbent firms, together with the processes of entry and exit.

**Table 5.5. Total Sales and Number of Firms in Fortune Global 500 (2003)
for Each Country. Sales are in Billions of U. S. Dollars**

Country	Total Sales	Number of Firms	Country	Total Sales	Number of Firms
United States	5841	189	Russia	62	3
Japan	2181	82	Brazil	61	3
Germany	1363	34	Belgium	60	3
France	1246	37	Norway	60	2
United Kingdom	1079	35	India	60	4
The Netherlands	388	12	Belgium/The Netherlands	57	1
Switzerland	382	12	Mexico	49	1
China	358	15	Venezuela	46	1
Italy	300	8	Denmark	35	2
South Korea	266	11	Luxembourg	29	1
United Kingdom/ The Netherlands	250	2	Malaysia	26	1
Canada	185	13	Singapore	15	1
Spain	162	7	Taiwan	14	1
Australia	107	7	Ireland	12	1
Sweden	96	6	Thailand	12	1
Finland	71	4			
			Total	14,873	500

Concerning the former, a common starting point in the literature, and also a handy instrument to assess if and how size influences growth, is the so-called *Gibrat's law*.[15]

Let

$$s_i(t + 1) = \alpha + \theta_i s_i(t) + \varepsilon_i(t) \tag{7}$$

where $s_i(.)$ are the log-sizes of firm i at times t and $t+1$, and α is the sector-wide (both nominal and real) component of growth.

Gibrat's law in its strong form suggests that

(a) $\theta_i = 1$ for every i
(b) $\varepsilon_i(t)$ is an independent, identically and normally distributed random variable with zero mean.

Hypothesis (a) states the 'law of proportionate effect': growth is a *multiplicative* process independent of initial conditions. In other words, there are no systematical scale effects.

Figure 5.7. Histogram of the Distribution of Sales for Biggest Firms Worldwide per Geographic Origin. Our Elaboration on Bureau Van Dijk (2005)

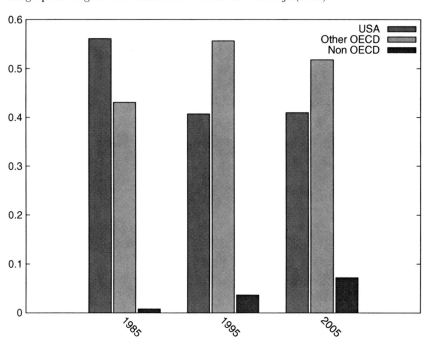

Note that were one to find $\theta_i > 1$, we ought to observe a persistent tendency toward monopoly. Conversely $\theta_i < 1$ would be evidence corroborating regression-to-the-mean, and, indirectly, witness of some underlying 'optimal size' attractor.

Overall, hypothesis (*a*), which is indeed the object of most inquiries, gets mixed support:

(1) most often, smaller firms – on average – grow faster (under the *caveat* that one generally considers small *surviving* firms).

(2) otherwise, no strikingly robust relationship appears between size and average rates of growth (see, among the others, Mansfield 1962; Hall 1987; Kumar 1985; Bottazzi et al. 2002; Bottazzi and Secchi 2003b), but the coefficient θ_i is generally quite close to one.

(3) the relationship between size and growth is modulated by the age of firms themselves, broadly speaking, with age exerting *negative* effects on growth rates, but *positive* effects on survival probabilities, at least after some post-infancy threshold (Evans, 1987b, 1987a).[16]

(4) Recent works have also highlighted a rich, non-Gaussian structure in the shocks $\varepsilon_i(t)$: cf. Bottazzi and Secchi (2006) on US firms and Bottazzi et al. (2007) on Italy; the discussion of this property would however take us too far away from the thrust of this work.

For our purposes here, let us retain the idea that corporate growth is (and has always been, as far back as our statistics go) a multiplicative process driven by factors that, on average, have little to do with size either way: that is, size does not seem, now as well as 40 years ago, either to foster or to hinder growth, at least above a certain threshold, with faster growth and higher mortality rates in the smaller cohorts.

Size, Innovativeness and Efficiency

As known, the influence of size upon innovative capabilities and/or revealed rates of innovation has long been debated in the literature, often under the misplaced heading of the so-called 'Schumpeterian hypothesis' according to which, size as such would confer an innovative advantage (for discussions, see Kamien and Schwartz,1982; Baldwin and Scott,1987; Cohen and Levin,1989; Cohen 1995; Symeonidis 1996).

The evidence, again, does not seem to support any strong relation between size and innovativeness. So, for example, Scherer (1965), well before the current technological revolution, analyses the relation between sales, R&D employment and patents over a few hundred big firms and finds an inverted U-shaped relation between sales and R&D intensities. However, on quite similar data, Soete (1979) identifies strong intersectoral differences, with several sectors displaying 'increasing returns' in the relation size-innovativeness. Yet later, Bound et al. (1984), on a larger sample, find again the inverted U, with the peak of innovativeness in the medium size cohorts. The sectoral specificities of the revealed correlation between innovativeness and size is explicitly addressed by Acs and Audretsch (1987, 1990), who find a positive correlation in 156 industrial sectors, a negative one in 122, and negligible rates of innovation – as they measure them – irrespective of size in 170 sectors. Pavitt et al. (1987) analyses innovativeness using a discrete innovation count from the Science Policy Research Unit (SPRU) database and find a U relation (not an inverted one!) with small-to-medium and very big firms displaying the highest propensity to innovate. Such a relation, however, shows strong sectoral specificities (cf. the already mentioned taxonomy in Pavitt, 1984). So, for instance, innovative firms are likely to be rather small in industrial machinery; big firms prevail in chemicals, metal working, aerospace and electrical equipment, while many 'science-based' sectors (such as electronics and pharmaceuticals) tend to display a bimodal distribution with high rates of innovation of small and very large firms.

The bottom line here, in agreement with Cohen and Levin (1989), is that the results on the relation between size and innovativeness are 'inconclusive' and 'fragile'. And, in fact, a good deal of the evidence on such relationship is further weakened, first, by endemic sample selection biases: quite often one compares the universe of medium to big firms with a biased sample of small ones, indeed, those that innovate. Second, even when one finds size-innovativeness correlations, one should be extremely careful in offering any causal interpretation. It could well be, for example, that in some circumstances, being bigger is conducive to innovation (aerospace is a good example), but the opposite direction of causation is generally at work too; a firm is big today precisely because it has been innovative in the past (for example, this is, a bit, the story of Intel).

What about the relationship between size and production efficiency as measured by inputs productivity? We discuss the issue at greater length in Dosi and Grazzi (2006) where we explore such a relation at disaggregated levels in the Italian case. Again, the data seem to suggest, roughly, either *constant returns to scale* or a mild evidence of a continuing role of *economies of scale*, plausibly associated with scale-biased forms of mechanization/automation of production.

Entry, Exit and Market Turbulence

The evidence discussed so far lends support to the existence of some powerful invariances in industrial structures (concerning, for example, size distribution and growth processes) that appear to hold throughout the current technological revolution. These persistent properties, however, should not be taken as evidence of 'business as usual', and even less of any sort of long-term equilibrium.

On the contrary, underlying the foregoing statistical regularities, one observes, indeed, the turbulent microeconomics that Metcalfe (2001) calls 'restless capitalism'. In fact, an extremely robust stylized fact that seems to apply irrespective of periods of observation of countries and sectors is the persistent turbulence in the profile of industrial evolution, due to persistent entry and exit flows and changes in the incumbents' market shares. For more details, see, among the others, Acs and Audretsch (1990), Beesley and Hamilton (1984), Baldwin (1998), Bartelsman and Doms (2000) and the comprehensive comparative analysis on the patterns of entry and exit in Bartelsman et al. (2005). Figure 5.8 and Table 5.6 offer a broad picture of the gross and net changes in employment in the US by firm size classes since the early '90's.

Note that relatively high rates of entry are pervasive phenomena even in high-capital-intensity industries (Acs and Audretsch 1989, 1991). The overwhelming majority of entrants begin with small size, with the partial exception of those 'entrants' that are actually new subsidiaries of incumbent, sometimes MNC, firms. Exit rates are quite high, too, of the same order of magnitude as entry

Figure 5.8. Net Change (Thousands) in Employment per Size Class, 3rd quarter 1992 to 1st quarter 2005, Seasonally Adjusted

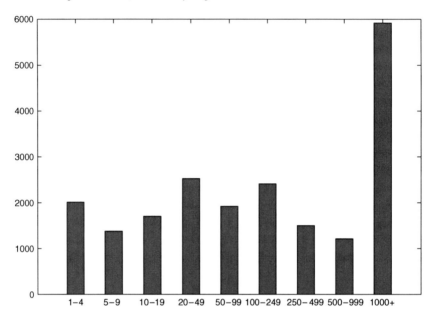

Source: *Business Employment Dynamics*, Bureau of Labor Statistics (2005).

flows. Roughly, around half of the entrants are dead after seven years in all OECD countries (Bartelsman et al. 2005). The evidence on churning ('rubbish in, rubbish out' dynamics) is quite robust and apparently uncorrelated with the appearance of a new techno-economic paradigm.

Certainly, a phenomenon that distinguishes the last three decades from the previous period is the apparent increase in the rates of entry of new firms, generally small start-ups. So, for example, *gross* entry flows in the US were around 50,000 per year in the early '50s and around 500,000 in the last decade (with a peak of 700,000 in 1988). It is hard to disentangle the drivers of such a phenomenon. Circumstantial evidence suggests that a significant share of new firms are in fact spin-offs from incumbent firms (on the characteristics of entrants, see Bhidé, 2000). Indeed, the emergence of a new technological paradigm is likely to have influenced entry dynamics. One should, however, avoid any strict identification of entry with 'innovative entrepreneurship', the latter being a small subset of the former (see also below).

Less effort has gone into the investigation of the degree of turbulence *in the oligopolistic core of individual industries.* Rather old studies (e.g., Kaplan, 1954; Collins and Preston, 1961; Mermelstein, 1969; Bond, 1975) suggest a relatively high

Table 5.6. **Average Per cent Shares**[a] **of Gross Job Gain and Gross Job Losses by Firm Size, 3rd Quarter 1992 to 1st Quarter 2005, in Thousands, Seasonally Adjusted**

Category	Firm Size Class (Number of Employees)								
	1–4	5–9	10–19	20–49	50–99	100–249	250–499	500–999	1000+
Gross job gains	14.3	11.5	11.9	14.2	9.1	9.8	5.9	4.9	18.4
Expanding firms	7.0	10.6	12.0	15.1	10.0	11.1	6.8	5.7	21.7
Opening firms	51.8	16.0	11.6	9.8	4.3	3.1	1.3	0.9	1.2
Gross job losses	14.6	11.8	12.2	14.4	9.1	9.7	5.8	4.8	17.6
Contracting firms	7.5	11.1	12.3	15.2	10.0	10.8	6.7	5.5	20.9
Closing firms	49.2	15.5	11.7	10.3	4.8	3.9	1.8	1.2	1.6
Net change	9.9	6.6	8.1	12.1	9.2	11.5	7.3	6.0	29.3

Source: *Business Employment Dynamics*, Bureau of Labor Statistics (2005).
[a] Share measures the per cent of the category represented by each firm size class.

stability in the membership and rankings within such a core itself. Broadly in the same vein, Chandler (1990) notes that 96 per cent of the top 200 firms in year 1924 were still present, albeit sometimes under different denominations, in 1958. Louçã and Mendonça (2002) use the Fortune 500 to extend the work of Chandler. They emphasize the long-term turnover of the membership of the largest-firms group, which is probably attributable to change in the dominant techno-economic paradigm. Come as it may, whatever chosen measure of 'turbulence' – including of course death rates – it appears to be much higher among small firms as compared to bigger cohorts (cf. Acs and Audretsch, 1991; Geroski and Toker, 1996).

In any case, one has to carefully distinguish the relative stability of the oligopolistic core in many industries from the dynamics in the relative size rankings of top firms over the whole economy. Anecdotal evidence goes both ways; examples that come to mind are, on the 'erosion of the oligopolistic leadership' side, General Motors or Westinghouse, and, on the 'oligopolistic emergence' side, Microsoft or Nokia. But note that the emergence of new oligopolists, like in the latter case, does not occur in incumbent sectors, but in new lines of business associated with the emergence of new technological paradigms. No doubt, more than two-thirds of the first Fortune 500 firms (year 1954) do not appear in current statistics (at least under the original name). However, it does not look to be a sign of an 'organizational revolution' specific to the currently emerging new techno-economic paradigms, but rather a long-term feature of 'restless capitalism' with its persistent emergence of new industrial activities and its changing weights among them.

A complementary angle from which to look at the organizational changes in contemporary industry is in terms of gross and net job flows conditional on firm-size classes. In the 'Fordist golden age' a good deal of employment creation occurred in medium-to-large companies. Over the last three decades the contribution of small firms to job creation seems to have increased; for much more detailed analyses on the '80s and early '90s, cf. Boeri and Cramer (1992) and Davis et al. (1996). This applies in different degrees to all OECD countries (OECD, 1994). So, for example in the period 1990–1995 new production units in the US accounted for 69 per cent of the total job creation (and 22 per cent of the total was due to new start-ups).

Interestingly, however, the bias toward small firms in employment creation seems to have become less pronounced or even reversed in the most recent years, at least in the US; bigger firms (with more than 1,000 employees) in the new century are by far the biggest net source of employment (cf. Table 5.6 and Figure 5.8). Small firms (especially start-ups) continue to be a major source of *gross* employment creation, but this is matched by impressive rates of employment *destruction*, too (cf. again Table 5.6). This is, in fact, the employment facet of the 'churning' discussed earlier in terms of entry and death of new firms. Italy – a country characterized by high rates of new firms formation – is a good case in point; new firms are born mainly in rather traditional industries and often display very low degrees of innovativeness and, as everywhere, many die young.

Note also that widespread entry is not a new phenomenon. As Chandler (1990) himself noted, large integrated firms were mostly concentrated in capital-intensive and technology-intensive industries, and in a handful of countries. Smaller firms have been the norm in labor-intensive activities in many regions of the world. Moreover, as already remarked, note that in both labor-intensive and capital-intensive industries, a good deal of entry and exit has always occurred. The novelty, if any, is the apparent relative increase in turbulence – with higher rates of both entry and exit – at the lower end of the size distribution.

Some Conclusions: The Major Stylized Facts

Let us summarize the historical patterns highlighted in this chapter:

1. A few OECD countries, especially European ones, display a decline in average firm size starting in the late 70's early 80's. Yet, the decline has not been dramatic. Large firms still play an important role in terms of output and employment. And, in fact, the importance of the largest firms seems to have increased in the US over the most recent period.
2. At the aggregate level, the size distribution of firms is still considerably skewed. In this respect, a well-established and persistent fact, which is robust

across countries, is that the overall firm size distribution is close to a Pareto one. The picture is more blurred at more disaggregate sectoral levels, but the skewness of the distribution remains a robust property.

3. The science-based industries and the scale-intensive ones, according to the classification by Pavitt (1984), exhibit a more asymmetric distribution. Circumstantial evidence confirms Pavitt's findings that science-based industries display a higher share of both very large and quite small firms.

4. The most important change compared to the earlier decades has been the notable increase in the number of new firm entries, especially in the US and partly in the UK, made of both new start-ups and on many occasions spin-offs from existing firms. The new firms account for a significant share of the increase in employment as measured by gross job flows and a positive but much lower share of net job gains.

5. Since the new entries are accompanied by corresponding high exit rates, the recent decades have exhibited an increase in industrial turbulence at least at the lower end of the size distribution.

6. Finally, while there has been a trend towards globalization, this has not implied greater oligopolistic concentration worldwide, and certainly not a greater concentration of international production in the US. However, our elaborations show that sectoral degrees of concentration have not fallen systematically either, with the mode of concentration measures falling from the '80s to the '90s (and remaining stable thereafter), but also with an increase in the number of highly concentrated sectors.

What does this evidence tells us about the possible emergence of a 'new regime' of industrial organization, possibly based on a different balance between small and big firms?

A while ago, Herbert Simon (Simon, 1991, 27–28) suggested the following thought experiment: Suppose that each intra-organizational interaction is flagged with a green colour and each market transaction with a red one. Allow some visitor from outer space to approach the earth. What will he see? Simon answer was: a lot of continents and islands with the green colour interlinked with many, thick and thin, red lines.

Has the picture changed since Simon's original answer? Our bird's-eye statistical answer is: not too much, if at all. Hence, if the question of whether there has been a 'Third Industrial Revolution' is posed in terms of overall balances between the activities that are integrated within organizations and those that occur through market interactions, the answer is largely negative. Of course, we do not know how to precisely measure the number of intra-organizational interactions. However, if we reasonably assume that the bigger a firm is, the higher the number of intra-organizational interactions it contains, then the evidence on the relative stability of size distributions offers strong support to the point.

At closer look, however, many things have changed, both as 'normal' outcomes of the processes of creative destruction/creative accumulation, and as specific features of the new techno-economic paradigm.

In the foregoing image, some continents have shrunk or even disappeared while some (old and new) islands have grown to the size of continents.

Hence, first, not too surprisingly, 'life cycle' phenomena imply that the seemingly dominant firms in 1900 (including, in the US, some associated with the distribution of Ice Bars in New England!) are almost entirely different from those one observes in say, Fortune 500 today (again cf. Louçã and Mendonça, 2002). At the same time, one observes the emergence of Intel, Microsoft (and also Boeing and Airbus, etc.) of the current world, indeed quite persistent leaders.

Second, at an even closer look, our outer-space observer will notice significant, persistent, fluctuations in the location of innovative activities among 'continents' and 'islands' of different sizes and ages.

Enough to corroborate the notion of a 'Third Industrial Revolution'? Certainly, the technological breakthroughs militate in favour of the 'revolutionary' hypothesis. However, the organization picture is rather more blurred. Within the co-evolutionary dynamics of technologies, sectors and firms, a 'revolution' can hardly be seen from the angle of the distribution of activities left respectively to the 'visible hand' of organizations and the 'invisible hand' of market interactions.

References

Acs, Z. J. and D. B. Audretsch. 1987. 'Innovation, Market Structure and Firm Size.' *Review of Economics and Statistics* 69, 567–575.

————. 1989. 'Small-Firm Entry in U. S. Manufacturing.' *Economica* 56, 255–265.

————. 1990. *Innovation and Small Firms*. Cambridge, MA: MIT Press.

————. 1991. 'R&D Firm Size and Innovative Activity.' In Z. J. Acs and D. B. Audretsch (eds). *Innovation and Technological Change: An International Comparison*. Ann Arbor: University of Michigan Press.

Antonelli, C. and P. A. David (eds). 1997. *International Journal of Industrial Organization* 15, Special Issue.

Armington, C. 1986. 'Entry and Exit of Firms: An International Comparison.' Economic Council of Canada.

Axtell, R. L. 2001. 'Zipf Distribution of US Firm Sizes.' *Science* 293, 1818–1820.

Baldwin, J. R. 1998. *The Dynamics of Industrial Competition: A North American Perspective*. Cambridge: Cambridge University Press.

Baldwin, W. L. and J. T. Scott. 1987. *Market Structure and Technological Change*. London/ New York: Harwood.

Bartelsman, E. J. and M. Doms. 2000. 'Understanding Productivity: Lessons from Longitudinal Microdata.' *Journal of Economic Literature* 38, 569–594.

Bartelsman, E. J., S. Scarpetta and F. Schivardi. 2005. 'Comparative Analysis of Firm Demographics and Survival: Micro-Level Evidence for the OECD Countries.' *Industrial and Corporate Change* 14, 365–391.

Beesley, M. E. and R. T. Hamilton. 1984. " 'Small firms" Seedbed Role and the Concept of Turbulence.' *Journal of Industrial Economics* 33, 217–232.

Bhidé, A. V. 2000. *The Origin and Evolution of New Businesses.* Oxford: Oxford University Press.

Boeri, T. and U. Cramer. 1992. 'Employment Growth, Incumbents and Entrants: Evidence from Germany.' *International Journal of Industrial Organization* 10, 545–565.

Bond, R. S. 1975. 'Mergers and Mobility among Largest Corporations, 1948–1968.' *Antitrust Bulletin* 20, 505–520.

Bottazzi, G., E. Cefis and G. Dosi. 2002. 'Corporate Growth and Industrial Structure. Some Evidence from the Italian Manufacturing Industry.' *Industrial and Corporate Change* 11, 705–723.

Bottazzi, G., E. Cefis, G. Dosi and A. Secchi. 2007. 'Invariances and Diversities in the Evolution of Italian Manufacturing Industry.' *Small Business Economics* 29, 137–159.

Bottazzi, G. and A. Secchi. 2003a. 'Properties and Sectoral Specificities in the Dynamics of U. S. Manufacturing Companies.' *Review of Industrial Organization* 23, 217–232.

_____. 2003b. 'Why Are Distributions of Firm Growth Rates Tent-Shaped?' *Economics Letters* 80, 415–420.

_____. 2006. 'Explaining the Distribution of Firms Growth Rates.' *RAND Journal of Economics* 37, 235–256.

Bound, J., C. Cummins, Z. Griliches and A. Jaffe. 1984. 'Who Does R&D and Who Patents?' In Z. Griliches (ed.). *R&D, Patents, and Productivity.* Chicago: University of Chicago Press.

Bureau of Labor Statistics. 2005. *Business Employment Dynamics.* Washington: Bureau of Labor Statistics. Available at http://www.bls.gov/bdm/

Bureau van Dijk. 2005. Osiris. Bureau Van Dijk Electronic Publishing. Available at http://www.bvdep.com

Cantwell, J. and S. Iammarino. 2001. 'EU Regions and Multinational Corporations: Change, Stability and Strengthening of Technological Comparative Advantages.' *Industrial and Corporate Change* 10, 1007–1037.

Chandler, A. D. 1990. *Scale and Scope: The Dynamics of Industrial Capitalism.* Cambridge, MA: Harvard University Press.

Cohen, W. M. 1995. 'Empirical Studies of Innovative Activity.' In P. Stoneman (ed.). *Handbook of the Economics of Innovation and Technological Change.* Oxford: Blackwell, 182–264.

Cohen, W. M. and R. C. Levin. 1989. 'Empirical Studies of Innovation and Market Structure.' In R. Schmalensee and R. D. Willig (eds). *Handbook of Industrial Organization,* vol. 2. Amsterdam: North-Holland, 1059–1107.

Collins, N. R. and L. E. Preston. 1961. 'The Size Structure of the Largest Industrial Firms, 1909–1958.' *American Economic Review* 51, 986–1011.

Davis, S. J., J. C. Haltiwanger and S. Schuh. 1996. *Job Creation and Destruction.* Cambridge, MA: MIT Press.

Dosi, G. 1988. 'Sources, Procedures, and Microeconomic Effects of Innovation.' *Journal of Economic Literature* 26, 1120–1171.

_____. 2007. 'Statistical Regularities in the Evolution of Industries: A Guide through some Evidence and Challenges for the Theory.' In F. Malerba and S. Brusoni (eds). *Perspectives on Innovation.* Cambridge: Cambridge University Press.

Dosi, G., A. Gambardella, M. Grazzi and L. Orsenigo. 2008. 'Technological Revolutions and the Evolution of Industrial Structures: Assessing the Impact of New Technologies upon the Size and Boundaries of Firms.' *Capitalism and Society* 3. Available at http://www.bepress.com/cas/vol3/iss1/art6

Dosi, G. and M. Grazzi. 2006. 'Technologies as Problem-Solving Procedures and Technologies as Input-Output Relations: Some Perspectives on the Theory of Production.' *Industrial and Corporate Change* 15, 173–202.

Dosi, G., F. Malerba and L. Orsenigo (eds). 1997. *Industrial and Corporate Change* 6, Special Issue.

Dosi, G., O. Marsili, L. Orsenigo and R. Salvatore. 1995. 'Learning, Market Selection and Evolution of Industrial Structures.' *Small Business Economics* 7, 411–436.

Dosi, G., L. Orsenigo and M. Sylos-Labini. 2005. 'Technology and the Economy.' In N. J. Smelser and R. Swedberg (eds). *The Handbook of Economic Sociology*. 2nd edn. Princeton / New York: Princeton University Press.

Eurostat. 2006. *Structural Business Statistics (Industry, Construction, Trade and Services)*. Luxembourg: Eurostat, Statistical Office of the European Communities. http://ec.europa.eu/eurostat

Evans, D. S. 1987a. 'The Relationship between Firm Growth, Size, and Age: Estimates for 100 Manufacturing Industries.' *Journal of Industrial Economics* 35, 567–581.

———. 1987b. 'Tests of Alternative Theories of Firm Growth.' *The Journal of Political Economy* 95, 657–674.

Freeman, C. and C. Perez. 1988. 'Structural Crises of Adjustment, Business Cycles and Investment Behaviour.' In G. Dosi et al. (eds). *Technical Change and Economic Theory*. London: Pinter, 38–66. [20.1]

Geroski, P. A. and M. Mazzucato. 2002. 'Learning and the Sources of Corporate Growth.' *Industrial and Corporate Change* 11, 623–644.

Geroski, P. A. and S. Toker. 1996. 'The Turnover of Market Leaders in UK Manufacturing Industry, 1979–86.' *International Journal of Industrial Organization* 14, 141–158.

Ghemawat, P. and F. Ghadar. 2006. 'Global Integration Global Concentration.' *Industrial and Corporate Change* 15, 595–623.

Hall, B. H. 1987. 'The Relationship Between Firm Size and Firm Growth in the US Manufacturing Sector.' *Journal of Industrial Economics* 35, 583–606.

Ijiri, Y. and H. A. Simon. 1977. *Skew Distributions and the Sizes of Business Firms*. Amsterdam: North-Holland.

Japan Statistical Bureau. 2006. *Establishment and Enterprise Census*. Tokyo: Statistical Bureau Japan. Available at http://www.stat.go.jp/

Kamien, M. I. and N. L. Schwartz. 1982. *Market Structure and Innovation*. Cambridge: Cambridge University Press.

Kaplan, A. D. 1954. *Big Enterprise in a Competitive System*. Washington, DC: Brookings Institution.

Kumar, M. S. 1985. 'Growth, Acquisition Activity and Firm Size: Evidence from the United Kingdom.' *Journal of Industrial Economics* 33, 327–338.

Langlois, R. N. 2003. 'The Vanishing Hand: The Changing Dynamics of Industrial Capitalism.' *Industrial and Corporate Change* 12, 351–385.

Lotti, F., E. Santarelli and M. Vivarelli. 2003. 'Does Gibrat's Law Hold among Young, Small Firms?' *Journal of Evolutionary Economics* 13, 213–235.

Louçã, F. and S. Mendonça. 2002. 'Steady Change: The 200 Largest US Manufacturing Firms throughout the 20th Century.' *Industrial and Corporate Change* 11, 817–845.

Malerba, F. and L. Orsenigo. 1995. 'Schumpeterian Patterns of Innovation.' *Cambridge Journal of Economics* 19, 47–65.

———. 1997. 'Technological Regimes and Sectoral Pattern of Innovative Activities.' *Industrial and Corporate Change* 6, 83–117.

Mansfield, E. 1962. 'Entry, Gibrat's Law, Innovation, and the Growth of Firms.' *The American Economic Review* 52, 1023–1051.

Marsili, O. 2005. 'Technology and the Size Distribution of Firms: Evidence from Dutch Manufacturing.' *Review of Industrial Organization* 27, 303–328.

Mermelstein, D. 1969. 'Large Industrial Corporations and Asset Shares.' *American Economic Review* 59, 531–541.

Metcalfe, S. J. 2001. 'Restless Capitalism: Increasing Returns and Growth in Enterprise Economies.' In A. Bartzokas (ed.). *Industrial Structure and Innovation Dynamics*. Cheltenham: Edward Elgar.

Newman, M. E. J. 2005. 'Power Laws, Pareto Distributions and Zipf's Law.' *Contemporary Physics* 46, 323–351.

OECD. 1994. *Employment Outlook*. Paris: OECD Publishing.

———. 1995. *Industrial Structure Statistics*. Paris: OECD Publishing.

———. 2006. *Structural Demographic and Business Statistics 1996–2003*. Paris: OECD Publishing.

Pavitt, K. 1984. 'Sectoral Pattern of Technical Change: Towards a Taxonomy and a Theory.' *Research Policy* 13, 343–373.

Pavitt, K., M. Robson and J. Townsend. 1987. 'The Size Distribution of Innovating Firms in the UK: 1945–1983.' *Journal of Industrial Economics* 35, 297–316.

Scherer, F. M. 1965. 'Market Structure, Opportunity, and the Output of Patented Inventions.' *American Economic Review* 55, 1097–1125.

Simon, H. A. 1991. 'Organizations and Markets.' *Journal of Economic Perspectives* 5, 25–44.

Soete, L. L. G. 1979. 'Firm Size and Inventive Activity: The Evidence Reconsidered.' *European Economic Review* 12, 319–340.

Storey, D. J. 1994. *Understanding the Small Business Sector*. London: Routledge.

Sutton, J. 1997. 'Gibrat's Legacy.' *Journal of Economic Literature* 35, 40–59.

Symeonidis, G. 1996. 'Innovation, Firm Size and Market Structure: Schumpeterian Hypotheses and Some New Themes.' *OECD Economics Department Working Papers* 161.

United States of the Census. 1976. '1972 Enterprise Statistics.' Washington: US Department of Commerce, Bureau of the Census.

———. 1981. '1977 Enterprise Statistics.' Washington, DC: US Department of Commerce, Bureau of the Census.

———. 1986. '1982 Enterprise Statistics.' Washington, DC: US Department of Commerce, Bureau of the Census.

———. 2006. 'Statistics of US Businesses.' Washington, DC: US Department of Commerce, Bureau of the Census. Available at http://www.census.gov/csd/susb/susb.htm

Chapter Six:

GOVERNANCE IN AND OF TECHNO-ECONOMIC PARADIGM SHIFTS: CONSIDERATIONS FOR AND FROM THE NANOTECHNOLOGY SURGE

Wolfgang Drechsler
Tallinn University of Technology

Task and Background[1]

The following considerations derive from Carlota Perez theory of techno-economic paradigms (TEPs).[2] They are intended to further explore the role of the state, both empirically and normatively, within the TEP model. They also propose that nanotechnology will very likely be the paradigm-leading technology for the sixth surge (see in detail Drechsler 2009); this is not necessary for the main argument but will facilitate a much more concrete and specific discussion, and hopefully will be interesting in its own right as well. In the present context, the model itself may be presumed known; for this reason, I only briefly reiterate those aspects that are specifically important for the current topic:

There have been five technological revolutions, five surges, in the last 250 years. We are now in the middle of the fifth, namely the age of information technology, knowledge and global telecommunication (Perez 2002, 10–12, 14) – in brief, ICT (information and communication technology, sometimes also referred to as just IT) – which started in 1971.

> [Next to] the new products, industries and technologies that characterize it, each technological revolution gives birth to a new set of generic all-purpose technologies and a new organizational common sense, or techno-economic paradigm, capable of modernizing all the existing economic activities. Thus, the entire economy is gradually brought to a higher productivity level (and not just the new industries). (Perez 2004b)

> Technological revolutions change the 'commonsense' criteria for engineering and business behaviour across the board. In fact, in my view, each technological revolution merits that name, not only for the importance of the new industries it ushers in and the new technical possibilities it opens, but also – and perhaps mainly – because it radically modifies the 'best practice frontier' for all sectors of the economy. (Perez 2004a, 227)

Not only the economy is transformed, however, but also state and society. This is due to the more general nature of TEPs, for they generate 'a set of best practice principles which serves as a conscious or unconscious paradigm for steering institutional change and for designing the social tools with which to master the new techno-economic potential' (Perez 2004a, 217). 'These principles can be said to conform to a techno-organizational paradigm.'[3]

And as a theory such as this is also intended to 'help see ahead to the next phase of the sequence, in order to design timely actions to make the best of the impending opportunities' (Perez 2002, 7; see 163) one is also compelled to look beyond the end of the ICT paradigm and to speculate about the sixth surge and thus, about the technology (or technology cluster) that will lead it. According to Perez, it 'has often been suggested that biotechnology, bioelectronics and nanotechnology might conform the next technological revolution.' She states that all these fields are developing; however, she purports that the 'key breakthrough' is far from even being predictable (Perez 2002, 13.) Also, it is possible – as is often said – that the sixth surge might be governed by a convergence of bio- and nanotechnology, or a larger convergence that also includes ICT (regarding convergence, see only Roco and Bainbridge 2003) – and of course, it might just as well be none of the above.

As we are in the middle of the fifth TEP, probably – since the Fall of 2008 – at the 'beginning of the end' of its turning-point, we can tentatively assume, on account of the inner structure of the TEP, that the next paradigm will make its breakthrough and begin to diffuse roughly by 2025–2035, not earlier.

Nanotechnology as a TEP

What are the reasons for assuming that it is nanotechnology that will be the paradigm-leading technology in the sixth surge, rather than biotechnology or convergence? Cons include:

1. The existence of alternatives such as the highly dynamic field of biotechnology and a placatory model of inclusive convergence, so that it is by no means certain that nanotechnology will indeed 'win the race'.

2. The fact that before the big bang, it is always uncertain which technology will lead the next paradigm – in the 1960s and 1970s, as can be seen from the classical indicators, such as contemporaneous visions of the futures and science fiction, the designated next leading technology was nuclear power, not any kind of ICT.

3. The fact that according to Arnold Gehlen's philosophy of technology – which is not the foundation for Perez theory, it is true, but which does seem to exhibit numerous parallels with it and to partially share its understanding of economy and society, and thus to provide an additional foundation to it (Gehlen 1957, 9)[4] – nanotechnology does not represent a further abstraction, a further disengagement from the human body, when compared to ICT, which means that, in effect, it would not constitute logical progress.[5]

Arguments in favour of nanotechnology as the leading one of the next TEP include:

1. The conceivability of nanotechnology as a paradigm, i.e., its potential to radically change and transform the *Lebenswelt* of mankind, not just the economy.[6]

2. The unattractiveness of the alternatives. In effect, convergence is a 'weasel word', evading the necessity to settle on one technology (and today rendering it possible to smuggle good old ICT into the new paradigm in a prominent or co-leading role, rather than as part of the infrastructure – a comfortable and comforting and thus tempting idea). Biotechnology, on the other hand, is much more limited than nanotechnology because in principle, any problem that can be solved by the former can also be handled with the latter – and a large amount of further problems on top of that (see, albeit with caution, Drexler 2007, Roco and Bainbridge 2003).[7]

3. The fact that the idea of nanotechnology as the leading technology is a realistic one, i.e., present solutions, patents, technologies, etc., make it seem possible from today's perspective.

4. Finally, nanotechnology's potential of solving the problems of the fourth surge, the paradigm of mass production – namely the problems of material and energy (which could not be solved by the fifth wave) – and also some of the problems of the fifth surge itself; for that reason, it represents logical progress.[8]

In sum, it may be said that the chances of nanotechnology indeed being the leading technology of the next TEP are fairly high, so that it at least seems sensible to focus on it and to ponder how to react to that scenario and what the consequences could be, from the perspectives of technology, economy and state and society.

NanoGov I

This insight takes us to the main question of the current considerations at last, the connection of TEPs and governance. (For a definition of governance see Drechsler 2003) What could or should governance look like in the nano-paradigm, the sixth TEP, an era that only begins in 20–30 years? To ask such a question, to even suggest an answer for it, may strike one as frivolous from many a perspective, but in light of the TEP model, the question can be discussed at least in the realm of speculation.

What are the odds of nanotechnology influencing governance at all, even if it will indeed 'take over' in a quarter of a century? According to the TEP model, the answer is that it is highly likely, for as we know, it is in the nature of the leading technology to influence and shape organization per se, general best practices and processes – this has to carefully be set apart from characteristics that are specific to the respective phases and periods. The current ICT paradigm is the best example, not only, but also with respect to the catchphrase 'e-governance'; the situation was the same in the previous paradigm of mass production.[9] Judging from the theoretical basis of TEPs, it would be impossible that there was no influence of this kind during the sixth surge.

What sort of influence could it be, though? Taking up Gehlen's argument again, we can attribute to nanotechnology a return to the physical, for what is central here is substance, material, things, everything that belongs to the 'real world', including the human body. This is precisely what ICT – and several theories from the ICT era – distanced itself from by overcoming space, privileging ideas and communication; the key word was frequently 'virtuality'.[10] The randomness of space, substance, the body and its dwelling-place, all but defining to ICT, would be revoked or even supplanted in a paradigm that centres on matter and the body.[11] This would speak for the formation of physical clustering of production as well as of life, for the necessity of gathering at specific places, and thus for matters of space and, in effect, their power, for bigger problems in the context of migration, demographic shifts, etc.[12] The relevance of a governance structure that coordinates, balances, but also conserves, in other words, that of a classical state of an Aristotelian conception (Arist. Pol.) is thus likely to grow remarkably.

Is it necessary though, to know today, or at least to think about, what governance might look like in the nano-paradigm? 'No' appears to be the proper answer here for – apart from the lack of recognizability – no precautions must or can be taken right now for this distant age; there is no impact on today.[13]

State and TEPS

But how about the role of the state in the TEP model generally? The idea of governance is an ICT approach per se, i.e., an approach significantly inspired and shaped by the ideas of networks, communication and information (see Castells 2001, Drechsler 2005); thus, it might not be a permanent 'acquisition' but rather a temporary phenomenon linked to the current paradigm. However, the following considerations are mainly concerned with govern*ment*, in other words, with the role of the state in its actual narrow sense (see Drechsler 2004, 2003), and government persists within governance and remains relevant or even grows regarding its tasks (Kattel 2004). In addition, it is always a central feature of a paradigm-leading technology that it achieves a political unity of the first, second and third sectors, i.e., classical governance, by influencing all of them in a significant way. So, the potential temporality of the phenomenon may be considered unharmful for our purposes.

These thoughts direct our considerations towards the role of the state in the gestation period of the next paradigm during the deployment period of the current one, i.e., its phases of synergy and maturity, at the end of which the preparations for the next surge and, soon after, the big bang of the new leading technology occur. How does, or should, the role of the state look like in this time?

It is highly relevant at this point to figure out which features belong to the paradigm, the period and the phase respectively. I would like to suggest that the regard in which the state and its power are held, the attitude towards the state *and thus* its power and standing – well beyond the state's engagement in the economy – and which we will call 'state closeness' (i.e., closeness to the state, *Staatsnähe*, for current lack of a better word), both on account of empirical evidence and the inner logic of the model, is indeed a matter of the period, not the paradigm. In the installation period, there is 'state distance' (*Staatsferne*) – there is general critique, indeed rejection of the state and its possibilities, which leads to a critique of the tasks of the state and their reduction, or at least an attempt thereof, while the deployment period is denoted by state closeness (see already Drechsler et al. 2006, 15–20).

As the following graph will show, I suggest that this is less so in the sense of stability, but, as was to be expected, in a dynamic form. Contrary to the surges themselves, which as Perez has noted and indeed discovered are precisely not waves or cycles (Perez 2006b), the degree of state closeness seems, by way of a hypothesis that I herewith offer, to change in a fairly genuinely wavelike trajectory that shows a sharp decline during installation, an often swift reversal with the crash (during the fall 2008 crash, the deciding time for it was one week), and a steady but weakening ascent during deployment.

Figure 6.1. Degree of State Closeness During a Surge (Perez/Drechsler)[14]

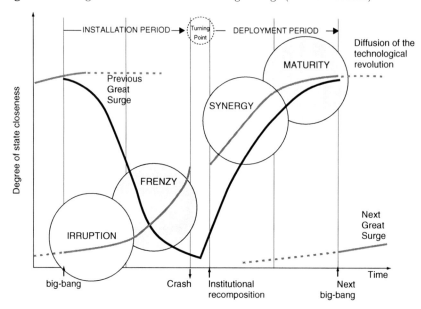

Of course, this graph is not 'scientific' in the sense of empirical validation, nor of a precise denotation of the y-axis; it only expresses a certain dynamic that can be less quantified than experienced, as is appropriate for the TEP theory – however, some further corroboration is surely required. Most certainly, the curve will look differently in different surges, as well as in different countries (the present one is altogether based on the development in the core country or countries), but the general trajectory should hold if the hypothesis were to be judged as correct or at least heuristically useful.

The active, competent, appreciated state would actually be an obstacle in the period of installation, which is characterized by focusing on the economy (and new technology), being speculative and having almost an 'anti-societal' stance and that *must* (both in the sense of 'will' and 'should') lead to a 'faulty result', while state distance is needed in the frenzy phase as well as for phasing out the old leading technology and for supporting and establishing the new one.

Yet, not only the end of the current paradigm requires the state in the sense of creative destruction management,[15] but also – and this is a key aspect for the entire considerations regarding state closeness – even especially, the implementation of the deployment period, particularly in the noneconomic realm, which for the most part is the foundation for the question of whether the synergy phase really gives rise to a 'golden' or merely a 'gilded' age (see Perez 2002, 53, 76, 167; Perez 2007).

Especially concerning the development of the new leading technology, it is the state's responsibility not only to support, but also to help shape it, because hardly anything happens 'just like that'; the market does not do so automatically. Some sort of risk socialization appears to be necessary if one does not want the new technology to pass one by.[16] Indeed, in the time when the new paradigm is being prepared, the state's specific role is to reduce the risk that the state in question misses out on progress or that its position is not sufficiently suitable for the new phase. Because of the central importance – in the context of innovation and surges – of the reorientation of the national economy towards the new leading technology, any other outcome would mean falling behind, with all its dire consequences.

NanoGov II

What does this mean for the role of the state regarding nanotechnology? If, as we have argued, the odds that it will turn into the new leading technology are high, it must not be neglected, even now. The state's task now would be to make big investments in the sector (both research and development); of course, other sectors and other technology (e.g., biotechnology) must also be kept in mind. It is relevant, though, that investments of this kind do take place, and especially in niches that the economy has shied away from (at least so far), i.e., basic research on the one hand and the range of products on the other that sound illusory and do not seem usable in any way – thus, by no means e.g., paint and varnish or medicine, areas where a crowding-out effect could be expected. What is relevant here is precisely the possibility for the state *not* to let its behaviour be governed by the urge to be lucrative, or rather, only lucrative in the long run, and subject to a high risk level.

Investments that might have a larger effect on economic growth and employment in maybe 20–30 years can only be made if the timeframe is clear and if there are no expectations of faster extensive effects (and, as an aside, if the present focus is on the current TEP, namely ICT) (Perez 2006a). On the part of the state actors, three fundamental qualities are necessary, which were neglected or even disparaged in the context of state critique and state pessimism typical of the installation period that prevailed in the last few decades:

1. A long-term strategy, which also includes long-term perspective, employment and responsibility, according to the given timeframe
2. A high level of competence among the actors, concerning both management abilities and the grasp of innovation and new technology
3. The permission to make big mistakes and bad investments, for what is important is precisely the support for developments that might turn out to be dead ends – otherwise, the state would not be needed

Thus, to be adequately prepared for a nanotechnology paradigm, a state is required that employs a long-term perspective, has enough competence at its disposal and tolerates mistakes. More precisely, it is not 'the state' that should have these distinctions but rather those state actors who are entrusted with the respective areas, i.e., the respective civil servants in charge of them.[17]

Conclusion

In sum, a push-pull effect can be detected from the perspective of the relationship between nanotechnology and governance: nanotechnology requires a well-working state to establish itself appropriately; in return, it supports state closeness by its implicit demand for state competence, a long-term focus and tolerance for mistakes. The same can be said for all paradigm-leading technologies, and therefore *in extenso* for the role of the state in the TEP model, which seems to be wave-like with the nadir in the turning point, and thus the zenith between the maturity of one and the irruption of the successive paradigm.

If this were so, it would significantly add to our understanding of why the state is evaluated differently at different times, and what the implications of this are. I also hope that these considerations have hinted at the immense framework-setting, heuristic, explanatory potential and applicability of Carlota Perez' theories in the general sphere of governance as well. Further studies along these lines – in either direction – would, surely, be most promising.

References

Castells, M. 2001. *The Internet Galaxy: Reflections on the Internet, Business, and Society*. New York: Oxford University Press.

Dolata, U. and R. Werle (eds). 2007. *Gesellschaft und die Macht der Technik: Sozioökonomischer und institutioneller Wandel durch Technisierung*. Frankfurt/Main/New York: Campus.

Drechsler, W. 1997. 'Carl Schmitt: *The Leviathan in the State Theory of Thomas Hobbes*.' *Perspectives on Political Science* 26, 125–126.

————. 2002. 'Darin Barney: *Prometheus Wired: The Hope for Democracy in the Age of Network Technology*, and Hubert L. Dreyfus: *On the Internet*.' *Philosophy in Review/Comptes Rendus Philosophiques* 22, 86–89.

————. 2003. 'Good Governance.' In [Hanno] Drechsler, Hilligen and Neumann (eds). *Gesellschaft und Staat. Lexikon der Politik*. 10th edn. München: Franz Vahlen (C. H. Beck).

————. 2004. 'Governance, Good Governance, and Government: The Case for Estonian Administrative Capacity.' *Governance and Good Governance, Trames* 8, 388–396.

————. 2005. 'eGovernment and Public Management Reform.' Plenary lecture, eGovernance Catalonia Forum '05: Public Administration in the age of the Internet.' Barcelona, 13 June. Available at http://www.gencat.net/forum-egovernance/2005/cat/ponencies.htm

———. 2009. 'NanoGov: Nanotechnologie, Innovation, Governance und Verwaltung aus der Perspektive der Techno-Ökonomischen Paradigmen.' In A. Scherzberg and J. Wendorff (eds). *Nanotechnologie: Grundlagen, Anwendungen, Risiken, Regulierung.* Berlin, New York: de Gruyter Recht, 307–325.

Drechsler, W. and R. Kattel. 2009. 'Conclusion: Towards the Neo-Weberian State? Perhaps, but Certainly Adieu, NPM!' In C. Pollitt et al. *A Distinctive European Model? The Neo-Weberian State. The NISPAcee Journal of Public Administration and Policy* 1, 2, 95–99.

Drechsler, W. et al. 2006. 'Creative Destruction Management in Central and Eastern Europe: Meeting the Challenges of the Techno-Economic Paradigm Shift.' In T. Kalvet and R. Kattel (eds). *Creative Destruction Management: Meeting the Challenges of the Techno-Economic Paradigm Shift.* Tallinn: PRAXIS Center for Policy Studies, 15–30.

Drexler, K. E. 2007. *Engines of Creation 2.0: The Coming Era of Nanotechnology.* Updated and expanded edn. WOWIO Books (www.wowio.com).

Gehlen, A. 1970 [1957]. *Die Seele im technischen Zeitalter: Sozialpsychologische Probleme in der industriellen Gesellschaft.* Hamburg: Rowohlt.

Kattel, R. 2004. 'Governance of Innovation Policy: The Case of Estonia.' *Governance and Good Governance, Trames* 8, 397–418.

Nelson, R. R. 2003. Review of Perez 2002. *Journal of Socio-Economics* 2, 467–469.

Nordmann, A., J. Schummer and A. Schwarz (eds). 2006. *Nanotechnologien im Kontext: Philosophische, ethische und gesellschaftliche Perspektiven.* Berlin: Akademischen Verlagsgesellschaft.

Perez, C. 2002. *Technological Revolutions and Financial Capital: The Dynamics of Bubbles and Golden Ages,* Cheltenham: Edward Elgar. [74.1]

———. 2004a. 'Technological Revolutions, Paradigm Shifts and Socio-Institutional Change.' In E. S. Reinert (ed.). *Globalization, Economic Development and Inequality: An Alternative Perspective.* Cheltenham: Edward Elgar, 217–242. [75.1]

———. 2004b. 'The Context for Innovation Policies and Strategies after the Financial Frenzy of the 1990s.' Keynote address, 4th European Forum for Innovative Enterprises, Stuttgart, 6 December (ppt).

———. 2006a. 'Respecialisation and the Deployment of the ICT Paradigm: An Essay on the Present Challenges of Globalization.' In R. Compañó et al. (eds). *The Future of the Information Society in Europe: Contributions to the Debate,* [Seville:] IPTS/Luxembourg: OOPEC, EUR 22353 EN, 33–66. [77.2]

———. 2006b. 'The Turning Point: An Open Stage for Socio-Political Choice.' Lecture, 40th Anniversary of the Research Policy Institute/CIRCLE, Lund University, Lund, September (ppt).

———. 2007. 'Technological Revolutions, Paradigm Shifts, and Social Goals.' The 2007 Marie Jahoda Annual Lecture, SPRU, University of Sussex, Brighton, October (ppt).

Perez, C. and C. Freeman. 1988. 'Structural Crises of Adjustment, Business Cycles and Investment Behaviour.' In G. Dosi et al. (eds). *Technical Change and Economic Theory.* London: Pinter, 38–66. [20.1]

Pollitt, C. and G. Bouckaert. 2004. *Public Management Reform: A Comparative Analysis.* 2nd edn. Oxford: Oxford University Press.

Pollitt, C. et al. 2009. *A Distinctive European Model? The Neo-Weberian State. The NISPAcee Journal of Public Administration and Policy* 1, 2.

Reinert, E. S. 1999. 'The Role of the State in Economic Growth.' *Journal of Economic Studies* 26, 268–326.

Rochet, C. 2007. *L'innovation, une affaire d'Etat: Gagnants et perdants de la IIIe révolution industrielle.* Paris: L'Harmattan.

Roco, M. C. and W. S. Bainbridge (eds). 2003. *Converging Technologies for Improving Human Performance: Nanotechnology, Biotechnology, Information Technology and the Cognitive Science.* Dordrecht: Kluwer.

Schummer, J. and D. Baird. 2006. *Nanotechnology Challenges: Implications for Philosophy, Ethics and Society.* Singapore: World Scientific.

Smith, M. R. and L. Marx. 1994. *Does Technology Drive History? The Dilemma of Technological Determinism.* Cambridge, MA: MIT Press.

Wade, R. 2003. *Governing the Market: Economic Theory and the Role of Government in East Asian Industrialization.* Reprint. Princeton, NJ: Princeton University Press.

Chapter Seven:

INNOVATION POLICY AND INCENTIVES STRUCTURE: LEARNING FROM THE MEXICAN CASE

Gabriela Dutrénit
and
Alexandre O. Vera-Cruz
Universidad Autónoma Metropolitana-Xochimilco, Mexico City

Introduction

Carlota Perez has reflected broadly about the diffusion of technological revolutions, the way in which technologies and technological capabilities determine the growth potential of countries, and the way in which the global technological context shifts windows of opportunity for the development of countries and regions. In this direction, the document titled 'A vision for Latin America: a resource-based strategy for technological dynamism and social inclusion', elaborated for CEPAL, reflects about Latin America's opportunities during the deployment stage of the Information and Communications Technology (ICT) paradigm, and the installation stage of a new paradigm, which seems to be oriented towards biotechnology, nanotechnology, new materials and new energy sources. It presents a proposal that suggests a dual development strategy for Latin American countries – 'dual integrated model' – based on science, technology and innovation (STI) for building robust resource based-processing industries and specializing on high-added-value products. Such a model integrates a top-down strategy of development, which aims at achieving competitiveness on world markets for specialized natural resources, with a bottom-up strategy, which seeks to identify and promote wealth-creation activities amongst localities.

As it has been broadly discussed in her work (Perez 1985, 2002 and 2008), each paradigm implies not only technological change but also new ways of thinking or a new common sense towards efficiency and innovation, new ways of acting and new institutions. In this sense, in order to establish a strategy that benefits from the deployment of a paradigm or takes advantage of the installation stage, it requires the emergence of new social norms and new forms of agents' behaviour. In this proposal of a dual strategy, social norms related to STI and forms of behaviour acquire a particular relevance.

Social norms are built and shift at a slow pace. They are inserted into the social systems that operate inside society, and even more, they influence the forms of behaviour from academics, entrepreneurs and other agents, and even society's perception regarding the STI community.[1] The behaviour of agents obeys to social norms, and therefore, while facing paradigm shifts and even other changes of minor depth, agents tend to reproduce old ways of doing things and observe difficulties in changing their behaviours.

Social norms are influenced by existing incentives. In this way, policy should generate a range of incentives consistent with the paradigm, in order to foster new opportunities, and stimulate change in agents' behaviour. Difficulties in generating a new coherent incentives structure could restrict the shift towards new behaviours and therefore, towards the diffusion of new technologies and the taking advantage of a new window of opportunity. This is why a reflection oriented towards taking advantage of a window of opportunity should include the issue of the incentives structure required to induce change in agents' behaviour and promote new ways of thinking and acting. There is limited knowledge regarding the influence of public policy over the shift in established social norms and the behaviour of the STI community.

The aim of this paper is to contribute to the discussion of the dual strategy based on natural resources for Latin America proposed by Carlota Perez. It focuses on the required changes of the existing incentives to promote new behaviours among STI agents according to the mentioned strategy, and on other issues related to the viability of such strategy, such as leadership and the building of consensus and governance. This reflection draws on the Mexican case.

The Mexican experience is interesting for different reasons: there are abundant natural resources, and important technological capabilities in resource-based processing industries; also it has been built capabilities in other manufacturing industries; and there has been a huge effort devoted to the formation of human resources, and recently, STI is flourishing in several regions of the country. Additionally, since 2001, a change has been introduced in the design of STI policy oriented to accelerating the building of technological capabilities and stimulating innovation. The experience of this STI policy and the problems that it has confronted allow the identification of some focuses of attention when a new strategy is being designed and implemented.

The content of this document is as follows: after this introduction, the section on natural resource-based strategy presents a brief description of Carlota Perez proposal of the dual strategy of development based on natural resources; the section on the Mexican case synthesizes efforts that have taken place in Mexico during the last decade to design and implement a new STI strategy; the section following that reflects over such experience on topics related to the structure of incentives and the behaviour of agents, the definition of leadership, the conditions to ensure the governance of the National System of Innovation (NSI) and the construction of consensus between agents; and the concluding section contains final reflections.

A Natural Resource-Based Strategy for the Development of Latin America

In the document titled 'A vision for Latin America', Carlota Perez examines actual trends in globalization and in the diffusion of the ICT revolution, and discusses Latin America's potential to enter into a new paradigm, which has begun to be installed. She proposes a dual strategy for development. This section outlines her ideas.

Carlota Perez points out that given globalization's recent evolution, Latin America faces two important challenges: The first one is competition with China and other Asian countries in global markets, and the second is the uneven distribution of income, and the high poverty levels that rule the region.

Asia is a very densely populated continent with a relatively low endowment of natural resources. It has several advantages over Latin America in the fabrication of high-volume and low-cost products, generally produced through cheap labour-intensive assembly processes. In contrast, Latin America has abundant natural resources and energy, which offers the opportunity to specialize, from these resources, in processes industries. In the face of the scarcity of raw materials in Asian countries relative to their need of growth (e.g., China and India) and the increase in international food prices (cereals, processed food, etc.), Latin America could become the supplier of raw materials, food and other agricultural goods (from the standard to the most sophisticated, custom-made products) for the rest of the world.

The ICT paradigm is in the deployment stage; the globalization process and the ICT revolution have brought with them the hypersegmentation of three key areas: markets, value chains and technologies. These processes are the bases of the proposed strategy.

The hypersegmentation of markets refers to the fact that 'the ICT revolution has led to a refined fragmentation of all markets, not only in manufacturing, but also in raw materials and services'. This is expressed in the appearance of upper layers of products in most markets, which are produced under conditions that allows associating them to the 'special', the 'unique' or the 'custom made'. From the standpoint of production, the ICT open opportunities to produce at lower scales than those allowed by mass production. This creates quasi-monopolistic conditions that would allow the steady maintenance of high prices. Carlota Perez argues that new opportunities are opened to specialize on 'premium' products directed to local and global niches, particularly based on natural resources.

The hypersegmentation of value chains refers to the fact that ICT have created optimal conditions to allow the coordination of activities of different firms integrated into global chains. This greater ease of coordination generates, as a counterpart, higher motivation of global corporations to grant autonomy and incentives to their subsidiaries to innovate, foster local advantages, achieve higher positions in the value chains and shift the export profile of countries. She asserts that this opens spaces for mutually beneficial negotiations with host governments to increase the quality of employment and of activities locally developed.

The hypersegmentation of technologies is associated with an increase of specialization in high technologies and its coexistence with traditional methods. In other words, ICT allows the coexistence of a greater diversity of technologies. This opens spaces for global corporations to focus on their core technologies and outsource with specialized suppliers the components they do not wish to produce. She argues that this unlocks many opportunities for small local firms, which supply specialized services.

As Carlota Perez (2008) argued, today, in the deployment stage of the ICT paradigm, it seems that future revolutionary industries will be a mixture of biotechnology, nanotechnology, bioelectronics, new materials and new energy sources, modelled socially by increased interest and concern about the environment. These technologies can be broadly related to process industries based on natural resources. During the actual period of installation of the new paradigm, these technologies would tend to develop in connection with some existent leading industries.

In front of the challenges and opportunities put forward by the new paradigm, as well as by the hypersegmentation processes associated with the ICT, Carlota Perez states that a window of opportunity for Latin America appears. She argues that there exists a quite clear possibility to now start a capability improvement process aimed at preparing to enter the next technological revolution by using current raw material exports as a platform and source of funding. In order to grasp this opportunity she proposes a 'dual integrated model' for Latin America, based on two strategies. The first one is to promote, from the top, competitiveness in world markets. This strategy would be oriented to the activation and strengthening of the economies' growth engines by providing the resources that make the model viable. The second is to support, from the bottom, wealth-creation activities at the local level to generate employment and reduce poverty. This dual strategy cannot be implemented only by means of the market; even though it cannot be imposed with efficacy by the government, it requires strong governmental leadership.

As with every development strategy, it demands a long-term effort. The objectives should consider the gradual migration towards products with increasing added value, with characteristics each time more specialized and custom-made for the client, and the establishment of strong innovation networks (with participation of firms and local, national, continental and international universities).

In order to accomplish all of the objectives, the strategy demands a complementary effort amongst different agents to promote some labour-intensive industries, such as construction, health and personal services. To achieve this, it is required to strengthen the knowledge and the accumulated 'know-how' of each country regarding their current export products to move technologically upstream, downstream and laterally.

Perez recognizes that this dual strategy also requires the development of a process of consensus building amongst agents aimed at the convergence of actions. According to her, the 'State or Market' dichotomy is obsolete and the results counterproductive.

The proposal is suggestive, and as such, it needs to be discussed broadly in the region. There is a set of critical issues that emerge, looking at the design and implementation of such a dual development strategy, which would allow Latin America to take advantage of the window of opportunity that emerges from the future paradigm:

- The 'dual integrated model' is a dual long-term development strategy. It requires the integration of several objectives that historically have been regarded as a trade-off: those oriented towards increasing competitiveness and those oriented towards reducing poverty. Both should be articulated from the set-up.
- It is required to reorient technological capabilities and the formation of human capital. The accumulated technological capabilities should be reoriented towards export markets of the process industries, and towards local, national and global niches. This requires an intensive learning process at three complementary levels: learning in the public sector to develop capabilities to lead the process; learning in the business sector to gradually increase its innovative capabilities; and learning, updating and adapting of the education and public research systems. The knowledge production and the formation of human capital have to be reoriented to the needs of new markets.

- As Carlota Perez points out, 'development opportunities are a moving target, and development strategies are temporary.' In this sense, there is an urge to discuss, generate agreement and reorient institutional and technological capabilities to seize them. This is why it is fundamental to generate consensus amongst agents, which implies the creation of effective policies to ensure cooperation of all the involved agents (public and private, scientists and entrepreneurs, local and national), as well as the coordination of policies and the negotiation of mutually beneficial agreements.
- In the new paradigm, key knowledge areas seem to be biotechnology, nanotechnology, bioelectronics, new materials and new energy sources. The building of capabilities in these areas requires a shift in the way of thinking and acting; behaviours characterized by cooperation, work inside networks, multidisciplinary efforts and teamwork appear to be appropriate and should be promoted.
- Even though she argues that the source for funding could come from the increase in raw materials prices, commitments of public and private funds are required.[2]

Efforts to Build a New STI Strategy: The Mexican Case

Recent experience in designing and implementing a new STI policy in Mexico may contribute to reflect on some of the challenges that the introduction of a new strategy in Latin American countries may confront.

The main efforts of STI policies directed toward the construction of STI capabilities in Mexico are connected with the creation in 1970 of CONACyT (Consejo Nacional de Ciencia y Tecnología–National Council of Science and Technology), as the agency responsible of promoting STI activities in the country. As in the case of many other similar agencies in the world, the regulatory framework assigns it two roles: policymaker and funding agency. In spite of occupying a crucial position in the NSI, in practice and since its foundation, its intermediary role between the principal (government) and the agent (STI community) has been complicated because of the weakness of the social contract regarding STI in Mexico.[3]

Such weaknesses result, on one hand from CONACyT's 'weak political position' inside the government structure, and on the other, from the historically low public investment in these activities.

Recent Changes of the STI Policy

A number of studies have documented that Mexico, similar to several Latin American countries, has exhibited weaknesses in STI policy design and implementation (FCCT 2006; Velho 2005; Chudnovsky, Niosi and Bercovich 2000; Vonortas 2002). However, the Mexican STI policy has evolved over time. The design of STI policy during the period 2000–2006 benefited from several changes on the regulatory framework and cumulative learning processes from previous experiences, as well as from the adaptation of applied instruments in other countries, particularly from the OECD and Brazil.

Amongst the most significant legal reforms we could highlight, the Law for the Foment of Scientific Research and Technological Development in 1999, the publication during the year 2002 of the Special Program of Science and technology 2001–2006 (PECYT 2001–2006) as the main document that guidelines STI policy in Mexico, and later the Science and Technology Law and the new CONACyT's Organic Law in 2002. These laws include a set of vertical and horizontal mechanisms for the coordination of policies and decisions, such as the budget inter-secretarial committee integrated by vice-ministries with scientific and technological activities, and the National Conference on Science and Technology integrated by STI organisms from state and municipal governments. In addition, during 2002 the Advisory Forum for Science and Technology (FCCT – Foro Consultivo Científico y Tecnológico) was created, associated with CONACyT's Organic Law, an organism integrated by representatives from communities of agents (associations of private industrial and agriculture sectors, and of academics, the most important universities, etc.) to propose policies, programs and budget orientation to CONACyT and hence, contribute to the generation of the required consensus for the installation of a modern institutional framework.

The Science and Technology Law of 2002 created the base for a 'State Policy' on the matter; STI received a greater priority under the assumption of an increasing investment and commitment from governmental organisms, as well as the adoption of an integrated budget for STI at federal level. In this manner, reforms from 2002 granted CONACyT greater autonomy and independence from the Ministry of Public Education, where it was previously located, as well as greater coordination powers as head of the NSI. The new CONACyT Organic Law in particular, located it under the direct command of the President of Mexico, as the head of the National Council of Scientific Research and Technological Development.

The principles that shape the new STI model include: (1) the adoption of tighter quality standards and the pursuit of pertinence amongst research and development (R&D) activities in the public research system, which is perceived as a greater orientation towards the solution of national economic and social issues, (2) the explicit intention to promote interactivity and coordination amongst NSI agents, (3) compromise towards the regionalization of country-wide STI capabilities, (4) the promotion of innovation activities, particularly in the private sector, and finally, (5) the creation of spaces for the participation of large groups of the Mexican society. (PECYT 2001–2006)

Such objectives translated into the introduction of 60 funds and programs operated by CONACyT, individually or in connection with other organisms and entities. The policy mix includes:

- 17 Sectoral Funds: Operated jointly by CONACyT and ministries or other governmental institutions, which promote the development and the consolidation of STI capabilities according to the strategic needs of each of the participating sectors (e.g., basic research, innovation, energy, agriculture, etc.); they operate as competitive funds.
- 30 Regional Funds: Operated jointly by CONACyT and state and municipal governments, which aim to develop local STI capabilities and fund projects oriented to local needs and conditions; they also operate as competitive funds.
- Institutional Funds: This category includes a wide range of instruments – from the development of human resources to strategic projects – under CONACyT's direct control. The most important has been the AVANCE program, which seeks to promote innovation amongst private firms (last mile).
- The National System of Researchers: It is one of the STI instruments with more tradition in the country. It was created in 1984 and its main objectives include the promotion of formation, development and consolidation of a critical mass of high-level researchers, mainly inside the public system. It grants pecuniary incentives (monthly compensation) and non-pecuniary (status and recognition) to researchers based on their productivity and quality of their research.
- Postgraduate Scholarships Program: This program was created in 1971 and it grants scholarships to postgraduate students in Mexico and abroad.
- R&D Fiscal Incentives: This has been the most successful instrument to promote R&D activities amongst the private sector between 2001and 2008. The Ministry of Finances has decided the granted amount, which has grown throughout the period to reach 450 million dollars.
- Direct Support to Innovation. During 2009 R&D Fiscal Incentives were substituted by direct support to R&D activities.

The Special Program for Science, Technology and Innovation (PECiTI 2007–2012), introduced by the new administration, provides continuity to the efforts to redirect STI activities. The document, with vision to the year 2030, defines the steps to follow in order to achieve gradual development and consolidation of NSI in four stages: (1) 2007–2012, strengthen STI capabilities, (2) 2013–2018, accelerate development, (3) 2019–2024, competitive consolidation, and (4) 2024–2030, NSI maturity. This program provides continuity to the strategy from the previous administration, reinforcing weak points. However, there are no significant changes in the funding commitments, which sustain the previous historical trends towards low investment levels in STI.

According to the goals established on the PECYT 2001–2006, gross expenditures in research and experimental development (GERD) in relation to GDP should reach 1.0 per cent. However, recent data obtained from CONACyT (2007) shows the persistence of a significant gap in relation to this target. Both the Federal Expenditures on Science and Technology (FES&T) and the GERD as a percentage of the GDP have leveled at below 0.5 per cent. Figures for 2007 were 3,500 and 4,000 million dollars respectively. The ministries of Public Education and Energy appear to have a greater control over the NSI, since their individual participations inside FEST are 33 per cent and 18 per cent, respectively, while CONACyT's amount represents 17 per cent (Dutrénit et al. 2008). This has weakened CONACyT's role as coordinator of the NSI.

Aside from budget deficiencies, there are certain remarkable achievements, such as the emergence of new actors and the NSI reconfiguration, the existence of STI capabilities built throughout the country, universities in every state and public research centres in several areas of technology and different states, an increase in the amount of R&D financed by the business sector (from 14.3 per cent in 1993 to 41 per cent in 2005), and successful performances in some specific areas. Actually, recent evidence shows greater technology incorporation by the business sector, with a group of firms achieving some commercial and innovative successes (FCCT 2006; Dutrénit et al. 2008). The emergence of knowledge-based regional productive clusters is also apparent. The system has proved the absorptive capacity for new public funding and the STI policy has shown capabilities to introduce changes in agent behaviour; in this sense, sectoral and regional funds have stimulated the reorientation of research groups towards the solution of sectoral and regional problems. R&D fiscal incentives have helped increase firms' R&D, and the use of competitive funds has stimulated the generation of country-wide capabilities to define demands, evaluate and manage projects.

In spite of the achievements, assessment of the Mexican NSI suggests that this system is still rather small and is mainly derived from the 'aggregation' of a number of institutions and public and private organizations operating in a poorly articulated fashion. In spite of improvements in some performance indicators, the bulk of Mexican firms observe their competitiveness to be threatened, given their poor performance in knowledge production and transfer. Similarly, firms face strong difficulties for absorbing knowledge generated by universities, public research centres, and from abroad. The dearth of linkages between knowledge producers and users hinders the articulation required to produce positive and cumulative effects. In addition, current programs in support of innovation remain weak, poorly integrated, and only in 2009 will provide direct subsidies for R&D. Likewise, there is a bias of the public funds towards large firms for which investment in these activities appears more attractive. Resources available to promote innovative capabilities among small and medium-size firms remain limited.

Challenges

In spite of accumulated improvements since 1999, STI policy faces several important challenges: (1) slowness regarding the institutional reform related to the public research system, (2) limited public investment in STI activities, (3) insufficient empowerment of CONACyT as the agent responsible for NSI governance, (4) inertias associated with the operation of policy instruments from previous administrations, which hold a large share of the STI budget, (5) a policy mix design that has not contributed to a coherent incentives structure, thus contradictory incentives allow for opportunistic behaviours, and (6) slow learning processes inside CONACyT due largely to an orientation towards implementation.

Additionally, there have been observed difficulties to building consensus, when STI resources are extremely small and the budget does not grow. There have been, of particular importance, the tensions generated between funding to science versus funding to innovation, between curiosity-driven science and problem-oriented science, and between funds managed by federal and regional governments.

According to van der Meulen (2003, 325), we could characterize CONACyT amongst the agencies that 'strongly identify with the scientific community, and monitoring is organized through the evaluation of peers denominated by the scientific community, which also request funding. In such configuration, even when the governments transfer resources, in practice scientists keep control of actions'. This has demanded great lobbying work and generation of consensus in the scientific community to change the composition of the budget, which has not been enough.

Recent reforms and the – albeit limited – transformations recorded in the NSI suggest that the current environment may be potentially more conducive to the development of STI activities. There is also a growing awareness and willingness of specific sectors of Mexican society to tap into STI activities in order to achieve some of their long-term socioeconomic development goals. There is strong evidence to suggest that agents are sensitive to the necessity of generating consensus. The Mixed Funds are the result of a concern to favour the regionalization of STI capabilities, and have allowed for learning amongst regions. Further than the observed deficiencies in its design and implementation, since 2000 the STI policy has shifted the incentives, which seek to build new social norms able to lay foundations for strategic behaviours amongst agents.

Lessons from the Mexican Case

This section draws on FCCT (2006) and Dutrénit et al. (2008). The experience of introducing new STI policy design in Mexico throughout this decade allows the extraction of a set of lessons in relation to the construction of a coherent incentives structure that stimulates shifts amongst agents' behaviour, the definition of the leadership for the strategy, the conditions to ensure governance of the NSI and the building of consensus. Such elements should enter into the discussion of any new strategy for Latin American countries.

Incentives Structure and Agents' Strategic Behaviour

The Mexican case shows that putting in practice a new STI policy strategy requires that the agents – individuals as well as organizations – that integrate the academic, entrepreneurial, and governmental sectors adopt new patterns of behaviour. In order to accomplish the emergence and reinforcement of such patterns, it is necessary to modify the incentives structure and introduce some changes into formal institutions. Both types of changes should be based on the existing legal framework, which should be reformed and operated in a consistent manner. However, a slow pace for change in the legal framework and institutions delays the emergence of new social norms in relation to STI and the new strategic behaviours required.

Features of Strategic Behaviour from Agents

The characteristics of the deployment stage of the ICT paradigm, and in the face of possibilities to seize windows of opportunity that could open during the installation stage of a new paradigm, demand changes of the agents' behaviour. The Mexican case suggests that some strategic behaviour that appears to be relevant is the following:

- The *business sector*. Assume business risks implied in R&D investment, post-R&D and innovation to accent the observed transformation in some segments that tend to link with universities and public research centres in order to generate knowledge; improve the way in which public funding is taken advantage of; and implement new strategies to develop managerial capabilities and business know-how in the case of the small and medium-size firms (e.g., elaboration of business plans, capabilities of negotiation, etc.)

- The *academic sector*. Reinforce the commitment to attend human resources and knowledge-generation demands from the business sector and society; improve research's social commitment; and keep and deepen excellence evaluation processes.
- *Public administrations at every level (federal, state, municipal)*: Increase the strategic capacity to design policy; change significantly the coordination with other agents and the global coherence of the policy mix; provide close follow-through to the implementation of policy and prevent changes that could affect the context, the rules and the policies in every required moment; design institutions and incentives in order to make more flexible public intervention according to swaps in the demands and requirements from the different agents; and at state level, to design and implement more and better instruments to foster STI according to each region. Additionally, the proposal of a dual strategy requires the mixture of top-down and bottom-up policies emanating from regions and localities, which should be compatible and interactive.
- Jointly, *the academic sector and public administrations*: Develop science education programs at the primary level, and science divulgation and other activities to increase the sensitivity of society in relation to achievements obtained by scientific and technological knowledge.
- *Every agent in the NSI*: Build strategic intelligence capabilities, comprehend its position on the system, develop cooperative strategic behaviour with other agents and seek for collective learning from experience. The success of fostering STI will largely depend on developing collaborative modes amongst agents and overcoming distrust inherited from past experience, which is particularly relevant amongst universities and public research centres.

The initial conditions to breed and induce these behaviours are diverse in agent type and country. In the Mexican case, there are observed behaviours that point out, in some cases, incipient movements, and in others, more decisive action towards strategic behaviours. These shifts have been encouraged and should be reinforced by formal institutions and the incentives structure. These gradual shifts also require an understanding of the strategy by the agents in order to continually adjust their behaviour.

Incentives Structure and Social Norms

In order for strategic behaviour features to emerge or reinforce, it is necessary to modify the incentives structure. This refers to a set of mechanisms – penalties and rewards – that shape social norms, and determine a set of accepted social norms, in this case associated to STI, over which agents' behaviour is built. Some of these norms refer to ways of funding, contracting, promoting and rewarding researchers and firms.

Social conducts are very complex, norms and behaviours that have been taught or have developed through time play an important role in the construction of a society (Laffont and Martimort 2002). In face of the design and implementation of a new strategy, it is to be expected that agents tend to replicate behaviours that they have learned as a result of a particular conception of the role of STI in society. This makes difficult the transformation of behaviours towards strategic ones, when STI policies are introduced with new objectives and instruments. However, as agents respond to incentives, their modifications may induce shifts amongst agents' behaviour. There are several types of incentives that influence the behaviour of the STI community (Puchet 2008):

1. Economic incentives associated with the policy mix and the budgetary assignation of resources.
2. Incentives that change the rules of the game relative to specific STI activities.
3. Incentives that modify general aspects of the regulatory framework.

Economic incentives related to the policy mix and budgetary assignations of resources emerge from government intervention based on financial resources, which tend to induce certain social behaviours amongst agents. There is a set of these incentives that change the behaviour of agents and hence generate permanent guidelines or behaviour (e.g., productivity-based rewards to researchers), in other words, they change premises from agents' decision making processes, and therefore become unquestionable. There are other incentives that only change opportunity costs from decisions related to the realization of an activity, but the conduct disappears if the incentive related to the activity is gone (e.g., scholarships). It is necessary to modify the incentives structure, particularly those incentives that contribute to building new premises for action.

It is necessary to stimulate strategic behaviours for the design and implementation of a new strategy. The Mexican experience suggests that in the case of rewards for researchers, based on productivity (so popular today in Mexico and other Latin American countries), it would be convenient to migrate towards the constitution of specific stimulus systems that distinguish several types of activity – scientific research, technological development, high-level human resource formation – with more precise orientation and less generic evaluations. These stimuli should be incorporated in the lines of action defined for the new strategy.

In the case of incentives for universities and public research centres, private firms and state-owned firms, the foment funds could be reoriented towards programs in several stages and aspects of technological development, as the adaptation, diffusion and transfer of technologies, privileging the assignation of resources towards projects of collaboration and cooperation amongst agents from the academic and productive sectors, and amongst agents of different regions. In the case of incentives for firms that perform R&D and innovation, it could be appropriate to emphasize the support of small and medium-size firms and processing industries.

The incentives that shift the rules relative to specific STI activities, and those that modify general aspects of the regulatory framework, are normative; they materialize in the introduction of specific norms, which tend to change the rules to which NSI agents are subject. The vast majority of such norms emanate from legal ordinances different from the STI ones, and do not articulate coherently with those incentives associated with the policy mix. They include aspects related to intellectual property, governance, evaluation of universities and public research centres, the creation of technology-based firms with the participation of researchers, as well as other normative incentives that emerge from a more general environment, and influence not only STI agents, but also those that participate in a wider range of economic activities. Included in these sets are: capital markets regulation relative to portfolio investment and the introduction of risk capital instruments into the stock exchange; labour markets regulatory framework relative to employment stability and qualification of labour; norms that rule the aperture of firms; fiscal operation and the deduction of investment expenditures; regulations related to the use of ICT; and the criteria for public purchases (Puchet 2008).

The economic and normative incentives configure the incentives structure and regulatory framework for STI, which in turn condition agents' behaviour and contribute to the generation of strategic behaviours. The analysis of the integration and the consequences of these normative frameworks over the mentioned behaviours appear to be a crucial task for the implementation of a successful strategy.

Leadership, Governance and the Generation of Consensus

The Mexican case shows a set of difficulties that emerge for the coordination between local/regional and federal levels, different ministries, academy and private sectors, and even within CONACyT between different directions. It was quite difficult to build the required consensus to support the process of change. Efforts to introduce modifications in the incentives structure to generate certain agents' strategic behaviours should have been accompanied by changes in formal institutions and forms of governance.

It seemed particularly important to define more clearly the required features of the regulatory framework, introduce a coherent set of legal reforms and generate consensus about the composition of the organisms in charge of the orientation, approval and implementation of the strategy.

The distinction between legal regulations and formal institutions is pertinent here. The regulatory framework around the NSI is seen as a structured set of rules and norms. Some components of this set emerge from pieces of laws, presidential decrees, regulations and other legal principles of secondary importance. These shape formal institutions as a subset of rules that is used and practiced by agents and organizations. In practice, such a subsystem is formed in an independent manner in relation to those written regulations of different kinds – legal, by decree, regulations, etc. To the formal institutions thus conceived, one should incorporate routines, habits, codes of conduct for both agents and organizations that shape the subsystem of informal institutions, referred to above as social norms.

In the Mexican case, the legal reforms from 1999 were a step forward, but are still insufficient to provide the formal institutions that could facilitate the new strategy. Even today, the regulatory framework remains insufficient and fragmented and interferes with NSI's consolidation and development.

A lesson learned from this experience is that it would be useful to distinguish between different roles of leadership. On one side, the representatives of NSI's main agents should be included as part of the *decision-takers*, and on the other, the *policymakers* should have the specialized function of designing and implementing the strategy. This distinction has a double purpose: (1) to improve the forms of harmonization between representatives of the main agents and government officials, and (2) to separate two different arenas, the political-strategic agreements and the design and operation of the policies.

Three relevant lessons learned from the Mexican case are the following:

1. *On the regulatory framework.* An appropriate regulatory framework is required to facilitate the coordination between the regulations set specifically to govern STI activities and the regulations to other activities that somehow overlap (or even comprise) those related to STI, to improve the government organisms, and to facilitate the coordination mechanisms between agents to agree around the strategy's objectives and lines of action and to interact.

2. *On the leader team.* The process of change should be led by a team integrated by the main decision-takers in STI from the government (ministries with the highest investment in STI), the main universities, the states or cities with larger expenditures in STI, and large private and public-owned firms with large R&D centres. They can have the political and financial capacity to encourage a process of change. This composition of the leader team would empower the strategic decisions with the required autonomy from short-term policies or measures decided by the Executive. At the same time, the involvement of the main agents in the decision about the strategic objectives

of the strategy would generate better conditions to induce changes in the agents' behaviour towards strategic ones. The leader team would take the long-term decisions.
3. *On the STI agency role*. The STI agency can play the role of policymaker of the strategy; experts in design and implementation of STI policies should be called for this role. This team would take the short-term decisions and would be responsible for the implementation and operation side of the strategy. The STI agency, as CONACyT in the Mexican case, should take the strategic coordination of NSI, which overcome the usual role of a funding agency.

As the installation period of the new paradigm could be short, conditions for rapid learning from the agents are essential. In this sense, the decision-takers should be convinced about the opportunity for such strategy and, as highlighted by Perez (2008), understand 'that development opportunities are a moving target, and that development strategies are temporary and must be updated and reshaped accordingly'. In parallel, policymakers should develop and continuously improve certain skills, such as: interpreting trends; designing an appropriate policy mix, with the flexibility to redesign it as the strategy evolves; understanding the variety of firms, sectors and technologies, and their productive and technological chains, and therefore be able to intervene in the weak points in each moment; and inducing changes within the incentives structure to stimulate new social norms and then to foster the strategic behaviours required in each stage. All these entail a good system of indicators, monitoring and evaluation.

Firms and academy should also develop a learning capacity to adapt to the moving targets. Firms should react promptly to the new policy instruments and academy should develop the capability of response to new demands generated by the new instruments.

As asserted by Carlota Perez in her document, such a strategy requires the generation of consensus between agents, both for the design and start-up as for its sustainability over time. But, such a consensus demands that each agent has a clear idea of what it could win and lose, and of his commitments. The strategy should promote the participation of all the stakeholders through forums, seminars and other activities to take into account their opinions on the results in each strategy stage. The idea of generating a participative society could be called for again. The generation of consensus should be the main feature in the decision making process, which requires an evolution toward efficient and horizontal forms of NSI governance. In this respect, different levels of coordination are essential: academic sector, business sector and government; national/federal and regional/local policies; private and public sector; objectives of both branches of the strategy; and STI policies amongst other policy arenas.

Even though the generation of consensus and the emergence of new forms of governance are a difficult task and can be seen as a key challenge, what is clear is that only long-term policies based on consensus and the agents' commitments can reach cumulative effects and generate the necessary changes in agents' behaviours.

Another challenge refers to the dual feature of the proposed strategy and the need for combining the objectives of the top-down strategy with those related to the bottom-up one. In this sense, the challenge is to be able to articulate an integrative vision of all the national potentialities and demands.

Resources and Viability of the Strategy

The recent Mexican experience also illustrates that a successful change of incentives to induce modification in the agents' behaviour should go hand in hand with a substantial increase in the STI budget. Changes in the composition of an invariable budget affect agents' interests, and generate tensions that militate against the process of change. Thus, to avoid confrontation in the initial period, it would be better to keep the traditional resources allocation and reorient the additional resources to the new targets of the strategy.

In this context, a successful strategy requires a commitment from the government to increase the budget for STI. Certainly, the private sector should assign concurrent funds; however, it is hard to believe that most of the additional resources could come from the private sector, at least during the initial stage.

If additional public funds are imperative in the initial stage, the Ministry of Finance is called on to be involved in this process from the very beginning. It should be involved not only to ensure the increase of public resources and the reorientation of these resources as the strategy evolves along different stages, but also to support the required institutional reforms of NSI. In other words, the Ministry of Finance should be involved in the governance of NSI. In the Mexican experience, the lobbying with the Ministry of Finance was not successful in convincing it about the future increase of public income associated with an investment in the designed strategy.

Final Reflections

Latin American governments have not believed that STI can stimulate economic growth and solve its problems of unemployment and poverty. There is no clear social contract for STI, and the investment in STI has been extremely reduced over time. In the last decade, agents have observed gradual changes towards the strategic behaviours described above. This suggests the emergence of the minimum conditions to rethink the role that STI and knowledge can play in satisfying social needs and creating welfare. However, it seems that governments lack clarity about the appropriate strategies and the required consensus.

The dual development strategy based on both STI for building robust resource-based processing industries and attending the employment generation in the localities proposed by Carlota Perez is very suggestive. First, because it looks at Latin America's endowments, and second, because it positions these endowments as potentialities to the new technological paradigm.

However, the design and implementation of this strategy requires breaking inertias and acquiring a long-term vision, generating consensus between the main agents, and taking risks by the local and national governments. This strategy should be supported in the formulation of a long-term public policy, where coordination and governance mechanisms acquire relevance to allow the participation of society. This policy should be designed and implemented with the participation of all the agents – academy, business sector and governments at national, federal and local levels. Its implementation has to be independent of the different administrations in order to give certainty to STI's development.

This new strategy requires additional public resources. The increase in the budget would be the way to reorient fresh resources to new targets while avoiding tensions that could emerge when the same budget is allocated in a different way.

A flexible incentives structure has to be built and it has to evolve according to the moving targets to avoid opportunist behaviours that can come out when contradictory incentives coexist. A slow rhythm of change of the general framework conditions delays the emergence of new social norms in relation to STI and of the strategic behaviours required for the success of the strategy.

Leadership, consensus and commitments seem to be key features to initiate and sustain a process of change led by a dual strategy of development for Latin America. If the main agents are involved in the decision making process, it is more likely that they are going to fulfil the required commitments. Long-term policies based on leadership, consensus and commitments of the main agents can breed cumulative effects and generate changes in agents' behaviours, which give feedback to this process and produce endogenous dynamics.

Thus, the emergence and evolution of such a strategy depend on the initial commitments, the joint efforts of the main agents and the building of a cooperative dynamic between them. Four aspects seem to be extremely important for the success of this process:

1. An explicit agreement between all the agents about the objectives and lines of actions of the dual strategy
2. An agreement between the main agents and the government about the composition and role that the leader team of the strategy can play

3. A commitment of the Executive, jointly with the Ministry of Finance, to assign additional resources to the STI budget and to allow the reorientation of these resources according to the stages of the strategy
4. An agreement with the Congress to approve the budget suggested by the Executive

Gradually over time, the progress of the strategy will generate a reduction of the need for additional public resources, as innovation is endogenized and catalytic attributes of the STI policy emerge (Teubal 1997; Avnimelech and Teubal 2008). In addition, an increase in tax collection is expected, associated with the increase of the economic activity. All this will reduce the pressure on the public resources, changing the composition of the STI budget on the private sector.

References

Antonelli, C. 2005. 'Models of Knowledge and Systems of Governance.' *Journal of Institutional Economics* 1, 51–73.

Avnimelech, G. and M. Teubal. 2008. 'From Direct Support of Business Sector R&D/Innovation to Targeting Venture Capital/Private Equity: A Catching-Up Innovation and Technology Policy Life Cycle Perspective.' *Economics of Innovation and New Technology* 17, 153–172.

Braun, D. 1993. 'Who Governs Intermediary Agencies? Principal-Agent Relations in Research Policy-Making.' *Journal of Public Policy* 13, 135–162.

Casas, R. 2005. 'Exchange and Knowledge Flows between Large Firms and Research Institutions.' *Innovation: Management, Policy and Practice* 7, 188–199.

Chudnovsky, D., J. Niosi and N. Bercovich. 2000. 'Sistemas nacionales de innovación, procesos de aprendizaje y política tecnológica: una comparación de Canadá y Argentina.' *Desarrollo Económico* 40, 158, 213–252.

CONACyT. 2002. Programa Especial de Ciencia y Tecnología (PECYT), 2001–2006. Mexico: CONACyT.

———. 2007. Programa Especial de Ciencia, Tecnología e Innovación (PECYT), 2007–2012. Mexico: CONACyT.

Dutrénit, G., F. Santiago and A. O. Vera-Cruz. 2006. 'Influencia de la política de ciencia, tecnología e innovación, sobre los incentivos y comportamiento de los agentes: Lecciones del caso mexicano.' *Economía, Teoría y Práctica* 24, 93–118.

Dutrénit, G. et al. 2007. 'Coevolution of Science and Technology and Innovation: A Three Stage Model of Policies Based on the Mexican Case.' In S. E. Cozzens and E. Berger Harari (eds). *Atlanta Conference on Science, Technology, and Innovation Policy*, Piscataway, NJ: IEEE.

———. 2008. *The Mexican National System of Innovation: Structures, Policies, Performance and Challenges*. Background Report to the OECD Country Review of Mexico's National System of Innovation. Technical Report. Mexico: CONACYT.

FCCT. 2006. *Diagnóstico de la política científica, tecnológica y de fomento a la innovación en México (2000–2006)*. Mexico: Foro Consultivo Científico y Tecnológico.

Katz, J. 2000. *Reformas Estructurales, Productividad y Conducta Tecnológica en América Latina*. Santiago de Chile: CEPAL/Fondo de Cultura Económica.

Katz, J. and G. Stumpo. 2001. 'Regímenes sectoriales, productividad y competitividad internacional.' *Revista de la CEPAL* 75, 137–159.

Laffont, J. J. and D. Martimort. 2002. *The Theory of Incentives: The Principal-Agent Model.* Princeton, NJ: Princeton University Press.

Larédo, P. and P. Mustar (eds). 2001. *Research and Innovation Policies in the New Global Economy.* Cheltenham: Edward Elgar.

Morris, N. 2003. 'Academic Researchers as "Agents" of Science Policy.' *Science and Public Policy* 30, 359–370.

Murmann, J. P. 2003. 'The Coevolution of Industries and Academic Disciplines.' Northwestern University, Kellogg School of Management, Working paper WP03–1.

Nelson, R. 1995. 'Coevolution of Industry Structure, Technology and Supporting Institutions, and the Making of Comparative Advantage.' *International Journal of the Economics of Business* 2, 171–184.

Perez, C. 1985. 'Microelectronics, Long Waves and World Structural Change: New Perspectives for Developing Countries.' *World Development* 13, 441–463. [9.1]

———. 1996. 'La modernización industrial en América Latina y la herencia de la sustitución de importaciones.' *Comercio Exterior* 46, 347–363. [52]

———. 2001. 'El cambio tecnológico y las oportunidades de desarrollo como blanco móvil.' *Revista de la CEPAL* 75, 115–136. [72.1.1]

———. 2002. *Technological Revolutions and Financial Capital: The Dynamics of Bubbles and Golden Ages.* Cheltenham: Edward Elgar. [74.1]

———. 2008. 'A Vision for Latin America: A Resource-Based Strategy for Technological Dynamism and Social Inclusion.' Paper prepared under contract with the ECLAC Program on Technology Policy and Development in Latin America, CEPAL, Santiago de Chile. [84.1.1]

Puchet Anyul, M. 2008. 'Incentivos, mecanismos e instituciones económicas presupuestas en el ordenamiento legal mexicano vigente para la ciencia y la tecnología.' In G. Valenti (ed.). *Ciencia, tecnología e innovación: Hacia una agenda de política pública.* Mexico: FLACSO, 169–190.

Puchet Anyul, M. and P. Ruiz. 2008. 'Aspectos económico institucionales del marco regulatorio mexicano del sistema nacional de innovación.' *Revista REDES,* forthcoming.

Sanz-Menéndez, L. et al. 2007. Evaluación de la política de I+D e innovación de México (2001–2006), Informe final del Panel Internacional Independiente. México: CONACyT/ADIAT.

Smits, R. and S. Kuhlmann. 2004. 'The Rise of Systemic Instruments in Innovation Policy.' *International Journal of Foresight and Innovation Policy* 1, 4–32.

Teubal, M. 1997. 'A Catalytic and Evolutionary Approach to Horizontal Technological Policies.' *Research Policy* 25, 1161–1188.

———. 2002. 'What Is the Systems of Innovation (SI) Perspective to Innovation and Technology Policy (ITP) and how Can We Apply It to Developing and Industrialized Economies?' *Journal of Evolutionary Economics* 12, 233–257.

van der Meulen, B. 2003. 'New Roles and Strategies of a Research Council: Intermediation of the Principal-Agent relationship.' *Science and Public Policy* 30, 323–336.

Velho, L. 2005. 'S&T Institutions in Latin America and the Caribbean: An Overview.' *Science and Public Policy* 32, 95–108.

Volberda, H. W. and A. Y. Lewin. 2003. 'Coevolutionary Dynamics within and between Firms: From Evolution to Coevolution.' *Journal of Management Studies* 8, 2111–2136.

Vonortas, N. S. 2002. 'Building Competitive Firms: Technology Policy Initiatives in Latin America.' *Technology in Society* 24, 433–459.

Chapter Eight:

SCHUMPETER'S BUSINESS CYCLES AND TECHNO-ECONOMIC PARADIGMS

Christopher Freeman
SPRU, University of Sussex

It seems probable that Schumpeter thought of 'Business Cycles', at least before publication, as his *magnum opus*. It was, of course, immediately recognized, at least in the United States, as a major contribution to business cycle theory and economic theory more generally, and was accorded a major review article by Kuznets (1940) in the *American Economic Review*. Yet, half a century later it cannot be said that *Business Cycles* occupies a place in the history of economic thought comparable to the major works of Marx, Keynes or Ricardo, or even other works of Schumpeter himself.

The ambitious scope of the book is evident from the full title: *Business Cycles: A Theoretical, Historical and Statistical Analysis of the Capitalist Process* and its two volumes, comprising more than a thousand pages, bear further witness to the magnitude of the enterprise. Schumpeter always regarded business cycles not as a sideline or a speciality, but as a major manifestation of his theory of economic development and growth in capitalist economies. Already in the *Theory of Economic Development* he included a chapter on business cycles that foreshadowed his later work. Moreover, although he greatly admired Marx's intellectual achievement and gave him credit for being one of the first theorists to recognize cycles and address these problems, he nevertheless chided Marx (Schumpeter 1943, 36–39) for supposedly failing to develop any systematic theoretical explanation of crises and for holding an eclectic view embracing many possible causes. There is little doubt therefore that Schumpeter thought of *Business Cycles as* one of his most important contributions to economics, if not *the* most important.

Schumpeter remains the rogue elephant amongst twentieth century economists and although he has commanded the respect of the profession, he certainly has not won their allegiance.

Whereas some elements of his theory have earned a place at the centre of economic debate, such as his ideas on concentration, or on technological competition, it would still be difficult to make this claim for his business cycle theory.

This may of course simply be due to the myopic attitudes of much of the profession and to the continuing neglect of structural change. Even the central point of his whole life work: that capitalism can only be understood as an evolutionary process of continuous innovation and 'creative destruction' is still not taken into the bosom of mainstream theory, although many now pay lip service to it.

It will be argued in this paper that, although Schumpeter certainly faced lack of receptivity for most of his major ideas, there were also some weaknesses in the book itself that have contributed to its relative lack of success. It is not just a question of style, although *Business Cycles* was not a well written book. The history of economic thought has conclusively shown that it is possible to write even longer and more indigestible books than *Business Cycles*, which are nevertheless influential both inside and outside the profession.

Nor is it just a question of statistics. The debate on the statistical evidence for long cycles is likely to continue indefinitely. Despite the best efforts of economic historians the evidence for the first and second Kondratieff cycles is bound to remain weak and controversial and relates in any case mainly to one country – Britain. Schumpeter already anticipated and answered that type of critic such as Weinstock (1964) or Solomou (1987), who maintained that aggregative statistical time series did not consistently demonstrate the existence of long cycles. Louçã (1997) made a devastating critique of the purely econometric 'refutations' of long cycle theory and documented how uneasy Schumpeter was about the trend of econometric analysis in the Society that he helped to establish.

Schumpeter pointed out that his theory was concerned with the *qualitative* changes in the structure of the economy and that aggregative long time series could often obscure rather than reveal these changes:

> Since the development generated by the economic system is 'cyclical' by nature, the task to be accomplished goes far beyond the description of spectacular breakdowns on the one hand, and of the behaviour of aggregate quantities on the other, into the formidable one of describing in detail the industrial processes behind them. Historians of crises primarily talk about stock exchange events, banking, price level, failures, unemployment, total production and so on – all of which are readily

recognised as surface phenomena or as compounds which sum up underlying processes in such a way as to hide their real features. (1939, 221)

In my view, Schumpeter cannot be faulted for this approach and for concentrating attention on this underlying explanation of the spring tides and ebb tides of economic development. There *have been* periods of deep structural adjustment in the 1830s, 1880s, 1930s and 1980s, which were regarded at the time and by historians since, as unusually difficult times for the economy. These periods cannot be treated in just the same way as the minor recessions of the 1950s and the 1960s or similar recessions in other periods of high boom, such as the 1850s and 1860s or the 1890s to 1913. Nor can the sense of these long boom periods as 'belles époques' or golden ages of growth ('*les trente glorieuses*') be dismissed as collective self-deception because the untidy, uneven and imperfect measures of aggregate growth that we have do not always conform to the ideal requirements of some statisticians.

The criticisms of Schumpeter's *Business Cycles* that follow therefore do not refer to this 'statistical' critique, nor to matters of style or presentation but to the fundamental concepts, i.e. to his theory of equilibrium, his theory of innovation and entrepreneurship and his theory of technology.

Schumpeter, Walras and Keynes

One of the problems that Schumpeter faced was the ascendancy of Keynesian ideas in the 1930s and 1940s and their greater policy relevance. Many people have puzzled over the apparent inconsistency between various statements of Schumpeter about equilibrium. On the one hand, he said that the system never was and never could be in equilibrium and stressed the inherently disequilibrating effects of the stream of innovations characteristic of capitalism. On the other hand, he consistently praised Walras for his theory of general equilibrium and insisted not only that this was the greatest achievement of economic theory, but that it was close to reality. Precisely in Volume I of *Business Cycles* he insists that:

Common sense tells us that the mechanism for establishing or re-establishing equilibrium is not a figment devised as an exercise in the pure logic of economics but is actually operative in the reality around us. (1939, 47)

Some critics have attempted to resolve this apparent inconsistency by arguing that he used the model of static general equilibrium simply as an expositional device to *contrast* with his own dynamic model, and to make this more intelligible to the reader. But, as the quotation above suggests, this cannot be reconciled with the fact that Schumpeter constantly emphasized the importance of equilibrium throughout his life from the first chapter of *Theory of Economic Development* (and his earlier book on economic doctrine and method) to his final work *History of Economic Analysis.* Shionoya (1986) is therefore right to insist that Schumpeter's admiration for Walras was no mere formal acknowledgement or passing phase, but was an integral part of his entire theory.

Both in *Theory of Economic Development* and in *Business Cycles* Schumpeter represents *boom* as a departure from equilibrium and recession as a return to equilibrium in largely Walrasian terms. In *Business Cycles* he also represents *depression* as a departure from equilibrium and the revival from depression as a return to equilibrium. He said of long cycles: 'The phenomenon becomes understandable only if we start with the neighbourhood of equilibrium preceding prosperity and end up with the neighbourhood of equilibrium following revival.' (1939, 156)

Whilst in *Business Cycles* Schumpeter regarded depression as an 'unnecessary' and pathological departure from equilibrium (1939, 150–155) that could be aggravated by scares or panics and whose depth could not be predicted, he nevertheless continued to stress the 'natural' equilibrating tendencies of the system. Moreover, he believed that these equilibrating tendencies were inherent in the behaviour of the economy. Paradoxically, therefore, he had greater faith in the resilience of the economy than Keynes and devoted very little attention either to the role of institutions or to the role of technology in achieving a more stable dynamic equilibrium.

In the 1930s, Schumpeter took up the position of the detached academic partly because he did not think that there was very much that should be done about the depression, or indeed could be done. Keynes took up the position of the scourge of 'laissez-faire' theories because he thought that there was a great deal that could and should be done to counteract depressive forces in the British and in the world economy.

Already long before the publication of his own *General Theory* in 1936 in a BBC broadcast he was quite explicit (quoted in Eatwell, 1982):

On the one side are those who believe that the existing economic system is, in the long run, a self-adjusting mechanism, though with creaks and groans and jerks and interrupted by the time lags, outside interference and mistakes ... on the other side of the gulf are those who reject the idea that the existing economic system is, in any significant sense, self-adjusting ... I range myself with the heretics.

As is well known, Schumpeter wrote a highly critical, even vitriolic review of the *General Theory*. Paradoxically, despite his own reputation as a heretic, he was in some respects closer to the 'self-adjusting' school, although he believed that the equilibrating mechanism operated through cycles of varying length. However, lack of immediate political applications would not in itself have prevented Schumpeter's theory of business cycles from becoming more influential, if the central ideas had proved themselves in the long term.

Schumpeter's Theory of Innovation and Entrepreneurship

It might seem strange to criticize Schumpeter's concept of innovation and entrepreneurship that was after all his most distinctive contribution to economics generally and not just to the theory of business cycles. There is no serious disagreement on my part with his insistence that innovation incessantly revolutionizes the economic structure and that 'this process of creative destruction' is an essential fact about capitalism (1943, 83).

What is at issue is not this part of his vision, which does indeed give him a unique position among 20th Century economists. The problem lies rather in the abstract generalizations about innovation and diffusion that predominate in the basic theory of *Business Cycles*, although much less so in the historical sections. This abstract 'pure theory' of innovation is closely related to his theory of entrepreneurship since an entrepreneur is defined as the individual responsible for an innovation. Both his theory of innovation and of entrepreneurship were carried over directly from the *Theory of Economic Development*.

In some ways Schumpeter's definition of innovation was a wide one. He included not only technical innovations, but organizational and managerial innovations, new markets, new sources of supply, financial innovations and 'new combinations'. There are passages in *Business Cycles* where he appears to accept the introduction of a new product into another country or another region as 'innovation' (1939, 374) rather than 'imitation', although elsewhere he is dismissive of 'imitators' as mere routine managers rather than genuine entrepreneurs.

But despite the breadth of his definition and the occasional extension of the concept to some aspects of diffusion his conceptualization of innovation was in other ways very limited. He scarcely discussed the origins of innovation, had virtually nothing to say about the interactions of science and technology and largely neglected the cumulative nature of technology, despite his earlier recognition in 1928 of the role of industrial R&D departments in large corporations. He substituted a theory of entrepreneurship both for a theory of the firm and for a theory of innovation. It is almost as though his vision of innovation and entrepreneurship was frozen at the level of the first formulation in *Theory of Economic Development* in 1912. Shionoya (1986) was justified in describing this formulation as failing to explain what circumstances determine innovation and in commenting that 'innovation remained an exogenous factor to the economic system despite his contrary assertion.' Ruttan (1959) put the matter more bluntly when he said:

> Neither in *Business Cycles* nor in Schumpeter's other work is there anything that can be identified as a theory of innovation. The business cycle in Schumpeter's system is a direct consequence of the appearance of clusters of innovations. But no real explanation is provided as to why innovations appear in clusters or why the clusters possess the particular types of periodicity which Schumpeter identified ...

Tsuru (1993) makes the interesting point that for Schumpeter it was this business cycle theory that determined his theory of capitalism itself, since profit was defined as arising only from entrepreneurship that disturbed equilibrium. For Marx it was the other way about: his theory of business cycles was derived from his theory of the instability and conflicts of interest engendered by capitalist relationships.

Instead of discussing the circumstances that may encourage or hinder innovations, and why they cluster together, Schumpeter simply insists that they are the product of super-normal individuals with exceptional intelligence and energy. Innovation is described as 'an act of will' rather than of intellect. Whilst there is certainly an element of truth in Schumpeter's perception of the exceptional difficulties facing many innovators and the exceptional persistence that is often needed to see them through, this conceptualization is lacking in depth and, surprisingly, in historical perspective. Moreover, it leads to relative neglect of some of the elements that are actually essential for a satisfactory theory of the business cycle itself: the interdependence of many innovations both technologically and economically and the existence of technological trajectories. It also leads to a relative neglect of incremental innovations, which are less obviously the product of 'heroic' entrepreneurship but whose cumulative effect is nevertheless extraordinarily important. Finally, it fails to focus attention on the specific features of each new wave of technical change, which is supposedly the driving force of each long cycle of economic development.

These are harsh comments but it was these weaknesses that made it possible for Kuznets (1940) and others to make two basic criticisms of Schumpeter's *Business Cycles* to which he had no adequate response.

1. Which innovations were so big in their scale that they could possibly drive long cycles of the entire world economy? There are tens of thousands of

inventions and innovations every year. Surely some theory of the clustering of innovations would be necessary to relate innovations to major waves of investment and long cycles of development?

2. Why should a long cycle last about half a century? If it is entrepreneurial energy that drives the whole system, then Kuznets asked ironically, did the heroic entrepreneurs get tired every 50 years?

The answer to the first criticism is actually *implicit* in much that Schumpeter wrote in *Business Cycles* and *Capitalism, Socialism and Democracy* and in some passages, it is explicit as for example, in the following:

> When some innovation has been successfully carried into effect, the next wave is much more likely to start in the same or a neighbouring field than anywhere else. Major innovations hardly ever emerge in their final form or cover in one throw the whole field that will ultimately be their own. The railroadization, the electrification, the motorization of the world are instances. (1939, 167)

But although in this and other passages, there is the embryo of a full-fledged theory of the long-term diffusion of interdependent clusters of technical and organizational innovations, elsewhere the approach is far more discursive and resembles a listing of various scattered innovations, rather than a more systematic account of constellations of technologically, economically and socially interrelated innovations connected by cumulative advances in science and technology and knowledge accumulation in specific types of firm and leading sectors.

In *Business Cycles*, Schumpeter does use the expression 'industrial revolution' both to describe the first Kondratieff wave in eighteenth Century Britain and to characterize the changes in the third Kondratieff cycle, but he does not develop the concept systematically in either case.

This failure may be attributed partly to the fact that he was actually far more interested in the financial side of business cycles than in the technology. Only about a hundred out of a thousand pages in the book deal mainly with inventions and innovations. But this was not the main problem. More important was his preoccupation with the *individual* entrepreneur and the individual innovation and his reluctance to conceptualize invention, innovation and technology accumulation as a social process. This is related to his theory of diffusion with its sharp distinction between true entrepreneurs and routine managers and imitators.

Schumpeter's threefold distinction between invention, innovation and diffusion of innovations has been widely adopted by economists and there is no doubt that it has been analytically valuable. At least conceptually, it *is* essential to distinguish between the original *idea* for a new product or process (which may often be patented) and the translation of this idea into a commercially realizable innovation. The capacity of an enterprise to design, develop, produce and market a *new* product is *not* identical with inventive activities, and nor do the two activities necessarily coexist in the same organization. Schumpeter's insistence on this point was a major contribution to the understanding of innovation, even though there is an important overlap and interaction between inventive and innovative activities, and the very process of design, development, production and marketing may often give rise to further inventions.

Similarly, in the case of the distinction between innovation and diffusion of innovations, there *is* a difference between the very first commercial introduction of a new product or process and the subsequent process of diffusion (or 'swarming', as Schumpeter so aptly named it). But again, this distinction can be overdone. Economists who have studied diffusion processes in depth (e.g., Rosenberg, 1976) have emphasized very strongly that the product or process that is diffusing through an adopter population, at the end of the diffusion often bears little resemblance to the one that started the whole process.

Schumpeter was certainly aware of this point. He emphasized himself that 'the motorcar would never have acquired its present importance and become so potent a reformer of life if it had remained what it was thirty years ago and if it had failed to shape the environmental conditions – roads among them – for its own further development' (1939, 167).

Nevertheless, as so often in his work, there was a coexistence of two apparently contradictory elements. On the one hand, there was an insistence on looking at technical journals and company histories to understand the real process of technical change, and a real appreciation of many features of technical innovation. But on the other hand, this existed side by side with a theory of entrepreneurship that is largely ahistorical.

If we look at the history of science, technology, invention, innovation and diffusion of innovations, then we find, of course, recognition of the contribution of outstanding individuals in all parts of the system. But we also usually find recognition of innumerable minor contributions and of the role of institutions in the accumulation, dissemination and application of new knowledge.

At one end of the spectrum are some historians who put the main emphasis on outstanding individuals, and at the other end of the spectrum are those who stress the innumerable, sometimes anonymous contributions of a wide variety of scientists, technologists, engineers, workers, managers and users. Examples of the latter are theories of 'learning by doing' and 'learning by using', Gilfillan's (1935) theory of invention as proposed in his book on *Sociology of Invention* and Hessen's (1931) theory of scientific discovery. Examples of the former are the study of the 'sources of invention' by Jewkes et al. (1958) and Schumpeter's own theory of entrepreneurship.

In both these cases, there is of course some recognition that 'pygmies' as well as 'giants' play some part in the process and some recognition that social institutions, such as research laboratories, design departments, universities and firms may facilitate the activities of inventors and innovators.

Schumpeter did recognize (1939, 346) that the function of entrepreneurship could be performed within public institutions and he also recognized that it could be split between a number of individuals (1939, 327). Jewkes also recognized that some important inventions did emerge from the R&D laboratories of large firms and that it was sometimes hard to ascribe them to any single individual or even to several. Schumpeter went further and maintained that large oligopolistic or even monopolistic firms would have a competitive advantage in research and innovation. It may therefore seem strange to classify him with the 'heroic' individualist school. His position was contradictory, since he also maintained that the bureaucratization of innovation would lead to the death of entrepreneurship and of capitalism itself.

Despite the later developments in his theory in the 1920s and 1930s (Schumpeter's 'Mark II'), his basic theory of entrepreneurship was scarcely modified in *Business Cycles* compared with the *Theory of Economic Development*. He failed to develop the notion that the *function* of entrepreneurship could be exercised differently in different types of firms and with different types of innovation in each successive industrial revolution. He had a theory of entrepreneurship without a theory of the firm. This prevented him from recognizing the full significance of the 'partnership' form of company organization in the first Kondratieff wave (the original 'industrial revolution') as well as later changes in company structure, culminating in the 'networking' organizations of today.

Numerous empirical studies of innovation have confirmed Schumpeter's recognition of the importance of the entrepreneurial *function* in taking an invention to the market. They have confirmed his view that an entrepreneur is not the same as a capitalist. But they have also shown that the way in which the function of entrepreneurship is performed varies across different types of firms, different countries, different technologies and different historical periods.

Characteristically they also show multiple sources of information inputs from within and from outside the innovating organization and the importance of the 'national systems of innovation' – the supporting network of scientific and technical institutions, the infrastructure and the social environment. These things are surprisingly lacking in Schumpeter's theory of innovative entrepreneurship.

Thus, although his theory went beyond the mainstream theory of the firm as a rational profit-maximising agency, operating with perfect information and foresight in any country, any culture and any period of history, it suffered to some degree from the same tendency to postulate from pure logic a single universal essence for entrepreneurship.

This was important for his theory of 'business cycles', because it meant that he made little or no attempt to examine the changing pattern of international technological leadership and related patterns of entrepreneurship or the influence of innovation on patterns of international trade. Thus, the disequilibrating effects of international technological competition were largely unexplored in *Business Cycles* as were the issues of underdevelopment and international trade.

A New Theory of Innovation and Long Cycles

It would be impossible in this paper to do justice to the enormous range of empirical and theoretical work on innovation, diffusion, entrepreneurship, and their relationship to business cycles, which has been carried out since Schumpeter's death. Much of it was inspired directly or indirectly by Schumpeter's own work, and this is the best tribute to his achievement. It is possible here only to select and condense from a few contributions, some of the results that seem most relevant to this discussion and to indicate some elements of a new theory.

One of the difficulties that Schumpeter confronted was precisely the lack of empirical and theoretical studies in his field of investigation. Rogers (1962) and Rosenberg (1976) have pointed out that there were scarcely any studies of diffusion of innovations in industry before the 1960s. There were also very few case studies of innovation that took into account technological, economic and entrepreneurial aspects. The history of technology was a relatively neglected area, even by comparison with the history of science. Today, the situation is undoubtedly much improved, although this improvement relates mainly to the period since the Second World War rather than to the long-term historical studies. Nevertheless, it is now possible to make tentative generalizations about some aspects of innovation, diffusion and entrepreneurship with a little more confidence than was possible in Schumpeter's time. The task of economic theory has been to develop a theory of the firm that does not assume as its foundation either hyperrationality of individual entrepreneurs or groups, nor supernormal intelligence and energy (Dosi and Orsenigo 1988). This research programme is sometimes described as 'neo-Schumpeterian'.

Technical innovation emerges from this research not only as a disequilibrating, uncertain, disturbing element, but also quite often as an element of continuity, with rather well-defined trajectories, and sometimes offering rather clear-cut investment opportunities for future development of new products, processes, systems and markets. It remains true that in other circumstances, described so vividly by Schumpeter, technical innovations and their diffusion can be a severe shock to the system. This means, however, that it is not necessary to found a theory of business cycles on the supposed dichotomy between the destabilizing effects of innovation and the supposed equilibrating effects of 'normal' economic behaviour in absorbing these shocks in recession and recovery periods. Rather, is it important to identify in what circumstances *technical innovation itself* may stimulate and restore business confidence, and in what circumstances the reverse may occur (Freeman and Perez 1988).

This analysis cannot be restricted to the level of the individual innovation or to counting of numbers of innovations; the qualitative aspects and the systems inter-relatedness of innovations must be taken into account. Furthermore, it must recognize that it is *diffusion* of innovations that underlies waves of investment, not the first attempts. Under favourable conditions, the Schumpeterian bandwagons roll and business confidence improves, leading to an atmosphere of 'boom' in which, although there are still risks and uncertainties attached to all investment decisions, animal spirits rise. Such favourable conditions include complementarities between equipment, materials and component innovations and the emergence of an appropriate infrastructure, as well as some degree of political stability and institutions that promote, or at least do not hinder too much, the diffusion of new technologies. In these favourable circumstances, the growth of new markets and the profitability of new investments appear to offer a fairly stable prospect of future growth, despite the uncertainties, which are always present.

But there are also circumstances when technical change can initially have the opposite effect and can destabilize investment by undermining confidence in the future prospects for the growth of some firms, industries or economies. Moreover, as technologies and industries mature over a long period, diminishing returns and declining profitability may set in, leading to sluggish investment behaviour. If this is at all widespread, it may take major social and political changes to restore confidence in the future growth of the system on the basis of new technologies. The 'natural' equilibrating tendencies of the economy are not sufficient, as they involve a complex process of institutional and structural change, now commonly described as 'structural adjustment'.

On several of these problems, Carlota Perez (1983, 1985, 1986, 2002, 2004) has made an important contribution to formulating a new and more plausible theory of the relationship between innovation and long cycles of development. In particular, she has provided a convincing answer to Ruttan's point about clusters of innovations and Kuznets' original criticisms of *Business Cycles*, by suggesting the notion of a pervasive change in technology underlying each of Schumpeter's 'successive industrial revolutions'. As we have seen, Schumpeter himself hinted at such a concept, but failed to provide any empirical or theoretical foundation for his idea. A number of authors, such as Keirstead (1948) with his 'constellations' of innovations or Freeman, Clark and Soete (1982) with their 'new technology systems' or Dosi (1982) with his 'technological paradigms', have demonstrated both a technological and an economic basis for the clustering of innovations. But Perez went beyond these formulations in several important respects. Her concept is that of a 'meta-paradigm' change affecting all or almost all branches of the economy, directly or indirectly.

She uses the expression 'techno-economic' rather than 'technological paradigm' (Dosi 1982) because the changes involved go beyond engineering trajectories for specific product or process technologies and affect the conditions of production and distribution throughout the system, and because the glue that links the innovations together is not merely technology. Her concept corresponds more to Nelson and Winter's concept of 'general natural trajectories' and once established as the dominant influence on engineers, designers and managers, becomes a 'technological regime' or common sense best practice for several decades and across the whole economy. From this it is evident that she views Schumpeter's successive industrial revolutions as providing a succession of 'techno-economic paradigms'.

A new techno-economic paradigm develops initially within the old, already showing its decisive advantages during the 'downswing' phase of the previous Kondratieff cycle. However, it becomes established as a dominant technological regime only after a period of great turbulence (a crisis of structural adjustment) involving deep social and institutional changes, as well as the replacement of the motive branches of the economy by new leading sectors. This point is an important one, as several theories have suggested that Kondratieff upswings were based on a cluster of innovations introduced immediately before the upswing (Mensch 1975). Schumpeter, on the other hand, pointed several times to the long gestation period for the diffusion of key innovations and to the fact that they were sometimes made long before the upswing in which they became predominant, as in the case of railways (1939, 254–255) or the related case of steam engines (von Tunzelmann 1978), which became the predominant technological regime only in the second and not the first Kondratieff cycle.

As has already been made clear, Perez' conception of a 'techno-economic paradigm' is much wider than 'clusters' of innovations or even of 'technology systems'. She is referring to a combination of interrelated product and process, technical, organizational and managerial innovations, opening up an unusually wide range of new investment and profit opportunities. Such a paradigm change implies a unique new combination of decisive technical *and* economic advantages.

The organizing principle of each successive paradigm and the justification for the expression 'techno-economic paradigm' is to be found not only in a new range of products and systems, but most of all in the dynamics of the relative *cost* structure of all possible inputs to production. In each techno-economic paradigm, a particular input or set of inputs, which may be described as the 'key factors' or 'core inputs' of that paradigm, fulfil the following conditions:

1. Clearly perceived low and rapidly falling relative cost. As Rosenberg (1976) and other economists have pointed out, small changes in the relative input cost structure have little or no effect on the behaviour of engineers, designers and researchers. Only major and persistent changes have the power to transform the decision rules and 'common sense' procedures for engineers and managers (Perez 1985; Freeman and Soete 1987).
2. Apparently, almost unlimited availability of supply over long periods. Temporary shortages may, of course, occur in a period of rapid build-up in demand for the new key factor, but the prospect must be clear that there are no major barriers to an enormous long-term increase in supply. This is an essential condition for the confidence to take major investment decisions that depend on this long-term availability.
3. Clear potential for the use or incorporation of the new key factor or factors in many products and processes throughout the economic system; either directly or (more commonly) through a set of related innovations, which both reduce the cost and change the quality of capital equipment, labour inputs and other inputs to the system.

Perez maintains that this combination of characteristics holds today for microelectronics and few would deny this. It held until recently for oil, which underlay the post-war boom (the 'fourth Kondratieff' upswing). Before that, she suggests that the role of key factor was played by cotton in the first, by coal and iron in the second and by low cost steel in the third Kondratieff (Tables 8.1–8.4 illustrate the trends during the corresponding periods).

Again, Schumpeter already commented on the enormous range of innovations in machinery and metal products that were facilitated by the universal availability of cheap steel in *Business Cycles*:

[Bessemer's] real genius, but of the typically entrepreneurial kind, was in the vision of the vast possibilities for *cheap* steel … The revolution which it wrought … extended to practically all parts of the economic organism … the increase in the efficiency of steam-driven machinery and of tools in general which it induced: better plates, rails, and structural material, and so on were only a part … Armstrong's hydraulic machinery—elevators, drawbridges, cranes, pumps … maritime armament…Ordnance, rifles,

Table 8.1. Key Factors: Price Behaviour
Coal Prices in Britain by Region – 1800–1850
(Shillings per ton)

Year	London	Birmingham	Manchester
1800	48	9	16
1810	36	12	13 (1813)
1820	31	13	10 (1823)
1830	26	6 (1832)	10 (1833)
1840	22	8	7 (1841)
1850	21	5	6

Source: von Tunzelmann 1978.

Table 8.2. Key Factors: Price Behaviour
Price of Steel Rails in the US – 1870–1930
($ per ton)

Year	Steel Rails	Consumer Price Index
1870	107	38
1875	69	33
1880	68	29
1885	29	27
1890	32	27
1893	28	27
1895	24	25
1898	18	25
1910	28	28
1920	54	60
1930	43	50

Source: US Historical Statistics.

small arms, and munitions ... Woodworking, textile, grain-milling machinery ... tin-canning and refrigeration, hence food preservation, the sewing machine... self-acting screw machinery ... the bicycle ... and a thousand other things that gave the reins to steam were partly or wholly the effect of steel... in part conditioned by the steel innovations. Several quite new departures—the dynamo, for instance, or the internal combustion engine ... the increase in exactness and standardization, and in the use of interchangeable parts... greatly improved quality and facilitated mass production at rapidly falling costs. (1939, 372–375)

**Table 8.3. Key Factors: Price and Volume
Crude Oil 'Real' Price Per Barrel**

(1991 = Base Year; Price 1991 = $ 18.1)	
1860	30
1870	34
1880	10
1900	12
1910	7
1920	10
1940	8
1960	7
1970	3

World Crude Oil Production

(Billion of Barrels)	
1939	2.1
1950	3.8
1960	7.7
1973	20.4
1991	22.6

Source: Cambridge Energy Research Associates quoted in '*The Prize*', Yergin (1991).

Every one of the inputs identified as 'key factors' existed (and was in use) long before the new paradigm developed. However, its full potential was only recognized and made capable of fulfilling the four conditions above when the previous key factors and their related constellation of technologies gave strong signals of diminishing returns and of approaching limits to their potential for further increasing productivity or for new profitable investment. This point complements Schumpeter's analysis in terms of the erosion of profitability through the swarming process.

Perez argues that from a purely technical point of view, the explosive surge of interrelated innovations involved in a technological revolution, could probably have occurred even earlier and in a more gradual manner (2002, 27–32). But there are strong economic and social factors at play that serve as prolonged containment first and as unleashing forces later. The massive externalities created to favour the diffusion and generalization of the prevailing paradigm act as a powerful deterrent to change for a prolonged period. Paul David (1985) demonstrated some of the ways in which the economy may become 'locked in' to a particular technology and Brian Arthur (1988) has provided convincing evidence of the strength of these

**Table 8.4. Key Factors: Volume, Price and Potential
Estimates of Increase in ICT Capacity and Decreasing Cost**

Area of Change	(1) Late 1940s Early 1970s	(2) Early 1970s- Mid 1990s	(3) Mid 1990s Onwards 'Optimistic' Scenario	Relative accuracy (*) of the 1994 predictions (with hindsight)
OECD Installed Computer Base (Number of machines)	30.000 (1965)	Millions (1985)	Hundred Millions (2005)	Probably Underestimated: There were 263 million internet subscribers in 2005 (and the number of computers is much greater than that of Internet subscriptions) 1 Billion PCs in 2008
Components per Micro-electronics circuit	32 bits (1965)	1 Megabit (1987)	256 Megabits (late 1990s)	Overestimated: 128 Megabits (in 2000)
Leading Representative Computer: Instructions per second	10^3 (1955)	10^7 (1989)	10^9 (2000)	Somewhat Underestimated: 3.5×10^9 (in 2000)
Cost: Operations per Thousand $US	10^5 (1960s)	10^0 (1980s)	10^{10} (2005)	Within the Range: Between 10^9 and 10^{12} (2005)

(*) In terms of decision making and of how the key factor reassures innovators and investors into venturing in the new technologies and their applications, the trend and the predictions at the time are more relevant than their eventual accuracy.
Source: Freeman and Soete (1994) for the first four columns and various sources for the last.

'containment' forces in his theory of path-dependent processes. It is only when productivity along the old trajectories shows persistent limits to growth and future profits are seriously threatened that the high risks and costs of trying the new technologies appear as clearly justified. And it is only after many of these trials have been obviously successful that further applications become easier and less risky investment choices.

The new key factor does not appear as an isolated input, but rather at the core of a rapidly growing system of technical, social and managerial innovations, some related to the production of the key factor itself and others to its utilization. At first, these innovations may appear (and may be in fact pursued) as a means of overcoming the specific bottlenecks of the old technologies, but the new key factors and related sectors soon acquire their own dynamics and successive innovations take place through an intensive interactive process, spurred by the limits to growth that are increasingly apparent under the old paradigm. In this way, the most successful new technology systems gradually crystallize as an ideal new type of production organization that becomes the common sense of management and design, embodying new rules of thumb, restoring confidence to investment decision makers after a long period of hesitation. This process can be seen very clearly today with the interrelated growth of microelectronic components, computers, telecommunications, the Internet and a wide range of new services and manufactured products.

The full constellation – once crystallized – goes far beyond the key factor(s) and beyond technical change itself. It brings with it a restructuring of the whole productive system.

Among other things, as it crystallizes, the new techno-economic paradigm involves:

1. A new 'best practice' form of organization in the firm and at the plant level (Table 8.5)
2. A new skill profile in the labour force, affecting both quality and quantity of labour and corresponding patterns of income distribution
3. A new product mix in the sense that those products that make intensive use of the low-cost key factor will be the preferred choice for investment and will represent, therefore, a growing proportion of GNP
4. New trends in both radical and incremental innovation geared to substituting more intensive use of the new key factor(s) for other relatively high cost elements
5. New trends in the location of investment both nationally and internationally as the change in the relative cost structure transforms comparative advantages
6. A particular wave of infrastructural investment designed to provide appropriate externalities throughout the system and facilitate the use of the new products and processes everywhere (Antonelli 1992)
7. A tendency for new innovator-entrepreneur type small firms also to enter the new rapidly expanding branches of the economy and in some cases to initiate entirely new sectors of production

As a consequence, what for Schumpeter is the downswing and depression of the long wave can be seen as the difficult and turbulent period of introduction

Table 8.5. **Change of Techno-Economic Paradigm**

Mass Production Old	ICT-Flexible Production New
Energy-Intensive	Information-Intensive
Design and engineering in 'drawing' offices	Computer-aided design and engineering
Sequential designs and production	Concurrent engineering
Standardized	Customized
Rather stable product mix	Rapid changes in product mix
Dedicated plant and equipment	Flexible production systems
Single firm	Networks
Hierarchical structures	Flat horizontal structures
Departmental	Integrated
Product with service	Service with products
Centralization	Distributed intelligence
Specialized skills	Multi-skilling
'Planning's-fixed strategies	'Vision' – flexible adaptable strategy

Source: Adapted from Perez (1983).

of a new paradigm where the previous one is maturing and declining and the new is forcing its way with the help of finance. It is the period of transition, characterized by deep structural change in the economy, and such changes require an equally profound transformation of the institutional and social framework. The process leads to a financial bubble, then a collapse and the onset of prolonged recessionary trends indicating an increasing degree of *mismatch* between the techno-economic subsystem and the old socio-institutional framework. It shows the need for a full-scale re-accommodation of social behaviour and institutions to suit the requirements and the potential of a shift that has already taken place to a considerable extent in many areas of the techno-economic sphere. This re-accommodation occurs as a result of a process of political search, experimentation and adaptation, but when it has been achieved, by a variety of social and political changes at the national and international level, the resulting 'good match' facilitates the upswing phase of the long wave. A climate of confidence for a surge of new investment is created through an appropriate combination of regulatory mechanisms that foster the full deployment of the new paradigm.

Since the achievement of a 'good match' is a conflict-ridden process and proceeds very unevenly in differing national political and cultural contexts, this may exert a considerable influence on the changing pattern of international technological leadership and international patterns of diffusion. (Freeman and Louçã 2001)

The uneven and varied response of governments, firms and industries to the threats and opportunities posed by a new wave of technology tends to accentuate the uneven process of development. Newcomers are sometimes more able to make the necessary social and institutional innovations than the more arthritic social structures of established leaders. This means that changes of techno-economic paradigms are likely to be associated with the temporary aggravation of instability problems in relation to the flow of international investment, trade and payments as well as with catching-up processes and changes in the relative ranking of nations (Perez and Soete 1988).

For the occasion of the current *Festschrift*, this paper has concentrated on Carlota Perez' contribution to the theory of innovation and long cycles. This has, during the past quarter of a century, proven to offer the genuine possibility of overcoming some of the weaknesses in Schumpeter's pioneering formulation. It has been, in some sense, the best tribute to the spirit of his work, and at the same time, testimony for the significance of hers.

References

Antonelli, C. 1992. *The Economics of Information Networks*. Amsterdam: Elsevier.

Arthur, W. B. 1988. 'Competing Technologies: An Overview.' In G. Dosi et al. (eds). *Technical Change and Economic Theory*. London: Pinter.

David, P. A. 1985. 'Clio and the Economics of QWERTY.' *American Economic Review* 75, 332–337.

Dosi, G. 1982. 'Technological Paradigms and Technological Trajectories.' *Research Policy* 11, 147–162.

———. 1984. *Technical Change and Industrial Transformation*. London, Macmillan.

Dosi, G. and L. Orsenigo. 1988. 'Coordination and Transformation: An Overview of Structures, Behaviour and Change in Evolutionary Environments.' In G. Dosi et al. *Technical Change and Economic Theory*. London: Pinter.

Dosi, G. et al. (eds). 1988. *Technical Change and Economic Theory*. London: Pinter.

Eatwell, J. 1982. *Whatever Happened to Britain?* London: Duckworth.

Elliott, J. E. 1985. 'Schumpeter's Theory of Economic Development and Social Change: Exposition and Assessment.' *International Journal of Social Economics* 12, 6/7, 6–33.

Freeman, C. (ed.). 1996. *Long Wave Theory*. Elgar Critical Writings in Economics 69. Aldershot: Edward Elgar.

Freeman, C., J. Clark and L. Soete. 1982. *Unemployment and Technical Innovation: A Study of Long Waves in Economic Development*. London: Pinter.

Freeman, C. and F. Louçã. 2001. *As Time Goes By: From the Industrial Revolutions to the Information Revolution*. Oxford: Oxford University Press.

Freeman, C. and C. Perez. 1988. 'Structural Crises of Adjustment, Business Cycles and Investment Behaviour.' In G. Dosi et al. (eds). *Technical Change and Economic Theory*. London: Pinter, 38–66. [20.1]

Freeman, C. and L. Soete (eds). 1987. *Technical Change and Full Employment*. Oxford: Blackwell.

———. 1997. *The Economics of Industrial Innovation*. 3rd edn. London: Pinter.

Gilfillan, S. 1935. *The Sociology of Invention*, Chicago: Follett.

Hessen, B. 1931. 'The Social and Economic Roots of Newton's "Principia".' In N. Bukharin (ed.). *Science at the Crossroads*. London: Frank Cass.

Jewkes, J., D. Sawers and J. Stillerman. 1958. *The Sources of Invention*. London: Macmillan.

Keirstead, B. 1948. *The Theory of Economic Change*. Toronto: Macmillan.

Keynes, J. M. 1936. *General Theory of Employment, Interest and Money*. New York: Harcourt Brace.

Kuznets, S. 1940. 'Schumpeter's Business Cycles.' *American Economic Review* 30, 257–271.

Louçã, F. 1997. *Turbulence in Economics*. Cheltenham: Edward Elgar.

Mensch, G. 1975. *Das technologische Patt: Innovationen überwinden die Depression*. Frankfurt: Umschau. [English trsl. 1979: *Stalemate in Technology*. New York: Ballinger.]

Nelson, R. and S. Winter. 1977. 'In Search of a Useful Theory of Innovation.' *Research Policy* 6, 36–75.

―――. 1982. *An Evolutionary Theory of Economic Change*. Cambridge, MA: Harvard University Press.

Perez, C. 1983. 'Structural Change and Assimilation of New Technologies in the Economic and Social System.' *Futures* 15, 357–375. [3.1]

―――. 1985. 'Microelectronics, Long Waves and World Structural Change: New Perspectives for Developing Countries.' *World Development* 13, 441–463. [9.1]

―――. 1986. 'Las Nuevas Tecnologías: Una Visión de Conjunto.' In C. Ominami (ed.). *La Tercera Revolución Industrial: Impactos Internacionales del Actual Viraje Tecnológico*. Buenos Aires: Grupo Editor Latinoamericano, 43–90. [12.1]

―――. 2002. *Technological Revolutions and Financial Capital: The Dynamics of Bubbles and Golden Ages*. Cheltenham: Edward Elgar. [74.1]

―――. 2004. 'Technological Revolutions, Paradigm Shifts and Socio-Institutional Change.' In E. S. Reinert (ed.). *Globalization, Economic Development and Inequality: An Alternative Perspective*. Cheltenham: Edward Elgar, 217–242. [75.1]

Perez, C. and L. Soete. 1988. 'Catching up in Technology: Entry Barriers and Windows of Opportunity.' In G. Dosi et al. (eds). *Technical Change and Economic Theory*. London: Pinter. [23]

Rogers, E. 1962. *Diffusion of Innovations*. New York: Free Press.

Rosenberg, N. 1976. *Perspectives on Technology*. Cambridge: Cambridge University Press.

―――. 1982. *Inside the Black Box*. Cambridge: Cambridge University Press.

Ruttan, V. 1959. 'Usher and Schumpeter on Invention, Innovation and Technological Change.' *Quarterly Journal of Economics* 73, 596–606.

Schumpeter, J. A. 1908. *Das Wesen und der Hauptinhalt der Theoretischen Nationalökonomie*. Leipzig: Duncker & Humblot.

―――. 1912. *Theorie der wirtschaftlichen Entwicklung*. Munich/Leipzig: Duncker & Humblot. [English trsl. 1934: *The Theory of Economic Development*. Cambridge, MA: Harvard University Press.]

―――. 1928. 'The Instability of Capitalism.' *Economic Journal* 38 (151), 361–386.

―――. 1939. *Business Cycles*. New York: McGraw-Hill.

―――. 1943. *Capitalism, Socialism and Democracy*. London: Allen and Unwin.

Shionoya, Y. 1986. 'The Science and Ideology of Schumpeter.' *Revista Internazionale di Scienze Economiche e Commerciale* 33, 729–762.

Solomou, S. 1987. *Phases of Economic Growth, 1850–1973: Kondratieff Waves and Kuznets Swings*. Cambridge: Cambridge University Press.

Tsuru, S. 1993. *Institutional Economics Revisited*. Cambridge: Cambridge University Press.

v. Tunzelmann, N. 1978. *Steam Power and British Industrialisation to 1860*. Oxford: Clarendon.

Weinstock, U. 1964. *Das Problem der Kondratieff-Zyklen*. Berlin: Duncker & Humblot.

Chapter Nine:

ASIAN INNOVATION EXPERIENCES AND LATIN AMERICAN VISIONS: EXPLOITING SHIFTS IN TECHNO-ECONOMIC PARADIGMS

Michael Hobday
University of Brighton

Introduction

Carlota Perez' intellectual development and research interests have been well covered in other papers in this volume. This paper focuses on one lesser-known dimension of Perez' life long work, namely, her leading role in translating academic research into practical strategies and ways forward (called visions) for Latin America. Carlota's recent work in this area builds on substantial early working experience in carrying out import-substitution policies in Venezuela and her subsequent observations of (largely unsuccessful) attempts to move to export-led growth paths on the part of Latin American countries under 'neoliberal' or Washington Consensus policies.[1]

Carlota Perez' working experience is very impressive. From 1975 to 1977, Carlota worked for the Institute of Foreign Trade (in the Ministry of Foreign Affairs in Venezuela) in charge of technology issues, then from 1980 to 1983 as director of technological development in the Ministry of Industry. From 1985 to 1987 she worked with members of CENTRIM, training innovation consultants in Venezuela. After this (until 1999) her work included various projects for both the Industry and S&T Ministries (including one for the Institute of Engineering that involved benchmarking S&T institutes around the world). Then from 1999 to 2002, Carlota worked as consultant to the Venezuelan oil holding company PDVSA, focusing on the R&D company INTEVEP. In addition, Carlota has advised the top management of major corporations, including IBM, on future techno-economic paradigms. This rich practical experience has fed back in to Carlota's research, giving it enormous practical resonance and relevance.

In particular, by linking her research on paradigms to the practical challenges of economic and technological development within Latin America, Carlota has made important strategic contributions, the most recent of which has been the beginning of an articulation of a vision for Latin America (called 'LA Vision'), which is based on opportunities for exploiting shifts in techno-economic paradigms (Perez 2008). This paper makes two arguments about this work. First, it argues that the LA Vision programme has the potential for being significant for the next phase of Latin American development. Second, it argues that LA Vision is also entirely consistent with the historical experiences of innovation and growth in East and South East Asia. In contrast to the recommendations of many policy observers (see Part 2 below), a key message from Carlota's recent work is that Latin American countries cannot, and should not, attempt to imitate or follow the paths of the successful Asian economies – and they certainly should not attempt to compete with them directly. Instead, LA should seek to complement, not copy, the growth paths of the Asian economies. Rather than imitating the Asian economies, the countries of Latin America should build on their own distinctive experiences, resources and capabilities to forge distinctive new development paths that can cope with the economic and social challenges facing Latin America – and take advantage of recent movements in frontier techno-economic paradigms.

The paper is organized as follows: Part 1 discusses the Asian innovation experience that was based on the development of the (then) new electronics industries that constituted the early stage of the current information and communications technology (ICT) paradigm. This paradigm gave rise to a massive, ever-increasing demand for electronics and information technology systems, product, components and other manufactured hardware. At the early stages, the Asian economies responded to this new demand through the production of huge volumes of fairly standard, mature products, based initially on low-cost labour and simple technical inputs. Subsequent shifts in the ICT paradigm towards advanced information systems, multimedia, software and Internet-based services enabled leading firms in the West, the EU and Japan (such as IBM, Hewlett-Packard, Ericsson and Sony) to further relinquish hardware manufacturing and move into high-value, information-intensive services, and bundles of hardware, software and services, sometimes called 'solutions' (Davies et al. 2006). This process of vacating the hardware sector and moving up the ICT value chain has provided further space for the Asian latecomers to upgrade their now formidable hardware manufacturing capabilities, prompting further large investment in new process technology, product design and R&D.

Part 2 examines the conventional, neo-liberal (or Washington Consensus) policy models and lessons that commonly arise from analyses of East Asia's growth. Although many policy analysts believe that the developing countries of Latin America (and other regions) can and should learn lessons from the experiences of successful Asian economies (especially Korea, Taiwan and China), Part 2 argues that such proposals are fundamentally misleading.[2]

Part 3 substantiates this argument by delving into the views of leading historical figures in the field of growth and development, including Gerschenkron (1962, 1963), Kuznets (1958, 1966), Abramovitz (1986) and more recently, Nelson (1998). This section argues that it is both analytically wrong and empirically flawed to draw direct policy lessons from Asia in this way.

Part 4 turns to Carlota Perez' recent LA vision work, arguing that it is entirely consistent with the views of the 'great' development economists of the past – and with the recent Asian growth and innovation experiences, Carlota's work presents new, exciting and practical ways of thinking about previous successful developers that could prove instrumental in charting new paths of industrialization in Latin America, and perhaps other regions. Indeed, this re-thinking of how techno-economic paradigms relate to industrialization could open up a new development agenda for the future.

Part 1: Patterns of Asian Innovation

Asian Exploitation of the ICT Paradigm

Asia's growth over the past 30 years or so has been largely the result of its response to the new techno-economic paradigm initially called electronic, then microelectronic, then semiconductor, then digital and now ICT, reflecting the progressive development of this technology from isolated and fairly simple hardware products (e.g., consumer electronics) towards advanced and integrated computing, software and Internet-based services and solutions. The changes in terminology reflect the development, transformation and growth of the paradigm that still, and increasingly, calls for the manufacture of enormous quantities of hardware to underpin the infrastructure of the new digital ICT-internet paradigm.

What this evolving paradigm did was to transform the global innovation and economic system during its successive phases of its growth (Perez 1985). Each new wave of product and system design, based on ever-more sophisticated semiconductor technology gave rise to increasingly complex demands by the advanced nations for further types of electronic components and systems. Asian hardware leadership, which began first with Japan, moved gradually out to lower-cost Asian countries, stimulating rapid export-led growth in the region.

As leading firms move into highly sophisticated ICTs, with firms such as IBM and Hewlett Packard supplying service-based 'solutions' (Davies et al. 2006), further vacating the hardware sector and, with it, the product design and process innovation capabilities required to develop hardware. The most advanced Western and Japanese ICT producers are now highly dependent on innovative, low-cost electronics hardware produced by Asian manufacturers, with China adding to the capacity of the region for innovation and production.

Broad Patterns of Catching Up in Asia

While the part played by the shifting ICT techno-economic paradigm is often overlooked in discussions of Asian development, another oft-ignored feature is the diversity of Asian development, not only in terms of policy but also in industrial structure, ownership and corporate strategy. While there were, indeed, some features of similarity (see below), the overall development process did not occur in a uniform way across Asia, but was subject to a great deal of variety.

In the case of Korea and Taiwan, there was considerable institutional and policy learning from the Japanese model. With it, there was also a rejection of the conventional Western policies of the day. Korea and Taiwan rejected free-market comparative-advantage policies and the recommendations of conventional economists (Vogel 1991), choosing instead to deliberately engineer development and avoid continuing dependence on low cost labour and commodity production.

To demonstrate the success of the region, it is worth briefly recalling the position of Asia in the late 1950s and early 1960s and their subsequent growth success. In 1962, Taiwan and Korea had GNP per capita levels similar to those of the poorer African nations. By 1986 the two countries had moved up rankings by 47 and 55 places respectively, with average GDP growth of 8 per cent to 10 per cent per annum. Company growth rates were much faster, often reaching 20 per cent to 30 per cent per annum for sustained periods of time.[3]

Hong Kong and Singapore in the 1960s were bedevilled by poverty, unemployment and poor housing, with little manufacturing base. By the 1980s, as a result of average growth rates of up to 10 per cent per annum, both countries had achieved full employment with rapidly rising wages and higher value added production. As a result, assembly activities had progressively shifted to lower cost Asian economies including Malaysia, Indonesia, Thailand, Vietnam, Philippines and China, leading to their rapid export-led growth. As a result of these advances, by the early 1990s much of world growth, trade and manufacturing had shifted to the East and Southeast Asian regions.

East Asian Local Firms

While much of the debate on Asia has focused on macroeconomic, trade and government policy issues, research on firm-level innovation strategy reveals some common approaches to technology acquisition and provides insights into the micro dynamics of Asia's catching up. So how did local firms in East Asia (i.e., Korea, Taiwan and Hong Kong) acquire technology and begin to catch up with the leaders?[4] These so-called latecomer firms can be defined by two sets of typical developing country disadvantages: First, they were dislocated from international sources of technology, science and R&D; second, they were cut off from advanced markets and with them, demanding users, user-producer links, and the clusters and networks usually viewed as critical to competitiveness. As a category, latecomer firms are not only distinct from Western and Japanese leaders, but also followers. Followers, unlike latecomers, are located within advanced country markets and have access to leading edge technology. In fact, they often benefit from the heavy technology investments of the leading firms, becoming fast followers in their markets (Freeman, 1974).

Samsung entered transistor radio and black and white TV production in a joint venture with Sanyo in 1969 (diversifying from insurance, property and paper and other products). By 2007 Samsung Electronics registered 2,725 patents in the US, second only to IBM with 3,148. In 2006 it was spending US$5.6 billion on R&D, employed around 123,000 workers and boasted 17 R&D Centres around the world. The firm had moved up the value chain to become a world leader in semiconductors, mobile phones, laptop computers and other high-technology electronic products.

Three very approximate phases of Samsung's catch-up provide a glimpse into the general progress of Korean and Taiwanese firms in electronics. Although very few of these firms have achieved the advanced status of Samsung, other major Korean firms such as Hyundai and LG followed a similar pattern. Phase 1, from the early 1960s to the mid-1970s, can be called the *basic assembly* stage. Firms such as Samsung, Hyundai, LG of Korea and Tatung of Taiwan began the assembly of standard, simple goods, supplying foreign TNCs (mostly from Japan and the US). Often, this export production occurred within the subcontracting arrangement called OEM (original equipment manufacture) whereby the foreign TNCs buyer supplies the design, technology, training (and brands) and then distributes the product in the developed country markets. This began in areas such as basic consumer electronics, simple computing and telecommunications products, and electrical appliances.

Phase 2, from the mid-1970s to mid-1990s, can be called the *manufacturing innovation stage*. By the mid-1970s Samsung and others had mastered manufacturing process innovation and also learned product improvement skills. At the start, Samsung needed to learn more about product design in order to improve the manufacturing process (so called design-for-manufacture). Building on this, Samsung and others learned to make improvements to design and then to design new products usually to offer to the TNC buyers. The TNCs, in turn, benefited from the low-cost design and assembly and would brand and distribute the products in the US and other western markets, gaining most of the value added.

Phase 3, from the mid-1990s onwards, can be called the *design and R&D innovation stage*. Having learned more about design and having invested in R&D for many years to support manufacturing and design, Samsung increasingly produced its own new product designs, based on in-house R&D and its own design engineering skills. A parallel process of learning about marketing enabled Samsung to organize its own distribution network and build up its brand image. At this stage, Samsung had caught up with the world leaders in high technology products such as mobile phones, semiconductors and PCs.

While one cannot generalize from a few firms to others, and some firms may well have followed other paths, the case of Samsung demonstrates some interesting firm-level innovation features. Firms like Samsung engaged in a 20–30-year hard slog of technological learning, beginning with simple mechanical assembly. There was no overnight success or leapfrogging, and the source of technology was largely from within the firm and from foreign customers and suppliers of technology, rather than local public research institutes or universities. The OEM subcontracting system, which accounted for 70 per cent to 80 per cent of total Korean electronics exports as recently as the early 1990s, provided a valuable channel for technology transfer from abroad and technology learning at home. It also provided a mechanism for exporting and helped firms overcome marketing and brand barriers to entry. OEM allowed for economies of scale in production, and the TNC buyers were motivated by low costs to provide advice on capital equipment, engineering, training and management.

Innovation was incremental – not radical – focusing on improvements in manufacturing and products. Until recently, most innovation was low cost, behind the R&D frontier innovation, including improved designs for manufacture and new product models. Also the process was not just learning or imitation. We can see novel business models and technology specializations (e.g., TSMC in Taiwan is a world leader in chip fabrication only while ANAM of Korea is a world leader in chip assembly/test only). Research also shows that despite all this success, firms are still weak in software, basic research, and capital goods (most capital goods continue to be imported from Japan and the USA).

The Samsung case allows us to compare Asian innovation patterns with that of western leadership innovation (see Figure 9.1). Firms such as

Figure 9.1. Comparing Asian Firms with Standard (MIT) Model

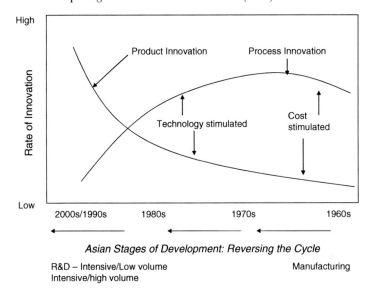

Source: Derived from the four-country study of Asian electronics (Hobday 1995, 188 and 194).[5]

Samsung typically began with relatively stable, mature products and technologies and they then moved 'backwards' along the cycle of innovation, from assembly to manufacturing innovation, to design, ultimately to R&D, reversing the 'normal', Schumpeterian path of development that is supposed to begin with R&D. This Asian innovation path was highly innovative in strategic terms. While Japan had also pursued this type of entry strategy, never before had a group of poor developing countries managed to achieve such large-scale economic development through this kind of behind-the-frontier innovation.

Southeast Asian TNC-led Growth

In some respects, the Southeast Asian path of innovation is very different from that of the East Asian countries, emphasizing the variety in the region. In Southeast Asia, in stark contrast to East Asia, Governments looked to foreign direct investment (FDI) and the subsidiaries of transnational corporations (TNCs) to lead export growth. In Singapore, the Government believed, rightly or wrongly, that local capitalists were not strong or experienced enough to lead industrialization. The Government therefore invited in foreign TNCs, giving them a degree of freedom of operation seldom witnessed in the developing world. This policy proved highly successful, with TNCs exporting from subsidized economic zones. At the time, this was a major policy innovation. Today, many countries compete for FDI.

The success of Singapore led to imitation by Malaysia, Thailand and later Indonesia, Philippines and Vietnam), all pursuing a path of development based on FDI, rather than local firms. In China, FDI conducted by foreign affiliates is responsible for a large and growing proportion of export growth, with US and European TNCs in particular investing heavily in China both for exports and to supply local markets. As Gaulier et al. (2004) note, in 2003 FDI accounted for more that 55 per cent of total exports, compared with only 20 per cent in 1992. However, within the processing zone activities, FDI accounted for around 80 per cent in 2003. Foreign TNC affiliates also account for a large proportion of high-technology exports. Interestingly, FDI into China comes now mainly from Asian Countries, with Japan and the newly industrialized countries relocating their labour-intensive production into China. Other Asian firms and countries therefore benefit considerably from China as a low-cost export platform in a complex regional system of production and innovation.

Innovation in Southeast Asia can be understood within the context of the global strategies of individual competing TNCs. Figure 9.2 presents the typical

Figure 9.2. TNC Subsidiaries: South East Asian Model of Technology Catch Up

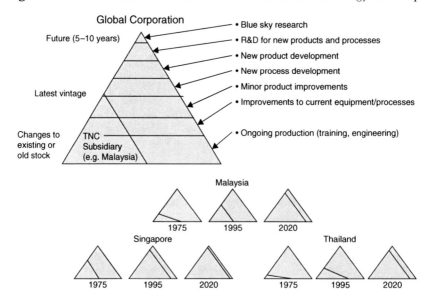

Source: Adapted from Hobday (1996, 78), which provides evidence in support of this interpretation.

range of technological activities carried out by TNCs and their subsidiaries, ranging from basic research at the tip of the triangle through to simple technical improvement activities at the base of the triangle. Most R&D and core product design (the top of the triangle) is carried out within the TNC host country. However, the technological activities of the subsidiaries in Southeast Asia (e.g., see the Malaysian profile in Figure 9.2) should not be dismissed as unimportant. R&D, although often stressed, amounts to the 'tip of the iceberg', usually well under 15 per cent of corporate turnover and often less than 10 per cent. Other vital technological activities include design, engineering, technician and operating tasks. These activities are essential for productivity, quality and competitiveness and their requirements often shape corporate R&D strategy and provide the demand for longer term R&D.

The technology activities of TNC subsidiaries in countries such as Malaysia and Thailand constitute one essential part of the overall operation. Through time, subsidiaries in Southeast Asia progressed from basic assembly to higher stages of technological activity, such as process engineering and minor product design. This process requires substantial investment in facilities, skills, training and education. At the present time, typical Malaysian and Thai subsidiaries are situated between higher-technology operations in countries such as the US, the UK and Singapore and lower-cost operations in countries such as China. This reflects the general level of development and the relative factor costs of each economy. To progress further, the TNC subsidiaries in Malaysia (and their suppliers) have to build up further capabilities in precision engineering, prototype building, product design and R&D.

Recent research reveals various approximate stages of development with Singapore in the lead, followed by Malaysia and Thailand, with others lagging behind, still conducting basic assembly (Hobday 1996; 2000). Over time, technology activities have expanded outwards as shown in the mini-triangles in Figure 9.2. Subsidiaries have shifted from cheap-labour assembly tasks to high-technology activities. Firms such as Seagate in Thailand have made huge investments in advanced manufacturing technology in high-technology products such as hard disk drives. Other firms produce PCs, semiconductors and a multitude of other devices. As in the East Asian region, these firms exploited the demand for electronics hardware created by the expansion and evolution of the ICT techno-economic paradigm rooted in the advanced economies.

China appears to be following a similar path to the Southeast Asian region, but with both local firm *and* TNC-led growth. China has the added advantages of (1) a very large local market, not present in the other Asian countries and (2) a massive cheap and technically sound labour supply. The conditions facing China today are very different from those facing Korea and Taiwan in the past. Increased mobility of capital, people, ideas and business models means that

China has more to draw upon and can innovate in new ways, sometimes in partnership with foreign firms eager to gain shares of the local market. Through its powerful learning capacity, China appears to compressing the stages of catch-up by moving far more swiftly across the triangle than the earlier entrants such as Singapore and Malaysia.

Diversity and Innovation in Policy

In addition to the different business strategies followed across the region, we also see variety in policy mechanisms, industrial structure and firm size. For example, in terms of the degree of direct government intervention, in the early stages of development (i.e., in the 1960s and 1970s) there was a great deal of intervention in South Korea and Singapore, but much less in Taiwan and a more-or-less *laissez faire* approach in Hong Kong. In South Korea the Government directly supported the large *chaebol* with financial subsidies and other privileges (Amsden 1989). In Singapore, the Government supported the large foreign TNCs with incentives, tax holidays and export processing zones, allowing them a freedom to operate rarely seen before in the developing world (Yue 1985).

By contrast, much of Taiwanese early export development in electronics was led by small and medium-size companies that exported *via* a multitude of traders (Chou 1992). Many of these were fearful of government and therefore operated in the 'underground' economy (Chaponniere and Fouqin 1989). Only later on did the Taiwanese government become directly involved through large scale investments, notably in the Hsinchu industrial park.

Regarding economic openness, Korea and Taiwan were fairly closed to FDI for much of the 1960s, 1970s and 1980s, whereas Singapore and Hong Kong were very open. During the 1980 to 1988 period, total FDI from the two largest investors (Japan and the US) amounted to US$14.3 billion in the four countries, with Hong Kong receiving the largest amount (US$6.3 billion) and Singapore second with US$3.6 billion. By contrast South Korea, a much larger economy, only received US$2.3 billion and Taiwan only US$2.1 billion (James 1990, 15). Policy-wise, Singapore and Hong Kong placed few restrictions on FDI, whereas Taiwan and South Korea tightly controlled FDI, protecting local industries from foreign competition and encouraging domestic firms to supplant foreign ones wherever possible.

With respect to industrial policy, while Hong Kong and Singapore pursued export-led policies, South Korea and Taiwan combined export incentives with controls or outright bans on imports to protect domestic markets for local firms. South Korea was very restrictive, banning most consumer goods and raw materials that did not have to be imported. The Taiwanese Government often negotiated the terms of FDI and tied TNCs to local content rules and export targets.

There was also variety in company size and patterns of ownership that led to, and resulted from, particular government policies. While Taiwan and Hong Kong depended to a high degree on small (and a few large) Chinese-owned family businesses, the South Korean government supported the *chaebol*, leading to highly concentrated industrial structures in Korea. By contrast, in Hong Kong and Taiwan small firms proliferated and grew, resulting in dispersed and pluralistic industrial structures with some large firms and many SMEs. When comparing industrial concentration we see a remarkably stark contrast between South Korea and Taiwan.

Government policies and company strategies were closely entwined. In Taiwan, SMEs relied on speed and flexibility, whereas the South Korean giant firms invested in high-volume, process-intensive electronics sectors. Taiwanese and Hong Kong SMEs tended to specialize in fast-changing market niches, while the South Korean conglomerates, in some respects, imitated the Japanese *keiretsu*, emphasising scale and very high degrees of vertical integration. With respect to ownership, Taiwan and South Korea relied mostly on locally-owned firms, while Singapore depended almost entirely on foreign TNCs for electronics exports, with Hong Kong relying on a mixture of local and foreign firms.

Variety was an important feature of government policy in East and Southeast Asia promoted for the simple reason that each country began with different resources and capabilities so that policies needed to be tailored to these initial starting conditions. Each country developed a local capitalist class in somewhat different ways. Each followed a different path of industrial development – but all focused on using exports to lead economic growth and technology accumulation.

Part 2: The Fallacy of Policy Imitation

Typical Policymaking Processes

It is tempting, but highly misleading, to think that other developing nations should imitate the Asian growth success. Simple catch-up theory and 'common sense' lead many agencies, including the World Bank, OECD, UNIDO, UNCTAD, EU, consultants, governments and academics, to draw on Asian experience to suggest policies, paths and lessons for other developing countries. However, while there may be some insights from the Asian experience, direct lessons and models cannot be transferred.

For example, IBRD 2008 is a major study by the Commission on Growth and Development sponsored by The International Bank for Reconstruction and

Development and The World Bank. This report develops lessons from 13 successful economies, 9 of which are Asian (the others are, curiously, Botswana, Brazil, Malta and Oman). The report draws lessons arguing that modern institutions and 'good practices' (e.g., privatization, liberalization, property rights and enforceable contract law) are needed for growth and development (rather than a consequence as in much of Asia). The report also assumes the standard historical 'agriculture to manufacturing' model still applies (e.g., IBRD 2008, 6) whereas, for example, recent Indian growth has been fuelled by domestic services rather than manufacturing or exports (Singh 2005; Gordon and Gupta 2003; Hansda 2001).

Similarly, the World Bank's 'Doing Business' programme argues that poorer countries should adopt policies of the leading nations of the world including the most advanced Asian countries (again identifying 'best practices' from developed economies) in, for example, owning property, starting-up businesses and liberalizing markets. The programme argues that more than 2 per cent could be added to the growth of the 'most difficult countries to do business' if they adopted the practices of the leading nations (World Bank 2004, 3). However, even if such policy groups had the experience of Asia right (which they often do not), it would still be wrong to recommend 'follow the leader' policies.

The 'Doing Business' approach can be seen as a sub-set of the wider package of 'Washington Consensus' conventional wisdom, presented as 'rules of good behaviour for promoting economic growth' (see Rodrik 2004, 20). Typical policy recommendations include: export-led growth paths; more open markets (to foreign investment and imports); privatization, deregulation and business-friendly policies; high technology production (e.g., ICT, biotechnology and new materials); government support for knowledge-based industries and industrial clusters; and the construction of science and technology parks.

This kind of policy making reflects a deeply flawed and ahistorical understanding of how latecomer development occurs. Perhaps even worse, many of the 'lessons' run contrary to the Asian evidence. Some of the 'explanations' and 'best practices' occurred well after the take off (e.g., science and industrial parks and policies towards clusters). Others are highly misleading. For example, Korea and Taiwan were highly restrictive towards FDI and operated very closed internal markets (and still do in many sectors), only allowing in capital goods, materials and products that could not be produced locally. In contrast to high technology and knowledge intensive production, the focus of exporting for at least the first 20 years was 'low technology' products based on fairly simple manufacturing processes.

However, even if the Asian diagnosis would have been correct, it would still be a mistake to draw lessons in this way. To demonstrate this point, it is useful to examine an earlier version of this policy debate that occurred in the post-war period.

Part 3: Learning from Earlier Generations of Development Economists

Modern day lesson-making is a new version of an old discourse typified in the pointed debate between Rostow and other leading development economists, most notably Gerschenkron (see below). W. W. Rostow (1916–2003), like today's policymakers, also proposed a 'follow the leader' approach. His classic text *The Stages of Economic Growth: a Non-Communist Manifesto* (1960) sold more than 260,000 copies in the first edition and became the conventional policy wisdom of the day. Rostow's main contribution was a prescriptive growth model for developing countries based on stages of economic development and takeoff of the then-developed countries.

In terms of policymaking, Rostow argued, 'It is useful, as well as roughly accurate to regard the process of development now going forward in Asia, the Middle East, Africa and Latin America as analogies to the stages of the preconditions and take off of other societies in the late eighteenth, nineteenth, and early twentieth centuries' (Rostow 1960, 153). This is a remarkably similar agenda to that of today's policy imitators: i.e. the lessons of past industrializers (e.g., Asia) should be applied directly to the developing countries of today. However, several other economists at the time were highly sceptical of this approach. Most notably Alexander Gerschenkron (1904–1978) a Russian-born, Austrian-trained Harvard economic historian, completely rejected the ideas of Rostow as ill-conceived and ahistorical. Gerschenkron researched European latecomer industrialization and also viewed industrialization as a 'stage like' process, but disagreed fundamentally with Rostow, arguing that: (1) there were (and could be) no automatic stages of development; and (2) latecomers did not/could not pass through the same stages as previous industrializers, because others had passed through them changing the market and technological circumstances facing new industrializers.

Gerschenkron argued that each country has its own distinctive resources related to its own particular stage of backwardness, and this would strongly influence any potential growth path. In his text of 1962, *Economic Backwardness in Historical Perspective*, he argued, 'this [Gerschenkron's interpretation of stages] differs essentially from the various efforts in "stage-making" [typified by Rostow], the common feature of which was the assumption that all economies were supposed regularly to pass through the same individual stages as they moved along the road of economic progress… Thus, Rostow was at pains to assert that the process of industrialization repeated itself from country to country' (355).[6]

Simon Kuznets (1958; 1966), a Nobel prize-winner for economics, made similar points. Kuznets argued that the developing economies of his era possessed distinctive characteristics compared with earlier developers, disputing the conventional view that countries tended to go through the same stages in their development history. He argued that 'Examination of similarities and differences [of industrialization experiences] should be particularly instructive [for today's developing countries] since it would suggest the different role of various factors as the conditions, set by the changing world scene and the historical heritages of each country, modify the process of adjustment to the industrial system.' (Kuznets 1958, 152). Kuznets' cross-sectional and time-series empirical evidence on the characteristics of developing countries showed that developing countries possessed very different structural characteristics compared with the industrialized countries at the time they developed. There could be no simple predictable paths or stages. As a result, he helped establish the field of development economics, the main task of which was to illustrate the distinctive paths and experiences of contemporary developing countries.

Another highly respected observer of growth, Moses Abramovitz, made similar points. In his famous paper 'Catching Up, Forging Ahead and Falling Behind', Abramovitz (1986, 405–406) stressed the shaping role of the initial conditions of developing nations for their growth and development potential, arguing that the prevailing institutions and educational attainment levels were key factors in shaping the conditions that govern the diffusion of knowledge and the mobility of resources. He argued that 'The state of a country's capability to exploit emerging technological opportunity depends on a social history that is particular to itself and that may not be closely bound to its existing level of productivity. And there are changes in the character of technological advance that make it more congruent with the resources and institutional outfits of some countries but less congruent with those of others (1986, 405).

More recently, Richard Nelson (1998) argued the case for much more sophisticated and history-friendly growth models to reflect observed historical patterns. In his paper 'The Agenda for Growth Theory: A Different Point of View', Nelson criticizes evidence and history-free modern growth models. He reflects on the need to understand and differentiate between different kinds of national systems of innovation in developing countries, stressing variety. To be of value, theories need to understand the nature of institutions and technological processes as well as the different capabilities of firms. Nelson makes the point that growth and technological advance are disequilibrium processes that are not (and perhaps cannot be) captured in existing formal growth models.

Returning to Gerschenkron, there are several other highly instructive insights from Gerschenkron's analysis of European latecomer development that chime with Carlota Perez' contemporary analysis of Latin American industrialization and the above analysis of Asian industrialization. Gerschenkron argued, 'the industrial development of Europe appears not as a series of mere repetitions of the "first" industrialization but as an orderly system of graduated deviations from that industrialization' and 'the higher degree of backwardness, the more discontinuous the development is likely to be' (1962, 44 and 45), suggesting variety and discontinuity in patterns of development.

This idea of graduated deviation in Europe conforms to the experience of Asian industrialization. Japan was the first to develop, followed by the four 'dragons', South Korea, Taiwan, Hong Kong and Singapore (with significant differences). The four dragons were then followed by the second-tier countries of Southeast Asia (including Malaysia, Thailand, Indonesia, and Thailand). China's economy then took off, combining many of the 'old' strategies of East and Southeast Asia (e.g., exports *via* foreign multinationals, and large scale sub-contracting) but with radical new features including a very large local market and huge supplies of cheap technical labour. China's development must also be viewed in the context of the latest phase of increasingly fluid internationalization of capital, managerial labour and productive and innovative activity, which was quite different from the conditions facing the four dragons in the 1960s.

Gerschenkron also argued that rather than a process of imitation of prior industrializers, modern latecomers should engage in the 'substitution of missing prerequisites'. He argued, against Rostow, that it should not be a case of

Figure 9.3. Substitutes for Missing Prerequisites in Asia

Missing Prerequisite for growth (e.g. as evident in US and Japan)	Asian Substitute for missing prerequisite
Strong entrepreneurial and managerial capacity	Korea – state sponsorship of the *chaebol – helped grow a new 'class' of managers*
	Singapore – subsidies for TNC subsidiaries – created investment and an industrial base
Large internal markets	Korea, Taiwan, Hong Kong – sub-contracting system allowed access to US/European export markets
Access to advanced technology/ R&D resources	Singapore/Malaysia/Thailand – through foreign direct investment TNC subsidiaries brought technology
	Korea, Taiwan – sub-contracting provided access to technology

Source: Amended from Hobday (2003)

latecomers investing in a standard set of prerequisites or preconditions – but, on the contrary, substituting for missing prerequisites. Gerschenkron pointed out that European history should be seen as a pattern of substitution of missing prerequisites, governed by the prevailing and changing degree of backwardness. This again indicates that the policies of past, successful industrializers, cannot be a guide to late industrializers.

Regarding the idea of substituting missing prerequisites, Gerschenkron stressed the importance of innovation and the inability of conventional historical research on its own to guide strategy: 'the very concept of substitution is premised upon creative innovating activity, that is to say, upon something that is inherently unpredictable with the help of our normal apparatus of research' (1962, 359–360). As far as translating this analytical method or insight into development lessons or policies, Gerschenkron was very cautious. Regarding actual deliberate policies for development, he argued, 'There is no intention to suggest that backward countries necessarily engaged in deliberate acts of "substitution" for something that had been in evidence in more advanced countries. Men in a less developed country may have simply groped for and found solutions that were consonant with the existing conditions of backwardness.' Gerschenkron (1962, 359).

This has two important implications that Perez' LA Vision approach attempts to address: First, the inherently unpredictable and innovative nature of latecomer paths to development. Second, the inability of the 'normal' apparatus of research to grapple with and shape contemporary latecomer development. Carlota Perez, in my view, helps overcome these problems by providing a method for articulating a broad and inclusive vision for Latin American and the role of the vision in shaping future activity, to which we now turn.

Part 4: LA Vision – A New Apparatus of Development Thinking for Latin America

The above lines of reasoning call for a new agenda for developing countries of the kind Perez offers, and not just for Latin America. There are at least two reasons for this. First, there may be few (if any) direct historical lessons or models to imitate from Asia or other successful cases. Second, Asian export-led growth based on electronics hardware, initially based on the early stage of the ICT paradigm, is now likely to be closed for most other countries. The hardware sector is now highly advanced and probably already too 'crowded' with the entry of China (Mexico with its history of electronics exports may prove to be an exception).

Therefore, it may well be useful to think of the 'missing prerequisites' facing other countries, and how they can be substituted for, using specific local resources and skills to develop possible future scenarios for growth. This line of reasoning is consistent with Carlota's recent work. The LA Vision idea accepts the differences between the wide and varied group of countries that constitute Latin America. It calls for the development of a sustainable, productive way forward that complements existing centres of growth (e.g., in Asia) and offers methods to help shape a positive future for the region, and which ensure policy makers are involved and engaged in the vision making process. Carlota's work provides a substantial first attempt at this task.

For example, in her paper 'A Vision for Latin America', Perez (2008) analyses the region's natural resource endowments as a potential platform for a technologically dynamic and socially cohesive future.[7] The vision involves building on LA's distinctive technological capabilities and resources, within the external context of recent shifts in the ICT techno-economic paradigm. Carlota's approach combines (1) rigorous empirical research, (2) creative thinking about possible futures and (3) policy engagement, especially in the development of visions. The paper (implicitly) rejects 'follow the leader' policy thinking, opening up the search for new innovative growth paths that complement, rather than copy, the Asian economies and the older developed countries. As we see below, the approach builds on each country's (and the region's) history, capabilities and opportunities and expects (perhaps unpredictable forms of) innovation and distinctiveness to be a dimension of any future growth path – consistent with the Asian experience.

To begin, the paper analyses recent trends in the diffusion of what began as the electronics paradigm and is now more commonly called the ICT paradigm, which embraces the Internet, IT-based services and advanced software, developed mostly by leading firms mostly in the West. It also includes all the hardware that supports the services. Whereas in Asia, the process of exploiting the paradigm occurred out of experimentation and trial-and-error, today Perez offers a detailed analysis of the paradigm and its likely future direction, from which policy makers and analysts can together construct a vision, or several visions, of successful development futures for Latin America. This approach provides a new way of 'framing' the issue of Latin American development as a whole, amenable to empirical research (see below), while at the same time recognizing the wide variety of resources endowments and challenges facing the many countries within the region. It is both an analytical framework and a mechanism to stimulate practical policy debate on possible futures that can then, hopefully, be realized through strategy and policy. The overall vision incorporates not only an understanding of the current changing techno-economic environment, which earlier Asian policy did not have, but also mechanisms by which local and regional technological, institutional and policy capabilities may be deployed to underpin future growth paths.

The Asian development phase in the 1950s and 1960s largely took place in the 'dark' through trial-and-error learning, and often contrary to world development institutions and mainstream economists who recommended the pursuit of conventional static comparative advantage theory (Vogel 1991). By contrast, Carlota's approach calls for an agreed 'sense of direction' that can enable countries to embark on purposeful and dynamic development paths.

Carlota's analysis shows that the recent rising prices of raw materials, fuelled by Asian growth, have led to higher growth rates in several LA countries, based on commodity exports. However, her analysis also warns that underpinning technological capabilities have not generally followed suit. Severe weaknesses in domestic capabilities exist, for example, in the process exporting industries, which need to be addressed by business strategy and government policy. Carlota also emphasizes the deep and worrisome economic and social inequalities that persist across the region and, in some cases, have intensified due to export-led growth-restructuring programmes of the 1980s, which were accompanied by huge growth in unemployment, underemployment and informal employment.

Governments, academic and other observers in the region are becoming aware of the need to develop new, long-term growth opportunities that address social inequalities and provide for genuine development, rather than innovation and growth 'for its own sake' that excludes large sections of the population. However, Perez shows that shifts in the ICT paradigm provide important new process and commodity upgrading opportunities. A key challenge presented by this window of opportunity is how to rapidly develop the special technological capabilities needed to progressively upgrade the process industries in order to underpin a range of new growth paths for Latin America.

Rather than imitate or compete with Asia, Carlota argues that in the prevailing and rapidly changing techno-economic conditions, the most appropriate approach is to identify untapped technological potential where Latin America has a comparative advantage over fast-growing Asia and that, in many cases, complements Asian growth. This is a very different approach to the most conventional wisdom of the Washington Consensus and recent IBRD and World Bank guidance (see Part 2 above).

Several of the high-growth Asian countries (e.g., Korea, Taiwan, Singapore and Hong Kong) are densely populated with low endowments of natural resources. Other countries such as China, Malaysia and Indonesia are abundant in some natural resources but cannot supply their rapid growth needs without major imports, producing new demands that have recently driven up prices.[8] In addition, natural resource upgrading has not been the core of the growth of any of these countries and they remain relatively technologically weak in these sectors. By contrast, manufacturing exports have been at the core of Asia's development over the past three or four decades, led by exports of electronics hardware. Much of Latin America is rich in natural resources and firms have long experience in natural resource development and exporting – but are relatively weak in manufacturing exports. Broadly speaking, as Perez argues, these 'complementary' positions give Asia the advantage in labour- and technology-intensive manufacturing (or *fabricating* industries), while Latin America has dynamic comparative advantages in resource-based *processing* industries. Latin America as a whole has extremely varied resource endowments and capabilities so that, within this broad new thrust of development, specialization can be achieved within and between economies.

What are the resource-based processing industries and how to approach them? Perez' strategy aims at competitiveness in world export markets through the development of frontier technologies in process industries. Product areas cannot be specified or predicted in advance, but have to be shaped by policy makers and business leaders. What is clear, is that at the heart of the LA Vision is the idea that the continent could become one of the world's leading and most flexible sources of low, medium and high technology material inputs, food and other agricultural goods to the rest of the world and, in particular, to Asia, where demand is currently outstripping supply. While the future scale of demand may well fluctuate, the structure and quality of demand is likely to persist and grow in the medium to long term.

The vision entails a rapid technological upgrading of resource-based activities coupled with improved export performance through continuous innovation in products and processes. Recent research by Teixeira (2008) on Brazil shows that, although largely unrecognized and unsupported by policy, this process has already begun in some sectors, with strong Brazilian exports in medium-technology areas, and evidence of a transformation of the capabilities of leading local suppliers from local- to export-market competitiveness. This process of transition from import-substitution to export-led growth in Brazil has involved the creation of new capabilities within leading firms characterized by continuous innovation and the growth of significant export-market competencies, leading to successes in various high-value export niches, above and beyond traditional low-cost commodity markets.

However, Teixeira's work also emphasizes that this advance is limited to a relatively small number of leading firms and that policies have not sufficiently grasped, understood or supported progress in this area. Most firms lack awareness of this new opportunity. As a result, many other exporters that might have joined a growth 'bandwagon' have failed to do so. The Perez vision sees a gradual transformation of the whole economy as more and more firms learn to master and upgrade the processing industries. Each country contributes through its own technology and sector and specialties ranging from aluminium, to paper, to refining, to alcohol production, to petrochemicals to food.

Carlota also stresses variety in size of enterprise, which includes not only large-scale producers, but also medium-scale specialties (e.g., in chemicals, biotechnology and nanotechnology), small-scale customized materials and specialized chemicals, niche products, capital goods and high-technology support services. In some cases, these activities have taken root in the specific capabilities required in metallurgy, chemistry and food processing. But the vision is far wider and more ambitious, bringing in the development of advanced ICT trajectories, themselves based on scientific and research capabilities in the region. The thrust of the vision is to move increasingly towards higher value-added products supported by new technologies capable of creating further specialized products, more customized features and export-led innovative developments.

Of course, as Carlota makes clear in her paper, manufacturing could not and would not be abandoned. However, much of the specialization in manufacturing (or fabrication) would be applied to the growing needs of processing industries (for example, downstream capital goods) or alternatively in various high-value, low-volume niches that are now emerging as a result of the ICT paradigm, which Carlota calls 'hypersegmentation'. This applies especially to the largest Latin American economies (e.g., Brazil, Mexico and Argentina) where competitive capabilities in various manufacturing areas already exists.

Acquiring capabilities in processing and resource-based industries has great technological upgrading potential *via* ICT, biotechnology and new materials. Building process-based capabilities could enable Latin America to gain important footholds in forthcoming technological paradigms that might involve combinations of ICTs, biotechnology, nanotechnology, new materials and energy technologies.

Regarding socioeconomic inclusion, as Perez recognizes, the process industries are capital-intensive and tend to require a high proportion of skilled and highly skilled personnel. This suggests that alternative, complementary forms of growth capable of addressing unemployment, underemployment, informality and poverty need to be sought. 'Trickle down' has seldom brought about wide social benefits, so Carlota recommends a two-pronged policy approach to development; one focusing on growth, centred on process industries and resource-based specialization, the other addressing poverty and unemployment, amounting to what Perez terms 'a dual integrated model'.

The social inclusion dimension of the approach acts at the municipal and local levels by promoting and supporting wealth-creating activities, not only for traditional local markets but also regional and global markets. Perez recommends the development of specialized clusters targeting specific niche markets, based on local advantages operating within national and international value networks. The antipoverty half of the strategy is, so far, less well articulated in Carlota's model, but no less important than the core growth strategy. Both dimensions of the strategy need to linked and integrated; the antipoverty strategy improving the quality of life – the process strategy developing the core engines of growth for the economy.

An important argument of Perez is that this kind of model can only function within a socially and politically shared vision. Clearly, the various groups involved will act autonomously in their domains, but somehow a dynamic and effective institutional framework is needed to integrate and support both elements of the strategy. Carlota points to the need for consensus-building among groups in business, universities, nongovernmental organizations, and many other local groups – but clearly very little will happen without a strong government lead, supported by clear and forceful policy measures and incentives that induce the right kind of market behaviour. This is the kind of experimentation hinted at by Gerschenkron (1962) in his pioneering development studies of European industrialization. However, unlike the latter, Perez believes in the value of deliberate consensus-building and institutional shaping towards economic and social goals, creating a positive-sum strategy directed at well-specified windows of opportunity, framed by new global techno-economic paradigms.

Carlota's approach involves both research and action to bring about change. For example, research can identify cases where the above processes are already happening, how firms confront and overcome processes problems, how they are innovating and exporting in niche markets (e.g., Teixeira 2008). There may well be different kinds of resource-based specialization routes and strategies that research can identify and learn from, preparing the ground for an expansion of such activities, supported by policies and business strategies.

A key strength of Carlota's approach is that it goes beyond research, using research evidence to promote new policies and strategies that bring about practical changes towards a shared vision. Clearly, many aspects of the model need further development and research-iteration during the process of developing a vision. For example, as Perez stresses, we need to understand how to further the social and environmental dimensions of the model, demonstrating how society will benefit, through concrete examples, models and theorizing, in order to systematically address poverty and unemployment within Perez' dual integrated model.

There is also a pressing need to develop and apply the practical tools and processes that are able to convert research ideas, models, and examples into visions and policies. Many of these exist in the area of futures and visioning within industry, but they need to be absorbed and integrated into LA Vision in order to facilitate policy collaboration and change.[9] Visioning and implementation tools need to be co-developed with the research through all its the stages, not just at the end of the research as academics typically do. In other words, the research needs to be co-developed with decision makers in government, business and other social groups. They must be fully engaged in the vision process – as they are responsible for bringing about changes.

Conclusion

Research on the Asian economies reveals huge variety in sources of catch-up growth, industrial structure, government policies, scale of FDI, firm size and patterns of corporate ownership. In today's developing world, the idea of simple 'catch-up' can be quite misleading. As revealed in the Asian experience, there was not only variety but also substantial innovation in the methods, policies and strategies of catching up – perhaps as much variety in catch-up as in the ways leaders compete at the R&D frontier itself, as Abramovitz, Gerschenkron, Kuznets and Nelson all suggested in their work. We probably need a variety of growth models to capture all of this, especially, the symbiotic growth and technology relationships between catching-up economies and their partners in the 'developed world'.

Indeed, the conventional notion of 'catch-up' needs serious questioning, especially when thought of as a linear progression of latecomers toward a technological and market 'frontier' defined by leaders. Instead, we need a new conceptualization that recognizes and focuses on the various patterns of innovation that can and do occur during economic development, and that can lead to leadership, alternative positions, new markets, and a variety of unpredictable paths of growth.

The Asian cases revealed new growth paths centred on highly specific and symbiotic international relationships of technology, trade and investment. All this occurred within the context of a new, fast-growing techno-economic paradigm that created massive demand for various forms of electronics and information technology hardware that Asian firms learned to supply in partnership with their foreign buyers. Asian export-led growth was based on demand from the US and Europe and specific technology flows, mostly from the US and Japan, creating new, symbiotic, sustained forms of growth in Asia and in the partner countries such as the US.

Carlota's LA vision embraces these dynamics, linking Latin America with the developed market economies, the Asian countries including China, and other countries around the world. Rather than compete with Asia, Perez' model calls for *complementary* strategies that can exploit international demands and imbalances in technology, trade and investment of the kind Albert Hirschman and Charles Lindblom (1962) argued for.[10] Understanding how techno-economic paradigms emerge and transform can also help us identify market imbalances and bottlenecks and develop visions, based on likely poles of techno-economic growth occurring between countries, developed and developing.

In the context of Latin America, and for that matter other developing economies, there can be no direct Asian model to follow or copy. Other countries need to identify, build and exploit their own distinctive advantages and competencies as Asia did in the past. The electronics manufacturing boat may well have sailed as a development option, given the advanced stage of this ICT paradigm, the maturity and competence of Asian suppliers and the entry of new Asian economies, especially China. However, by complementing Asian growth paths and the new demands they produce, Latin America can create and exploit new growth poles by progressively moving up the value-added chain of resource-based activities, using cheap labour and low-cost advantages, only ever an 'entry ticket' to a path of sustained growth.

Despite Perez' progress with visions, their limits also need to be recognized. No one can guarantee a future vision and, therefore, flexibility, experimentation and the ability to learn rapidly and react to changes, problems and new opportunities is essential – perhaps more important than getting the vision 'right' or narrowly defined. Asia had no foresight regarding export-led growth, but swiftly exploited the ICT-led demand for electronics hardware in new innovative ways. Innovation in its widest sense (in technology, in institutions and policy) was fundamental to Asian success, consistent with the hypothesis of Gerschenkron (1962). To realize these new opportunities, LA governments need to work with industry and other partners, at home and abroad. Policymakers should not only involve themselves in vision building, but also in removing bureaucratic and other obstacles to growth, stimulating entrepreneurship in all its forms.

The value of Carlota's vision for Latin America is that it recognizes that, within the context of a new paradigm, any successful strategy must both build upon local and national advantages (or potential ones) – and complement prevailing external market and technological directions – thereby producing a positive-sum, highly engaged, national-international strategy, much the same way as Asia did in the past. 'Catching up' is a misnomer in this context. It is not a question of imitating or 'following the leader' but, instead, a matter of profound innovation on the part of the growing economy. Only by developing a new and distinctive approach to development did the economies of East and Southeast Asia grow rapidly for three decades. The same could be true for Latin America in the future. So, policy groups can be assured that the 'conventional wisdom' that continues to recommend packages of 'best practice' based on a single model of development should be rejected.

One of Carlota's chief contributions in this area is to provide the beginnings of the 'new apparatus' called for by Gerschenkron (1962, 359–360). This new approach goes beyond research to embrace a range of tools designed to develop a much clearer understanding of the opportunities created by new techno-economic paradigms within the world economy. Policymakers and researchers together need to chart possible new paths to development that combine local resource advantages with high-value-added opportunities and thereby achieve growth that embodies employment creation, fairness and sustainability. Carlota shows how these tools can be used to identify opportunities within Latin America and to elaborate how development strategies can be identified and pursued by firms and nations across the region, relying on human choice, experimentation and, ultimately, innovation.

References

Abramovitz, M. 1986. 'Catching Up, Forging Ahead and Falling Behind.' *The Journal of Economic History* 46, 385–406.

Amsden, A. 1989. *Asia's Next Giant: South Korea and Late Industrialization.* New York: Oxford University Press.

Chaponniere, J.-R. and M. Fouquin. 1989. *Technological Change and the Electronics Sector: Perspectives and Policy Options for Taiwan.* Report prepared for Development Centre Project. Paris: OECD.

Chou, T.-C. 1992. 'The Experience of SMEs' Development in Taiwan: High Export-Contribution and Export-Intensity.' *Rivista Internazionale di Scienze Economiche e Commerciali* 39, 12, 1067–1084.

Davies, A., T. Brady and M. Hobday. 2006. 'Charting a Path Towards Integrated Solutions.' *MIT Sloan Management Review* 47, 39-48.

de Geus, A. 1988. 'Planning as Learning.' *Harvard Business Review* 66, 70–74.

———. 1999. *The Living Company: Growth, Learning and Longevity in Business.* London: Nicholas Brealey.

Freeman, C. 1974. *The Economics of Industrial Innovation.* Middlesex: Penguin.

Gaulier, G., F. Lemoine and D. Unal-Kesenci. 2004. 'China's Integration in Asian Production Networks and Its Implications.' Paper, CEPII (Centre D'Etudes Prospectives Et D'Informations Internationales, Paris, France) Conference, 'Resolving New Global and Regional Imbalances in an Era of Asian Integration.' Tokyo, 17–18 June.

Gerschenkron, A. 1962. *Economic Backwardness in Historical Perspective: A Book of Essays.* Cambridge, MA: Belknap.

———. 1963. 'The Early Phases of Industrialisation in Russia.' In Walt W. Rostow (ed.). *The Economics of Take-off into Sustained Growth.* London: Macmillan.

Gordon, J. and P. Gupta. 2003. 'Understanding India's Services Revolution.' IMF Working Paper WP/04/171, Washington.

Hansda, S. 2001. 'Sustainability of Services-Led Growth: An Input Output Analysis of the Indian Economy.' Reserve Bank of India Occasional Paper 22, (1, 2 and 3).

Hirschman, A.-O. and C. E. Lindblom. 1962. 'Economic Development, Research and Development, Policy Making: Some Converging Views.' *Behavioural Science* 2, 211–222.

Hobday, M. 1995. *Innovation in East Asia: The Challenge to Japan.* London: Edward Elgar.

————. 1996. 'Innovation in South East Asia: Lessons for Europe?' *Management Decision* 34, 71–82.

————. 2000. 'East versus Southeast Asian Innovation Systems: Comparing OEM and TNC-led Growth in Electronics.' In L. Kim and R. R. Nelson (eds). *Technology, Learning and Innovation: Experiences of Newly Industrialising Economies.* New York: Cambridge University Press.

————. 2003. 'Innovation in Asian Industrialisation: A Gerschenkronian Perspective.' *Oxford Development Studies* 31, 293–314.

IBRD. 2008. *The Growth Report: Strategies for Sustained Growth and Inclusive Development.* Washington, DC: The World Bank, Commission on Growth and Development, The International Bank for Reconstruction and Development.

James, William. 1990. 'Basic Directions and Areas for Cooperation: Structural Issues of the Asia-Pacific Economies.' Asia Pacific Cooperation Forum, Session 2, June 21–22, Korea Institute for International Economic Policy, Seoul.

Kim, L. 1980. 'Stages of Development of Industrial Technology in a Less Developed Country: A Model.' *Research Policy* 9, 254–277.

————. 1997. *Imitation to Innovation: The Dynamics of Korea's Technological Learning,* Boston, MA: Harvard Business School Press.

Kuznets, S. 1958. 'The Pre-Industrial Phase in Advanced Countries: an Attempt at Comparison.' In A. N. Agarwala and S. P. Singh (eds). *The Economics of Underdevelopment.* London: Oxford University Press.

————. 1966. *Modern Economic Growth: Rate, Structure, and Spread.* New Haven, CT: Yale University Press.

Lee, J., Z.-T. Bae and D.-K. Choi. 1988. 'Technology Development Processes: A Model for a Developing Country with a Global Perspective.' *R&D Management* 18, 235–250.

Nelson, R. R. 1998. 'The Agenda for Growth Theory: A Different Point of View.' *Cambridge Journal of Economics* 22, 497–520.

Perez, C. 1985. 'Microelectronics, Long-Waves and World Structural Change: New Perspectives for Developing Countries.' *World Development* 13, 441–463. [9.1]

————. 2008. 'A Vision for Latin America: A Resource-Based Strategy for Technological Dynamism and Social Inclusion.' Presented to the ECLAC Program on Technology Policy and Development in Latin America, Santiago, Chile. [84.1.1]

Pfeffer, J. and R. I. Sutton. 2000. *The Knowing Doing Gap: How Smart Companies Turn Knowledge into Action.* Boston, MA: Harvard Business School Press.

Rodrik, D. 2004. 'Rethinking Growth Policies in the Developing World.' The Luca d'Agliano Lecture in Development Economics, Turin. http://ksghome.harvard.edu/~drodrik/luca_d_agliano_lecture_oct_2004.pdf

Rostow, W. W. 1960. *The Stages of Economic Growth: A Non-Communist Manifesto.* Cambridge: Cambridge University Press.

Schwartz, P. 1991. *The Art of the Long View: Paths to Strategic Insight for Yourself and Your Company.* New York: Currency Doubleday.

Singh, A. 2005. 'The Past, Present and Future of Industrial Policy in India: Adapting to Changing Domestic and International Environment.' Paper presented at New Delhi Industrial Policy Meeting, 13–14 December, Faculty of Economics, University of Cambridge, England.

Teixeira, A. 2008. *Latecomer Transition Capabilities: The Case of Brazilian Export Firms.* DPhil thesis, SPRU, University of Sussex, England.

Utterback, J. M. and W. J. Abernathy. 1975. 'A Dynamic Model of Process and Product Innovation.' *OMEGA, The International Journal of Management Science* 3, 639–656.

Vogel, E. F. 1991. *The Four Little Dragons: The Spread of Industrialisation in East Asia.* Cambridge, MA: Harvard University Press.

World Bank. 2004. *Doing Business in 2000.* Washington, DC: World Bank.

Yue, C. S. 1985. 'The Role of Foreign Trade and Investment in the Development of Singapore.' In W. Galenson (ed.). *Foreign Trade and Investment: Economic Development in the Newly Industrialising Asian Countries.* Madison, WI: University of Wisconsin Press.

Chapter Ten:

DOING CAPITALISM: NOTES ON THE PRACTICE OF VENTURE CAPITALISM (REVISED AND EXTENDED)

Warburg Pincus
and
Centre for Financial Analysis and Policy, University of Cambridge

Preface

I could not ignore the invitation to contribute to a *Festschrift* in honour of Carlota Perez. For Carlota's work stands at the hinge of my own career-long engagement at the interface of finance and technology. In *Technological Revolutions and Financial Capital* (Perez 2002), she defined an agenda too neglected in the history of economic development and in the analysis of the dynamics of capitalism. In doing so, she provided a framework for understanding the complex feedback loops that link technological innovations, embodied both in physical assets and business models, with the financial assets created to fund them and the necessarily speculative trading of those assets that follows on their distribution.

In her working paper on 'Finance and Technology: A Neo-Schumpeterian Perspective', Carlota Perez wrote:

> In Schumpeter's basic definition of capitalism as 'that form of private property economy in which innovations are carried out by means of borrowed money', we find his characteristic separation of borrower and lender, entrepreneur and banker, as the two faces of the innovation coin. This is not, however, how his legacy has been interpreted and enriched by the great majority of Neo-Schumpeterians. The accent has almost invariably been on the entrepreneur to the neglect of the financial agent,

no matter how obviously indispensable this agent may be to innovation. (Perez 2004, 2)

This contribution is intended to put some flesh on the bones of that abstract 'financial agent'.

The original of the revised and extended essay[1] to which this is a preface was instigated by Hyman Minsky in 1985, what today seems like another age. While it reads – and was intended so to do – as a measured reflection based on extended experience as an active venture capitalist (VC), in fact, it was rather more of a prospectus for what I hoped to be able to accomplish. It was written at the moment that my partners and I were completing the sale of our specialist Wall Street investment banking firm, F. Eberstadt & Co., Inc., to Robert Fleming PLC, a substantial British asset management and merchant banking firm. I myself was almost three years away from joining Warburg Pincus with a mandate to attempt to translate the propositions of the essay into a coherent investment strategy and an active investment portfolio. What follows is the original essay, whose text is in italics, into which I have interpolated comments drawn both from my own subsequent experience and from the burgeoning academic literature on the practice of venture capital.

Introduction

This paper originated in a shock of recognition. In the second volume of his discourse on Civilization and Capitalism *Fernand Braudel muses on the 'eclecticism' of 'the most advanced kind of capitalism':*

> *as if the characteristic advantage of standing at the commanding heights of the economy … consisted precisely of not having to confine oneself to a single choice, of being able, as today's businessmen would put it, to keep one's options open. (Braudel 1982, 381).*

My colleagues and I work as venture capitalists and as investment bankers of a specialized kind, engaged in raising capital to support the growth of technology-based companies and in realizing liquidity for their founding investors – often ourselves – by managing public offerings of their shares or by merging them into much larger companies. A primary virtue of our practice is the opportunity to choose with broad discretion where to commit our own and our clients' capital across what Braudel calls 'the differential geography of profit'. (Braudel 1982, 433)

The immediate relevance of Braudel's insight made me seek to recall how other primary explorers of the dynamics of economic society had characterized the role of 'the capitalist'. This paper, accordingly, begins with a discussion of what capitalists do in the worlds of Braudel and Marx and Keynes and Schumpeter. The second section of the paper is a report from the front: what do the venture capitalists I know actually try to do with the capital and other resources they control. My conclusions reflect both the contemporary relevance of the authorities and a desire to find out how much, if at all, the professional practice of venture capital today represents a novel extension of capitalism.

What Capitalists Do: Four Views

Braudel: *In Braudel's synoptic view, the 'unlimited flexibility' of capitalists in their search for profit is the 'essential feature' that establishes a 'certain unity in capitalism from thirteenth-century Italy to the present-day West':*

> *One's impression then ... is that there were always sectors in economic life where high profits could be made,* but that these sectors varied. *Every time one of these shifts occurred, under the pressure of economic developments, capital was quick to seek them out, to move into the new sector and prosper ... (Braudel 1982, 433–434)*

The telling point is Braudel's grasp of the capitalist's unchanging goal: to escape from the 'world of transparence and regularity,' as he defines the 'economy', where the possibility of profit is constrained and even eliminated by the regulations of the traditional market or the competition of the emerging free market: 'the capitalist game only concerned the unusual, the very special, or the very long distance connection ...' (Braudel 1982, 456). It was in long distance trade where Braudel's capitalists truly flourished:

> *Long-distance trade certainly made super profits; it was after all based on the price difference between two markets very far apart, with supply and demand in complete ignorance of each other and brought into contact only by the activity of middlemen ... If in the fullness of time competition did appear, if super-profits vanished from one line, it was always possible to find them again on another route with different commodities ... (Braudel 1982, 405)*

If the domain and context is vastly different, yet the activity remains recognizable: to put surplus cash to work, again and again, wherever the potential return is effectively unlimited either by established economic and other institutional structures or by competition. But to pioneer in establishing 'the long distance connection' was, literally, to sail uncharted seas in primitive boats with rudimentary instruments for navigation and for defence. The magnitude of the possible reward was commensurate with the risk ... of sailing off the edge of the world.

The notion of 'arbitrage' as the essence of investment retains a powerful resonance. For Braudel's capitalist, the arbitrage opportunity was created by geographical distance. For the modern, technology-oriented VC, the arbitrage is between an innovation and its transformation into a commercialized product or service. My experience suggests that too much weight is given to management of the process of technical transformation – 'research and development' – and too little to the selection of the target output. For Braudel's capitalist, the question asked of the sea captain would be: 'Why are you setting your course *there*?' For a modern VC, the corresponding question of the entrepreneur would be: 'Just *whose* problem are you proposing to solve?' It took me some twenty years to fully absorb this principle.

The domains where 'super profits' have been available for capture by professional venture capitalists, in fact, have proven to be quite limited. Information technology, broadly defined, and secondarily, biotechnology, have accounted for a substantial majority of all of US venture capital activity since the 1960s (Gompers and Lerner 2004, 12–13, Table 1.2). I discuss below some reasons why VCs have found success in such a limited 'geography of profit'. But even within the limited range of industries where VCs have found success, there is a trade-off between industry specialization and the flexibility to shift investment focus across industries. A recent academic study has found the highest returns to be associated with 'generalist firms with specialized' investors (Gompers, Kovner, Lerner and Scharfstein 2006a), that is, a firm equipped to respond at least partially to Braudel's observation that 'high profit' opportunities move from sector to sector over time.

Marx: While Marx' principal theoretical concern is with the generation of surplus value through the process of industrial production, he defines 'the capitalist' in terms as general as Braudel might wish. The creation of capital arises from the capitalist's inversion of the circulation of commodities, 'C-M-C' – 'selling in order to buy' – into 'M-C-M' – 'buying in order to sell.' (Marx 1961, vol. I, 152–153) The generality of the capitalist's role as the embodiment of accumulation again, as for Braudel, crosses the nominal phases of capitalism:

> *Buying in order to sell, or more accurately, buying in order to sell dearer, M-C-M',*
> *appears certainly to be a form peculiar to one kind of capital alone, merchants' capital.*
> *But industrial capital too is money that is changed into commodities, and by the sale*
> *of these commodities is re-converted into more money. The events that take place outside*
> *the sphere of circulation, in the interval between the buying and the selling, do not*
> *affect the form of this movement … (Marx 1961, vol. 1, 155)*

But those 'events' decisively affect the substance; in fact, they create the very reason for the circulation of capital in the first place. The increase in money, which drives the process, arises from the capitalist's purchase and exploitation of the commodity that alone can create value, namely labor. So the capitalist exists as the omnipotent human link in the endless chain of accumulation, converting cash into 'means of production and labor-power' in order to produce commodities which he then sells for more cash 'over and over again.' (Marx 1961, vol. 1, 564)

The power that Marx' capitalist enjoys to command labor power in order to create surplus-value distinguishes him from Braudel's capitalist, who finances a venture which, literally, sails beyond his own control. At least until 'the law of the tendency of the rate of profit to fall' asserts itself (Marx 1961, vol. 3, chapters 13–14), Marx does not allow for the uncertainty inherent in the capitalist process of production, by which I mean the certainty that at every moment for some capitalists – and at some moment for all capitalists – the never-ending circle will be broken and they will lose money. There is, however, one intriguing reference in Capital *to what might be broadly recognized as venture capital in a distinctive, if unflattering, guise:*

> *If the rate of profit falls ... there appears swindling and a general promotion of swindling by recourse to frenzied ventures with new methods of production, new investments of capital, new adventures, all for the sake of securing a shred of extra profit which is independent of the general average and rises above it (Marx 1961, vol. III, 253–5).*

The intriguing aspect of this insight, of course, is the fact that the venture capital boom of the 1980s, funded by billions of dollars committed from institutional and corporate sources of capital, has indeed followed on more than a decade of secular disappointment, if not depression, in the profitability of established industry. And yet, Marx' simple and profound spiral remains: from M to C to more M. Substitute 'company' for 'commodity' and you have in brief the charter of the professional venture capitalist.

Marx's capitalist exists in order, successively, to build independent businesses of ever greater scale and scope. By contrast, the venture capitalist manages successive portfolios of investments, fund by fund, distributing risk across 'multiple shots on goal'. And the outcome of a successful venture capital investment is often sale of the venture to an established company ('trade sale') rather than the public offering of its stock ('IPO'). In fact, much of venture capital investing can be thought of as funding 'distributed research and development' for large enterprises. Contrariwise, Cisco represents but one, if the largest and most successful technological enterprise, deliberately to drive growth through acquisition of innovative ventures. We shall see below how dependent venture capital returns are on the availability of a receptive IPO market. Here it is sufficient to note that success in funding a sustainable business to positive cash flow from operations is only one and, at that, the rarest of the distribution of outcomes professional venture capitalists may enjoy across their portfolios. But, as Marx's capitalists would recognize, it is only success in returning more capital to their limited partners than originally committed that buys for VCs the opportunity to keep playing the game.

Keynes: *The capitalist of Keynes' General Theory inhabits a world hardly recognizable to Marx, one in which 'the outstanding fact is the extreme precariousness of the basis of knowledge on which our estimates of prospective yield have to be made'. (Keynes 1961, 149) The maturing of capitalism has produced both the separation of ownership* *and management and the development of organized security markets. The result represents a radical break with capitalist experience:*

> *[T]he daily revaluations of the Stock Exchange … inevitably exert a decisive influence on the rate of current investment. For there is no sense in building a new enterprise at a cost greater than that at which a similar existing enterprise can be purchased; whilst there is an inducement to spend on a new project what may seem an extravagant sum, if it can be floated off in the Stock Exchange at an immediate profit. Thus certain classes of investment are governed by the average expectation of those who deal in the Stock Exchange as revealed in the price of shares, rather than by the genuine expectation of the professional entrepreneur. (Keynes 1961, 151)*

For Keynes, the separation of ownership and management has turned the capitalist into an investor, and the development of organized security markets all but inevitably turns the investor into a speculator. (Keynes 1961, 154–155)

Against speculation, 'the activity of forecasting the psychology of the market', stands enterprise, 'the activity of forecasting the prospective yield of assets over their whole life.' (Keynes 1961, 158) But the capitalist engaged in enterprise is as far from the embodiment of calculating maximization as may be imagined. Though derived in order to explain the failure of capitalist enterprise to spur economic recovery from the bottom of the Great Depression, Keynes' characterization of the capitalist as an instinctual animal operating within the speculative casino of the Stock Exchange has remarkable resonance for the venture capitalist today. (Keynes 1961, 161–162) The venture capital boom of the past several years was directly driven by the extraordinary 'high-tech' speculation in the new issue market in 1983. And the collapse of 'animal spirits' among professional venture capitalists apparent in 1985 has followed upon the inevitable collapse both of the stock market speculation and of many of the ventures that were funded under the influence of that speculation. More broadly, in contrast with the capitalist as prime mover in Braudel and Marx, Keynes' capitalist is utterly passive when it comes to the actual commitment of capital to new profit-promising enterprise. Secondary dealing in shares has arisen as a substitute for forging a long-distance bridge between supply and demand or direct engagement in the creation of value.

The 'boom' of 1983 and the 'collapse' of 1985 have a quaint ring to all who have survived the dot-com/telecom Great Bubble of 1999–2000 and its aftermath. The excesses, including the excess returns captured by venture capitalists during the latter episode, dwarf the profits available in the earlier one. As one crude measure, the total amount of capital raised in all venture-backed IPOs in the mini-Bubble year of 1983 (calculated in 2002 dollars) was approximately $4.25 billion; the amount raised in each of 1999 and 2000, the years of the maxi-Bubble, approximated $21 billion, or ten times as much (Gompers and Lerner 2004, 12–13, Table 1.2). But here we have a signal of great significance for differentiating the contingencies facing the modern VC from Braudel's and Marx's model capitalists. For indeed, the risk that dominates venture returns over the past generation is the state of the public equity markets, the financial environment, versus the operational risks to which Braudel's financiers were exposed and that challenged even Marx's protagonist.

Perhaps the most tempting path to perdition for a modern VC has been to attempt to read from current market signals the appropriate loci of new venture investments. Keynes explicitly cites the 'inducement' to invest an 'extravagant sum' if the projects 'can be floated off in the Stock Exchange at an immediate profit'. But, almost invariably, the latency in the venture investment process is simply too great. There were new ventures that were conceived and floated to the public markets within the span of the Great Bubble of 1999–2000, but the reckoning generally came too soon for the venture investors to realize liquidity before first the shares and then the putative business collapsed. As the global financial crisis that began in 2007 deepens and extends the relative IPO drought that has existed since 2001, this risk is not of current concern. What is of concern is the stark alternative that VCs and entrepreneurs jointly face in the absence of an active IPO market: to focus a new venture on proving the commercial utility of an innovation with the goal of delivering it into the hands of a large enterprise that already owns all the other components of a business (distribution, marketing, production, financial administration and compliance), or to take on the much greater challenge of attempting to build an independent business that can fund itself from internally generated cash flow. Those who succeed on the latter path will, no doubt, eventually be rewarded; the risk/reward calculus is bound to favour the former path for most.

Schumpeter: *Schumpeter likewise sets a reduced, secondary role for the modern capitalist owner against the distinctive emphasis he places on the entrepreneur, as Perez noted in her 2004 paper. Innovation – 'any 'doing things differently' in the realm of economic life' (Schumpeter 1939, 84) – drives the course of economic evolution. And innovations in turn are embodied in New Plant, in New Firms and, above all, in New Men (Schumpeter 1939, 93-96) – the entrepreneurs who carry out innovations:*

> *… [T]he entrepreneur may, but need not, be the person who furnishes the capital … In the institutional pattern of capitalism there is machinery, the presence of which forms an essential characteristic of it, which makes it possible for people to function as entrepreneurs without having previously acquired the necessary means. It is leadership rather than ownership that matters. (Schumpeter 1939, 103)*

The capitalist, in his prime role as owner of surplus cash available for investment, has been relegated in remarkable fashion:

> *[R]isk bearing is no part of the entrepreneurial function. It is the capitalist who bears the risk. The entrepreneur does so only to the extent to which, besides being an*

entrepreneur, he is also a capitalist, but qua entrepreneur he loses other people's money *(emphasis added) … (Schumpeter 1939, 104)*

Turnabout is fair play, as capitalists are the heirs of the successful entrepreneurs of previous generations and are thereby endowed with the opportunity to redistribute their wealth by placing it at the disposal of new entrepreneurs. (Schumpeter 1939, 106)

Schumpeter is at pains to separate out the entrepreneurial function as against the variety of individuals who may fill the role. In the old competitive capitalism, it is easy to find the entrepreneur 'among the heads of firms.' It is in the modern capitalism of 'giant concerns' that the entrepreneur's identity – as manager, salaried employee or major stockholder – has become problematic. Schumpeter extends his search further, finally touching on what appears to be the proto-venture capitalist:

Although company promoters are not as a rule entrepreneurs, a promoter may fill that function occasionally and then come near to presenting the only instance there is of a type which is entrepreneur by profession and nothing else. *(Schumpeter 1939, 103; emphasis added)*

The very process which transforms, historically and conceptually, the aggressive owner of surplus wealth into the passive candidate for entrepreneurial exploitation in turn creates the space into which the professional venture capitalist can move.

This article was written relatively early in my career, when I still was in transition from investment banking to venture capital. While I had grasped the iron law of cash flow, I had not fully comprehended the logic of hedging illiquid investments in an uncertain world. At this writing, investors the world over have been discovering that the promise of quantitative risk management through hedging strategies implemented in purportedly liquid markets can prove catastrophically illusory. But such strategies are not even theoretically available to the venture capitalist. Two instruments are available to the venture capitalist when things go awry, cash and control: cash to buy time to fix things and control to use the time thus bought. In terms of the relationship between the entrepreneur and the venture capitalist, the simple, brutal rule is: 'If you cannot sell your shares, you better be able to fire the CEO'. And yet, in the long history of the innovation economy, there is much evidence that Schumpeter's emphasis on the entrepreneurs versus their source of funding was well placed.

The dynamic relationship between entrepreneur and venture capitalist has generated a rich literature over the past 20-plus years, both academic (e.g., Lerner 1995, 301–318) and non-academic (e.g., Ferguson 2001). The most comprehensive study of the respective contributions of entrepreneurs and venture capitalists to successful outcomes concludes that '…previously successful entrepreneurs derive no benefits from the value-added services of more experienced venture capital firms....' (Gompers, Kovner, Lerner and Scharfstein 2006b, 2–3). Contrariwise, '[w]here venture capital firm experience does matter is the performance of first-time entrepreneurs and serial entrepreneurs with histories of failure (Gompers, Kovner, Lerner and Scharfstein 2006b,16). When properly seasoned, Schumpeter's entrepreneur thus trumps even the experienced venture capitalist. Yet every entrepreneur was once a novice....

What Venture Capitalists Do: One Experience

The single most salient canonical fact to emerge from the academic study of venture capital returns is the extreme skew they exhibit. A landmark study of venture capital performance documents a large differential between internal rates of return at the 75th and the 25th percentile of 23 per cent versus 3 per cent (Kaplan and Schoar 2007, 1798 (Table II). My own research draws upon a sample of funds with performance roughly twice that of the industry as a whole; it indicates that, excluding the top decile of funds, performance failed to match that of the relevant public markets over more than two decades since 1980. On the other hand, the top decile of funds showed extraordinary performance relative to any benchmark; their median return from 1980 to roughly 2003 was no less than 193 per cent; even excluding the Bubble period, the top decile of funds delivered a median IRR of 93 per cent. (McKenzie and Janeway 2008, Table V)

Both Kaplan and Schoar, and MacKenzie and Janeway also find evidence of persistence in VC returns; performance of a given fund is a predictor of performance of the next (MacKenzie and Janeway 2008, 33–34) and the next two (Kaplan and Schoar 2007, 1805–1809) funds. This is arguably the only class of financial assets in which such persistence has been documented. It may testify to the scarcity of the skills on which success in venture investing is based, whose importance is enough to outweigh the volatility of the markets in which the output of those skills are valued. In what follows, the venture capitalist, 'taken at his own aspiration', may be deemed to be one of that 'talented (and persistent) tenth' responsible for the industry's excess returns.

Let us first take the professional venture capitalist at his own aspiration. For analytical purposes, I abstract his practice into four categories of activity: selection of investment, working with entrepreneurs, providing financial autonomy and declaring victory.

Selection of Investment: *As ever in the history of capitalism, from the furthest frontier of Braudel's research on down, the goal is to compete as little as* necessary, *not as little as possible. The distinction here reflects the conflict between being first in successfully exploiting a new technology versus being so much the first that no market exists for the product. The history of venture capital is littered with examples of technological 'solutions' in search* *of commercially identifiable problems; the history of venture capital is also littered with sets of 'me-too' start-ups seeking to follow where others have already proven a market to exist. The point is that the selection of interesting investment opportunities requires the matching of evolving technological capabilities with evolving market needs.*

Keynes wrote fifty years ago that 'investment based on genuine long-term expectation is so difficult today as to be scarcely practical', contrasting it with the speculative game of guessing 'better than the crowd how the crowd will behave.' (Keynes 196, 104) The venture capitalist elevates the task into another dimension, for he is attempting to form a genuine long-term expectation at the most problematic frontier, where rapidly evolving technologies and barely emergent markets intersect. No wonder that venture capitalists should search for the 'unfair advantages' that a particular entrepreneurial team brings to attack a particular market/technology window or that most venture capitalists should spend most of their time playing follow the leader (Braudel's merchant venturers only financed the pioneering of new trade routes when excessive competition forced them to). In either case, the venture capitalist is assuming the secondary role assigned by Schumpeter, betting on an entrepreneur.

In addressing the challenge of investment selection in 1985, I ignored perhaps the single most economically significant aspect of the issue. As asserted by Andrew Metrick, 'large companies are the optimal place for the majority of high-tech innovations' (Metrick 2007, 14). A bit of lore available to ingest at my original firm, F. Eberstadt, was the history of how 'plastic' – endowed with a special status in the universe of innovation, courtesy of the movie *The Graduate* – actually came to be commercialized. It took each of General Electric and DuPont twenty years and more than one billion of vintage 1955–1975 dollars to bring engineered polymers to mass-market acceptance, and success depended in good part on the intervention of OPEC, whose price revolution in the early 1970s induced auto companies to substitute plastics for steel in order to reduce the weight of cars. Technical problems of production scale-up were only part of the problem. Investment in application marketing and product engineering – that is, identification in parallel of those whose problems plastics could solve and development of the specific product as the solution – were necessary across a broad spectrum and over years, requiring resources beyond the scope of any collection of venture capitalists and on a time frame beyond the lifetime of any VC fund. More generally, materials science has generated countless innovations of enormous commercial significance and a vanishingly small number of successful ventures. I am reasonably confident that the lesson of plastics will be relearned in the domain of nanotechnology.

In this context, the paradox of biotechnology requires some consideration. In 1977, I received a phone call from Bob Swanson, the VC co-founder of Genentech who had previously known the Eberstadt firm in his role as an analyst at Citibank. This led to an intense focus on the part of my colleagues and me on the nascent biotechnology industry. Our conclusion was clear: biotechnology was an inappropriate domain for venture investing because the time from laboratory to clinic by way of the FDA was certain to exceed the 10–12 year life of a venture fund. As it was not possible to generate operating revenues, a successful investment would be dependent, inevitably and decisively, on the generosity of the public equity markets both for intermediate funding and for ultimate liquidity. As 1973–1980 was one of those seemingly endless epochs when there was effectively no IPO market, such a risk profile was unacceptable.

Even in retrospect, reflecting on the observable existence of some five windows for biotech IPOs over the past thirty years, I remain unconvinced that we were wrong. The transient availability for public investment in no-revenue/cash-negative biotech ventures appears to me to have been an episodic function of some event – FDA approval of a 'miracle drug' – that induces enough investors to ignore the objectively available Bayesian prior on the number of candidate molecules that actually reach market and, instead, to execute the following algorithm:

- There are two available states of the world:
  (1) The molecule succeeds and we make a 'gazillion' dollars
  (2) The molecule fails and we lose everything….
- 'Half a gazillion is good enough for me!'

That the aggregate net return on both venture and public investment in biotech is a substantial negative number – notwithstanding Genentech, Amgen and a few others – is common wisdom in the venture industry. On the other hand, the fact that a handful of VC firms, such as Venrock, have recorded repeated success in biotech investments over several decades provides evidence for the limited stock of skill that drives both the extreme skew and the distinctive persistence in venture capital returns.

Working with Entrepreneurs: *Venture capitalists do not, by and large, plan to be the pawns of rapacious entrepreneurs. Sooner or later, nonetheless, the venture capitalist learns this law of life: entrepreneurs lie. It comes with the territory, as Arthur Miller put it in a not wholly different context. For the innovating entrepreneur would have the world become by his efforts other than as, by definition, it now is. And the world is often recalcitrant. When the world resists, the accuracy of reported results is likely to suffer.*

A tenacious grasp on the realities of the cash cycle is the venture capitalist's defence. When entrepreneurs are able to lie, it is generally because the venture capitalist is about to be taught the difference between the Income Statement, as defined within the flexible standards of Generally Accepted Accounting Principles, and Cash Flow, as inflexibly defined by the bank statement of receipts and disbursements. Countless are the ventures which have run out of money while reporting record profits as they accelerate reported revenues by hook and by crook.

It is a tribute to Marx that 'M-C-M', the flow of cash – out, to purchase labor services and materials; in, from the collection of receivables for the sale of products – should remain the basis for policing the financial integrity of the capitalist venture.

By insisting on the direct expression of all operating decisions in terms of cash in/cash out the venture capitalist participates as active partner in the entrepreneurial process. It is as if he has signed on to one of Braudel's voyages, if not as navigator then as paymaster. And, when a venture stumbles, it is generally the venture capitalist who gets to insist on the final law of cash flow: there are no fixed costs, only a definable period of time – and a corresponding cash requirement to buy the time – during which to translate high-and-fixed into low-and-variable expenses.

In working with entrepreneurs over a generation, I have found a near absolute, binary distinction between those whose strategic purpose is to build a business and those whose all-encompassing engagement is with the technology. My own contrarian approach has begun with the observation that, at any point in time, there is far more technology available than anyone knows what to do with. Further, merely adding to the stock of available technology creates no economic value, which brings us back to the question that brings the marketplace into the conversation: Just whose problem are you proposing to solve?

There is a corollary to this observation: the best technology need not win in the marketplace. In fact, a number of salient turning points in the competitive dynamics of the Information Technology industry over the past generation would suggest that the best technology is likely to lose:

- Intel won dominance in the market for 16-bit microprocessors
- Microsoft won dominance in the market for PC operating systems
- Oracle won dominance in the market for relational database management systems

In each case, technically inferior offerings beat technically superior offerings from Zilog, IBM and Ingres, respectively, as the losers in each case knew that they had delivered 'the best' and did not believe they had much more to do, while the winners in each case won through commercial focus and marketing prowess.

While the 'successful serial entrepreneur' may need no help in integrating between market needs and technological capabilities, it is often the VC who begins the conversation by insisting that the problematic gap be addressed. It is also the VC who inevitably, at the inception of any venture, and episodically whenever new capital is raised, insists on consideration of exit alternatives. That is to say, the VC represents the external reality that it is the entrepreneur's mission in some way to alter.

Providing Financial Autonomy: *With rights go responsibilities. In return for the right to participate in building a venture, the venture capitalist accepts the responsibility for providing finance. Both to fulfil this responsibility and to share risks in pursuit of the best deals, venture capitalists travel in packs. Just as with the merchant financiers whose networks Braudel traces across pre-modern Europe, professional venture capitalists work in identifiable cliques and coteries, a small number as leaders – and in some cases allies – and a vastly large number as followers. Beyond the ranks of the self-proclaimed, risk-seeking venture capitalists, the lead venture capitalist seeks to establish access to consistent support for the ventures he sponsors among the relatively small number of institutional investors gaited for long-term illiquid private equity investments, among potential corporate 'partners', among commercial bank 'venture lenders', among leasing companies, throughout the established structure of finance and industry. The duty of the venture capitalist, in short, is to be rich ... in relationships, even more than cash.*

The emergence of professional venture capitalists over the post-war generation has been punctuated by waves of speculative fever which have swept through the securities markets and deluged new ventures of every sort and description with literally (though momentarily) limitless funds: 1983 was only the most recent. But the bubbles are the exception; their lifetimes are measurable in months. The venture capitalist earns his return in good part by securing the financial resources to support his ventures during the years in between. From the day I joined my firm in 1970 until the explosion that began in the winter of 1982–3, 1 should note, there were no more than six to eight quarters out of more than fifty during which the equity market in New York was reasonably accessible to initial public offerings for new companies.

The value of being 'rich in relationships' has been definitively documented by a recent academic study of venture capital networks. Applying graph theory to data on US venture capital investment syndicates and returns, the authors conclude that 'VCs that are better networked at the time a fund is raised subsequently enjoy significantly better fund performance' (Hochberg, Lungqvist and Lu 2007, 253). But even the best networked VC cannot protect a venture from the consequences of a bear market and the closing of the IPO window. Finally, the overriding significance of the financial environment in which venture capitalists and entrepreneurs exist demands assessment.

Declaring Victory: *A new issue market such as that of 1983 makes it easy, so easy that the problematic question of what constitutes 'victory' can be ignored. Going public at extraordinary values – multiples of what Keynes' long-term investor would consider appropriate – becomes a substitute for victory. For an enterprise, victory might be considered to be the achievement of such a position of market franchise and technological security as to allow management effective discretion in trading off profitability versus growth, while also conferring on management the discretionary' power to generate positive cash flow from operations. No amount of capital is enough if these operating goals are not attainable, and they are not attained often.*

For the venture capitalist, as distinct from the enterprise, the case is even clearer. Victory for today's venture capitalist is identical with what it has always been, as chronicled by Braudel and as proclaimed by Marx: to realize his investment – at a rate of return that fully compensates for the risk accepted – in the form of cash which is then available for new investments. The new issue market of 1983 allowed liquidity to be nominally created for stockholders in a host of ventures. The regulations under the securities laws and the restrictions imposed by underwriters generally combined to keep the venture investors locked in until the bubble had burst and the world and the marketplace had done a reasonable job of separating out the sheep from the goats.

Effective victory is more certainly available, as a venture matures, by merging it into an established company. As maturity expresses itself – whether in incipient price-taking or incipient technological exhaustion or incipient organizational inflexibility – it is generally more attractive to realize all of one's investment at one fell swoop than to hope to cash out bit by bit, ever dependent upon the vagaries of the public market and its assessment of value. For very few new ventures of any sort, at any time, 'go all the way'. The quintessential representative of Keynes' professional class of speculators should have the last word on the subject. When asked how he had made his money, Bernard Baruch legendarily replied: 'By selling too soon.'

Of course, the new issue market of 1982–1983 was the trailer for the full-length feature of 1999–2000. But looking across the entire span from 1980 to the post-Bubble era, the dependence of venture capital returns on access to the IPO market is clear. My own research characterizes each quarter since the start of 1980 by the number of venture-backed IPOs and the proportion of them that were for companies not yet profitable, thereby generating an index of IPO market speculation (or lack thereof). The median internal rate of return for the funds in our sample when distributions back to their investors coincided with superior IPO market conditions was no less than 76 per cent, while under poor IPO market conditions the median IRR was only 9 per cent; eliminating the top decile only reduces these median returns to 69 per cent and 7 per cent respectively (McKenzie and Janeway 2008, Table XI).

In the absence of a hot IPO market, theory would suggest that the alternative of a trade sale can be expected to yield lowers returns, as elimination of the 'outside option' of going public reduces the joint bargaining power of the entrepreneur and VC (Metrick 2007, 100). One study of some 12,000 venture exits estimates that the valuations achieved in IPOs exceed those in trade sales, as theory would suggest (Das, Jaganathan, Sarin 2003). Since the end of the Bubble in 2001, venture-backed IPOs declined precipitously and, since the onset in 2007 of the financial crisis, the IPO market has effectively closed across all geographies. The consequences for venture capital returns, for the venture capital industry and, indeed, for the innovation economy more broadly, will be substantial.

Some Conclusions: The Capitalist as Entrepreneur

For my part, the original shock of recognition remains. Schumpeter writes of entrepreneurial innovations creating 'New Economic Space.' (Schumpeter 1939, 134) It is across this space, as across the ocean challenged by Braudel's capitalists, that today's venture capitalists are chartered to explore a like 'differential geography of profit'. As innovators breaking free from the structured world of mature capitalism, they are supposed to be throwbacks in spirit to an earlier age, while mastering simultaneously the commercial potential of a range of frontier technologies. In fact, reality is less romantic, and the operating significance of Keynes' sermon on enterprise and speculation remains profound. I would judge that the great majority of venture investments made by the great majority of professional venture capitalists only one and two years ago have already proved not to have been based on 'superior long-term-forecasts of the probable yield of an investment over its whole life' but rather were attempts, more or less witting, 'to guess better than the crowd how the crowd will behave.' (Keynes, 1961, 154–5) And some victories will always be a function of dumb luck. The observation that Braudel cites from Jean de La Bruyere is telling:

> *there ... are stupid men and I dare even say imbeciles who find themselves good places and are able to die rich without one having any reason to suspect that they have contributed to this by their labor or the slightest industry: someone simply took them to the source of a river, or perhaps mere chance put them in its way; they were asked 'Do you want water? Take it.' And they took it. (Braudel 1982, 402)*

Yet the relationship between risk and reward remains as critical as it is problematic. Marx' all powerful capitalist operates free from the risk which Schumpeter's exploited capitalist passively bears. The venture capitalist both bears risk and is supposed to work to reduce it. While this contributed labor, indeed, is intended to generate value and potentially surplus value, much of it is bound to run to waste and loss. But note: by and large, it is not the venture capitalist's loss. For, as Schumpeter remarked in his passing reference to the 'company promoter', today's professional venture capitalists are themselves generally entrepreneurs, working to earn a carried interest in the funds they have secured from wealthy families, pension funds, insurance companies, industrial corporations, banks and even in some instances the retail investing public. In a broad-gauged effort to pursue higher returns than have been available in established industry by emulating the success of a relatively small number of individuals and partnerships whose activities date from the 1950s and 1960s, such institutions have committed billions of dollars under contract to a host of professional venture capitalists in the past few years. In this phenomenon there is something novel.

The venture capitalist as entrepreneurial fund manager seeks to reduce his risk actuarially by spreading it across a portfolio of investments, each carefully screened for technological innovation, market relevance and managerial leadership. This, at least, is the prospectus he offers his investors. In truth, every investment to some extent represents its own gamble on the wind and the tides and the current incidence of piracy and scurvy and the most feared of all threats, competition. Throughout the history of capitalist enterprise, there have emerged rules to reduce the odds: counting the cash at the end of every day and before and after every decision is still the most important, which in turn means that no spread of commitments is an effective substitute for sailing as an active partner on every vessel that you back.

In the current epoch of dimmed animal spirits and faltering spontaneous optimism for high technology ventures, there is a certain comfort in observing speculative enthusiasm shift – as Braudel might have foreseen – to the opposite end of the spectrum, the leveraged buy-out of the industrial dinosaur. Less visibly, the professional venture capitalists are proceeding in their efforts to prove, if they can, their durability as a hybrid species of capitalist and entrepreneur. But building companies is hard work and much presumption underlies the venture capitalist's promise. He is, after all, himself an entrepreneur, and we know that entrepreneurs lie. The possibility does exist that, in retrospective fact, the emergence of the professional venture capitalist as a generic actor in our economic society will represent an ephemeral, epiphenomenal flourish marking the peak of our generation's great speculation. And yet, and yet ... how great was the presumption in travelling East for spices eight hundred years ago!

Undoubtedly, the best was yet to come for the 'financial agents' whose capital fed the great wave of technological innovation that initiated and drove the deployment of the global Internet. And this is precisely where these reflections on 'Doing Capitalism' intersect Carlota Perez' innovative contribution. For me, her signal achievement has been to explain the necessary endogeneity of speculative financial bubbles at the core of the process through which fundamental, networked technologies are deployed and through which the new economic space thereby created is explored. The professional venture capital industry, whose existence and characteristics my 1985 paper considered, came into its spectacular fulfilment, alongside the entrepreneurial segment of the equity markets, precisely as the dot-com/telecom Bubble emerged in the late 1990s. The venture capital industry provided critical funding for deployment of the physical infrastructure of the Internet before anyone could observe the economic benefits and cash flow returns that it would generate and, likewise, for the Darwinian explosion of hopeful monsters competing to deliver those benefits and to generate that positive cash flow. This, precisely, is what Bubbles are for!

The numbers are staggering; capital committed to member firms of the National Venture Capital Association (NVCA) rose from $4 billion in 1985, the year of my original paper, to $9.9 billion in 1995 and then onward and upward; $20 billion in 1997, $30 billion in 1998, $56 billion in 1999 and no less than $105 billion in 2000. Capital, under the management of NVCA members, grew from $18 billion in 1985 to $225 billion in 2000. After the Bubble burst, annual commitments of new capital dropped to $10 billion per year in 2002 and 2003, but then rose back to $20 billion in 2004, $30 billion in each of 2005 and 2006 and reached $40 billion in 2007 (NVCA 2008, Tables 1.02 and 2.02). And this resurgence took place even as the market for

IPOs remained constrained and haphazardly accessible at best, before it effectively disappeared with the onset of the Financial Crisis in 2007. If, indeed, the economic role for venture capitalists in the foreseeable future is to fund distributed R&D, in the absence of a vibrant IPO market, then I hypothesize that the industry is hugely overcapitalized. One may note that in 1981, out of aggregate VC investments of $1.2 billion, $343 million went to 'seed/start-up' investments; in 2004, out of aggregate VC investments of $21 billion, the amount committed to 'seed/start-up' investments was all of $348 million (Metrick 207, 15). And, as new investments have risen with the resurgence in funding of VCs, the proportion of early-stage investments to the total has stayed below that 3 per cent level.

All this is to suggest that returns to the venture capital 'industry' are likely to be disappointing relative to historical, pre-Bubble norms (of course, the returns of the Bubble years were unsustainable in the extreme). We can expect to see extended attrition among VC firms and a gradual but ultimately substantial reallocation of capital away from venture capital. The set of best firms, the top decile, will remain and renew itself. The professional venture capitalist will remain as today's embodiment of the 'financial agent', even as the venture capital 'industry', scaled as it became to Bubble proportions, does indeed prove to have been '*an ephemeral, epiphenomenal flourish marking the peak of our generation's great speculation*'.

References

Braudel, F. 1982. *The Wheels of Commerce*. New York: Harper & Row.

Das, S. R., M. Jaganathan and A. Sarin. 2003. 'The Private Equity Discount: An Empirical Examination of the Exit of Venture Backed Companies.' *Journal of Investment Management* 1, 1–26.

Ferguson, C. 2001. *High Stakes, No Prisoners: A Winner's Tale of Greed and Glory in the Internet Wars*. New York: Norton.

Gompers, P., A. Kovner, J. Lerner and D. Scharfstein. 2006a. 'Specialization and Success: Evidence from Venture Capital.' Mimeo.

———. 2006b. 'Skill vs. Luck in Entrepreneurship and Venture Capital: Evidence from Serial Entrepreneurs.' National Bureau of Economic Research working paper 12592.

Gompers, P. and J. Lerner. 2004. *The Venture Capital Cycle*. 2nd edn. Cambridge, MA: MIT Press.

Hochberg, Y., A. Ljungqvist and Y. Lu. 2007. 'Whom You Know Matters: Venture Capital Networks and Investment Performance.' *Journal of Finance* 62, 251–301.

Janeway, W. H. 1986. 'Doing Capitalism: Notes on the Practice of Venture Capitalism.' *Journal of Economic Issues* 20, 431–441.

Kaplan, S. N. and A. Schoar. 2007. 'Private Equity Performance: Returns, Persistence and Cash Flows.' *Journal of Finance* 60, 1791–1823.

Keynes, J. M. 1961. *The General Theory of Employment, Interest and Money*. New York: Macmillan.

Lerner, J. 1995. 'Venture Capitalists and the Oversight of Private Firms.' *Journal of Financial Economics* 50, 301–318.

Marx, K. 1961. *Capital* 1 and 3. Moscow: Foreign Languages Publishing House.

McKenzie, D. M. and W. H. Janeway. 2008. 'Venture Capital Fund Performance and the IPO Market.' Cambridge University Centre for Financial Analysis and Policy working paper.

Metrick, Andrew. 2007. *Venture Capital and the Finance of Innovation.* New York: Wiley.

National Venture Capital Association. 2008. *Yearbook.* Washington, DC: NVCA.

Perez, C. 2002. *Technological Revolutions and Financial Capital: The Dynamics of Bubbles and Golden Age.* Cheltenham: Edward Elgar. [74.1]

Schumpeter, J. A. 1939. *Business Cycles* 1. New York: McGraw-Hill.

Chapter Eleven:

SMALL STATES, INNOVATION AND TECHNO-ECONOMIC PARADIGMS

Rainer Kattel
Tallinn University of Technology

Introduction

Innovation, and economic development for that matter, was born in small and, by today's standards, even in microstates like Renaissance city-states.[1] Cities like Venice, Florence, Delft, and others were extraordinarily successful at innovation – using knowledge to create economic gains – and in out-competing nations much larger in geographic, demographic or almost any other measure of size (Hall 1999; Landes 1999, 45–59; Reinert 2007). In these cities, it can be argued that smallness was one of the key factors that contributed to an institutionally highly embedded and yet diversified economy – both then already seen as pivotal ingredients of sustained growth. Indeed, early key political economists such as Giovanni Botero (1590) and Antonio Serra (1613) juxtaposed small city-states with great economic and often military power to natural resource-rich large areas that were economically backward. Today's wisdom seems, instead, to regard smallness as a source of multiple constraints on innovation and economic development in general (e.g., Armstrong and Reid 2003; contrast with Easterly and Kraay 2000). These constraints can be summarized as follows (Walsh 1988; Freeman and Lundvall 1988; also earlier, Robinson 1963):

1) Almost by definition, small states (particularly the less-developed ones) have small home markets that limit the possibilities for economies of scale and geographical agglomerations.
2) Small home markets and dependence on exports threaten small states with overspecialization, lock-in, and low diversification of the economic structure.

3) Small states do not have the financial capabilities or human resources to invest into cutting-edge science, research and development, which makes prioritization, selectivity and adaptability key in policy design.

This paper looks at the question how techno-economic paradigms as a key feature of capitalism is influencing small states in terms of innovation and economic development in general. The paper argues that a number of new challenges and risks in the international economy have emerged during recent decades that reemphasize the issue of size.[2] One of the key reasons for this shift is the change in techno-economic paradigm from mass production to ICT-based networks. Unlike much of the twentieth century, state size is now again one of the key determinants of how and why companies innovate (state size impacts company-level innovation, although the impact changes somewhat with the level of development). Successful small economies learned to overcome issues arising from size. New challenges in the international economy transform size into one of the key tempo-spatial dynamic characteristics of a polity.

This paper uses the relational understanding of small states that has been used relatively widely in recent small-states literature. According to this definition, 'being a small state is tied to a specific spatio-temporal context, not a general characteristic of the state. A small state is not defined by indicators such as its absolute population size or size of GDP relative to other states. Instead, a small state is defined by being the weak part in an asymmetric relationship'. (Steinmetz, Thorallsson and Wivel 2009; also Thorallsson and Wivel 2006) Smallness or size is a dynamic characteristic of a country, its impact changes in time, and it is best understood as a relatively important determinant in welfare of that particular country.

New Challenges and Risks

While innovations and technological change are often seen as key drivers of economic growth and development, it is seldom recognized that many innovations can bring significant adverse side effects as well. There are two key reasons for such effects:

1) Innovations and technological change often work through a process that Schumpeter described as creative destruction, where new products, activities, jobs, and industries are created and old ones evaporate (Schumpeter 1912, 1942).
2) Many innovations create dynamics, such as economies of scale, that become, as Arthur and others have shown, powerful enforcers of learning mechanisms and of various feedback linkages among value-chain actors

that all lead up to strong path dependencies and barriers of entry for competitors (companies, regions, countries) (Nelson and Winter 1982; Arthur 1994).

These aspects of innovation necessitate a public sector-led process that can be called creative destruction management (following the original Schumpeterian idea), where public policies support creation of new knowledge, companies, and jobs and alleviate the destructive effects (Drechsler et al. 2006; Kregel and Burlamaqui 2006). During much of the twentieth century successful instances of creative destruction management were greatly helped by the particular nature of the then prevailing techno-economic paradigm.

Mass-production or the Fordist system of production used huge hierarchical organizations and long-term planning that were both directed at creating stability in production and reaping economies of scale and scope (Chandler 1990). Increasing real wages and living standards that guaranteed stable consumption patterns became effectively part of that production and planning system. While first realized probably by Henry Ford when he more than doubled his workers' salaries, this system, was perfected by the small Nordic welfare states during the 1960s and the 1970s (Katzenstein 1985; Mjoset 2000). The rise of the East Asian economies can also be understood as an exemplary case of using the mass production paradigm (see also Hobday in this volume). The then small economies of Asia developed via strong state-led industrialization efforts that were based on creating strong government-owned enterprises and networks of enterprises in order to create economies of scale (e.g., Amsden 1989; Wade 2004). Essentially, the Nordic welfare states and the Asian tigers showed that size does not matter as long as one was able to capture the logic of the paradigm: mass production assumes mass consumption that in turn feeds on mass employment that is not interrupted by sickness, old age or any other similar circumstance (i.e., welfare-state regulations, other forms of regulation, or customs such as long-term employment that socializes unemployment risks).

The Fordist paradigm was thus 'naturally' prone to agglomeration effects (as integration into large hierarchies was its fundamental principle) that in turn created middle-income jobs (significantly helped by the welfare state type regulations), not only in developed countries, but also increasingly in the developing world (for instance, Mexico's real wages were continuously increasing precisely until the end of the Fordist paradigm in the mid-1970s; see Palma (2005)). The Fordist paradigm also worked similarly for regions as economic agglomerations and the welfare state also carried the fruits of innovation to geographically remote areas.

The breakdown of this system has been hastened by three developments: (1) change in the techno-economic paradigm following the new ICT-based technological revolution coming to its full force during the 1990s; (2) adoption of the Washington Consensus economic policies; and (3) growing financial instability.

Techno-Economic Paradigm Shift

According to Perez, paradigms last somewhere around a half century and consist of a 'common sense' about how the capitalism of that particular period works and develops (2002, 2006). The paradigms form around a set of key innovations and technologies that then encompass and transform the whole economy. The current ICT-based techno-economic paradigm goes back to key innovations in the 1970s and has engendered fundamental changes in production processes in almost all industries (including many services and agriculture). Perhaps the most profound feature of the ICT-paradigm is the growing use of outsourcing and the breaking up of various production functions that have, in turn, created strong de-agglomeration pressures, both in highly industrialized as well in developing countries (for discussion, Samuelson 2004; Krugman 2008). Gains from technological change and innovation do not disperse within regional or national geographic boundaries so easily anymore (see also Palley 2006; Gomory and Baumol 2004). Large production units and mass employment are substituted by highly specialized networks that operate and source production and knowledge, often supra-regionally or even globally – creating a vicious circle of increasing competition, pressure to cut costs and lower wages, luring foreign investors who often bring few fruits to the specific location with extensive concessions (in taxes, etc.), and as a result, enclave economies and de-linkaging effects emerge (Gallagher and Zarsky 2007). At the same time, the ICT-led paradigm also enables creation of niche production that has a potential to become supra-regional or even global, for instance, hospitals specializing into specific heart surgery (Prahalad 2006).

The ICT-led paradigm increases pressures for de-agglomeration, de-linkaging, and de-diversifying. This has become the key challenge to many smaller or peripheral nations/areas where such pressures are already quite strong. It is not so much the issue of size as such (e.g., scarcity in human capital) that has become important but, rather, a combination of geographic location and economic specialization patterns. This can be summarized as a position a nation holds in international value chains. For instance, while Finland is both geographically peripheral and demographically relatively small (ca. 5 million inhabitants), its place in the international mobile electronics-production value chain is distinctly very high. Yet, Finland is also seeing a growing outflow of R&D activities into regions with lower costs and larger agglomeration effects such as India.

Finland's position, however, has little if any positive bearing on Finland's neighbouring country Estonia (80 km to the south, ca. 1.4 million inhabitants). In the mass-production paradigm, Estonia could have devised relatively simple strategies to reap the benefits from its proximity to highly developed markets via specializing into lower end products/markets and moving up the value ladder. National policymaking could have created successful catching-up strategies. Instead, Estonia's electronics industry specializes today in simple production and assembly of products with low wages and substantial de-linkaging effects (Kalvet 2004; Högselius 2005). The ICT-led global production paradigm makes such strategies highly temporary and largely futile as upgrading in such sectors does not happen very often (Giuliani et al. 2005).

While the ICT-led paradigm significantly amplifies de-agglomerations, larger nations/regions are somewhat more hedged against risks imminent in the current paradigm. This means that smaller (and especially developing) countries have a growing dependency on international markets and production networks. Second, for smaller nations it can be argued that the policy space needs to be redefined. If local and foreign companies have growing incentives to de-link production, R&D, etc., from a given geographic position, then investing more into education, creating more cultural possibilities and better social programs only seems to delay the inevitable (Cimoli et al. 2005). Small state policymaking needs to become supra-regional (for instance, within the European Union). Size in terms of political influence and power – of having the necessary human resources able to negotiate supra-regional policies – is becoming key to the economic success of small states. While it can be argued that this concept is generally known in small-state literature (see, e.g., Ingebritsen et al. 2006 for a collection of useful discussions), the key new understanding here is that this concept also affects innovation. Indeed, when mass-production innovation policy is local (creating local technological capabilities and markets, and then moving to exports), the ICT-paradigm innovation policy of small states has to be supra-regional from the start. In fact, hardly any small country in Europe or elsewhere is capable of or is practising such policies yet.

It has been argued that such a logic of dispersion of global production networks that create de-agglomeration and de-linkaging effects is not necessarily inevitable to the ICT-paradigm (Perez 2006). Still, the global macroeconomic environment – namely, the Washington Consensus policies – create significant incentives to instate policies that enable the adverse effects of the ICT-paradigm and innovations to be particularly strong. While these policies might seem to be precisely supra-national in nature as demanded by the new techno-economic paradigm, in many areas such policies have enlarged de-agglomeration effects and not the opposite. While for many small countries economic openness has become the key economic policy mantra, this situation might in fact increase and not lower the challenges these countries face in global competition.

The Washington Consensus

Initially a list of 'ten policy instruments about whose proper deployment Washington can muster a reasonable degree of consensus' (Williamson 1990), the Washington Consensus may have failed, in light of the mainly negative experience many developing countries had with these policies (World Bank 2006; Rodrik 2007). It has given way to 'Washington Confusion' (Rodrik 2007). On the level of actual policy-making, however, the Washington Consensus still seems to be in full force, coming in many new disguises. While the simple battle cry of the 1990s – stabilize, privatize, liberalize – has given way to more intricate phrases and policy advice, they still boil down to the same core ideas.

Two observations are crucial: First, whatever its intellectual roots and its current health, the Washington Consensus essentially became the vehicle delivering the techno-economic paradigm change globally. Second, the main policy vehicles of the consensus, such as financial globalization and foreign direct investments based growth policies, have failed to deliver growth (Rodrik and Subramanian 2008) and, instead, have magnified the negative effects of the ICT paradigm. In combination, both observations have a huge impact on the way innovation takes place in many companies, especially in developing countries and poorer regions, and the way most countries see and define the policy space available to them. Indeed, one of the most fundamental characteristics of industrial change in developing countries such as the Central and Eastern Europe during 1990s has been that a majority of companies have actually engaged in process innovation (e.g., in the form of acquisition of new machinery) in seeking to become more cost-effective in the new marketplace.

Since the main emphasis of the Washington Consensus policies is on both macroeconomic stability (low inflation, low government deficits, stable exchange and interests rates) and on open markets (low, if any, trade barriers, common technical standards, etc.), these policies have two main assumptions: (1) increased foreign direct investments (that should thrive in stable economic environments) bring foreign competencies, know-how, linkages and increased competition for domestic producers, that (2) create more pressures to innovate in the form of better and cheaper products and services. If these assumptions are coupled with the real changes taking place in production networks due to the changing paradigm, however, we get highly dynamic forces engendering structural change in more vulnerable areas. Indeed, these changes were largely the reason for the consensus policies in the first place (Kregel 2008a, 2008b). Yet, as economic performance of the 1990s shows, the dynamic changes in (developing) countries following the Washington Consensus policies have been highly surprising, not to say disappointing (World Bank 2006; Amsden 2007; Chang 2007). The policies were highly effective in destroying admittedly outdated industrial capacities in the developing world, yet they were also similarly spectacularly ineffective in creating new capabilities and opportunities.

In sum, the international policy environment created is a highly fertile ground for the negative effects of the techno-economic paradigm change to come into full force without counterbalancing by international policy initiatives. For small states this situation significantly increases the challenges brought on by the ICT-led globalization of production networks. While there are clear gains from trade, economic specialization and trade patterns become key determinants in the way a small country integrates into the world economy (e.g., the clear difference in the way Finland's and Estonia's electronics sectors are integrated into world markets). Small developing countries have to keep in mind that waving the flag of rather simple liberalization and openness might just as easily undermine their own competitiveness in the long run because of de-industrialization and de-agglomeration. Under these circumstances, smallness becomes a crucial factor in designing innovation policies. How can the combined potentially negative impact of the ICT-paradigm and the global environment, as defined by the Washington Consensus policies, be counteracted? Innovation and industrial policy measures that have been accepted during the last 500 years, such as infant-industry protection, (also included in Willamson's 1990 article, but not enforced under the Washington Consensus) are not only discredited and politically hardly acceptable (for instance, within the EU), but it is also unlikely that such measures (or R&D tax breaks) would work, for instance, in the case of Estonia's electronics industry. Existing specialization patterns and global dynamics are simply too strong for such measures to gain any significant traction. Small states in particular, both highly developed and developing, should reconsider their innovation, industrial, fiscal and monetary policies in order to counterbalance the potential negative dynamics.

Financial Instability

Financial instability as a concept originates from Keynesian economic theory and was further developed by Hyman Minsky (in particular 1982, 2008). While Minsky used the concept only in the nation-state framework, Jan Kregel's work (especially 1998a, 1998b, 2004, 2008a and 2008b) has extended Minsky's analytical tools to international economy. The basic idea behind the Minsky-Kregel framework is relatively straightforward: a free-market economy is inherently unstable because stability itself leads to relaxed financing criteria (lower margins of safety) that in turn engender a growing number of businesses that have difficulties meeting their financial commitments, resulting in financial instability or crises.

Three distinct financing positions exist for assets in a free-market system: hedge, speculative, and Ponzi finance (Minsky 2008: 230–238). All positions are defined according a business unit being able to meet its financial commitments. In the hedge position, cash flow from operating activities is enough to cover all outstanding debts and other financial commitments. In other words, all of them are hedged. In the speculative position, cash flows do not cover all commitments, and thus the business unit needs to sell some of the assets or cut costs, etc., in order to meet commitments. Ponzi finance is a position where it is clear that the business unit is not able to meet all commitments, which are larger than assets owned. In essence, the unit is insolvent because 'financing costs are greater than income' (Minsky 2008, 231).

Clearly, when one adds the Schumpeterian framework of innovation and creative destruction (as Kregel and Burlamaqui (2006) do), we have a theoretical toolbox to understand how innovation coupled with competition (both in the industry and the financial sector) can create all of the financing positions (e.g., speculative or Ponzi positions can result from successful innovations by the competitors or by failed product development). The toolbox also explains how these financing positions can impact a business unit's incentives to innovate in order to create a hedged financing position or not, as dangers of sliding into speculative or Ponzi position loom.

As Kregel (2004) has shown, the Minsky framework can also be used to analyze country positions in the international economy. Similar to businesses, sovereign countries can also have hedge, speculative, or Ponzi finance positions. Adding Schumpeterian concepts of creative destruction and innovation to this construction allows us to understand how innovation at the company level and sovereign financial stability or instability are not only connected, but also have a fundamental impact on each other.

Such linkages become crucial for economic development in small countries, as they have relatively small cushions with which to absorb various external and internal financial shocks and fluctuations (e.g., in terms of the central bank's ability to guarantee private banking deposits). Again, a huge difference exists between the mass-production paradigm and the current globalized and open financial markets. To understand the difference, here we look at two typical cases: small state Type A being a Nordic economy existing within the mass-production paradigm, and small state Type B being a Baltic economy operating under open financial markets.

Under the Bretton Woods international financial system (that lasted until the early 1970s), it was relatively common to have more or less closed capital markets (further discussion in Kregel 2004, 2008b). Most Nordic (Type A) economies operated under economic policy regimes that included (in one form or other) wage agreements (and wage indexing), closed capital markets and strong export dependency that resulted in rapid industrialization and productivity growth. (Mjoset 2000 is an excellent overview of postwar Nordic economic policy regimes.) This, in turn, brought strong growth not only in wages and profits, but also in inflation, resulting in periodic loss of export competitiveness through high wages. Such a situation can be described as a highly speculative position, because loss of export competitiveness means a lessened ability to meet financial commitments (by both private and sovereign borrowers). What a typical Nordic country did during the postwar era to return to a hedge position and to increase export competitiveness was to devaluate its currency. This action generally returned the country into a hedge position, and the wage/profit growth started all over again. As devaluation hit both profits and wages, such managed boom-bust cycles were also socially accepted. The typical Nordic country avoided prolonged financial instability and thus being in a Ponzi finance position (e.g., runs on its currency, banks, wave of insolvencies). The type A small country used all the aspects of the mass-production paradigm extremely well and managed wage, export, and profit growth in a more or less systematic way. Via mechanisms that absorbed internal and external shocks relatively well, such a policy framework created strong incentives for (high risk) innovations at the company level as it socialized the risk of sliding into a Ponzi finance position. In addition, under continuous wage growth and welfare-state regulations, home markets for highly sophisticated products also expanded rapidly and again socialized risks for prolonged and high-risk product development and innovation.

Under the Washington Consensus policy framework, Baltic economies (Type B) followed a distinctly different path where avoiding instability and boom-bust cycles was one of the key policy determinants from the very beginning. These economies were seeking to create stability and international trust through a currency peg, an open economy, a balanced public budget, low tax and administrative burdens, and generally weak power by labour to negotiate wages. This allowed for furious restructuring of the economy through direct foreign investments (Tiits et al. 2008). However, particularly during early 2000s, large amounts of foreign investment and private lending financed consumption and real estate booms (e.g., Fitch 2007a, 2007b, 2007c), driving wage growth into double-digit territory. This forced Baltic economies to face precisely the same kind of speculative position where export competitiveness was threatened and endangered their abilities to meet all liabilities (mostly in the private sector and households because public borrowing remains low). This is the situation that the Baltic economies face in 2009.

A key change that made devaluation under these circumstances an almost impossible policy option was brought through open (capital) markets and a currency peg. Large amounts of private borrowing in the Baltic economies are done in euros. In addition, many export industries, being part of international value chains and often involved in outsourcing activities, pay for their inputs in euros as well. This means that devaluation would hit wages, input prices, and consumption, affecting, in turn, the public budget through lower revenues from taxing turnover. Devaluation would not necessarily lead Baltic economies back to a hedge position; rather, they would remain speculative and need new financing (investments, borrowing) in order to meet current commitments. This means trying to attract new foreign funds through low taxes, lax labour regulations, etc., causing less public funding for investment into productivity-increasing activities.

In order to ensure that the speculative position does not become a Ponzi finance position, Baltic economies need to constrain wage growth. This can happen either through increased unemployment or bankruptcies or both. Becoming an euro-area country can serve as an exit strategy out of a possible Ponzi position, but the dangers of remaining in a speculative position would not change. Such economies are bound to become or remain highly unequal in terms of income distribution, and home markets remain imports-based and strongly segmented – rather hostile to high-risk product development and innovation.

Under condition of financial liberalization, Washington Consensus policies that stress macroeconomic stability and outsourcing nature of industry under the ICT-led paradigm, type B small developing countries become highly vulnerable to financial instability. This, in turn, is directly related to the way innovation happens at the company level in these economies (innovation as outsourcing, cost-cutting machinery acquisitions that demand less labour, etc.). Financial instability in effect locks type B small economies into specific innovations that target low value-added sectors and activities. Type B countries face constant de-diversification pressures. Product and other high-risk innovations remain very costly to finance as there are almost no public policy options to socialize these risks without creating high rent-seeking incentives (e.g., prolonged dependence on public subsidies, lock-in into dead-end technological platforms, etc.). Small home markets cannot serve as tests beds for new products/innovations.

As type A countries thrived under the mass-production paradigm that is no longer there, and as type B countries face prolonged financial instability, both need to reinvent economic policy regimes to create conditions for sustained growth in the ICT-led techno-economic paradigm.

Death of Distance, Rebirth of Size?

The ICT revolution, and the enormous reshaping of industries it enables, has been called the 'death of distance'. This paper argues that the same revolution, along with the impact of Washington Consensus policies and growth of financial fragility, has led to a rebirth of size as a key factor for geopolitical units to take into account while devising innovation and economic policies for growth and development.

Indeed, size matters enormously for innovation. While the logic of the previous techno-economic paradigm, that of mass production, was in itself highly conducive for agglomeration and linkaging effects to emerge – key factors driving innovation and sustained economic growth – then under ICT paradigm that is amplified through Washington Consensus type of globalization, these effects are turned into reverse for many countries. Mass production paradigm thrived under top-down policymaking framework: welfare state policies and/or state-led industrialization policies could carry the positive spillovers of innovation and technological change also to remote areas of distinct geopolitical entities. This seems to be increasingly difficult.

This means, this paper argues, that country size matters again as it is one of the key determinants for company-level innovations (the kind of innovations that prevail in the private sector).

The implications for innovation policy are that these policies should be built following bottom-up logic: creating local networks and scaling them up into wider networks, which is essentially the opposite of the mass-production paradigm where creation of national or supra-regional economies of scale was key.

References

Amsden, A. 1989. *Asia's Next Giant: South Korea and Late Industrialization*. Oxford, England: Oxford University Press.

————. 2007. *Escape from Empire: The Developing World's Journey through Heaven and Hell*. Cambridge, MA: MIT Press.

Armstrong, H. W., and R. Read. 2003. 'The Determinants of Economic Growth in Small States.' *The Round Table* 368, 99–124.

Arthur, B. W. 1994. *Increasing Returns and Path Dependence in the Economy*. Ann Arbor: University of Michigan Press.

Botero, G. 1590. *Delle cause della grandezza delle città*. Rome.

Chandler, A. D. 1990. *Scale and Scope: The Dynamics of Industrial Capitalism*. Cambridge, MA: Harvard University Press.

Chang, H-J. 2007. *Bad Samaritans: Rich Nations, Poor Policies, and the Threat to the Developing World*. London: Random House.

Cimoli, M., J. C. Ferraz and A. Primi. 2005. *Science and Technology Policies in Open Economies: The Case of Latin America and the Caribbean*. Santiago: ECLAC. Available at http://www.cepal.org

Drechsler, W. et al. 2006. 'Creative Destruction Management in Central and Eastern Europe: Meeting the Challenges of the Techno-Economic Paradigm Shift.' In T. Kalvet and R. Kattel (eds). *Creative Destruction Management: Meeting the Challenges of the Techno-Economic Paradigm Shift.* Tallinn: PRAXIS Center for Policy Studies, 15–30.

Easterly W. and A. Kraay. 2000. 'Small States, Small Problems? Income, Growth and Volatility in Small States.' *World Development* 28, 2013–2027.

Edquist, C. and L. Hommen. 2008. *Small Economy Innovation Systems: Comparing Globalisation, Change, and Policy in Asia and Europe.* Cheltenham: Edward Elgar.

Fitch. 2007a. *Risks Rising in the Baltic States?* Special report, 6 March.

―――. 2007b. *Bulgaria, Croatia, Romania: How Sustainable are External Imbalances?* Special report, 20 March.

―――. 2007c. *The Baltic States: Risks Rising in the Trailblazers of Emerging Europe?* Special report, 8 June.

Freeman, C. and B-Å Lundvall (eds). 1988. *Small Countries Facing Technological Revolution.* London: Pinter.

Gallagher, K. P. and L. Zarsky. 2007. *The Enclave Economy. Foreign Investment and Sustainable Development in Mexico's Silicon Valley.* Cambridge, MA: MIT Press.

Giuliani, E., C. Pietrobelli and R. Rabellotti. 2005. 'Upgrading in Global Value Chains: Lessons from Latin American Clusters.' *World Development* 33, 549–573.

Gomory, R. E. and W. J. Baumol. 2004. 'Globalization: Prospects, Promise and Problems.' *Journal of Policy Modeling* 26, 425–438.

Hall, P. 1999. *Cities in Civilisation: Culture, Innovation, and Urban Order.* London: Phoenix.

Högselius, P. 2005. *The Dynamics of Innovation in Eastern Europe: Lessons from Estonia.* Cheltenham: Edward Elgar.

Ingebritsen, C., I. Neumann, S. Gstöhl and J. Beyer (eds). 2006. *Small States in International Relations.* Seattle: University of Washington Press.

Kalvet, T. 2004. *The Estonian ICT Manufacturing and Software Industry: Current State and Future Outlook.* Seville: Institute for Prospective Technological Studies – Directorate General Joint Research Centre, European Commission.

Kattel, R., T. Kalvet and T. Randma-Liiv. 2009. 'Small States and Innovation.' In Steinmetz, Thorhallsson and Wivel (eds). *Small States inside and outside the European Union: The Lisbon Treaty and Beyond,* forthcoming.

Katzenstein, P. J. 1985. *Small States in World Markets. Industrial Policy in Europe.* Ithaca: Cornell University Press.

Kregel, J. A. 1998a. 'East Asia Is Not Mexico: The Difference between Balance of Payment Crises and Debt Deflations.' The Levy Economics Institute of Bard College Working Paper, No 235. Available at http://www.levy.org/pubs/wp235.pdf

―――. 1998b. 'Yes, 'It' Did Happen Again. A Minsky Crisis Happened in Asia.' The Levy Economics Institute of Bard College Working Paper, No 234. Available at http://www.levy.org/pubs/wp234.pdf

―――. 2004. 'External Financing for Development and International Financial Instability.' G-24 Discussion Paper Series, United Nations. Available at http://www.unctad.org/en/docs/gdsmdpbg2420048_en.pdf

―――. 2008a. 'The Discrete Charm of the Washington Consensus.' The Levy Economics Institute of Bard College Working Paper, No 533. Available at http://www.levy.org/pubs/wp_533.pdf

―――. 2008b. 'Financial Flows and International Imbalances: The Role of Catching Up by Late-Industrializing Developing Countries.' The Levy Economics Institute of Bard College Working Paper, No 528. Available at http://www.levy.org/pubs/wp_528.pdf

Kregel J. A. and L. Burlamaqui. 2006. 'Finance, Competition, Instability, and Development Microfoundations and Financial Scaffolding of the Economy.' *The Other Canon Foundation and Tallinn University of Technology Working Papers in Technology Governance and Economic Dynamics 4.*

Krugman, P. 2008. 'Trade and Wage, Reconsidered'. Available at http://www. princeton. edu/~pkrugman/pk-bpea-draft.pdf

Landes, D. S. 1999. *The Wealth and Poverty of Nations: Why Some Are So Rich and Some So Poor.* New York: Norton.

Minsky, H. P. 1982. *Can 'It' Happen Again? Essays on Instability and Finance.* New York: Sharpe.

––––––. 2008. *Stabilizing an Unstable Economy.* New York: Yale University Press.

Mjøset, L. 2000. 'The Nordic Economies 1945-1980.' *ARENA Working Paper Series,* No 6. Available at http://www.arena.uio.no/publications/wp00_6.htm

Nelson, R. and S. Winter. 1982. *An Evolutionary Theory of Economic Change.* Cambridge, MA: Harvard University Press.

OECD and Eurostat. 2005. *Guidelines for Collecting and Interpreting Innovation Data, Oslo Manual.* 3rd edn. Paris: OECD Publishing.

Palley, T. 2006. *Rethinking Trade and Trade Policy: Gomory, Baumol, and Samuelson on Comparative Advantage.* The Levy Economics Institute of Bard College, Policy Brief 86.

Palma, J. G. 2005. 'The Seven Main "Stylized Facts" of the Mexican Economy Since Trade Liberalization and NAFTA.' *Industrial and Corporate Change* 14, 941–991.

Perez, C. 2002. *Technological Revolutions and Financial Capital: The Dynamics of Bubbles and Golden Ages.* Cheltenham: Edward Elgar. [74.1]

––––––. 2006. 'Respecialisation and the Deployment of the ICT Paradigm: An Essay on the Present Challenges of Globalization.' In R. Compañó et al. (eds). *The Future of the Information Society in Europe: Contributions to the Debate.* Seville, Spain: European Commission, Directorate General Joint Research Centre. [77.2]

Prahalad, C. K. 2006. 'The Innovation Sandbox.' *strategy+business* (Fall). Available at http://www.strategy-business.com/press/freearticle/06306

Reinert, E. S. 2007. *How Rich Countries Got Rich ... and Why Poor Countries Stay Poor.* London: Constable & Robinson.

Robinson, E. A. G. (ed.). 1963. *Economic Consequences of the Size of Nations.* London: Macmillan.

Rodrik, D. 2007. *One Economics, Many Recipes: Globalization, Institutions, and Economic Growth.* Princeton: Princeton University Press.

Rodrik, D. and A. Subramanian. 2008. 'Why Did Financial Globalization Disappoint?' Available at http://ksghome.harvard.edu/~drodrik/Why_Did_FG_Disappoint_March_24_2008.pdf

Samuelson, P. A. 2004. 'Where Ricardo and Mill Rebut and Confirm Arguments of Mainstream Economists Supporting Globalization.' *Journal of Economic Perspectives* 18, 135–146.

Schumpeter, J. A. 1912. *Theorie der wirtschaftlichen Entwicklung.* Munich / Leipzig: Duncker & Humblot.

––––––. 1942. *Capitalism, Socialism, and Democracy.* New York: Harper.

Serra, A. 1613. *Breve trattato delle cause che possono far abbondare li regni d'oro e d'argento dove non sono miniere.* Naples: Lazzaro Scorriggio.

Steinmetz, R., B. Thorhallsson and A. Wivel (eds). 2009. *Small States inside and outside the European Union: The Lisbon Treaty and Beyond,* forthcoming.

Thorallsson, B. and A. Wivel. 2006. 'Small States in the European Union: What Do We Know and What Would We Like to Know?' *Cambridge Review of International Affairs* 19, 651–668.

Tiits, M., R. Kattel, T. Kalvet, and D. Tamm, 2008. 'Catching Up, Pressing Forward or Falling Behind? Central and Eastern European Development in 1990–2005.' *The European Journal of Social Science Research* 21, 1, 65–85.

Wade, R. 2004. *Governing the Market: Economic Theory and the Role of Government in East Asian Industrialization.* 2nd edn. Princeton: Princeton University Press.

Walsh, V. 1988. 'Technology and Competitiveness of Small Countries: A Review'. In C. Freeman and B-Å Lundvall (eds). *Small Countries Facing Technological Revolution.* London: Pinter, 37–66.

Williamson, J. 1990. What Washington Means by Policy Reform. Available at http://www.iie.com/publications/papers/paper.cfm?ResearchID = 486

World Bank. 2006. *Economic Growth in the 1990s: Learning from a Decade of Reform.* Washington, DC: World Bank.

Chapter Twelve:

FINANCIAL EXPERIMENTATION, TECHNOLOGICAL PARADIGM REVOLUTIONS AND FINANCIAL CRISES

Jan Kregel

Levy Economics Institute of Bard College
and
Tallinn University of Technology

Ever since Schumpeter's *Theory of Economic Development* (Schumpeter 1934), economists have been aware of the importance of finance as the enabling agent of the creative destruction that is necessary for the dissemination of innovation and capitalist wealth creation.[1] In Carlota Perez' explanation (Perez 2002) of the technological developments as the instigators of surges of development, it is financial capital that commands this process in the 'installation period', leading the way to the hyperinflation of asset values and the creation of a bubble that allows for the full exploration of the attributes of the new technological paradigm. But the resulting bubble-driven inflation of paper values relative to real values eventually becomes an obstacle to further development as financial capital resists longer-term investment and instead increasingly focuses on short-term gains, diverting funds from production into financial speculation, 'quasi-gambling', seeking financial gains for gains sake. The full deployment of the installed paradigm thus requires the elimination of the excessive financial layering through a financial collapse, and increased regulation of the financial system through more rigorous government control in a way that does not prevent the full deployment of the new technology led by production capital reaping the full economic and social potential of the now prevailing paradigm.

There are a number of familiar features in this description of the role of finance in the development process. It resembles closely the description of financial fragility developed by another student of Schumpeter, Hyman Minsky. Both approaches take as given the inevitability of the cyclical behaviour of the economy, but also reject the idea that cycles repeat – each one is new and idiosyncratic. This is basically because the crucial element determining the evolution of each cycle is the technological innovations that characterize it.

However, in Minsky's view, the denouement of financial excess and the aftermath of the financial crisis lead not only to government regulation, but to a reversion to risk-averse behaviour. Thus, in the period of increasing fragility and layering, agents do not recognize their behaviour as leading to increasing risk, while in its aftermath they become excessively risk averse. Thus, it is not only regulation that reins in their speculative activity; it is also the desire to avoid returning to conditions of fragility. In Minsky's terminology this is represented by a return to hedge financing structures in which lenders require excessively large cushions of safety and only the safest, routine projects obtain financing. It is in conditions of increased government control and regulation as well as the increasing risk aversion that the deployment of the new technological paradigm takes place. But, the characterization of this period should be one in which the activities are of declining risk and increasing profitability as firms realize their first-mover advantage and thus, much of the financing is from internal funding. In this period firms seek to establish long-term strategies and make long-term investments for expansion, to form alliances or oligopolies to extend its market reach and moderate competition, and to enable the full deployment of the installed paradigm by regulating finance, expanding the appropriate markets (often through direct or indirect income redistribution).

Yet, there is a more basic difference in approach. For the Perez cycle, the driving force is a new technological paradigm in the productive sector. Finance is simply the handmaiden that allows the new technology to be explored, exploited and installed before it is fully deployed, at which point the financial sector is reined in by regulation introduced after a financial collapse linked to the overextension of financing in the installation period. However, for Minsky, the important innovations occur in the financial sector and join with the natural tendency for periods of economic expansion and stability to lead to declining margins of safety and increasing financial layering. The ensuing collapse is the same, but the motive force is quite different.

The relations between the two approaches might be put as follows: Financial regulation that is introduced in response to the crisis in the installation period provides the financing for the deployment period, and at the same time lays the seeds of financial innovation in the form of regulatory arbitrage that provides the financing for the installation period of the emerging paradigm. The most recent crisis episode has a new feature, as the ICT paradigm itself became a powerful tool of financial innovation leading to the current crisis, raising the question of whether the anticipated regulation will provide the basis for the completion of the deployment period, and whether financial and technological innovation is a coincidence or systematic factor. The creation of a mass market for corporate equity in the 1920s that financed the mass-production paradigm suggests that it may be the latter.

This raises the question of whether it is possible to combine the two approaches to the generation of financial crisis – innovation in the provision of finance and the introduction of a new technological paradigm. In particular, it raises the question of whether it is financial innovation in the financial sector that provides the increased financing that allows for the exploration and installation of the new technological paradigm. In the Perez cycle, there is little discussion of the structure of the financial system, or of the possibility of innovation in that sector driving the introduction of technology. Equally, in Minsky's elaboration of financial fragility there is little discussion of how technological change in the productive sector might influence this process. Likewise, there is little discussion of the difference between financial innovation and technological paradigms in finance, although at the end of his life, Minsky was concerned by the rise of what he called 'money manager capitalism' (Minsky 1988), which he defined as the increased concentration of financial investment decisions in the hands of a small number of professional managers of pension funds, mutual funds, insurance companies and other institutional investors, as well as the role of securitization in creating an increasingly integrated and layered global capital market (Minsky 1987).

It is clearly beyond the scope of this essay to verify the correspondence between technological paradigms in the financial sector and the real sector for each of the five technological paradigm cyclical expansions that have been identified in Perez' work.[2] Instead, attention is given to the two paradigms that have taken place in the twentieth century. This is because there is evidence of a major paradigm shift in the technology of financial markets that can be discerned in the 1970s. This was associated, as the theory would suggest, with the response to that last crisis and the regulation that was imposed in the aftermath of the 1930s depression. It is also of interest because the new paradigm in the real sector provides a decisive influence on the development of the new paradigm in the financial sector. We thus start with a rendition of the role of financial innovation in the early post-war recovery and its transformation in the 1980s to a new financial paradigm.

Minsky and Schumpeter

Although Hyman Minsky has written extensively on the economics of Keynes, he was a graduate student of Joseph Schumpeter at Harvard. From Keynes he learned the importance of money and expectations in the determination of the performance of the economy. From Schumpeter he learned the crucial role of banks and other financial institutions in supporting entrepreneurs' access to the resources they required to introduce new methods of production that were the source of economic progress through creative destruction. He also learned the crucial role of technical innovation in creating a dynamic of imperfect competition that allowed Chandlerian 'first movers' to gain dominance in their markets that could be used to generate above market returns. For Schumpeter, competitive markets, if they existed, could never exist for long; technical innovation by first movers is continuously creating a dynamic, imperfectly competitive advantage. While Schumpeter, and Perez, following Schumpeter, viewed this as a process that took place primarily in the world of manufacturing firms, for Minsky it was a process that also referred to the production of financial innovations by financial institutions.

There is a key difference in Schumpeter's view of the role played by money in the liberation of resources to be invested in new technology from that of his predecessors and contemporaries and is very close to the approach taken by Keynes. The traditional view is that investment is financed by prior saving of real income, that finance is simply real resources in monetary form that is free capital to be converted into new and more productive uses. But Schumpeter was working in the tradition of Wicksell, who recognized that in modern financial systems of the time, banks could create credit quite independently of the decisions to save out of income. It was this approach that allowed the banks to arm entrepreneurs with the power to commandeer resources for their new, innovative projects without the need for prior saving or converting existing capital investments into a new form. Schumpeter's system is a Wicksellian pure-credit money system. In Keynesian terms, the role of the financial system in the process of creative destruction is to create liquidity.

Minsky's focus is on the way in which the financial system creates liquidity. Here, there are two basic forces at work that determine financial innovation in the creation of liquidity. The first is regulation, for economic policy purposes, that is designed to limit the ability of financial institutions to create liquidity. In general, he believed that most innovations were the result of banks' responses to the imposition of regulations for monetary policy purposes. It was for this reason that he argued that such policy measures would reinforce the natural tendency to financial fragility rather than promoting economic stability (Minsky [1957] 1982).

In particular, those policy measures that restricted credit would lead to what he called 'experiments' with the structure of the balance sheets of financial institutions. Indeed, he was particularly critical of the role of the Federal Reserve in failing to recognize the impact of policy actions that used punitive interest rates to control inflation on financial structure and financial innovation. However, recent experience suggests that Federal Reserve policy to support the economy through extremely low interest rates, generating a search for yield, may be just as potent in producing experimentation by institutions as periods of monetary restriction.

The second was from a perceived potential profit from introducing new financial innovations – or what has come to be called 'financial engineering'. From a lifetime of study and participation in financial institutions, Minsky learned that just like other profit-maximizing firms, financial institutions such as commercial and investment banks create first-mover advantages through experimentation that allows them to gain competitive advantage through the creation of market imperfection. However, financial and manufacturing firms differ in one important respect. They do not benefit from intellectual property protection. Dominant market position due to innovation is easily contestable.

Thus from a Minsky-Schumpeter point of view, financial markets will always be imperfectly competitive dynamic markets characterized by the creation of imperfect information. But, in difference from manufacturing firms, their evolutionary change due to innovation will be more rapid because technological innovation can be easily replicated. The focus of this innovation is the creation of new methods of liquidity creation. Thus, the conjunction of the Perez cycle and the Minsky cycle must be sought in the concomitance of financial innovation producing new methods of liquidity creation that provide the financing for the installation of the new technology through creative destruction.

Innovation for Market Competition or Regulatory Competition

The stock market collapse of the 1930s provides an example of the turning point at the end of the installation stage of the age of oil, automobile and mass production that started around the turn of the century. This period is punctuated by the 1914–1918 war, and a short recession that ushered in the excesses of the roaring twenties boom that eventually expanded into Florida real estate speculation and then equity market excesses. The innovation that took place in this period is the operation of investment banks in providing the funding for installation.

'The most spectacular financial developments of the decade, however, occurred in the securities industry. They were the result of several circumstances, some indicating fundamental changes in financial practices. During the 1920s, as business profits rose, corporations increasingly relied on the security markets not only for their long-term capital requirements, but for their current needs as well. Rising profits, moreover, made many businesses less dependent than previously on short-term bank credit.... During the 1920s the yearly total issues of domestic corporate securities more than triples, soaring form about $ 2.8 billion in 1920 to over $ 9 billion in 1929' (Carosso 1970, 2423).

Thus, the increase in liquidity was provided by the expansion in the volume of transactions, turning long-term financing commitments into assets that could be realized through sale in the market at short notice, and the extension of sales to the general public. Whereas investment banks before the war had dealt only with the wealthy, their major innovation was to extend their market to the entire populace. Thus, through the magic of financial intermediation by investment banks, the productive sector received permanent equity financing while investors believed that they had liquid assets. The higher the market went, the cheaper the funding for the corporations issuing stock. Difficulties arose once the financial wizards discovered that they did not need actual productive enterprises to earn their fees and started to sell bonds of foreign governments, especially of Latin America, and nonexistent companies.[3]

The Glass-Steagall regulation that was introduced in 1933 was designed to restrict the operations of bank affiliates dealing in capital market activities that had become both highly speculative and often fraudulent as the stock market boom progressed. The regulation was meant to restrict deposit-taking banks, in the US known as 'commercial banks', from undertaking such capital market activities or owning affiliated companies that did so. These activities were restricted to a special category of non-deposit-taking financial institutions known generically as investment banks or stockbroker-dealers. It was this system that financed the 'golden age' of growth and expansion in the 1950s and 1960s – the deployment period. But while the financial system was under control and regulation, and in general is presented as serving the needs of a dominant productive sector, this did not mean that innovation was absent.

Under the Glass-Steagall system, commercial banks provided transactions deposit accounts and lent short-term to commercial and industrial borrowers. Regulation Q set a maximum interest rate of 0 per cent payable on transactions demand deposits and 2.5 per cent (raised in 1957 to 3 per cent) on savings deposits and time deposits with maturities over 180 days held with commercial banks. Since many commercial banks had opened affiliates to undertake capital market activities to offset declining income due to the increased borrowing by their clients directly in the stock market, the aim of the regulations was twofold. First, to prevent banks from raising interest rates to compete for deposits that had been used to fund the speculative activities of their securities affiliates. Second, it was to ensure commercial banks sufficient income to make it unnecessary for them to pursue such activities.

For a commercial bank operating under the Glass-Steagall regulations, profitability was determined by the net interest margin, the difference between its regulated core deposit rates and the lending rate. Banking costs (Minsky thought that they required around 450 basis points to be competitive) limited competition for borrowers, so lending volume and profits could only be increased by balance sheet experimentation. This included using incentives to shift deposits from liquid sight deposits to less liquid savings or time deposits, by reducing their secondary reserve holdings of US government securities that had ballooned during the war, or reducing their capital ratios. Indeed, both of the latter declined rapidly in the post-war period. But, these were static improvements with clear limits (buying reserves had to wait the development of the inter-bank market – see below).

In addition, banks could also increase profitability by reducing costs, in particular nonperforming loans and losses through improved monitoring of the creditworthiness of borrowers. Indeed, it has traditionally been thought that banks exist because of the informational advantage that they have over their depositors in assessing the credit risks of borrowers. Minsky always considered the most important part of banking the conversation between the borrower and the lender in which the banker posed the Basic Question to the borrower: *How Are You Going To Repay Me?*

Credit assessment was important because it was a key method of improving profitability given the constraints imposed by bank regulation on price or interest rate competition. According to Robert Morris Associates, 'Given the fact that banks rarely achieve return on assets greater than 1 per cent, the charge-off of even a relatively small amount of assets can quickly eliminate bank earnings and eat up capital or reserves.'[4] Commercial banks thus had limited incentives to compete amongst themselves on price terms, and increasing profits depended on good credit assessment and innovation to generate sources of funding that fell outside the interest rate limitations set by regulations. The basic form of innovative competition was thus in improving credit assessment and attempts to elude regulations, rather than competing with other commercial banks. Innovation in the Glass-Steagall era was thus dominated by 'regulatory competition' or 'regulatory arbitrage'.[5] Thus, in Perez' framework, the period up to the early 1970s would coincide with technological maturity and falling productivity of the mass-production paradigm while after that date, the increasing innovation to circumvent regulation laid the basis for financing the new technological breakthrough in the IT sectors.

Minsky's theory of financial fragility is based on the idea of endogenous instability generated by periods of financial stability in which lenders and borrowers take on increasingly risky lending contracts. Indeed, the post-war deployment period produced such a period of sustained, stable expansion in which cushions of safety were reduced as perceptions of risk were reduced. This change in perception takes place primarily in the credit assessment process that is the primary determinant of profitability – the conversation in which the banker assesses the borrower pro forma and decides how much to lend relative to the prospective cash flow.

But it is also important to note that the regulatory structure limiting competition contributed to the reduction in cushions of safety as secondary reserves and capital were drawn down in order to increase earnings. All these factors driving increased profitability led to decreasing cushions of safety that could be justified by the sustained period of growth and loan repayment performance.

Because segmentation restricted financial institutions by function, there was little scope for competition with the other forms of financial institutions. Investment banks could provide capital market financing and services to business firms with little formal restriction. Those that were public companies were subject to regulation by the Securities and Exchange Commission, which employed the 'sunshine' principle that full disclosure of information was the best form of market regulation. Until the 1980s, however, most were private partnerships. Since investment banks were involved in all aspects of corporate finance, their activities covered sales (corporate banking), primary (initial pricing and underwriting) and secondary distribution (trading to provide information of pricing) and research. But, since investment banks generally had access to confidential corporate information in providing financial and underwriting advice, they operated as house banks and remained tied to particular firms. There was thus little incentive to compete amongst each other for client business.

Savings and loans banks provided mortgage financing without limitation on rates that could be paid on deposits or mutual shares, but the FHA guarantee that was applied to most home loans meant that they had a clear competitive advantage in this type of lending. Thus, in addition, for commercial banks there was little incentive to price or service competition in the other main areas of the financial market.

'Regulatory Competition'

Innovation to remove activities from coverage by regulations limiting price thus became the primary form of indirect competition with other financial institutions. Such activity was initiated early in the post-war period when market rates on Treasury Bills rose above the regulated interest rates. Since banks could not offer corporate clients higher deposit rates and could only offer illiquid 180-day time deposits at Regulation Q rates, the banks started to lose their large corporate deposits. In addition, they started to face competition across their client base from savings banks that were not at that time covered by Regulation Q limits.

The response was innovation in the form of the negotiable certificate of deposit created by Walter Wriston at First National City Bank. It was a $1million certificate of deposit with a 180-day maturity (subject to Regulation Q limits on time deposit rates) that Wriston had convinced government security dealers, with the support of the bank, to discount and thus provide a liquid (negotiable) secondary market. As a result, banks could offer time deposit rates on instruments that were as liquid as demand deposits.

The negotiable CD thus provided a competitive advantage for the bank relative to other banks and gave it a competitive advantage in attracting corporate accounts. The advantage was short-lived, as other banks soon offered similar instruments, but the innovation was successful, defeating the regulation and providing the formal equivalent of a demand deposit that paid positive interest rates. However, the advantage was limited, for it depended on the Regulation Q rate for time deposits remaining above the Treasury Bill rate.

Competition for Retail Deposits

As noted above, thrifts were not covered by Regulation Q and could thus compete with banks for smaller retail deposits. Thrifts used high-profile marketing techniques to attract deposits, in particular through national newspaper advertisements. Some California thrifts offered premium rates for postal savings accounts in competition with bank savings and time deposits, offering rates in late 1962 that were even higher than long-term Treasury rates and near the rates paid on new corporate issues.

Again, the response was innovation by commercial banks to create an instrument that could compete with competition from thrifts. As noted above, there were separate rates set under Regulation Q for bank savings and time deposits. In 1962 the maximum rate on time deposits rose above the savings deposit rate, and by end 1965 the maximum rate payable on time deposits, and thus on CDs, was 150 basis points above equivalent rates on savings deposits.

Since time deposits could be offered to both corporate and individual accounts, while savings deposits could only be held by individuals, Franklin National Bank of Long Island started to offer individual savings depositors $1,000 time deposit certificates paying the higher CD interest rate. The result was a shift from savings to time certificates for banks' clients, but more importantly, a shift out of thrift accounts to bank time deposits. The resulting decline in financing for housing caused a collapse in house prices – especially in California, where the thrifts had been most aggressive in attracting national deposits.

These 'consumer' CDs allowed banks to counter the competitive advantage for savings deposits that that thrifts enjoyed because of their exemption from Regulation Q. However, the impact on the construction industry led to a special, maximum Regulation Q limitation for 'consumer' time deposits set below the CD rate, and the extension of to extending Regulation Q to thrifts, but with a 25 basis point margin to ensure them a competitive advantage relative to banks. In addition, to restrict the access by retail clients, a $100,000 minimum size was placed on negotiable CDs.

However, this special advantage relative to commercial banks did nothing to shield the thrifts from competition from non-bank money market instruments when market rates exceeded Regulation Q limits. This would eventually lead to the Thrift Crisis of 1980s.

The 1966 Credit Crunch and the End of Glass-Steagall

In the Spring of 1966 market rates rose above Regulation Q maximum rates for thrifts, and outflows of funds exceeds inflows of funds for thrifts as consumer deposits were offered by banks. The additional margin on regulated interest rates provided a 'rescue' for the thrifts that reversed this trend and caused banks to lose deposits. Until 1966 the Fed had always adjusted the maximum rate payable on time CDs to stay above the prevailing market rates. This was the condition required to make them competitive with Treasury Bills. However, in the attempt to restore the relative competitive advantage of thrifts, CD rates were allowed to fall behind rising market rates. The predictable result was a collapse of bank sales of CDs to corporate clients and a shift of retail clients' time and savings deposits back to thrifts. To stem their deposit drain and meet existing lending commitments to corporate borrowers, banks cut back sharply on new lending and were forced into distress sales of their secondary reserve holdings of government securities, forcing prices down and producing large losses.

The fall in prices and the decline in funding caused a liquidity crisis for government securities dealers who normally finance their inventory with bank lending. The dealers thus suffered from both a reluctance of banks to continue lending and a decline in prices of their inventory that served as the collateral behind the loans. The dealers thus joined the banks as distress sellers of securities, driving prices down and interest rates further upwards, making negotiable CDs and bank deposits even less attractive. This was a classic Minsky crisis – both the banks and the dealers were selling position to make position, and the more they sold, the more they had to sell to cover their exposure. The crisis quickly spread to the stock market as banks reduced call loans to specialist market makers and the entire financial system risked going into a stall due to lack of liquidity. Sounds familiar? Summer of 1998? Autumn of 2008? All provide similar scenarios.

The shift of funds out of the banks and thrifts was described as 'disintermediation' and it was generally believed that it would be followed again by a process of 're-intermediation' as depositors returned their funds to bank and savings deposits. However, conditions did not return to 'normal'. The credit crunch caused banks and thrifts to reassess their funding strategies. It was at this time that banks started a new experiment that would eventually lead to the downfall of the Glass-Steagall regime and lay the basis for the financing of the new age of what would be baptized high tech – computers, information technology and communications. In this experiment, banks shifted from what was called Asset Management (basically managing funding through changes in the secondary reserve portfolio and the loan book) to Liability Management, the search for new sources of funding by creating liabilities that were outside government reserve regulations. Thrifts did this through the creation of Negotiated Orders of Withdrawal (NOW) accounts that made thrift deposits as liquid as bank deposits.

Escape Abroad – Eurobanking

This period was also characterized by a number of ad hoc regulations on financial institutions to limit borrowing by non-residents that was believed to be at the source of the international weakness of the dollar. Controls on capital market activities such as the shift from a voluntary to an obligatory lending restraint and the interest equalization tax, plus the fear of another funding crisis similar to the 1966 crunch led banks to seek offshore sources of funding in the Eurodollar markets because they were not considered regulated deposits. Thus, the activity of US banks in the London Eurodollar market dates from the 1966 crunch. From 1965 to 1970 Federal Reserve System banks with foreign branches grew from 13 to 79. It also led to a resuscitation of the interbank market for reserves. After 1963 interbank loans were considered as the sale and repurchase of an asset, and, as such, not subject to the then prevailing limitation on loans to a single borrower to 10 per cent of capital. This is what is now known as the 'federal funds' market.

The fear of lack of funding from banks led corporate borrowers to seek non-bank sources of funds, and many started to issue commercial paper. Banks also formed bank holding companies to issue commercial paper with the proceeds used to purchase loans from the bank, thus removing them from the balance sheet and freeing reserves. This was a process that would again be exploited after the introduction of Basle capital adequacy requirement with the creation of variable interest entities that acted as repositories for bank assets and reduced bank capital requirements.

The Fed quickly acted to classify the proceeds from the sales of loans to bank holding companies as 'deposits' and, as such, subject to reserving and Regulation Q interest rate limits. The result was a rejuvenation of the Federal Funds market for interbank lending.

The Thrift Crisis – a Crisis of Deregulation

As a result of the increasing experimentation by commercial banks and saving and loans, Congress eventually tried to resolve the matter through deregulation in the Depository Institutions Deregulation and Monetary Control Act of 1980. While maintaining segmentation of the financial system, it sought to reduce and harmonize regulations for banks and thrifts. The Act called for the elimination of Regulation Q by 1986 (in fact, this was anticipated to 1984) and the creation of uniform regulations for all deposit takers, including thrifts. In addition, it gave Federal regulation precedence over state usury laws on certain types of lending, such as mortgages (making possible adjustable rate mortgages that were to play a role in the subprime crisis).

These regulations, meant to save the thrift industry, provided for its rapid demise. It is not necessary to recount the entire episode that is, in any case, now well documented. It is sufficient to recall that by removing limitations on deposit rates, financial institutions could compete on the basis of price and interest rates. However, in difference from banks who held short-term revolving consumer and business loans, thrifts held thirty-year fixed rate residential mortgages. The new regulations thus created an instant balance sheet mismatch in which the duration of the liabilities fell dramatically relative to the duration of the assets. To avoid insolvency, the only possibility was to expand into alternative investment opportunities with higher, and thus more risky, rates of return. The result was the loss of the industry.[6]

Computers and Innovation

By the 1980s the new innovative paradigm in the real economy started to have an impact on the financing sector. As an example of the impact of this factor, consider the compounding of interest on time deposits. The use of computers made it possible for banks to provide continuous compounding for a large number of accounts that would not have been feasible using hand calculation or even mechanical calculating machines.

Another example is the development of the commercial-paper market. It has already been mentioned that both banks and firms had started to issue commercial paper to provide non-bank sources of funding.[7] Initially, the issue of commercial paper by firms was underwritten by investment banks, and much like CDs, they were sold in large size to institutions and banks, excluding retail clients. However, the introduction of the computer allowed the creation of a money market mutual fund investing in commercial paper and paying market interest rates, because it made possible the daily calculation of the investments required to maintain the redemption value of a share in the fund equal to $1.00. Since it could be bought or sold at the fixed price of one dollar, the money market mutual fund share became the formal equivalent of a bank deposit, but paying short-term market interest rates.

Deregulation and Disintermediation

The deregulation that started in the US financial system in the mid-1970s thus provided the basis for the installation phase of the new wave of innovation by restoring price competition to the funding market across all deposit takers, as well as competition on lending rates and for borrowers. It also brought about an innovation paradigm shift that would eliminate credit assessment as the most important business of bankers – as was shown in the thrift crisis and the subsequent commercial bank real estate crisis at the end of the 1980s. The driving force was the negative impact on profits of the disintermediation that was the result of deregulation. The deregulation that was supposed to save banks and thrifts brought the extinction of the latter and questions about the survival of the former. A popular book and article title around this period became "Can Banks Survive?"

An indication of the crisis caused by bank disintermediation is the fall in banks' share of all financial assets from around 50 per cent in the 1950s to around 25 per cent in the 1990s. Financial disintermediation represents a process in which the number of intermediary agents involved in financial transactions is reduced. In particular, transactions take place directly between original contracting counter-parties in the market, rather than being arranged by banks acting as intermediaries. This is clearly the case of firms issuing commercial paper that is sold directly to the public. While changes have clearly taken place in the activities of banks after deregulation it is not clear that this has necessarily led to a decrease in bank intermediation.

Thus, in the US in the 1990s many commercial banks that were formally restricted from activities such as the sale and management of trust and investment funds, availed themselves of the Section 20 exemption that allowed them to generate up to 5 per cent of net earnings (increased to 10 per cent, and in 1997 to 25 per cent). Section 20 refers to part of the Glass-Steagall Act of 1933 that separated commercial and investment banking. While banks retained the ability to handle certain securities, such as Treasury securities, Section 20 prohibits banks from affiliating with firms 'engaged principally' in underwriting and dealing in securities, like corporate bonds and equity. Appropriate interpretation by regulators of the phrase 'engaged principally' left room for a bank holding company to form a subsidiary that conducted a large portion of permissible activities and a smaller portion of otherwise prohibited activities. The Federal Reserve first authorized such a subsidiary in 1987 and banking organizations eventually came to operate 51 securities subsidiaries, including some well-known securities firms such as Citigroup's acquisition of Solomon Smith Barney.

This expansion has also worked in the opposite direction with securities firms and insurance companies linking up with certain types of depository institutions known as 'nonbank banks' such as industrial loan banks, credit card banks, or to link with deposit units through the acquisition of a single thrift, known as a 'unitary thrift'. For example, American Express owned an industrial loan bank with about $12 billion in assets.

Financial Engineering

The combination of increased computing power and deregulation provided the basis for a new form of financial innovation called financial engineering. Two examples represent this trend. The first is Sidney Homer and Martin Liebowitz' *Inside the Yield Book* published in 1972. The book extended Irving Fisher's insistence that there are an infinite number of interest rates expressed in terms of different *numeraire*, and for different future periods. Thus, interest rates can be in terms of money, or gold, or any commodity, just as interest rates can be for a period running from today to an infinite number of future periods, or from any one of an infinite number of future periods to an infinite number of subsequent future periods.

The book also rediscovered the importance of Macauley 'duration'. Thus, bond traders who had been accustomed to searching the pages of the yield book that gave all bond values for a wide range of combinations of interest rates and maturities, could now assess the price responsiveness of fixed interest instruments with similar prices but different terms and maturities. It made fixed-interest securities into arbitageable securities. It also made possible the unbundling of the various cash flows represented in a fixed-interest bond, and led to the 'stripping' of interest coupons from fixed-interest securities to create discount bonds. Market imperfections in the pricing of any one of the implicit interest rates offered the possibility of an arbitrage profit by either unbundling or bundling the pieces of a single coupon bond. All of which could only be done with the advent of sufficient computer power. Once the two were joined, the trading function became dominant and the main source of profits for investment banks.

This expertise in financial engineering led to a different form of intermediation. An example is given by Bankers Trust, a commercial bank that could not survive in the NY market and thus decided to change its business plan to generate a 20 per cent return on equity. It started with seeking a more efficient distribution of capital across its different activities through the introduction of Risk Adjusted Return on Capital (RAROC). It recognized that there were no Fed limitations on earnings from proprietary trading, at precisely the time when Bretton Woods had broken down and currency markets were extremely volatile. It further sought to compete by creating lending vehicles that used the innovative combinations of leveraged financial instruments. Again, an activity not precluded to regulated commercial banks.

The below-prime structured lending instrument sold to Procter and Gamble in 1994 based on the sale of an interest rate option that provided the income to reduce the interest rate is now well known.[8] While it was clear that if the written option ended in the money there was no limit to the losses that could be incurred and thus to the loss of capital that was involved, in court P&G argued that they did not understand the degree of leverage that was attached to the negative outcome, despite the fact that they had already purchased similar instruments in the past. Again, the design of these instruments required the combination of the knowledge of how to unbundle revenue streams and computer power to calculate their values.

But the main point here is that innovation was used to create a profit for the bank by creating imperfect and asymmetric information for its clients at the same time that it provided additional sources of liquidity. The bank clearly knew the parameters of the contract, while the client did not. It could thus be sold at a much higher price than if it had been properly evaluated. Thus, in the new world of deregulation, regulatory innovation is replaced by innovation that creates a competitive advantage for the bank in trading with its clients.[9] At the same time, these instruments provided an increase in liquidity in the market since the structures were highly levered and they usually contained derivatives that are also highly levered since the possession of a derivative contract only requires a margin payment.

The Changing Source of Bank Profits

The erosion of Glass-Steagall regulation under the continued pressure of regulatory innovation not only opened up new areas of activity for banks, it changed the major source of their profits. While the elimination of

Regulation Q allowed more direct competition with other banks over active and passive interest rates, this did not lead to an increase in the share of bank profits resulting from intermediation. Instead, banks moved to increase their fee and commission incomes and their income from the proprietary trading of securities. As a result, the focus of the banks' activities shifted away from credit quality assessment towards the creation of activities that produced commissions and fees, and towards the creation of products that could be traded by the banks' proprietary trading desk or sold to clients. This meant a large increase in financial layering, that is, an increase in the degree of intermediation associated with the closing phases of the new wave of financial innovation. Largely as a result of this erosion of the segmentation between deposit and loan banks and investment banks, in 1999 Congress approved the Gramm-Leach-Bliley (GLB) Act that allowed banks to expand the range of their business opportunities. The new legislation repealed key provisions of the Glass-Steagall Act to permit a form of universal banking, modifying the Bank Holding Company Act of 1956 to permit the holding company owners of commercial banks to engage in any type of financial activity. At the same time it allowed banks to own subsidiaries engaged in a broad range of financial activities not permitted to banks themselves. As a result, banks of all sizes gained the ability to engage in a much wider range of financial activities and to provide a full range of products and services without regulatory restraint.

An important current example of how financial institutions have taken advantage of the new regulations is Countrywide Financial Corporation. GLB allowed a mortgage company to own a thrift (that eventually was converted into a bank) bank (overseen by the OTS), a broker-dealer trading US government securities and mortgage-backed securities, a mortgage servicing firm, a real estate closing services company, an insurance company, three special-purpose vehicles to issue short-term commercial paper backed by mortgages originated by Countrywide. For the holding company as a whole, mortgage banking generated 48 per cent, banking 32 per cent, capital markets 13 per cent and insurance 6 per cent of its pre-tax earnings in 2006.

New Form of Bank Intermediation

GLB did little to halt the decline in the share of assets intermediated by banks proper. It simply shifted these activities to other units of bank holding companies or to subsidiaries. This has been most recently noted by Ben Bernanke, the Chairman of the Board of Governors of the Federal Reserve, who indicates that 'nonbank lenders have become increasingly important in many credit markets, and relatively few borrowers are restricted to banks as sources of credit. Of course, nonbank lenders do not have access to insured deposits. However, they can fund loans by borrowing on capital markets or by selling loans to securitizers.' He notes, however, that 'Banks do continue to play a central role in credit markets; in particular, because of the burgeoning market for loan sales, banks originate considerably more loans than they keep on their books' (Bernanke 2007).

Thus, the major activity of banks is no longer to provide direct financing for businesses or households. Instead of holding loans and the associated risk on their balance sheets they have become 'originators' that create financial assets that they then sell to a subsidiary that in turn sells them in the capital market to non-bank financial institutions such as pension funds or insurance companies, or to the general public. This is a major change from the kind of bank activity that Minsky had originally referred to. The banker's basic question is now: *To Whom Can I Sell This Loan?* The credit quality assessment and monitoring function usually attributed to banks is no longer necessary to ensure profitability. Again, computer applications of statistical techniques were crucial in providing models of credit scoring that banks used in place of their traditional assessment of creditworthiness of borrowers.[10] Increasing profitability now comes from increasing, as fast as possible, the volume of assets originated, securitized and sold to capital markets. Thus, it is no longer the banks that provide liquidity by taking loans onto the asset side of their balance sheets. It is the capital markets and the derivative structures that provide the liquidity required to fund the creative destruction of the productive sector.

While attention has been focused on the mortgage industry and the use of securitization to fund subprime borrowers, the important point is not the assets that are financed. The mortgage market may be seen as simply part of the froth as the financial sector enters its frothy stage of gambling rather than financing the installation of the new technology. What is important is the new technological paradigm of liquidity creation that was created through structured lending vehicles and its interaction with the introduction of the new technological IT paradigm in both the financial and the productive sector.

We now know that that paradigm was not sustainable, and that there will be another period of re-regulation, accompanied by a period of Minskyian retrenching in which financial institutions become hedge units and stop lending. This will certainly produce a global recession, if not depression, and call into question the deployment of the new technology unless the government acts to shore up aggregate demand as well as introducing new financial regulation. Up to the end of 2008, however, government has been more interested in shoring up financial institutions than in supporting households who will be crucial to the expansion of demand for the deployment of the IT technological paradigm.

References

Auger, P. 2005. *The Greed Merchants: How the Investment Banks Played the Free Market Game.* New York: Penguin.

Bernanke, B. 2007. 'Remarks.' Federal Reserve Bank of Atlanta's 2007 Financial Markets Conference, Sea Island, Georgia. 15 May.

Black, W. K. 2005. *The Best Way to Rob a Bank is to Own One.* Austin, TX: University of Texas Press.

Carosso, V. P. 1970. *Investment Banking in America: A History.* Cambridge, MA: Harvard University Press.

Chew, L. 1996. *Managing Derivative Risks: The Use and Abuse of Leverage.* New York: Wiley.

Golin, J. 2001. *The Bank Credit Analysis Handbook: A Guide for Analysts, Bankers, and Investors.* New York: Wiley.

Homer, S. and M. Leibowitz. 1972. *Inside the Yield Book.* New York: Prentice-Hall.

Kregel, J. A. and L. Burlamaqui. 2005. 'Banking and the Financing of Development: A Schumpeterian and Minskyian Approach.' In S. de Paula and G. A. Dimsky (eds). *Reimagining Growth: Towards a Renewal of Development Theory.* London, New York: Zed, 141–167.

Mayer, M. 1990. *The Greatest Ever Bank Robbery: The Collapse of the Savings and Loan Industry.* New York: Macmillan.

———. 1998. *The Bankers: The Next Generation.* New York: Penguin Putnam.

Minsky, H. P. 1982 [1957]. 'Central Banking and Money Market Changes.' Reprinted in *Can 'It' Happen Again?* Armonk, NY: Sharpe.

———. 1986. *Stabilizing an Unstable Economy.* New Haven: Yale University Press.

———. 1988. 'Money Manager Capitalism, Fiscal Independence and International Monetary Reconstruction.' Paper prepared for a Round Table Conference: The Relationship between International Economic Activity (Trade and Employment) and International Monetary Reconstruction. Castle Szirak, Hungary. 25–26 August 1988. [Levy Economics Institute Minsky Archives (A209.17B).]

———. 2008 [1987]. 'Securitization. Handout Econ 335A. Fall 1987.' Reprinted as Levy Economics Institute Policy Note 2008–2.

Perez, C. 2002. *Technological Revolutions and Financial Capital: The Dynamics of Bubbles and Golden Ages.* Cheltenham: Edward Elgar. [74.1]

Schumpeter, J. A. 1934. *Theory of Economic Development.* Cambridge: Harvard University Press.

Winkler, M. 1929. *Investments of the United States in Latin America.* Boston, MA: World Peace Foundation.

———. 1999 (1933). *Foreign Bonds: An Autopsy.* Washington DC: Beard Books.

Chapter Thirteen:

WHY THE NEW ECONOMY IS A LEARNING ECONOMY

Bengt-Åke Lundvall
Aalborg University

Foreword and Postscript

When I was invited to give a contribution to the *Festschrift* for Carlota Perez, I proposed that my contribution should be based upon a paper on 'the new economy' and its crisis that I started to draft before Christopher Freeman's 80th birthday, September 2001. This choice was quite natural, since the original paper was written in honour of both Chris Freeman and Carlota Perez. In the light of the current crisis, this choice of an 'old paper' has become even more appropriate. Much of the argument in the paper relating to the ICT bubble is highly relevant also for the current crisis. I have therefore decided to leave the text in its original shape while adding this postscript as a foreword.[1]

The basic message in the paper is that while Information and Communication Technologies (ICT) offer a great potential for productivity growth, it was naïve to assume that it could bolster permanent high rates of noninflationary economic growth. What Greenspan and others neglected was the central insight in Carlota Perez' work that the productivity potential can be fully exploited only after a sequence of radical institutional changes. The institutional changes that did take place – the weakening of trade unions, the deregulation of financial markets, the increased used of share options and, in general, the increased freedom for capitalists to move capital across borders and to change the form of capital through leveraging – was highly biased and it certainly did not establish a framework supportive for technical, organizational and institutional learning.

Some of the points made in the paper on the difficulty to exit from a deflationary crisis through traditional monetary policy and through reducing taxes for the rich, are even more relevant in the current crisis. After the crisis of 2000, economic policy aimed at low rates of inflation on the basis of the assumption that they represent stability. The fact that deregulation of financial markets and the redistribution of income in favour of the rich led to unprecedented rates of 'asset inflation', making the rich richer, did not worry economists – most of them actually saw it as a sign of economic health.

At the end of the paper, I point to the need for a new kind of Keynesianism that involves massive investment in the upgrading of the competencies of the low-skilled workers and in programs that stimulate firms to engage in organizational change and in market-oriented innovation. These recommendations are even more relevant in the current situation where the alternative seems to be to subsidize big banks responsible for the crisis and industries that have not been prepared to adjust to the new reality where low-carbon technological trajectories are necessary.

Upgrading the skills of workers and delegating responsibility to them should be seen as one important component of innovation policy strategies. In recent research we have demonstrated that innovation thrives in firms that combine science-based learning (STI) with experience-based learning based upon doing, using and interacting (DUI) (Jensen et al. 2007). Narrow interpretations of innovation assuming it to be rooted directly science explains why current attempts to harness science for innovation – including making universities into profit-oriented institutions – has resulted in 'innovation paradoxes' everywhere (Lundvall et al. 2008).

In the paper I make the point that 'hype' played an important role in sustaining the growth of the economy in the 1990s. Today, this point may be deepened and extended. With the rapid growth of a profit-oriented sector engaged in 'symbol analysis', 'ethical business', 'story-telling' and 'image-nursing', the gap between the reality and the pictures of this reality that are produced by this industry has been growing. The Enron affair was just one symptom of a much broader and deeper capitalist malaise. One of the neglected consequences is that the very foundation of the knowledge-based or learning economy is at stake.

Today *trust* is the scarcest of all resources in the economy. Kenneth Arrow once wrote that 'you cannot buy trust and if you could buy it, it would have no value whatsoever.' The current phase of the crisis where governments offer gigantic injections of cash and credit into financial institutions without getting much response in terms of increase in their willingness to lend money to enterprises and families adds to this insight. It also demonstrates that 'you cannot impose trust upon others'.

This has serious implications for the possibilities to stimulate a short-term financial revival but the implications for the long-term production and use of knowledge may be even more fundamental.

In a knowledge-based economy, transacting information and knowledge is at the very core of the system and it is well known that when it comes to information, market failure is the rule rather than the exception (Foray and Lundvall 1996). When all institutions engaged in the production, validation and diffusion of knowledge, including accounting firms, universities and think tanks, have been made subservient to the principles of profit making, there is no instance left that can act 'as central bank of last resort for knowledge'. The current efforts everywhere to make universities profit-oriented and to make them the obedient servants of private industry will bring down some of the last defences against the establishment of general distrust (Caraça et al. 2009).

The title of the paper refers not to the knowledge-based, but to 'the learning economy'. This reflects our understanding of the current era as being one where change in technologies, markets and organizational forms are rapid and where the competitiveness of people, organizations, regions and nations will reflect the capacity to forget old and to learn new competences. It is obvious that the most interesting forms of learning involve an interaction and communication between people and that trust is a prerequisite for successful interactive learning (Lundvall and Johnson 1994; Lundvall 1996).

This is true in institutions specialized in teaching, but it is equally true for the learning taking place within organizations and across organizational borders. Economies based exclusively upon legal control where you expect everybody to act exclusively in his short- or long-term own interest will not offer good opportunities to learn. To realize the full economic and social potential of information and communication technologies, institutional reforms need to focus upon how to re-establish trust. Here, current proposals to strengthen government regulation are necessary, but far from sufficient. An economy ruled only by law and profit is not a learning economy. Principles of solidarity and respect for the relative autonomy of 'non-capitalist' institutions supporting the knowledge society need to be re-established. In recent research we have been able to show that in Europe, national systems with a broad participation in processes of learning at the workplace, rooted in egalitarian societies, have a stronger national innovation performance than the ones with less broad participation and more social inequality (Arundel et al. 2007).

In a globalizing world these principles also need to be extended from the national to the global communities. One of the reasons for the current global financial crisis is that the financial system has become global in terms of interdependencies and repercussions, while the real economy, and especially the access to knowledge and learning, remains national.[2] The very limited effort to give financial development assistance to poor countries is problematic in the current crisis where an increasing number of people will be starving the coming years. In the long run the uneven playing field in terms of access to knowledge and learning is more detrimental for the possibilities to create a more stable world economy. There is a need for a 'new new deal' with focus upon the distribution of access to learning both within and across national borders.

In the paper I point to the possibility of the crisis triggering a change in policy strategies giving more attention to the need for new institutions supporting interactive and organizational learning at the national and the global levels. But in the wake of the crisis of 2000, most of the old patterns were re-established. New global mechanisms made it possible to move out of the crisis without any major changes in public policy. Among the most important new mechanisms were the role of China and its outstanding rate of capital accumulation on the one hand, and the uncontrolled expansion of negative saving, especially in the US and the UK. This illustrates that there is no automatic 'policy learning' taking place that guarantees that this crisis will not be just one more step toward global destruction. Small events and political battles will determine the outcome.

Introduction

One interesting difference among different social science disciplines is their respective willingness to recognize that 'a new era has arrived'. Historians are sceptical because they can always remember that what most of us see as new has been seen before. Economists belonging to the neoclassical mainstream school share this scepticism because they work with general tools and with tools that are not easily applied to qualitative change. Management theorists operating as consultants have the opposite interest – if they can convince customers that we have entered a new era, they have also created a market for new management tools. In this paper, we will accept the idea of a new era as our working hypothesis. We will criticize the concept of the new economy for its simplistic understanding of what is going on, but we share its basic assumption that the widened and deeper use of ICT represents a fundamental change in the economy and society.

When I started to work at OECD in 1992, I tried to convince the Secretary General (Jean Claude Paye) and his chief of staff (John Llewellyn) that ICT was bringing fundamental change into the working of the economy. I also argued that the OECD economists no longer could allow themselves to neglect this fact and leave it to a handful of ICT experts in the organization to reflect upon its broader implications. To begin with, the response was scepticism, until one day (as far as I remember it happened in 1994), they came back converted to 'the new economy' after a meeting in Washington with Alan Greenspan. Since then, 'the new economy' has established itself at the very centre of the OECD discourse. The OECD ministerial meetings in 2000 and 2001 both had 'economic growth in the new economy' as their major theme (OECD 2000; OECD 2001).

Here we will argue that it is useful to rethink the concept 'the new economy' in Chris Freeman's and Carlota Perez' analytical schemes as a shift in the techno-economic paradigm (Perez 1983; Freeman and Perez 1984). Seen in this light, the real challenge is much broader and more difficult than that signalled by the new economy. The important message is that today there is an enormous untapped growth potential that could be mobilized to solve social and economic problems if our societies engaged in institutional reforms and organizational change to promote learning processes.

Defining the New Economy

While Chris Freeman and Carlota Perez emphasize the difficulties with passing from one techno-economic paradigm to another, the new-economy discourse, as pushed by Alan Greenspan and others, emphasizes the productivity-enhancing effects of ICT. The acceleration in productivity growth is assumed to lie behind a new kind of macroeconomic development where long-term growth goes on undisturbed by inflation and uninterrupted by recessions. You might say that this is 'the end of history applied to macroeconomics.'

There is also the other side of the new-economy discourse, referring to a new family of firms whose characteristics are assumed to signal the future. These firms are typically producing Internet services or other advanced knowledge-intensive products and services. They have been presented as the 'role model' for all firms. Absence of trade unions, focus on stock options instead of wage increases, e-commerce instead of snail-mail commerce combined with the youthfulness of the entrepreneurs have been seen as elements signalling the future. The expectations about their future growth and profitability have certainly been 'irrationally exuberant'. They have been at the very core of the financial bubble in the United States.

The two parallel discourses have reinforced each other not only as ideological messages, but also in their interplay in the real economy. The macro discourse, and the laxity of monetary policy it allowed for, stimulated speculation in the stock market and directed the speculation toward 'new-economy stocks'. The increase in the value of NASDAQ stocks tended, until the bubble burst, to bolster growth in demand from households.

ICT and Productivity Growth

One weakness with the macro discourse is that it has never been made quite clear how one jumps from the assumption of higher productivity growth at the micro level to the assumption of eternal stable growth. The 'transmission mechanism' has not been made explicit. *Ceteris paribus*, a speed-up of productivity growth, will certainly help to keep inflation down for a period. But in the long run, the impact on inflation will certainly depend as much on how the behaviour of financial markets, firms, trade unions and raw-material producers responds to a speed-up of productivity growth.

Further, there has been little discussion about the consequences of the fact that the productivity increase has been very unevenly distributed in the economy. If the productivity increase primarily takes place in sectors producing investment goods or consumer goods, it could, for instance, make a major difference in what kind of economic growth pattern we should expect.

To assume the effect from wider use of ICT to be more or less eternal stable growth may be characterized as 'economic political hubris' and Greenspan has certainly been one of those guilty preaching this sermon in the 90s. He did send out cautioning signals from time to time – as in December 1996 – when he warned against 'irrational exuberance' in stock markets. But these warnings were drowned in optimistic signals.

Another critical issue addressed in this paper is whether the assumptions regarding the positive productivity impact of ICT can be taken for given. Actually, a very different view can find support in historical and empirical analysis. Paul David has made one of the most important contributions to explaining the Solow Paradox – 'we see computers everywhere but in the productivity statistics'. At the 1990 OECD seminar bringing together leading experts on technology and growth to debate the causes of the productivity slowdown, he drew a parallel to the slow and uneven productivity impact of the diffusion of electricity in the industrial system (David 1991). He argued that the period of institutional and organizational adaptation always would be long for any radically new technology.

The Danish Experience

At about the same time as the OECD conference (1990), I was involved in summarizing the results from the so-called PIKE project where the objective was to explain *a fall in manufacturing productivity* of 1984–1986 in Denmark. We found the most prominent explanation of this extreme version of the Solow Paradox at the firm level, and it certainly had to do with the implementation of ICT. We found that firms that introduced ICT *without combining it with investments in the training of employees, with change in management and with change in work organization, got a negative effect on productivity growth that lasted several years* (Gjerding et al. 1990). These results were confirmed later on (with much more detail and precision) by the Danish Ministry of Business and Industry (Ministry of Business and Industry, 1996, 94–99).

The alternative perspective indicated by Paul David's analysis and the Danish studies points in a very different direction than the new-economy hypothesis. Paradoxically, it may be argued that *as long as the economy remains new, it will be much more difficult to obtain productivity growth than in an old economy.* In OECD countries, the highest rates of productivity growth ever were those registered in the '60s when the OECD economies already had moved far ahead on the Fordist scale-intensive trajectory. The very maturity of the technologies used made the rapid growth of productivity possible.

The fact that in recent years high productivity rates have been registered predominantly within the sectors producing ICT, reflects that *for these sectors, ICT is not representing a new, but rather an old and well-established paradigm.* And, for Silicon Valley and some of the Asian NICs, the absence of 'old economy' sectors has been a key factor making it possible to rapidly transform the 'new economy' sectors from being 'new' to becoming 'old'.

This is one reason why it is adequate to call the current era 'a learning economy' (Lundvall and Johnson 1994; Archibugi and Lundvall 2001). What is at stake is the capacity of people, organizations, networks and regions to learn. Learning to cope with and use the full potential of the new technologies is, in a sense, to transform them from being new to being old.

The OECD Evidence of a New Economy

Given this background, it is not surprising that OECD has had great difficulties in finding evidence, in growth and productivity data, for the existence of a new economy. Out of 26 OECD countries there was an acceleration of growth only in a minority of 10 from the '80s to the '90s. Among these, the only big ones were the US and Canada, and the increase in growth rates for these two countries were miniscule (OECD 2001, 7). In 9 out of 17 listed countries, 'multifactor productivity' accelerated. Again, the increase in the US was very small. The UK and Spain experienced the most dramatic fall in multifactor productivity growth, while the six countries with the most significant acceleration were Finland, Australia, Ireland, Canada, Sweden and Denmark (OECD 2001, 8).

It should also be considered that the US productivity data have been inflated by new statistical practices. The level of registered productivity growth in the US and elsewhere increasingly reflects attempts made to take *quality increases* into account. These 'corrections' are especially important when it comes to assess the real value of new generations of computers. Such corrections based on the concept of 'hedonic indexes' may be meaningful for consumer goods – the consumer may be willing to pay for extra capacity (big and rapid cars) even when they cannot use it (because of lack of parking space and because of speed limits) – consumers have the privilege to enjoy irrational pleasures. Their meaningfulness when the users are professional organizations is much more debatable. What makes a 'real difference' for professional users is the value of the computer in actual use. It is not obvious that an increased potential that cannot be realized because of lack of skills and old forms of organization should be taken into account as increasing the value of the product.

Beyond the Hype?

The title of the 2001 OECD report is 'The new economy: Beyond the hype'. I find this rather misleading, since 'the hype' has played a major role in shaping the actual dynamics of the new economy over the last couple of years, especially in the US. It has certainly affected the kind of upturn we have seen. And the 'hype' will play a role also in determining how difficult it will be to establish a new upswing after the bubble has burst.

A whole industry of media has been built around promoting popular shareholding, and those working in this industry have a strong vested interest in promoting hype to the extreme. Business journals have produced enormous amounts of success stories. Ordinary people have got hooked on buying shares – some of them for the same reasons they engage in gambling and lotteries. Naïve policymakers used young new-economy entrepreneurs as 'wise men', asking them to be their guides into the promising but uncertain e-future. Even sober social democrats in the Nordic countries have been captured by this hyping wave.

One major result of all this was the spectacular rise in high-tech shares in the US as well as in Europe. In its turn, this rise contributed to the illusion of rapidly growing wealth among households and created the basis for growth in private consumption and a reduction of savings ratios in the US. In this sense, the hype is one of the factors explaining the relative success of long-term growth in the US. Without the hype, growth rates would have been more modest.

Keynesianism for Rich People?

When speculative bubbles burst in Asia or Latin America, there is quick agreement in international financial institutions, such as the IMF, that at the root of the problem are fundamental structural and institutional weaknesses that need to be corrected before any macroeconomic stimulation policy could be made effective. It is interesting to note that when there is a 'hype bubble' in the US, no such critical insights are forthcoming. There is no request for 'structural reform'. Instead, the bursting of the bubble triggers strong demands for expansionary monetary policies and even for expansionary finance policy. This is actually the opposite of the cure that has been imposed upon Asian and Latin American bubble economies.

Another interesting aspect of the debate on macroeconomic policy is that while Keynes recommended expansionary policies primarily because he was worried about workers losing their jobs and ending in misery, the present concern is more with speculative capitalists losing some of their capital. When the bubble began to burst, there was a queue of financial experts, normally quite critical to active government intervention, who asked for reductions in interest rates. In the financial pages, increases in unemployment rates were actually welcomed, since they signalled that it was possible to move ahead with more expansionary monetary and financial policies that might, at the end, give a boost in profits without causing inflation.

A question of dramatic importance is how far monetary policies are at all effective in a period characterized by a combination of extreme uncertainty and low inflation rates. When inflation is high, there is ample room to get very low and even negative real interest rates. As the Japanese experience indicates, it is much more difficult to avoid the liquidity trap in a situation with deflation. It will therefore be interesting to see if the interest rate reductions in the US will result in the stimulation aimed at. A popular complement is to reduce taxes in order to give a financial stimulus to the economy. Again, the Japanese example gives rather limited ground for optimism regarding the effectiveness of such a policy. If uncertainty is strong both in the household sector and among investors, the main result may be an increase in savings rather than an increase in effective demand.

This would leave us with classical Keynesian policy in the form of public investment. Building roads and bridges with public funds may have a real impact, but the ideological unwillingness to expand public expenditures is strong. Perhaps the US promotion of the Star Wars program should be seen as an alternative to building Keynesian Pyramids. The military meaningfulness is difficult to see when the potential for small-scale terrorism and biological warfare are considered. But, of course, it would give a complementary injection of effective demand for the now-suffering high-technology sectors. And in the US, it might be easier to create a strong alliance around such a policy than one that focused on environmental or social problems.

The hype and the speculative bubble have resulted in a situation where old monetarist recipes tend to come into disrepute and where Keynesian ideas are taken aboard in the US. The European Bank, with its loose connection to national government, seems to be especially slow to adapt to the new reality.

Also, in the more structural policy field, Europe tends to misinterpret the reality of the new economy in the US.

What About the US Success?

One major argument for pushing for a neoliberal model of the new economy and to call for 'structural reform' (meaning primarily a weakening of the protection of workers) has been the assumption that the United States economy performs better than the major European economies and Japan (it is neglected that the most successful countries in the nineties have been small and socially homogenous countries with strong welfare states and equal distributions of income). Therefore, it is important to reflect upon how far the relative United States success in terms of high and stable growth reflects that its market-dominated institutional set-up is especially conducive to the effective use of ICT.

The major reason for slow growth in the United Kingdom in the '50s in terms of volume as well as productivity was, according to Kaldor, that it had emptied its reserves of labour in agriculture before the rest of Europe and Japan. I believe that ample access to labour on the supply side and Kaldorian dynamics may go a long way in explaining the noninflationary United States growth in the 1990s. On the demand side, the major factor has been the unique position of the dollar and the US financial market. This unique position created the room for the expansionary demand policy that was overlayered by the hype and the financial speculative dynamics.

On the supply side, there have been factors making expansion possible without labour market bottlenecks. At the bottom of the skill pyramid, the easy access to a 'hidden' reserve of nonemployed illegal immigrant workers has made noninflationary expansion possible in the service sector. At the top of the skill pyramid, the unique position of the US university system has attracted bright and hardworking young people from all over the world to science and engineering studies. This has reduced the barriers for rapid growth of the ICT-producing sectors that have a higher-than-average growth in terms of both volume and productivity.

If this analysis is correct, the idea of using the US as 'a benchmark' for Europe implies much more ambitious policy strategies than those debated today in Europe. Stimulating more entrepreneurship, venture capital and numerical flexibility in the labour market will not challenge the US hegemony in the global financial system, and it will not make the university system a competitive alternative to what the US can offer today. If these challenges should be taken up, the focus should be moved to the role of an emancipation of the European financial markets and university system. Much more ambitious and less ideological approaches to the European Bank and the European Research Area would be called for.

Back to the Solow Paradox

In order to develop a 'no regret' policy strategy where the potential of ICT is realized, it is useful to go back to the Solow Paradox and ask once again why the growth performance of 'the new economy' is so weak in spite of great and promising technological opportunities. The response would have to take into account the complexities reflected in the Perez-Freeman techno-economic paradigm analysis. It would call for a much more critical assessment than OECD has produced so far. OECD remains handicapped by its ideological prejudices in favour of private ownership, unregulated markets and against collective and solidarity-based solutions.

There are some minor openings in new directions in the OECD reports, but they tend to be drowned by the standard sermons. For instance, 'getting fundamentals right' has in earlier documents only referred to macroeconomic stability, while in the latest report it is referred to as 'fundamental economic and *social* stability' and in the ensuing analysis there are some considerations about distributional issues. But these considerations end up with references to the UK as a model and to its 'make work pay' programs. The fact that the Nordic countries with their highly egalitarian societies come out as successes while the UK appears as the outstanding looser according to OECD's own ranking, is not at all reflected in the policy recommendations.

The fact that the 'new economy' discourse has been so strongly infiltrated by a general ideological pro-market and antigovernment stance may actually be one reason why the Solow Paradox will be valid also for the new communication and media technologies and for Internet services. A more pragmatic approach would have recognized that collective initiatives and regulations are necessary to make sure that there is a certain quality in the content of what is distributed through the new media. The historical success of radio and television might have been less impressive if service content had been left completely to private-market competition.

Europe's Next Step

High degree of competition in telecommunication, ample access to venture capital and a culture of entrepreneurship in the US have at EU gatherings been seen as setting a benchmark model for Europe, and it has been neglected that most policy prescriptions are double-edged with negative side effects. For instance, there might be too much as well as too little individual entrepreneurship, given the general institutional framework. The calls for more 'entrepreneurship' in Europe have as much to do with ideology as with concerns for economic growth and well-being.

More important than stimulating a great number of new firms that tend to disappear and primarily bring with them a temporary misallocation of resources – as illustrated by the many Internet entrepreneurs who now have become unemployed or ordinary wage earners – is the transformation of existing organizations. This intuition was behind the ambitious title of the book *Europe's Next Step* edited by Andreasen, Coriat, den Hertog and Kaplinsky (Andreasen et al. 1995). Recent research in the IKE group in Aalborg gives a unique opportunity to link organizational change at the workplace level and product innovation to job creation in the whole economy. For further information on the data and the project see (Lund and Gjerding 1996; Lund 1998; Lundvall 2002).

Employment Development in Static and Dynamic Firms

In what follows we will compare the aggregate employment in two types of firms. Dynamic firms are characterized by the fact that they combine more advanced organizational traits with market-related innovations. The static firms are characterized by traditional form of organization and low activity in terms of market-related innovation. The firms have been characterized on the basis of data from 1993–1995. To begin with, we examine the ability of the two types of firms to create jobs during the period 1992–1997.

Table 13.1 shows that firms that combine new forms of organization with the introduction of new products 1993–1995 create many more jobs than those that do neither. Between 1992 and 1997 there was a total gain of about 3,400 jobs in the subset of all DISKO-firms. In the same period, there was a gain of about 4,600 jobs in the dynamic firms and a loss of 1,650 in the static firms in this period. Again, it is worth noting that the divergence between the employment trends is modest to begin with, but that it keeps growing as time goes by. This might reflect that radical change in technology and organization

***Table 13.1.* Employment in Respectively Dynamic and Static Firms 1992–1997**

	Nov 92	Nov 94	Nov 96	Nov 97
Dynamic firms	70,227 = 100	103.5	103.5	106.6
Static firms	24,983 = 100	99.7	96.0	93.4
Entire DISKO subset	137,445 = 100	103.0	101.4	102.5

Source: Lundvall (2002), 181.

has a positive impact on performance only after a period of organizational learning. The data show that the dynamic firms were much more successful in creating jobs than the static firms in Denmark in the '90s.

The data set also makes it possible to divide the workforce into a core workforce and a more loosely attached workforce. Our criterion for belonging to the core is full-time continuous employment in the firm for more than one year and a maximum degree of unemployment of 15 per cent during the calendar year in question. The use of this criterion means that the 'more loosely attached' employees make up about one third of the DISKO subset for the year 1994.

Table 13.2 shows that the core workforce makes up a larger percentage in the dynamic firms than in the average for all firms.

Thus, it is characteristic that the dynamic firms – the firms that have implemented extensive organizational and technical changes – have less pronounced cyclical variation in employment and that they have a larger core workforce. To the extent that the share of the labour force employed in dynamic firms grows – and this is a tendency in Denmark, both because more firms introduced new organizational traits and because the dynamic firms increase their employment – we should, everything equal, expect a certain reduction in the very high Danish labour market mobility. This would, in itself, function as a stabilizing factor in relation to the cyclical development in the entire economy.

Another important issue is to what extent the movement towards learning organizations tends to contribute to the polarization in the labour market between skilled and unskilled workers. In order to analyse this issue, it is relevant to take into account also the competition pressure. A strong transformation pressure may be expected to expose unskilled workers more than skilled workers. Therefore table 13.3 includes only unskilled workers divided in four groups reflecting the type of firm they belong to. Firms have been grouped according to how they have responded to questions about the change in competition pressure they experienced 1993–1995 and according to if they belong to the category of dynamic or static firms (Lundvall and Nielsen 1999).

Table 13.3 shows that the dynamic firms in the longer run (between 1992 and 1997) were able to compensate for the negative impact on employment of much

Table 13.2. **Share of Core Work Force in Dynamic and Static Firms 1994**

	Dynamic	Static	All Firms
Share of core workforce	66.8 per cent	60.7 per cent	64.3 per cent

Source: Nielsen (1999), IDA data combined with DISKO survey.

Table 13.3. **Employment of Unskilled Workers in Dynamic and Static firms 1992–1997**

	Nov 92	Nov 94	Nov 96	Nov 97
Strongly increased competition				
Dynamic firms				
Static firms	16,500 = 100	100.3	96.9	102.1
	4,218 = 100	92.3	81.9	75.0
Somewhat increased or milder competition				
Dynamic firms	11,262 = 100	101.5	98.5	102.0
Static firms	5,862 = 100	99.3	97.0	93.5

Source: IDA data combined with DISKO survey.

stronger competition. The strongly exposed dynamic firms did as well as those less exposed to intensified competition. But most interesting, the table shows massive job losses (25 per cent over five years) for unskilled workers in those firms exposed to much stronger competition that neither used new forms of organization nor introduced new product. More highly developed organizational forms do not in themselves make the unskilled workers more vulnerable. They are, however, vulnerable to strongly increased competition on their product markets. Unskilled workers that work in firms and industries strongly exposed to competition where the opportunities or ability to engage in change are limited, are the ones most strongly at risk for losing their jobs. Policies aiming at promoting competition need, thus, to be combined with policies enhancing the capability to innovate and introduce organizational change.

The DISKO Data and the Distinction Between Static and Dynamic Firms

The data to be presented here emanates from a big project on the Danish innovation system – DISKO. In 1996 we made a survey addressed to 4,000 firms in the private sector – services as well as manufacturing firms – and we got responses on technical innovation, organizational change and competence building from around 2,000 firms. The questions focused especially on what kind of changes the firms had introduced in these areas in the period 1993–1995.

Then we linked register data on employment for the same firms to the qualitative information 1990–1994. Recently, we have been able to update the employment data for the survey firms until 1997. There are some technical difficulties involved since the surveys were addressed to 'firms' as legal units, while the employment data refer to 'production units' that may constitute a part of a 'firm'. To solve this problem, we linked the questionnaire addressed to a specific firm to the register data referring to the biggest of the production units belonging to the firm. Since we are considering change in employment rather than levels of employment, this should not undermine the validity of the analysis.

On the basis of the survey data, we developed a classification of firms in which we combined their degree of organizational development with their activity in terms of the development of products and markets. In this way, we could differentiate between firms that did not meet either demand (we characterize these as 'static' firms), those who met one of the two demands ('flexible' and 'innovative' firms, respectively) and finally, those that met both demands (these we characterize as 'dynamic'). In the following discussion, in order to maintain a certain degree of clarity, we shall concentrate on comparing the two extremes—that is, the static and dynamic firms—with each other and with the average of all the firms in the survey.

The most important results from the DISKO data analysis are:

- That firms introducing new products and new forms of organization characterized by functional flexibility (dynamic organizations) create more jobs than the average firms. The positive impact on employment works itself out over a period of three years.
- That dynamic organizations create more stable jobs (the core labour force is bigger).
- That both these results hold also for unskilled workers.
- That there are job losses for unskilled workers both in static and dynamic organizations, but the massive job losses for this category of workers take place in those organizations exposed to intensified product competition that do not engage in technical innovation and organizational change.

These results tend to support the basic assumption behind *Europe's Next Step* and they point to whole new set of policies that have much more to do with organizational change – establishing learning organizations – than with just accelerating the diffusion of information technology (Coriat 2001; Nyholm et al. 2001). As long as NASDAQ was booming and everything beginning with 'e' was believed to bring us into economic paradise, it was not easy to get policymakers to listen to such a message, but after the bursting of the bubble, things might have changed somewhat.

Summing Up

The current situation of extreme uncertainty can easily develop into global economic stagnation, and the traditional stimulation policies might be either blocked by ideological and institutional barriers (the anti-inflation stance of the European Central Bank) or limited in impact because of the low inflation rates. In this situation, it might be useful to start thinking about a new kind of Keynesianism where public expenditures aim at upgrading human resources and promoting organizational change. The Danish data presented here indicates that the socioeconomic rate of return on investments in adult training and organizational change is especially high in this period characterized by ample unexploited technological opportunities. Therefore, what has been assumed to be 'a new economy' should rather be seen as an era where the demand for a new type of economic policy is especially strong. To agree on defining and the implementing such a new type of economic policy will probably prove to be as difficult as it was in the 1930s.

References

Andreasen, L. E., B. Coriat, F. den Hertog and R. Kaplinsky (eds). 1995. *Europe's Next Step: Organizational Innovation, Competition and Employment*. London: Frank Cass.

Archibugi, D. and B.-Å. Lundvall (eds). 2001. *Europe in the Globalizing Learning Economy*. Oxford: Oxford University Press.

Arundel, A., E. Lorenz, B.-Å. Lundvall and A. Valeyre. 2007. 'How Europe's Economies Learn: A Comparison of Work Organization and Innovation Mode for the EU-15.' *Industrial and Corporate Change* 16, 1175–1210.

Caraça, J., B.-Å. Lundvall and S. Mendonça. 2009. 'The Changing Role of Science in the Innovation Process: From Queen to Cinderella?' *Technological Forecasting & Social Change* 76, 861–867.

Coriat, B. 2001. 'Organizational Innovation in European Firms: A Critical Overview of the Survey Evidence.' In D. Archibugi and B.-Å. Lundvall (eds). *The Globalizing Learning Economy*. Guildford, King's Lynn: Oxford University Press, 195–218.

David, P. A. 1991. 'Computer and Dynamo: The Modern Productivity Paradox in a Not-Too-Distant Mirror.' In OECD. *Technology and Productivity*. Paris: OECD.

Foray, D. and B.-Å. Lundvall. 1996. 'The Knowledge-Based Economy: From the Economics of Knowledge to the Learning Economy.' In D. Foray and B.-Å. Lundvall (eds). *Employment and Growth in the Knowledge-Based Economy*. OECD Documents. Paris: OECD.

Freeman, C. and C. Perez. 1984. 'Long Waves and New Technology.' *Nordisk Tidsskrift for Politisk Ekonomi* 17, 5–14. [5]

Gjerding, A. N., L. Kallehauge, B.-Å. Lundvall and P. T. Madsen. 1992. *Den forsvundne produktivitet* [Productivity lost: Danish industrial development in the middle of the eighties]. Copenhagen: DJØF Forlag.

Jensen, M. B., B. Johnson, E. Lorenz and B.-Å. Lundvall. 2007. 'Forms of Knowledge and Modes of Innovation.' *Research Policy* 36, 680–693.

Lund, R. 1998. 'Organizational and Innovative Flexibility Mechanisms and Their Impact upon Organizational Effectiveness.' DRUID Working Paper 98, 23, Department of Business Studies, Aalborg: Aalborg University.

Lund, R. and A.N. Gjerding. 1996. 'The Flexible Company, Innovation, Work Organisation and Human Resource Management.' DRUID Working Paper 96, 17, Department of Business Studies, Aalborg: Aalborg University.

Lundvall, B.-Å. 1996. 'The Social Dimension of the Learning Economy.' DRUID Working Paper 1, Aalborg University, Department of Business Studies.

———. 2002. *Innovation, Growth and Social Cohesion: The Danish Model.* Cheltenham: Edward Elgar.

Lundvall, B.-Å. and B. Johnson. 1994. 'The Learning Economy.' *Journal of Industry Studies* 1, 23–42.

Lundvall, B.-Å., E. Lorenz and P. Rasmussen. 2008. 'Education in the Learning Economy: A European Perspective.' *Policy Futures in Education* 6, 681–700.

Lundvall, B.-Å. and P. Nielsen. 1999. 'Competition and Transformation in the Learning Economy: the Danish Case.' *Revue d'Economie Industrielle* 88, 67–90.

Ministry of Business and Industry. 1996. 'Technological and Organisational Change. The OECD Jobs Strategy, Country Report, Denmark.' Copenhagen: Ministry of Business and Industry.

Nielsen, P. 1999. *Personale og produktion: Menneskelige ressourcer i udvikling af nye fleksible produktionssystemer.* Aalborg: Aalborg University.

Nyholm, J., L. Normann, C. Frelle-Petersen, M. Riis and P. Torstensen. 2001. 'Innovation Policy in the Knowledge-Based Economy: Can Theory Guide Policy-Making?' In Archibugi and Lundvall (eds). *Europe in the Globalizing Learning Economy.* Oxford: Oxford University Press, 253–272.

OECD. 2000. *A New Economy: The Changing Role of Innovation and Information Technology in Growth.* Paris: OECD.

———. 2001. *The New Economy: Beyond the Hype. Final Report on the OECD Growth Project.* Paris: OECD.

Perez, C. 1983. 'Structural Change and Assimilation of New Technologies in the Economic and Social System.' *Futures* 15, 357–75. [3.1]

Chapter Fourteen:

THE ART OF MACRO-QUALITATIVE MODELLING: AN EXPLORATION OF PEREZ' SEQUENCE MODEL OF GREAT SURGES

Lars Mjøset
University of Oslo

Technological Revolutions and Financial Capital is one of the most important books written on capitalism. Historically *and* theoretically! How can such a statement be made on Carlota Perez' first and (so far) only book? How can a slim volume of about 180 pages be mentioned together with works such as the 2,350 page *Das Kapital* by Marx, Schumpeter's 1,400 pages of *Business Cycles* or Åkerman's 930 pages of *Ekonomisk Teori*?

Åkerman? Why mention a scarcely-ever-quoted Swedish economist (1896–1982) together with always-quoted scholars such as Marx and Schumpeter? One reason is that I happen to know that Carlota Perez appreciates his main book (Åkerman 1944, which was translated into Spanish in 1960) above Schumpeter's work, although she – like most others (except Kindleberger 1978, Goldstein 1988) – commits the sin of not quoting it. But a more important reason is this: There is a close connection between the claim that Perez' work is *theoretically* important, and the paradoxical fact that most of Åkerman's work entitled 'Economic Theory' contains an empirical analysis of the core capitalist countries in the 1820–1940 period.

Åkerman and Perez share the same basic substantive research problem: How can patterns in the development of the core capitalist group of countries since the late eighteenth century be reconstructed in a way that serves the analysis of present economic developments? Åkerman was a founding member of the Econometric society, but rather than converting to the econometric program of statistical inference (the Cowles commission approach as pioneered by Haavelmo and others), he continued to pursue a 'low tech' approach to the analysis of economic time series. To mainstream economists, he remained stuck in an outdated 'barometer' approach to business cycle analysis, an early kind of applied economics that had been superseded by econometrics. But in an institutionalist perspective, Åkerman held sway against the economics mainstream throughout his career, exploring the relationship between economic structures and cycles by means of what we can today define as a contextualist methodological approach (Mjøset 2009). In this essay, we show that the methodology implied in Perez' book is also a contextualist one. Tracing parallels between Åkerman's and Perez' work allows us to spell out how the contextualist approach can deal with methodological challenges in macro-qualitative studies.

Great Surges and their Four Phases

Technological Revolutions and Financial Capital (Perez 2002) analyses industrial capitalism from the late eighteenth century onwards. Perez' (1983 and 1985) point of departure is the Schumpeterian study of long (Kondratiev) waves of about 50-years duration. She redefines these as *great surges of development*, following an orderly sequence of four phases: irruption – frenzy – synergy – maturity. This focus converges with Åkerman's, whose 1928 dissertation was entitled *On the Rhythms of Economic Life*.

A great surge starts in the *irruption* phase as a 'love affair' emerges between a revolutionary technology (cotton spinning, steam-driven railways, heavy engineering, auto-industrial complex, information/communication technology) and finance capital. The latter searches for new sources of high returns in a situation where old technologies have matured. As the potentials of a new technology become visible, financial capital dissociates itself from productive capital through a *frenzy* phase in which the paper value of the new activities explodes. Although financial capital helps establish adequate infrastructure for the new technologies, the decoupling becomes increasingly extreme. The evolving casino capitalism ends in bubble and crash. A depression then leads through a turning point in which new regulations are introduced. With reference to the excesses of the crash, finance capital is strictly controlled. The long-term interests of production capital are promoted through the 'happy marriage' of the *synergy* phase, a Golden Age that broadly generalizes the new technologies. Finally, there are 'signs of separation' during the *maturity* phase, as markets saturate. Finance capital no longer expects huge gains from the old technology, and parts of it flow as idle money in search of another revolutionary technology.

This is indeed a very 'economic' account of the history of capitalism! No chapter is longer than 15 pages. The book contains no narrative of each long surge (but see Freeman and Louçã 2001, chapters 5–9). The historian would be provoked by the lack of narrative beyond the rather formal sequence. Most social science theorists, in contrast, would sceptically note the absence of high-level theory. How is it possible to claim that the sequence model is a crucial contribution to theoretically informed historical analysis of capitalism?

We shall treat the sequence model as a theoretical model, specifying it with reference to other varieties of such models. Following Achinstein (1968, 212ff) we define a theoretical model as (1) a set of assumptions about some object or system, (2) to which it attributes 'an inner structure, composition, or mechanism' intended to explain properties exhibited by it. The model is (3) 'a simplified approximation useful for certain purposes', it is (4) proposed within a broader framework of basic theories, and (5) it is often developed on the basis of an analogy between the target object/system and some other object/system. Below, we shall compare three types of such theoretical models.

Methodological Reflection in Early Twentieth-Century Economics

In 1950, Åkerman's most famous student, Swedish economist Erik Dahmén (1950, 9–11) based his analysis of economic development on three 'lines of thought': The first was Veblen's criticism of the dominant classical/neoclassical schools. The second was Åkerman's analysis of economic transformations, as well as his methodological reflections regarding the 'fundamental dualism' between causal analysis and economic plans. The third was Schumpeter's focus on entrepreneurial activity as a search for new combinations of production factors, as well as his (anti-Keynesian) scepticism against analysis based entirely on aggregated concepts.

Schumpeter in 1908 analysed in detail the Walras version of the axiomatized general equilibrium system in his first book, but in his theory of economic development (1911) and later in *Business Cycles* (1939/1982), he pursued a wholly different line of study, taking economic transformation as the point of departure. Andersen (2004) recently emphasized that the notion of entrepreneurship was Schumpeter's application of a quite aristocratic notion of 'elites' that he drew from Pareto and even from the sociological theories of elites.

Typically, all three economists mentioned by Dahmén pursued the 'history and methodology of economics' as a side activity to their empirical studies. The 'aristocrat' Schumpeter may have regarded this as a luxury. To Veblen and Åkerman it was a necessity, as they were torn between frustration with the weight of neoclassical convictions in economics and optimism that economics would eventually become an 'evolutionary science'. Åkerman (1960) showed how economics could start from a time/space-specifying causal analysis and then go on to model the plans of the relevant collective actors.

In essays published between 1898 and 1908, Veblen noted that static neoclassical models of price formation were unable to grasp actual developments over time, driving forces of development and changing institutions. These models isolated the hedonistic economic actor as eternal human nature: a self-centred, consumption-focused, non-socialized spectator, passively calculating optimizing strategies, incapable of creating anything new, and without habits. Such models formalized Bentham's hedonism, which again rooted in classical natural-order thinking. The environment determines all things; human nature is seen as 'substantially uniform, passive and unalterable in respect of men's capacity for sensuous affection', pursuing greatest gain or least sacrifice, measured in 'hedonistic magnitudes'. Psychological effect is equated with expenditure of kinetic energy, forming a 'theory of costs in terms of discomfort' (Veblen 1919, 134f).

Veblen's alternative was in line with pragmatist philosophy, especially Dewey's pursuit of a psychology that analyses mental life in active terms and thinking as a collective activity, focusing on impulses and their development rather than on the mere feeling of pleasure and pain. Veblen also suggested an alternative view on regularities, as the result of habitual action (Hodgson 2004).

While Veblen's methodological reflections related to the earliest generation of neoclassical scholars (J. B. Clark, I. Fischer, A. Marshall), Åkerman's philosophy of economic knowledge critically reflected on the attempts to turn the neoclassical models into tools of dynamic empirical analysis through the turbulent interwar period. The neoclassical starting point, wrote Åkerman (1939), was 'a (seemingly) always valid logical theory'. He claimed that 'central theory in economics' was at a crossroads:

One may either follow the classical and neoclassical tradition and more or less consciously accept its natural-philosophical and utilitarian preconceptions, building on this basis a construction that may roughly fit even the contemporary institutional system. Alternatively, one must realize that such a program is bound to fail, and that the only secure way goes through a complete reassessment of the assumptions and methods of economic theory. (Åkerman 1939, 7)

Following Veblen, Åkerman held that survival of the idea of a natural order leads equilibrium theory to *fuse* the 'logical definition of concepts, the drawing up of actors' plans, description of the total economic process as well as the laying down of norms both for individuals and for society as a whole'. This 'aprioristic synthesis' was met with mounting criticism in the interwar period. The economic mainstream responded by attempting 'to "complete" equilibrium economics by additions drawn from the theory of anticipations, the theory of business cycles, and from dynamic analysis'. Åkerman scrutinized these attempts (and particularly the local Swedish variety, the Stockholm school), finding that they scarcely were 'thoroughly founded in philosophy and the theory of knowledge'. Since they largely disregarded the question of 'the logical and methodological *connection* between the various strands of research', economics became fragmented into axiomatized 'central theory', a number of attempts to make it dynamic, econometrics based on ever larger datasets, economic history and sociological studies of the collective actors.

Åkerman's alternative was to explicitly think in philosophical and methodological terms, thereby synthesizing economics with elements from the other social sciences in a non-fragmenting way. Such explicit reflection led to the insight that economics relies on a fundamental dualism between theory and reality, as well as between economic plans and causal reconstruction. Only by accepting this dualism, could one work towards 'a realistic synthesis free of contradictions' (1939, 8).

Few listened to him. When Åkerman retired in the 1960s, Dahmén was one of the few scholars who would still quote him. Mainstream economics became even more dominated by the unrealistic synthesis. The situation is the same today. Among the three economists mentioned by Dahmén, Schumpeter is the only one who is now widely celebrated. Åkerman is entirely forgotten, Veblen is only a classic among sociologists, and increasingly recognized in science studies and anthropology. Dahmén's work is popular among economic historians and business school economists.

The Contextualist Framework and the Specificity of Macro-Qualitative Studies

In contemporary philosophy of the social sciences, the distinction between a standard position, emphasizing parallels to natural science, and a social-philosophical position, with similarities to the humanities, is well established. We shall here define a third position, the contextualist framework (Mjøset 2009).

This methodological framework has been developed with reference to research in areas distant from macro-historical political economy. Its roots are in micro-sociological interactionism, network-research and participatory action-research. Some scholars believe that this methodology is only relevant in micro-sociology. But the crucial feature is not the level or the scope, but that cases at any level are accepted as interesting in and of themselves. The neo-Kantian term 'historical individuals' (frequently used by Weber) indicates such a focus.

This methodology reflects the fact that social scientists gain much of their knowledge through interactions with humans that are the same kind as ourselves. Social scientists participate in what they study. This is particularly obvious in micro-sociological fieldwork, which has therefore been the core reference for the development of qualitative methodologies. The interaction through which we gain knowledge about people also involves us in people's pursuit of outcomes that matter in and of themselves. This is similar to a number of other walks of life: treatment of a medical case, procedures in court cases, therapy with a client and social work. These are all concrete relations between people, and the expert is committed to getting specific results that make a difference for the other person(s) involved. Experiment is not an option. But contextualism is not a methodology of historical narratives as such. It is not averse to generalization. It requires contextualized generalizations developed bottom-up, from the substantive, explanatory analyses of relevant developments. This is the notion of explanation-based theory. In the following, we relate to grounded theory (Glaser and Strauss 1967) as the so far most systematic specification (but not the only one) of such a notion of theory.

The generalized contextualist approach to methodology (Mjøset 2009) applies such lessons to macroscopic and historical kinds of study as well. All qualitative research is grounded in studies of cases; it is 'small-n' research, but the size and complexity of cases may differ dramatically. We shall spell out four ways in which macro-qualitative analyses differ from micro-qualitative ones:

1. *Macro-qualitative studies do not work with 'raw' field data, but with data that are mostly 'secondary' in some way.* In macro-studies, fieldwork is mostly impossible. In historical macro-studies, it is always impossible. The equivalent to fieldwork is to tap into relevant earlier research: this 'field' consists of various printed sources, information-seeking interviews (e.g., with experts of various kinds) as well as earlier analyses relating to the field, from the relevant local research frontiers down to detailed historical monographs. The historian's most classical craftwork – finding, classifying and reading archives – is the most obvious parallel to fieldwork in research on the past. Macro-historians may rely on archival research, but they must employ a much wider set of sources. This may well include quantitative data, but mostly in descriptive forms (possibly including techniques of data-mining). More generally, scholars who conduct macro-qualitative studies must learn to sift through large amounts of so-called 'secondary' sources. Nobody takes up the study of large, significant cases without preconceptions. There is already a huge literature and a lot of views on such cases. Some competence in the sociology of knowledge is therefore required. One must learn to recover grounded elements (Mjøset 2006, 356) from research based on ungrounded perspectives (such as

philosophies of history). Glaser and Strauss' (1967) book title is *The Discovery of Grounded Theory*, but here the more relevant formula in macro-qualitative studies is *the improvement of grounded theory*! Improvement is not adequately understood as testing; it may entail one or more of the following: deepening, reformulation, extension, etc. – all of which may be considered contributions to accumulated knowledge in specific areas.

2. *In macro-qualitative studies, the fewer the cases, the more the resulting grounded theory is substantive only.* The larger the cases, the fewer they are. There are some 200 nation states, but only one case of world capitalism. Grounded theory mostly starts by studying selected cases, followed by the theoretical sampling of more cases. Studies of very large cases, however, may rather have to divide their cases into smaller parts. Perez – as we shall see – divides her one big case into a periodization of four-five long surges, searches for patterns in each of these periods, *and then* moves back to look at the whole. Glaser and Strauss' distinction between substantive and formal grounded theory is an important one, but it is really relevant only in research that works with a medium to large number of relatively 'small' cases. Theory on huge cases is always substantive. (Formal grounded theory is 'modules' that may aid explanation, patterns that recur in many different areas of social research (see Glaser and Strauss 1967, Ch. IV; Mjøset 2009, 54–59). As for Perez' four-phase sequence model, this implies that we cannot interpret it as formal grounded theory).

3. *In macro-qualitative studies, the use of theoretical models is more explicit than in micro-qualitative studies.* Dealing with huge and complex cases, the use of quite stylized models seems unavoidable. There is not an explicit notion of models in Glaser and Strauss (1967). But in their notion of theory as a process, there are several steps on the way to an integrated grounded theory. In field notes and memos, the researcher codes the empirical material collected in the field, spelling out concepts and relations between these. Memos contain temporary conclusions. Thus, it makes sense to state that memos imply several theoretical models (relationships between concepts) that guide later fieldwork; such models can be seen as parts of the process of theory formation. We shall see that Perez' sequence model can be seen as such a memo, intermediate between two 'fieldworks'. We can turn existing grounded theory – both substantive and formal – into theoretical models. If we form a theoretical model without reference to earlier substantive grounded theory, we use internal analogies developed from our peculiar field of research. If we use a theoretical model based on formal grounded theory, the analogy may be borrowed from another field of social research (e.g., 'divide and rule', a mechanism that can be distinguished in many walks of life).

4. *Macro-qualitative studies often study topics that form the context for many other studies.* A huge case is general in a substantive way! The world economy is a crucial

part of the context for all nation-states; a nation-state is context for many smaller cases. When there is a choice of many cases, we may doubt the value of studying just one case, but studying the one case of capitalism is clearly relevant. The capitalist world economy is a kind of super-context, influencing most of the topics, at whatever level, that social scientists study. Neither mathematical modelling, statistical inquiry, nor theories based on a program of micro-reduction can give an adequate notion of this context. A separate macro-qualitative analysis is necessary. In this sense, macro-qualitative analysis of 'grand' contexts is indispensable for any social science.

One of the important roots of macro-qualitative studies lies in earlier philosophies of history. There is no space here to discuss whether present-day social philosophy (especially its theories of modernity and globalization) continues to generate such philosophies, understood as ungrounded imposition of grand narratives. But it must be stated that if scholars who specialize in macro-qualitative research are to live up to their responsibility and provide knowledge about a context of importance to all of social science, it is crucial that they take care to avoid any philosophy of history. Perez resists any such temptations. Her sequence model is grounded in empirical material from the economic history of the relevant core countries.

The Neoclassical Methodological 'Package'

Mainstream economics is formulated within the *standard* methodological framework, which judges knowledge in the social sciences with reference to a modified experimental logic (Mjøset 2009): neoclassical models are thought experiments, econometrics emulate an experimental logic using non-experimental data. We shall treat such models as a specific variety of theoretical models. That notion (Achinstein 1968) was originally developed with reference to natural science, and we shall later also rely on a comparison with physics. We then have three types of theoretical models to compare: one type linked to physics experiments, another one represented by the neoclassical economics, and one macro-qualitative type. Perez' sequence model is a case of the latter.

Schumpeter is the one economist who is important both to the neoclassical school and to the neo-Schumpeterian tradition that is Perez' starting point. Despite his dynamic turn, namely, Schumpeter continued to endorse – although in quite ambivalent statements – the neoclassical methodological 'package': At a high level of *abstraction*, a theoretical model that *isolates* the passive 'optimizer under constraint' is formulated. The model is then projected upon an axiomatized system, a set of mathematical concepts. A number of *idealizations* such as perfect foresight, perfect divisibility, symmetric information, and so on, are necessary given the axiomatic relations of such a mathematical model. This understanding fuses Black's (1962, 223) definition of a mathematical model with Black's (1962, 226) and Achinstein's (1968) notion of a theoretical model (cf. also Mäki 2001). The fusion of economic theory and axiomatization can be read out of terms like 'the consumption function', 'the production function', function being understood in the mathematical sense. Drawing on the prestige of mathematics as the privileged tool of science, the discipline canonizes this axiomatized model as an overall, basic reference point. This leads to whole families of models called 'toy economies' or 'analogue economies'.

This kind of model is involved in mainstream treatment of the same research problems as Perez addresses. As Erixon (2007) notes, the leading neoclassical theories of economic development (*new growth theory*; Helpman 2004) are entirely divorced from theories of economic cycles (the real business cycle (RBC) approach; Lucas 2004). There are important differences between the two approaches, one of which is that new growth theory is very interested in the modelling of 'Schumpeterian' dynamics. But they both agree that any *theoretically sound* economic argument proceed through some version of the axiomatized, basic model, held to represent a general high-level research frontier. This is crucial to the professional identity of mainstream economists; any complex topic of contemporary relevance must be approached *through* a mathematically idealized high theory of constrained maximization. Both modelling traditions aim to 'complete' equilibrium theory – making it a dynamic theory.

This was the project that Veblen and Åkerman doubted. To the extent such doubts are still voiced, mainstream economists mostly respond with reference to the fact that economics today can model any kind of outcome. The real beauty of economic modelling, they claim, emerges when the strict idealizations are relaxed. Introducing asymmetric information, Akerlof and Stiglitz became post-war pioneers of this approach. However, the main message of the criticism is not about the assumption of some kind of rationality, but about the epistemological status of the idealized toy economy. Let us therefore consider somewhat more closely the 'original' of the thought experiment analogy – the physics experiment.

A natural science experiment can be described as a set of practical isolations (shielding and other ways of cancelling the impact of potentially confounding causal factors) and idealizations (as Galileo made his inclined plane as slippery as possible, friction approaching zero allowed the idealization friction = 0, which simplified the mathematical expression; Harré 1983). Galilean idealizations eliminate confounding factors. A successful experiment thus insulates the 'pure' workings of one causal mechanism – understood as a 'law-like regularity'. De-idealization can be conceived as a dismantling of experimental controls, allowing definition of more complex formulas, useful for engineering in real, non-experimental situations. (Based on the work of L. Nowak, the Poznan school in the philosophy of science has developed such an interpretation with reference both to the social and natural sciences; Hamminga 2004.) In this way, high, basic theory is related to more 'phenomenological', real life situations. The crux of the standard approach in economics is the claim that axiomatized thought experiment models follow a similar logic.

Within the philosophy of the natural sciences, the status of such experimentally generated regularities (their 'external validity') in non-experimental settings has been discussed (Cartwright 2007, 39). We need not take a position in this debate, but it should be noted that recent arguments posit that this problem is even more severe in neoclassical thought experiments. Cartwright (2007, 233f) claims that toy economy models also rely on non-Galielean idealizations. These 'do not eliminate confounding factors, but rather provide a simple enough structure to make a deductive study possible.' The absence of physical experimenting makes it impossible to distinguish Galilean and non-Galilean idealizations. The thought experiment model is thereby isolated from empirical experience. Its *goal* becomes self-referential: to confirm the high theory reference point. De-idealization of non-Galilean idealizations does not approach the real world; it just generates more complex toy economies. The models are qualitative ones, but they only show us the workings of a highly idiosyncratic and specific model world. The relevance to 'engineering', e.g., of economic policies, is not at all clear. This dilemma, by the way, was noted by Åkerman in a major position paper:

> If in such a conceptual system one attempts to approach reality by dropping the atomistic premises of equilibrium economics, logical coherence is sacrificed without increased realism, because in such a deductive analysis with its alleged lowering of the level of abstraction the data of reality will not come into contact with the method and result of the analysis. (Åkerman 1954 [1942], 181)

There is no space here to discuss further the problems involved in the attempts to bridge this gap by calibrating the representative actor toy economy models by inclusion of selected time series to explain cyclical movements (Hoover 2001 and 2008; Mjøset and Cappelen 2009). Let us just note that the standard framework is often invoked to legitimate both this, as well as other formulas about basic factors underlying the flow of empirical events.

Using another element of Cartwright's (1999) terminology, theoretical models in physics can be seen as a blueprint for the building of an experimental set-up that will serve as a nomological machine producing law-like regularities. The Åkerman / Veblen criticism can then be rephrased as a criticism of toy economy thought experiments; this is a theoretical model that can be built in a computer, and it can only produce toy economies (see also Hoover's (2002, 164) rejection of Cartwright's (1999, Ch. 7) claim that also neoclassical economic models are nomological machines).

The Sequence Model as a Theoretical Model

We are now ready to specify a third type of theoretical model, one that reflects the four particularities of macro-qualitative studies, as noted above. As a theoretical model (3), it models the highly significant, huge case of industrial capitalism (4), the model is related to a set of theories that all are substantive ones (2), and the empirical material is a variety of 'secondary' sources (1). We shall see that even such a model uses idealizations, but these are conceived within a contextualist, non-experimental framework. In order to distinguish them from mathematical idealizations, we shall call them isolations (cf. also Mäki 2001).

Contextualist methodology requires prior causal analysis, paying 'attention to the different decision units of importance *within definitely specified institutional frameworks*' as 'the setting of the models of calculation' (Åkerman 1960, 15). No theoretical model is given a privileged position as an overall, basic reference point. Rather, the scholar is content with a number of theories at the lower level, connected in *local* research frontiers. This approach is neither driven by high theory, nor by methods. The methodological choices made depend on the research problems.

Perez develops her sequence model with reference to accumulated knowledge that has emerged from earlier efforts to explain the dynamics of capitalism. Broadly, she draws both on the history of technology (historical studies of specific technologies, their origins and diffusion), communication infrastructures, principles of organization, institutions, regulations and economic policies. She also relies on empirical and theoretical work on patterns of interaction between production and financial capital, as well as studies on the relationship between social mobilization, formation of institutions and implementation of regulations in the most important core capitalist countries. Space does not permit a more detailed account of these various interrelated local research frontiers. It is sufficient here to note that at the outset, her strongest commitment is to the neo-Schumpeterian tradition, as already noted, and as further specified below.

With reference to pragmatist philosophy, the contextualist position considers formation and improvement of theory as a process. In this process, initial theoretical models guide reconstructions of relevant empirical material ('fieldwork'); this leads to formation of more integrated theoretical models, which, in the next turn, guides reanalysis as well as more empirical research. Perez first sketches the historical specificity of industrial capitalism. We call this her first investigation. She then turns to isolations in order to conduct partial reconstructions in her *second* investigation.

Consider the difference between a reconstruction of something that has happened, and the experiment, which makes something happen here and now. (Remember that even in quantitative social science, data are overwhelmingly about events in the past.) Even with reference to an outcome of particular interest, a reconstruction is never a complete one. Descriptively complete reconstructions are impossible, and also unnecessary. In line with pragmatist philosophy, we conceive of thinking as collective, and of knowledge as participating in processes of developing human society. Reconstructions select explanatory factors, organizing them into complex (and thus cumulative) causal processes, with reference to a sense of adequate explanation. In the world created by industrial capitalism, judgments on adequate explanation are basically made in two settings: in research collectives and in various networks of decision-makers. These two environments may or may not overlap. Mostly, they overlap only partially. The account in this section mostly relates to reconstruction and theoretical models established by researchers; we return to decision-makers in our conclusion.

The analyst conducts partial reconstructions linked to selected factors that earlier cumulative research has shown to be of importance, separated from other factors. Building an experiment, idealization can be approximated. Concerning macro-qualitative partial reconstructions, Perez isolates what research has so far has found to be the main 'forces'. Isolation is a better word for this, since it is about relating to the history of a large system 'in operation' out there. This system cannot be built. It is already there, being 'built' by ongoing interactions. In grounded theory terms, isolations may be described as reconstructions focused on certain core concepts that emerge from the coding of a huge qualitative empirical material. These theoretical models serve as 'memos' connecting earlier and later fieldwork.

In her third investigation, Perez drops one of her initial isolations, developing the sequence model as one that is more integrated than the earlier neo-Schumpeterian theoretical models. Let us compare it to a neoclassical toy economy. The scopes differ vastly. Neoclassical models start from human conduct in an allegedly universal sense, while Perez models phases within periods during industrial capitalism. In the basic neoclassical view, human nature is unchanging, while the context is changing. But the models are mathematically idealized. There is thus no room for empirical knowledge about real-life context. Assumptions about the context are made as the modeller plays around with the toys of the model. Perez also gives a stylized account of her context, but it is, as Åkerman suggested, the result of a causal analysis. Her modelling is qualitative; it does not rely on mathematics, but on analogies (life cycle, recurrence) from inside the study of social interaction. It is also directly set at the macro level, thus avoiding the grave problems of micro-reduction that haunt representative actor macro-models, particularly the real business cycle models (Hoover 2001).

We are back to our threefold contrast: In a physics experiment, idealizations are built in real life and real time to produce a regularity. This regularity then serves as a 'basic' one, while the dropping of idealizations leads towards more adequate mathematical formulas and more adequate engineering formulas. In the neoclassical thought experiment, a high-level research frontier (already established to facilitate mathematical expression) developed from ideas about natural order is the point of departure. This set of idealizations defines a model world with model time, and if it satisfies logical criteria of consistency, the researchers may play with this toy economy. They have many options in terms of de-idealizations, but one can never be sure that the calculated regularities are real ones.

From a contextualist perspective, one may claim that neoclassical thought experiments pay the price for trying to save an experimental perspective in a field of science where few experiments can be set up. In contrast, then, macro-qualitative study explicitly lets experiments 'disintegrate' into the two separate but connected strategies of causal analysis and forecasting. The relationship to the real world is not as in physics, where engineering is related to fundamental experimentally generated knowledge via de-idealization. In economic life, various experts rely on partial reconstructions; they develop forecasting techniques that influence planning, which directs the strategic choices of decision-makers. Further reconstructions try to explain how the strategies interact with other influential processes to produce economic development. Implementation of strategies and causal reconstruction cannot be unified in any experiment. To the extent social science participates in social development, this participation takes the form of a back-and-forth movement between causal reconstructions and economic plans. This was the profound insight behind what Åkerman termed the dualism between causal analysis and economic plans (he also used the terms 'analysis of alternatives' and 'models of calculation' – the Swedish term was *kalkyl*, which means calculation). He emphasized that the relationship between causal analysis and forecasting will remain a dualism, but one that can be narrowed down. The important point about theoretical models, such as the sequence model, is that they can serve both different activities. (We return to this in the conclusion.) In Perez' fourth investigation, the model allows her to develop more explanatory reconstructions, which is what Perez does in her fourth investigation.

Such improved analysis may imply a dropping of isolations, but this does not yield better mathematical statement for engineering use. Even improved theoretical models can never be blueprints for a constructible machine that can produce regularities. De-isolation of a contextualist theoretical model brings in more context, and it brings in specific processes to be traced. Depending on our explanatory needs, these may be further decomposed into specific mechanisms that enter into conjunctions. Engineering statements are general, to be related to many cases, while these process-tracings approach historical individuality. No future cases may be exactly similar to the ones reconstructed. Still, if researchers do a good job, presenting bounded generalizations based on thorough case reconstructions, better planning may also follow. The cases studied in macro-qualitative research are, after all, cases of importance to most of us.

Perez' four investigations illustrate theory as a process; it starts with the state of knowledge in relevant research frontiers, proceeds by partial reconstructions depending on various isolations, discovers a more integrated theoretical model that is both substantive and grounded. This allows improved reconstructions, with more focus on causal chains and causal conjunctures. Isolations are partly dropped, but the analysis is still analytical, thanks to the model. The result is historically individual process-tracings.

At one point (Perez 2002, 151) Perez 'roughly' ranges her interdisciplinary study within evolutionary economics. Such a methodology can accommodate important features such as bounded rationality and path dependence. The reference to neo-Darwinian evolutionary theory emphasizes parallels to a non-experimental field of natural science. Philosophy of science aspects of such an approach have been explored (Hodgson 1993). A full discussion of limitations and possibilities requires another paper. Here we shall only note that even if Veblen (1919, 56 ff) insisted that economics had to become an evolutionary science, and even if Åkerman (e.g., 1939, 74) developed Veblen's notion of cumulative causation further, we hold that the contextualist framework suits Perez' project the best. While both frameworks converge in their interest in process-tracing, the contextualist framework has the advantage of being legitimated by reference to social science only.

We have specified the meaning of isolation in macro-qualitative models. The target system of Perez' sequence model is the industrial capitalist core of the world economy. Table 14.1 now suggests three isolations that constitute this target system, they relate to economic area, layers of that area, and to the functions of capital. Table 14.2 then specifies how these isolations relate to the four investigations out of which Perez' book is composed.

In the next four sections, we take a closer look at the four investigations, paying particular attention to the empirical grounding. We distinguish pure illustrations from systematic comparison, emphasizing – with reference to the notion of mechanisms – that only the latter can lead towards an adequate level of explanation.

Table 14.1. Three Isolations Behind Perez' Sequence Model

I1: *Area* –	Isolation *of* the core of the world economy, that is, isolation *from* non-core areas (periphery). The core is the economic areas in which the technological revolutions of industrialism emerge, as well as areas with conditions for development and catch-up processes, areas in which the new technologies are rapidly diffused. (Perez 2002, 47)
I2: *Layer* –	The techno-economic, economic and national institutional layers are isolated. They are isolated *from* any impact that may follow from the organization of economic areas into an international system of states.
I3: *Functional* –	Isolation of production capital. That is, isolation from the specific roles and interests of financial capital.

First Investigation – A Basic Context Based on Earlier Research

One of the reasons why Perez' book is shorter than most books on the huge case of capitalism, is that she – unlike both the Marxian and Weberian traditions – never defines capitalism with reference to its historical contrasts to other modes of production or civilizations. Perez states that 'the sequence technological revolution – financial bubble – collapse – golden age – political unrest' is 'based on causal mechanisms that are in the nature of capitalism' (Perez 2002, 3). These mechanisms 'stem from' three integrative 'features of the system': (1) that 'technological change occurs by clusters of radical innovations forming successive and distinct revolutions that modernize the whole productive structure', (2) 'the functional separation between financial and production capital, each pursuing profits by different means', (3) 'the much greater inertia and resistance to change of the socio-institutional framework in comparison with the techno-economic sphere, which is spurred by competitive pressures' (Perez 2002, 6). If we call these three driving forces, the logic is as follows: *driving forces* → *mechanisms* → *IFSM sequence.*

Since the mechanisms 'stem from' the driving forces, Perez' definition of industrial capitalism must be inferred from her account of these: It is a social formation in which technological change has gained relative autonomy, under the pressure of competition, it is wound up with the interaction between production and financial capital, and formed also by socio-institutional forces.

The 'fieldwork' leading to this definition is *not* explicated in the book. It is not shown that these driving forces are specific to capitalism. Actually, Åkerman (1960, 14) started his final synthetic work in the same way. He noted the obvious insight that any selection of data and presentation of facts 'presupposes some theory', and when one starts by presenting 'the trends of industrialism', one

Table 14.2. Perez' Analytic Strategy

	Driving Forces			Chapter	The three isolations			Sequence	Periodization Comparison	Number of Cases
	TR/TEP	K	SIF		Area	Layer	Functional			
First investigation – The historical specificity of industrial capitalism										
	+	+	+	1	–	–	–	–	–	One (industrial capitalism)
Second investigation – Long wave periodization redefined as great surges										
	+	÷	÷	2	+	+	+	5 periods/Per		Four and a half (surges)
	÷	÷	+	3	+	+	+	Life cycle of TR		
	+	PK	+	4	+	+	+	2 phases (IN/D)		
Third investigation – Finding the sequence model in all the surges										
	+	PK/FK	+	5	+	+	÷	5.1 IFSM/5.2 IFSM/Per		Four and a half (surges)
	+	÷	÷	6	÷	+	+	–		
	+	+	+	7	+	+	÷	7.1 IFSM/7.2 IFSM/Per		
Fourth investigation – Further study of industrial capitalism in the light of the sequence model										
	+	+	+	8	+	+	+	M phase	Compare M1-5	One
	+	+	+	9	+	+	÷	I phase	Compare I1-5	(some
	+	+	+	10	+	+	÷	F phase	Compare F1-5	trends).
	+	+	+	11	+	+	÷	Turning point	Compare TPs	Potential
	+	+	+	12	+	+	÷	S phase	Compare S1-5	typology
	+	+	+	13	+	+	÷	Typology of FI	Typology of FI and II	
	+	+	+	14	+	+	–	14.1 Formal model		
	–	–	–	15	–	–	–	–	–	–

Abbreviations: TR/TEP – Technological revolution/Techno-economic paradigm; K – Capital (PK – production capital; FK – financial capital); SIF – Socio-institutional framework; Per – periodization (as given in Tables 2.1, 2.2 and 2.3 in Perez 2002); 1–5 – the five great surges defined by the periodization; IN/D – Installation/deployment; IFSM – *the four phase sequence:* Irruption, Frenzy, Synergy, Maturity; FI – Financial innovations; II – Institutional innovations. *The three isolations:* See Table 14.1.

'inevitably to some extent anticipates the subsequent analytical, more or less deductive, exposition'. Once we conceive theory as a process, this procedure is easily understood. Explanation-based theory is compatible with the view that all observations are theory-loaded. Starting their respective accounts, both Perez and Åkerman relate to a cluster of local research frontiers, defining a set of driving forces that are specific to industrial capitalism. In Perez' case, her first and second investigations mainly relate to earlier theoretical models in the neo-Schumpeterian tradition.

Second Investigation – Isolations Yield Partial Reconstructions

The neo-Schumpeterian tradition had for some decades focused on long waves. Perez rejects preconceptions contained in the theoretical models developed in this tradition: that long waves are explained by endogenous economic causes (e.g., in terms of an economic model), that they appear as regular up- and downswings in aggregate variables (e.g., using econometric approaches), and that they appear as world-wide phenomena (Perez 2002, 60). Thus she reconceptualizes the 'long waves' as 'great surges'.

Perez' second investigation reconstructs the development of industrial capitalism by partial reconstructions of the impact of the three groups of driving forces in a system defined by the three isolations. In Chapter 2, she studies the technological driving forces independently of their interactions with the two other driving forces. The analysis is summed up in three tables. The first (2.1) specifies five technological revolutions. The second (2.2) specifies five constellations of industries and infrastructures, focusing on large network structures from canals/waterways to digital telecommunications (Perez 2002, 14). The third (2.3) lists the five techno-economic paradigms considered as five changes in organizational 'common-sense'. The three tables support the periodization of 50 to 60 year periods between technological big bangs. Perez has here given a qualitative reformulation of a number of basic 'stylized facts' summed up in neo-Schumpeterian theoretical models.

The macro-qualitative focus requires certain new concepts. Besides 'great surges', a techno-economic paradigm (cf. Perez 1983) is understood as 'sort of a mental map of best-practice options' (Perez 2002, 16) that are 'abstracted from the logic of the generic technologies of the period and from the behaviour of firms'. This notion depicts how techno-economic patterns shape and interact with socioeconomic relations as an 'organizational paradigm'.

From Chapter 3 onwards, Perez sets out to search for patterns in the way the driving forces operate through each of these periods. These reconstructions are summed up in two partial sequence models. Chapter 3 considers only the role of the institutional framework, which links techno-economic features to 'society-wide processes' (Perez 2002, 23). The diffusion of a technological revolution is conceived as a threat that generates resistance. A mismatch emerges between 'the economy and the social and regulatory systems' (Perez 2002, 26). The full potential of the new technologies can only be realized through 'institutional recomposition'. Conflicts and struggles lead to new regulations within which technology and institutions then match. The first partial sequence model thus has four phases: First, the paradigm is configured, involving dynamic growth in a few early new products/industries. Second, the full potential of the technology is understood and an infrastructure for its use is developed. Third, the potential for innovation and market creation is fully realized, and fourth, this potential is weakened as ever fewer products and industries are free of market saturation tendencies (Perez 2002, 30).

In Chapter 4, this sequence is specified as the life cycle of a *paradigm*. Still considering only the real economy, this yields a two-phase sequence model of the *installation* and *deployment* periods (Fig 4.1) of the 'best practice principles' contained in each paradigm.

In sum, Chapters 2 to 4 can be considered a report from a round of 'fieldwork' in which observations are to some extent directed by neo-Schumpeterian theoretical models. The periodization and the partial sequence models are 'memos' from this fieldwork. Given her determination to write a short book, the empirical material takes the form of illustrations. When we know the rest of the book, we clearly realize that the illustrations are based on the full sequence model. Driving forces do not explain by themselves; the sequence model is needed to specify how they interact.

Third Investigation – Defining the Full Sequence Model

In Chapters 5 and 7, the functional isolation is dropped and remains so through the rest of the book. The interaction of technological, economic and institutional driving forces is studied at a less abstract level, defined only by the area- and layer-isolations. Thereby, a dimension not often covered in the technology-oriented neo-Schumpeterian analyses is emphasized: the possibility that financial activities dissociate from the real economic sphere. Thus, Perez now relates to an additional set of relevant local research frontiers. These are more in Veblen's than in Schumpeter's line of thinking. They range from the more theoretical treatment of financial instabilities (Minsky 1986) to the specialized economic history (summarized, e.g., in Kindleberger 1978) of such instabilities.

The distinction between production and financial capital allows Perez to define the sequence model with reference to the specific roles played by financial capital. Installation starts with *irruption*, which turns into *frenzy*.

After the turning point, deployment implies first *synergy*, then *maturity* (Figures 5.1, 7.1, 14.1). The phases are roughly dated in Figures 5.2 and 7.2, 1771 to 2002, following the periodization confirmed in the second investigation. The average length of each surge is 51 years. The one case of industrial capitalism has been divided into five great surges of capitalist development.

Chapter 6 is an excursus; it drops the area isolation (introducing peripheral areas of the world economy), focusing (as in Chapter 2) on the dynamics of the technological driving force separately. The chapter serves as a preparation for later analyses of how peripheral areas became parts of the core through catch-up industrialization (the topic of Perez 1983, 1985), or are in other ways influenced by the core.

Macro-qualitative research, as noted above, should overcome philosophies of history. Marx developed a philosophy of history reflecting a political philosophy. The 'basic contradictions of capitalism' would lead to class polarization, misery, breakdown and political struggles on the organization of society. Perez has social institutions as one out of three sets of driving forces. Institutional change in core capitalism has a lot to do with working class mobilization, but also with the concerns of farmers, middle classes, elite factions, etc. Perez implicitly rejects the Marxian idea that relations of production in and of themselves generate a historical trajectory into crisis. Relations of production are seen as influenced, especially at turning points, by regulations reflecting politicians' and regulators' concern for social consensus and stability. The response to the interwar recession, for instance, gave rise to different types of political regimes: New Deal, social democracy and fascism – but all of them brought about extensive regulation of capitalism in the core area.

Perez comes out against any fundamental theories of secular change. She implies no teleology in terms of development towards either Utopia or breakdown. Her model is thus different from the many models of stages (e.g., early/late capitalism). She is not averse to defining secular trends, but statements on this must be grounded in the specificity of cycles, as her fourth investigation shows. The only implication is the recurrence of an orderly sequence. There will be bubbles, crashes and depressions at the turning points, but there will be future 'Golden Ages' too.

As for empirical substance, Chapters 5 and 7 contain few illustrations and no comparisons, only the sequence model and the periodization. The Chapter 6 excursus also has little space for comparisons or illustrations.

Since Perez studies huge cases, formal grounded theory cannot play any role. The most formal elements she involves are common sense terms such as 'life cycle', describing the sequences as a love affair (a first romance, decoupling, recoupling and maturity). Concerning the link between sequences, she invokes recurrence. Despite these formal elements, we suggest that the sequence model is a theoretical model that is intermediate between less and more integrated *substantive* grounded theory. If, however, as we stated earlier, mechanisms are in between the driving forces and the sequence model, we still have not found the level at which Perez will introduce the mechanisms that explain the developments through the phases of each surge. Irruption, frenzy, synergy and maturity cannot be turned into *grand mechanisms*. The real mechanisms are smaller ones. Thus, a fourth investigation is needed.

Fourth Investigation – Reanalysing the One Case of Capitalism, With Reference to the Sequence Model

Chapters 8–12 work towards an integrated substantive grounded theory of the great surges of industrial capitalism. The question is whether empirically, the four-and-a-half great surges have gone through the four phases, always in that specific order. This investigation leads towards a level of specification at which we will accept that the model yields an explanatory theory.

Perez now makes new observations with direct reference to the model. This is comparable to the fieldworker who returns to the field equipped with a theoretical memo (the sequence model) based on field notes from earlier fieldwork (second and third investigation). Observations are here theory-loaded, as they are directed by a macro-qualitative theoretical model developed from earlier substantive grounded theory.

If the model stands the challenge of historical specification, it will be accepted as accumulated knowledge and will influence and become part of the relevant local research frontiers. But through this final and most empirical investigation, we note a tension between the general nature of the theoretical model and the specificity needed when detailing the mechanisms. Perez (2002, 159f) includes both generalization and specification when stating that the power of her interpretation will be obvious to those who are 'willing to accept *recurrence* as a frame of reference and the uniqueness of each period as the object of study'. She recounts how 'the historical record became a laboratory for testing of the hypotheses of the model'. Her 'genuine experiments in regularity' involve a listing of phenomena that 'could be part of the recurrent sequence', followed by a 'test': do such phenomena appear 'again and again in each similar historical phase, following the preliminary model'?

The five chapters contain comparisons that are guided by the model, one chapter per phase, and a separate one on the turning point (see Table 14.2). But we find that Perez not always fills in empirical observations for all four-and-a-half surges. She does not tell the reader whether the missing information is left out because it is easily explained by the model, uninteresting or deviant. Thus, she only partly achieves comparative specification towards the adequate level of explanation. Summarizing the most notable deviations from her model, Perez concludes:

> A model built on the basis of four-and-a-half cases requires bold stylization and open-minded testing. Naturally, the job is far from complete and further research is likely to help modify and strengthen these tentative results. ... Obviously, any dogmatic or rigid application of the model will defeat its purpose. Its main value is serving as a tool to help organize the richness of real life but not to hammer facts into tight boxes. (Perez 2002, 160)

We see how theory is conceived as a process. Perez recounts that the potential deviations made her reshape and enrich her hypotheses, claiming that the deviant features can be explained in ways that are compatible with the model. We have suggested that the general features are taken care of in the theoretical model, whereas the explanatory substantive grounded theory is something that is emerging. Rather than viewing history as a laboratory, history should be viewed as a field. Rather than 'genuine experiments', the formulation 'pursuit of contextualizing generalization' fits better the idea of improving grounded theory, which is how Perez relates to the neo-Schumpeterian tradition that she started out with. The model is general, since it is a simplified approximation (no tool is tailor-made for one task), whereas the focus on the mechanisms at work in each period is part of the process of improving the substantive grounded theory as an explanation-based theory.

In connection with deviating patterns in the third surge, Perez notes:

> There is no mechanical sequence to be found, without looking at the actual behavior of financial and production capital and to the specific manner and rhythm in which the technological revolution is being installed and where. In the end, all the techno-economic phenomena will be very much conditioned by the institutional and political context of the specific moment in the countries involved. And this is particularly important in cases of falling behind and forging ahead. What is significant, in terms of the value of the model, is that there are causal chains and identifying features that can help the analysis and the interpretation not only of the regularities but also of some of the deviations from the basic pattern. (Perez 2002, 123)

Perez does a better job than most scholars in balancing generalization and specification in social science. But the quote conceives the relationship between model and explanation in terms of a basic model and explainable deviations.

In our conclusion, we shall suggest another way of looking at this: the sequence model remains a model (and there may be other overlapping ones), while the explanations generated by using the model as a tool may, in a next round, lead to various kinds of contextual generalizations that are more specific than the sequence model. Such a future fifth investigation would require a combination of typology and historically specified mechanisms. Such further development of macro-grounded theory would be a task for researchers. Perez' invocation of 'causal chains and identifying features' hints to this, but the statement is vague since these are assumed to help the analysis of regularities and 'some of the deviations'. Our alternative indicates that they may also explain deviations, but without supporting the model.

The sequence model, however, may not be outdated. To understand why, we shall again relate to Åkerman's dualism – mentioned several times already – between causal analysis and economic plans. But the sequence model should not be taken as the only one. There is a hierarchy of local research frontiers, giving rise to more than just one theoretical model in the study of core industrial capitalism. Also when discussing how Perez' theoretical model relates to other, quite parallel models, Åkerman's dualism will prove useful.

Conclusions

The sequence model, Perez tells us, should be employed as a tool. There are two quite different kinds of users: social scientists and decision-makers. Perez is familiar with both. She makes her living out of the combination of two part-time activities: research and consultancy. In fact, Åkerman had a similar experience. In 1922–1923 he was employed in a public office publishing quarterly economic surveys. Between 1928 and 1933 he was the scientist in charge of the business cycle reports published by the Swedish Employers Association (Mjøset 1997, 33f). But while Åkerman turned from full-time consultancy to full-time research, Perez has maintained a double connection throughout her career. While many researchers renounce on their commitment to science when practicing consultancy for a longer period, Perez has managed to combine the two.

It is not a far-fetched speculation that both scholars developed some of their main ideas from this double relationship. We have noted that theoretical models such as Perez' sequence model can be useful for both causal analysis and economic plans (Åkerman 1954). We have also noted that Åkerman emphasized a connection that is often downplayed in the philosophy of economic modelling: these models are in various ways connected to and implied in the forecasting and planning activities that influential collective actors engage in. Thus, Åkerman's pursuit of a contextualist approach in economics does not imply a rejection of mathematical modelling. However, he rejects the idea that one must necessarily proceed through a model of one grand plan for the coordination of all economic activities. Like Veblen, Åkerman suspected that neoclassical theorists turned a particular style of mathematical idealization into a modern, secular substitute for older, morally based ideas of natural order.

Also like Veblen, he pointed to reconstructions of processes of cumulative causation as the alternative. Through his reconstructions of industrialism, as well as the Swedish experience, he had learned how actual developments follow as the unanticipated consequences of the interplay of plans pursued by influential collective actors with different planning horizons and interests. At the time of the industrial revolution, the farmers' seasonal perspective was still dominant, while in the 1930s, the much longer-term planning horizon of the state also put its mark on the industrial economies (and the big boost to techniques of business cycle analysis and economic forecasting came in this period). In Perez, we find the same insight, but she employs a cruder distinction between production and finance capital (long- and short-term horizons), and she also includes the very long-term perspective of the state. Åkerman (1939) held that mathematization in economics should relate to such group-specific plans. Thereby, economics 'models of calculation' could be made more grounded.

The reason why the sequence model may persist, then, is that it may turn out to be useful for groups of social actors. Forecasters and decision-makers rely on stylized facts, disciplinary styles of reasoning, and experience with (and information networks extending to) the particular field covered. Perez' sequence model would seem a useful tool to many types of decision-makers (firms, organizations, state bureaucracies), since there are limits to how much information they can process to back up their forecasts and strategy choices.

The model does not yield forecasts in and of itself, but it may help the forecasters to contextualize the situation they are in. In core states, for instance, it provides a framework for decisions on innovation and industrial policies – already central on the neo-Schumpeterian agenda. For states in the periphery, it invites reflections on strategies of catch-up industrialization. For many states and other international actors it gives a context for discussing economic policies and institutional redesign to counter disaster scenarios following from, e.g., turning-point situations.

At the time of writing – late 2008, the year of the most far-reaching financial meltdown since the 1930s – the world economy is clearly at a turning point in Perez' sense. Her model suggests that the two last phases of the fifth surge will follow orderly. But the model yields no precise timing. When the book was published in 2002, Perez had reasons to believe that the turning point was already imminent. To understand why there was such a long time span between the Asian (1997) and NASDAQ (1999) crises, researchers would have to engage in more specified process-tracing, aided by systematic comparisons with reference to the sequence model. That study may also bring out more widely applicable mechanisms, as we note below.

The model further indicates that following financial crash and depression, there will be a new 'Golden age'. Perez notes in Chapter 13 that the principles of a 'new economy' can be discerned in each frenzy phase. The 1990s was just one out of five cases of this. Still, secular changes across surges require that the policy responses, institutional innovations and regulatory strategies that generate synergy differ from surge to surge. Responses to the present recession cannot simply reproduce the Keynesian strategies that brought the world economy out of the 1930s great depression (Perez 2002, 146). More precise planning/forecasting requires a more specifying analysis. Doing this, researchers may pursue systematic comparisons directed by Perez' sequence model. But they may also relate to a number of other relevant theoretical models.

In this respect, we shall limit ourselves to relevant research frontiers within political economy. There is, of course, the more empirically oriented part of the economics mainstream, econometric research based on large data sets. It should have a place for qualitative contextualization. One can, for instance, see traces of this in Maddison's (2007) work. We have noted that Åkerman, for one, followed the development of econometrics, and saw his own approach as an important addition. However, econometrics has largely remained true to the methodological 'package' prevailing in the economics mainstream. No strong links to macro-qualitative research have been forged, and we must also remember that macro-qualitative studies, with their strongly interdisciplinary orientation, are no strong part of any social science.

In political economy, however, at least since its renaissance in the 1960s, there are many non-mainstream scholars with an interdisciplinary orientation. In this literature, there is some amount of macro-qualitative research, involving theoretical models reflecting research problems similar to those of Perez and Åkerman. Briefly listing some of these, we shall relate to the layer isolations and area isolations (Table 14.1).

Let us first relate to the *layer isolation*. During the third surge, relations of hegemony between the great powers were in flux. Technological dynamics, institutional innovations and finance/production connections differed in Britain, Germany, and the US. The latter two caught up and challenged British hegemonic dominance in international relations. At several points in her fourth investigation, Perez drops the layer isolation, relating to features of the inter-state system, particularly great power relations. She also compares this multi-polarization of the European great powers with the more united Cold War state system during the fourth surge. Thus, for some questions, models relating to great-power relations may guide us towards mechanisms that explain the development within surges. Both the international currency system, international transfers and multilaterals organizations organizing trade and security are heavily influenced by relations of hegemony. There are many such theoretical models in international political economy and international relations. Some of these are models of war cycles and others deal with cycles of hegemonies (an extensive overview is Goldstein 1988).

Let us then turn to the *area isolation*. As part of the fourth investigation, Perez drops the area isolation, analyzing a pattern in which the periphery plays a role in several surges. Idle money flows from the core into specific peripheral areas during the irruption/frenzy phases. The last case was the Asian bubble and crash in 1997, and guided by her model, Perez notes the parallel to the Argentine boom that led to the 1908 Baring crisis, and possibly also to US railway manias and panics during the frenzy phase (1830s and 1840s) of the second surge. British capital was attracted by specific objects in the periphery, faced major losses, but left parts of the periphery with an infrastructure that would play an important role in future surges. There are many models that include centre/periphery dynamics as central to world capitalism. The most ambitious one is certainly Wallerstein's attempt to devise a *dependencia* model that generates both long wave Kondratiev cycles and hegemony shifts (again, Goldstein 1988 contains an overview).

Concerning the relationship between different theoretical models aimed at the same target system, consider these two alternatives: Should we pursue an integration of clusters of related theoretical models into more synthetic models? Or should we use the models as separate tools, applying them to analyse our empirical material from slightly different, but related angles? This relates to the two alternative ways of bridging generalization and specification, sketched at the end of the preceding section. The first option can be combined with a search for one theoretical model allegedly more fundamental than any other theoretical models. The second option would be compatible with a notion of problem-related hierarchies of local research frontiers. This would retain the specificity of each modelling tradition. It would support accumulation of knowledge in terms of typologies and process-tracings rather than in terms of fundamental models that explain through modifications. One would then see the third surge as another *type* – another case of a surge, e.g., a surge marked by great-power fragmentation rather than hegemony.

So far, we have discussed cyclical patterns, but there are also questions of secular trends. Using her sequence model through the fourth investigation, Perez shows how a variety of developments and trends can be demonstrated. Some cover a few, but not all phases, some relates to financial capital in the phases when it dissociates from production capital, etc. Many of these disaggregations are useful, although the analysis is not very systematic. Other approaches, however, emphasizes secular changes more than Perez.

We have no space to pursue a more detailed comparison with Åkerman's (1944, 1960) own theory of industrialism. It has another way of appreciating national specificities; it relies on analysis of a fixed set of four countries, and it pays more exclusive attention to secular patterns. Åkerman's account reminds of more recent sketches by the regulation school (a recent statement close to Perez' research questions is Boyer 2004). Although by now a nation-state-focused research program, the regulation school started out with ideas about nineteenth century competitive regulation being superseded by twentieth century administrated regulation. No detail can be given here, except for the point that like Åkerman, these schemes deemphasize similarities of sequence, emphasizing patterns of secular change and irreversible change across surges. The fourth surge, then, is primarily the emergence of the US mass-consumption-driven capitalist system ('Fordism'). This aspect is well taken care of in Perez' account, but her overall perspective is more on recurrence. This gives somewhat different emphasis in the present period. The regulation school would argue that when frenzy and crash recurs today, the core of the world economy is historically unique in the degree to which wage earners have claims on welfare-state-based or private-association-based welfare (e.g., retirement benefits). Mobilizing both perspectives (but not integrating them) would probably yield a thicker analysis of the present.

Finally, there is the question of what the model can do in terms of more formal generalizations. Recall the topic briefly commented above, the delay of the recent turning point 2002–2008. One possible explanation is that the depression was delayed until 2008–2009 because dissociated financial capital switched to speculation objects – the US subprime loans – in areas not related to the new technology. This may be a mechanism that can be explored in formal theorizing about speculative ventures in many walks of life. Another such mechanism is visible ahead of financial crashes at the end of frenzy periods: there is plenty of evidence that the financial house of cards will soon crumble; still, too few actors listen to the warnings. This can be seen as a formal grounded theory of manias (Kindleberger 1978, Minsky 1986).

Another kind of formalization is typologies concerning specific areas of the economy. In her Chapter 13, Perez presents a typology of financial innovations. It is drawn from the core cases, but is relevant in analyses at many levels, for instance in analyses of particular developments within nation-states. She also relates it to the sequence model, showing how the type of financial innovation differs from phase to phase, and from paradigm to paradigm.

Also, in other important macro-qualitative projects, we find that broad frameworks are used to generate typologies. In Senghaas (Mjøset 2007), an implicit model of 'peripherization pressure' is related to a typology of different third world states in terms of their potential for catching up. Use of Perez' sequence model would enrich this research frontier, since it could provide disaggregation of peripherization pressure relative to phases. In the study of state formation and nation building, Rokkan's 'conceptual map of Europe' (Mjøset 2000) serves as a broad 'typology-generating' instrument. Rokkan reaches further back than Perez, but his model would also benefit from specification in the light of Perez' sequence model for the periods following his industrial revolution dividing line.

We have mentioned the relevance of international hegemonic relations to Perez' model: When the financial crisis of 2008 looses its grip, there will be depression, but from this depression – which economic unit or region will rise as the one that will exert hegemonic influence? Regions of Asia have caught up for many decades. They now have a well-developed infrastructure relevant to the ICT fifth surge. That facilitates further industrial development and social modernization. On the other hand, even though the US has aided the Chinese catching-up strategy for thirty years, as Britain earlier aided the US, that country's development is different in many important ways. This serves as warning against using the third surge as a direct analogy for the coming fifth surge. We must consider parallel use of models of hegemony, and researchers must work in the process-tracing mode.

Åkerman writes that a synthesis of reconstruction and forecast is necessary, but it cannot be achieved! There is here an unbridgeable dualism: forecasting can never rely entirely on updated causal accounts. The synthesis between causal analysis and 'analysis of alternatives' (calculation/plans) between the two is a 'task that can never be solved, but that can be imagined as an asymptotic approximation – coming from opposite sides – towards a common line' (Åkerman 1938, 307).

Social research participates in social development by switching between the two sides – causal analysis and plans. Tools such as Perez' sequence model are indispensable to anyone who wants to know and act in the context of industrial capitalism, a context none of us can escape.

References

Achinstein, P. 1968. *Concepts of Science: A Philosophical Analysis.* Baltimore: Johns Hopkins Press.
Åkerman, J. 1928. *Om det ekonomiska livets rytmik.* Stockholm: Nordiska Bokhandeln.
_____. 1938. *Das Problem der sozialökonomischen Synthese.* Lund: Gleerups.
_____. 1939. *Ekonomisk teori 1.* Lund: Gleerups.
_____. 1944. *Ekonomisk teori 2.* Lund: Gleerups. [Spanish edition: *Estructuras y cieclos economicos.* Madrid: Aguilar, 1960].
_____. 1954 [1942]. 'Economic Plans and Causal Analysis.' *International Economic Papers* 4. London: Macmillan.
_____. 1960. *Theory of Industrialism.* Lund: Gleerups.
Andersen, E. S. 2004. *Joseph A. Schumpeter.* Copenhagen: Jurist- og Økonomforbundets forlag.
Black, M. 1962. *Models and Metaphors.* Ithaca: Cornell University Press.

Boyer, R. 1999. *The Dappled World*. Cambridge: Cambridge University Press.

———. 2004. *The Future of Economic Growth*. Cheltenham: Edward Elgar.

———. 2007. *Hunting Causes and Using Them*. Cambridge: Cambridge University Press.

Dahmén, E. 1950. *Svensk industriell företagarverksamhet: Kausalanalys av den industriella utvecklingen 1919–1939*. Stockholm: IUI.

Erixon, L. 2007. 'En skördetid för Dahmén? Den svenska tillväxtskolan i dagens nationalekonomi.' In N. Karlson et al. (eds). *Erik Dahmén och det industriella företagandet*. Stockholm: Ratio, 151–191.

Freeman, C. and F. Louçã. 2001. *As Time Goes By: From the Industrial Revolution to the Information Revolution*. Oxford: Oxford University Press.

Glaser, B. and A. Strauss. 1967. *The Discovery of Grounded Theory*. New York: Aldine de Gruyter.

Goldstein, J. S. 1988. *Long Cycles*. New Haven: Yale University Press.

Hamminga, B. 2004. 'The Poznan Approach.' In J. B. Davis, D. W. Hands and U. Mäki (eds). *The Handbook of Economic Methodology*. Cheltenham: Edward Elgar, 388–391.

Harré, R. 1983. *Great Scientific Experiments: Twenty Experiments that Changed Our View of the World*. Oxford: Oxford University Press.

Helpman, E. 2004. *The Mystery of Economic Growth*. Cambridge, MA: Belknap Press.

Hodgson, G. M. 1993. *Economics and Evolution*. London: Routledge.

———. 2004. *The Evolution of Institutional Economics*. London: Routledge.

Hoover, K. D. 2001. *The Methodology of Empirical Macroeconomics*. Cambridge: Cambridge University Press.

———. 2002. 'Econometrics and Reality.' In U. Mäki (ed.). *Fact and Faction in Economics*. Cambridge: Cambridge University Press.

———. 2008. 'Idealizing Reduction: The Micro-Foundations of Macroeconomics.' In press; available at http://www.econ.duke.edu/~kdh9/.

Kindleberger, C. P. 1978. *Manias, Panics, Crises*. New York: Basic Books.

Lucas, R. E., Jr. 2004. 'My Keynesian Education.' In M. De Vroey and K. Hoover (eds). *The IS-LM Model: Its Rise, Fall and Strange Persistence*. Durham: Duke University Press, 12–24.

Maddison, A. 2007. *Contours of the World Economy, 1–2030 AD*. Oxford: Oxford University Press.

Mäki, U. 2001. 'Models, Metaphors, Narrative, and Rhetoric: Philosophical Aspects.' In N. J. Smelser and P. B. Baltes (eds). *International Encyclopedia of the Social & Behavioral Sciences* 15. Amsterdam: Elsevier, 9931–9937.

Minsky, H. P. 1986. *Stabilizing an Unstable Economy*. New Haven: Yale University Press.

Mjøset, L. 1997. 'Johan Åkerman's dualistische Synthese.' In G. Eisermann, G. M. Hodgson and L. Mjøset (eds). *Johan Åkermans Das Problem der sozialökonomischen Synthese: Vademecum zu einem Klassiker des skandinavischen Institutionalismus*. Düsseldorf: Verlag Wirtschaft und Finanzen, 31–55.

———. 2000. 'Stein Rokkan's Thick Comparisons.' *Acta Sociologica* 43, 381–398.

———. 2006. 'No Fear of Comparisons or Context: On the Foundations of Historical Sociology.' *Comparative Education* 42, 337–362.

———. 2007. 'An Early Approach to the Varieties of World Capitalism: Methodological and Substantive Lessons from the Senghaas/Menzel-Project.' *Comparative Social Research* 24, 123–176.

———. 2009. 'The Contextualist Approach to Social Science Methodology.' In D. Byrne and C. Ragin (eds). *The Sage Handbook of Case-based Methods*. London: Sage, 39–69.

Mjøset, L. and Å. Cappelen. 2009. 'Economics and the Others.' *Nordic Journal of Political Economy*, forthcoming.

Perez, C. 1983. 'Structural Change and Assimilation of New Technologies in the Economic and Social Systems.' *Futures* 15, 357–375. [3.1]

———. 1985. 'Microelectronics, Long Waves and World Structural Change: New Perspectives for Developing Countries.' *World Development* 13, 441–463. [9.1]

———. 2002. *Technological Revolutions and Financial Capital: The Dynamics of Bubbles and Golden Ages.* Cheltenham: Edward Elgar. [74.1]

Schumpeter, J. A. 1982 [1939]. *Business Cycles.* Philadelphia: Porcupine.

Veblen, T. 1919. *The Place of Science in Modern Civilization.* New York: Huebsch.

Chapter Fifteen:

TECHNOLOGY, INSTITUTIONS AND ECONOMIC DEVELOPMENT

Richard R. Nelson
Columbia University
and
University of Manchester

Introduction

Carlota Perez (1983, 2002, and with Freeman 1988) has been in the vanguard of a small group of economists and other social scientists who have been arguing that the driving force behind the economic development that has taken place over the last two centuries has been the co-evolution of technologies and institutions. I use the term 'development' here rather than 'growth' to connote that, under this view, an essential feature of the process has been the rise over time of new technologies, institutions, and industries, and the decline or radical reshaping of others, and to think of the economic progress as simply being able to produce more, and using aggregate statistics like GNP or GNP per worker as an indicator of what has happened, is to miss the heart of the story.

As we know, the latter perspective is a hallmark of the neoclassical economic growth theory that grew up in the 1950s and remains the basic story about economic growth taught in mainline economics departments. From its genesis, neoclassical growth theory has recognized technological advance as a key driving force. However, even its modern versions do not come to grips with the processes by which technology advances, as these have been documented by empirical scholarship, and while a few recent models do incorporate a characterization of 'creative destruction', that characterization is not just highly stylized, but, from the point of view of Perez and her colleagues, misses most of the action.

It was Schumpeter (1942), of course, who sharply articulated the argument that, under capitalism, economic development involves a process of creative destruction, as new technologies and new firms take the place of established ones. In his *Business Cycles* (1939), he presented a view of economic development as involving a series of 'long waves', with each wave associated with a particular set of technologies whose development drives and shapes how the economy progresses during that era. This perception is central in the writings of Perez and her colleagues. But Schumpeter gives little play to the fact that the effective development of new technologies often requires an institutional structure that is quite different from that which supported the development of the technologies of the prior wave. It is that understanding that has provided the particular shape to the development theory espoused by Perez, Christopher Freeman (with Perez, 1988, and with Louçã, 2001), Alfred Chandler (1962, 1977), Peter Murmann (2003), and in some of my own recent writings (particularly 2008).

In recent years there has been a strong revival of interest in institutions in economics and the other social sciences. Indeed scholars like Douglass North (1990) have argued that the key to economic growth has been in having the right institutions. However, for the most part, the literature on institutions and economic growth has not related institutions and institutional change to the evolution of the technologies driving economic growth. The importance of the theorizing that Perez has pioneered is that it has tied together technological advance and institutional change as a co-evolutionary process.

In this essay I will summarize two of my contributions to this evolving body of economic development theory.[1] The first is a conception of the 'social technologies' that complement 'physical technologies', a perspective that, I believe, fits very nicely with Perez' concept of a 'techno-economic paradigm'. The social technologies concept helps to bring more order to the concept of institutions, and to the notion that technologies and institutions co-evolve. The second is my argument as to why fruitful institutional evolution seems to be much more difficult than fruitful evolution of physical technologies.

Techno-Economic Paradigms, Social Technologies, and Institutions

A key concept in Carlota Perez' writings in this area is that of a techno-economic paradigm. For Perez, a techno-economic paradigm, as with Thomas Kuhn's scientific paradigm (1962) and Giovanni Dosi's technological paradigm (1982), centrally involves a set of beliefs regarding how things ought to be done. In Perez' argument, the dominant technologies of an era are fundamental in shaping the paradigm of that era. But there clearly is more to 'the way things are done' than technology in any narrow sense of that term. And it is these other aspects that lead Perez to write about the institutions that are needed before a new technology can be exploited and developed effectively.

I want to propose that the concept of 'social technologies' that complement 'physical technologies' that Bhaven Sampat and I have developed (2001), provides a useful way of thinking about techno-economic paradigms. And that concept leads naturally to a way of analysing the 'institutions' that are needed to support physical technologies.

Our social technologies concept involved a broadening of the way economists conceptualize an economic 'activity'. In its standard use in economics, an activity is thought of as a way of producing something, or more generally doing something useful; Sampat and I take a broad view of what the term encompasses. Undertaking an activity or a set of them – producing a radio, growing rice, performing a surgery, baking a cake, procuring a needed item, starting a new business – involves a set of actions or procedures that need to be done, for example, as specified in a recipe for the preparation of a cake. These steps or procedures may require particular inputs (like flour and sugar for the cake, cash or a credit card to procure the ingredients for the cake), and perhaps some equipment (something to stir with, a stove, a vehicle to go to the store). Economists are prone to use the term 'technology' to denote the procedures that need to be done to get the desired result.

However, a recipe characterization of what needs to be done represses the fact that many economic activities involve multiple actors, and require some kind of a coordinating mechanism to assure that the various aspects of the recipe are performed in the relationships to each other needed to make the recipe work. The standard notion of a recipe is mute about how this is done. Sampat and I proposed that it might be useful to call the recipe aspect of an activity its 'physical' technology, and the way work is divided and coordinated its 'social' technology.

From this perspective, virtually all economic activities involve the use of both physical technologies and social technologies. The productivity or effectiveness of an activity is determined by both aspects.

One central aspect of Perez' argument is that in any economic era, certain 'physical' technologies orient the thinking of technologists regarding effective ways of doing things. Another central aspect, or at least my interpretation of it here, is that to be effective, a physical technology needs to be complemented by an appropriate 'social' technology. Sampat and I have argued that social technologies are enabled and held in place by things like laws, norms, expectations, notions of legitimate governing structures and mechanisms, customary modes of organizing and transacting. All of these tend to support certain social technologies and make others difficult or infeasible within a society. Sampat and I have suggested that the term 'institutions' is used by most of the writers on the subject to denote structures and forces like these, that mould and hold in place prevalent social technologies.

If that conception is accepted, then there generally will be a number of different 'institutions' that support and constrain particular social technologies, and they operate in different ways. Some institutions have a broad and somewhat diffuse effect on the social technologies that are used or not used. Thus, if one considers the structure of modern biotech in the United States, a topic that I will deal with at some length later, belief in the value of university entrepreneurship is largely atmospheric, affecting a wide range of activities and the social technologies used in them. Other institutions are more specific to the particular social technologies under study, as strong patent rights in the field of biotechnology.

Some institutions, for example laws bearing on particular activities are, in a sense, external to social technologies, and mould them. Others are broad organizational forms used to structure and manage a technology, as we will explore in Alfred Chandler's analysis of the rise of mass production. Situations like these clearly are what are in the minds of scholars who want to distinguish sharply between institutions, in the sense of rules or governing structures, constraining and supporting a particular pattern of behaviour, and the behaviour itself.

However, social technologies also can be self-institutionalized, if I may use that term. This is an important reason why the lines often are blurred between a prevalent practice and the 'institutional' supports for that practice.

Social technologies can be self-institutionalized in several ways. First, customary behaviours, modes of interacting, organizing, tend to be self-reinforcing because they are expected and familiar, and doing something different may require going against the grain. Second, social technologies tend to exist in systems, with one tuned to another, and self-supporting. This may make going against the grain in one social technology especially difficult, because it involves losing touch with complementary social technologies. Third, social technologies, like physical technologies, tend to progress over time, as experience is accumulated, and shared deliberately or inadvertently. Trying a new social technology, like pioneering a new physical technology, is risky, and involves abandoning the fruits of what may be considerable prior experience. I note that these forces of self-institutionalization are important reasons why a society's ability to control the social technologies in use through conscious designing of institutions may be limited.

Institutions clearly have certain stability. Yet economic growth, as we have experienced it, has seen old social technologies fade away, sometimes abruptly, sometimes slowly, and be replaced by new ones. It is time to explore more deeply the role of institutions and institutional change in the process of economic growth.

The Co-Evolution of Technologies and Institutions

Today economists studying economic growth are in accord that technological innovation is the key driving force. The 'technology' on which attention has been focused almost always has been 'physical' technology, in the sense that I laid out in the previous section. The basic argument of Carlota Perez, and her colleagues arguing a similar theme, has been that to operate effectively and to develop new physical technologies often require the emergence and development of new social technologies.

Below, I briefly describe three historical episodes that nicely illustrate the dynamic connections: the rise of mass production in the United States in the last part of the nineteenth century, the development of the first science-based industry – synthetic dyestuffs – in Germany during roughly the same period, and the development of specialized research firms and of strong university-industry interactions that have marked the rise of pharmaceutical biotech in the US over the last quarter century. My treatment of the first two cases will be very compressed, since I have described them in other places (Nelson and Sampat 2001, Nelson 2008). My discussion of biotech will be more extended.

Alfred Chandler's work (1962, 1977) is central to my telling of the first story. Under his analysis, the processes that led to mass production in a range of industries were initiated by the development of the technologies that enabled the establishment of the telegraph and the railroad, which in turn made it possible for business firms to market their products over a much larger geographical area. At the same time, advances were being made in the ability to design and manufacture highly productive machinery. Together, these developments opened the possibility for significant economies of scale and scope.

However, to exploit these opportunities, firms had to be much larger than had been the norm, and large size posed significant problems of both organization and management. The organizational problem was partly solved by the emergence of the modern hierarchically organized company, and later by the multidivisional form of organization (the M form). I note, with Chandler, that the railroad and telegraph companies themselves had to deal with this organizational problem.

New modes of business organization were only a start. To manage these huge companies required many more high-level managers than an owner could garner by canvassing family and friends, which had been the usual practice. The notion of professional management came into being, and shortly after, business schools emerged as the institutional mechanism for training professional managers. The financial needs of the giant companies were beyond what could be met through existing financial institutions, and both modern investment banks, and modern stock markets, emerged to meet the needs.

All of these developments raised complicated issues of corporate, labour, and financial law. Gradually these were worked out. At the same time, the market power of the new large firms and their tendency to collude with each other gave rise to new regulatory law and antitrust.

Peter Murmann (2003) provides the most detailed and analytic account of the rise of the industry producing synthetic dyestuffs. Here, the initiating event was a breakthrough in the science of organic chemistry. As a result, persons with advanced training in the theory and techniques of chemistry had a special capability for developing synthetic dyestuffs. In order to take advantage of this new capability, business firms had to develop the concept and structure of the industrial research laboratory, as a place where university-trained scientists could work with their peers in discovering and developing new products. German patent law was tightened up, better enabling German firms to protect the new dyestuffs they created. Also, in the new regime involving hired scientists, new law also had to be developed to establish who had patent rights on products coming out of the labs.

And the German university system had to gear itself up to train significant numbers of chemists inclined to work for industry. The various German governments provided significant funding to enable this latter development to happen.

Turning to my third case, the rise during the 1960s and 1970s of molecular biology as a strong science, and the creation of the basic processes used in modern biotechnology, clearly was a watershed for the American pharmaceutical industry. These developments opened up a new route to pharmaceuticals discovery and development, one in which, at least at the start, established pharmaceutical companies had no particular competences, and at the same time, one where certain academic researchers had expertise. Several lines of university-based research began to appear very promising commercially. A number of new biotech firms were formed, staffed by university researchers and their students, with plans to develop new pharmaceuticals, and either license the successful results to established pharmaceuticals companies, or go further downstream themselves into the pharmaceuticals business.

Several prevailing broad institutional factors enabled and encouraged these developments. One was the traditional openness of American universities to entrepreneurial activity on the part of their researchers. Another was an established venture capital industry, which quickly came to see the finance of biotech start-ups as a potentially profitable business. These two features of the prevailing institutional framework in the United States should be regarded as part and parcel of a general institutional friendliness toward entrepreneurship. However, the emergence of firms specializing in research, and of university researchers closely linked to these firms, was a quite new institutional development (for a history see Mowery et al. 2005).

To make this arrangement viable commercially required that the research firms have control over the new products and techniques they developed. Here, a key legal decision in 1980 assured sceptics that the products of biotechnology could be patented. At about the same time, Congress passed the Bayh-Dole Act, which encouraged universities to take out patents on the results of government-funded research projects, and to try aggressively to commercialize those results. While the language of the act is not specifically focused on biotech, an important part of the argument that led Congress to believe that technology transfer from universities to industry would be encouraged if universities had strong patent rights and could grant exclusive licenses to a firm to develop their embryonic products was specifically concerned with pharmaceuticals.

In all of these cases one can see clearly the intertwining of the development of new physical technologies, and the emergence and development of new social technologies. Various general aspects of the broad institutional environment clearly were necessary for the innovations that drove developments in these cases to proceed effectively.

First of all, the economic and social cultures had to encourage entrepreneurship, and the risk taking that is inevitable when new activities are launched. The relevant 'institutions' here probably mostly involved norms, and expectations, although the legal system had to be such that potential entrepreneurs could expect to get rich if they succeeded. Second, in all of these cases, developments involved sharp breaks from the 'circular flow' of economic activity, and finance needed to be available to support new firms doing new things. Again, the supporting institutions involved a mix of norms and expectations, laws providing some security for investors, and appropriate organizational structures. Third, labour market institutions had to be compatible with new firms being able to attract workers with suitable skills.

In each of these cases, new social technologies came into place, and new institutions to enable and support them. Many of the institutional developments that occurred came about largely as a result of private actions, but a number required collective action, generally involving government and the political process. The latter two cases involved new government programs. All three saw the writing of new law.

Note that institutions enter these stories in two ways. First, as background preconditions that enable the developments to arise in the first place and take the shape they do. Here the relevant institutions tend to be associated with broad economy-wide context conditions, like a legal system that defines and enforces contracts, a financial system capable of funding new enterprises, flexible labour markets, and in the dyestuffs and biotech cases, a strong university research system. But second, as the case studies show, the dynamics of development often require old institutions to change or new ones to emerge. Here, the institutions in our stories are more technology or industry specific, like bodies of law tailored to a technology or industry, or the development of university research and training in particular fields.

Many contemporary writers attempting to describe effective institutions have proposed that economies are productive and progressive when institutions support market mechanisms. In each of the cases sketched above, one can see the central role market organization of economic activity plays in fostering productivity and progressiveness. However, the advantages of market organization, and the disadvantages of trying to plan and control economic development from a central authority, are not those highlighted by the neoclassical theory of market organization and its virtues. It is the fundamental uncertainties involved in innovation, the inability of economic actors to see clearly the best things to be doing, that make the pluralism, the competition, which is associated with market organization of economic activity so important. Competition also often tends to keep prices from getting completely out of line with costs. But as Schumpeter (1942) argued long ago, by far the principal benefit that society gets from market organization of economic activity and competition is innovation and economic progress. Also, as I have stressed, non-market institutions play key roles in each of these case studies.

My discussion above has focused on particular technologies and industries, rather than the economy as a whole. I noted above that, following along the lines laid out by Schumpeter, Perez has argued that in any economic era, a relatively small set of technologies and industries are driving economic growth. I do not want to take a stand on this argument, because it raises a whole new set of empirical issues. However, I do note that, from this point of view, the Chandler and Murmann stories are particularly interesting because mass production undertaken by large hierarchical firms, and industrial R&D tied to firms engaged in production and marketing, are the hallmarks (sometimes combined and sometimes not) of the industries that drove economic growth in the advanced industrial nations during the first two-thirds of the twentieth century. Biotech has been forecast by many people to be a key technology of the twenty-first century.

However, the social technologies and the institutions needed to support them that are needed for effective use and development of new physical technologies are not easy to discern or put in place. I next turn to this issue.

The Processes of Institutional Change

How do a country's institutions come to be what they are? To what extent can salutary institutional reform be subject to deliberate analysis, planning, and implementation?

There is a longstanding divide about these issues in the writings of institutional economists. In the early part of the twentieth century, John R. Commons (1924, 1934), focusing on the evolution of the law, staked out a position that, to a considerable extent, the institutions that a society had were the ones it had deliberately put in place, wisely or not. Friedrich A. v. Hayek's theory (1967, 1973) of why societies had the institutions that they had was different, stressing 'private orders' that changed over time through a relatively blind evolutionary process. There is a similar divide among the 'new institutional economists' regarding this matter. Indeed, Douglass North himself has taken both views, starting from a position that institutions were the result of a deliberate, rational choice processes (Davis and North 1971), and later moving to a position very similar to Hayek's (North 1990, 1999), that institutions could not be effectively planned, and that the societies that had good ones should regard themselves as fortunate. Thrainn Eggertsson has followed a similar intellectual traverse.

Partly, the difference here relates to the assumed influence and effectiveness of human purpose, intelligence and forward-looking planning, versus more or less random change and ex-post selection. Partly, the difference is in regard to whether institutional change is seen as occurring largely through collective – generally governmental – action, or whether the process is seen as being largely decentralized, involving many actors. The position I espouse here is that on both counts the contrast often is drawn too sharply. I want to agree strongly with the economists and other social scientists who argue that institutions evolve rather than being largely planned. However, I also want to argue that beliefs about what is feasible, and what is appropriate, often play a major role in the evolution of institutions. Human purpose and human beliefs play important roles, both in the generation of the institutional alternatives on which selection works, and in determining what survives and what does not. And in many cases, the process involves both decentralized and collective action.

The mix, of course, depends on the kind of institution one is analyzing. The development of formal law obviously involves deliberate governmental action. Generally, there is debate about what the law should be, and some kind of a formal decision process. On the other hand, the evolution of custom generally is highly decentralized and whatever conscious deliberation there is tends to be myopic. But, it may be a mistake to see the processes here as completely separated. Thus, Commons noted explicitly that, particularly in common-law countries, the development of formal bodies of law tended to be strongly influenced by the customs of the land that were broadly deemed appropriate. And Hayek, too, recognized that formal law often was developed to support custom, while warning of the dangers of putting in place formal law, or public policies more generally, that were not based on the wisdom of custom.

In the cases described earlier, the development of new organizational forms was an important part of the story. While Chandler's account of the emergence and development of the organizational structure of the modern corporation highlights innovation by individual companies, a body of corporate and financial law developed along with, responsive to, and supporting and constraining these private developments. Murmann's account of the development of the modern industrial laboratory involves a mix of private experimentation and decision-making, and the formation of laws and public programs responsive to the emergence of industrial research. The rise of the industrial structure in biotech that we see now in the US clearly has been developed by a mix of private and public actions.

While each of these cases shows an evolutionary process that is sensitive to changing needs and conditions, I now want to argue that the process of evolution of social technologies and their supporting institutions is erratic, compared with the way physical technologies evolve. The ability to design institutions that work as planned is much more limited than the ability to design new physical technologies. Selection forces, including the ability of the human agents involved to learn from experience what works well and what doesn't, usually are significantly weaker for institutions and social technologies than for physical technologies. And usually there is much less ability to compare alternative institutions analytically.

One important reason is that physical technologies are more amenable to sharp specification and control, and are easier to replicate and imitate more or less exactly, than are social technologies. The performance of physical technologies, including the nature of the output they produce, tends to be relatively tightly constrained by the physical inputs and processing equipment used in their operation. On the other hand, social technologies are much more open to the vagaries of human motivations and an understanding regarding what is to be done, which seldom can be controlled tightly. Granovetter (1985) has argued against the 'over-institutionalization' of theories of human behaviour.

Certainly, the institutions that can be consciously designed tend to mould behaviours only relatively loosely, and themselves often are difficult to specify and control tightly. Thus, it is clear from Chandler's discussion of the multi-divisional form (the M form) of business organization that arose in the early twentieth century and became 'standard' among companies producing a range of products and selling them in different areas, that there was very considerable variation among firms. The variation involved both formal structure and the actual division of decision-making between the central office and the branches, which were only partly a matter of managerial choice. Indeed, there was a certain fuzziness to the general concept, and even individuals in the companies who were nominally in charge seemed not to have known in any detail just how the system they had actually worked.

As I have noted, physical and social technologies sometimes are tightly intertwined. Mass-production methods, of the sort that Chandler argued were an important part of the reason for the development of the modern corporation, is a good example, involving both specialized machinery and a complex division of labour and management and control system. Over the years, empirical studies have consistently shown large differences in productivity between establishments of the same corporation producing the same things and using the same production machinery. (Perhaps the best of these studies remains the old one by Pratten 1976.) The differences here clearly were due to different social technologies that management was not able to control in any detail.

A second important difference is that in most cases, but not always, it is far more difficult to get reliable evidence on the efficacy of a new institution or social technology than for a new physical technology. In part, this is a consequence of the phenomena just discussed. For a company contemplating adoption, the problem of estimating the efficacy of the M form of organization surely was made more difficult by the fact that what the M form actually was and how it actually worked differed significantly from firm to firm, and within a particular firm, tended to change over time. But even without this complication, it tends to be very difficult to sort out the effects of a particular institution or social technology from the influences of a wide variety of other variables that bear on the profitability of a firm, or to estimate reliably the benefits and costs reaped by society from a complex of strongly interacting policies and laws. In contrast, it is much easier to gain a reliable assessment of the efficacy of a new pharmaceutical, or the performance of a new aircraft design.

Both of these differences are related to the fact that a lot can be learned about physical technologies, product designs or modes of production, by building prototypes and doing controlled experimentation 'offline', as it were, in research and development. It is much harder to do this for institutions. Thomke (2003) provides a convincing and detailed analysis of the role of deliberate experimentation in the design and development of physical technologies. If a physical technology can be made to work in a controlled setting, it often is possible to routinize and imbed it in physical hardware, and in this and other ways, shield it from environmental influences that could be different online from experimental conditions. The looser the coupling of institutions that can be designed and the behaviours they generate means that transfer from controlled setting to actual practice does not work nearly as well, even if the institution as a whole could be operated in an experimental setting.

Another important difference is that because of the ability to routinize, shield and control, it often is possible to experiment with a part of a physical technology offline, and to transfer an improved version of that piece to the larger system with confidence that it will work in that context and in actual practice. In contrast, the likelihood that a piece of an institution or social technology that works well in an offline experimental setting will work well when imbedded in an online system is small.

This is not to deny the important role of learning by doing and using regarding the efficacy of physical technologies. However, virtually all learning regarding social technologies and the institutions that mould and support them has to proceed online. And for the reasons suggested above, even that learning is difficult and uncertain.

Relatedly, 'scientific' understanding bearing on institutions, and indicating ways that they might be improved, generally is much weaker than the scientific understanding bearing on physical technologies. The applications-oriented natural sciences and engineering disciplines often can provide very helpful illumination of prevailing practice and potential roads to improvement of physical technologies. They can point relatively sharply to what is essential to the performance of a product design, or production process, and what is likely peripheral. While Vernon Ruttan (2003, 2006) has proposed otherwise, I would argue that the behavioural and social sciences provide much less light on how present institutions work and how to improve them. In trying to understand why, it is important to recognize that the productive knowledge of applied scientists and engineers comes not only from the underlying basic sciences, but also from observation, experiment, and analysis of prevailing practices and artefacts, or models of these that are built expressly for experimentation and analysis. For the reasons discussed above, the kind of knowledge about institutional effectiveness, and the key institutional elements that determine effectiveness, that behavioural and social scientists can achieve is relatively limited.

The emergence and adoption of new social technologies can proceed rapidly and fruitfully if there is a reasonably well-defined problem that needs some solution; one can readily identify a new social technology that solves that problem at least broadly, and the needed institutional supports for that social technology are relatively obvious. Under these conditions, the needed new institutions can come relatively quickly into place, at least if those who are in a position to make the institutional changes have an interest in doing so. Thus, in the United States, the M form spread relatively rapidly among multi-product multi-market firms. The M form did at least mitigate the problem of overload of decisions to be made by top management of such firms. The industrial research laboratory provided a way for firms to hire groups of scientists and put them to the task of inventing, and relatively quickly became an 'institution' in industries where the competitiveness of firms depended on their prowess at creating new products and manufacturing processes.

On the other hand, the history of both the M form and the industrial research laboratory is one of firms continuing to struggle to fine-tune the structures so that they would work well in their particular context. It is illuminating to contrast the experience here with the evolution of mass-production machinery. In the latter, many engineers were involved in designing machines, and getting relatively reliable information on performance from their own testing, and from feedback from users. Efforts to improve design could be guided by that user feedback and by the ability of designers to experiment offline, with reasonable confidence that what they learned from that experimentation would hold up in actual practice. And designers could learn from studying the characteristics and performance of the machines made by other designers.

There is little evidence of anything like this progressive, cumulative learning regarding business or research organization. The evolution of social technologies and the institutions that support them is a difficult, uncertain process, compared with the evolution of physical technologies. Indeed, as noted earlier, corporations running different establishments producing the same things with the same physical equipment often find it very difficult to establish a common set of 'social technologies' for the different establishments.

Indeed, in some circumstances, institutional evolution can result in building into place social technologies that are quite ineffective, or worse. For the most part, evidence of the benefits and costs of using new physical technologies is sharp enough so that few really bad ones ever get into widespread use (although there unfortunately are a number of cases where deleterious side-effects, or problems that arose in particular contexts, were discovered only after a technology was around for a while). In contrast, the introduction and spread of social technologies can be driven by fad, or ideology. Given the difficulties in getting reliable feedback on actual performance, social technologies and the institutions supporting them, once in place, may be difficult to dislodge, even if there is little evidence that they are accomplishing what they were established to do.

This just might be the case regarding the institutions that have been put in place in the United States in support of the development of biotech. I am not arguing here that this is the case, but there are some worrying signs.

There is, first of all, the question of whether firms that specialize in biotech research, and aim to make profit by licensing their research products to other firms, are commercially viable. It is somewhat curious, and I think highly relevant, that the notion that a biotech firm could be profitable simply by doing research, without having close organizational linkages to production and marketing, gained enthusiastic credence so readily. This proposition was inconsistent with the history of industrial research that was recounted above, where firms making and selling products learned the advantages of doing R&D internally. While there were a few earlier exceptions, by and large, firms that tried to make profit by specializing in R&D were not successful. Regarding the present case, it has been recognized widely for some time that most biotech firms who have specialized in research, and have not moved themselves into production and marketing, are not making any money. However, until relatively recently, this problem has been treated as something that time would cure, and not an indication that the business plans and expectations involved in this structure possibly were not viable, except in quite special circumstances. Recently, there has been more recognition of this possibility. Gary Pisano's new book (2006) makes this argument forcefully.

There also are good reasons to be open-minded or even sceptical about the economic value, and more generally, of the wisdom of the new policies encouraging universities to patent what they can out of what comes out of their research, an institutional development that, while not tied to biotech, has been exercised especially vigorously in this field. It is clear that since the 1970s, many important new products and processes have been made possible by academic research. Over this period, university patenting has increased greatly, as has university revenues from technology licensing. These facts have led some sophisticated observers to argue that Bayh-Dole has amply met its goals. Thus, *The Economist* (2002) opined that 'possibly the most inspired piece of legislation in America over the past half century was the Bayh-Dole act of 1980'.

However, the enthusiasts for Bayh-Dole generally have suffered from a historical myopia. University research was contributing importantly to industrial innovation long before Bayh-Dole, and much of what industry was drawing on was in the public domain, not patented. Bayh-Dole was brought into a university research system that already was strongly oriented to spurring innovation, and quite successful at it. Thus it is not clear that the new university patenting has been as important in facilitating technology transfer as the advocates have claimed. Put another way, contrary to the message of the quote from *The Economist*, it is quite possible that much of the university contribution would have occurred without university patents.

On the other hand, the downsides of Bayh-Dole, and the policies of universities to patent as much as they can, and earn as much money as they can from their patents, are now more visible than they were a few years back.

Recently, there has been some backing off from the enthusiasm for university patenting that marked the 1980s and 1990s. A recent issue of *The Economist* (2005) focused on many of the issues raised above, implicitly arguing that the costs of university patenting, and often exclusive licensing, needed to be weighed against the benefits. The National Institutes of Health (NIH) has issued guidelines calling for its grantees to license their patented inventions widely, not narrowly.

Both the attractiveness to investors of the business plans of specialized research firms, and in many cases, the ability of universities to patent the results of their research, have been dependent of the tendency of the US Patent Office to give patents on material far upstream from a viable commercial product, and for the courts to uphold these patents. Recently, concerns have been expressed that these kinds of patents, which control paths of future research, can seriously interfere with the progress of science (for a discussion see Nelson 2004).

In sum, the effectiveness of the institutions that have grown up in the US in support of biotech is quite uncertain. There are major uncertainties regarding the effectiveness, or the economic viability, of firms that specialize in research and do not themselves get into production and distribution. It is uncertain whether on not Bayh-Dole, or rather the set of incentives and practices symbolized as well as reinforced by Bayh-Dole, has been a plus or a minus. The practice of granting patents on research results some distance from a practical product is generating growing resistance. The uncertainties here show clearly how difficult it often is to evaluate new social technologies, and the institutions supporting them. Mistakes can be made, and can last a long time.

Concluding Remarks

The basic arguments put forth in this essay are these: The employment of 'physical' technologies requires the use of complementary 'social' technologies, and the latter, in turn, require a set of supporting institutions. This perspective helps flesh out the argument put forth by Perez and 'fellow-travellers' that new technologies often call for new institutions. But identification and establishment of the institutions needed to enable society to gain as much as it can from promising new physical technologies is not easy. I would add that the institutions that work effectively in one social-political economy are often difficult to transfer and adapt to the conditions of another.

These observations lead me to the conclusion that understanding institutions and their dynamics better is the most challenging task facing economists and other social scientists studying economic development.

References

Chandler, A. D. 1962. *Strategy and Structure: Chapters in the History of the Industrial Enterprise.* Cambridge: MIT Press.

————. 1977. *The Visible Hand: The Managerial Revolution in American Business.* Cambridge: Harvard University Press.

Commons, J. 1924. *Legal Foundations of Capitalism.* New York: Macmillan.

————. 1934. *Institutional Economics.* Madison: University of Wisconsin Press.

Davis, L. and D. North. 1971. *Institutional Change and American Economic Growth.* Cambridge: Cambridge University Press.

Dosi, G. 1982. 'Technological Paradigms and Technological Trajectories.' *Research Policy* 11, 147–162.

Dosi, G. et al. (eds). 1988. *Technical Change and Economic Theory.* London: Pinter.

The Economist. 2002. 'Innovation's Golden Goose.' December 12.

————. 2005. 'Bayhing For Blood or Doling for Cash?' December 24.

Freeman, C. and F. Louçã. 2001. *As Time Goes By: From the Industrial Revolution to the Information Revolution.* Oxford: Oxford University Press.

Freeman, C. and C. Perez. 1988. 'Structural Crises of Adjustment, Business Cycles and Investment Behavior.' In G. Dosi et al. (eds). *Technical Change and Economic Theory.* London: Pinter, 38–66. [20.1]

Granovetter, M. 1985. 'Economic Action and Social Structure: The Problem of Embeddedness.' *American Journal of Sociology* 91, 481–510.

v. Hayek, F. A. 1967. *Studies in Philosophy, Politics, and Economics.* London: Routledge and Kegan Paul.

————. 1973. *Law, Legislation, and Liberty.* Vol. 1: *Rules and Order.* London: Routledge and Kegan Paul.

Kuhn, T. 1962. *The Structure of Scientific Revolutions.* Chicago: University of Chicago Press.

Mowery, D., R. Nelson, B. Sampat and A. Ziedonis. 2005. *Ivory Tower And Industrial Innovation.* Stanford: Stanford Business School Press.

Murmann, P. 2003. *Knowledge and Competitive Advantage: The Coevolution of Firms, Technologies, and National Institutions.* Cambridge: Cambridge University Press.

Nelson. R. 2004. 'The Market Economy and the Scientific Commons.' *Research Policy* 33, 455–471.

————. 2008. 'What Enables Rapid Economic Progress: What are the Needed Institutions?' *Research Policy* 37, 1–11.

Nelson R. and B. Sampat. 2001. 'Making Sense of Institutions as a Factor Shaping Economic Performance.' *Journal of Economic Behavior and Organization* 44, 31–54.

Nelson, R. and S. Winter. 1982. *An Evolutionary Theory of Economic Change.* Cambridge, MA: Harvard University Press.

North, D. C. 1990. *Institutions, Institutional Change, and Economic Performance.* Cambridge, MA: Harvard University Press.

————. 1999. *Understanding the Process of Economic Change.* London: Institute of Economic Affairs.

Perez, C. 1983. 'Structural Change and Assimilation of New Technologies in the Economic and Social Systems.' *Futures* 15, 357–375. [3.1]

————. 2002. *Technological Revolutions and Financial Capital: The Dynamics of Bubbles and Golden Ages.* Cheltenham: Edward Elgar. [74.1]

Pisano, G. 2006. *Science Business: Promise, Reality, and the Future of Biotechnology.* Boston: Harvard Business School Press.

Pratten, C. 1976. *Labor Productivity Differentials within International Companies*. Cambridge: Cambridge University Press.

Ruttan, V. 2003. *Social Science Knowledge and Economic Development*. Ann Arbor: University of Michigan Press.

———. 2006. 'Social Science Knowledge and Induced Institutional Innovation: An Institutional Design Perspective.' Staff Paper P02-07, Department of Applied Economics, University of Minnesota.

Schumpeter, J. A. 1939. *Business Cycles*. New York: McGraw-Hill.

———. 1942. *Capitalism, Socialism, and Democracy*. New York: Harper & Row.

Thomke, S. 2003. *Experimentation Matters*. Boston: Harvard Business School Press.

Chapter Sixteen:

TECHNO-ECONOMIC PARADIGMS AND THE MIGRATION (RELOCATION) OF INDUSTRIES TO THE PERIPHERIES

Keith Nurse
University of the West Indies, Barbados

Introduction

The development of capitalist world economy has exhibited discontinuous or wave-like patterns of rapid expansion (upswings), which in turn are followed by periods of relative stagnation or 'crisis' (downturns) and vice versa, in successive phases. This cyclical rhythm is captured in the theory of long cycles or waves of 40-60 years, first articulated by Nikolai Kondratiev.[1] Kondratiev's theory on cyclical rhythms in capitalist development argues that these patterns are constitutive of the logic of the world economy, and that they are a response to the contradictions inherent in the endless pursuit of capital accumulation. This is most evident during periods of stagnation or downturn when the world economy faces 'crises' in accumulation. It is these periods of tension that gives capitalism its dynamic, or what Schumpeter has described so lucidly as the paradox of 'creative destruction'.[2]

Shifts in the techno-economic paradigms are a key feature of the long waves of the capitalist world economy in that they indicate the arrival of an innovation-rich phase that gives rise not only to new leading sectors (e.g., product and process innovations), but also to new organizational and managerial innovations that ultimately have a pervasive effect on how business is conducted throughout the world economy (Freeman and Perez 1988; Perez 2002, 2004). The arrival of new techno-economic paradigms is not just economic and business phenomena, as it triggers transformations in socio-institutional and political structures both at the national, regional and global level. In the inter-state system, shifts in the techno-economic paradigm provokes a reshuffling of geo-economic and political roles: former hegemons (e.g., the Netherlands, Britain and currently the US) may become victims of their earlier success, and semi-core and semi-peripheral countries may erect trade barriers and industrial policies to foster domestic industry along neo-mercantilist lines (Hopkins and Wallerstein 1982). In such periods, Freeman and Perez (1988, 64) argue that 'newcomers are sometimes more able to make the necessary social and institutional innovations than the more arthritic social structures of established leaders.'

The emergence of new techno-economic paradigms and leading sectors, however, are insufficient by themselves to overcome downturns. The process by which the world economy comes out of a downturn is far more complex. Downturn phases involve the reorganization of production processes in those former leading sectors that have matured and declined in terms of profitability. These ailing sectors have tended to gain an extension in their life cycle (a boost in their profitability) through two strategies: (1) the rationalization of production processes at existing sites (e.g., mergers, acquisitions, buyouts, strategic alliances, etc.) resulting in increased concentration in sectors (e.g., oligopolies); and, (2) through the migration or relocation of industrial production to more favourable locations in the peripheries where the cost of doing business is cheaper or the profitability rates are higher (Frobel, Heinrichs and Kreye 1981).

Carlota Perez (1985, 2001, 2002) is one among few long wave theorists (Hopkins and Wallerstein 1982; Lewis 1978; Nurse 1998; Wallerstein 1984) to analyze the migration of industries from the core economies to the peripheries during long wave downturns as a key feature of the world economy. For example, Perez (2002, 83) argues that

This outspreading of infrastructures and mature processes has been one of the forces diffusing capitalism throughout the world and widening its potential markets, at the same time as it is one of the mechanisms fuelling the catching-up efforts of lagging countries. Additionally, successful redeployment also creates the conditions for financial capital to invest in other activities in the destination territories, by reducing the risks and increasing the knowledge about possible distant investment. So, both productive and financial capital tend to arrive in peripheral countries at the same time when the diffusing revolution is in the last phase of its life cycle, moving the dynamics of the system outwards from its 'home bases'.

This recurring pattern has received little attention in the literature. Hubert Schmitz (1984, 2) refers to this gap in the literature as an 'uncomfortable lacuna in the map of knowledge'. He notes that the connection between systemic crises and the surge of industrialization in the periphery is far from clear. In response, the objective of this paper is to illuminate the key processes involved in the changing structure of the world division of labour by mapping the migration of industrial production across the globe, in long wave phases, from the emergence of the Industrial Revolution in Europe to the present. In each successive long wave phase there have been extensive transformations in the geo-economic structure, techno-economic paradigms and socio-institutional and political framework of the world system (see Table 16.1). A major element of these transformations has been the shifting and broadening of geographic loci of economic roles. More precisely, what has occurred is a succession of transformations in the division of labour on a worldwide scale, incorporating more and more new zones into the capitalist mode of production via the migration or relocation of industries from the core to the semi-peripheries and later to the peripheries (see Figure 16.1).

The First Kondratiev (1782–1845)

Historically, industry has migrated from region to region, from country to country via several modes. It is noted by Cairncross, for instance, 'the trader from abroad, the internationally minded scientist, and the immigrant artisan have been the main channel for the importation of foreign techniques' (1962, 180). As an example, he points out that 'at the beginning of the Industrial Revolution in the eighteenth century, there can have been scarcely an industry in England that did not owe its origin to immigrants from abroad, many of them refugees' (1962, 180). By the middle of the nineteenth century Britain had become the 'workshop of the world' and the economic hegemon. In this period, the export of British capital made a significant contribution to continental industry. According to Hobson, 'there was hardly a factory in the whole of Europe where Englishmen were not employed, and many works were owned by Englishmen' (1914, 107).

The migration of British capital to Continental Europe was sparked by a depression that occurred after the Napoleonic wars. The British economy was faced with bankruptcies, bank closures, industrial shutdowns, swelling unemployment and growing social inequalities that the wartime prosperity had concealed (Jenks 1927, 26). The response of British capital under these conditions was to seek new opportunities abroad through relocation or foreign investment. Jenks (1927, 23) explains:

> Not because she must, but because she was used to doing it, Great Britain after the war sought to continue to produce at the old speed. And because of the same habituation, she sought outlet for her energies in seeking another foreign market to replace that which government contracts had provided abroad. Foreign investment throve as a means to foreign trade.

Table 16.1. Long Waves in Historical Perspective[3]

Kondratiev Phases	Hegemon/Major State Actors	Techno-Economic Paradigms/Leading Sectors	Socio-Institutional & Political Framework
Upswing 1782–1825 Downturn 1825–1845	Great Britain/Germany, US	Mechanization of Production/Textile Industry; Steam Engine, Locomotive Engines	Industrial Revolution in Europe, US, French & Haitian Revolutions, Napoleonic Wars → Pax Britannica Deindustrialization of India & China; Decolonization of L. Amer. *Wealth of Nations* (1776)
Upswing 1845–1873 Downturn 1873–1892	Great Britain/Germany, US	Capital Equipment Production/Railroadization, Iron & Steel, Textile, Machinery, Steam Ship	Era of Free Trade (1840s–1870s) American Civil War, Formation of German Empire, Italian Unification/Meiji Restoration/Dominion of Canada, Scramble for Colonies in Africa, Asia, Pacific → Age of Imperialism, Monopoly Capitalism. *Das Kapital* (1867)
Upswing 1892–1929 Downturn 1929–1948	U.S./W. Europe, Japan, USSR	Fordism/Taylorism → Assembly Line Production/Electrification Internal Combustion Engine → Automobile, Aircraft; Chemicals, Petroleum	Core Rivalry → World Wars I & II, the Russian & Chinese Revolutions, Fascism in Italy/Nazism in Germany; Japan's Greater East Asian Co-Prosperity Sphere
Upswing 1948–1973 Downturn 1973–2000?	U.S./W. Europe, Japan, USSR, NICs	Mass Production → Automation/Electronics, Petrochemicals, Nuclear Energy, Computers → Motor Car Industry, Consumer Durables	Pax Americana → Cold War Decolonization of Third World Multilateralism: UN Systems, IMF, IBRD, GATT, NATO, OECD, G7, EEC, Third World Solidarity: NAM, NIEO, UNCTAD-G77, OPEC Transnational Corporation: Free Enterprise/Trade → Welfare State NIDL/EOI: EPZs & WMFs
Upswing 2000?	EEC, Japan, US, NICs, Russia, China, E. Europe	Knowledge Intensive Production ICTs, Microelectronics, Flexible Manufacturing, Robotics, Telecoms, Informatics, Bio-technology, Nano-technology	Core Rivalry → Neoprotectionism, Regional Trading Blocs, Bilateralism → Recolonization of Third World: Structural Adjustment, End of Cold War → Decline of Actually Existing Socialism, Fragmentation of Soviet Bloc, Reunification of Germany Supranational Monopoly Capitalism

Figure 16.1. Shares of World Manufacturing Output by Region, 1750–2002

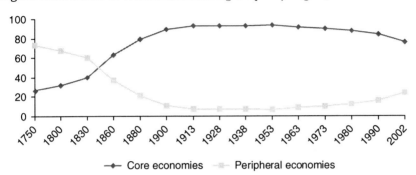

Source: Bairoch (1982); UNIDO (2005).

It blazed the trail for cosmopolitan specialization, for the extension of the Industrial Revolution, the expansion of British economy to embrace the world.

Jenks notes further that an important impetus to the relocation of industries was the protectionist tendencies of Britain's neighbours and the possible threat of competition:

> Survivals of mercantilist legislation were to a great extent responsible for the establishment of English factories in Belgium, France, the Germanies and Russia. On the one hand there were tariffs imposed by these countries against British goods, often with the intention of promoting domestic industry. On the other a British embargo on the export of machinery, in the vain attempt to limit the knowledge of technical improvements to the Isles, compelled British manufactures of engines and machines to procure patents and erect factories abroad to forestall pirating of their products. For there was no effective way of preventing the smuggling of designs and of machines in parts. (1927, 179)

An estimation of the value or volume of relocations for this period is understandably challenging, as Jenks explains:

> It is impossible to make any sort of quantitative statement of the volume of British capital which at various times engaged directly in the development of manufactures upon the Continent. The scattering instances which can be assembled do not exhaust its scope, we may be sure. It is pre-eminently the joint-stock form of enterprise which secures publicity. And the joint-stock principle was invoked in very small degree in the beginnings of the

Industrial Revolution in France as well as in Great Britain. Yet there had been migrations of British capital, British enterprise, skill and inventiveness, of which the stock and share lists knew very little, since early in the nineteenth century. And in some respects these movements had been of importance in domesticating the Industrial Revolution upon the Continent (1927, 178–179).

In the United States, because of its geographic separateness, the relocation of British firms was not a major factor in its industrial development. Instead, much of the industrial impetus was stirred indirectly by the 'expenditure of British capital upon public work' (Jenks 1927, 84). US industrial growth after 1816, however, was largely influenced by changes in the external environment:

> The Panic of 1819 followed the post-war boom. The price of agricultural commodities fell rapidly and unemployment in the cities of the North reached alarming proportions. The last great Corn Law was passed by Parliament in 1815 to protect English agriculture from foreign imports. This and the recovery of agriculture in Europe caused American exports of grain to fall. The declining price of their produce induced the farmers of Pennsylvania and other Northern states to rally to the cause of industrial protection. (Chase-Dunn 1980, 204)

This protectionist movement played an important role in transforming the U.S. economy from an 'agricultural and mercantile economy that existed before 1815 to the more diversified manufacturing economy that developed thereafter' (Chase Dunn 1980, 207). The initial industrial expansion was concentrated in the New England region. The strategy of import-substitution proved successful, for between 1820 and 1830 the US economy was able to expand the share of cotton cloth consumption supplied locally from 30 per cent to 80 per cent. By the late 1820s the protectionist mode was no longer necessary and by 1832 US textiles were competing with British products as far away as the Far East (Chase Dunn 1980, 207).

These examples demonstrate that the relocation of industrial production has its beginnings very early in industrial capitalism. It is true that the earlier forms were less formalized and so, less quantifiable, but this does not minimize their significance.

The Second Kondratiev (1845–1892)

The second Kondratiev phase began with an expansionary phase from 1845–1873. This period saw an unparalleled growth in industrial capitalism in

Britain. By 1865, during the era of 'Victorian prosperity', Jevons, an English economist, described the international division of labour this way:

> The plains of North America and Russia are our corn fields; Chicago and Odessa our granaries; Canada and Baltic are our timber forests; Australasia contains our sheep farms, and in Argentina and on the western prairies of North America are our herds of oxen; Peru sends her silver, and the gold of South Africa and Australia flows to London; the Hindus and the Chinese grow tea for us, and our coffee, sugar, and spice plantations are in all the Indies. Spain and France are our vineyards and the Mediterranean our fruit garden; and our cotton grounds, which for long have occupied the Southern United States, are now being extended everywhere in the warm regions of the earth. (Quoted in Kennedy 1987, 151–152)

Industrial expansion also occurred on the European Continent, as well as in the United States. By 1880 Britain's share of world manufacturing output reached a peak of 22.9 per cent; the US share had more than doubled from its 1860 level; and France and Germany's growth was steadily increasing. Hobsbawm (1975) has aptly referred to the period as the 'Age of Capital'. This upswing phase was based on an institutional framework of British free-trade imperialism, and a new technological paradigm of capital goods production (the manufacture of machines by machines) and a revolution in transport through railroadization.

The arrival of the downturn of 1873–1892, referred to as the 'Great Depression', changed the air of optimism. World markets and world trade stagnated. Increasing inter-firm rivalry led to an increase in merger movements that created large oligopolies, trusts and cartels. The unfavourable world economic climate sparked a new round of protectionism throughout Europe and North America. It was only Britain, Holland and Denmark that adhered to free-trade principles after 1880 (Kenwood and Lougheed 1971, 84).

One of the main effects of the downturn was the stimulation of the relocation of industry. American and European firms jumped tariff barriers and established branches and subsidiaries in each other's markets. American capital was by far more dominant and throughout Europe, one heard cries of the 'American invasion' (Wilkins 1970, 70). These relocations came in the form of overseas 'branch' factories geared to supply foreign markets. The emergence of these branch factories signalled the arrival of the multinational firm or today's transnational corporation.

Singer Sewing Machine Company was the first American firm to successfully relocate part of its operations abroad. Singer's first overseas factory was established in Glasgow in 1867. The rationale given for the establishment of the overseas factory was the appreciating United States currency, rising domestic wages, and the 'enormous freight bills, storage and various incidental expenses' that were being incurred in supplying the British market. Singer made subsequent investment in its overseas branches. These investments proved so fruitful that by 1874, Singer was producing and selling more than half of its sewing machines abroad (Wilkins 1970, 42).

Other American firms followed in the footsteps of Singer and established branches abroad. In the pre-1914 period there were 122 subsidiaries of American firms that had manufacturing operations scattered throughout Europe, Canada, Latin America and Asia, investments totalling approximately 530 million pounds. Similarly, by this date there were 60 subsidiaries of British manufacturing firms that were operating abroad with as much as 250 million pounds invested. Continental European multinational firms were far more transnationalized and had 167 subsidiaries established abroad. Most were from Germany and Switzerland;[4] the remainder were from France, Holland, Belgium and Sweden. Most of these subsidiaries were located within Europe while eight firms had branches in the United States.[5] One of the top destinations for this flow of foreign direct investment was Russia, where between 1880 and 1900 approximately '50 per cent of all new capital invested in industrial corporations doing business in Russia was of foreign origin' (Mc Kay 1975, 345). As the following quote illustrates, the rationale behind these investments contains a logic that is sympathetic to the relocation thesis:

> Saturation of the home market or the existence of surplus output capacity during periods of depressed domestic economic activity led to the growth of exports, and eventually to foreign production when export markets were threatened by local competition, tariffs, or some such other development. (Kenwood and Lougheed 1982, 162)

In the new growth sectors, steel and metalworking, Britain was an important innovation centre (for example, the Bessemer converter, Siemens' open hearth in 1866, and the Thomas process in 1878), but lost out in the exploitation of these new innovations to Germany (Soete 1985, 223). As a result, by the end of the nineteenth century the speed of American industrial expansion was second only to Germany.

The Third Kondratiev (1892–1948)

The close of the century saw a new expansionary phase (1892–1914). This third Kondratiev phase saw the eclipse of British industrial prowess with the technological lead going to both the United States and Germany. Both of these countries emerged as major growth and innovation poles in the new leading sectors of assembly line mass production, the automobile, and electricity. Britain was clearly lagging behind in these new sectors.

This third Kondratiev phase, which contained two major world wars, also saw the ascent of Japan, Russia, Italy and the European settler colonies of Canada and Australia into core status. The arrival of the third Kondratiev downturn, the longest and most severe of the crises experienced to date, extends in real terms from World War I to the end of World War II (1914–1948). It is often referred to as the 'long economic crisis'.[6]

In the 1920s the relocation process moved to a new intensity. This was especially the case with American companies. As Mira Wilkins puts it, American firms were 'building more plants, manufacturing more end products, investing in a greater degree of integration, and diversifying on a worldwide basis' (Wilkins 1974, 138). In this period the number of overseas manufacturing subsidiaries of UK and Continental European firms declined while the number of US subsidiaries abroad increased. For example, it is estimated that US FDI in Latin America increased by 28.4 per cent between 1929 and 1950. Investments from the UK, on the other hand, declined by 60 per cent and investments from other European countries declined even more significantly (UNECLAC 1965, 33). The decline in investments from these countries is partly attributable to the war in Europe.

An interesting dimension of the relocation process had begun to emerge during this period. Firms were relocating and exporting to third markets. For example, Singer's operations in Scotland were servicing its European market. American firms were also relocating to Canada to take advantage of the tariff preferences that Canadian products enjoyed in the protected markets of the British Empire and elsewhere (e.g., Canadian Singer in the 1920s supplied Singer's outlets in Latin America without any tariff advantage) (Wilkins 1974, 140–142).

Another major transformation in the international division of labour during this period was the arrival of industrial production in the large peripheral countries of Brazil, Argentina, Mexico and India under the banner of import-substitution industrialization (ISI). The industrialization of these countries was based on large inflows of foreign capital as exemplified by the fact that as many as 200 subsidiaries of US and European TNCs had established manufacturing operations in Latin America by 1939. In the rest of the newly industrializing countries, only some 100 manufacturing subsidiaries had been established by this time, most firms being located in India (Jenkins 1987, 5–6).

The production relocated by US capital to Latin America was primarily in food processing (mostly meat packaging), light industry (phonographs and radios), petroleum, automobiles and tires, construction materials (including cement) and pharmaceuticals. D. M. Phelps' study of American investments in Argentina, Brazil, Uruguay and Chile provides information on the value of these industrial investments. Of the 66 subsidiaries listed, 75 per cent of these operations were relocated after 1921. However, before 1920, there were 16 branch plants in operation, 9 of them meat-packing plants (Phelps 1969, 14).

The significance of the import-substitution thrust is reflected in the changed composition of commodity imports among these semi-industrial countries in the period 1899 to 1959. As a consequence, there was a fall in demand for consumer goods imports (i.e., textiles and clothing and other light manufactures) and a rise in imports of capital goods and intermediate inputs (metals, chemicals, and machinery and transport equipment). The latter increased by over 450 per cent during the period. The change in imports reflects the development of the ISI mode of specialization in these economies (Baerresen 1965, 21).

The migration of industrial production to these areas was triggered by the long economic crisis of the 1930s. As Albert Hirschman argues, the timing of the arrival of such production in Latin America is not coincidental to systemic change:

> Wars and depressions have historically no doubt been most important in bringing industries to countries of the 'periphery' which up to then had firmly remained in the nonindustrial category. The crucial role of the two world wars and of the Great Depression in undermining acceptance of traditional ideas about the international division of labour between advanced and backward countries is well known. (Hirschman 1978, 343–344)

These observations refer to 'demand pull' factors such as the shortage of imports due to the war or balance of payments problems. This climate does much to make imports less attractive and to foster domestic industry. But in the analysis of the relocation phenomenon, it is equally important to understand the rationale behind the 'supply push' factors that encourages firms from the core to migrate to peripheral areas. This is because in most cases, the introduction of ISI in Latin America and other areas was externally propelled. From this perspective, Dudley Phelps (1969, 30) outlines the motives behind the migration of American firms to Latin America:

> Surely the migration movement as a whole cannot be dated by the war. Rather, the impetus behind the movement is to be found in our [American] maturing industrial economy. Concerns which have migrated are, in general, those which occupy a strong if not dominant position in the domestic market. Furthermore, they are the mass-production industries in which there is a constant incentive to increase the volume of output in order

to decrease unit costs of production. Often there appeared to be little chance to secure additional business in the domestic market. Hence, foreign markets were cultivated, for they were newer and less saturated, and competition was likely to be less severe.

After World War II, ISI became more of a nationalist-state strategy, but even then it was largely externally propelled. Maxfield and Nolt (1990) show that ISI was sponsored to a large extent by the US administration: US technical aid missions were sent to most developing countries to help draft and implement ISI development plans. They cite the rationale behind the sponsorship as being related to Cold War concerns but also to the concerns of the powerful internationalist bloc of US business. They argue that:

> Subsidized branch plant investment behind ISI trade barriers was an acceptable alternative to freer trade. Thus U.S. sponsorship of ISI was necessarily linked to vigorous efforts to secure favourable conditions for US FDI. This ensured that ISI protectionism stimulated the internationalization of large US firms rather than the loss of these foreign markets. (1990, 50)

The Fourth Kondratiev (1948–2000?)

The fourth Kondratiev phase saw the greatest expansionary boom in the history of global capitalism. This expansion was based on the absolute ascent of the United States as the new hegemonic leader; the automation revolution and the new leading sectors of electronics, nuclear energy, petrochemicals, and plastics; a model of accumulation based on mass consumerism, social welfare, Keynesian economics and a multilateral system that promoted transnational corporatism. However, by the mid-1960s this model of accumulation had run into serious bottlenecks. This crisis in the world economy, was evident in the decline in economic growth rates in the industrialized countries and the world economy as a whole. The crisis is also indicated by the breakdown of the Bretton Woods Agreement; the rise of structural unemployment and neoprotectionism in the developed countries; the growth of bankruptcies, merger movements and takeovers; the Third World debt crisis and innovations in automation, computerization, digitalization and information and communication technologies.

The emergence of a downturn in the late 1960s, early 1970s, ushered in a new international division of labour. Japan and West Germany recovered from World War II devastation to rival the US in world merchandise trade. These economies proved to be competitive with the US in the former leading sectors such as steel, cars, electronics and consumer durables, as well as in the new wave of knowledge-intensive technologies such as microelectronics, telecommunications and biotechnology. The newly industrializing countries of Latin America (Brazil and Mexico) and East Asia (South Korea, Taiwan, Singapore and Hong Kong) also emerged as competitive exporters on the world market under the regime of export-oriented industrialization (EOI). This shift in economic loci is reflected in the rising share of developing countries in world merchandise trade from 4.4 per cent in 1955 to 7 per cent in the early 1970s and to over 12 per cent by the 1980s. The extent of the advance in manufactured exports is such that manufactures surpassed primary products as the main export of developing countries for the first time (Frobel, Heinrichs and Kreye 1980). However, the export of manufactured goods from these countries is highly concentrated in a few countries, namely the Asian NICs. These countries account for as much as two-thirds of the manufactured exports of the developing world.

The nature of production under EOI is generally in those industries that have passed the innovation stage and have achieved a high level of standardization and are facing a wage-productivity squeeze in the developed countries, for example, textiles and clothing, household appliances, office and telecommunications equipment, machinery and transport equipment, and other engineering products and semi-manufactures. This trend is also evident in some capital-intensive industries such as automobiles, iron and steel and chemicals as well as service and knowledge-intensive industries where aspects of the value chain can be outsourced to cheaper locations. By far, however, the most significant advance in manufactured exports from the developing countries has been in the industries of textiles and clothing where shares in world exports in 1985 was approximately 25 per cent and 43 per cent, respectively (Frobel 1988).

These advances were the result of the relocation of mature industrial sectors from high-wage areas of the core economies and the establishment of export-oriented industrial policies in peripheral economies (e.g., *maquiladoras* in Mexico). These trends are exemplified by the emergence of a world market for labour power and a world market for production sites. The growth of EOI is also reflected in the spread of export processing zones (EPZs) and world market factories (WMFs) throughout the developing world. It is estimated that in 1975, 25 developing countries operated 79 zones employing just over 800,000 persons (see Table 16.2). By 1986 the number of developing countries with EPZs had risen to 47, with 176 zones and over 1.9 million persons employed. By the late 1990s the number of countries had doubled to 93 with employment levels of 22.5 million. In recent years the growth has been spectacular with 130 countries having EPZs and employment levels of 66 million. China alone is estimated to contribute over 60 per cent of the employment.

Table 16.2. **Estimates of the Development of Export Processing Zones**

Years	1975	1986	1997	2002	2006
Number of countries with EPZs	25	47	93	116	130
Number of EPZs or similar types of zones	79	176	845	3000	3500
Employment (millions)	n.a.	n.a.	22.5	43	66
Of which, China	n.a.	n.a.	18	30	40
Of which, other countries with figures available	0.8	1.9	4.5	13	26

Source: Boyenge (2007, 1).

By and large, the production occurring under EOI is driven by foreign capital. Foreign equity participation and control in developing countries exports have grown as these economies have become more integrated into global value chains (Nurse 1995). FDI inflows to developing countries have expanded since the 1980s from 5.4 per cent of GDP to 27.3 per cent in 2005. The importance of FDI inflows is reflected in a range of export industries from mineral extractive sectors to garment manufacturing (UNCTAD 2007). However, FDI only presents part of the picture. Much of the EOI is being carried on by independent Third World firms, but under a variety of forms of TNC investment relationships, for example, joint ventures, licensing arrangements, international subcontracting, original equipment manufacturing, management contracts and restrictive marketing arrangements. The choice of investment relationship is often linked to the absorptive capacity of the firms in the country as well as industrial policies. The data suggests that the best performing export economies (e.g., South Korea and Taiwan) are those that choose more arms-length technology arrangements such as original equipment manufacture as opposed to FDI (UNIDO 2003, 42). For most other developing countries the conclusions are that 'there is little evidence of a significant contribution by FDI to technological capability accumulation in LDCs' (UNCTAD 2007, 41).

Theorizing Relocation

A long view of industrialization illustrates the global development problem in stark terms. Figure 16.2 shows the relative shares of world manufacturing outputs for the core economies and the periphery from 1750 to 2002.

In broad outline, the major observable changes are: first, the relative decline in the periphery's share of manufacturing and the emergence of a

Figure 16.2. Long Wave Movement, Technological Diffusion and the Periphery

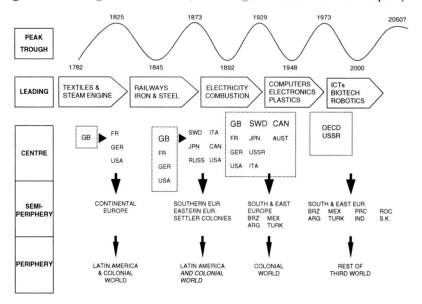

'technology gap' between the 'Third World' and the 'West' after the 1840s on account of the deindustrialization of countries like India, China and Pakistan and the consequent rapid growth of industrialization in Europe and North America (Williamson 2006). The second observation is the apparent reindustrialization of the periphery since the 1950s/1960s, largely reflected in the growth of China, the Asian NICs and a small group of exporters through technological and industrial upgrading. Other peripheral regions (e.g., South Asia, Latin America and the Caribbean, Africa, Middle East) that applied more passive approaches to technological development have underperformed, as exemplified in declining shares of world manufacturing value added (UNIDO 2005). How can this long-term trend be explained by long wave theory?

The historical analysis above suggests that during a downturn, when core markets are saturated and the innovation potential and profit rates have declined, the tendency is for firms and technologies to be exported to the peripheral areas of the world-economy where the organic composition of capital is lower, labour power is cheaper and the exploitation of labour or the environment is less regulated (Mandel 1984). Relocation is thus a mechanism for the resolution of the crisis of valorisation in the core economies during a downturn as well as a mechanism for industrial catch-up in the peripheries. Ranjit Sau argues that 'it is the possibility of selling the near-obsolete machinery to the capitalists in the Third World that helps stabilize the profit rate in the metropolis; it also paves the way for continuous technological

advancement there, which again keeps the rate of profit from tumbling down'
(Sau 1978, 75). He explains that

> In the Third World, the wage rate is much lower and the profit rate
> considerably higher in comparison with the advanced capitalist countries;
> besides, technical progress and rising wages in the latter are continuously
> taking their toll on obsolescence. Under such circumstances, the class
> interests of the bourgeoisie of the advanced capitalist countries neatly
> converge with those of the bourgeoisie of the Third World. The
> metropolitan bourgeoisie is eager to dispose of its old, obsolete plant and
> equipment, and its counterpart in the outer periphery of world capitalism
> is equally interested in welcoming the outmoded, second-hand stuff.
> (Sau 1978, 81–82)

The historical record suggests that with each successive downturn, there have
been spurts in capital exports and the parallel integration of new zones into
the product cycle of the declining sectors of a long wave. These capital
exports however, have been restricted generally to semi-peripheral countries.
This is because they possess the necessary 'absorptive capacity', for example,
human resources, business infrastructure and credit rating, to effectively use
the technical and capital resources. This explains the limited nature of
industrial relocation in each long wave. For example, before 1913 almost
two-thirds of the total foreign investment undertaken during the nineteenth
century was concentrated in the United States, Canada, Australia, Argentina
Brazil and some European countries (Kenwood and Lougheed 1982,
160–162). A similar pattern emerged during the 1970s with private bank
lending to developing countries. The six largest borrowers accounted for close
to 60 per cent of total capital receipts (Freiden 1981, 412).

The main recipients of capital during a long wave downturn – the semi-
peripheral countries – also end up being the main debtors when a debt crisis
erupts in the peripheries. And so, not only do the manufacturing firms of the
core benefit from the extension of the profitability cycle through relocation,
the financiers of peripheral industrialization also make a significant return
(Stewart 1993). In the last 200 years these debt crises have occurred with such
regularity in Latin America that Carlota Perez notes, 'every 50 to 60 years,
from the independence period through the 1960s and 1970s, plentiful credit
poured into the periphery, as soon as opportunities in the core countries
began to wane' (2002, 86). She goes on to explain that the problem relates in
large part to the cyclical rhythm of the long-waves:

> As regards debtors in peripheral countries, many of the loans taken one or
> two decades earlier were meant for redeployment of the established

paradigm. In other words, they propelled the last thin splash of the previous surge. Those were investments in mature technologies serving stagnant markets or in old infrastructures, probably still needed, but no longer very profitable. The economic benefits from these activities are insufficient to amortize debt and their levels of efficiency soon become inadequate to operate in markets increasingly governed by the superior productivity of the new technological revolution. (Perez 2002, 102)

Perez deepens the argument by illustrating that the problem for the peripheries is also one of overlap between the old paradigm in its dying stages and the emergence of the new. The thesis is that the long wave has six phases wherein the fifth and sixth phases in the old techno-economic paradigm coincide with the first two phases of the new paradigm, thereby annulling 'some of the advances made in the periphery' in the prior phases (Perez 2002, 64–65).

In many respects, what Perez offers here is a theory of why the migration of industries to the peripheries has limited transformational possibilities for industrial catching-up. In short, Perez (2001) argues that catching-up via mature technologies is a failed strategy as techno-economic paradigms are moving targets that rewards innovators. In many respects, the argument is that the countries that are able to avoid the relocation/debt trap are those that are proactive and have developed the requisite technological capabilities and industrial infrastructure to seize the windows of opportunity in the long wave transition from one techno-economic paradigm to another.

Conclusion

The key conclusion is that the relocation of industries into the peripheral economies has more often than not led to the establishment of enclave sectors, particularly in those countries that have been passive adopters of technology. These enclave sectors generally operate under technologically superior standards of production, have limited linkages with the rest of the economy and generate new forms of technological dependence. In short, relocation, while providing a spurt of industrial production in peripheral areas, reinforces the extraverted and dependent nature of peripheral capitalist structures under ever more constraining conditions as techno-economic paradigms advance.

Perez is clear to make the distinction between technology creation and acquisition (innovation) and technology imitation or diffusion (e.g., through passive relocation) in explaining the logic intrinsic in peripheral industrialization that perpetuates dependency and extraversion. From this perspective, the long wave framework and the mapping of techno-economic paradigms speak not only to the issue of conjunctural shifts in the world economy; it also highlights the issues of structures of accumulation as well as the geo-cultures of development. In this regard, Carlota Perez has made a critical contribution to the historiography of development by developing a methodology for understanding technological change that elaborates on the intrinsic relation between the core and peripheral economies in a long-term, large-scale context.

References

Baerresen, D. 1965. *Latin American Trade Patterns*. Washington, DC: Brookings Institution.

Bairoch, P. 1982. 'International Industrialization Levels from 1750 to 1980.' *Journal of European Economic History* 11, 269–334.

Boyenge, J.-P. S. 2007. ILO Database on Export Processing Zones (Revised). Geneva: ILO.

Cairncross, A. K. 1962. *Factors in Economic Development*. London: Allen.

Chase-Dunn, C. 1980. 'The Development of Core Capitalism in the Antebellum United States: Tariff Politics and Class Struggles in an Upwardly Mobile Semiperiphery.' In A. Bergesen (ed.). *Studies of the Modern World-System*. New York: Academic Press, 189–230.

Feis, H. 1930. *Europe: The World's Banker, 1870–1914*. London: Kelley.

Franko, L. 1974. 'The Origins of Multinational Manufacturing by Continental European Firms.' *Business History Review* 158, 277–301.

Freeman, C. and C. Perez. 1988. 'Structural Crises of Adjustment, Business Cycles and Investment Behaviour.' In G. Dosi et al. (eds). *Technical Change and Economic Theory*. London: Pinter, 38–66. [20.1]

Freiden, J. 1981. 'Third World Indebted Industrialization: International Finance and State Capitalism in Mexico, Brazil, Algeria and South Korea.' *International Organization* 35, 407–431.

Frobel, F. 1988. 'Perspectives on the New International Division of Labour.' Paper presented at conference on 'The Future of the Caribbean in the World System.' Kingston, Jamaica, May.

Frobel, F., J. Heinrichs and O. Kreye. 1981. *The New International Division of Labour*. Cambridge: Cambridge University Press.

Hirschman, A. 1978. 'The Political Economy of Import-Substitution Industrialization in Latin America.' In S. P. Singh (ed.). *Underdevelopment to Developing Economies*. New York: Oxford University Press, 340–374.

Hobsbawm, E. 1975. *The Age of Capital*. London: Weidenfeld & Nicholson.

Hobson, C. K. 1914. *The Export of Capital*. London: Constable.

Hopkins, T. and I. Wallerstein. 1982. *World-System Analysis: Theory and Methodology*. Beverly Hills, CA: Sage.

———. 1987. 'Capitalism and the Incorporation of New Zones into the World-Economy.' *Review* 10, 763–779.

Hymer, S. 1976. *The International Operations of National Firms: A Study of Direct Foreign Investment*. Cambridge: MIT Press.

Jenkins, R. 1984. *Transnational Corporations and Industrial Transformation in Latin America*. New York: St. Martin's Press.

———. 1987. *Transnational Corporations and Uneven Development*. London: Methuen.

Jenks, L. 1927. *The Migration of British Capital to 1875*. New York: Knopf.

Kennedy, P. 1987. *The Rise and Fall of the Great Powers*. New York: Random House.

Kenwood, A. G. and A. L. Lougheed. 1971. *The Growth of the International Economy, 1820–1960*. London: Allen.

————. 1982. *Technical Diffusion and Industrialization before 1914*. New York: St. Martins.

Kondratiev, N. 1984. *The Long Wave Cycle*. Guy Daniels (trans.). New York: Richardson & Snyder.

Lewis, A. 1978. *Growth and Fluctuations 1870–1913*. London: Allen & Unwin.

Mandel, E. 1984. 'Explaining Long Waves of Capitalist Development.' In C. Freeman et al. (eds). *Long Waves in the World Economy*. London: Pinter, 195–201.

Maxfield, S. and J. Nolt. 1990. 'Protectionism and the Internationalization of Capital: U.S. Sponsorship of Import Substitution Industrialization in the Philippines, Turkey and Argentina.' *International Studies Quarterly* 34, 49–81.

McKay, J. 1975. 'Foreign Enterprise in Russian and Soviet Industry: A Long Term Perspective.' *Business History Review* 158, 336–356.

Nurse, Keith. 1995. 'The Developmental Efficacy of the Export-Oriented Clothing Industry: The Jamaican Case.' *Social and Economic Studies* 44, 195–227.

————. 1998. 'Third World Industrialization and the Reproduction of Underdevelopment.' *Marronnage* 1, 69–97.

Oman, C. 1984. *New Forms of Investment in Developing Countries*. Paris: Development Centre of the OECD.

Perez, C. 1985. 'Microelectronics, Long Waves and World Structural Change: New Perspectives for Developing Countries.' *World Development* 13, 441–463. [9.1]

————. 2001. 'Technological Change and Opportunities for Development as a Moving Target.' *Cepal Review* 75, December, 109–130. [72.2.1]

————. 2002. *Technological Revolutions and Financial Capital: The Dynamics of Bubbles and Golden Ages*. Cheltenham: Edward Elgar. [74.1]

————. 2004. 'Technological Revolutions, Paradigm Shifts and Socio-Institutional Change.' In E. S. Reinert (ed.). *Globalization, Economic Development and Inequality. An Alternative Perspective*. Cheltenham: Edward Elgar, 217–242. [75.1]

Phelps, D. 1969. *The Migration of Industry to South America*. York, PA: Maple Press.

Raffer, K. 1987. *Unequal Exchange and the Evolution of the World System*. Houndmills: Macmillan.

Sau, R. 1978. *Unequal Exchange, Imperialism and Underdevelopment: An Essay on the Political Economy of World Capitalism*. Calcutta: Oxford University Press.

Schmitz, H. 1984. 'Industrialization Strategies in Less Developed Countries: Some Lessons of Historical Experience.' In R. Kaplinsky (ed.). *Third World Industrialization in the 1980s: Open Economies in a Closing World*. London: Frank Cass, 1–21.

Schumpeter, J. A. 1939. *Business Cycles*. New York: McGraw-Hill.

Soete, L. 1985. 'Long Cycles and the International Diffusion of Technology.' In C. Freeman (ed.). *Design, Innovation and Long Cycles in Economic Development*. London: Pinter.

Stewart, T. 1993. 'The Third World Debt Crisis: A Long Waves Perspective.' *Review* 16, 117–171.

Stopford, J. 1974. 'The Origins of British-Based Multinational Manufacturing Enterprises.' *Business History Review* 158, 303–335.

UNCTAD. 2007. *The Least Developed Countries Report, 2007: Knowledge, Technological Learning and Innovation for Development*. Geneva: United Nations.

UNECLAC. 1965. *External Financing in Latin America*. New York: United Nations.

UNIDO. 2005. *Industrial Development Report 2005. Capacity Building for Catching-up: Historical, Empirical and Policy Dimensions*. Vienna: UNIDO Publication.

van Roon, G. 1985. 'Cycles, Turning Phases, and Societal Structures: Historical Perspectives and Current Problems.' In C. Freeman (ed.). *Design, Innovation and the Long Cycle.* London: Pinter.

Wallerstein, I. 1984. 'Long Waves as Capitalist Process.' *Review* 7, 559–574.

Wilkins, M. 1970. *The Emergence of the Multinational Enterprise: American Business Abroad from the Colonial Era to 1914.* Cambridge, MA: Harvard University Press.

———. 1974. *The Maturing of Multinational Enterprises: American Business Abroad from 1914 to 1970.* Cambridge, MA: Harvard University Press.

Williamson, G. J. 2006. *Globalization and The Poor Periphery Before 1950.* London: MIT Press.

Chapter Seventeen:

ON THE DISCREET CHARM OF THE (RENTIER) BOURGEOISIE: THE CONTRADICTORY NATURE OF THE INSTALLATION PERIOD OF A NEW TECHNO-ECONOMIC PARADIGM

José Gabriel Palma
University of Cambridge

Introduction

This chapter analyses one of Carlota Perez' main insights regarding the contradictory nature of the 'installation' period of the current new techno-economic paradigm, as well as the role of these contradictions in the genesis of the ongoing financial crisis.[1] Basically, despite the enormous potential for increased productivity growth unleashed by the current technological revolution, productivity growth in industrialized countries (and in most of the developing world) has actually declined since the irruption of the new 'Age of Information Technology and Telecommunications' (for the case of the US, see Figure 17.18). In essence, the period of 'installation' not only creates all the conditions for unleashing economic progress, but also generates 'tensions' of an economic, social and political nature that can turn into formidable obstacles to economic growth.[2]

Perez identifies three main 'tensions' that are bound to arise during the period of 'installation' of a technological revolution: the first is the tension between 'the paper economy and the real economy' (i.e., between financial capital and productive capital); the second is the tension between 'the size and profile of effective demand and those of potential supply' (i.e., the real-economy effects of increased inequality); and the third is the political tension between 'the poorer poor and the richer rich' (Perez 2005, 16–19).

The first 'tension' relates to the very essence of the technological bubble that characterizes the period of 'installation' (see Figure 17.15); according to Perez: '[this is] a process of asset inflation in which the stock market (paper) values decouple from the real value of the companies they represent. Thus, ... profit gains come from reselling the assets or from participating in the many instruments (futures, derivatives, hedge funds or others) that are created in the casino economy that builds up during Installation' (2005, 16).

Although once the bubble has collapsed, this first tension might fade away – bringing 'values' back into line with 'fundamentals' (as losses bring financial investors back to the real economy, and the losers are likely to press for more effective regulation) – according to Perez, the collapse of the NASDAQ bubble was not big enough to reshape the relationship between financial and productive capital (in favour of the latter). As a result, even after the dot-com bubble burst, a healthy investment climate was not re-established; furthermore, there was no real punishment for fraud, or proper development of the necessary remedial regulation. Thus, the distorting influence of the 'short termism' of the financial world continued to weigh upon the real economy, acting as a constraint on productive investment and productivity growth.[3]

In sum, even after the NASDAQ bubble had been ruptured, the CEOs of production companies found it extremely difficult and risky to embark upon long-term projects; and this was not due to constraints created by competitive struggles in the real economy, heightened uncertainty or tight profit margins – let alone by lack of finance – but due to continued pressures for increased short-term profit coming from the world of finance.

The second 'tension' relates to the real-economy consequences of the process of income polarization that tends to characterize the period of 'installation' of a new technological revolution.[4] This increased inequality is responsible for the fact that the effective demand for the new products associated with the technological revolution becomes insufficient to unleash the full potential supplies for them. In other words, due to income polarization the range of products and services that become available with a new technological paradigm are much narrower than those actually feasible during a period of 'installation'. Thus, increased inequality leads to 'premature market saturation' (Perez 2005, 17). And one way to break (at least temporarily) this demand constraint in an increasingly unequal economy is through increased household debt (see Figures 17.8 and 17.10).

Finally, the third 'tension' is found in the inevitable political consequences of income polarization. Although this strain is primarily of a social and political nature, it is bound to create further constraint on economic growth. As mentioned above, one of the main characteristics of a period of 'installation' is that a disproportionate share of the benefits of economic growth and financial developments accrue to those at the top of the income scale, leading to a growing abyss between the rich and the poor. In fact, the income of those not at the top of the distribution tend to stagnate, or even to fall towards the lower ranks of the distribution (see Figures 17.2–17.6). So, what a period of 'installation' leaves in its wake is 'the resentment stemming from downward mobility in the face of affluence' (Perez 2005, 18). This, in turn, results in a loss of hope and increased anger, violence, problems of governance and migratory pressures from the South.

This chapter will look at the above 'tensions' – and the peculiar (and not very sustainable) forms by which they were dealt with – during the period of 'installation' of the fifth techno-economic paradigm, that of the age of information and telecommunications, in its 'core' country – the US. It will also look at how these 'tensions', and the dynamics they generated, are a crucial component in the genesis of the current financial crisis. In particular, this chapter will analyse how during the 'installation' period the massive potentials for increased productivity growth of the new technological revolution were not realized due to the fact that the huge income polarization that it produced fuelled the process of increased 'financialization' rather than one of increased investment and productivity growth (see Figures 17.12–17.18).

Income Polarization During the Period of 'Installation' of a New Techno-Economic Paradigm

Figure 17.1 shows that (as in the case of the previous technological revolution, especially after the end of the First World War) the period of 'installation' of the current techno-economic paradigm, which started around the mid-1970s, was followed by a remarkable process of income polarization.

As is evident from Figure 17.1, the fortunes of the richest one per cent in the US took a rather remarkable turn after the 'irruption' of the new technological revolution in the late-1970s, the appointment of Paul Volker to the Fed in 1979 (and his flamboyant monetarism), and the election of Reagan as president a year later: including realized capital gains, the share in national income of this group (1.4 million 'tax units' by 2006) increased from 8.9 per cent to 22.8 per cent between then and 2006 – or from 8 per cent to 18 per cent if capital gains are excluded.[5] A relatively similar scenario is found in the UK after the election of Mrs Thatcher in 1979 (see Atkinson 2007).

In fact, by 2006 the share of the top one per cent in the US had already returned to its pre-1929 level, reversing in a short period the entire previous 50-years of relatively steady decline.[6] Figure 17.2 indicates that this was possible because the key characteristic of the distributive outcome of this 'installation' period was its 'winner-takes-all' nature.[7]

Figure 17.1. US: Income Share of the Top 1%, 1913–2006

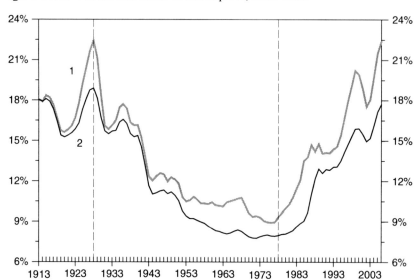

[1] = including realized capital gains; and [2] = excluding capital gains. Three-year moving averages.
Source: Piketty and Sáez (2003, 2006).[8] In [1] taxpayers are ranked by gross income including capital gains; and in [2] they are ranked excluding capital gains.[9]

Figure 17.2. US: Average Income of the Bottom 90% and of the Top 1%, 1933–2006

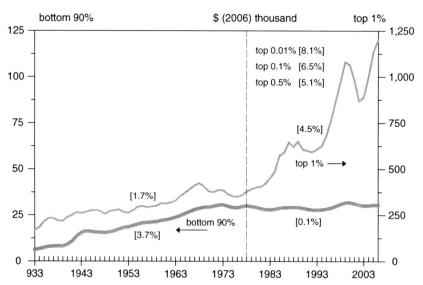

Percentages shown in the graph are average annual real rates of growth between 1933–1978 and 1978–2006. Three-year moving averages.
Source: as in Figure 1 (includes capital gains).

According to the source, while in real terms (i.e., dollars of 2006 value) the average income of the bottom 90 per cent actually fell between 1973 and 2006 (from $31.3 thousand to $30.7 thousand), that of the top 1 per cent increased *3.2-fold* (from $386 thousand to $1.2 million). And in the case of the top 0.5 per cent, it jumped *3.8-fold*; in the case of the top 0.1 per cent, *5.4-fold*; and in that of the top 0.01 per cent, *7.5-fold*.[10] What a difference from the previous decades of 'liberal-Keynesianism' (the 'deployment' period of the previous techno-economic paradigm – that of 'Age of the Automobile, Oil, Petrochemicals and Mass Production'), when the average income of the bottom 90 per cent grew twice as fast as that of the top 1 per cent.

Furthermore, if one compares these two groups from the point of view of their own cycles, the reversal of the income-growth asymmetries is even more remarkable (see Figure 17.3).

In fact, as Kalecki had envisaged (1943) both liberal-Keynesianism and neo-liberalism became countercyclical, but each for a different phase of the cycle. In a way, both seek to change the balance of power between income groups – Keynesianism in order to prevent the disrupting effects of crisis-ridden capitalism; neo-liberalism in order to return power and control to their 'rightful owners' (capital). (See also Wood 1999, 23)

Figure 17.4 shows the similarity of the Clinton and Bush administrations during the latter period. During the seven-year period of economic expansion of the Clinton administration (1993–2000), and the four-year period of expansion of Bush's (2002–2006), 'average' real family incomes grew by 4 per cent and 2.9 per cent annually, respectively. However, these averages disguise remarkable asymmetries: in fact the overall 'average' corresponds to that of percentiles 95–99 (something that did not happen even in Pinochet's Chile; see Palma, 2007).

As a result, during the seven-year period of economic expansion of the Clinton administration the top 1 per cent of income earners captured 45 per cent of the total growth in (pre-tax) income, while during Bush's four-year period of expansion no less than *73 per cent* of total income growth accrued to the top 1 per cent. Perhaps the neoliberal ideology associated with this period of 'installation' of the new techno-economic paradigm is just shorthand for 'the art of getting away with such a remarkably asymmetric distributional outcome *within a democracy*'…[11]

Figure 17.5 shows how the contrast between the fortunes of the great majority and that of the powerful minority gets even more extreme when the comparison is made with the very few at very top of the income distribution.

While the average income of about 120 million families remained roughly stagnant during this 28-year period, 0.01 per cent of the total had their average income multiplied *8.5 times* – including periods in which their annual income

Figure 17.3. US: Average Income Top 1% and Bottom 90%, 1933–2006

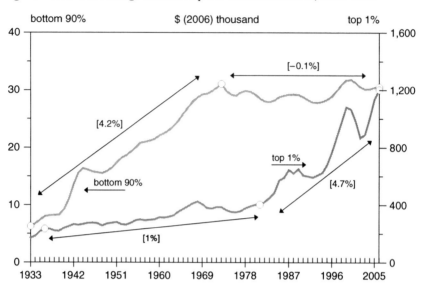

Percentages shown in the graph are average annual real rates of growth in respective periods (1933–1973 and 1973–2006 for the bottom 90 per cent, and 1936–1980 and 1980–2006 for the top 1 per cent). Three-year moving averages.
Source: as in Figure 17.1 (includes capital gains).

Figure 17.4. US: Average Income Growth by Income Groups, 1993–2000 and 2002–2006

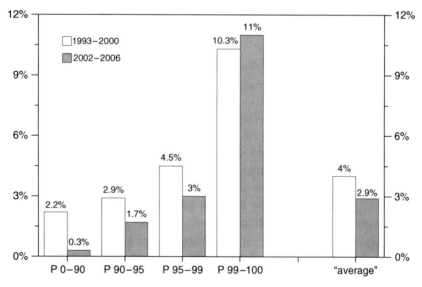

P = percentiles.
Source: as in Figure 17.1 (includes capital gains).

Figure 17.5. US: Average Income of the Top 0.01% and of the Bottom 90%, 1978–2006

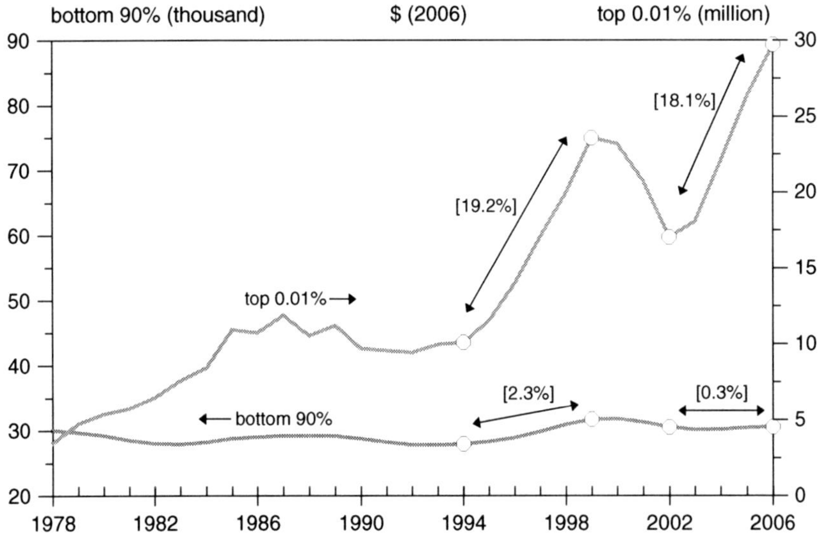

Percentages shown in the graph are average annual real rates of growth in respective periods (1994–2000 and 2002–2006). Three-year moving averages.
Source: as in Figure 17.1 (includes capital gains).

grew at no less than 19.2 per cent (the six last years of the Clinton administration) and 18.1 per cent (four of the years of the Bush administration). No such luck for the bottom 90 per cent who during these respective periods had their annual average income grow by only 2.3 per cent and 0.3 per cent. That is (very roughly, and in dollars of 2006 value) from 1978 to 2006 the gap between the average income of these two groups of families jumps from a difference between $30 thousand and $3 million to one of between $30 thousand and $30 million.

Figure 17.6 shows the contrasting fortunes of these two groups of families in the long run, where the disparity between the 'Keynesian-liberal' 'deployment' period and the two 'installation' periods (before 1929 and after the mid-1970s) becomes even clearer.

Including realized capital gains, and after a long period of decline, this multiple shoots up in a way that 'defies gravity' – from its lowest point in the 1970s to its peak in 2006, it jumped from 115 to 970.[12] In sum, if during the 'deployment' period of the fourth techno-economic paradigm the 'American Dream' seemed to belong to the majority of the US population, since the 'irruption' of the fifth technological revolution towards the end of the 1970s it has been highjacked by a rather tiny minority – for the rest, it has only been available on credit...

Figure 17.6. US: Average Income Top 0.01% as a Multiple of Average Income bottom 90%, 1917–2006

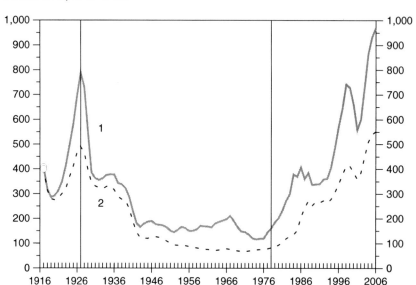

[1] = including capital gains; and [2] = excluding capital gains. Three-year moving averages. *Source*: as in Figure 17.1 (data available only from 1917).

At the same time, this huge income polarisation since the 'irruption' of the latest technological revolution – between 1980 and 2006 just the taxable income of the top 1% increased by nearly US$2 trillion, and that the top 10% by US$3.5 trillion – obviously became one of the major contributors (and one probably more important than the Asian 'savings glut') to the increased liquidity in the US financial markets (the abundance of which transformed financial markets into fundamentally unstable institutions, totally unable to self-correct. In fact, the current crisis may have many roots, but a crucial one relates to income polarisation. In particular, as Figure 17.7 indicates (and as good old-fashioned Keynesian economics has always emphasised) the current crisis has again shown that developments in financial markets are closely related to the distribution of income, so the latter is a crucial component in the understanding of the crisis and in the planning of how to get out of it.

It could be argued, however, that this is a case of simultaneous causation; the rich own most financial assets, and anything that causes the value of financial assets to raise rapidly will also cause inequality to raise fast. However, this close relationship stands even when capital gains are *excluded* from tax-payers' income (see Palma, 2009b).

Figure 17.7. US: Income Share of the Top 10% and value of Financial assets as % of GDP, 1947–2007

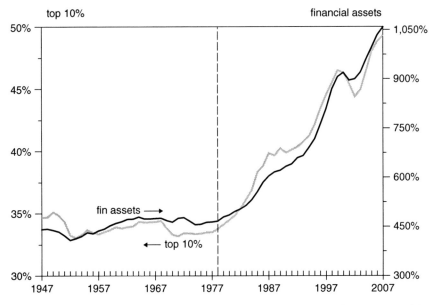

Fin assets = value of financial assets as percentage of GDP; and top 10% = income share of the top 10% (includes capital gains). 3-year moving averages.
Sources: as in Figure 17.1, and Fed (2009).

Two 'Post-Modern' Rent-Seeking Economic Laws that Emerged During the Period of 'Installation' of the Fifth Techno-Economic Paradigm

Some of the 'tensions' discussed above (which characterize the period of 'installation' of the new techno-economic paradigm – and which had a direct impact on the genesis of the current financial crisis) meant that income polarization not only contributed significantly to the increase in financial markets liquidity, but was also associated with a huge increase in the level of public and household debt.[13]

The Increase of Public Sector Debt

As is well known, during the recent period of 'installation', the huge increase of the pre-tax income share of the top income earners was actually accompanied by a remarkable fall in their tax rates. For example, according to an IRS report obtained by the *Wall Street Journal*, in 2005 the top 400 income tax payers (with a combined gross income of more than $100 billion) controlled 1.2 per cent of the nation's total taxable income – twice the share they had in 1995. As if this huge increase in taxable income was not enough, this group also had their effective income tax rate cut by nearly half (from 30 per cent to 18 per cent).[14]

Taxes on corporate profits also declined remarkably; for example, these taxes as a percentage of public expenditure fell from 15 per cent of the total in 1978 to just 6 per cent in 1982, while at the same time the public deficit grew by an almost identical converse amount (from 6 per cent to 16 per cent of public expenditure). Again, by 2002 taxes on corporate profits were back at 6 per cent of public expenditure, while the deficits went up again to 16 per cent. In fact, the share of taxes on corporate profits in total public expenditure fell below even the level reached by this ratio during the difficult (and low-profit) years of the 1930s recession (9%).[15] In all, it has been estimated that the Bush tax cuts amounted to $1.8 trillion (Krugman 2009b); and that amount is almost identical to the US$ 1.7 trillion increase in the debt of the Federal Government between the beginning of the first Bush administration in 2001 and 2007 (and the start of the financial crisis; see Fed 2009).

So, basically this neo-liberal rentier economic law that emerged during the period of 'installation' of the new technological revolution could be summarised in the following terms: rather than paying taxes to get free public goods, it was much more fun for the top income earners and big corporations to 'part-pay/part-lend' these taxes to the government...

The Increase in Household Debt

Much has been said regarding the increase in household debt before the 2007 financial crisis, and the huge dead weight that it is bound to bring to the eventual recovery. However, not enough attention has been paid to the fact that this debt was essential to sustain the growth of aggregate demand in the face of stagnant average incomes in the bottom 90 per cent of the population (see Figure 17.8).

As Figure 17.8 indicates, the fall in the rate of growth of the gross income of the bottom 90 per cent (from 3.5 per cent between 1950 and 1980 to 1.8 per cent between 1980 and 2006) is associated with *the same rate of growth of personal consumption expenditure in both periods* (3.5 per cent). No prizes for guessing what made up the difference!

This gives rise to the second of the 'post-modern' rent-seeking economic laws that emerged during the period of 'installation' of the new techno-economic paradigm; it could be summarized in the following terms: rather than paying the level of wages that were required to achieve the growth of aggregate demand necessary to sustain the process of capital accumulation,

Figure 17.8. US: Gross Income of the Bottom 90% and personal Consumption expenditure, 1950–1980 and 1980–2006

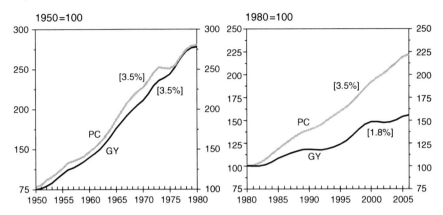

PC = Personal Consumption Expenditure; and GY = gross income of the bottom 90 per cent.[16] Three-year moving averages. Percentages shown in the graph are average annual real rates of growth in respective periods.
Sources: as in Figure 17.1, and US Census Bureau (2008).

it was much more fun for the capitalist élite to 'part-pay/part-lend' these wages... Figure 17.9 indicates the resulting huge increase in the level of household debt (both consumer credit and home mortgage debt) after the election of Reagan.

As Figure 17.9 shows, consumer credit of the household sector jumped from 25 per cent to over 40 per cent of wages and salaries between the early 1980s and 2007. In turn, home mortgage debt also soared from 65 per cent to 166 per cent, respectively. And as is well known, a significant component of the increase in mortgage debt was devoted to finance consumption as US households were allowed to transform the capital gains in their homes into ATM machines – home equity withdrawal reached US$700 billion in 2005 (see Roubini 2009).

Figure 17.10 illustrates the effects of the capitalist élite's preference to 'part-pay/part-lend' the required level of wages on household debt, and the mirage of an ever increasing households' net worth. The latter not only provided the foundations for the ever-increasing access to credit, but probably was also a fundamental component of the material foundations of the neo-liberal 'spontaneous consensus'-type of hegemony found in the US since 1980 – with its ever increasing tolerance for inequality.

During the 25-year period prior to 2007, household sector debt more than doubled as a share of disposable income (it jumped from 65% to 136%), while real household net worth increased (as a share of personal disposable income)

Figure 17.9. US: Debt Outstanding of the Household Sector as a % of Wages and Salaries, 1965–2007

Con cred = consumer credit of the household sector; and h mortg = home mortgage debt of the household sector. Three-year moving averages.
Sources: US Census Bureau (2008) and Fed (2009).

from 450% to 615%, having peaked at 645% in 2006. The US was not alone in this boom of household debt; in many other industrialised countries, especially in the UK and Iceland, households were also allowed, indeed encouraged, to accumulate an excessive amount of debt. In the UK the latter reached roughly 1.7 times the level of household disposable income and in Iceland more than 2 times. In the process, households have accumulated an amount of financial risk that has proved to be at levels that are obviously not privately efficient, let alone socially efficient. This excessive amount of risk has become evident in the alternate phase of the cycle, that of the 'sudden stop' to their access to additional financing. In all, the average household in the US is currently carrying US$122,000 in personal debts; added to this, its share in federal debt already amounts to US$547,000 (*USA Today* 2009).

In turn, Figure 17.11 illustrates that within the non-financial sector of the US economy households were not the only ones to increase rapidly their 'financial depth' after 1980.

In the meantime, the debt of the financial sector was climbing even faster than that of the non-financial sector – between 1980 and 2007 it

Figure 17.10. US: Household Sector Debt and Net Worth as a Share of Personal Disposable Income, 1965–2007

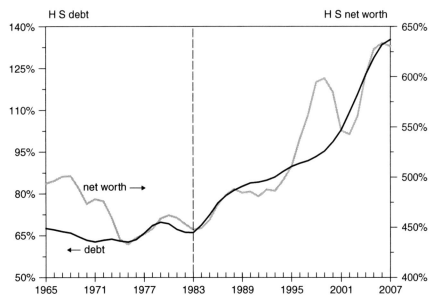

H S debt = Household sector debt; and H S net worth = Household sector net worth. Three-year moving averages.
Source: US Census Bureau (2008), and Fed (2009, flow of funds accounts).

jumped from 20% to 116% of GDP. Overall, during this period the ratio of debt to GDP more than doubled (from 168% to over 350%). How could anybody believe that a debt-fuelled bubble of asset-price inflation was actually about real wealth creation? And how could anyone think that such remarkable increases in the level of debt by both the financial and the non-financial sectors could be sustainable in the long run? Or how could anyone think that if banks could not dazzle investors and regulators with might, it was perfectly acceptable that they puzzle them with fudged balance sheets?[17] How anyone could think that markets would never call this blatant bluff is anybody's guess.

We are now clearly paying the price for the delusional optimism of policymakers and regulators, who believed that they could happily close their eyes to the risks associated with asset bubbles and credit booms – 'how can you be sure it is a bubble? Do you know better than the market'? In fact, no policy maker was willing to call the debt-fuelled 'irrational exuberance' of asset prices a bubble since according to the efficient market hypothesis to call a bubble a bubble is a contradiction in terms.

Figure 17.11. US: Debt Outstanding by the Non-Financial Sector, 1950–2007

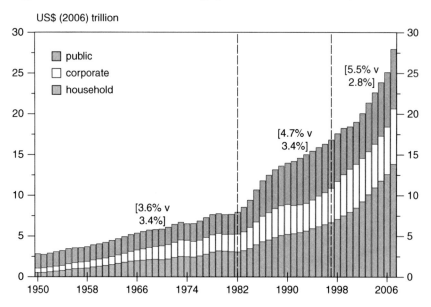

Household = total household debt (consumer and mortgage debt); corporate = total non-financial corporate debt; public = total public sector debt (local and federal). Percentages shown in the graph are average annual real rates of growth of debt and of GDP in each period, respectively.
Source: Fed (2009).

Income Polarization Leading to Greater 'Financialization' and Lower Levels of Saving, Investment and Productivity Growth

From a macroeconomic point of view, the crucial aspect of the huge increase in inequality and in financial 'deepening' was that they were associated with a meagre-macro. In particular, they are linked to a disappointing rate of productivity growth; an ever increasing level of 'financialisation'; a massive drop in the overall level of private savings; and a particularly poor rate of private investment – poor especially since increased inequality took place side by side with a relative dynamic increase in personal consumption, high profit rates, easy finance and social tranquillity. Perhaps the least surprising part of this story is the collapse in the level of personal saving (see Figure 17.12). Obviously, three decades of stagnant average real income for the bottom 90 per cent coupled with a relatively fast rate of growth of personal consumption expenditure is not the best recipe for dynamic personal saving (at least, as traditionally measured in national accounts).[18]

Figure 17.12. US: Income Share of the Top 1% and Personal Saving as a % of DPY 1913–2006

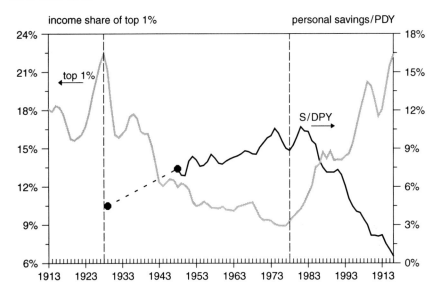

Top 1 per cent = income share of the top 1 per cent; S/DPY = personal saving as a percentage of Disposable Personal Income. Three-year moving averages. Data on personal savings between 1929 and 1948 are not shown due to sharp fluctuations during both the 1930s recession and the Second World War (the same will be the case for other data on saving and on investment below). *Sources:* as in Figure 17.1, and US Census Bureau (2008).

Furthermore, contrary to what was widely predicted by the 'supply-siders' of the Washington Consensus, in this new neo-liberal-type capitalism a remarkable fall in corporate taxation led to a decline in corporate saving as a share of corporate profits (as opposed to what had happened for most of the 'financially repressed' Keynesian period; see Figure 17.13).

So, on the remarkably positive things that were to happen if taxes on high-income groups and big corporations were to be cut, this is further evidence that (at best) '[i]t turns out that when you cut taxes on the rich, the rich pay less taxes; when you raise taxes on the rich, they pay more taxes – end of story' (Krugman 2007). The combined effect of the collapse of personal savings and the decline in corporate saving led, of course, to a huge decline in the overall level of private saving – as a share of gross national income net private savings fell from 11.2% in 1984 to 3.3% in 2006.

However, the really contradictory nature of this 'installation'-type capitalism is revealed in the relationship between income polarization and private investment (see Figure 17.14).

Figure 17.13. US: Undistributed Corporate Profits and Corporate Taxes as % of Corporate Profits, 1950–2007

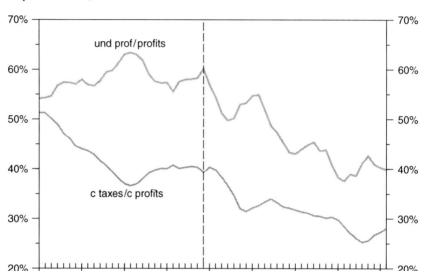

Und profits/profits = undistributed corporate profits as a share of corporate profits; and c taxes/c profits = corporate taxes as a share of corporate profits. 5-year moving averages. *Sources:* US Census Bureau (2008).

Even having said all of the above, it is still truly remarkable to see how private investment failed to respond positively to the combined incentives of huge income polarisation cum political stability and dynamic growth of personal consumption, high profit rates, and overabundance of finance. Private investment instead actually declined as a share of GDP, falling cyclically from its peak of 18.5% of GDP in 1979, to just 15.5% in 2007.[19] In fact, what happened to investment during the neo-liberal period challenges all available economic theories of investment.[20] That is, and not for the first time, we are faced with a 'macro' that only makes analytical sense if examined within the framework of the political settlement and distributional outcome in which it operates. Figure 17.14 helps us in this direction by revealing the changing nature of the process of accumulation between the Keynesian and the neo-liberal periods. While in the former, the increased 'compulsions' for big business and the declining shares of income for top earners had forced the capitalist élite to accumulate via increasing productive capacities and moving away from sheer surplus extraction, the latter period is characterised by a ('scissor') movement in reverse. Figure 17.15 also shows how the increased process of 'financialisation' led to a remarkable decoupling between the real and financial worlds.

Figure 17.14. US: Income Share of the Top 1% and Share of Private Investment in GDP, 1913–2006

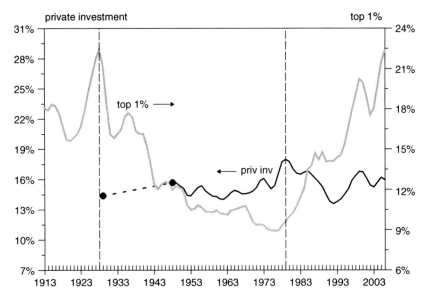

Top 1 per cent = income share of the top 1 per cent; priv inv = private investment as a percentage of Gross Domestic Product (current prices; excludes private inventories). Three-year moving averages.
Sources: as in Figure 17.1, and US Census Bureau (2008).

During the period of 'deployment' of the fourth techno-economic paradigm (otherwise known in the financial literature as the period of financial 'repression') total financial assets remained relatively stable as a share of GDP (at a level below 500 per cent), while private investment experienced some acceleration (from 13.8 per cent of GDP in 1961 to 18.5 per cent in 1979). In the subsequent period of 'installation' of the new techno-economic paradigm (otherwise known as the period of financial 'liberalization'), a period of huge asset inflation (that more than doubled the value of total financial assets as a share of GDP) was accompanied by a slowdown of the rate of private investment (from 18.5 per cent of GDP in 1979 to 15.5 per cent in 2007). During this period the value of financial assets not only decoupled from the real economy, but the abundance of finance and the associated asset-price-led (not so) 'irrational exuberance', instead of having a positive pulling effect on private investment, had instead the effect of 'friendly fire'. Therefore, there is not much evidence here to support the McKinnon and Shaw-type argument in favour of financial liberalisation – one of the most influential ideas behind the emergence of the Washington Consensus.

Figure 17.15. US: Total Financial Assets (All Sectors) and Private Investment as % of GDP, 1947–2007

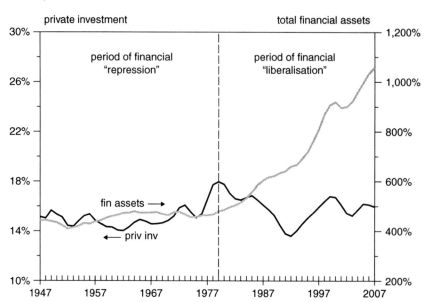

Fin assets = total financial assets (all sectors); and priv inv = private investment (excludes private inventories). Three-year moving averages.
Sources: US Census Bureau (2008) and Fed (2009).

As Figure 17.15 also indicates, maybe financial 'liberalisation' was just an attempt at introducing a 'unit root' into the post-Bretton Woods stationary financial processes, so that it could then be 'shocked' with (hopefully) permanent upward effects!

Furthermore, how could policy makers have ignored the damage that the disproportionate growth of the financial sector was inflicting on the real economy via a special version of the 'Dutch disease' – in this case, the crowding out of the non-financial tradable sector (both export- and import-competing) by the excessive growth of the financial sector (and construction)?[21] In fact, financial markets were allowed to expand to such an extent that industrialized countries moved from a situation in which banks and other financial institutions were 'too large to fail' (e.g., LTCM in 1998), to one in which they became almost 'too large to be rescued'.[22]

In turn, Figures 17.16 and 17 show how the relationship between income distribution and private investment has changed through the long technological cycle.

This statistic could be understood as a proxy for the changing nature of the process of accumulation; i.e., for the changing relationship between what top income earners take away from the economy, and what they put back into it

Figure 17.16. US: Income Share of the Top 1% as a Multiple of Private Investment in GDP, 1929–2006

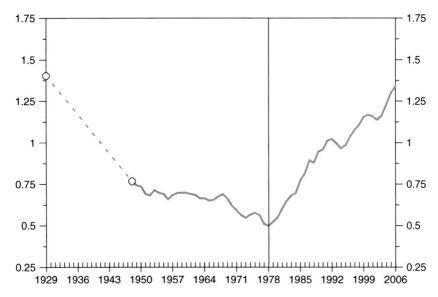

Three-year moving averages.
Sources: as in Figure 17.1, and US Census Bureau (2008).

Figure. 17.17. US: Income Share of the Top 10% as a Multiple of Private Investment in GDP, 1929–2006

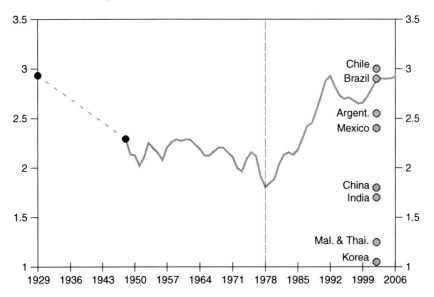

Argent. = Argentina; Mal. & Thai. = Malaysia and Thailand. Three-year moving averages.
Sources: as in Figure 17.1; the US Census Bureau (2008); and World Bank (2008).[23]

in terms of improved productive capacities. In fact, towards the end of the period this relationship had changed so much that even the income share of the top 0.5% (i.e., only about seven hundred thousand families, earning 18.6% of the total in 2006) ended up well above the share of all private investment in GDP (15.5%). Finally, probably no other statistic communicates better the increasingly rent-seeking nature of the capitalist élite during the neo-liberal period in the US than that in Figure 17.17.

It seems that the main aim of the neo-liberal capitalist élite in the US was to create a 'post-industrial' capitalism – with only carrots but no sticks for the capitalist élite. That is, one without 'compulsions', where, among other things, productive investment becomes an optional extra on top of assured rent-earnings opportunities and increased surplus extraction.[24] And also probably no other statistic demonstrate better than that in Figure 17.17 how the US seems to be increasingly in some sort of 'projective identification' with Latin American-style capitalism (see Palma, 2009c). That is, neo-liberalism also ended up as a de facto mechanism for bringing middle-income developing countries' institutional structures and distributional outcomes into industrialised countries.[25] In sum, US rentiers did certainly succeed in their attempt to get rid of practically all obstacles on their greed. When eventually the market called their bluff, it became evident how self-destructive and short-sighted this strategy had been.

As the income distribution and investment data above show, like 'rentier aristocrats' whose wealth depends on their capacity to squeeze surpluses out of peasants, the post-1980 neo-liberal capitalist élite in the US also preferred to increase its wealth mainly by developing a more effective technology of dispossession. That is, by improving its own coercive powers (on top of its remarkable talents for creating virtual financial wealth), rather than by increasing its capacities for developing further the productive forces of society. From this perspective, neo-liberalism could also be understood as a new form of moral hazard: one characterized by the fundamental distortion of incentives.

Moreover, since capitalism without 'compulsions' is probably as efficient as Communism without workers' control over the bureaucracy, it should probably come as no surprise that the 'collateral damage' of all of the above is productivity growth (see Figure 17.18).

Although the decline in the annual average rate of growth of productivity in the US since the irruption of the new 'Age of Information Technology and Telecommunications' was less sharp than in most other industrialized countries (between 1950–73 and 1973–2008 it fell from an average of 2.3% to one of 1.4%), this was only due to a disappointing rate before 1973.[26] In fact, as Figure 17.18 indicates, the much heralded acceleration of productivity growth in the US after 1983 (from an average of 1% between 1966–1983 to one of just 1.7%

Figure 17.18. US: Output, Employment and Productivity, 1950–2008

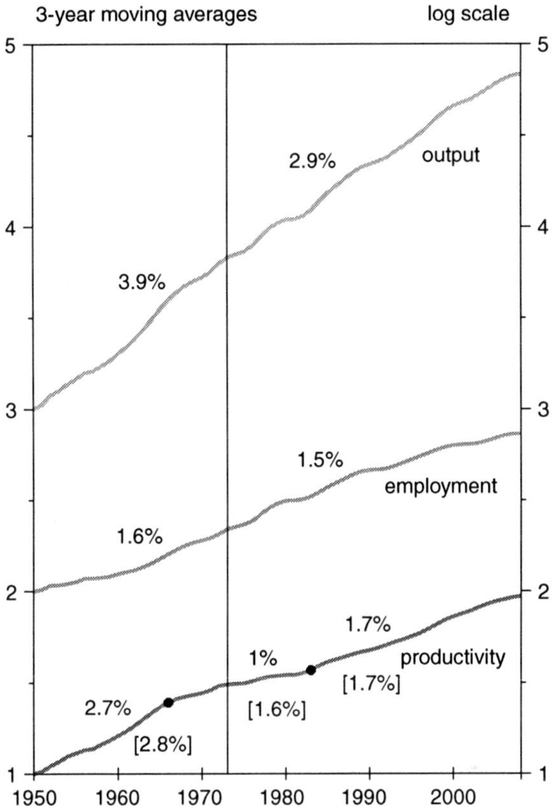

Three-year moving averages. Percentages shown in the graph are average annual real rates of growth in respective periods (1950–1973, and 1973–2008); however, as the productivity cycle was slightly different, the rates of growth for this variable are shown for the periods 1950–1966, 1966–1983, and 1983–2008; percentages in brackets correspond to productivity per-hour worked for the same periods.
Source: GGDC (2009).

between then and 2008) practically disappears when productivity is measured as output per hour-worked (rather than per worker).

Conclusions

In sum, in addition to Schumpeterian innovators in the new information technologies, some of the venture capital essential for their operations, and massive investment in infrastructure for telecommunications, what emerged during the period of 'installation' of the current techno-economic paradigm was also a new type of capitalism; one that is not only extremely unequal and highly rent-based, but also one in which large segments of the capitalist elite wanted to have all the benefits that capitalism could possibly offer them without having to struggle with the 'compulsions' that normally come with these benefits – while doing exactly the opposite to workers and small firms.[27]

In other words, what emerged during the latest period of 'installation' was a new type of capitalism characterized by the coexistence of the progressive elements of the 'installation' period with others 'not-so-progressive', characterized by large segments of the capitalist elite attempting to create an economic, political and social environment in which they could have their cake and eat it: call it 'neo-liberal neo-Darwinism'; i.e., a deliberate attempt (especially from financial capital, and from the 'mature' and the most polluting industries of the previous techno-economic paradigm) to create the economic and political environment best suited to the survival of the un-fittest – i.e., un-fittest vis-à-vis what was required for a successful 'deployment' of the new techno-economic paradigm.[28]

What also emerged was a new neo-liberal ideology that *de facto* provided the required legitimisation needed by financial groups and segments of productive capital both to block the necessary progressive transformations, and to identify and exploit every imaginable new source of rent – so that productive investment could become an optional extra on top of assured rent-earnings opportunities. It also provided the technologies of power with the required degree of sophistication for accomplishing the most remarkable 'dispossession feat' ever within a democracy.[29] It also provided the necessary façade of 'modernity', which, as Adorno reminded us, can easily be used as a disguise: 'Today the appeal to newness, of no matter what kind, provided only that it is archaic enough, has become universal' (1974, 85). Undoubtedly the key issue to understand is the role of democracy itself – especially the unmasking of the material basis for the 'spontaneous consensus-type of hegemony' that allowed all this.

It can even be argued that, when became unchallenged, post-industrial, 'geriatric' capitalism nearly brought to an end its specific cultural formation: the Enlightenment – especially that crucial aspect that requires the submission of all authority to the scrutiny of critical reason.

There are, of course, many lessons to be learned from the current financial crisis, such as those regarding the need for intelligent global and domestic financial regulation and effective capital controls in intrinsically unstable and fast-changing financial markets – Keynes argued strongly for an international financial and payments system that would insulate nations at least partially from the economic maladies of other nations, and from the predatory nature of international finance. This crisis also shows us the need for an economic environment that would favour 'stickers' rather than 'snatchers' (in Hicks' sense). However, the main lesson is that it exposed the high degree of toxicity of the neo-liberal ideology when it became uncontested and put to the test by an intrinsically rent-seeking capitalist élite, and by an intrinsically compliant political class. From this perspective, the roots of current financial crisis can be found in a mostly rent-seeking and politically unchallenged capitalist élite transforming neo-liberalism into a toxic ideology capable of generating a monsoon of toxic assets.

Yet, Perez (and those who look at this crisis from the perspective of repeated long technological cycles) tells us that things are bound to change for the better in the incoming phase of 'deployment' of the current techno-economic paradigm – a phase that normally follows the financial crisis and economic recession that usually marks the end of the 'installation' period. In the past, this new phase has been characterized mostly by the reversal of the relationship between financial and productive capital, which allows the latter to take the lead and unleash all the potential of the new technological paradigm – including the considerable 'creative destruction' forces of the 'deployment' phase.[30] And, in this reversal, productive capital can benefit enormously from the 'overinvestment' in new infrastructures (telecommunications) characteristic of the bubble during the 'installation' period (the dot-com bubble). In fact, periods of 'deployment' tend to bring about 'Golden Ages'.[31]

However, I think that this time this shift from the 'installation' to the successful 'deployment' phase may prove more complex than in previous techno-economic paradigms – and certainly more problematic than in the last one (1930s). Basically, this time capitalism faces a crisis 'without an enemy' – either from within (e.g., organized labour), or from the outside. That is, it is unlikely that FDR would have been able to carry out in the 1930s all the political and economic transformations that were necessary for a successful shift towards the 'deployment' period – including the necessary regulation of financial capital (not just to control its excesses, but also to help shift its orientation towards financing productive investment), the remarkable increase in the marginal rate of income taxation, and the movement towards a welfare state – without the combined threat of increased domestic instability and growing external challenge from the Soviet Union and Nazi Germany. In other words, the successful transformations of the 1930s had as much to do with the objective requirements of the 'deployment' period of the fourth technological paradigm (e.g., mass production needing mass consumption fuelled by a fast growing income of the bottom 90 per cent), as with the political imperative to come out of the recession. One provided the logic; the other facilitated its implementation (and hugely reduced the political and economic transaction costs of this transition).

The same goes for the remarkable common sense of the Bretton Woods accord and the rapid development of the welfare state in many industrialized countries after the Second World War – Keynes' task would have certainly been more difficult if the participants of that 1947 meeting at Bretton Woods had not desperately wanted some sanity after the madness of the war; and Churchill and his Conservative Party could have hardly offered unemployment, poverty and destitution to returning soldiers by completely opposing the welfare reforms of the new post-war Labour administration.

Furthermore, current problems are compounded by the fact that both financial and productive capital will probably emerge from the current crisis with an even higher degree of oligopolistic power. Therefore, it is difficult to imagine how it will be politically feasible for the state even to start doing the necessary 'disciplining' of the capitalist élite along the lines of increased 'compulsions' for big business (needed for a successful transformation of the process of accumulation from its current mostly rent-seeking nature to one based on increased productive capacities). In fact, in Foucault's terms, what is required even to start injecting some efficiency into the system is a shift from the current neo-liberal state of affairs – in which 'the state is under the surveillance of the market' – to a Keynesian one where 'it is the market that is under the surveillance of the state'.[32] Unless the severity of the current crisis is such that it finally ends up making an effective transition possible, perhaps the current technological paradigm will be remembered for the unique difficulties of its transition towards a successful 'deployment' phase – and for the length of time that was necessary in order to come out from the financial crisis that took place at the beginning of this transition.

So far, the signs are not very promising. The current economic crisis seems to be changing everything except the fundamental ways in which those in power and academia think about economics and politics. Perhaps nothing is more revealing in this regard than the delusion that showering money with little or no conditionality into the financial system (mostly rewarding 'principals' of financial institutions for their failure to oversee that their 'agents' run financial institutions in the shareholders' long-term interests) means that 'we are all Keynesians again'.[33] Or the prevailing idea that the current financial crisis does not represent the failure of both a whole model of banking and finance (in which an overgrown financial sector did an untold amount of harm), and of a whole model of policy-making (in which the fundamental role for the state ended up being one of a facilitator of the rent-seeking practices of big business).

In this respect, it is rather depressing to see how the current Geithner-Summers plan for rescuing the US financial system, and the Brown-Darling one for the British system, have as their underlying vision that the post-crisis financial system will be more or less the same as it was before the 2007-crisis, although somewhat tamed by prudent market-friendly regulations – and anyone who disagrees, of course, is just politically naïve. And (as supposedly the current crisis is just one of illiquidity and confidence) it is also depressing to see how their plan for getting from A to B consists just of easy money and a massive fiscal stimulus – so far, in the US alone the latter is worth US$12 trillion in terms of liquidity support and public guarantees, insurances and recapitalisations. So finance ministers and central bankers are prepared to become lenders of first and only resort, spenders of first and only resort, and insurers of first and last resort – but not financial architects of any resort.

References

Adorno, T. 1974. Minima Moralia: Reflections from Damaged Life. London: New Left Books.

Atkinson, A. B. 2007. 'The Distribution of Top Incomes in the United Kingdom, 1908–2000.' In A. B. Atkinson and T. Piketty (ed.). *Top Income Over the Twentieth Century: A Contrast between European and English-Speaking Countries.* Oxford: Oxford University Press.

Buiter, W. 2009. 'Can the UK Government Stop the UK Banking System Going down without Risking a Sovereign Debt Crisis?' *Financial Times*, 20 January 20.

Fed = Board of Governors of the Federal Reserve System of the United States of America. 2009. 'Flow Of Funds accounts of the United States.' Available at http://www.federalreserve.gov/datadownload/

Feldstein, M. 1995. 'The Effect of Marginal Tax Rates on Taxable Income: A Panel Study of the 1986 Tax Reform Act.' *Journal of Political Economy* 103, 551–572.

Foucault, M. 2004. *Naissance de la Biopolitique: Cours au Collège de France, 1978–1979.* Paris: Hautes Etudes, Gallimard Seuil.

Francis, D. R. 2008. 'Tax Havens in US Cross Hairs. With $345 Billion in Lost Revenue, Tolerance for off-Shore Avoidance Fades.' *CS Monitor*, 9 June.

Frangie, S. 2008. *The Good Governance Agenda, Weak States and Economic Development: The 'Political Economy of Consensus' in Post-Civil War Lebanon, 1993–2005.* PhD thesis, University of Cambridge.

GGDC. 2009. Groningen Growth and Development Centre Database. Available at http://www.ggdc.net, and http://www.conference-board.org/economics

Gordon, M. 2009. 'UBS Says 47,000 Accounts Held by Americans Avoiding Taxes.' *Associated Press*, 4 March.

Kalecki, M. 1943. 'Political Aspects of Full Employment.' *Political Quarterly* 14, 322–331.

Keynes, J. M. 1931. 'The Grand Slump of 1930.' In *Essays in Persuasion*. London: Macmillan, 135–147.

Khan, M. H. 2005. 'The Capitalist Transformation.' In K. S. Jomo and E. S. Reinert (eds). *The Origins of Development Economics: How Schools of Economic Thought Have Addressed Development.* Delhi: Tulika/London: Zed.

Krugman, P. 2007. 'Where's My Trickle?' *The New York Times*, 10 September.

———. 2009a. 'The Market Mystique.' *The New York Times*, 27 March.

———. 2009b. 'Health Care Showdown.' *The New York Times*, 22 June.

Lewis, M. 2009. 'Wall Street on the Tundra.' *Vanity Fair*, April. http://www.vanityfair.com/politics/features/2009/04/iceland200904

Markopolos, H. 2005. 'The World's Largest Hedge Fund Is A Fraud.' In Blodget, H. 'Busting Bernie Madoff: One Man's 10 Year Crusade.' *The Business Insider*, 17 December 2008. Available at http://www.businessinsider.com/2008/12/busting-bernie-madoff-one-mans-10-year-crusade

Marx, K. 1867. *Capital* 1. Available at http://www.marxists.org/archive/marx/works/1867-c1/index.htm

Palma, J. G. 2007. 'Globalising Inequality: The "Centrifugal" and "Centripetal" Forces at Work.' In K. S. Jomo (ed.). *Flat Worlds, Big Gaps*. London: Zed.

————. 2008a. 'From Fundamentalism to Idolatry: Why Mainstream Economics Switched from the "Worship of a Concept" (The Faultless Efficiency of Free Markets) to the "Worship of a Thing" (Mathematics).' Mimeo.

————. 2008b. 'De-Industrialisation, Premature De-Industrialisation and the Dutch Disease.' *The New Palgrave Dictionary of Economics*. 2nd edn. London: Palgrave Macmillan.

————. 2009a. 'Why Did the Latin American Critical Tradition in the Social Sciences Become Practically Extinct?' In M. Blyth (ed.). *The Handbook of International Political Economy*. London: Routledge, forthcoming.

————. 2009b. 'The Revenge of the Market on the Rentiers. Why Neo-Liberal Reports of the End of History Turned out to Be Premature.' *Cambridge Journal of Economics* 33, 829–869.

————. 2009c. 'Flying-Geese and Waddling-Ducks: The Different Capabilities of East Asia and Latin America to "Demand-Adapt" and "Supply-Upgrade" their Export Productive Capacity.' In J. E. Stiglitz, M. Cimoli and G. Dosi (eds). *Industrial Policy in Developing Countries*. New York: Oxford University Press.

Perez, C. 2002. *Technological Revolutions and Financial Capital: The Dynamics of Bubbles and Golden Ages*. Cheltenham: Edward Elgar. [74.1]

————. 2005. 'Respecialisation and the Deployment of the ICT Paradigm.' Working Paper, FISTERA (Foresight on Information Society Technologies in the European Research Area) Project. Seville: EU/IPTS. [77.1]

Piketty, T. and E. Sáez. 2003. 'Income Inequality in the United States, 1913–1998.' *Quarterly Journal of Economics* 118, 1–39. Data updated to 2006: http://berkeley.edu/~saez/TabFig2006.xls

Reilly, D. 2009. 'Banks' Hidden Junk Menaces $1 Trillion Purge.' *Bloomberg News*, 25 March. Available at http://www.bloomberg.com/apps/news?pid = 20601110&sid = akv_p6LBNIdw

Roubini, N. 2009. 'Ten Risks To Global Growth.' *Forbes*, 25 May. Available at http://www.forbes.com/2009/05/27/recession-depression-global-economy-growth-opinions-columnists-nouriel-roubini.html

Rove, K. 2009. 'Bush Was Right When It Mattered Most.' *Wall Street Journal*, 22 January.

Rusbridger, A. 2009. 'A Chill on "The Guardian".' *The New York Review of Books* 15 January–11 February.

Skidelsky, R. 2009. 'The Myth of the Business Cycle.' Project Syndicate, 22 January. Available at http://www.realclearmarkets.com/articles/2009/01/the_myth_of_the_business_cycle.html

Stiglitz, J. E. 2009. "Capitalist Fools." *Vanity Fair*, January. Available at http://www.vanityfair.com/magazine/2009/01/stiglitz200901

US Census Bureau. 2008. http://www.census.gov/compendia/statab/hist_stats.html

USA Today. 2009. 'Leap in U.S. debt hits taxpayers with 12% more red ink.' 29 May. Available at http://www.usatoday.com/news/washington/2009-05-28-debt_N.htm

Wall Street Journal. 2008. 'Madoff Misled SEC in '06, Got Off.' 18 December. Available at http://online.wsj.com/article/SB122956182184616625.html

Wood, E. M. 1999. 'The Politics of Capitalism.' *Monthly Review* 51. Available at http://www.monthlyreview.org/999wood.htm

World Bank. 2008. *World Development Indicators 2008*. Available at www.worldbank.org/data/wdi2005/index.html

Chapter Eighteen:

PRODUCTION-BASED ECONOMIC THEORY AND THE STAGES OF ECONOMIC DEVELOPMENT: FROM TACITUS TO CARLOTA PEREZ

Erik S. Reinert
Tallinn University of Technology
and
The Other Canon Foundation, Norway

'In every inquiry concerning the operations of men when united together in society, the first object of attention should be their mode of subsistence. Accordingly as that varies, their laws and policies must be different.'

William Robertson (1721–1793), *The History of America*, 1777.

The Idea of Stages

History – it has been said – was created to prevent everything from happening simultaneously.[1] History obviously implies that events happen in a sequence, and stage theories are attempts, based on different criteria, to organize the historical process in sequential stages. In their most general form, stage theories postulate that a key factor in the process of socioeconomic development is the mode of subsistence, i.e., what, how and with which tools a society produces. Stage theories are tools that can be used to study both the qualitative changes in the division of labour over time, and the processes of institutional design and change that accompany these changes. Stage theories point towards areas where the focus of human learning is concentrated at any point in time, and as such, they serve as a basis for a qualitative understanding of processes of techno-economic change and of income inequality. It is to this ancient tradition of organizing history that Carlota Perez has made the most original and path-breaking contribution of the last 100 years.

As I see it, understanding the qualitative differences between economic stages – the relationship between technology, social organization, and wealth – is a prerequisite for understanding, designing and implementing appropriate institutions and mechanisms both for the technology policy and for income distribution in a society. This general point is made by Joseph Schumpeter, who sees stage theories as 'a simple explanatory device for impressing upon beginners (or the public) the lesson that economic policy has to do with changing economic structures and therefore cannot consist of a set of unchanging recipes' (Schumpeter 1954, 442). This short phrase represents a strong critique of the 'one size fits all' development policies of the Washington Consensus over the last decades.[2]

Schumpeter is otherwise not very positive to the use of stage theories, which is somewhat surprising, because his 'long waves' essentially picture a similar phenomenon. In this chapter I argue that Carlota Perez, inspired by Schumpeter's long waves, has added the qualitative changes to organizational life and to society at large that are by-products of radical technological change. In doing this, I argue, her work is situated closer to that of the German Historical School, from which Schumpeter's thinking emerged, than to Schumpeter himself. By doing this, she has converted Schumpeter's 'long waves' of different growth intensities into 'great surges of development'. Her 'great surges', I argue, are very similar to the 'stage theories' of economic development that have their origins in antiquity, that played an important role during the formative period of classical economics, and survived well into the twentieth century in both German and US economics. When Schumpeter published the second edition of his *Theory of Economic Development* in 1926, he made the important decision of leaving out what in the first edition (Schumpeter 1912) had been chapter 7, 'The Economy as a Whole'. By putting back the effects of innovation and technological change to 'The Economy as a Whole' Carlota Perez has enriched the Schumpeterian tradition by bringing back the ideal of economics as embedded in, rather than separate from, society at large. The way academic fashion was moving at the time, Schumpeter made his 1912 book more 'trendy' by leaving out chapter 7. The fact that for some time the very idea of stages and 'modes of production' tended to be closely associated with Marxist economics may have deterred Schumpeter from embracing stages, but all this is only speculation.

Theories of periods and stages have been used in most of the social sciences. In the history profession the material from which Man's tools were made (e.g., stone or bronze) has become universally accepted as the basis for establishing early historical periods: the Stone Age (Mesolithic, Neolithic), the Bronze Age. Other criteria could have been used, e.g., based on social organization, but *the technology variable* was chosen. Not only in the history profession, but also in anthropology, the idea that technology is an important determinant for society is an old one; the discussion of the relationship between irrigation and centralized government being a classical example. In political science, the idea of stages of Man's development is born – with Jean Bodin's (1530–1596) study of the Republic – with the commencing of the science itself. If we define sociology as starting with Auguste Comte (1798–1857), the idea of stages was there from the very beginning of that science as well. In economics, theories of stages were central both to the important French economist and statesman Robert Jacques Turgot (1727–1781) and in the teachings of Adam Smith (1723–1790). In his book on the early stage theories from 1750 to 1800, Ronald Meek goes so far as to suggest that 'there was a certain sense ... in which the great eighteenth-century systems of 'classical' political economy in fact *arose out* of the four stage theories' (Meek 1976, 219). In spite of this, the idea of economic stages grew more and more peripheral after 1900, only to be revived by Carlota Perez and her partner Christopher Freeman starting in the 1980s.

Incipient ideas of stage theories are found in antiquity, both in Greece and in Rome. One may read Tacitus' (55?-after 117 AD) *Germania* in such a way that 'the relative degree of civilization of the different German tribes depended upon the extent to which agriculture and pasturage, rather than hunting, preponderated in their mode of subsistence' (Meek 1976, 12). The idea of stages grew out of the idea of cycles, which in political history is an old one. Cycle theories are given importance both by the influential Arab historian Ibn-Khaldun (1332–1406) and by Machiavelli (1469–1527). With Jean Bodin, one of the path-breakers of the Renaissance, comes the idea that historical cycles may have a cumulative and upward trend: the idea of progress. With Bodin, the idea of progressive stages is born as a child of the optimistic spirit of the Renaissance. Bodin, at the same time, discusses the embryonic nation-state (the Republic), its institutions, laws and taxation.

Whereas Bodin puts much emphasis on geographical and climatic conditions, Francis Bacon (1561–1626) in his *Novum Organum* gives a different explanation when discussing the startling difference between the conditions of life in the various parts of the world. Bacon postulates that 'this difference comes not from soil, not from climate, not from race, but from the arts.'[3] Bacon is probably the true founder of what we shall label the production-based and activity-specific theory of economic welfare. As we shall see, his idea that the material condition of a people is determined by its arts – i.e., by the professions exercised – is central to the nineteenth century German and North American conflict with England over economic theory and industrial policy.

During the Enlightenment, particularly between 1750 and 1800, stage theories were – so to say – at centre stage, particularly in England and France. During the expansion and geographical extension of industrial society from the 1840s onward, stage theories again became part of the economists' toolbox – this time particularly in the US and Germany. At the time, the fundamental changes that could be observed made it obvious that the world was entering a historical period that was qualitatively different from all previous ones.

The stage theories born during the First Industrial Revolution – those of Turgot and of the early Adam Smith teaching in the 1750s – follow Man first as a hunter and gatherer, then as a shepherd of domesticated animals, then as a farmer, finally to reach the stage of commerce. Most significantly, English classical economists tended from the late eighteenth century on to concentrate their analysis on the last stage of evolution, on commerce – on supply and demand and on prices – rather than on production. A German economist at the time wryly commented that English economists looked upon the economy as a kind of 'freight terminal' of goods already produced. During the nineteenth century, German and US economists insisted on a very different interpretation of the development stages. To them, the previous stages were all built on ways of producing goods, and they saw it as a grave mistake to classify the next stage of development in terms of commerce rather than in terms of production. This theoretical difference of opinion essentially laid the foundation for how nineteenth-century German and US economic policy came to differ from that prescribed by English theory.

English Stage Theories (Eighteenth Century) (Adam Smith)	German/US Stage Theories (Nineteenth Century) (Friedrich List/Richard Ely)
1. Age of Hunters	1. Age of Hunting
2. Age of Shepherds	2. Age of Pasturage
3. Age of Agriculture	3. Age of Agriculture
4. Age of Commerce	4. Age of Agriculture and Manufacturing

This kind of stage theories is useful, also, in order to understand the important issues of population and sustainable development. The pre-Columbian population of North America – consisting essentially of hunters and gatherers – has been estimated as low as 3 million people, whereas the pre-Columbian population of the Andes, having reached the agricultural stage, has been calculated at 12 million. This gives a population density 30–40 times higher in the apparently inhospitable Andes than on the fertile prairies. The concept of sustainability is not very meaningful until the technology variable is introduced.

Because the focus of analysis was to be trade and commerce, and not production, English and, later, neoclassical economic theory slowly came to see all economic activities as being qualitatively alike. One example of this is David Ricardo's trade theory, upon which our present world order rests, which models world trade as bartering labour hours, be they in the Stone Age or in Silicon Valley. Theories of production which were later added into this Anglo-Saxon tradition of economics – today's standard theory – essentially came to regard production as a process of adding capital to labour in a rather mechanical way, similar to that of adding water to genetically identical plants growing under identical conditions. In this theoretical tradition, no considerations are made as to how the availability of technology varies the potential which different activities – at any point in time – present in terms of adding capital to labour in a potentially profitable way. The standard economics tradition also came to disregard completely the 'soil' in which the process of adding water to the plant (capital to labour) took place, i.e., the historical, political and institutional context of the process of development. Standard economic theory considers neither the obvious focusing of technical change at any point in time, i.e., the extreme variation in what Carlota Perez calls 'windows of opportunity' between different economic activities resulting from this changing focus, nor the context in which this process takes place. In my view, this blind spot of conventional economic theory is a major cause of our failure to come to grips with the extremely inequitable distribution of income on a world scale.

Classical, neo-classical and today's standard economics all stand in sharp contrast to the German/US tradition – which we can say lasted until and including the theories of Simon Kuznets (1901–1985) – in which economic growth is seen as activity specific, i.e., the potential to create wealth varies enormously between economic activities. In this setting, stage theories serve as a focusing devise which singles out the area of human activity where learning was focused, pointing at the frontier of human learning. As I have argued elsewhere (Reinert 2007, chapter 3), emulating the nations at the frontier of knowledge – protecting and nourishing the activities of the ruling techno-economic paradigm – has been the mandatory passage point through which all presently wealthy nations have passed before converting to a strategy of 'comparative advantage'.

In 1949 Paul Samuelson – using the standard assumptions of neo-classical economic theory – showed that international trade would lead towards an equalization of wages all over the world (factor-prize equalization). In the alternative German/US production-based tradition, the equalization of wages between a society solely specialised in herding animals – in pasturage – trading with one specialised in advanced industrial production is an absurd proposition. Because the core of its theory was based on barter rather than production, neoclassical economics created what Lionel Robbins has called a *Harmonielehre* (Robbins 1952, 22–29) – a theory of automatic harmony – where free trade automatically tended to create an equalization of wages throughout the world economy, regardless of the economic activity in which the nation specializes. In my opinion, it is difficult to overestimate the fundamental importance of the late seventeenth-century schism in economic theory that was created by the two different interpretations of the next stage in Man's evolution. Whether one saw this next stage as the *Age of Commerce* – thus creating barter-based theory – or as the *Age of Agriculture and Manufacturing* – creating a production-based theory – resulted in completely different *Weltanschauungen* and in completely different ideas on what causes economic development and welfare.

Francis Bacon was essentially right: the choice of profession still determines the way of life more than do geography, climate, race or religion. Andean pastoral societies are organised in a way similar to Saami reindeer herders in Northern Fenno-Scandia. The basic pre-Columbian social organization in the Andes, the *Ayllu*, is very similar to the Saami *Siida*, a type of society that the German stage theorists called *Sippenwirtschaft* or Clan Economy. Similarly, a stockbroker in Lima, Peru will have a lifestyle that has much more in common with a stockbroker in Oslo than with a Peruvian who makes his living cutting sugar cane. This activity-specific aspect of economic life has, however, been lost in today's standard textbook economics. Today's world economic order essentially functions on the assumption that in a world of free trade, a nation of cane cutters will be as wealthy as a nation of stockbrokers. As already indicated, I feel that the loss of Bacon's insight accounts for our inability to understand the unequal distribution of wealth on a world scale. In other words, our incomplete understanding of production is at the core of our inability to understand income inequalities. Carlota Perez' work has assisted in re-Baconizing economics: moving its base away from abstract assumptions towards observations of empirically based facts.[4]

Stage theories are 'ideal types' in a Weberian sense. In Kaldor's terminology, each stage would constitute a cluster of 'stylized facts' about one particular type of society. Fixed points of transition between stages are, of course, not easily established. Points of transition between childhood, adult life and old age are equally difficult to establish, but few would argue that this problem makes 'childhood' and 'old age' useless concepts. Stage theories are not iron laws, and there are no automatic mechanisms that carry nations from one stage to the next. During the nineteenth and early twentieth century both conservatives and Marxists saw the spread of industrial society across the globe as an inevitable process. The last 50 years have taught us otherwise. Not only is there no automatic upgrading and promotion in the system, the possibilities of being downgraded, of 'falling behind' in Moses Abramowitz' framework, are definitely present. There are also instances when the historical sequence is different; before having tamed animals, American Indian women of some tribes were growing a few plants of corn around their dwellings. Keeping all the limitations of stage theories in mind, however, they constitute an instrument that deserves being put back into the tool shed of economic theory.

Today the world economy is well into a transition from a society based on Fordist mass production to a society where information technology sets the standard, and – as Carlota Perez has argued – on which a new organizational common sense has been created. With their concept of techno-economic paradigms, Carlota Perez and Christopher Freeman offer us an analysis within what List and Ely would call the manufacturing stage. Alternatively, it may be argued that the incipient information society with its dematerialization of consumption represents a brand new fifth stage in the history of mankind. German economist Karl Bücher treated the geographical dimension of this transition – globalization – already in his book *Die Entstehung der Volkswirtschaft* first published in 1893 (Bücher 1919a).

Stages, Postmodernity, and Harmony in Economic Theory

Profound changes in the structure of society seem, then, to create a demand for broader perspectives, for a qualitative and dynamic understanding of 'the bigger issues'. In the history profession, the present paradigm shift has again recently awoken interest in 'global history', including a journal dedicated to the issue. Although the idea of global history is easy to dismiss from the depths of archival studies, long-term history has a professional tradition dating back to the Renaissance and is still seen as compatible with the tools that historians use. During the nineteenth-century process of industrialization, also in the economics profession, theories of economic stages were seen as 'an indispensable part of the toolbox of economics'.[5]

From the standpoint of today's standard theory, however, stage theories bring together three key aspects which were the most important casualties of the neoclassical process of formalizing economic theory, i.e., the three conspicuously absent factors: time, space (geography) and human knowledge. In today's economics there is no longer such a compatibility with stage theories as can be found in the history profession. Standard economic theory is fundamentally quantitative, static and ahistorical, and the historical school of economics – which had produced the nineteenth-century stage theories – virtually died out with the 1950s. In the first section of this paper I have already pointed to a most important watershed in economic theory: how and when the English classical school – by no longer defining stages according to production – separates itself from previous economic tradition and from nineteenth-century US and German economic theory and policy. As I see it, this schism is of great importance in order to understand the economics of 'leader' and 'laggard' nations to this very day. My 2007 book *How Rich Countries got Rich … and Why Poor Countries Stay Poor* employs Carlota Perez' stage theories in proposing a theory of global uneven development.

Stage theories are typically not products of Anglo-Saxon economics, where Adam Smith brought production and trade together into the category of 'labour hours'. This, in turn, made it possible for David Ricardo to construct the trade theory upon which our present world order rests: The world economy is modelled on the bartering of qualitatively identical labour hours. This made the present abstraction from production possible. Stage theories, on the other hand, are all children of a dynamic and holistic, all-inclusive view of economics as involving all social sciences. Stage theories are dynamic and *modernist* in the sense that the Renaissance philosophers, like Francis Bacon in England and Leibniz in Germany, were modernists. A stage theory in the neoclassical tradition of Paul Samuelson would be a contradiction in terms, because this is a theory void not only of time (and consequently of any historical sequence), but also largely of empirical facts from the realm of production.

As opposed to *modernist* dynamism and its resulting 'stages' – cumulative, progressive, retrogressive or cyclical – neoclassical economics, containing no learning and no novelty, has clear *postmodernist* qualities[6]. Neoclassical economics with its innumerable equilibrium points takes on a quality of indeterminacy, of 'undecidability', which is seen as typical also of postmodernist poetry; of Gertrude Stein and Ezra Pound.[7] Like postmodernist poetry, the neoclassical world view seems to describe a world where 'innovation no longer seems possible, or even desirable.'[8] When their extreme static generalizations and determinacy – like factor-price equalization – are queried, today's standard economists tend to retreat to the opposite standpoint, to the extreme unpredictability of theories of complexity and chaos theory. From the safe haven of a theory predicting and proving automatic universal harmony in the equalization of factor prices – a *Harmonielehre* – standard economic theory at times retreats to the opposite extreme, to a model with a complete lack of predictability. In other words, modern economics tends to treat all economic activities as either being qualitatively *all alike* or *all different*. The intermediate levels of abstraction – where 'some economic activities are more equal than others' (with apologies to George Orwell) – which offer clues to understanding world income distribution, are generally absent. Frank Graham's 1923 model, which will be discussed later in this chapter, is an example of the middle level of abstraction that is often missing today.

Today's equivalent of the 'invisible hand' is that 'the economy is like the weather', or like hurricanes and earthquakes (Krugman 1996). These two types of metaphors are, in a sense, opposites – the automatic harmony and predictability created by the 'invisible hand' on the one hand, and the chaotic complex diversity created by the weather on the other. What is interesting from the point of view of economic policy is that these counterpart metaphors lead to the same policy conclusions: in both cases Man is at the mercy of some uncontrollable force. Both in the case of the invisible hand and of hurricanes and earthquakes, human will, skills, knowledge, intuition and leadership can do precious little to change the course of history. Adam Smith's invisible hand and Paul Krugman's metaphor about the economy being like the weather at their very core share the role of man as a passive being in the hands of 'Providence', as is discussed in Jacob Viner's interesting book on this subject.[9]

In contrast to this strategy, where a passive Man is at the mercy of external forces – be they invisible hands or the forces of the weather – stand the stage theories, where history is 'the result of human action, but not the execution of any human design'.[10] The contrast with Krugman, when he describes the great Depression, is clear: '…most booms and slumps have had no obvious external cause. Most notably, the mother of all economic slumps, the contraction from 1929 to 1933, came as it were out of a clear blue sky. But then, so do hurricanes.' Krugman's alternative metaphor, if there is no such thing as a 'typical recession', is that 'recessions are more like earthquakes than like hurricanes.' (Krugman 1996, 5) It seems that Krugman considers economic slumps to be outside the influence of human beings, just like hurricanes or earthquakes. Just as with Adam Smith's invisible hand, Mankind is again, in Krugman's world view, at the mercy of a pre-Renaissance type of 'Providence' or 'Faith'. *Entzauberung* – the *de*-mystification of the world as a prerequisite for development – almost yields to *re*-mystification or *Wiederverzauberung* of mainstream economics.

The idea that neoclassical economics is postmodernist is not new. According to McCloskey, Friedman's 1953 essay 'was more postmodernist than one might suppose from slight acquaintance with the text' (McCloskey 1985, 9) or, as another author puts it, 'Postmodernism is immanent in modern economics.'[11] Postmodernism and standard economics indeed seem to meet in their quality of static 'undecidability' – in contrast to the cumulative dynamics of the historical school of economics. Krugman's 1996 book makes economics into *dynamic* undecidability. The contrast between this 'postmodernist' standard economics of today and the 'modernist' historical school can be traced back through the centuries to their very origins; to the Renaissance and the Enlightenment respectively.[12] Standard economic theory is an exaggeration of the mechanical and quantifiable view of the world representing the least constructive elements of the Enlightenment, the mechanization of the world picture. Here aporia (indecision) is a result of a rationality that, in the absence of novelty, 'will eventually enslave us to rules' (McCloskey 1985, 72). Stage theories, on the other hand, are products of the Renaissance where new ideas, knowledge and leadership move history along, building and un-building structures and stages in a Schumpeterian process of creative destruction.

Stage theories are typical products of German economic theory,[13] of a type of theory which Werner Sombart (Sombart 1928) calls *verstehende*, as opposed to *ordnende* economic theory, or what Nelson and Winter (Nelson and Winter 1982) call *appreciative economics*. Perez clearly writes in this tradition. Such theories were at the core of German economics, but were also influential in the United States in the period when US economics was heavily influenced by German economics, a period which ended after WW II. Before 1900, most US economists were educated in Germany. Stage theories are framed in an attitude of *Zuerst war die Ganzheit:* in the beginning there was 'the whole', from a time where reality was still interpreted as obviously being interdisciplinary, from before scientists started fragmenting their approach to the world around them into different professions with scant communication between them. In this holistic approach to economics, whatever seems relevant – regardless of what academic tribe a particular fact narrowly belongs to – is part of that profession. If, for example, it seems that nutrition in a particular time and place seems important for economic development, then the relevant part of nutritional theory is most obviously a part of economics. As is readily admitted by philosophers of economics today, this type of qualitative understanding has been lost in post-WW II economics: 'Scientism has damaged the ability to understand' (McCloskey 1985, 50).

The stage theories – as well as traditional German economics in general – also internalize what Alfred Chandler (1990) put on the map of business economics in 1990: scale and scope. Stage theories are theories of non-equilibrium economics. They are fundamentally histories of various aspects of the cumulative growth of human knowledge – of novelty – and its impact on *division of labour and its impact on scale, scope and geography* of economies over time.

It would probably be correct to say that stage theories are all *economic interpretations of history*, although they may not all be *materialistic interpretations of history* in the Marxian sense. Edwin Seligman, the American social scientist, defined the economic interpretation of history as follows: 'We understand, then, by the theory of the economic interpretation of history, not that all history is to be explained in economic terms alone, but that the chief considerations in human progress are the social considerations, and that the important factor in the social change is the economic factor. The economic interpretation of history means not that the economic relations exert an exclusive influence, but that they exert a preponderant influence in shaping the progress of society' (quoted in Ely 1903, 25–26). Marx and Engels focused on one particular aspect of the economic stages, on the conflict between social classes. As we shall see, this is only one of many aspects of which stage theories lend themselves to analysis.

I personally tend to look at both the economics profession and political development in general as having been stuck now during more than 100 years in an unrelenting fight between what, with time, no doubt will be seen as two very strange and unproductive theoretical angles. One set of theories, what we call today's 'standard theory', which, because it was fundamentally based on barter, created a theory of automatic social and economic harmony. In this theoretical model all economic activities are alike, and free trade will tend to equalize the factor prices across the world. The other set of theories – the Marxist ones – focused on one particular aspect of the economic stages, on the fight between the social classes, and on a perceived inherent impossibility of social and economic harmony, except in a hypothetical stage following the dictatorship of the proletariat. During the nineteenth century a third set of economic theories claimed that it was not primarily the economic system that caused social injustice, but rather the extra-economic, political and social factors that intervene in all economic processes. Existing property relationships, and the consequent class struggles, were seen to be the result of historical-political development, not an automatic outcome of the mode of production itself. Social and economic harmony could be *created* under any mode of production, but this required conscious design of economic institutions, of trade policy and of elaborate mechanisms of income distribution. Main theorists in this third, now defunct, type of economic theory were Henry Carey in the United States and Friedrich List and Eugen Dühring in Germany. Their view corresponds today to Carlota Perez' interpretation of the social challenges as the world economy moves away from the Fordist mass-production stage of economic development and into a new stage based on information technology (Perez 2002, Perez 2004).

The alternative nineteenth century economic theories – the 'Third Way' – which refused both English classical, Anglo-Saxon neoclassical economics and Marxism, became in very short supply during the Cold War period following World War II. Ricardian economics came to dominate the whole political axis from left to right, making the Cold War into a civil war between different fractions of Ricardian economics. Social democrats tended to convert to neoclassical mainstream economics, and the theories that had built social democracy – originating in the German *Verein für Sozialpolitik* or 'Organization for Social Policy' (1872–1932) – died out. Alternative 'Third Way' theories partly continued to live on in the pragmatic economic policies of social democracy, but the economic theory of social democracy most unfortunately too often became neoclassical economics. This made it virtually impossible to export practically functioning social democracy to the Third World – the production-based theories which were at the roots of the political 'Third Way' had been unlearned by the economics profession as barter-based, neoclassical economics took over. The 2008 financial crisis made the absence of less abstract and more empirically based economic theory evident once again.

Anthropocentric Economics: *Man and His Needs* as the Core of Economics

Karl Bücher's *Die Entstehung der Volkswirtschaft* (The Genesis (or Formation) of the National Economy), first published in 1893, is a classical stage theory book written in the German tradition. Just like Carlota Perez' work, it focuses on different technological systems of production rather than on trade. On fundamental points Bücher's and Perez' books are in strong conflict with the world view represented by standard Anglo-Saxon economics, the brand of economics which completely dominates in 'the global village' of today. While public opinion today is increasingly worried about maintaining the biological diversity of the planet – opposing cloning – few seem to care about the lack of diversity in approaches to economics. The coming of the financial crisis – seen only by a few economists knowing the work of Hyman Minsky – amply testifies to the risk of theoretical monoculture. In their core assumptions about what their profession is all about, virtually all of today's living economists are cloned in a mode of thinking which is fundamentally different from that of Bücher's and Perez' production-based tradition. I shall here briefly contrast Bücher's conception of economics with that of today's barter-based economics.

First of all, the very title of the book – The Genesis of the National Economy – is an affront to English economics at the time (and later, as in Margaret Thatcher's phrase, 'There is no such thing as society.'). In German economics, the *Volkswirtschaft* – the National Economy – is a fundamental unit of analysis, while, as Friedrich List pointed out, English economics is *cosmo*political economics. The factors that cause the nation-state to be of any importance tend to be assumed away in English economic theory as well as later in neoclassical and today's standard theories. The core assumptions of Anglo-Saxon economics tend to create automatic harmony and equilibrium, but it is probably fair to say that this end product of harmony is already built into the assumptions on which the theory is based. One basic assumption creating social harmony in neoclassical theory is the fact that neoclassical economics made all economic activities qualitatively alike as carriers of economic development. This is what Buchanan calls *the equality assumption*, without which mainstream economics would lose its analytical power. Like all stage theories, Bücher's theory functions at a different, and lower, level of abstraction. Compared to mainstream economics, Bücher and Perez are both *praxisnah* – near to reality. Bücher scorns what he sees as '*die verschimmelte Schulweisheiten*' – the mouldy school truths – of theoretical economics (Bücher 1919b, 197), and I know Carlota would agree to this term.

Secondly, as already mentioned, English economics was fundamentally a theory of *barter*, and not of *production*.[14] Very early in his *Wealth of Nations*, Adam

Smith defines 'his propensity to barter' as the main difference between Man and other animals (Smith 1976, 17). Bücher goes very clearly against Smith on this: 'Primitive Man, rather than having a innate propensity to barter, has – to the contrary – a propensity against bartering (*eine Abneigung*).' In the old language, Bücher says, the verbs for *barter* (*tauschen*) and *cheat* (*täuschen*) are the same. There is plenty of evidence to support the idea that trading was an occupation of very low prestige in many ancient cultures. On discovering that his wife owned a ship trading grain, one Byzantine emperor had the whole ship and its cargo burned in order to distance himself as much as possible from such 'vulgar' activities (Nicol 1990). We can assume that with 'imperfect information' and few standard methods for measuring value existing, early bartering carried with it a high risk of being cheated. Anthropological research into processes of barter points to stable value relationships existing over long periods of time, e.g., 'a sheep for a sack of potatoes'. Bücher mentions, however, von Thünen as a German economist who in his *Isolierte Staat* starts from the assumption of a barter economy (Bücher 1919a, 90). This makes it natural that von Thünen – out of a huge number of German economists who wrote on economics and geography – is quoted in Paul Krugman's papers on economics and geography. However, also von Thünen saw the need for protecting the city activities – the increasing returns activities – in his 'isolated state'. Von Thünen was also quoted by the Nobel Committee when Krugman received the Swedish Central Bank's Prize in the Memory of Alfred Nobel in 2008.

To Adam Smith, then, 'in the beginning there were barter and markets'; to Karl Bücher, 'in the beginning there were production and social relations'. To Bücher – as well as later to Karl Polanyi (Polanyi 1944) who was inspired by him – during the early stages of civilization the processes of production and consumption are so intertwined that the concept of barter makes no sense. As already mentioned, I consider the neglect of production – combined with *the equality assumption* discussed above – to be the main reason why Anglo-Saxon economics produces theories of harmony, like Samuelson's factor-price equalization. Standard economic theory ignores (1) the difference between production processes in their ability to absorb new knowledge and (2) the historical increasing returns that are created by this new knowledge, producing a 'national rent' to economies engaged in the economic activities which carry the new economic stage or techno-economic paradigm.

Thirdly, Bücher squarely places himself in the German tradition of Christian Wolff (1679–1754), in which the Human Being and its Needs (*Der Mensch und seine Bedürfnisse*) are at the core of economic theory. This contrasts with English theory, which came to be built around a utility-maximizing Homo Economicus. Bücher's definition of *Volkswirtschaft*, which includes also all institutional aspects of economic life, shows this clearly: '*Die Gesamtheit der*

Veranstaltungen, Einrichtungen und Vorgänge, welche die Bedürfnisbefriedigung eines ganzen Volkes hervorruft, bildet die Volkswirtschaft (Bücher 1919a, 85), which I would attempt, not quite literally, to translate as 'The totality of institutions, measures and processes which are called upon to satisfy the needs of a nation form the National Economy.' It is evident that both policy and law – founded in national institutions, measures, and processes – are at the core of the National Economy in Bücher's system. The concept of a National Innovation System, originating with Christopher Freeman, fits neatly with Bücher's conception of a *Volkswirtschaft*.

This third contrast is why we call classical German economics *anthropocentric* economics, rather than the *barter- and capital-centred* English political economy. In the Anglo-Saxon tradition the Human Being is generally reduced to being a factor of production – an input. In the German and continental tradition meeting the needs of this factor of production was the whole object of the exercise of economics, whereas in Anglo-Saxon tradition the reward to the Human Being as a factor of production is hardly an issue other than a 'cost'.

Stage Theories and Economic Development: An Overview

Early Theories – from Cycles to Stages

When trying to put order in the concept of time, the idea of ordering history chronologically obviously suggests itself. A system of ordering periods according to the rulers of the reign also seems a 'natural' system. The idea that human history alternatively may be divided into *qualitatively different periods* or *stages* has been with us since the Bible. Mankind's first stage, Paradise, gives way to a period when Man shall only eat his bread 'in the sweat of his face' (Genesis 3: 19). In this first 'stage theory' there is no natural improvement from one stage to the next, there is indeed a qualitative retrogression. Only towards the end of his stay on Earth may Mankind again aspire to repossess the qualities that he was forced to leave behind in the first stage.

As I have already mentioned, the idea of dividing human history into qualitatively different stages was essentially born with the idea of progress itself, with the Renaissance. The idea of the Renaissance – Rebirth – was itself a consequence of an acute awareness of retrogression: Mankind, compared to previous achievements, had 'fallen behind', but could 'forge ahead' if a social system encouraging and ordering Man's creativity could be created. Jean Bodin (1530–1596), French, and Hugo Grotius (1583–1645), Dutch – both lawyers – share a historical view emphasising changing division of labour in different historical periods. (Kuczynski 1978, 69–71). The first division of labour, as Bücher would point out, was that inside the household, between husbandry and what was for a long time called housewifery. The very name 'economics', of course, comes from a Greek word describing this 'household management'. The idea of a further division of labour is found in Plato's *Republic* and *Laws* and, less spelt out, in Aristotle's *Ideal City*.[15] Grotius sees the first division as being between agriculture and husbandry (Kuczynski 1978, 71).[16]

Stage theories of history differ from their predecessors – cyclical theories of history – in that they offer continuous improvement as a possibility, but not as a necessary outcome. In all stage theories it is understood that different areas of the world will normally be at different stages, and some of them specify the possibility for retrogression.

The fourteenth century is considered a 'dark' age in most of Europe, except for an early Renaissance blooming in Sienna. This century produced a prolific Muslim historian and philosopher, Ibn-Khaldun (1332–1406, called Abenjaldún in the Spanish literature). Born in Tunisia, and serving various of the potentates who divided Muslim North Africa and Spain between them, Ibn-Khaldun served as a professor of law and a judge in Cairo. Based on the studies of the Arab peoples, he emphasizes the distinction between nomads and town dwellers, but – typically of pre-Renaissance thought – he saw history developing in cycles, advancing only to later fall back to the previous stage. Ibn-Khaldun describes the nomadic tribes of the desert, organized in clans originating in blood relationships. The cycle of human societies is described as follows:

'The need for justice in the clan causes leaders to arise, and when the groups become sufficiently numerous, they migrate to fertile lands and ultimately change into town dwellers or subdue already existing town communities, adopting the previously established civilization. The town dwellers become luxurious and lose their capacity for self-defence. The rulers, as their wants increase, must resort to constantly increasing taxation; and resenting the claims of their clansmen to equality with themselves they rely for aid on foreign supporters, who become necessary moreover because of the decline of clansmen as warriors. Thus the state grows decrepit and becomes the prey of a fresh group of nomads, who undergo the same experience' (Margoliouth 1932, 564–565).

Ibn-Khaldun fixes the duration of the cycle of human societies to 120 years, or 4 generations of 30 years. In the fourteenth century Ibn-Khaldun describes societal retrogression based on a mechanism similar to the one described by Michael Porter in his 1990 book *The Competitive Advantage of Nations*. Porter's cycle of retrogression is described below. The Perez-Freeman framework of techno-economic paradigms also expressly includes the possibility that a paradigm shift not only opens windows of opportunity for improvement, but also opens 'a back door' which leaves some nations to fall behind. In today's process of globalization, the possibilities of retrogression merit, in my view, a much closer scrutiny (Reinert 2007, Ch. 5).

Pre-Renaissance Europe was acutely aware of the historical cycles of violence that would operate. During the Renaissance, therefore, an important argument was that economic growth was a way of channelling Man's energy away from warfare and destruction and into wealth creation.[17] Created in the image of God, it was Man's pleasurable duty to invent, to continue the creation that the Lord had initiated (Reinert and Daastøl 1997, 233–283). Today's Africa reminds us of the possibility of retrogression; we observe genocides of shattering cruelty, the collapse of nation-states and 'Somalization' of nations into fiefdoms run by warlords. In a way we are reinventing 'private colonialism', with today's mining companies operating with private armies in ways similar to Sir Walter Raleigh's during the times of Elizabeth I.

Underlying all stage theories is a more or less well-expressed tendency towards an ever-increasing division of labour. Within this framework, the stage theories focus on different aspects, which I shall discuss in detail later. Friedrich List focused on the type of production, Karl Bücher on the geographical dimension, Karl Marx on the social conflicts, Bruno Hildebrand on a trend towards a more abstract system of payments, and Carlota Perez and Christopher Freeman today focus on the technological aspects. As Richard Ely (1903) and Franz Oppenheimer (1923) point out, these approaches are highly complementary and correlated; they focus on different aspects of the same process of development or what some authors used to call 'modernization'.

Stage theories, then, are theories chartering the *degree of division of labour* and *core technologies* over time. Until the fall of Fordism, it is probably fair to say that this degree of division of labour was accompanied by ever-increasing scale of production in ever-larger units of production. Post-Fordism opens up a potential for increasing returns in very small niches, thereby simultaneously reducing the scale of operations and increasing variety through flexible specialization. However, if our unit of analysis is division of labour – not scale – post-Fordism continues the trend from the ancient household economy until today.

By tracing the degree of division of labour as human knowledge advances, stage theories also trace the minimum efficient size of human societies, from the household economy, via town economies and national economies, to the global economies. The division of labour – although it is probably the most celebrated of all Adam Smith's concepts – finds no place either in classical or neoclassical economics. As we shall discuss later, we have today no theory of the division of labour. In my view, this is because the division of labour is essentially a tool of production-based economics, of mercantilism. As early as in 1613 Antonio Serra used the division of labour in order to divide activities into those subject to increasing returns[18] – which caused wealth – and other activities, which kept states in poverty. To Serra increasing returns and a high degree of division of labour were both at the basis of the synergy which mercantilist economists called The Common Weal (*Das Gemeinwohl, il bene comune*). Frank Graham's 1923 model, referred to later, is built on the same principle as Serra's.

The division of labour is fundamentally based on the existence of fixed costs – either in tools or in human knowledge – which create synergies. Mercantilists would consistently refer to economic policies, e.g., the establishment of factories, which was done to 'promote the common weal'. The increase in the common weal was, in my view, caused by increasing returns from an ever-greater division of labour driven to a large extent by mechanization. The assumption of constant returns to scale – which in practice denies the existence of fixed costs – is at the core of the individualist Anglo-Saxon approach to economics. The inclusion of the division of labour and also its consequences causes German economics to naturally include society – as nations and/or labour markets – as well as the individual in economic theory.

To Bücher, stage theories are 'the only way that economic theory may make use of the research of economic history'. But, these stages of development must not be confused with the periods in which the historian divides his material. 'The historian must not in any period forget any important aspects of the period he studies, whereas the stages of the theoretician only have to cover what was normal.' In these aspects it seems to me that Bücher's stages have much in common with Perez and Freeman's techno-economic paradigms. Bücher and Perez both emphasize what Bücher calls 'the so called periods of transition (*Übergangsperioden*) when everything is in flux (*wenn alle Erscheinungen sich im Flusse befinden*)'.

Friedrich List and Bruno Hildebrand – The First Modern Stage Theories (1840s)

Bücher himself (1919a, 88) lists two alternative stage theories, those of Friedrich List and Bruno Hildebrand. The first stage theory in German economics was that of List, as already mentioned in this chapter. List divides history in the following stages: (1) The hunting period, (2) The pastoral period, (3) The farming period, (4) The agricultural-manufacturing period and (5) The agricultural-manufacturing-trading period. Another similar early stage theory was that of Carl Rodbertus-Jagetzow.[19]

Bruno Hildebrand, the first economist of the German Historical School, uses the mode of exchange as his criterion for the establishment of stages. His stages are: natural economy, money economy, and credit economy.[20] The theory as such was published in 1864, but the fundamental ideas are already in

Hildebrand's 1848 book *Economics at Present and in the Future (Die Nationalökonomie der Gegenwart und Zukunft)*. The revolutionary date 1848 puts his theory into the right perspective; it was a contribution to address the social problems of the day. Whereas Marx and Engels wanted to turn the social pyramid upside down, Hildebrand wants to make *Bürger* out of the workers. In this sense his agenda is very similar to that of Eugen Dühring, who some years later also sees the de-proletarization (*Entproletarisierung*) of the workers as the only solution to the social problems of the day.

Hildebrand sees the natural economy as a system that keeps Man to the cultivation of the soil. The creation of a money economy was a necessary condition for a division of labour, and consequently for the market economy which freed Man from toiling the ground. This development would not have been possible if money had not been available as a way to store value and as a common denominator of value. To Hildebrand, the modes of exchange are the fundamental powers that enable economy, society and culture to change. The money economy allowed for improvements, but in the long run, the advantages of the money economy developed into disadvantages. The worker, freed from the land, became vulnerable in the ensuing competition in an atomistic society in which the ties of family and kinship that kept people together tended to break up. To Hildebrand, the credit economy would solve this problem by re-establishing trust and human interaction in qualitatively better relationships in process of exchange and investment.

Richard Ely – The Main US Stage Theorist – and His Comparison of Stages (1903)

US economist Richard Ely – a student of Karl Knies in Heidelberg – has a good survey of stage theories in his 1903 book *Studies in the Evolution of Industrial Society*. Ely (1854–1943) was one of several German-educated Christian US Economists who were very influential in the United States up until, and including, The New Deal. According to *The International Encyclopaedia of Social Sciences*, Richard Ely 'probably exerted a greater influence upon American economics during its vital formative period than any other individual'. The fact that he is normally labelled a Christian socialist shows how the mental forces that built US society were very far away from what today is standard Anglo-Saxon economics. Rather than dividing economics in macro and micro, Ely seems to have income creation and income distribution as the two important facets of economics.

Ely's own stages are similar to those of List: (1) The hunting and fishing stage, (2) The pastoral stage, (3) The agricultural stage, (4) The handicraft stage, and (5) The industrial stage. More interestingly, however, Ely provides a comparative chart of five different types of stage theories, all displaying different aspects of

Table 18.1. **The Economic Stages**

From the Standpoint of Production	From Bücher's Standpoint	From Hildebrand's Standpoint	From the Labour Standpoint	From Giddings' Standpoint
1. Hunting and Fishing	Independent Domestic Economy	Truck Economy	Slaughter of Enemies, Women's Labour, and Beginning of Slavery	Luck Magic Sacrificial
2. Pastoral				
3. Agricultural			Slavery and Serfdom	Slave Labour
4. Handicraft	Town Economy	Money Economy	Free Labour Governed by Custom	Trade
5. Industrial (1) Universal Competition as an Ideal	National Economy	Credit Economy	Individual Contract with Increasing Regulation by Statute	Capitalistic
(2) Concentration	(World Economy)		Group Contract and Regulation by Statute	
(3) Integration				

Source: Ely (1903).

the societal development of Mankind: from the point of view of production (his own stage theory), from Bücher's standpoint, from Hildebrand's standpoint, from labour's standpoint, and from economist and sociologist Franklin Henry Giddings' standpoint. Giddings' main stages are Ceremonial and Business economics. These both have three sub-stages: Luck, magic and sacrificial economies, and slave, trade and capitalistic economies. These different types of stages would, of course, often not overlap in time. In this framework, Table 18.1, Carlota Perez' techno-economic paradigms fit like a natural sixth type of stage theory, based on the fundamental technologies carrying each period. Taken in conjunction, these stage theories emphasize different aspects, each of them representing a necessary but not sufficient condition for economic development.

Oppenheimer's Typology of Typologies

In the third volume, tome one, of his *System der Soziologie* from 1923, Franz Oppenheimer (Oppenheimer 1923, 254–309) has an excellent systematic discussion of stage theories from several angles. Oppenheimer starts by discussing two factors which contribute to the stages: *Die Differentierung* (i.e., the division of labour), *Die Integrierung* (i.e., the integration), which he divides into both their political and trade aspects. Oppenheimer introduces a special chapter on what he calls *Transportwiderstand* – i.e., the resistance to integration that is formed by geographical distance and consequent costs in terms of time and transportation cost. His *Transportwiderstand* lends itself perfectly as a concept through which the role of infrastructure may be introduced into the discussion of techno-economic paradigms. A related concept is Alfred Chandler's *economies of speed* (Chandler 1990).

Oppenheimer thoroughly discusses the combined effects of his two main factors (division of labour and integration) on the evolution of the following types of stages of societies: (1) The Stages of Division of Labour, (2) The Stages of Integration (essentially Bücher's), (3) The Phases of Evolution (scale of operation seen from the business point of view; i.e., handicraft, manufacturing, factories and trusts), and finally (4) Phases of Means of Circulation (the stages of monetary sophistication, i.e., Hildebrand's stages). One interesting aspect of previous stage theories in the light of the present transition into a new techno-economic paradigm, is that the 'natural' tendency towards an ever-increasing scale of operation may, in some industries, have been modified following the Fordist mass-production paradigm. To follow Chandler's terminology, economies of scope may have increased in importance at the expense of economies of scale. But the overall scale is still extremely important, a fact of which Microsoft and Amazon are just two examples.

Rostow's Non-Communist Manifesto (1960)

One of the latest stage theories to gain prominence was the five-stage theory of development presented by W. W. Rostow in his book *The Stages of Economic Growth* (1960). The subtitle *A Non-Communist Manifesto* hints at an agenda for the book that is clearly spelled out on the dust jacket: 'to offer a comprehensive, realistic and soundly based alternative to Marx' theory of how societies evolve'.

Rostow's stages are (1) The traditional society, (2) The preconditions for take-off, (3) The take-off, (4) The drive to maturity, and (5) The age of high mass consumption. However, Rostow fundamentally traces these stages as they are reflected in the relationship between two ratios: the proportion of income saved (the savings ratio) and the productivity of new investments (the output-capital ratio). His model is typical for the rather simplistic views about economic growth which were prevalent for many years following World War II, and which are still deeply embedded in the world economic order. Rostow's model clearly represents what Schumpeter calls 'the pedestrian view that it is capital per se which propels the capitalist engine'. He very much underestimates the mechanisms whereby society converts savings into investments and production: Man's intuition, skills, tools, will and leadership, Nietzsche's 'capital of wit and will' *(Geist- und Willenskapital)*.

Porter and the Possibility of Retrogression (1990)

As already mentioned, Michael Porter's book *The Competitive Advantage of Nations* (1990) contains an interesting example of a stage theory where the possibility for retrogression is clearly present – almost unavoidable if great care is not taken to prevent it. The model is clearly of a Schumpeterian brand, where society passes through the following stages of progress: (1) The factor-driven stage, (2) The investment-driven stage, and (3) The innovation-driven stage. The fourth stage – representing retrogression – Porter calls the wealth-driven stage.

This stage of decline sets in when the wealth created in the past is not able to create new wealth. The motivation of investors, managers, and individuals in general shifts in ways that undermine sustained innovation. Powerful companies are able to protect themselves – often with the help of government – from the need to innovate. Management-labour relations harden as each side strives to keep its share of a shrinking pie. At the same time, the social burdens increase, and ultimately outgrow society's ability to sustain them.

Porter's book received worldwide attention in the early 1990s, much as Rostow's book had in the early 1960s. However, Porter's ideas of industry clusters – already known under different names from Alfred Marshall, Francois Perroux and from Swedish economist Erik Dahmén – received most of the attention. His Schumpeterian stage theories deserved much more attention than they got, particularly because he opens up for retrogression and 'falling behind'. Porter's 'falling behind' is of the Mancur Olson type that nations may distribute themselves to poverty (Olson 1982).

The shifting power relations in today's world, intensified by the financial crisis, indeed open for much deeper studies of the decay of nations of the kind that was fashionable during the latter part of the 1700s, when the decay of city-states and the rise of the nation-states became evident. Economists Johann Heinrich Gottlob von Justi and Jakob Friedrich Bielfeld were influential Enlightenment economists contributing to the 'decay of nations' literature.[21] The faith of the losers – nations or regions – of a historical process consisting of relentless new surges of new techno-economic paradigms is as yet very much under-researched.

Techno-Economic Paradigms – Perez and Freeman (from 1983)

Carlota Perez and Christopher Freeman have broken down the historical period since the industrial revolution into different periods: techno-economic paradigms. As mentioned in the introduction, I see them as continuing the historical tradition of dividing history of Mankind into historical periods named after the technologies that dominated the period: e.g., stone-cutting technology in the Stone Age and iron technology in the Iron Age.

I see Carlota Perez' techno-economic paradigms as a continuation of Bacon's insight that the arts – the professions – are the most important factor determining Man's conditions of life. These periods may be looked upon as different modes – different methods – of increasing Man's material standard of living. Towards the end of each period it becomes increasingly clear that the previous technology is 'used up', its potentials are exhausted. There is no more room for improvements along the previous technological path – the world does not change anymore without fundamental changes to the technological base. Whereas the classical economists expected to arrive at a 'stationary state', in Carlota Perez' theory the perfect stone axe only represented the end of the Stone Age, not the end of technical change. Her perspective corresponds with the Renaissance 'duty to invent' as the Sisyphean task of Humanity (Reinert and Daastøl 1997).

Techno-economic paradigms are clearly a stage theory in the same way that Bücher's is, but focusing on the basic technologies driving the economy. They can clearly be interpreted as a continuation of List's and Ely's stage theories. In modern history, Perez and Freeman distinguish between five such different ways of increasing the standard of living, all of which dominated a long historical period. Table 18.2 shows, after Perez and Freeman, an overview of the characteristics of these periods, the industries that carry the paradigm, the inexpensive resources that become available in seemingly unlimited supply at rapidly falling prices, and the necessary infrastructure that is needed to reduce the *Transportwiderstand*.

***Table 18.2*. The Historical Techno-Economic Paradigms**

Name of Period	Important Industries	Inexpensive Resource	Infra-Structure	From-To
1. 1770–1840	Early mechanization	Textiles Wool	Water power Cotton	Canals Roads
2. 1830–1890	Steam and railway	Iron Transportation	Steam Coal	Railroad Steam ships
3. 1880–1940	Electricity and heavy industry	Electr. machinery Chemical ind.	Electricity Steel	Ships Roads
4. 1930–1990	Mass production (Fordism)	Cars Synthetic matter	Oil	Roads, Planes Cables
5. 1990–?	Information and communication	Data/Software Biotechnology	Micro-electronics	Digital telecom Satellites

The Perez/Freeman model is vaguely compatible with Porter's 1990 stages – both models are fundamentally Schumpeterian and innovation-driven. Porter clearly has a much less comprehensive understanding of the processes at work. However, in both cases the risk of falling behind is acknowledged: the Schumpeterian process of creative destruction may easily develop in such a way, that the creation takes place in one nation and the destruction in another.

The fundamental driving force behind the changing techno-economic paradigms is the changing level of Man's knowledge. Only by assuming away this factor – or building knowledge into the factor 'capital' – standard textbook economics tends to predict international harmony through international trade. One consequence of the Perez models is that nations exporting products based on old and commonplace knowledge will have a lower standard of living than nations exporting products containing advanced, new and scarce knowledge – regardless of their relative efficiency. The world's most efficient producers of baseballs for the American sport, who are in Haiti, make 50 US cents per hour. They are the world's most efficient producers in an industry that all the capital of the United States has not managed to mechanize. Baseballs are sewn by hand everywhere. The world's most efficient producers of golf balls – made by machines – have a nominal wage which is about 30 times higher. The uneven advances of mechanization produce huge inequities in world income, and lock many poor nations into a comparative advantage of being poor and ignorant.[22] This fact was not lost on US economists and politicians of the nineteenth century, but today its absence forms the most important blind spot on the cornea of mainstream economic theory. Until we include knowledge – Man's 'wit and will' – as a factor in economic theory, we shall continue, in vain, to throw money at the *symptoms* of poverty, rather than address its *causes*.

Using a Schumpeterian term, Carlota Perez' *vision* is clearly neo-Schumpeterian, and based on extremely thorough readings of his *Business Cycles* (Schumpeter 1939). Her great surges, however, differ considerable from Schumpeter's long waves. Table 18.3 is adapted from one of Carlota's own presentations:

In short, Schumpeter fundamentally tried to explain why growth took place in a wave-like pattern, pointing to the clustering of radical innovations. Perez delves into the qualitative aspects and huge impact of these radical innovations on society, on organizations, on the shifts between the domination of financial capital in one period and production capital in another, and on the changes in economic policy that must accompany the different phases of the surges.

Schumpeter has confused his students somewhat by presenting two theories of entrepreneurship, often called Mark I and Mark II. In the first one, in his early writings, Schumpeter argued that a nation's innovation and technological change originate with individual entrepreneurs. His Mark II version, developed later,

Table 18.3. Schumpeter's *Long Waves* in Economic Growth Compared to Perez' *Great Surges* of Technological Development

Definition	SCHUMPETER'S LONG WAVES in economic growth	PEREZ' GREAT SURGES of technological development
Focus	Variations in growth of GDP	Process of diffusion of the potential of successive technological revolutions
Method	Historical statistical analysis of economic variables (with technological underpinning)	Historical observation of technological, economic and socio-institutional behaviour (with statistical illustrations)
Object of Observation	The behaviour of the economy	The behaviour of the whole social system, with emphasis on the mutual influence of the techno-economic and the socio-institutional spheres
Role of Society and Politics	Out of the explanatory picture (though deeply affected)	Essential part of the explanation

Source: Perez (2007).

states that the actors that drive innovation and the economy are big companies which have the resources and capital to invest in research and development. Seen in a Perezian perspective, this apparent contradiction can be explained by the fact that Schumpeter's early writings took place at an early stage of the Fordist paradigm, when all surges tend to be products of innovating strong personalities, while when the Mark II version was written the paradigm was already installed and free competition was being replaced by oligopolistic structures (as is happening now). Radically new technologies originate in strong individuals – Andrew Carnegie in steel, Henry Ford in automobiles and Bill Gates in software – but as the companies they create become giants they join other giants in powerful industry structures that innovate in an organized way, but are destined to bureaucratize as they mature. This idea is already found in the writings of Harvard Business School's first dean, Edwin Gay, and is quoted in Perez (2002).

Techno-Economic Stages and Geography

The geographical dimension is not at the core of Carlota Perez' theories, and opening up for the geographical dimension also opens up for the discussion of income distribution in the various economic stages. On the other hand, some previous stage theories, such as Karl Bücher (1919a) have geography at their very core. The increasingly uneven development of the nations of the world, particularly the growing number of FFF-states, fragile, failed, and failing states (Reinert, Kattel and Amaïzo, 2009), signals the urgency of reintroducing this important relationship between techno-economic paradigms and geography.

Changing technologies carry with them qualitative changes in many aspects. Technologies and technological systems create particular spheres of gravity. They have their own geographical 'footprints'; each different technology creates its own geographical sphere much as each fluvial basin has its unique area of precipitation. Bücher's study, of course, also differentiates itself from that of Perez also by taking a much longer historical view.

Techno-economic stages develop according to Adam Smith's fundamental insight that the division of labour is dependent on the size of the market. Underlying this statement from Smith is an understanding that the division of labour is influenced by scale. The size of the market cannot be of importance for any other reason than scale: the division of labour is concomitant with increasing fixed costs and consequently with increasing returns to scale. Neo-classical economics, based on constant or diminishing returns to scale, has never been able to incorporate Adam Smith's basic insight about the extent of the market in its theory – no theory of the division of labour exists in modern economics. As George Stigler says, 'Almost no one used or now uses the theory of division of labour, for the excellent reason that there is scarcely such a theory... There is no standard, operable theory to describe what Smith argued to be the mainstream of economic progress.'[23] The diminishing- and constant-return assumptions of standard economics have erected a barrier preventing standard economic theory from absorbing what Adam Smith – as well as William Petty 100 years earlier – saw as the fundamental source of progress. When Paul Krugman recently put increasing returns on the map again, he initially did so by resurrecting Frank Graham's classical 1923 article at the core of which was the increasing- diminishing-returns dichotomy started by Serra in 1613. Very soon, however, the diminishing returns aspect disappeared from Krugman's work, and with it the key element in explaining Third World poverty (Reinert 2007).

Family Economy (Hauswirtschaft)

In Bücher's system, the first geographical sphere of human development is the family economy. In this economic stage the whole cycle from production to consumption takes place in the closed circle of family and kin. In the family economy it is not possible to separate production from consumption, Bücher says.[24] Exchange is by what modern anthropologists call reciprocity (*gegenseitige Hilfeleistung*). Karl Polanyi – who was clearly much inspired by Bücher – describes the income distribution systems in such societies as follows: 'In nonmarket economies these two forms of integration – reciprocity and redistribution – occur in effect usually together' (Polanyi 1971, 253).

At this stage society is very dependent on the soil (Bücher 1919a, 94), and collective labour (*Arbeitsgemeinschaft*) is important, rather than division of labour. The basic political units are clans (*Sippen*), where property is collective (*Gesamteigentum*). Houses are common (*Gemeinschaftshäuser*). Bücher here refers to Africa at the time of his writing. The lack of individualism is very clear, in some societies even death penalty can be taken over by another member of the tribe. Specialized labour – like a village shepherd – works for everybody and is fed by everybody (as is still the case even today in the Swiss Alps).

Within the same tribe, food is almost common property (Bücher 1919a, 62).[25] Some long-distance trade exists, e.g, in salt. As Polanyi has shown with the long-distance traders in pre-Colombian Mexico, the little trade that existed was to a large extent done on behalf of the clan. There is no industry outside the household at this stage in Bücher's system, artisans are household slaves (*Handwerkssklaven*). Bücher emphasizes that this system opens up for a large amount of division of labour – he names a lot of professions within the same Roman household – but this division of labour is not accompanied by trade.

Town Economy (Stadtwirtschaft)

The next evolutionary stage is the town economy. This stage is characterized by trade without intermediaries between specialized artisans and the public at town markets. The towns were often built around castles that provided refuge for the townspeople and people from the surrounding countryside in times of war. A person enjoying this privilege was a *Burger* (Burgensis). The need arose for economic institutions, for codifying laws and regulations for exchange that were not needed in earlier types of societies. Town markets required standards for weight and measure. In Mediaeval Europe, the towns had different standards of measurements, and an important part of early economic manuals was to list these weights and measures and to give their equivalents in the weights and measures of other towns. Still today, these local standards of measurement are found on old church walls in Italian towns.

Towns arose in ports, at river crossings, at trading posts for an increasing trade in goods like salt and iron. Markets grew in symbiosis with religious celebrations: accumulation of people always favours trade. The town specializes in arts and crafts and exchanges this for food from the surrounding countryside. Infrastructure is improved to reduce what Oppenheimer calls the *Transportwiderstand*.

National Economy (Volkswirtschaft)

This stage is characterized by a slow transfer of the institutions and synergies that had been seen as productive at the town level to a whole nation. This stage involves large-scale manufacturing, and trade is no longer direct between producer and consumer, but through intermediaries.

Bücher clearly sees the importance of mercantilist policies in order to create a national economy: 'Mercantilism is not a dead dogma, but the living *praxis* of all statesmen of any importance, from Charles V to Friedrich the Great. The typical economic policy of mercantilism was that of Colbert.' It is worth noting that no nation of any size – with the exception of tiny states like San Marino – has created a high standard of living without going through a stage of economic policy of the Colbert type (Reinert 2007).

The national economy became a very important unit for income distribution through labour mobility, and through common education, language, skills and values. Wages and – after the gold standard was abandoned – also money supply were increased at the pace of physical productivity of the economy. The barber raised his prices at the rate of productivity increase in the economy, and in this way the service workers in the industrialized countries came to have a much higher living standard than their Third World counterparts. This way of distributing the fruits of technological progress is what the French regulation school in economics refer to as 'Fordism' – a corollary to Fordism as a system of mass production in the theory of Perez and Freeman. This mechanism is what I have referred to as a *collusive* spread of the gains from technological change – a spread that to a large extent takes place inside a national labour market. The national economy became a *Burg* for the defence of a high living standard, just like the *Burg* in the town economy defended the *Burger* from enemy attacks.

The Global Economy

When reading Bücher's *Entstehung* today, one is struck by the thought that this book gives the account of Mankind's road toward a globalized economy. Bücher himself hints at the possibility of a global economy (*Weltwirtschaft*), but he sees it far into the future (Bücher 1919a, 149). Using Bücher's framework in his *Studies in the Evolution of Industrial Society*, Richard Ely makes the point about globalization very clear already in 1903: 'We are now in this stage (of national economies); and one may add, the next stage, according to this view, would be world economy. The money market is truly a world market' (Ely 1903, 68–69).

As in the previous stages, trade and technology lead the way, but institutional inertia slows and hinders society from achieving the full potential of new technological possibilities. In a sense the 'economies' of all Bücher's four spheres are still with is. We make sandwiches and brush our teeth in the Family Economy, we shop and buy services from the plumber in the Regional Economy, we participate in an educational and health system that is part of the National Economy, and we buy computers and watch movies that are part of the Global Economy. The global economy opens a new set of challenges for human institutions to create the 'good' society. In my view, there are particular problems in the area of income distribution, to which I shall return below.

Income Distribution Issues in the Different Techno-Economic Stages

Stage theories open up insights into both international trade theory and a better understanding of world income distribution. Friedrich List's theory of international trade – which set the standard for non-English trade policy in the nineteenth century – was based on his understanding of the stages of human evolution. Richard Ely says the following about List's 'National System of Political Economy':

> He (List) was interested especially in the problem of the protective tariff, holding that the policy which was suitable for one period in a nation's growth could not be safely followed in a subsequent period. In other words, he taught clearly that no one could properly describe himself either as a free trader or a protectionist, but that a man might be rationally a free trader at one period of development (of a nation), a protectionist at a later period, and again, at a subsequent period … a free trader. (Ely 1903, 21–22)

In this perspective, any nation dominating the new stage or paradigm would benefit from free trade, but nations risking to get stuck specialized in the activities of the former paradigm would need temporary protection. In my view, this is an observation still valid, but not much discussed, as regards the Freeman/Perez paradigm shifts. Both eighteenth- and nineteenth-century common sense (in the nineteenth century, with the exception of England) was that free trade was beneficial to nations at the same level of evolution, but only in the interest of the richer nations if trade was between nations at different stages of evolution. At the core of List's strategy was the idea that the production process engaged in the ruling techno-economic paradigm has to be present in all nation states. This was not only the basis for the industrialization of the United States and Continental Europe following England in the nineteenth century, it was also the basis of the Marshall Plan that rebuilt Europe after WW II. It can be said that it also forms

Table 18.4. Bücher's Stages of Development of Economics and Geography

Type of Economy	Mechanisms of Income Distribution
I. Household Economy	Family: According to need 'social relations' not 'markets'.
II. Town/Regional Economy	Family + labour mobility in small area + church.
III. National Economy	All of the above + distributing paradigm-carrying activity (= 'the industrial system') to all nations + State (taxation, schooling, health, 'welfare state')
IV. Global Economy	None of the above, but 'development aid'

the core idea of the Asian 'Flying Geese' method of sequentially upgrading industrial nations (Reinert 2007).

All Bücher's stages have their own mechanisms of income distribution. In Table 18.4, I have tried to summarize the stages and their respective mechanisms of income distribution. In all stages the regional or national labour market – in a system of free labour mobility – has provided what was probably the most important mechanism of income distribution. The income of the barber in the United States rose at the pace of productivity increase of the whole US economy – not at the pace of increase of productivity of the barber. For this reason the income of barbers, bus drivers, waiters and most traditional service workers are so much higher in the First World than in the Third – this in spite of the fact that the barbers and bus drivers in the Third World are just as productive and efficient as their colleagues in the First World.

A key feature of the paradigm-carrying economic activities is that the successful firms collect huge rents, as did the companies of Andrew Carnegie, Henry Ford and Bill Gates, each in their own paradigm. The presence of these rents in the labour marked made it possible to create collusion – through a Galbraithian balance of countervailing powers – between capital, labour and the tax state. What we call 'economic development' is in a sense a collectivization of industrial rents. The service sector shares in the increasing income by increasing their wages in parallel with the increasing wages of the industrial sector, which has been protected by huge barriers to entry and dynamic imperfect competition. Agriculture lives in a different world with perfect competition and diminishing returns, so even the most efficient farmers of the world – those of the United States and the European Union – need tariff protection from their colleagues in the poor world.

The global economy as we know it today differs fundamentally from all previous stages of economic geography in that labour mobility is – for the first time – restricted inside the prevalent sphere of the economic system. Since free labour mobility is not part of the globalized economy, it is – in my opinion – even more important than before to distribute productive activities of the new paradigm between nations. If not, in the globalized economy we will risk – even more than in the Fordist paradigm – that a large number of nations specialize in being poor and ignorant in the international division of labour. I shall discuss this problem more in detail in the next section.

Techno-Economic Stages: A Not So Optimistic View

As already discussed, stage theories do not pretend to present iron laws. Bücher clearly describes their passage as 'what is normal' – they are, says Oppenheimer, 'ideal types' in the Weberian sense. Stage theories do not represent the Whig conception of history that everything invariably improves. In my view they tend to conform to Carlota Perez' view that all stages or modes of production both socially and economically present a wide range of options.

There are, however, several aspects of stage theories that suggest that their *sequence* is mandatory, although retrogression – both self-induced and induced from the outside – is clearly possible. What Carlota Perez sees as a paradigm shift not only opens new windows of opportunity, but also opens back doors to retrogression. The whole idea of the Renaissance was to catch up to a previous stage which had been lost after what was – at the time – clearly perceived as a long period of retrogression.

All authors tie the stages to a cumulativeness of human knowledge that carries with it an increasing division of labour. Both Bücher and other authors are very conscious about the role of an increasing division of labour in the historical stages. As already mentioned, Oppenheimer calls the degrees of division of labour *The Stages of Differentiation*, which he ties to the geographical dimension (Bücher's stages) in *The Stages of Integration*, where the global economy is the last stage (ahead of a possible interplanetary economy).

Clearly, the duration of paradigms and stages can be drastically cut in time. Korea's 'leapfrogging' over a brief period of 40 years is perhaps the most remarkable example of how an industrial revolution may be compressed in time. In Korea, having eliminated a feudal landholding pattern seems to have been a prerequisite for this leapfrogging. The elimination of most of the feudal land holding structure in Bolivia after 1952 and in Peru after 1968 proves, however, that this is only one of many necessary conditions for 'take-off'.

The following two aspects would – in my view – point to stages being what historians of technology call 'mandatory passage points' – points that the evolution seemingly has to go through:

1. The cumulative nature of human knowledge. This cumulative aspect is evident when it comes to education; most people start in grade one and follow every grade up through university, although shortcuts – skipping one grade – are sometimes possible, but still the exception rather than the rule. In the same manner, there seems to be a natural sequence of technological change. An age based on nature's materials, like the Stone Age, is likely to precede an age dominated by a material produced by Man, like the Iron Age. But shortcuts are certainly possible. A country can skip the age of steam, just as in certain areas it will be possible to go directly to wireless telephony, skipping 'the age of cables'. So I would not like to push the 'naturalness' of any sequence too far. I believe that a wide range of possible trajectories exists, and that many end up not being optimal. This, however, does not subtract from a degree of cumulativeness: the Stone Age is not likely to follow an age of aluminium.

   Human knowledge may be seen – as Leibniz saw it – as a conscious climbing in a hierarchy of monads towards ever-higher levels of knowledge. In the Renaissance world view, since Man was created in the image of an incredibly creative God, it was his pleasurable duty to climb the hierarchy of monads towards ever-higher levels of knowledge: a 'duty to invent' (Reinert and Daastøl 1997). Leibniz' monadology in this sense points to the cumulative aspect of the growth of human knowledge towards higher degrees of perfection.

2. There are clearly connections between the stages of economic evolution and Man's hierarchy of needs. A hierarchy of human needs must, through the demand mechanism, to some extent determine the sequence of technological change; it is not feasible to think of a paradigm carried by sophisticated consumer services if people have not covered their basic needs for food, shelter and clothing. The German stage theorists make it very clear that an agricultural surplus was an absolute 'mandatory passage point' for human evolution to pass on to a further stage. The agricultural revolution was the first one, providing Man with food, his most basic need. Next came the industrial revolution, where production of textiles and clothing carried a succession of techno-economic paradigms – from the early industrialization of Venice in the fourteenth century all the way through nineteenth-century Manchester. But here lies a crucial point in history: only the production of clothing – the first industrial revolution – did provide the increasing returns, scale, scope, productivity explosions, barriers to entry and Schumpeterian dynamic and imperfect competition that made the triple rents of economic development possible: profits, higher wages and a larger tax base.[26] Agriculture did not.

There is, then, something organic in the process of evolutionary stages, whatever the criteria for the stages may be. This does, in my view, apply also to Perez' techno-economic paradigms. A nation needs to have been through a stage where mass production has created mass demand and mass welfare in order to move on to the next evolutionary stage in a healthy economic and social state. The alternative is retrogression and 'falling behind'. In my view, this is why Fordism has been, and still is, a mandatory passage point in order to create a post-Fordist society with a necessary purchasing power and a reasonable income distribution. This is also why the de-industrialization of so many small countries – Mongolia and Peru have been mentioned – may prove to have been a real disaster that will be very difficult to amend, except in the very long run. Spain's de-industrialization during the 1500s that only started to be repaired almost 300 years later comes to mind as a grim example.

There seem to be several reasons why Fordism was so special:

1. In my view, the Fordist paradigm was, and may remain, unique in its potential for large-scale income distribution within labour markets. The large scale of operations and the political power of a large number of workers allowed a rapid increase in the price of labour compared to the price of capital. This speeded up mechanization, which – in a virtuous circle – again increased the price of labour, and so on. This is what I have referred to as *collusive* distribution of the gains from technical change, in a three-layer rent-seeking where both capitalists, workers and the government in the producing nation 'collude' and keep a large share of the technological gains in their own nation (Reinert 2007 and 2009). This contrasts with the classical distribution of gains from technical change as it is assumed in economic theory: to the consumer as lowered prices.

2. The scale and geographical spread of operations in the network society of post-Fordism seem to make collusive distribution of gains from technical change much more difficult than before: we now get richer more from lower prices than from higher nominal wages. This relates to *scope* substituting for (and/or adding to) *scale* as previously discussed. US Steel workers were generally skilled workers agglomerated together and employed by one company, which created unionization and labour market power. McDonald workers are geographically spread, employed by different franchisees, and less skilled than traditional industrial workers. These factors tend to create lower wages as labour shifts from the Secondary to the Tertiary sector.

3. Fordism was the golden age for nations to catch up through reverse engineering. The Japanese could pull a US car apart and build a better one. Future techno-economic paradigms – be they based on bioengineering or

microtechnology – are likely to be much more patent-intensive, thus making catching up more difficult in the future.

4. The combination of Fordist mass production as the *techno-economic stage* and the nation-state as the *geographic stage* provided an enormous potential for raising real wages. Most competitors were national, and because a wage increase to one company also tended to be a wage increase for all its competitors, wage increases were not very threatening to a company. By making capital cheaper compared to labour, wage increases provided an enormous incentive for companies to mechanize. Today's global competition and weakened labour unions invite a downward spiral of real wages and real demand. We are likely to see more of this.

5. This tendency is reinforced by the sheer size of global markets, creating a new situation of 'the winner takes it all' markets. In my opinion it is therefore likely that societies going directly from semi-feudalism to post-Fordism may maintain the feudal structure of income distribution, albeit based on other criteria. I am much in agreement with Carlota Perez' view that all stages and techno-economic paradigms open for a whole range of possible types of societies. However, I fear that the establishment of a nation-wide distributive justice will be very difficult without passing through the nation-state-based Fordist mass-production society as an obligatory passage point. The scale of operations under the mass-production paradigm may have had as its most important effect that labour was needed on such a large scale that their bargaining power for the first time in history made a more equitable income distribution politically feasible.

6. One important aspect of Fordism was – as Carlota Perez points out – that, influenced by the technologies of mass production, large categories of objects became standardized and 'alike'. The typical example of this age is Henry Ford's statement that 'You can have your car any colour you want as long as it is black'. In Northern European social democracies it was stressed that human beings are equal. Under Maoism all individuals were even supposed to dress equally. Even under Hitler, all Aryans were seen as being alike, as well as all Jews and Gypsies in their categories. All human beings, or groups of human beings, came to be seen as 'equal' and 'alike'. Most societies now face a transition from seeing all human beings as being alike, to a stage where – if all goes well – all human beings are seen as being different – unique – but of equal value. Is it likely that cultures which have not passed through this stage of 'all human beings are equal' are able to build a consensus that all Men are different, but of equal value? Can such a consensus be built in places where native populations are still considered not much higher than animals? Is, in some cumulative sense, a notion that 'all Men are equal' an obligatory

Figure 18.1. Peru: Deindustrialization and falling wages as a percentage of GDP. 1950–1990

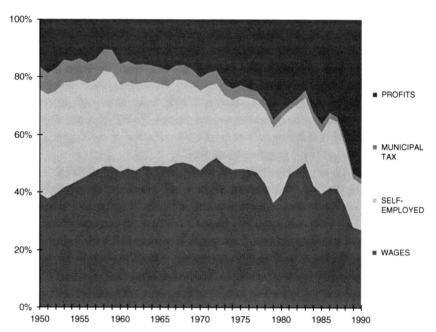

Legend, from top: profits, municipal tax, income of the self-employed, wages.
Source: *Banco Central de Reserva del Perú*. This breakdown of GDP by source was not published after 1990.

passage point in order that the idea that all Men are different – but of equal value – may be created?

Figure 18.1 illustrates how the presence of a 'Fordist' sector in an economy influences the distribution of GDP between the factors of production. Import substitution industrialization peaked in Peru in the early 1970s, and the collapse of this model also led to a collapse in real wages, which in fact were reduced by more than 50 per cent in real terms. I have also documented the same development in Mongolia (Reinert 2004).

At the height of the industrial age in Peru, in 1972, wages amounted to 51.2 per cent of GDP and the income of the self-employed, 26.5 per cent, a total of 77.7 per cent of GDP. Figure 18.1 shows how wages, salaries and the income of the self-employed shrank rapidly as the country prematurely opened up to free trade. In 1990, the last year the Peruvian Central Bank provided a breakdown of GDP in this way, the share of wages in GDP had almost been halved, to 26.5 per cent, and the share of the income of the self-employed had fallen to 15.9 per cent. In total, 'normal' people's share of GDP – wages, salaries and income of the self-employed – had shrunk by 45 per cent, from 77.7 per cent to 54.9 per cent of GDP as a result of Washington Consensus policies from the mid-1970s to 1990.

The Fordist techno-economic regime created a ratchet wheel effect: a system where wages could only move upwards, not downwards. The strength of the ratchet wheel effect could be seen during the Great Depression of the 1930s, when workers who kept their jobs generally kept their wages. However, the structural adjustment programs of the Washington Institutions ruined the Fordist wage regime and destroyed this ratchet-wheel effect. The data from Peru show how the structural adjustment program, also by virtually eliminating union power, destroyed the industrial rents that flowed to the population at large. The big question is how such a rent can be re-created in countries, such as Peru, which have lost their industrial base.

Globalization – in effect a shock therapy of free trade – therefore divided the developing world in two groups: Those whose manufacturing sector had been protected long enough, was large enough, and who were exposed to free trade gradually enough to benefit from free trade, countries such as Brazil, China and India. These countries stood to benefit from globalization. The other group – a large number of countries from Peru via Africa to Moldova and Mongolia – clearly lost out in a 'race to the bottom' type of development. Had their budding manufacturing sectors only been allowed to be gradually exposed to more competition, to more close integration with neighbouring countries rather than with the US and Europe, they could also have prospered. It is not clear to me how these countries will ever be able to build the necessary increasing returns base that is needed to successfully face new techno-economic paradigms yet to come.

Conclusion

I would claim that the study of economic stages – keeping the *caveats* of such generalization in mind – is indeed useful for understanding today's world. Afghanistan probably still exhibits normal traits of a clan economy, and its structure of governance is not likely to change until the underlying economic structure changes. Today, agricultural labour performed by women is still a main characteristic of African economies. Agricultural production in Africa and the horrid genocide in Rwanda scarily echo Richard Ely's 1903 description of an early stage or 'mode of production': 'The slaughter of enemies and women's labour are characteristic features of the early stage in the development of labour' (Ely 1903, 72). The Washington Consensus views on Africa's problems have failed to consider the qualitative aspects of a society as a reflection of the type of productive structure. Time has now shown that Africa's problems must be solved in the sphere of production, not in the sphere of 'fiscal restraint', of 'openness' of the economy and of 'free trade', of 'getting the prices right', or through the palliative economics of 'development aid'.

Common to all stage theories during their 'Golden Age' – from the Enlightenment through the 1930s – is that it was evident that, at any point in time, different geographical areas live in different stages. This may not be so obvious today, when most consumers consume in the global supermarket. However, if we focus specifically on production rather than on consumption – in the tradition of List, Bücher, and Perez – it becomes clear that the industrial rents are collected in the producing countries rather that in the consuming countries. The only successful countries in the nation-based stage of economic growth were those that managed to establish a Fordist manufacturing sector. Some of them, like Peru and Mongolia, lost this manufacturing sector again, which in both cases resulted in losses in real wages of more than 50 per cent.

Afghanistan, Liberia, Rwanda and Somalia are recent examples of total collapse of the nation-state,[27] and of a step back into tribal economies, back into Karl Bücher's clan economies. By reintroducing what Bücher saw as the 'indispensable tool' of stage theories – of production-based (as opposed to barter-based) economic theories – will we be able to better understand why globalization on the one hand is producing unprecedented wealth in some nations, but on the other hand also has the power to create increased poverty in other parts. We now risk a breakdown of civilized society in an increasing number of states which are absolutely uncompetitive and unemployable – at any wage level – in the globalized economy.

Although consumers in Somalia or Haiti – if they can afford it – have access to state-of-the art goods, their own *productive sector* is, to a large extent, locked into a specialization in activities operating under previous technological paradigms. They do not share in the rent that accrues to the consumer countries. Haiti was, for very long, the world's largest exporter and most efficient producer of baseballs, a product that all the capital of the United States so far has not managed to mechanize. All baseballs are hand-sewn, steeped in a techno-economic paradigm which otherwise died out over 100 years ago. Because they are specialized in leftover activities from former paradigms, the Haitians are increasingly reinforcing their comparative advantage in international trade: they are specialized in being poor and ignorant.

The failure of the 'Washington Consensus' in promoting development may be seen as a result of a failure to grasp the importance of stage theories and techno-economic paradigms. Today's success stories – India and China – are countries that consciously entered the Fordist industrialization paradigm in the late 1940s, and then slowly (perhaps too slowly) opened up.

As already mentioned, future techno-economic paradigms are likely to be more research-intensive and more patentable than previous ones. Very few countries have a positive balance of payments in royalties and patent fees, so world income is likely to be more concentrated than now. As I see it, once the manufacturing rent has been eroded – as shown in the case of Peru – no type of raw-material-based strategies will be able to re-create it. Creating such a national rent, in my view, necessitates the kind of dynamic, imperfect competition that only increasing-returns activities are able to provide. Pressure on migration from the poor world to the rich world is increasing sharply, and we seem to be faced with two options: Either we move the inhabitants of poor countries to countries where Fordist mass production has created generalized wealth (if so, to the detriment of the living standards there), or we establish the type of Fordist (and post-Fordist) mass production that made the rich countries rich also in the Third World.

The 2009 financial crisis has already started to erode real wages in the European periphery – e.g., in the Baltic – and is likely to do the same in countries like the United States, that are no longer heavily unionized. This may give rise to a new wave of protectionism by the rich countries. This may, in turn, make it feasible for those countries that seem to be destined to enter the next techno-economic paradigm, not as producers of the new core technologies, but only as consumers, to re-industrialize selectively. Five hundred years of history shows that an inefficient manufacturing sector produces a much higher national living standard than not having any at all.

References

Bücher, K. 1919a. *Die Entstehung der Volkswirtschaft.* 11th edn. Tübingen: Laupp.

————. 1919b. *Lebenserinnerungen.* Tübingen: Laupp.

Chandler, A. D. 1990. *Scale and Scope: The Dynamics of Industrial Capitalism.* Cambridge, MA: Harvard University Press.

Drechsler, W. 2004. 'Natural vs. Social Sciences: On Understanding in Economics.' In E. S. Reinert (ed.). *Globalization, Economic Development and Inequality: An Alternative Perspective.* Cheltenham: Elgar, 71–87.

Ely, R. 1903. *Studies in the Evolution of Industrial Society.* New York: Chautauqua Press.

Freeman, C. 1991. 'The Nature of Innovation and the Evolution of the Productive System.' In *Technology and Productivity. The Challenge for Economic Policy.* Paris: OECD.

Gehrig, H. (ed.). 1922. *Die Nationalökonomie der Gegenwart und Zukunft und andere gesammelte Schriften von Bruno Hildebrand.* Jena: Fischer.

Graham, F. 1923. 'Some Aspects of Protection Further Considered.' *Quarterly Journal of Economics* 37, 199–227.

Hildebrand, B. 1864. 'Natural-, Geld- und Kreditwirtschaft.' *Jahrbücher für Nationalökonomie und Statistik,* 2, 1–24.

Hirschman, A. O. 1977. *The Passions and the Interests. Political Arguments for Capitalism before Its Triumph*. Princeton, NJ: Princeton University Press.

Hoover, P. (ed.). 1994. *Postmodern American Poetry*. New York: Norton.

Kalveram, G. 1933. *Die Theorien von den Wirtschaftsstufen*. Leipzig: Hans Buske.

Krugman, P. 1996. *The Self-Organizing Economy*. Cambridge, MA: Blackwell.

Kuczynski, J. 1978. *Studien zu einer Geschichte der Gesellschaftswissenschaften* 8. Berlin: Akademie-Verlag.

Laistner, M. L. W. 1923. *Greek Economics*. London: Dent.

Margoliouth, D. S. 1932. 'Ibn-Khaldun.' In E. Seligman (ed.). *The Encyclopaedia of Social Sciences* 7. New York: Macmillan.

McCloskey, D. 1985. *The Rhetoric of Economics*. Madison: University of Wisconsin Press.

————. 1994. *Knowledge and Persuasion in Economics*. Cambridge: Cambridge University Press.

McCraw, T. 1992. 'The Trouble with Adam Smith.' *The American Scholar* 61, 353–373.

Meek, R. 1976. *Social Science and the Ignoble Savage*. Cambridge: Cambridge University Press.

Nelson, R. and S. Winter. 1982. *An Evolutionary Theory of Economic Change*. Cambridge, MA: Harvard University Press.

Nicol, D. M. 1990. *Venezia e Bisanzio*. Milan: Rusconi.

Olson, M. 1982. *The Rise and Decline of Nations: Economic Growth, Stagflation and Social Rigidities*. New Haven: Yale University Press.

Oppenheimer, F. 1923. *System der Soziologie* 3/1. 5th edn. Jena: Fischer.

Perez, C. 1983. 'Structural Change and Assimilation of New Technologies in the Economic and Social System.' *Futures* 15, 357–375. [3.1]

————. 2002. *Technological Revolutions and Financial Capital: The Dynamics of Bubbles and Golden Ages*. Cheltenham: Elgar. [74.1]

————. 2004. 'Technological Revolutions, Paradigm Shifts and Socio-Institutional Change.' In E. S. Reinert (ed.). *Globalization, Economic Development and Inequality: An Alternative Perspective*. Cheltenham: Elgar, 217–242. [75.1]

————. 2007. 'Globalisation at the Turning Point: A Perspective from the Great Surges Model.' Presentation at the Freeman Centre Seminar Series 2006–7 (1) 257, SPRU-CENTRIM, Universities of Sussex and Brighton. Available at http://www.sussex.ac.uk/spru/documents/perez_spru-centrim_april-07_def.ppt#257

Pigou, A. C. 1949. *The Veil of Money*. London: Macmillan.

Polanyi, K. 1944. *The Great Transformation*. New York: Rinehart.

————. 1971. 'The Economy as an Instituted Process.' In K. Polanyi, C. M. Arensberg and H. Pearson (eds). *Trade and Markets in the Early Empires*. Chicago: Gateway.

Porter, M. 1990. *The Competitive Advantage of Nations*. London: Macmillan.

Reinert, E. S. 1999. 'The Role of the State in Economic Growth.' *Journal of Economic Studies* 26, 268–326.

————. 2000. 'Karl Bücher and the Geographical Dimensions of Techno-Economic Change.' In J. Backhaus (ed.). *Karl Bücher. Theory, History, Anthropology, Non Market Economies*. Marburg: Metropolis.

————. 2004. 'Globalization in the Periphery as a Morgenthau Plan: The Underdevelopment of Mongolia in the 1990s.' In E. S. Reinert (ed.). *Globalization, Economic Development and Inequality. An Alternative Perspective*. Cheltenham: Elgar.

————. 2007. *How Rich Countries Got Rich ... and Why Poor Countries Stay Poor*. London: Constable & Robinson.

————. 2009. 'Emulating Success: Contemporary Views of the Dutch Economy before 1800.' In O. Gelderblom (ed.). *The Political Economy of the Dutch Republic*. Aldershot: Ashgate.

Reinert, E. S., Y. E. Amaïzo and R. Kattel. 2009. 'The Economics of Failed, Failing and Fragile States: Productive Structure as the Missing Link.' *The Other Canon Foundation and Tallinn University of Technology Working Papers in Technology Governance and Economic Dynamics*, 18.

Reinert, E. S. and A. Daastøl. 1997. 'Exploring the Genesis of Economic Innovations: the Religious Gestalt-Switch and the Duty to Invent as Preconditions for Economic Growth.' *European Journal of Law and Economics* 4, 233–283.

Reinert, S. (ed.). 2010. *Antonio Serra. A Short Treatise on the Causes that Can Make Kingdoms Abound in Gold and Silver even in the Absence of Mines (1613)*. London: Anthem, forthcoming.

Robbins, L. 1952. *The Theory of Economic Policy in English Classical Economics*. London: Macmillan.

Rostow, W. W. 1960. *The Stages of Economic Growth: A Non-Communist Manifesto*. Cambridge: Cambridge University Press.

Schumpeter, J. A. 1912. *Theorie der wirtschaftlichen Entwicklung*. Munich / Leipzig: Duncker & Humblot.

————. 1939. *Business Cycles*. New York: McGraw-Hill.

————. 1954. *History of Economic Analysis*. New York: Oxford University Press.

Serra, A. 1613. *Breve trattato delle cause che possono far abbondare li regni d'oro e d'argento dove non sono miniere*. Naples: Lazzaro Scoriggio.

Smith, A. 1976. *The Wealth of Nations*. Chicago: University of Chicago Press.

Sombart, W. 1928. *Der moderne Kapitalismus*. Munich / Leipzig: Duncker & Humblot.

Sommer, A. 1948. 'Über Inhalt, Rahmen und Sinn älterer Stufentheorien (List und Hildebrand).' In E. Salin (ed.). 1948. *Synopsis: Festgabe für Alfred Weber*. Heidelberg: Lambert Schneider.

Viner, J. 1972. *The Role of Providence in the Social Order*. Philadelphia: American Philosophical Society.

Chapter Nineteen:

CARLOTA PEREZ' CONTRIBUTION TO THE RESEARCH PROGRAMME IN PUBLIC MANAGEMENT: UNDERSTANDING AND MANAGING THE PROCESS OF CREATIVE DESTRUCTION IN PUBLIC INSTITUTIONS AND ORGANIZATIONS

Claude Rochet
IGPDE/CERGAM, Université Paul Cezanne, Aix-Marseille III

The publication of this book to crown the life and work of Carlota Perez in the service of research into technology cycles and their relationship with financial cycles comes at exactly the right time because, unfortunately, her analysis has proved to be absolutely right: about 30 years after the start of the fifth technology cycle based on information and communication technologies, the crisis is upon us. It is a global, systemic crisis similar to that of 1929, the one that separates the two phases of Kondratiev cycles (which do indeed always seem to last 50 to 60 years), even as those who waxed lyrical about the 'new economy' were predicting their disappearance. Carlota Perez steadfastly maintained in recent years that the dot-com bust in 2001 was not the 'real' crisis that, given the continuing split between the real and the virtual economy, was still to come. Her work helps give us a better understanding of the relationship between capitalism and society as a system based on disequilibrium, emphasizing the specific role of a financial capitalism that first fuels, then dampens, entrepreneurial ardour, this being the genuinely new anthropological model of capitalism as identified by Schumpeter.

The cyclical hypothesis having proved its worth, we can therefore look forward to a period of great turbulence, accompanied by social and political strife, if not war. October 2008 will go down in history as the time when the most orthodox of economic liberals were won over to the most radical state interventionism, to the point where *The Economist* (2008) was able to run the headline '*Re-bonjour, Monsieur Colbert*'.

It is, therefore, high time to return to the role of public management in response to these challenges. In the English-speaking world, it has centred on a single concept: the efficiency of organizations, which has become, in Fred Thompson's words (2006), the 'Holy Grail' of administrators and the sole measure of good and bad. In the real world, however, other criteria are needed, those of the value judgment from which the effectiveness and relevance of public action can be evaluated.

That does not mean neglecting efficiency; far from it. Public systems and organizations designed to regulate the world defined by the previous socioeconomic paradigm are now both unsuitable and expensive, creating a scissor effect between the cost of the state and its effectiveness at solving problems. The state's inability to deal with problems becomes a pretext for eliminating it, a process that I have dubbed the 'bureaucratic euthanasia' of the state.[1]

For Carlota Perez (2004), institutions are also subject to the process of Schumpeterian 'creative destruction', for which political leaders are ill prepared. She sets the scene very clearly in the conclusion of her major work (2002, 166):

> It is then possible to envisage the present model as an early-warning tool, providing criteria to guide policy making…. Could the bubble and its consequences be avoided? Could some institutional agent – or the capitalists themselves – identify the onset of maturity and facilitate the next revolution and its flourishing? Could the decline of the old industries be forestalled by conscious modernisation? Could the shift of power at the turning point be engineered without the recession and the social tension involved … The answers to those questions do not merely require research but a very deep understanding of the many human and social complexities involved.

But although the model gives us warning signs and the overall dynamic, there is no preordained strategy or universal recipe for managing the change.

Can the Time Lag in the Evolution of the State be Managed?

I summarize this problem in the following diagram, which I have taken from Carlota Perez. It shows two factors that introduce a time lag between the evolution of the state and change in the industrial sector.

Figure 19.1. Time Lag Between State and Industry Evolution

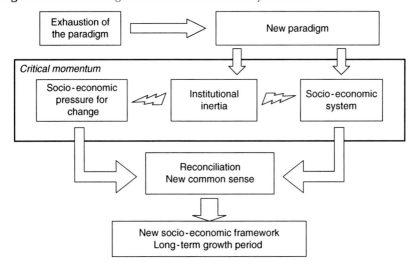

Source: Perez (2004).

The first factor is chronological. As far as the fifth Kondratiev cycle is concerned, information technologies affected firms' production methods first and the state later. In the second half of the 1990s, firms had to learn on the hoof how to rethink their business models and cope with innovation in products, in processes and, above all, in organization. Innovation marked a radical change in which old industries that found it difficult to evolve were eliminated in a context of fierce competition between the most innovative firms at the leading edge.

There is no value judgment involved in this first element of the time lag: the state and its organizations are merely affected later than the competitive sector. Another factor is that the state is a much bigger network of organizations than the competitive sector and, although broadly speaking, the problems of how organizational and technological architectures evolve alongside each other are equally complex, they differ in their intensity and timing.

The other element of the time lag, institutional inertia, is more problematical. Each paradigm shift is propagated at three interlinked levels (Perez 2004):

1. The new technological system rolled out in the productive sphere, in this case the impact of information technologies on production methods and the organization of work.
2. A set of better practices capable of reaping the benefit of the new technologies, which become standard practices that spread to all

productive activities and create the innovation framework (like Japanese production methods in the automobile industry)
3. The emergence of a new common sense, leading to the definition of a new institutional framework.

These three levels correspond to three partially overlapping waves. In order for the full potential of the new paradigm to be realized, it has to reach Level 3, the institutional level. That is the process of creative destruction at institutional level; the institutions of the previous technology wave no longer provide an environment in which all the possibilities of the new technology can flourish and have to be rethought.

In historical terms, it is a point of indetermination (Perez 2004) in the history of nations. Those that are able to re-forge the link between institutions and the techno-economic system see a considerable increase in their economic productivity, while the others are left behind. The time lag is critical to the evolution of the state in response to technological change. It is critical because creative destruction also marks the destruction of social consensus, the decline of alpha social groups and the emergence of new groups. Historically, it marked the replacement of the domination of the landed aristocracy by the industrial bourgeoisie, of peasant farmers by the working class. Today, it is the appearance of a new form of entrepreneurship and the emergence of 'knowledge workers' replacing workers who sold their physical strength.

This critical time is also one where the cards are redistributed between nations, as Alexander Gerschenkron rightly pointed out, giving backward nations an opportunity to catch up with dominant nations through a strategy of institutional innovation. The old nations, having constructed institutional frameworks suited to the former paradigm, have to change them. In doing so, they face institutional resistance that is all the stronger because the institutions concerned have spawned bureaucratic organizations that are difficult to change.

What History Teaches Us

In his *History of Economic Analysis*, Schumpeter describes with interest John Stuart Mill's position on the condition of British bureaucracy in the middle of the nineteenth century:

No serious administrator would have pretended at the time that [...], economic and social conditions and the agencies of public administration being what they were, any attempt to regulate the economy through State intervention would have resulted in anything but failure (Schumpeter 1986 2, 234).

British institutions had brought the country – the mighty fiscal and military state so well described by Patrick O'Brien – both prosperity and predominance. Because, contrary to what has become a stereotype, *plenty* derives from its interaction with *power*, and hence politics. Free-traders and laisser-faire theorists have presented mercantilist policies as being concerned solely with power, trade and industry being merely a means to an end.

On the contrary, the relationship between power and plenty has always been a balanced one in which neither power nor trade was an end in itself, assumed to be self-sufficient, but a self-sustaining dialectic with its roots in the first globalization, the *Pax Mongolica*, whose dynamic is described in Findlay and O'Rourke's monumental masterwork (2008).

Britain devoted 20 per cent of its GDP to the state budget (the state budget in France today, the butt of so much criticism, is only 16 per cent of GDP), and 80 per cent of that to the Royal Navy. The key to the Royal Navy's power was its capacity to keep up to 80 per cent of its fleet and sailors at sea, through clever management of the logistics chain – repairs, crewing, victualling (Findlay and O'Rourke 2008, 256) – a figure that neither the French nor the Dutch were able to match. Captains were expected to engage the enemy as soon as possible, so that young officers and crew would gain more experience. The Royal Navy had understood the strategic nature of knowledge; that benefited the Merchant Navy, which in turn became a reservoir of skill in peacetime that could easily be converted into military might.

As a country becomes more highly developed, institutional inertia is compounded by the formation of vested interests; but Britain proved astute in the management of this change. After the Glorious Revolution of 1688, Parliament changed the policy for granting monopolies so as to protect not a particular entity (like the Merchant Adventurers) but industrial sectors against the main rival of the day, the Netherlands, which practiced a policy of granting monopolies to particular interests in contempt of the general interest. It was the state's job to ensure national security and define the framework for competition between domestic entrepreneurs, a notion no different from the theory of educative protectionism that is at the heart of Friedrich List's 'national system of political economy'.[2]

The first need for adjustment between change in the socioeconomic sphere and change in the socio-institutional sphere arose in the first half of the nineteenth century, in the final phase of the first Kondratiev cycle. The prevailing winds clearly favoured the supporters of laissez-faire and free trade, for two reasons. From the standpoint of managing the administrative bureaucracy, Schumpeter's argument remains valid; mercantilist policies had generated large and costly bureaucracies at a time when those policies were no longer useful to a Britain that had reached the pinnacle of its power. The fact that there was no technique of 'public management' to reduce the bureaucracy justified John Stuart Mill's disillusioned stance in supporting laissez-faire, albeit unwillingly:

I confess I am not charmed with the ideal of life held out by those who think that the normal state of human beings is that of struggling to get on; that the trampling, crushing, elbowing, and treading on each other's heels, which form the existing type of social life, are the most desirable lot of human kind, or anything but the disagreeable symptoms of one of the phases of industrial progress. (1848, book 4, chapter 6)

But the shift towards laissez-faire and free trade had another cause; now that the country had acquired global supremacy, the residual protectionism of British policy had taken on a retrograde cast by defending the landed aristocracy against the assumption of power by industrialists.

The movement to repeal the Corn Laws was in fact a social movement against the high cost of living, reflecting the pressure for change emanating from the new socioeconomic system and directed against institutions. The Corn Laws had become extremely unpopular because they kept grain prices high and had been championed by Lord Castlereagh, an openly reactionary minister who displayed utter contempt for the working classes. In the midst of the recession that hit Britain after the Napoleonic wars, Castlereagh was the architect of laws to suspend habeas corpus and the freedom of the press, passed by a House packed with landowners whose interests the Corn Laws defended. Unemployment among the working population of Britain in the 1830s and 1840s rose to between 20 and 30 per cent even though the country had an abundance of wealth, albeit attended by a migration of economic activity from rural workshop to urban factory.

The agitation led by Richard Cobden and his Anti-Corn Law League raised public awareness of the issue. Created in 1840, the League had become a political movement with representatives in Parliament. A harvest ruined by rain in 1845 made it impossible to maintain the Corn Laws. The crisis of 1845–1847 was the last of the *Ancien Régime* type, a crop failure crisis that hit the whole of Europe (especially Ireland, where the potato famine left a million dead) and was a contributory factor to the political troubles of 1848 (Bairoch 1997). Cobden received the support of Daniel O'Connell and the Irish nationalists. In modern terms, the fight against the Corn Laws was a 'left wing' cause and the protectionists were the reactionaries. But it was truly intelligent management of the crisis of adjustment. The abolition of the Corn Laws in 1846, presented as a triumph of laissez-faire, can be seen in a radically different light. For Richard Cobden, abolishing the Corn Laws meant weakening rival countries' industry by opening up the British market to them and encouraging them to cling to activities with declining returns:

> The factory system would, in all probability, not have taken place in America and Germany. It most certainly could not have flourished, as it has done, both in these states, and in France, Belgium, and Switzerland, through the fostering bounties which the high-priced food of the British artisan has offered to the cheaper fed manufacturer of those countries. (Cobden 1868, 150.)

Free trade can therefore contribute to a policy of power; at the time it expressed Britain's national interests and was necessary for asserting the *Pax Britannica*. As history would have it, six months after the abolition of the Corn Laws in May 1846 Friedrich List, ill and beset by financial problems, committed suicide, helping to lend a symbolic dimension to the victory of free trade.

Free trade thus gained its credentials with a social alibi and scientific justification from the ideas of the classical economists, especially Ricardo, and the entire Saint-Simonian school. With the support of the Saint-Simonians, Richard Cobden was able to build up his network of treaties, first with Belgium, then (and more importantly) with the France of Napoleon III in 1860. Raymond Boudon (2006) argues that Cobden's policy can be regarded in the same light as today's 'Blairism', Cobden acting as a sort of latter-day Anthony Giddens with his 'third way' between liberalism and socialism, thanks to that historical convergence of the interests of social categories that were opposite in every other respect. Those were the conditions in which free trade became for Britain what Emmanuel Todd has called an 'identity myth'.

As far as public administration was concerned, the victory of laissez-faire did not lead to less state intervention. The administrative functions of the State mushroomed between 1830 and 1850. Even a supporter of laissez-faire like Chadwick (one of the two promoters of the 1832 Poor Laws reform) changed his position when faced with the expressions of hostility directed against him during the 1837 recession, the effects of which were considerably aggravated by the abolition of the Poor Laws. He was the author of a report on the health of the working classes in Britain, which recommended the establishment of a public health system, an idea initially rejected by the Tory government before being taken up by the Liberals in 1848.

The Return of the State

The issue here is not so much that of a return *per se*, for the state has never really gone away, but of its return into prevailing ideas about institutional strategies. What is at stake? Let us assume the hypothesis of Chris Freeman (2001) according to which economic growth results from the congruence of five sub-systems: science, technology, culture, economics and politics. Performance is therefore an emerging property linked to the quality of the interactions between these sub-systems. This idea can already be found in Fernand Braudel (1985, 6–68):

> Any dense society can be broken down into several 'sets': the economic, the political, the cultural, the socio-hierarchical. The economic set can be understood only in relation with the other sets, permeating them but also open to its neighbours. There is action and interaction. The particular and partial form of the economic set that is capitalism can be fully explained only in the light of those adjacencies and overlapping: there it will finally assume its true face.

At a time of technological disruption, performance will result from the emergence of a metasystem capable of incorporating and directing the complexity created by the appearance of a new technology. This process is at the heart of innovation.

Technology here should be taken in a broad sense to mean all the capital of operational knowledge available to create wealth through new processes, modes of organization and products. It is 'the measure of our ignorance', to use the expression of Moses Abramovitz who, in 1956, calculated that the accumulation of physical capital accounted for only 10 per cent to 20 per cent of growth (Abramovitz 1990).

The state plays several roles in this process. It defines the rules of the game even though it is also a player, as Douglass North has shown (1990). It defines the institutions that will reduce transaction costs between players and between sub-systems, through the efficacy of the rules it sets. At the same time, it is an organization which manages policies, like research and technology, the building of infrastructure and investment in education, that set the stage for all development and innovation.

Two options then arise: either progress is the result of a laissez-faire approach to innovation and the State is an infrastructure management cost that needs to be optimized, or it requires specific action by the state, a strategy whose cost-benefit ratio needs to be evaluated, and there is scope for proactive public policies.

The first option is that of the neoclassical school, which has engendered New Public Management, i.e., reform of the state reduced to reform of its administration by introducing market mechanisms into its operation.

The other option is found in the neo-Schumpeterian current of thought as represented by Freeman and Soete (1997) and Carlota Perez (2002), who show that technological disruptions are opportunities for redistributing the cards of comparative advantage between nations. It requires a proactive policy on the part of the State, or in other words, an industrial policy, anathema in European Commission doctrine until it suddenly found favour again after the global financial crisis in October 2008.

Forging Ahead, Catching Up or Falling Behind? The Role of Institutions

So there is scope for countries lagging behind to take deliberate action to catch up the leaders, whose institutions and social consensus are subject to pressures likely to threaten their internal equilibrium and balance of power and undermine their leading position (falling behind), whereas they need to constantly push forward the frontiers of technology (forging ahead). It is the quality of the interactions between the five sub-systems that will determine the technological path between these three options.

In economies like those of France and northern European countries, where the public sector accounts for more than half of GDP, the right use and management of these resources is all the more important, especially when public spending has been funded by borrowing for the last thirty years. Public spending can finance R&D, the acquisition of technological assets, advances in strategic areas, infrastructure, education and an increase in 'human capital' in general – in a nutshell, investment in the future. It matters little that the spending is deficit-financed since it helps to increase society's productive capacity, which can generate a surplus in better times. France's public sector deficit in 1946 was 145 per cent of GDP, but it was completely wiped out by the growth that took place in the *Trente Glorieuses*, accompanied by a sound level of inflation that reflected the general increase in prices and wages and negative interest rates.

If public organizations slump in torpor in their acquired positions, not only do they no longer help to increase human capital, but they see their impact diminish even as the overall cost of the state rises. If this effect is compounded by a lack of internal productivity in public administration, the scissor effect between cost and value produced becomes unfavourable.

The institutions of the *Trente Glorieuses* made it possible to reap the benefits of mass production, in Europe's case mainly after 1945. Taxation represented 9 per cent of GDP in France in 1913. By 1974, at the end of the cycle, that figure had risen to 35 per cent, and in 2004 to 54 per cent, though France could not be said to have entered the information society on a sound footing or to have come up with a suitable institutional framework for it. France devoted 6 per cent of GDP to research in the late 1960s, compared with just over 2 per cent now. Above all, 1974 marked the turning point at which the fall in industrial employment in mass production industries was not offset by job creation in other sectors, resulting in the emergence of structural unemployment. The disappearance of industrial policy under the influence of neoliberal thinking, combined with a policy of positive real interest rates, maintained sluggish growth, and what could and should have been a period of Schumpeterian creative destruction was nothing but a long and slow process of 'destructive destruction' (Aglietta and Berrebi 2007, chapter 4). *A scissor effect therefore exists between the growing cost of organizations and the decreasing yield of institutions.* It is in fact what amounts to a classic problem of obsolescence in a dynamic of adaptive systems: organizational entropy combines with institutional resistance to block the evolution of the state and uncouple it from the evolution of the other sub-systems. Positive action to reform the state could re-establish the synchronization, but that becomes impossible in practice because of the prevailing ideas about the State, derived from neoclassical theory, which give it merely a residual role of managing whatever the markets cannot do, the so-called 'market failures'.

Thus, *it is just when the state costs most that it becomes impossible to reform, because of the impossibility of redefining its role.* Public debate seems to reach an impasse; ultra-liberals seek to prove the need to do away with the state entirely at last, while the vested interests of the protected system guaranteed by the state defend the status quo and the bureaucracy in the name of 'defending public service'. It is that vicious circle which feeds the process of bureaucratic euthanasia.

To make this debate commensurable, we have to ask ourselves the question: *how can the state and public institutions in general create value?* It is interesting that part of the answer should come from a former scion of the neoclassical school, Douglass North, one of the founders of cliometrics, or 'New Economic History', a movement which sought to apply the mechanical and positivist principles of neoclassical economics to history (Freeman and Louçã 2001). North gradually abandoned his initial neoclassical orientation (North and Thomas 1973), in which the price mechanism served to eliminate obsolete institutions. He established that there can be inefficient institutions that are under no competitive pressure to reform, generally because they serve vested interests and not the public good (North 1981). North defines institutions as reducers of uncertainty, establishing stable structures within which players in society can interact (1990, 6) and, in Freeman's terminology, enabling the five sub-systems to converge towards a metasystem, i.e., a society capable of taking advantage of technological opportunities.

Institutions make it possible to identify opportunities (by creating the appropriate incentives), while organizations make it possible to exploit them; institutions and organizations are therefore linked in a process of co-evolution.[3]

How Do Institutions Evolve When Industrial Revolutions Occur?

But although North posits the link between institutions and organizations in an evolutionist model, he only partially defines the dynamics. His primary concern is to analyse which appropriate incentives institutions should introduce in order to have efficient organizations, thinking mainly of the United States, in terms of interactions between public institutions and private organizations. He supposes that learning by doing at an organizational level is sufficient, through feedback, to forge a new culture for those who conceive public institutions.

On the one hand, this view seems to be exclusively managerial and to ignore the cycle of ideas, which is autonomous in relation to that of organizations. Ideas may precede innovations and be a precondition for them, as in the Enlightenment. But when they congeal into ideologies, out of principle they take against the real so that dogma can prevail. The history of the nineteenth and twentieth century is there to remind us that this perfect system in which practical experience acquired in organizations feeds back into the design of institutions is the exception, generally due to periods of crisis or exceptional circumstances, and that ideology prevails.

In his recent work (2005), North moves his analysis forward by considering, like Aoki (2001), that institutions are self-sustaining systems of shared beliefs. The development of economic social systems is a succession of ergodic phases (in which the future state of a system can be predicted from its state at a given time) when it evolves within the same socioeconomic paradigm, and of non-ergodic phases when there is a paradigm shift resulting from industrial revolution. The key to change is in the capacity of the belief system to call itself into question.

On the other hand, it does not answer the fundamental question facing us: how can public institutions learn when faced with powerful professional state bureaucracies? Confronted with organizations regarded as unreformable, there is a strong temptation to enter into the rationale of the 'bureaucratic euthanasia of the state'. The public may be tempted, in the same movement, to reject not only the economic and social cost of an unbearable bureaucracy but also the very principle of public intervention. For managers, it is much easier to adopt the prevailing – and very convenient – ideas of laissez-faire than to devote time and energy to the difficult and unrewarding role of 'boss' of the public machine in order to reform it. Linked to the advance of individualism against the sense of the common good, it has been and still is the main factor of support for the 'liberal dogmatism' that Schumpeter denounces in his *History of Economic Analysis*. The State's management of the time lag is therefore the critical time in a nation's evolution.

Can the State Learn?

Let us start from the finding that private organizations do not have a specific genetic code that makes them more apt to learn and evolve than public organizations. I have shown (Rochet, 2007) that there is no bureaucratic fatality that makes the public sector incapable of evolving.

That being so, the evolution of the state becomes a locus of competition between nations: those that are better able to manage the evolution of their State, both institutionally and bureaucratically, and guide institutional innovation will be able to widen the gap. That is merely the reproduction, in new forms, of a historical process, the main constants of which have been accurately described by Erik Reinert (2007), and which follows in a direct line from Friedrich List's national system of political economy.

Shaping that evolution is a task to which we are called by the reference framework developed by Carlota Perez and which should be that of public management as an academic discipline.

Pragmatically, it comes down to asking whether the state, in its managerial methods, is lagging one industrial revolution behind. A classic example of this lag is the state's relationship with its information systems. The state still thinks in terms of 'computing', i.e., an accumulation of material capital, and not 'information systems' as a way of leveraging the transformation of organizations. It is a drain on the productivity of IT investment and a reason for the persistence of a 'Solow paradox' in public administration. In France, as in many other developed countries, the state has not set up an information systems department (Rougier 2003) responsible for defining a primary architecture and an interoperability policy, resulting in dissimilar systems that do not allow the necessary transition towards results-based management and, more importantly, in an anarchical procurement policy which, were it intelligently designed, could act as a lever of industrial policy and of support for innovative small businesses.

Many of these problems have been worked out in the industrial sector by trial and error. Lessons have been learnt and taken on board and could be applied to the public sector with little difficulty. The later the socio-institutional framework changes, the greater the gap and the more it costs to bridge.

In a nutshell, the fundamental question is this: does the state put itself into a position to learn in order to transform itself? Not knowing is a problem that can be solved by learning, but not knowing that one doesn't know and not putting oneself in a position to learn is a mistake. In those circumstances, the natural lag becomes a culpable one, the result of practical incompetence and a lack of political vision.

To explore the hypothesis that the State and technology evolve synchronously, we consider technology as a knowledge base in Joel Mokyr's meaning of the term. *Societies are adaptive systems whose capacity to change depends on the knowledge base.* It is the knowledge base that will manage change as a selection process of new technologies and new political and social combinations. The dominant powers are those that find the right combination to secure both their internal equilibrium and that of their relations with other national systems of political economy.

The real driver of growth is therefore the knowledge base, embodied in formal and informal institutions in the theories of North and Landes, who have updated this distinction made in the late nineteenth century by Veblen and Commons.

Our basic model starts with Mokyr's concept (2002) of useful knowledge and may be represented as follows in Figure 19.2.

Theoretical (or epistemic) knowledge consists of partly of the available scientific knowledge but above all of beliefs, i.e., what is considered plausible. It is knowledge for itself, produced by a small number of people for 'the love of knowledge', as David Hume puts it in his 1742 essay *Of the Rise and Progress of the Arts and Sciences* and is generally the fruit of happenstance:

> Avarice, or the desire of gain, is an universal passion, which operates at all times, in all places, and upon all persons: But curiosity, or the love of knowledge, has a very limited influence, and requires youth, leisure, education, genius, and example, to make it govern any person. You will never want booksellers, while there are buyers of books: But there may frequently be readers where there are no authors. Multitudes of people,

Figure 19.2. The Evolution of Knowledge According to Joel Mokyr

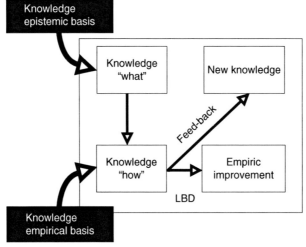

necessity and liberty, have begotten commerce in Holland: But study and application have scarcely produced any eminent writers. (Hume 1742)

It emerges before anyone knows how it may be used, which is the case with advances in science and technological progress. This process of knowledge generation itself follows an evolutionary selection process, which in turn will depend on the state of existing knowledge, in accordance with the principle of path dependence.

Empirical (or prescriptive) knowledge is the practical and operational knowledge engrammed in artefacts. There is limited scope for empirical improvement of this knowledge base (learning by doing). For example, I can empirically improve my mastery of the computer on which I am typing this text. But if I want to design an information system I need to have access to the epistemic knowledge base on which my practical ability is founded. It is what Pisano (2002) has called 'learning before doing'.

What evolutionary mechanism will underpin technological progress? For Mokyr, epistemic knowledge is the gene, while empirical knowledge is the phenotype. It is the capacity to establish interactions between the gene and the phenotype that drives technological evolution. Institutions as sets of rules are the reflection of this knowledge base gene, the belief system that underlies public action. Organizations are phenotypes that translate institutions into the real world. Unlike in pure biological evolution, the knowledge gene is less 'selfish', to use Richard Dawkins' term. There is a possibility of feedback from empirical knowledge to epistemic knowledge, starting off virtuous cycles that generate technological progress. *These cycles are doubly self-reinforcing*: the larger the epistemic base the more it develops of itself, while the more the empirical base feeds back into the epistemic base the more it stimulates its development.

The quality of institutions is central to the workings of this process. How do they co-evolve with the knowledge base?

- First, public institutions are based on organizations: public services, administrations, autonomous operators. The question is then whether the knowledge base of these organizations is able to evolve when they are confronted with a new technological paradigm. In other words, *are public organizations capable of learning and of behaving like adaptive systems?*
- Second, institutions as sets of formal rules have their own evolutionary cycles. David Landes (2003, 199) remarks that although the pace of their evolution is a decisive factor, especially in the short term, it is not necessarily quick: it took over a century, pretty much until the third quarter of the nineteenth century, for the capitalism of the first industrial revolution to forge the institutional framework within which it could truly flourish.

Thus, the evolution of institutions as formal rule sets depends on the evolution of informal rules, i.e., ideas (North 1990). We therefore need to study how these ideas evolve when confronted with the information technology revolution, since the issue at stake is quite clearly the capacity to build institutional comparative advantages (Amable and Petit, 2002).

Linking Evolution of the State and Evolution of Technology

The question of the link between the evolution of technology and the evolution of the state may seem incongruous nowadays, though it was self-evident during the Enlightenment. In her comparative study of relations between the State and invention in France and England, Liliane Hilaire-Pérez (2000) shows that it became a concern of the State at a very early stage. She identifies a genesis: policy in Venice, which, in 1474, became the first state to promulgate a law on inventors. It was seen differently in France and in England, demonstrating both the State's understanding of the importance of accumulating and safeguarding technology and the many different forms that the relationship between the state and technology could take. France, in the Venetian mould, maintained a very close link between policy and invention, whereas England took its distance in the seventeenth century with the royal prerogative. As Daniel Roche has said, 'the craftsman inventor at the end of the seventeenth century was a social hero, more technician than scientist in England, more scientist than technician in France', pronounced national characteristics even today.

But both countries shared the same concern to free the inventor, through political intervention by the state, from both academic thraldom and the cult of short-term gain. Likewise, the state does not only protect and promote the inventor, it also integrates technology in order to modernize its apparatus.

Not only do inventions consolidate the material foundations of power, for example, in war; their integration makes the administration more rational and favours the bureaucratization of a 'technostructure' state while also paving the way for the governmental project (Hilaire-Pérez 2000, 36).

The state, technology and modernization of the administration therefore very clearly evolve alongside each other to develop practices that would make a twenty-first century innovator and modernizer of public institutions green with envy, namely integration of the user into the process of validating the reality of the invention and its social utility and collegial work by administrations (inherited from Colbertism) to validate the exclusive privilege which is the inventor's reward. Inventions become the favoured means of reform. 'The Enlightenment inaugurated the era of political technology, the 'politicization of technology,' as Steven L. Kaplan has put it, and made invention an affair of state (Hilaire-Pérez

2000, 316). Whether English patents or French monopolies, in each case the state seeks to strike a balance between the monopoly that rewards the inventor and the spread of the invention.

This 'politicization of technology' is back on the agenda today with the development of national economic intelligence policies that seek to capture and protect a nation's tangible and intangible strategic assets.

The policy of technology clusters implemented in France since 2006, inspired by the success of such clusters elsewhere, helps to bring administrations closer to their role as architects of technological development. It is a radical change in the state's way of doing things. The success of a technology cluster results from the combination of two movements: one that is top-down, a national policy that provides strategic guidance and budgets, and one, doubtless more critical, that is bottom-up. In his analysis of Silicon Valley, Aoki identified the need for a player that would forge links between innovative small firms in a cluster, in this case the venture capitalist, and create synergies. How that goal is achieved depends on the local context, the culture, the quality of social relations, institutional incentives and the capacity to allocate responsibilities between the different levels involved, from national to local.

More importantly, when the game is being played at the frontiers of technology the dominant ideas that guide public action must be informed by the results of academic research. For instance, recent research by Roger Miller (2008) reveals that innovative practices cluster in a limited number of seven 'games of innovation' that are stable at the meso-economic level, while firms may play in different games at the microeconomic level. Miller shows that patents – a traditional focus of public policy for innovation in the former mass-production paradigm – play only a small role (8 per cent of players), that those who compete on costs (22 per cent of players) need to re-innovate if they want to survive, and that one of the keys in the game of innovation is the 'battle for architecture', i.e., the ability to define architectures, either closed or open, not only through technologies, but above all, through common standards, ideas, practices, norms, etc.

One lesson of Miller's research is that these games of innovation do not fit with the traditional categories of 'strategic activity domains' that group the same kinds of industrial activity. For instance, retail banking and corporate banking play in two different games that obey different rules. The traditional definition of a cluster is a grouping of activities pertaining to the same group of industries. However, Miller demonstrates that a cluster should not play in only one game but must include all the games of innovation so that firms can cooperate. Structuring these clusters in such a way that they include all the games is a matter for public policy.

Thus, a public policy for innovation may be represented as follows:

- At the macroeconomic level, the policy that sustains and funds a political strategy to lead the way in innovation. This includes basic research funding, cooperation between business and public institutions, initial and higher education, etc. and is the outline of what is commonly referred to as a 'national system of innovation.'
- At the meso-economic level, an organization of technological clusters that enables firms to understand the games of innovation and encourages them to cooperate.
- At the microeconomic level, a business intelligence policy that may help individual firms to understand the game of innovation they are playing in and the main opportunities and pitfalls they are confronted with. There is a particular need to support such an understanding of games of innovation within small businesses.

Can Public Management at the Present Time Help to Meet These Challenges?

Three different disciplines need to come together if the evolution of institutions and the evolution of organizations are to be combined

1. *Public policy evaluation* focuses on the value of the policy: are the impacts consistent with the strategic challenges of public policies and is the link between outputs and outcomes relevant and effective? The value of the policy is a matter of political judgment and, although an attempt may be made to construct strategic metrics, they will never ultimately be the key deciding factor
2. *Organizational efficiency* focuses on the strategic alignment of processes and, above all, on organizational learning so that public organizations can cope with their changing missions.
3. *Management control* is a form of steering centred on the best value policy: do outcomes meet expectations at the best cost, so that the cost/value ratio is optimized? The best value policy is a management matter and can be measured by a metric that, though more difficult to frame and implement than in the commercial sector, is not beyond reach.

These three dimensions can be interlinked by means of the increasingly widely used 'balanced scorecard', using information technologies that combine business-line architecture with technological architecture. The problem is that the academic discipline that has grown up under the title of 'public management', does so only to a very small extent.

The use of information technology in public administration is again revealing here. In the mainstream NPM framework, using IT is mainly conceived as a means of reducing costs. In an innovative and Schumpeterian framework, what is at stake is the ability to integrate the transformative potential of IT to foster a collective learning process within the public sector. One of the main failures of the NPM mainstream, especially in the UK and New Zealand, is its policy of outsourcing IT to the private sector, which has deprived the public sector of the strategic capabilities to manage IT and contributed to the constitution of provider oligopolies, with high costs and poor reliability as a result (Dunleavy and Margetts 2003). Technology is not a heaven-sent miracle cure but a means of stimulating innovation through learning (Rochet 2008).

I have shown that innovation is entirely possible in the public sector (Rochet 2007), especially by taking advantage of crises (Rochet 2008), provided that the 'one size fits all' recipes of NPM are avoided. Shunning NPM means returning to principles of organizational transformation based on human capital and a consideration of the context, integrating the potential of IT to make it a lever of endogenous transformation and not a sort of manna from heaven, as in the neoclassical view, that only needs to be adopted for problems to solve themselves.

So what NPM turned inside out has to be turned right way round again.

- That means first and foremost posing the question of value, in terms of the impact of public action by organizations on publics in the light of the political issues at stake in the context of the paradigm shift. Effectiveness must come before efficiency.
- Second, it means using the transformational potential of IT to come up with new processes of intervention, i.e., turning IT into an endogenous lever of innovation which makes things possible that otherwise would not have been, such as the modelling and automation of processes, the measurement of outcomes in real time and the possibility of building up a knowledge base. One of the most spectacular transformations of a professional activity has taken place in healthcare with the development of evidence-based medicine, in which decision-making is informed by research data (epistemic knowledge base), clinical experience (empirical knowledge base) and the preferences of the patient and his or her immediate circle (contextualization of the diagnosis and decision). Such innovations would be impossible if practitioners did not accept computerized knowledge management tools.
- Third, IT makes it possible to produce an overall design of processes and to align it with strategic objectives, thus enabling organizations to be efficient and reducing bureaucracy.

These tasks, in the conception of public mechanisms, are interactive but place the issue of the value of the policy at the forefront, whereas NPM puts efficiency first and neglects the process of endogenous innovation in administration.

The Fight to Manufacture Dominant Ideas

We come now to the last point to be included in the research programme in public management: the fight for dominant ideas. I have already pointed out that, unfortunately, although innovation in public organizations is entirely possible, it has little influence on dominant ideas, on the ideas embedded in institutions, and that hence, North's dynamic did not occur in this particular case. The minister at the head of an administration is not really a manager who knows his administration (which was one of NPM's basic pretexts for keeping the framing and the implementation of policy separate). It is always highly surprising, in discussions with politicians, to see how little they know about innovation in public administration and hence, prevent it[4]. Dominant ideas do not form through trial and error in contact with administrations, but in specific places where the great and good mingle (like Davos, where liberal thinking reigns supreme), with no concern for what really goes on in the day-to-day business of administrations or the innovation that takes place there despite everything.

The stakes are not insignificant. In conclusion, let us return to history. We have seen how Britain invented the 'myth of free trade' once it had become the dominant power, managing to pass off as a universal value what was merely the reflection of its own interests. The United States used the same strategy in the second half of the twentieth century. Manufacturing universal myths is one element of a domination strategy, but it can cut both ways.

The 'myth of free trade' has blurred these lessons of history. Much has been written about the subject in the last ten years (a recent Google search on the string turned up 40,000 entries). Its correspondent in public management is New Public Management, nourished by the rise of the 'public choice' school and neoclassical economics in contrast with the Weberian tradition.

While mythmaking may be a means of domination for incumbent countries standing on the technological frontier, allowing them to find commercial outlets for their products, it may also lead them to shoot themselves in the foot. Technological spillovers from leading countries to followers are increasing with globalization (Baumol 1986). Yet innovative activity consists mainly of imitation (Baumol, Litan, Schramm 2008), giving countries that are in the process of catching up an advantage, since through trade they are able to benefit from technology transfers from developed countries. That is clearly China's strategy today.

Britain was the first to pay the price of such a strategy. The United States had almost entirely caught up by the end of the nineteenth century and Britain's institutional vigour had wilted. David Landes (2000) identifies the main cause as 'entrepreneurial constipation'.

> The weakness of British enterprise reflected their combination of amateurism and complacency. Her merchants, who had once seized the markets of the world, took them for granted; the consular reports are full of the incompetence of British exporters, their refusal to suit their goods to the taste and pockets of the client, their unwillingness to try new products in new areas, their insistence that everyone in the world ought to read in English and count in pounds, shillings and pence. Similarly, the British manufacturer was notorious for his indifference to style, his conservatism in the face of new techniques, his reluctance to abandon the individuality of tradition for the conformity implicit in mass production. (Landes 2003, 337)

Nicholas Crafts (2004) sums up these causes, in addition to loss of the spirit of enterprise, as lack of investment in human capital, lack of investment in general, firms that were too small for mass production, crumbling social consensus and, above all, excessive faith in the market's capacity to regulate the economy. Britain had ended up believing an argument that it had previously used against its competitors in order to hamper them in their development. It applied to itself what Friedrich List called, in Ha-Joon Chang's nicely updated version (2007), the 'strategy of taking away the ladder' and 'shot itself in the foot'.

When the virtuous circle of organizational learning and institutional evolution is no longer sufficient to enable the State to cope with a paradigm shift, public management, looking beyond the management of organizations, must go back to the fundamental issues of political philosophy, those of the 'good society' and the common good, which question the possible impacts of technology and do not regard it as a universal revealed truth that defines a sacrosanct course of history.

References

Abramovitz, M. 1990. 'Economics of Growth.' In M. Abramovitz. *Thinking about Growth and Other Essays on Economic Growth and Welfare.* Cambridge, MA: Cambridge University Press.

Aglietta, M. and L. Berrebi. 2007. *Désordres dans le capitalisme mondial.* Paris: Odile Jacob.

Amable, B. and P. Petit. 2002. 'La diversité des systèmes sociaux d'innovation et de production dans les années 1990.' In J.-P. Touffut (ed.). *Institutions et innovation.* Centre Saint-Gobain pour la recherche en économie. Paris: Albin Michel.

Aoki, M. 2001. *Toward a Comparative Institutional Analysis.* Cambridge, MA: MIT Press.

Bairoch, P. 1997. *Victoires et déboires: Histoire économique et sociale du monde du XVIe siècle à nos jours.* Paris: Gallimard.

Baumol, W. J. 1986. 'Productivity Growth, Convergence, and Welfare: What the Long-Run Data Show.' *American Economic Review* 76, 1072–1085.

Baumol W. J., R. E. Litan and C. J. Schramm. 2008. *Good Capitalism, Bad Capitalism, and the Economics of Growth and Prosperity.* New Haven: Yale University Press.

Borins, S. 2008, *Innovations in Government: Research, Recognition, and Replication.* Washington, DC: Brookings.

Boudon, R. 2006. *Renouveler la démocratie, éloge du sens commun.* Paris: Odile Jacob.

Braudel, F. 1985. *La dynamique du capitalisme.* Paris: Champs, Flammarion.

Caron, F. 1997. *Les deux révolutions industrielles du XXe siècle.* Paris: Albin Michel.

Chang, H.-J. 2007. *Bad Samaritans: The Myth of Free Trade and the Secret History of Capitalism.* London: Bloomsbury.

Cobden, R. 1868. *The Political Writings of Richard Cobden.* Available at http://www.econlib.org/library/YPDBooks/Cobden/cbdPW.html

Crafts, N. 2004. 'Long Run Growth.' In R. Floud and P. Johnson (eds). *The Cambridge Economic History of Modern Britain.* Cambridge: Cambridge University Press.

Dunleavy, P. and H. Margetts. 2003. 'E-Government and Policy Innovation in Seven Liberal Democracies.' Paper, Political Studies Association's Annual Conference, Leicester University.

The Economist. 2008. "Re-bonjour, Monsieur Colbert." 23 October.

Findlay, R. and K. O'Rourke. 2008. *Power and Plenty.* Princeton: Princeton University Press.

Freeman, C. and F. Louçã. 2001. *As Time Goes By: From the Industrial Revolutions to the Information Revolution.* Oxford: Oxford University Press.

Freeman, C. and L. Soete (eds). 1997. *The Economics of Industrial Innovation.* Cambridge, MA: MIT Press.

Gerschenkron, A. 1969. *Economic Backwardness in Historical Perspective.* Cambridge, MA: Harvard University Press.

Hilaire-Pérez, L. 2000. *L'invention technique au siècle des lumières.* Paris: Albin Michel.

Hume, D. 1742. *Of the Rise and Progress of the Arts and Sciences.* 1875 Green and Grose edn. Available at http://infomotions.com/etexts/philosophy/1700-1799/hume-of-737.htm

Landes, D. S. 2000, *Richesse et pauvreté des nations: Pourquoi certains sont riches, pourquoi certains sont pauvres,* Paris: Albin Michel.

———. 2003. *The Unbound Prometheus: Technological Change and Industrial Development in Western Europe from 1750 to the Present.* 2nd edn. Cambridge: Cambridge University Press.

Mill, J. S. 1848. *The Principles of Political Economy.* Available at http://socserv.mcmaster.ca/econ/ugcm/3ll3/mill/prin/index.html

Miller, R. et al. 2008. 'Innovation Games: A New Approach to the Competitive Challenge.' *Long Range Planning,* in press.

Mokyr, J. 2002. *The Gifts of Athena: Historical Origins of the Knowledge Economy.* Princeton: Princeton University Press.

North, D. C. 1981. *Structure and Change in Economic History.* New York: Norton.

———. 1990. *Institutions, Institutional Change and Economic Performance.* Cambridge, MA: Harvard University Press.

———. 2005. *Understanding the Process of Economic Change.* Princeton, NJ: Princeton University Press.

North, D. C. and R. P. Thomas. 1973. *The Rise of the Western World: A New Economic History.* Cambridge: Cambridge University Press.

O'Brien, P. 1998. 'Inseparable Connexions: Trade Economy, Fiscal State and the Expansion of Empire, 1688–1815.' In P. Marshall (ed.). *The Oxford History of the British Empire* 2. Oxford: Oxford University Press.

O'Brien, P. and P. Hunt. 1999. *The Rise of the Fiscal State in Europe 1200–1815*. Oxford: Oxford University Press.

Perez, C. 2002. *Technological Revolutions and Financial Capital: The Dynamics of Bubbles and Golden Ages*. Cheltenham: Edward Elgar. [74.1]

———. 2004. 'Technological Revolutions Paradigm Shifts and Socio-Institutional Change.' In E. S. Reinert (ed.). *Globalization, Economic Development and Inequality: An Alternative Perspective*. Cheltenham: Edward Elgar. [75.1]

Pisano, G. P. 2002. 'In Search of Dynamic Capabilities.' In G. Dosi, R. Nelson and S. G. Winter (eds). *The Nature and Dynamics of Organizational Capabilities*. Oxford: Oxford University Press.

Reinert, E. S. 2007. *How Rich Countries Got Rich … and Why Poor Countries Stay Poor*. London: Constable & Robinson.

Rochet, C. 2007. *L'innovation, une affaire d'Etat: Gagnants et perdants de la IIIe révolution industrielle*. Paris: L'Harmattan.

———. 2008. 'The Common Good as an Invisible Hand: Machiavelli's Legacy to public Management.' *International Review of Administrative Sciences* 74, 497–521.

Rochet, C., O. Keramidas and L. Bout. 2008. 'Crisis as Change Strategy in Public Organizations.' *International Review of Administrative Sciences* 74, 65–77.

Rougier, H. 2003. *Economie du logiciel: renforcer la dynamique française*. Paris: Commissariat Général du Plan.

Schumpeter, J. A. 1986. *Histoire de l'analyse économique*. Paris: Gallimard.

Smith, A. 1904 [1776]. *An Inquiry into the Nature and Causes of the Wealth of Nations*. London: Methuen.

Thompson, F. 2006. "The Political Economy of Public Administration." In *Handbook of Public Administration*. Boca Raton, FL: CRC, Taylor & Francis.

CARLOTA PEREZ – HER BIOGRAPHY AND THE ORIGINS OF HER IDEAS

Erik S. Reinert
and
Benjamin Sagalovsky

Carlota Perez was born in Caracas, Venezuela, on 20 September 1939, the oldest of five children. Her father, Jose Henrique Perez Perez (1913-1978), was a very successful civil engineer as well as an international chess player who enjoyed playing up to twenty simultaneous games, including one in which he wasn't even allowed to look at the board. He devised a system for geographers to define the exact coastline in relation to tides, which was patented by the German company that built the equipment, and a method for scheduling his construction projects that predated PERT-CPM. Her mother, Carlota Perez Arenas (born 1919), is a painter and a determined, charming and courageous woman who, at ninety, drives a car and surfs the web.

The children were raised with very high expectations, and all, including the three girls, were expected to become engineers like their father. By the time Carlota entered kindergarten, at the age of three, she was already reading and writing. Her father's work took the family around the country, and Carlota ended up attending five different elementary schools.

The year Carlota turned eleven, the family got their first TV, she started high school and her parents divorced. Her mother, then 30, embarked for Buenos Aires with the five children – aged 6 to 11 – her sister, her aunt and her Oldsmobile. The Venezuelan petro-dollars were hard currency in Peron's Argentina and the children all went to private schools. Carlota had barely started high school anew in Argentina when, six months later, the family returned to Venezuela and she was sent to a Catholic boarding school in upstate New York.

Those were the early 1950s, and from the television set at the school dorm the young Carlota witnessed the rise of the 'American way of life' and the advance of mass production and mass consumption across society.

After graduation, reflecting the inclinations of both of her parents, Carlota decided to study architecture; she was one of only four women in the school of Architecture at the Illinois Institute of Technology. Led by Mies van der Rohe, the school was the epicentre of the Bauhaus movement in the United States, identified with Mies' signature glass-and-steel buildings. On her next visit to Caracas, where summer temperatures reign year around, Carlota thought that the first glass-and-steel building in Caracas would also be its last, and she decided to transfer to the more eclectic Pratt Institute in Brooklyn, New York. As Caracas eventually filled with glass office buildings and Venezuelans traded their light Caribbean clothes for gabardine jackets, shirts and ties, her wrong prediction taught her a valuable lesson: glass structures, northern clothing and cheap energy for air conditioning all came together to Venezuela as part of the same bundle of adoption without adaptation; all part of what she would later call the same techno-economic paradigm.

The study of architecture left a strong imprint on Carlota. Architects develop a capacity to analyze and integrate several contrasting but interrelated issues: the relationship between form and function; the shaping role of social, cultural, climatic and physical contexts; the difficult balance between structure and aesthetics; the need to fuse desires and feasibility, to blend beauty with the crude pragmatism of working wiring and plumbing. They also need to deal explicitly with the notions of design options and relative costs; a whole must be constructed as a combination not only of parts, but also of trade-offs. When she later turned her interest to the study of social structures, this background led her naturally to interdisciplinary endeavours and to the 'realm of the feasible' as a natural boundary for human action.

Carlota's increasing rejection of the restrictions and limits of individual disciplines brings echoes of the Faustian economics approach of the German Historical School, and of their dictum: *Zuerst war die Ganzheit* (in the beginning was the whole). Erik's paper in this volume points to more parallels between Carlota's thinking and pre-World War II German and United States economics.

In the early 1960s, when Carlota returned to Venezuela, she found herself in the middle of the revolutionary fervour aroused by the Cuban revolution, and the desire of so many young Latin Americans to follow that example. Marxism was at the top of everybody's reading list at the university and a central topic of discussion among intellectuals in every café. Engels' (1884) *The Origin of the Family, Private Property and the State* made a profound impression on Carlota, as the book resonated with her recent witnessing of how changes in technology can bring about transformations in economy and society.

The Venezuelan intellectuals' enamouring with 'real socialism' was crushed by the tanks that invaded Czechoslovakia in 1968. Carlota was impressed by the tragic outcome of an attempt to transform the Soviet system and replace the ruling *nomenklatura* with an intellectual elite capable of positive change and opening society to democracy and innovation. She was already appalled at the so-called 'Cultural' Revolution in China that enthroned inexperience and ignorance and tried to destroy all competence and accumulated knowledge, be it local or foreign. Her conviction was – and is – that a decent society can only be constructed through increased knowledge and ever-widening capabilities.

Carlota was by now determined to understand the role of knowledge and technology in the well-being of societies and the relationship, if any, between technology and social structures. She moved to France and embarked on a completely new career in Interdisciplinary Social Sciences at the University of Paris. One of her teachers, the young Benjamin Coriat, introduced her to the relationship between technical change and the changes in work organization, an idea that would become an essential contribution to her notion of paradigm shifts. She was also impressed by Radovan Richta's (1966) *Civilization at the Crossroads*, the manifesto of the Czech movement, whose main argument for a change of regime was based on the emergence of the computer and of information-based technologies, which demanded a different kind of power structure and a replacement of the bureaucrats with the intelligentsia.

A question that had long been troubling her was the fact that the technologies underlying both the capitalist and communist countries, as well as the failed Nazi and Fascist regimes, were essentially the same, and yet they were the basis for profoundly different social structures. Could the contrast between the Athenian and Spartan models provide a relevant historical parallel? Carlota submerged herself in the literature about the various Greek city-states and discovered that they did not fit the 'slavery mode of production' described by the Marxists. She identified not just two, but five different modes: from a patriarchal society with no slaves, through the Spartan caste system and its slave-centred economy, to the Athenian market-based democracy where the work of foreign slaves in mines and homes played a marginal role. This clearly suggested that the relationship between technology and society, while enormously relevant, was much more subtle and complex than what 'historical materialism' proposed.

Upon returning to Venezuela, she took an academic job as a researcher at the Central University in Caracas. She was tasked with reviewing the structural causes of the energy crisis of the 1970s and identifying its possible impact on the worldwide demand for oil. While researching these issues, she was startled to find out that at that point in time there was hardly any product or technology that was not energy intensive. The 1972 and 1976 reports of the *Club of Rome* had already highlighted the excessive use of materials and energy in relation to growth, while an article in *Fortune* magazine soon after the price hike (March 1974) calculated that six industries were responsible for 60 per cent of all industrial energy consumption (petrochemicals, oil refining, paper, cement, steel and aluminium), and yet the technologies existed that could help cut their consumption significantly. The reason why they did not bother to use them was clearly spelled out in one of the subtitles of the article: 'Too Cheap to Worry About'. This opened her eyes to the important role played by the low cost of oil in shaping the apparently varied technologies of the post-war era.

Around that time, the late 1970s, the all-pervasive promise of microelectronics was becoming apparent. A 1976 article in *Business Week* announced a 'Machine Revolution' that was 'Providing Products with Brainpower'. Not only were electronic instruments capable of controlling energy and materials use; these tiny and powerful chips could transform all sorts of products and processes, and create a host of new ones. Most of all, they were cheap and constantly getting cheaper and more powerful. The nature of the upcoming technological shift became clear to her: low-cost microelectronics would come to replace low-cost oil in shaping the technologies of the future.

It was in those years that Benjamin Sagalovsky met Carlota. With a background in electronics, and working at the time on a critical analysis of the Club of Rome's second model, he was soon drafted into Carlota's discussions about the oil-based economy and the nature and potential of microelectronics. Their dialog and friendship continued and deepened as they both pursued graduate studies in California, and extends to this date.

At the time of her insight into the role of microelectronics, Carlota had moved from the university to the Institute of Foreign Trade (ICE), a government department connected to the Ministry of International Economic Relations, headed by Manuel Perez Guerrero, the Co-Chairman of the North-South Dialogue. Carlota was in charge of technology issues, and thus was part of delegations to United Nations meetings on 'technology transfer' and on 'codes of conduct for transnational corporations' – part of what was then touted as a New International Economic Order. After years of great difficulty in gaining access to manufacturing technologies and export markets, developing countries were now able to buy licenses and set up factories, and produce not only for the home market but for export as well. The term in vogue was 'industrial redeployment', and these UN meetings were meant to regulate and improve the conditions for this transfer. Carlota was puzzled. Why had the situation changed? Why was it now profitable to sell the technologies outright, whereas before it had been difficult to get corporations to go beyond the fully owned foreign subsidiary? Why would the differential cost of labour suddenly become so important; hadn't it always been there? To answer these questions, she would need the notions of technological trajectories and maturity, which she would first learn about in Chris Freeman's (1974) classic text *The Economics of Industrial Innovation*. Now it was still a puzzle, but one thing was clear: the conditions for access to technology change substantially as time goes by.

She wondered whether such a shift might have happened before. Some university colleagues pointed her to Kondratiev's (1926) article on long waves and to Jevons' (1965) *The Coal Question*. Jevons' discussion of the consequences of dearer and less accessible coal for British growth in the 1860s clearly echoed the debates she was witnessing on the consequences of high-priced oil and the possible limits on world reserves. Moreover, Kondratiev's data about long waves and his cryptic suggestion that they were 'inherent in the essence of the capitalist economy' led her to a much wider formulation of her questions and to the intuition that such major changes in the direction and impact of technology might be a recurrent historical phenomenon.

As events further confirmed the depth of the changes taking place, Carlota decided to undertake formal research in the context of a postgraduate program. The ambition of the project and its overtly interdisciplinary nature made acceptance difficult in most conventional schools. She was warmly welcomed, though, at San Francisco State University, where a group of scholars had come together to set up a Department of Interdisciplinary Social Sciences. Raymond Miller, Stan Bailis and Don Barnhart became friendly guides in her ambitious and multidirectional endeavour. The location, near Silicon Valley, was an ideal place for witnessing the emergence of the information revolution and its exciting early years.

Some key readings during that time greatly contributed to consolidating her conceptual framework. Schumpeter's (1939) *Business Cycles* reinforced the importance of technology for economic growth and planted the seed for a future closer look at the important role of finance. That came together with Chris Freeman's (1974) book about the economics of innovation, Kuhn's (1962) *The Structure of Scientific Revolutions* and Kenneth Boulding's (1961) *The Image*. The latter was an odd book to come from an economist; it was essentially an argument about how worldviews (images) are formed in individuals and negotiated in society, and how they end up governing behaviour. Kuhn's theory provided three important insights about the impact of paradigm changes in science: how they redefined the criteria for the valid questions and the valid answers, the resistance this generates in the incumbents and the need to rewrite history to reinforce the belief in a continuous and uninterrupted process of advance. Major shifts in images or paradigms would face inertia precisely because the prior ones were strongly interwoven, were shared by the whole community and fulfilled expectations of security, stability and progress. All the main pieces thus came together for constructing the notion of a techno-economic paradigm, which would arise from the features and requirements of each particular technological revolution, and would set boundaries to the organization of production, the patterns of consumption and eventually the whole socio-institutional framework.

But Carlota didn't originally use the term paradigm in spite of having been impressed with Kuhn. At first she called it '*patrón tecnológico*,' which in Spanish implies a mixture of model to follow and regime. She didn't like the English translation as 'standard' as in the Gold Standard (*patrón oro*), and ended up choosing 'technological style'. This term, and Carlota's thinking in general, parallels the view in German economics – dating from long before Marx – that history revolves along qualitatively different stages (*Stufen*) of economic growth, what Marxists came to call 'modes of production' and what later, with Bertram Schefold, were to be called 'economic styles', or '*Wirtschaftsstile*'.

The structure was gradually coming together, but Carlota felt overwhelmed. She figured that in order to present these ideas, she would eventually have to write a major book, much like Schumpeter's *Business Cycles*. She was doing the research, amassing historical data, thinking through and writing what was shaping up as a full-fledged theory. Besides, as she recalls with unsuppressed fondness, her red portable Olivetti did not help – like today's computers would – with the many changes and rewritings required.

When Carlota returned to Venezuela in 1980 she decided to tackle the practical matters of technology policy armed with her new understanding. One of her contracts was the design of a new Technology Department for the Ministry of Development. She had long felt that the separate councils or ministries of science and technology in Latin America were inadequate for the task of promoting innovation in industry. They were always complaining about the lack of a bridge between research and industry, and she understood that this was so because they were what an architect would call a 'cantilever': a structure anchored on one side only. There were no pillars within industry to hold the other side of the bridge. She proposed to build those pillars and she worked on it herself; after designing the post of Director of Technological Development, she accepted to take it on as its first incumbent. The ensuing three years were priceless in furthering her understanding of the model of industrialization based on Import Substitution, and the underlying reasons for the lack of indigenous capability in the assembly industries. Paradoxically, there was more technological learning in natural resources, construction, electricity and the rest of the infrastructure that surrounded and provided services to the bare bones assembly plants.

She also gave active support to an indigenous electronics industry, started by Berkeley- and Stanford-trained PhDs. She saw how a fully digital PABX (local telephone exchange), the first in the world, was designed, built and exported by a small Venezuelan firm, as well as several other innovations. This was radically different from the rest of the local industries. In search of the deeper meaning of this anomaly, Carlota re-read Landes' (1969) *The Unbound Prometheus* and his depiction of how the United States and Germany, coming from behind, overtook Britain and gained leadership in the electrical and chemical technologies early in the twentieth century. Through her connections with other Latin Americans involved in Science and Technology policy, she found that in Brazil, Argentina and other countries, the electronics sector was innovating strongly as well, in stark contrast with the traditional, import-substituting electromechanical sectors. This brought her to Seev Hirsch's and Raymond Vernon's product cycle theory, and their analysis of how old technologies migrate at maturity. It became clear that there were two key periods in the evolution of a technology when it is accessible to laggards: at the beginning and at the end of its life cycle. This idea was to be developed in her 1988 article, together with Luc Soete, who had already advanced the concept of 'leapfrogging'. [23] It was further elaborated in an article originally written for the UNCTAD X meeting in 1999 and then published in the *Cepal Review* No. 75 in 2001. [72.1.1] Unfortunately, she also witnessed how the local electronics entrepreneurs lost their edge as better-located companies overtook them. That became another piece of the puzzle to investigate.

Her work entailed intense interaction with large and small firms, public and private, about the conditions and obstacles for technical change and innovation. This would prove highly valuable for her future consultancy work, and a solid groundwork for further elaboration. She became an avid reader of business publications: *Harvard Business Review, Business Week, Electronics*, and all the books of the business gurus so much in fashion at that time. She wanted to better understand and contrast what was happening to the companies in the developed world vis-à-vis what she was seeing in Venezuela as a result of the Import Substitution policies. To further understand these differences she spent the whole of 1993 (funded by the Canadian International Development Research Council) in a real-time case study of the modernization of a manufacturing company with 500 employees. Her paper on the Legacy of Import Substitution (published in Spanish in *Comercio Exterior* of Mexico in 1996, [52]) owed much to that intense and direct contact with the local industrial experience, and to her realization of how different it was from the cases described in the consultancy books and the international business press.

Another seminal insight arose from her experience founding FINTEC, the first venture capital government agency in Venezuela. It was based on models from Brazil and Israel, inspired by discussions with Morris Teubal, whom she had invited to visit Venezuela, and designed in collaboration with Sergio Barrio, a Peruvian colleague and a former researcher from SPRU, the Science

Policy Research Unit headed by Chris Freeman at the University of Sussex. The implementation of FINTEC was impaired by debates among all the government offices involved; when the agency was finally born, it ended up with too little money, too much interference and an inbuilt incapacity to take risks. The main practical problem was that it was illegal to lend public money without full collateral; this made the whole notion of government venture capital impossible and crippled the new institution. While government funding – and even direct public investment – had been very effective in helping set up the local production of traditional imports, and even in promoting mature export industries in some countries, it wasn't clear that it could do the same job for radical innovation. Could the private market be the only mechanism capable of bringing real risk-takers together with real innovators, at the particular time when this is badly needed? The answer to this question would take Carlota into an analysis of the role of financial capital, ultimately leading to her Great Surges theory.

But this was still 1983, and at that time Sergio Barrio suggested inviting Chris Freeman, Keith Pavitt, Roy Rothwell and Kurt Hoffman to come from SPRU and help convince the Venezuelan government of the importance of establishing a serious technology policy. Their visit was a big boost to many of the projects at hand, but the most important consequence for Carlota was meeting Chris. Catering to his interest in bird watching, she took him for lengthy walks in Parque del Este in Caracas and to Cata, a beautiful Caribbean beach at the edge of a rain forest. That scenery surrounded hours of conversation about technology and long waves, and Chris' proverbial generosity led him to pronounce that Carlota's views went even further than he had gone. He invited her to the seminar on Long Waves he was organizing in London, and suggested that she present a paper on the basic structure of her model.

Though Carlota doubted that such synthesis could be possible in the short space of an article, Chris insisted. He worked alongside her, reading through two reams of incomplete chapters and dozens of bits and pieces as they sorted them by theme and selected the clearest or simplest formulations. To her astonishment, the resulting outline was filled in one day from sections already written and a few connecting paragraphs. Two days later, she was presenting the paper at the Long Wave Seminar in London, and by the end of the year it was published. That is how the *Futures* article on 'Structural Change and Assimilation of New Technologies in the Economic and Social Systems' [3.1] came to be. Carlota remembers it as giving birth, with all the pain, the joy, and the relief.

To this day, Chris has been her colleague, partner and staunch supporter, through a long personal and professional relationship and a collaboration spanning a quarter of a century.

After the London seminar, Carlota secured funding from CLACSO (Latin American Social Sciences Council) to spend two years in SPRU as a visiting fellow. Chris Freeman introduced her ideas to the academic world, in particular to the evolutionary economics community. He cited her ideas in his own work, whenever relevant, and with his support, by the late 1980s, she was established as a researcher with her work gaining wider and wider recognition. They wrote various papers together for major conferences, culminating in their joint chapter in the 1988 book *Technical Change and Economic Theory*. [20.1]

Meantime, in 1985, having written four papers for publication and a major report about a strategy for the electronics industry in Venezuela [10], Carlota had gone back to work in Caracas. The 1980s were 'the lost decade' for Latin America, and even though high oil revenues allowed Venezuela to service the debt without yet having to follow IMF conditions on eliminating protective tariffs, it was clear to her that this could not last. Under the auspices of the United Nations Development Programme (UNDP), she set up a project in the Ministry of Industry to work with local companies and prepare them to better survive global competition. Also, and with support from the *Corporación Andina de Fomento CAF*, she brought a British team from the *Centre for Research in Innovation Management* CENTRIM, headed by John Bessant and Howard Rush, to train a local group of innovation consultants. Carlota's contributions to Science and Technology policy in her country earned her the Order of Andres Bello for outstanding service in Education and Science.

For several years, Carlota worked as a freelance consultant in different Latin American countries and lectured at university, government and business events. She immersed herself again in the actual problems of the agents of production, innovation and policy, while joining the conceptual dots of her model into what was gradually becoming a big picture. To keep her research efforts alive, Carlota kept her part-time visiting fellow status at SPRU, going there three times a year for a month or more. It was on one of those trips, during a conference in Maastricht, that Erik Reinert met Carlota. They discovered their common interest in the fate of Latin America, and immediately established a strong intellectual connection and a lasting friendship.

By the mid-nineties, Carlota wanted to devote more uninterrupted time to research and to write down a comprehensive account of her theories. She spent five months in SPRU and gathered enough evidence to begin writing what would become her book on *Technological Revolutions and Financial Capital*. [74.1] At that time, Erik was setting up The Other Canon, a network of economists rejecting the 'Physics envy' orthodoxy, reconnecting economics to history and to the *Praxisnähe* – the closeness to reality – of the former historical schools of economics. In 1997, in Oslo, Norsk Investorforum organized a conference on the turbulent relationship between finance and the real economy: 'Production

Capitalism vs. Financial Capitalism; Symbiosis and Parasitism: An Evolutionary Perspective.' (A prolegomenon and a 40-page bibliography on this subject, which has acquired increased actuality with the 2008 financial crisis, are found on www.othercanon.org.) The title seemed almost tailored to Carlota's own research programme.

After that seminar, she started looking for an opportunity to complete the book, which finally presented itself through a part-time contract with INTEVEP, the R&D arm of the Venezuelan oil company PDVSA. She stopped travelling – except to SPRU for research – and worked intensively in both reading and writing. She was finally able to read in depth, and with a clear purpose in mind, the works of Keynes, Kindleberger, Kuznets, Minsky, Hilferding, Veblen and so many others that had looked at the processes of growth, finance and cyclicality. Each contributed in a different way to structure, deepen and enrich the model that was taking shape.

Using Carlos Marichal's (1988) data on the Latin American debt crises across history she discovered an almost clockwork regularity since the Independence loans: money was lent at the maturity phase of each technological revolution and led to default some years after. Alfred Chandler's (1977) *Visible Hand* gave her a sequence in the structure of firms that coincided with the timing of the key paradigm changes. She found in David Wells' (1889) *Recent Economic Changes* strong and curious parallels with the Hoover Report (1929) on the frenzy of the 1920s, even though historically the 1880s were remembered as the 'Great Depression.' Could it be that the price declines of that earlier period were indeed a consequence of increased productivity in some important sectors, as Wells suggested? Could that supposed 'downswing' be a combination of an upswing in the new sectors, going through a productivity explosion, and a strong decline in the old sectors as they reached maturity and faced stagnant markets?

Carlota gradually began to question the Schumpeterian scheme of upswing and downswing in economic aggregates. She was convinced, for instance, that the 1950s represented the flourishing of all the technological potential that had been unleashed in the 1920s; it was the same technological revolution, the same paradigm. If that was the case, then the 1930s were not the end of a wave but just a parenthesis, as it were, in the process of diffusion. Working with Chris, she had already written a critique of Schumpeter's insistence on measuring the waves by the evolution of macroeconomic aggregates, which 'hid more than they revealed'. Now she realized that the proper object of study was not economic growth per se, but the process of technological diffusion and its various consequences. The focus had to be on the introduction and turbulent absorption by the economy and society of a new set of technologies and a new techno-economic paradigm and their deployment until maturity. With this way of looking at it, the timing and the regularities were revealed. She went back to all her history books, and the pendular movement of economic prominence from financial to production capital, with a stock market crash midway, became clearly visible in the long-term record. That completely changed the dating of each long wave and required a different concept. She chose 'great surge of development'.

The recurrence of a 'hiatus' of institutional recomposition after each crash not only helped understand the 1930s, but also suggested that once the new paradigm was established, finance had done its job of funding the new entrepreneurs and the infrastructure, and the resulting bubble had crashed, it was up to the various social forces to negotiate and establish the direction in which the economic potential unleashed would be focused, choosing from the wide range of the technically possible. The insights garnered in that initial review of Ancient Greece finally found a place in explaining the far more recent chapters of economic history.

Excited with the new findings, Carlota struggled with the appropriate naming for the periods and the phases, and worried about mechanical interpretations or excess determinism. But by now the puzzle was really solved and she just had to write it down. It was 1999.

When the NASDAQ stock market collapse occurred, Carlota was devastated. She thought she had lost the opportunity of (correctly) predicting it. On the bright side, this forced her to make the book independent of the specific historical moment; she had to describe the theory and the recurring sequence of diffusion of technological revolutions clearly enough as to be useful when read during any of its phases.

With the publication of *Technological Revolutions and Financial Capital* in 2002 [74.1], Carlota's theoretical edifice was basically complete. She was invited to do research in the Cambridge Endowment for Research in Finance (CERF) at the Judge Institute of the University of Cambridge. She soon became a consultant and lecturer to top global corporations. IBM has incorporated her theories into its global strategic thinking, Volkswagen invited her to be in the Scientific Board of its corporate university, Cisco regularly features her as a keynote speaker in its international events and so do other companies, governments and international organizations. She has been invited to give public lectures at Lund University, Sweden; the University of Oslo; the Instituto de Empresa and Universidad Complutense in Madrid; Deusto University in Bilbao; UC Berkeley in California; her own universities of Cambridge and Sussex and many others in Europe and Latin America.

In 2006, Carlota Perez was elected Professor of Technology and Socio-Economic Development at Tallinn University of Technology. She was to join the faculty of a Technology Governance graduate program set up by professors

Rainer Kattel, Wolfgang Drechsler, and Erik Reinert, who in 2004 had become Professor of Technology Governance and Development Strategies there. Carlota had met Wolfgang at the 1997 trailblazing Oslo conference and Rainer in 2002 in Tallinn at a workshop in the Estonian Ministry of Economics, and had since maintained a fruitful and frequent exchange of ideas with both of them. The new programme was in line with and partially based on her theories and on those of The Other Canon, in general. Tallinn University of Technology has since then become an intellectual hub for those theories.

As of this writing, her major research projects include the investigation of the nature and consequences of major technology and financial bubbles, the challenges posed by energy and environmental issues in shaping the deployment of Information and Communications Technologies, and the potential for combining technology and natural resources to re-launch the development effort in Latin America.

As should be evident from this sketch, Carlota's career is not that of the typical academic. Her theories have been developed through combining experience with study and through alternating roles as public servant, consultant, public lecturer and researcher. Her avid reading of theory is guided by her questions, and she often quips that the problem with the educational system is that if fills people with answers well before they have had the opportunity to formulate any of the questions. The bibliography at the end of this volume confirms the growth of important ideas from a strong connection to the practical world of policy making. It is her closeness to the real world – her *Praxisnähe* – building her theory from the facts towards a higher level of abstraction, rather than from assumptions, that makes her a worthy member of the German Historical School of Economics.

Carlota's architectural striving for integration and pragmatism, and for finding a structure that can maintain the whole together, has benefited us all and provides an overarching model that sheds some badly needed light on the challenges, opportunities and choices that we all need to face in these troubled times.

NOTES

Introduction: Carlota Perez and Evolutionary Economics

1 Sombart (1904) is still the best summary of nineteenth-century cycle and crisis theories. Regarding Keynes, see, e.g., Keynes (1997, 313–320).

2 Hobday in this volume shows how East Asian catching-up strategies during the twentieth century can be explained in a similar way.

3 In psychology, this is called 'selective perception' and goes back to the famous study by Hastorf and Cantril (1954) of a Dartmouth and Princeton football game and how respective supporters perceived the game. As they conclude, 'In brief, the data here indicate that there is no such 'thing' as a 'game' existing 'out there' in its own right which people merely 'observe'. The game 'exists' for a person and is experienced by him only insofar as certain happenings have significances in terms of his purpose' (133).

4 An excellent summary of Gadamer's thought in English is Lawn (2006).

5 Soros (2008), who calls this feedback loop 'reflexivity', shows how this describes how financial markets work.

6 The members of the German Historical School in general but especially Werner Sombart, the head of its 'Youngest' period, are key authors for the hermeneutical understanding of the economy. In English, see especially Sombart (1936); see also Drechsler (2000b).

7 Some evolutionary economists have attempted simulation models (e.g., Allen 1988) that do take reality into account and can incorporate at least some forms of structural change (as distinct from pure mathematical models). This might be a road worth pursuing further.

Developing Innovation Capability: Meeting the Policy Challenge

1 At the time, John Bessant and Howard Rush were head and deputy head, respectively, of CENTRIM.

2 This typology has previously been described in Hobday, Rush and Bessant (2001) and (2004) and Rush, Bessant and Lee (2008). It formed the basis of an audit tool developed by the authors for the World Bank Project on Korea and the Knowledge-Based Economy.

3 Reviews of the Microelectronic Applications Programme (see Northcott et al. 1986) and a more longitudinal evaluation of that programme by Rush et al. (2004) provide evidence for these types of learning.

4 Whilst providing financial support – for example contributions towards the cost of new equipment or preferential loans – can help accelerate diffusion there is also the risk that it creates dependency and a risk-averse approach on the part of firms. Instead of developing the internal capability to identify the need for new knowledge and the search, acquisition,

assimilation and exploitation associated with doing so effectively (absorptive capacity) they may remain externally dependent for support, guidance and strategic direction.

5 An interesting – and innovative – exception would be the use of the radio soap opera *The Archers* as a device to communicate information about good farming practice. Although the programme is now one of the longest-running in the world, it retains an 'Agricultural Story Editor' whose role is to continue to feed relevant updated information to the (comparatively few) farming listeners.

6 While such interventions can be important parts of governmental national or regional policy initiatives, they are also used by trade associations and value-chain benchmarking clubs.

7 We are grateful to Milady Parejo, one of the original members of the PAC team, for information regarding the programme and its follow-up.

Slow Food, Slow Growth ... Slow ICT: The Vision of Ambient Intelligence

1 The author has written this article in a personal capacity. He is indebted to all his colleagues at SMIT (VUB), IPTS (JRC-EC) TNO and DG INFSO with whom, over the past 15 years, he debated and worked on the future of the information society.

2 IPTS is one of the seven research hubs of the Joint Research Centre of the European Commission. ISTAG is a mixed industry-research-academia 'High Level Group' that advises the Directorate General responsible for European information society policy (DG INFSO) on research programs.

3 More specifically, the plans the United States developed on the Information Highways around the end of the 1990s, see Burgelman (1996a and 1996b).

4 For a more contextual version of the AmI storyline, I refer to Burgelman and Punie (2006).

5 The following five categories of requirement were used: (1) a seamless mobile/fixed web-based communications infrastructure; (2) very unobtrusive hardware; (3) dynamic and massively distributed device networks; (4) a natural feeling human interface, (5) dependability and security.

6 This was based on a number of internal reports that were only partially published; see, e.g., Pascu et al. (2006).

7 For a popular description see, e.g., Wikipedia entry, http://en.wikipedia.org/wiki/ Slow_food.

Technical Change and Structural Inequalities: Converging Approaches to Problems of Underdevelopment

1 Furtado (1961), for instance, established a direct relation between economic development and technological change pointing out that the growth of an economy was based on the accumulation of knowledge. He also defined development from a systemic and historically determined perspective. For details see Cassiolato and Lastres (2008).

2 It is important to stress that such neo-Schumpeterian work on technical change and innovation benefited also from earlier discussions that were basically taken in Latin America during the 1950s and 1960s. A significant advance resulted from the joint effort of several scholars at the University of Sussex in the late 1960s. The synthesis of this endeavor is the well-known Sussex Manifesto (Singer et al. 1970), prepared for the

debates of the UN Second Development Decade of the 1970s by Singer, Freeman, Cooper, Oldham and others.

3 In her better-known works, Perez distinguishes five cycles of capitalism associated with transformations in techno-economic paradigms. The last one corresponds to the diffusion of microelectronics and was analysed in more detail in several works by her and by Chris Freeman (Freeman 1987; Freeman and Perez, 1988; Perez 1983, 1985 and 1986).

4 Fiori (2001) notes that the most original contribution of LASA was its systemic vision of the capitalist development.

5 Translated from the Spanish by the authors.

6 Translated from the Spanish by the authors.

7 More recently, some authors (Chang 2002) used a similar line of reasoning when analysing changes in trade policy regimes and property rights regulations under the umbrella of WTO. They suggested that leader countries *kicked away the ladder* to prevent the upsurge of other countries using the same policy tools they extensively used in the past.

8 It is necessary to stress the difference between the LASA and the Theory of Dependency. LASA highlighted the relevance of structural relationships, within and between national economies and explains underdevelopment as a specific and differentiated condition in the global arena. The dependency theory, as posed by Cardoso and Faletto (1981), is a political theory about new colonialist relationship between rich and poor countries. It is not a development theory and its theoretical contributions are restricted to a stylized description of world power relations.

9 LASA explicitly suggested the inappropriateness of technology generated in advanced countries to cope with the problems of underdevelopment.

10 See also Prebisch (1949), Furtado (1961), Pinto (2000) and more recently Cimoli et al. (2005) and Porcile and Holland (2005).

11 Christopher Freeman's work is an important exception. See, for example, Freeman (2003).

12 Although this is a general problem, it assumes a larger dimension in the context of developing countries, where the inadequacy of both financial infrastructures and mechanisms for financing innovation (and in some cases even industrial development) is very often a marked characteristic. Most of these countries do not have *functional financial structures*, in the sense that private banks are not used to provide finance for long-term investment. For details, see Lastres, Cassiolato and Maciel (2003).

13 In a 1998 conference on policy alternatives for the new technological paradigm, Perez asked herself and gave an immediate answer: 'Am I proposing, by any chance, a form of technological determinism? Yes and no, because it is necessary to indicate the character of the range of options, and not the existence of a single path' (Perez 1998, 14).

14 For details, see also Cassiolato and Lastres (1999) and Arocena and Sutz (2003).

15 See, among others, Perez (1998), Cassiolato and Lastres (1999), Katz (2000) and Arocena and Sutz (2003).

16 See, among others, Furtado (1992); Katz (2000); Girvan (1997); Cassiolato and Lastres (1999); Cassiolato, Lastres and Maciel (2003).

17 LIPS basically represent a framework to understand processes of generation, diffusion and use of knowledge and the production and innovation dynamics. Such an approach offers a new tool to understand and orient technological and industrial development. Production and innovation are understood as systemic processes resulting from the articulation of distinct actors and competencies. This explains why new policies for production and innovation development aim at mobilizing these elements, with the objective of increasing the capacity to generate, assimilate and use such knowledge.

The New Techno-Economic Paradigm and its Impact on Industrial Structure

1 Part of this section borrows from Dosi et al. (1995); Dosi (2007). See also the special issues of *Industrial and Corporate Change* edited by Dosi et al. (1997) and that of *International Journal of Industrial Organization* edited by Antonelli and David (1997).

2 For a classical discussion see Ijiri and Simon (1977). More recent evidence is in Axtell (2001) and Marsili (2005).

3 The Zipf distribution is a discrete, one-parameter, univariate distribution that has been used to describe various physical and social phenomena that are highly skewed (Axtell, 2001; Newman, 2005).

4 The analysis on Italian firms has been performed on Micro.1 database and results on French firms make use of the EAE databank collected by SESSI and provided by the French Statistical Office (INSEE). The database has been made available to our team under the mandatory condition of censorship of any individual information. Two authors (G. D. and M. G.) gratefully acknowledge the Italian Statistical Office (Istat), and the French one (INSEE) for their invaluable support. The two databanks are described at length in Dosi et al. (2008).

5 Plots are produced on the logarithms of normalized values, so that the distribution is centered to zero, with densities presented in 64 equispaced points using an Epanenchnikov kernel.

6 On the stability over time of such asymmetric distributions, see also Armington (1986), Hall (1987), Storey (1994), Bottazzi and Secchi (2003a), among the others.

7 More on these issues in Dosi (1988); Malerba and Orsenigo (1995, 1997); Dosi et al. (2005).

8 Here one should, in fact, distinguish between 'discontinuous' complex-product industries such as automobiles, white goods and other consumer durables vs. 'continuous' flow industries such as refining or steelmaking.

9 In fact, in our case, the universe of all firms responding to the Central Statistical Office survey.

10 Refer to the Appendix in Dosi et al. (2008) for an accurate description of the mapping employed to relate a particular industrial activity, i.e., industrial classification code, into the corresponding 'Pavitt's group'.

11 Similar evidence on The Netherlands is discussed in Marsili (2005).

12 Firms in the 100–999 cohort.

13 Note that the percentage of publicly quoted companies over the total of the size cohort tend to fall with the latter.

14 With 'bigness' defined on the much larger meter of Osiris firms.

15 For discussions and reviews of the evidence, see Dosi (2007), Sutton (1997) and Lotti et al. (2003).

16 Moreover, the relationship between size and growth appears to be influenced by the stage of development of particular industries along their life cycles (Geroski and Mazzucato, 2002).

Governance in and of Techno-Economic Paradigm Shifts: Considerations for and from the Nanotechnology Surge

1 This essay is based on Drechsler (2009), but with a completely different focus (there, nanotechnology was the object; here, it is an illustration, and the interest was more in

PA than in governance). For general discussions of this topic throughout the years, and specifically of this essay, I am indebted to Rainer Kattel, Christopher Stillings and most of all Carlota Perez (who does not agree with many of the points of this paper, including central ones, including its evaluation of nanotechnology, convergence, and ICT), and for revisions of the manuscript to Benjamin Merkler and especially Ingbert Edenhofer. Research for this essay was partially funded by projects No. 5780 and 7577 of the Estonian Science Foundation ETF.

2 Perez 2002, also 2007, 2006a, 2006b, 2004a, 2004b, Perez and Freeman 1988.

3 Perez (2004a, 238; see 218, 223, 229, 236–238; 2002, 16–19, 24–25, 153); see also Gehlen (1957, 36, 76–77); *infra* notes 3 and 4. Thus, the TEP model certainly is a form of technological determinism, albeit 'in a mild form,' Perez (2007); see generally in this context Smith und Marx (1994); also Dolata and Werle (2007), esp. 9–104.

4 I hope to shed further light on the Gehlen-Perez relationship some time soon; for the time being, it must remain a mere assertion – one, however, that has been discussed with Perez (discussion of 27 September 2007).

5 According to Gehlen, the history of technology in the sense of 'organ replacement' is a result of a growing movement away from the body, from the organic to the inorganic (1957, 9–11). Regarding the higher level of abstraction in ICT as opposed to nanotechnology, however, Perez herself pointed out (discussion of 27 September 2007) that this is not the case if one considers abstraction in the sense of the possibility or impossibility of reverse engineering, which is much harder in the case of nanotechnology than in the case of ICT.

6 Nano-scenarios that have been suggested by industry, governments or in the context of technology assessment are frequently rather restrained and thought out for a short-term scope; thus, they take the further potential of nanotechnology only into account to a limited degree. It is noteworthy that the humanities' and social sciences' debate on nanotechnology – interesting as it may otherwise be – usually does not take aspects of innovation and general economy into consideration; see e.g., Schummer and Baird (2006), Nordmann et al. 2006.

7 The beginning of a TEP is always based on the preceding paradigm and develops from it, resulting in a kind of convergence; the important aspect regarding the new TEP, however, stems precisely from the specific elements of the leading technology, and the aspect of convergence rather makes it harder to recognize the latter. From today's perspective, it is hardly possible to envision a nano-paradigm without the enabling role of ICT. Perez herself, in fact, opts more for a convergence model (discussion of 30 November 2008).

8 See Perez and Freeman (1988), as suggested by Perez (discussion of 27 September 2007).

9 It must be conceded that empirical validation of this phenomenon for the earlier paradigms – an endeavour that is certainly cumbersome because of the documents and literature, but not impossible – has not taken place yet; on the contrary, it is rather a desideratum of TEP research, especially in relation to state and society. Richard Nelson (2003, 469) has pointed out that studies of this kind are to be expected.

10 The degree to which virtuality is connected to the ICT paradigm can be traced in the difficulty – even for those whose profession entails dealing with future, change, strategy and innovation – to imagine a world in which the net world, communication and information are not as important anymore as they are today.

11 Perez herself doubts this and rather sees ICT as 'likely to be the platform for a knowledge-based society for many decades to come' and 'as "manufacturing" was for the first four

surges; the underlying logic of several sets of technologies of increasing complexity and going deeper into the dynamics of matter' (Discussion of 30 November 2008).

12 Thus, also, the argument by my fellow editor Rainer Kattel. In such a case, Carl Schmitt's philosophical philosophy, contested as it well may be, seems to offer itself as an appropriate tool to grasp the paradigm (cf. Drechsler 1997).

13 It shall be said, however, that precisely because of the similarities with biotechnology, which also heavily focuses on the body, speculations regarding the nano-paradigm are certainly suitable at present to serve as a corrective for the absolutization of ICT – in other words, ICT also has an expiration date on it, at least as regards its dominant role (cf. Drechsler 2002).

14 Original graph supplied by Perez for Drechsler (2009) (23 November 2007), based on Perez (2002, 48), adapted by the author. Again adapted by the author for the current essay and adjusted after discussions with Perez (29–30 November 2008). © Carlota Perez (2002, 2007); this version © Wolfgang (Drechsler 2007, 2008). Perez herself did agree with the dynamics of the curve, but sees a slightly different shape, especially longer plateaus of state closeness and more steep descents and particularly ascents (discussion of 1 December 2008).

15 In the TEP model, creative destruction takes place both in the collapse before the turning-point and in the transition from one TEP to the next, i.e., roughly every 20–30 years, in different shapes, but in both instances as part of the installation period.

16 See Wade (2003); Reinert (1999); Rochet (2007).

17 Thus, at this point, the question regarding nanotechnology and public administration in the TEP context is brought up, i.e., the question of which model of organizing PA is ideal for the establishment of nanotechnology (for instance, such as it were) as a TEP. I have suggested that this is the Neo-Weberian State as conceived by Pollitt and Bouckaert (2004); Pollitt et al. (2009); and elsewhere (e.g., Drechsler 2009; Drechsler and Kattel 2009).

Innovation Policy and Incentives Structure: Learning from the Mexican Case

1 An example of existing social norms, which particularly affect the academic community, is the publication of articles in specialized journals of international circulation. Both the actual paradigm of ICT and the paradigm that is emerging require teamwork and a multidisciplinary approach to problems. This demands for other social norms, amongst which links with other agents is particularly relevant.

2 The present crisis has made the prices of raw materials drop; it is obviously too early to know the final impact.

3 See Braun (1993), van der Meulen (2003) and Morris (2003) about the role of intermediary agents, according to the principal-agent theory applied to STI policy.

Asian Innovation Experiences and Latin American Visions: Exploiting Shifts in Techno-Economic Paradigms

1 See Rodrik (2004) for a critical analysis of these economic and business reforms, referred to by Rodrik as the augmented Washington Consensus.

2 As shown in Part 2, agencies such as the World Bank, IMF, OECD, the UN and governments and consultancy companies often draw on the Asian experience to

recommend export-led growth paths, open markets, privatization, high technology production and government support for knowledge-based industries and industrial clusters, arguing that it is analytically wrong to draw lessons in this way (even worse, many of these policies had little or nothing to do with Asian development).

3 Unless otherwise stated this section is from Hobday (1996).

4 Differences with Southeast Asia are discussed below.

5 For the standard MIT model see Utterback and Abernathy (1975); for similar models that compare Asian with leadership paths covering a range of industries, see Kim (1997), 89, based on Kim (1980); and Lee et al. (1988).

6 For a full discussion see Hobday (2003).

7 'LA Vision' (Latin American Vision) – is a new programme of policy-engaged research centred at SPRU and CENTRIM. As of August 2008 it had a team of 29 academic members led by Carlota Perez, Martin Bell and others (including Matias Ramirez and Fernando Perini) with links to several international organizations and policy representatives of Latin America countries, bringing together country specialists, interdisciplinary skills and policy groups to identify credible new development paths for Latin American development.

8 Although this may change in the future (e.g., if there is a global economic downturn), the chances are that growth will resume at some stage and these long-term structural problems will re-emerge.

9 There are many useful tools and ideas from leading companies in the private sector that could be modified and applied to vision-building. For example, using the planning process to learn about and shape possible futures (based on the Royal Dutch Shell Experience, which helped to develop the concept of the learning organization) as provided by de Geus (1988 and 1999); Schwartz (1991) provides a range of tools for engagement and shaping the future; Pfeffer and Sutton (2000) provide tools for turning research 'knowledge' into action, arguing that there is little purpose for the accumulation of knowledge for its own sake.

10 Hirschman and Lindblom (1962) attacked the notion of balanced growth as either a likely process or a goal to be achieved by policy. Instead, they showed that sectoral imbalances are not only normal, but also that they can and should galvanize private entrepreneurs and policy makers into action.

Doing Capitalism: Notes on the Practice of Venture Capitalism (Revised and Extended)

1 The original version of this paper was presented to the Annual Meeting of The Association for Evolutionary Economics on 29 December 1985 and subsequently published as Janeway (1986). The original text has been slightly edited.

Small States, Innovation and Techno-Economic Paradigms

1 This paper builds on Kattel, Kalvet and Randma-Liiv (2009). Research for this essay was partially funded by the Estonian Ministry of Education and Research (targeted financing grant no. SF0140094s08) and by the Estonian Science Foundation (grant no. ETF7577). I would like thank Wolfgang Drechsler and Jan Kregel for their comments on an earlier version of this paper.

2 Interestingly, the last significant attempt to deal with small states and innovation is already 20 years old. *Small Countries Facing the Technological Revolution*, edited by Freeman and Lundvall, appeared in 1988. Yet, despite the title, the authors do not really deal so much with the issue of smallness as with the issue of innovation systems in general, as this concept was in its infancy at that time and was mainly developed by the same authors. Similarly, Edquist and Hommen (2008), while entitled *Small Country Innovation Systems*, hardly discusses size-specific issues as far as innovation is concerned either.

Financial Experimentation, Technological Paradigm Revolutions and Financial Crises

1 I am indebted to Rainer Kattel for helpful comments on an initial draft.
2 An assessment relating to different financial structures is undertaken in Kregel and Burlamaqui (2005).
3 See the accounts in Winkler [1933] (1999) and Winkler (1929) that suggest that fraudulent activities were well known before the market collapse.
4 Quoted in Golin (2001, 181).
5 The other major cost element is the management of cash and the operation of the transactions system – the deposit of funds and check clearing. The former deals with lobby costs and was met largely through the introduction of ATM machines, while the latter is operated through the Federal Reserve; neither offered possibilities for major innovations that allow for competitive advantage among commercial banks, but did create the possibility of non-commercial banks through credit cards and investment bank cash management accounts. See the discussion in Mayer (1998, Part I).
6 See Mayer (1990) and Black (2005).
7 Although commercial banks were thwarted by regulators from direct participation, they remained involved through the provision of contingent credit lines in the case of the failure of an issue by a business firm.
8 The deal is fully described in Chew (1996, 33 ff).
9 As Auger (2005, 11) notes, of these complex derivative products 'the clients were partly to blame but some investment banks cynically exploited their ignorance of this new and complicated product.'
10 These quantitative computer models were not only used in providing the FICO scores used to assess credit worthiness, they were also the basis of the assessment of credit ratings for the securitized asset structures rated by the credit agencies, as well as by the monoline insurers that provided credit enhancement for the structures.

Why the New Economy is a Learning Economy

1 The paper was presented on 22 January 2002, at the Conference on "Economie basée sur la connaissance et nouvelles technologies cognitives", Université Technologique de Compiegne.
2 A fundamental system failure emanates from the fact that this global system is managed nationally, and more specifically, from Wall Street in New York and the City in London. It was this peculiar set-up that made it possible for the United States and the United Kingdom to pursue economic strategies of beggar-thy-neighbour that would be out of reach for any other national economy.

Technology, Institutions and Economic Development

1 This paper draws extensively on an earlier article (Nelson 2008) where many of the arguments here are developed in a different context. The author is indebted to the Sloan Foundation for support of the background research.

Techno-Economic Paradigms and the Migration (Relocation) of Industries to the Peripheries

1 The literature on long waves generally credits N. D. Kondratiev, the Russian economist who headed the Conjuncture Institute in Moscow during the 1920s, with the discovery of long wave-like patterns in the world economy. Kondratiev estimated that these long waves last some 48–55 years, his calculations and empirical work dating from the 1780s, the beginning of the Industrial Revolution in Europe (see Kondratiev 1984).
2 See Schumpeter (1939). Like Kondratiev, Schumpeter argues that the capitalist world economy is always in a state of flux, expanding and contracting in what appears to be long waves or cycles.
3 This article follows Kondratiev's original dating of waves of development.
4 Between 1870 and 1914, many German firms had branches established overseas. For example, the great establishments (AEG, Siemens and Schuckert) had plants in Austria-Hungary, Russia, Italy, Spain and elsewhere, to make and install electrical equipment. Electrochemical works were established in Russia, Austria-Hungary, Spain, Sweden, Norway and Switzerland. See Feis (1930, 78).
5 The value of these investments is taken from Stopford (1974, 326) and the number of subsidiaries abroad from Franko (1974, 284).
6 van Roon (1985, 54) argues that the period should be seen as one big economic period because (1) 1913 saw the start of a protracted stagnation of the net social product; (2) even after the first world war one can speak of a general recovery only in a restricted sense; and (3) stagnation, unemployment, rationalization and concentration were notably striking characteristics of the 'golden twenties'.

On the Discreet Charm of the (Rentier) Bourgeoisie: The Contradictory Nature of the Installation Period of a New Techno-Economic Paradigm

1 As will be evident from the paper, Carlota's work, and the countless discussions we had for many years, have been extremely important to my own thinking.
2 See, for example, Perez (2005).
3 In a recent article, Robert Skidelsky explains that: 'in contrast to the dot-com boom, it is difficult to identify the technological 'shock' that set off the [subsequent] boom. Of course, the upswing was marked by superabundant credit. But this was not used to finance new inventions: it was the invention. It was called securitized mortgages. It left no monuments to human invention, only piles of financial ruin' (Skidelsky 2009, 2).
4 For the process of income polarization, see Figures 17.1–17.6 below; and for its effects on savings, investment and productivity growth, Figures 17.12–17.17. For a detailed analysis of the dynamic by which the period of 'installation' of a new techno-economic paradigm tends to lead to a process of income polarization, see Perez (2002).

5 In turn, including capital gains, the share of the richest 0.5 per cent increased from 6.2 per cent to 18.6 per cent; that of the top 0.1 per cent grew from 2.7 per cent to 12.6 per cent; and that of the 0.01 per cent jumped from 0.9 per cent to 5.5 per cent, respectively.

6 Remarkable as this income polarization may be, as these data are based on income tax statistics, it is likely that they even underestimate (perhaps significantly) the increase in the income share of the top one per cent after 1980. Financial liberalization, increased capital mobility and the proliferation of 'tax havens' made it much easier for this income group to evade taxes (see, for example, Rusbridger 2009). UBS has recently acknowledged that it helped 47,000 wealthy individuals in the US to evade taxes; see Gordon, 2009).

7 The same 'winner-takes-all-type distribution' is found in the South, especially in Latin America; see Palma (2007).

8 Computations by authors on tax return statistics (the number of tax returns in 2006 was 138.4 million). Income defined as annual *gross* income reported on tax returns, excluding all government transfers (such as social security, unemployment benefits, welfare payments, etc.), and before individual income taxes and employees' payroll taxes (but after employers' payroll taxes and corporate income taxes). Gross income includes all the income items reported on tax returns (and before all deductions); these are salaries and wages, small business and farm income, partnership and fiduciary income, dividends, interest, rents, royalties and other small items reported as 'other income'.

9 As the authors explain, realized capital gains are not a normal annual flow of income (in general, capital gains are realized by individuals in a lumpy way only once in a while) and form a volatile component of income with large aggregate variations from year to year depending on such things as changes in asset prices.

10 There does not seem to be much evidence in the US since the late 1970s to support a 'median voter' scenario!

11 An alternative formulation would be that it is shorthand for 'the art of generating a "spontaneous consensus"-type of hegemony (in the Gramscian sense) that such a remarkably asymmetric distributional outcome is the only game in town'. Alternatively, 'the art of transforming a particularly asymmetric set of distributive strategic choices, and the corresponding payoffs, into a Nash equilibrium' – as the majority becomes convinced that there was no point in trying to change such asymmetric distributive strategies while the all too powerful top income players kept theirs unchanged (despite the obvious fact that they could clearly improve their payoffs only if they could somehow agree on a strategy different from the current one – a rather good example of a Nash equilibrium that is not Pareto-optimal…). For an analysis of the neo-liberal ideology, politics and economics that characterize most of the developed and developing worlds after 1980, see Palma (2009a and b); see also Palma (2008a).

12 If capital gains are excluded, this multiple increases by a factor of 8.1; and if instead of the top 0.01 per cent, the comparison is made between the average income of the top 1 per cent and that of the bottom 90 per cent, during this period the respective multiple increases from 12 to 41.

13 There was, of course, also a massive increase in the level of corporate debt, but this process followed a different logic to that of the increase in the public and household sectors' debt.

14 See Francis (2008). It is important to note that the effective income tax rate of this group in 1995 (30 per cent) had already been reduced by the Tax Reform Act of 1986, which had cut drastically the top marginal income tax rates (see Feldstein 1995).

15 Furthermore, as tax cuts did very little to stimulate the economy, real stimulation was left to the Fed, which took up the task with unprecedented low-interest rates and liquidity (see Stiglitz 2009).

16 Note that due to lack of data, this graph compares the gross income of the bottom 90% with the level of personal consumption expenditure of the whole population. Also, note that in the right-hand panel the aggregate income of the bottom 90% grows at 1.8% only due to a growing population.

17 At the end of 2008 the US's four biggest banks by assets had not that much less assets in 'off-balance-sheet vehicles' than on their books (US$5.2 and US$7.2 trillion, respectively). As Reilly (2009) explains, '[o]ff-balance-sheet vehicles helped inflate the credit bubble by letting banks originate and sell loans without having to put aside much capital for them. So as lending soared, banks didn't have an adequate buffer against losses.'

18 As shown in Figure 17.10 above, households enjoyed a huge increase in net worth after 1980. As individuals feel richer, the may have well perceived that their 'permanent' income was growing rapidly as this includes unrealised asset appreciation as well as actual cash flow. That is, if individuals spend a relatively fixed proportion of their perceived income, their spending as a fraction of their flow income would rise. Thus, their conventionally GDP-measured savings rate would then fall.

19 In a recent assessment of the Bush administration, written as a column for the *Wall Street Journal*, Karl Rove states that: 'Mr. Bush ... cut taxes on capital, investment and savings. The result was 52 months of growth' (2009). Not much evidence that this growth was the result of the supposedly positive effects of tax cuts on private saving or investment...

20 Low levels of investment were also a key component of Greenspan 'conundrum'.

21 See Buiter (2009); for an analysis of the 'Dutch Disease', see Palma (2008b).

22 At the beginning of the current crisis finance and insurance accounted for 8% of GDP, more than twice their share in the 1960s. Also, the share of the financial sector in overall corporate profits increased from 10% to about one-third between 1986 and 2006. In turn, the list of stocks making up the Dow Jones Industrial Average did not contain a single financial company until 1982, while at the beginning of 2008, the Dow contained five – including such 'citadels' as AIG, Citigroup and Bank of America (see Krugman 2009a).

23 Note that the income distribution data from the US comes from a different source to those of the other countries shown in the graph – i.e., in the former from tax returns and in the latter from household surveys.

24 For an analysis of the role of 'compulsions' within capitalism, see Khan (2005). For him, 'capitalism is characterized not just by the presence of market opportunities, which have always been present in societies with markets, but also by a hitherto unknown introduction of market compulsions, which ensured that both capitalists and workers continuously had to strive to improve their performance just in order to survive. ... Only capitalist appropriation depends on market competition and therefore on the systematic improvement of labour productivity. Only capitalism, then, depends on constantly improving the forces of production. And only in capitalism is it necessary to grow just to stay in the same place' (2005, 72).

25 In the Preface to the first edition of *Das Kapital*, Marx says that "[t]he country that is more developed industrially only shows, to the less developed, the image of its own future" (Marx 1867). Well, maybe at that time – not any more...

26 Between these two periods, in Japan the annual average rate of growth of productivity fell from 7.5 per cent to 2 per cent; in West Germany from 4.7 per cent to 1.9 per cent

(the latter figure correspond to the period between 1973 and 1997); in France from 4.7 per cent to 1.6 per cent; and in Italy from 4.8 per cent to 1.4 per cent (see GGDC 2009).

27   Gore Vidal is reputed to have said that this type of political settlement could be best described as 'socialism for the rich and capitalism for the rest'.

28   Important components of that strategy were not just the abolition of most of the financial regulation erected during the 'New Deal' and the refusal of the Bush administration to join the 'Kyoto agreement', but also the lax implementation of the remaining environmental, competition and financial regulations. In financial spheres, for example, the Securities and Exchange Commission's enforcement staff actually shrunk 11 per cent in the two-year period prior to the onset of the sub-prime crisis, and the fines and other penalties it imposed dropped by more than half during the second term of the Bush administration. It also let Bernard Madoff keep operating even after having been alerted to his misdeeds by Harry Markopolos, an accountant and investment investigator who began pushing the SEC to investigate Madoff as early as 1999. – For a detailed analysis of Markopolos' quest and the documents he submitted to the SEC to show that Madoff's record of consistent low-double-digit returns simply couldn't be legitimate, see *Wall Street Journal* (2008), especially the 19-page document Markopolos sent to regulators in 2005, 'The World's Largest Hedge Fund Is a Fraud', where he concludes that 'I am pretty confident that BM [Bernard Madoff's hedge fund] is a Ponzi Scheme.' (Markopolos 2005). The *WSJ* article also explains how the SEC investigators had actually found as early as 2006 that Madoff had seriously misled the agency about how he managed customer money, yet the SEC decided not to take any action.

29   For example, after three decades of stagnant average real income for the bottom 90 per cent of the population, it took political genius during the 2004 presidential election to manage to avoid this issue altogether. Not only does neo-liberalism deserve an entry in the Guinness Book of Records under the heading 'degree of sophistication of technologies of power', but also, after the remarkable behaviour of 'free' agents in financial markets and the peculiarities of US politics during the recent past, mainstream economists and public-choice theorists should perhaps have another look at their concept of the 'rational agent'. For an analysis of what neo-liberalism is really about, see Palma (2009b).

30   According to Keynes, the reversal of the relationship between financial and productive capital was also essential for the recovery of the 1930s crisis: 'there cannot be a real recovery, in my judgment, until the ideas of lenders and the ideas of productive borrowers are brought together again … Seldom in modern history has the gap between the two been so wide and so difficult to bridge' (1931, -146; also quoted in Perez 2002, 167).

31   See Perez (2002).

32   On this issue, see Foucault (2004, 120), and Frangie (2008).

33   In October 2008 (in one of the most blatant cases of 'crony-capitalism' ever), the British Chancellor paid £20 billion for 60% of the shares of the Royal Bank of Scotland despite the fact that the stock market valuation of those shares at the time was less than half that amount – so, paraphrasing Joan Robinson, 'we are all "Bastard Keynesians" again…' Furthermore, as the net worth of that bank at the time was in all likelihood negligible, it is questionable whether he should have even paid the market value of those shares, as all that the market was probably doing in prizing those shares with a positive value was prizing the likely amount of the impending government subsidy (a bit of simultaneous causation here).

Production-Based Economic Theory and the Stages of Economic Development: From Tacitus to Carlota Perez

1 This paper builds on Reinert (2000).
2 I have argued that a country like Mongolia was 'bombed back' from an industrial stage to a pastoral stage by World Bank and IMF policies, with devastating results for wages, social conditions, and the environment (Reinert 2004).
3 *The Works of Francis Bacon,* quoted in Meek (1976, 13).
4 For a discussion of types of economics from this point of view, see Drechsler (2004).
5 *'Die Aufstellung solcher "Wirtschaftsstufen" gehört zu den unentbehrlichen methodischen Hilfsmitteln.'* (Bücher 1919a, 87)
6 I am indebted to Wolfgang Drechsler for the idea of connecting neoclassical economic theory with postmodernism.
7 For a discussion of postmodernism and indeterminacy, see Hoover (1994).
8 Art critic Suzi Gablik, quoted in Hoover (1994).
9 For a discussion of this intellectual tradition, see Viner (1972).
10 Adam Fergusson, in 1793, quoted in Meek (1976). This is close to the idea of history previously expressed by Neapolitan philosopher Giambattista Vico (1668–1744).
11 Paul Wendt quoted in McCloskey (1994, 72).
12 For a more general discussion of these issues, see Reinert and Daastøl (1997, 233–283).
13 For an overview of German stage theories, see Kalveram (1933).
14 Bücher says to this: 'English economics is therefore mainly a theory of exchange [*Die englische Nationalökonomie ist darum im wesentlichen Verkehrstheorie*]' (Bücher 1919a, 89).
15 The relevant original texts are found in Laistner 1923.
16 *'Hierbey ging bereits eine Art Theilung vor.'*
17 This is excellently argued in Hirschman (1977).
18 Serra (1613); see S. Reinert (2010).
19 For a discussion of early nineteenth century German stage theories, see Sommer (1948, 534–565).
20 Hildebrand's two articles on stage theory are also reprinted in Gehrig (1922).
21 The decay of nations is discussed in the context of the Dutch Republic in Reinert (2009).
22 Reinert (2007) elaborates extensively on these mechanisms.
23 Stigler quoted in McCraw (1992, 362).
24 *'Sie fließen in einander über.'*
25 The term used is *Gütergemeinschaft.*
26 For a discussion of the notion of 'triple rents', see Reinert (2009).
27 Reinert, Amaïzo and Kattel (2009).

Carlota Perez' Contribution to the Research Programme in Public Management: Understanding and Managing the Process of Creative Destruction in Public Institutions and Organizations

1 The first example of this type that I looked into was the reform of the Poor Laws in 1832 in response to the inefficiency and rent-seeking behaviour caused by the Speenhamland system; the inability to reform the system became the pretext for destroying it, with catastrophic consequences. See Rochet (2007).

2 Adam Smith also said that '*defence is of much more importance than opulence*' (Book IV of *The Wealth of Nations*, 464–465) and defended the Navigation Acts because he saw the Merchant Navy as a reservoir of seamen for the Royal Navy.

3 'Both what organizations come into existence and how they evolve are fundamentally influenced by the institutional framework. In turn, they influence how the institutional framework evolves' (North 1990,5).

4 In a fascinating collection of essays, Sandford Borins (2008) reviews innovation in North American administrations and finds that it is mostly incremental because of the lack of political support for radical innovation.

BIBLIOGRAPHY CARLOTA PEREZ

Classification Code

[B]	Book
[CA]	Academic conference proceedings
[CB]	Business conference proceedings
[CG]	Government or international organization conference proceedings
[Ch]	Chapter in book
[J]	Scholarly journal article
[M]	Magazine or opinion journal article
[L]	Lecture-mimeo
[P]	Pamphlet
[R]	Consultancy report
[WP]	Working paper

An asterisk (*) indicates the paper is, at the time of the preparation of this book, downloadable from the webpage www.carlotaperez.org

1. 1977. "Tecnología y Tendencias de la Economía Mundial: Apuntes para la Discusión" [Technology and Trends in the World Economy: Notes for Discussion]. Internal document. Caracas: I.C.E.-UPEI [Department of International Economic Policy of the Institute of Foreign Trade], August. [R]

2. 1980. "Prospectiva del ingreso fiscal petrolero 1980–2000: Análisis de cuatro estrategias alternativas" [Prospects for Fiscal Revenue from Oil 1980–2000: Analysis of Four Alternative Strategies]. Consultancy Report for *Alternativas para Venezuela Año 2000*. Caracas: CENDES-CORDIPLAN. [R]

3.1. 1983. "Structural Change and Assimilation of New Technologies in the Economic and Social Systems." *Futures* 15 (4), 357–375. [J] *

    3.2. Reprinted: 1996. In C. Freeman (ed.). *Long Wave Theory*. The International Library of Critical Writings in Economics 69. Cheltenham: Edward Elgar, 373–391. [Ch]

    3.3. Italian translation: 1985. "Cambiamento Strutturale e Assimilazione di Nuove Tecnologie nei Sistemi Economici e Sociali." In P. Bisogno (ed.). *Paradigmi Tecnologici: Saggi Sull Economia del Progresso Tecnico*. Milan: Prometheus, 155–186. [Ch]

    3.4. Spanish version: 1986 "Cambio Estructural y Asimilación de Nuevas Tecnologías en el Sistema Económico y Social." Mimeo. *

4. 1984. "Structural Change in Industry and Kondratiev Cycles." In C. Freeman (ed.). *Design, Innovation and Long Cycles in Economic Development.* London: Pinter, 27–47. [Ch]

5. 1985. With C. Freeman. "Long Waves and New Technology." *Nordisk Tidskrift för Politisk Ekonomi* 17, 5–14. [J]

6. 1985. "El Departamento de Política Tecnológica de la JUNAC: Contexto, Apreciaciones y Sugerencias" [The Department of Technology Policy of the Andean Pact: Context, Assessment and Suggestions]. Consultancy report to the Junta of the Andean Pact. Lima: JUNAC, November. [R]

7. 1985. "El Desarrollo de la Industria Electrónica e Informática en Venezuela: Necesidad y Posibilidad" [The Development of an Electronics and Software Industry in Venezuela: Necessity and Possibility]. Mimeo transcription of lecture at FUNDAVAC [Foundation for the Advancement of Science]. Caracas. [L]

8. 1985. "Towards a Comprehensive Theory of Long Waves." In G. Bianchi et al. (eds). *Long Waves, Depression and Innovation: Implications for National and Regional Economic Policy: Proceedings of the Siena/Florence Meeting October 1983.* Laxenburg: IIASA (International Institute for Applied Systems Analysis), 103–109. [CA]

9.1. 1985. "Microelectronics, Long Waves and World Structural Change: New Perspectives for Developing Countries." *World Development* 13 (3), 441–463. [J] *

9.2. Reprinted: 1990. In C. Freeman (ed.). *The Economics of Innovation, An Elgar Reference Collection.* Aldershot: Edward Elgar, 464–486. [Ch] *

10. 1985. "Hacia una Estrategia Integral para Venezuela en el Sector Electrónica e Informática" [Towards an Integrated Strategy for the Electronics and Software Sector in Venezuela]. Caracas: CONDIBIECA-UNIDO (Council for the Development of the Capital Goods Industry). [R]

11. 1985. "Long Waves and Changes in Socio-Economic Organisations." *IDS Bulletin* (Institute of Development Studies, Sussex, UK) 16 (1), 36–39. [J]

12.1. 1986. "Las Nuevas Tecnologías: Una Visión de Conjunto." In Carlos Ominami (ed.). *La Tercera Revolución Industrial: Impactos Internacionales del Actual Viraje Tecnológico.* Buenos Aires: Grupo Editor Latinoamericano, 43–90. [Ch] *

12.2. Reprinted: 1986. *Estudios Internacionales* (Santiago de Chile) 19 (76), 420–459. [J]

12.3. English translation: 2009. "The New Technologies: An Integrated View." *Working Papers in Technology Governance and Economic Dynamics*, The Other Canon Foundation and Tallinn University of Technology, 19. [WP] *

13. 1986. "El Impacto de la revolución Informática en la Política de Desarrollo Industrial de Venezuela" [The Impact of the Information Revolution on Industrial Development Policy in Venezuela]. Lecture transcription. Valencia: CAFADAE-CONINDUSTRIA (Electric and Electronic Industry Association-National Industry Council). [L]

14. 1986. "Hacia una Nueva Estrategia Industrial para Venezuela, Ante el Reto de la Revolución Electrónica" [Towards a New Industrial Strategy for Venezuela, Facing the Challenge of the Electronics Revolution]. Mimeo of consultancy Report. to CAFADAE (Chamber of electric and Electronic Industries, Venezuela) presented at the Annual Assembly of CONINDUSTRIA (National Industry Council). Caracas. [R]

15. 1986. With C. Freeman. "Innovazione, Diffusione e Nuovi Modelli Tecno-Economici" [Innovation, Diffusion and New Techno-Economic Models]. *L'Impresa* 2, 7–14. [M]

16.1. 1986. With C. Freeman. "The Diffusion of Technological Innovations and Changes in Techno-Economic Paradigm." In *Proceedings of the International Conference on Innovation Diffusion.* Venice: University of Venice. [CA]

16.2. Italian translation: 1987. "La Diffusione delle Innovazioni e il Cambiamento del Modello Tecno-economico." *Focus* 5, 17–40. [J]

17.   1986. "El Reto de la Revolución Electrónica" [The Challenge of the Electronics Revolution]. *Número* 7 (Caracas) (304), 99–112. [J]

18.1. 1987. "Revoluciones Tecnológicas y Transformaciones Socio-institucionales" [Technological Revolutions and Socio-Institutional transformations]. *David y Goliath* 12 (51, Special Issue on Technology). [J]

  18.2. Reprinted: 1988. In A. Cragnolini (ed.). *Cuestiones de Política Científica y Tecnológica*. Proceedings of the 2nd Jorge Sábato Seminar. Madrid: CSIC, 37–78. [CG]

19.   1988. "The Institutional Implications of the Present Wave of Technical Change for Developing Countries." Mimeo of paper for the Seminar on *Technology and Long-term Economic Growth Prospects*. Washington, D.C.: The World Bank. [L]

20.1. 1988. With C. Freeman. "Structural Crises of Adjustment, Business Cycles and Investment Behaviour." In G. Dosi et al. (eds). *Technical Change and Economic Theory*. London: Pinter, 38–66. [Ch]

  20.2. Reprinted: 1996. In C. Freeman (ed.). *Long Wave Theory*. Cheltenham: Edward Elgar, 242–270. [Ch]

  20.3. Reprinted: 1998. In H. Hanusch (ed.). *The Economic Legacy of Joseph Schumpeter* 2. Cheltenham: Edward Elgar, 86–114. [Ch]

21.1. 1988. "New Technologies and Development." In C. Freeman and B.-Å. Lundvall (eds). *Small Countries Facing the Technological Revolution*. London: Pinter, 85–97. [Ch]

  21.2. Reprinted: 2007. In L. Mytelka (ed.). *Innovation and Economic Development*. International Library of Critical Writings in Economics 213. Cheltenham: Edward Elgar, 16–28. [Ch]

  21.3. Italian translation: 1989. "Nuove Tecnologie e Sviluppo." In E. Bennedetti (ed.). *Mutazioni Tecnologiche e Condizionamenti Internazionali*. Milan: FrancoAngeli, 71–89. [Ch]

22.   1988. With C. Freeman. "Long Waves and Changes in Employment Patterns." In *Proceedings of Conference on Structural Change and Labour Market Policy* 1. Stockholm: ALC (Swedish Centre for Working Life), 1–12. [CA]

23.   1988. With L. Soete. "Catching Up in Technology: Entry Barriers and Windows of Opportunity." In G. Dosi et al. (eds). *Technical Change and Economic Theory*. London: Pinter, 458–479. [Ch]

24.   1988. With L. Vivas. "Creación de Condiciones Facilitadoras para la Modernización del Parque Industrial en Venezuela" [Establishment of Enabling Conditions for the Modernization of Industry in Venezuela]. Consultancy Report to UNIDO-Ministry of Development and FIM-Productividad (Research Fund for the Improvement of Quality, Productivity and Competitiveness). Caracas. [R]

25.   1988. "Una Nueva Estrategia Industrial Para Venezuela" [A New Industrial Strategy for Venezuela]. *Noti-Industria* 64, 8–15. [M]

26.   1988. "Tendencias en la Industria Mundial: Nuevos Elementos en la Competitividad" [Trends in World Industry: New Components of Competitiveness]. *Economía HOY* (Caracas) 8, 5–7. [M]

27.1. 1989. "Technical Change, Competitive Restructuring and Institutional Reform in Developing Countries." *SPR Discussion Paper* 4 (Strategic Planning and Review Department). Washington, D.C.: World Bank. [WP]

  27.2. Spanish version: 1992. "Cambio Técnico, Reestructuración Competitiva y Reforma Institucional en los Países en Desarrollo." *El Trimestre Económico* 59 (233), 23–64. [J]

28. 1989. "Equipment, Services and Organizational Change: Three Moving Frontiers for Telecommunications Managers." In *Proceedings 1989 of the Conference of the Caribbean Association of National Telecommunications Organizations*. Santo Domingo. [CB]

29. 1989. "Facing the Electronics Revolution in a Developing Country: The Case of Venezuela." Mimeo of paper prepared for the workshop on *Technological Change and the Electronics Sector: Perspectives and Policy Options for Newly Industrializing Countries*, 26–30 June. Paris: OECD. [L]

30. 1989. "Technology, Crisis and Opportunities for Development." Mimeo, transcription of a series of three lectures sponsored by the CPCT (Science and Technology Policy Council of Brazil). Brasilia: Central Bank of Brazil. [L]

31. 1989. "Tecnología, Competitividad Estructural y Mercado Interno" [Technology, Structural Competitiveness and the Role of Domestic Markets]. Mimeo of presentation at the Seminar on *Strategic Approaches for Latin American Integration in the 1990s*. Buenos Aires: IADB-INTAL. [L]

32. 1989. With C. Freeman. "Los Países del Pacto Andino y los Cambios en la Economía Mundial: Una Estrategia para la Modernización en la Década del Noventa" [The Countries of the Andean Pact and the Changes in the World Economy: A Strategy for Modernization in the 1990s]. Consultancy report to the JUNAC (Junta of the Cartagena Agreement or Andean Pact). Lima. [R]

33. 1990. "A Change in Paradigm for Competitiveness and Cooperation(Implications for South-South Linkages." Mimeo of presentation, Workshop on South-South Cooperation, November. Paris: OEDC Development Centre. [L]

34. 1990. "Electronics and Development in Venezuela: A User-Oriented Strategy and its Policy Implications." *Technical Paper* 25. Paris: OECD Development Centre. [WP]

35. 1990. "El Sector Energético ante el Nuevo Patrón Tecnológico" [The Energy Sector and the New Technological Regime]. In *Energía y Desarrollo* (Proceedings of the First National Energy Congress, School of Physical Sciences and Mathematics, April) 2. Santiago: Universidad de Chile, 25–37. [CA]

36. 1991. "El Nuevo Patrón Tecnológico: Microelectrónica y Organización" [New Technological Regime: Microelectronics and Organization]. In N. Carrasquero and M. Torres (eds). *Tópicos en Ingeniería de gestión*. Caracas: EDIT, 299–325. [Ch]

37.1. 1991. "Nuevo patrón tecnológico y educación superior: una aproximación desde la empresa." In G. López Ospina (ed.). *Retos Científicos y Tecnológicos* 3. Caracas: UNESCO-CRESALC, 23–49. [Ch]

37.2. English translation: 1992. "New Technological Model and Higher Education: A View from the Changing World of Work." In *Challenges and Options: Specific Proposals*. Caracas: UNESCO-CRESALC, 121–146. [Ch]

38. 1991. "La Empresa y la Competitividad" [The Firm and Competitiveness]. In *Proceedings of the Annual Assembly of ALAFACE* (Latin American Association of Beer Producers). Puerto la Cruz, Venezuela. [CB]

39. 1991. "Microelectrónica y Competitividad" [Microelectronics and Competitiveness]. In *Actas Simposio Actualidad Nacional e Internacional de la Electrónica y las Telecomunicaciones y su Impacto sobre el Desarrollo de Venezuela*. Caracas: FINTEC (Public Venture Capital Fund for Technological Innovation). [CG]

40. 1991. "National Systems of Innovation, Competitiveness and Technology: A Discussion of Some Relevant Concepts and their Practical Implications." Report to the University of Campinas. Sao Paulo. [R]

41. 1991. "Notas y Textos para Contribuir al Documento: Transformación Productiva y Recursos Humanos" [Notes and Texts to Contribute to the Document: Changing

Production Patterns and Human Resources]. Consultancy Report. Santiago de Chile: CEPAL. [R]

42. 1991. "Tecnología, Desarrollo y Sistema Nacional de Innovación" [Technology, Development and National System of Innovation]. In *Proceedings of the International Seminar New Context for Science and Technology Policies in Memory of Máximo Halty Carrere*. Montevideo: IDRC-OAS. [CG]

43. 1992. "Competitividad, Especialización y Cooperación" [Competitiveness, Specialization and Cooperation]. In *Actas Congreso Gerencia '92: Competir para Ganar 2*. Caracas: AVE, 33–38. [CB]

44. 1992. "Opciones para la Pequeña y Mediana Empresa en un Mundo Competitivo" [The Options Open to Small and Medium Firms in a Competitive World]. Lecture in *VII Jornadas de Análisis de la Industria de Bienes de Capital*. CONDIBIECA (Council for the Development of the Capital Goods Industry), Caracas. [L]

45.1. 1993. "Opciones para la PYME en un Ambiente Competitivo" [Options for SMEs in a Competitive Context]. In *Actas SLAMP '93* (Latin American Symposium on Small and Medium Industries). Caracas: CORPOINDUSTRIA. [CG]

45.2. Revised version: 2000. "Opciones para la Pequeña y Mediana Empresa en un Ambiente Competitivo" [Options for Small and Medium Firms in a Competitive Context]. *Revista Faces* (University of Carabobo, Valencia) 9 (19), 49–61. [J]

46.1. 1993. "Technology and Competitiveness in Latin America: Beyond the Legacy of Import Substitution Policies." Mimeo, workshop on *Globalization, Liberalization and Innovation Policy*. IDRC, Ottawa. [L]

46.2. Revised version: 2001. In G. Dutrénit, C. Garrido and G. Valenti (eds). *Sistema Nacional de Innovación Tecnológica: Temas para el Debate en México*. Mexico: UAM, 85–128. [Ch]

47. 1994. "Technical Change and the New Context for Development." In L. Mytelka (ed.). *South-South Co-operation in a Global Perspective*. Paris: OECD, 55–87. [Ch] *

48. 1994. "La Competitividad: Contexto y Concepto" [Competitiveness: Context and Concept]. Mimeo of presentation at the seminar *Communications for Competitiveness*. Venezuela Competitiva-UCAB, Caracas. [L]

49. 1994. With M. E. Corrales. "Estrategia de Relanzamiento del Instituto de Ingeniería." [A Strategy for Relaunching the Engineering Institute] Consultancy report. Sartenejas, Venezuela. [R]

50. 1994. With R. Rengifo, S. Parisca, P. Testa, J. Alfonso. "El Proceso de Modernización de una Empresa Venezolana" [The Modernization Process in a Venezuelan Firm]. Report of the pilot project on modernization after ISI. IDRC-FINTEC, Montevideo-Caracas. [R]

51. 1996. With M. E. Corrales, L. Rojas and R. Agudo. "La Empresa Venezolana en el Desarrollo Industrial" [Venezuelan Firms and Industrial Development]. Report to the project *Formulación de Estrategias Empresariales* [Designing Business Strategies]. CONICIT-CONINDUSTRIA, Caracas. [R]

52. 1996. "La Modernización Industrial en América Latina y la Herencia de la Sustitución de Importaciones" [Industrial Modernization in Latin America and the Legacy of Import Substitution]. *Comercio Exterior* (México) 46 (5), 347–363. [J] *

53. 1996. "Nueva Concepción de la Tecnología y Sistema Nacional de Innovación" [New Conceptualization of Technology and the National System of Innovation]. *Cuadernos de CENDES* 13 (31), 9–33. [J] *

54. 1997. "Neue Technologien und sozio-institutioneller Wandel" [New Technologies and Socio-Economic Change]. In H. Thomas and L. Nefiodow (eds.). *Kondratieffs*

Zyklen der Wirtschaft: An der Schwelle neuer Vollbeschäftigung? Köln – Herford: BusseSeewald, 17–52. [Ch]

55.   1997. "La Empresa Industrial Latinoamericana ante el Cambio Tecnológico" [The Latin American Industrial Firm Facing Technological Change]. Mimeo, *Second National Congress of Private Agents for the Development Corporation.* CORFO, Santiago de Chile. [L]

56.   1997. "The Social and Political Challenge of the Present Paradigm Shift." *Norsk Investorforum Working Paper* 2 (5). [WP] *

57.   1998. "Cambios Socio-políticos para Enfrentar los Nuevos Desafíos Empresariales y Sociales" [Socio-political Changes to Face the New Business and Social Challenges]. In *Creación de valor y gerencia, COEM97.* Lima: Ediciones ESAN, 193–220. [CA]

58.1. 1998. "Desafíos sociales y políticos del cambio de paradigma tecnológico" [Social and Political Challenges of the Techno-Economic Paradigm Shift]. In M. Pulido (ed.). *Venezuela: Desafíos y Propuestas.* Caracas: Editorial UCAB-SIC, 193–220. [Ch] *

58.2. Reprinted: 1999. *Desafíos sociales y políticos del cambio de paradigma tecnológico* (separate booklet). Caracas: UCAB. [P]

59.   1998. "Especialización y Alianzas para Posicionarse en los Mercados Locales y Globales" [Specialization and Alliances to Improve Positioning in Local and Global Markets]. Mimeo of transcription of public lecture. CVG (Venezuelan Corporation of Guyana), Puerto Ordaz. [L]

60.   1998. "La Reforma Educativa: Nuevo Paradigma, Nuevos Conceptos" [Educational Reform: New Paradigm, New Concepts]. In CNE (ed.). *Asamblea Nacional de Educación: Ponencias y Discursos* 2. Caracas: Editorial Laboratorio Educativo, 533–545. [CA]

61.   1998. "Opciones de la PYME: Una Vision Moderna" [Options for SMEs: A modern view]. Mimeo of presentation at the *International Congress of Managerial Strategies* AEEC-CEPROCA. [L]

62.   1998. *Innovaciones Socio-políticas para Enfrentar los Nuevos Desafíos Empresariales y Sociales* [Socio-political Innovations to Face the New Entrepreneurial and Social Challenges]. Caracas: Ediciones Eureka. [P]

63.   1999. "La Universidad en el Nuevo Paradigma: Formar para la Vida en la Sociedad del Conocimiento" [The University in the New Paradigm: Educating for Life in the Knowledge Society]. In J. M. Cadenas, M. Hanson and O. Rodríguez (eds.). *Reflexiones sobre la Educación Superior en América Latina.* Caracas: FAPUV-FUNDAYACUCHO, 144–158. [CA]

64.   1999. "Cambio de patrón tecnológico y oportunidades para el desarrollo sustentable" [Change of Technological Style and Opportunities for Sustainable Development]. *Colección Ideas para el Diálogo* 3. Caracas: Biblioteca Nacional de Venezuela. [WP] *

65.   1999. "Paradigm Shift and New Paths for Innovation and Governance." Mimeo of presentation at the Conference *Creating Wealth from Waste,* June. London: DEMOS. [L]

66.   1999. "Technological Change and Opportunities for Development as a Moving Target." Paper prepared for the *High Level Round Table on Trade and Development. UNCTAD X Working Paper* TD(X)RT1/9 (in English, French, Spanish, Chinese, Russian and Arabic). Geneva: UNCTAD. [WP]

67.   1999. "El Reto del Cambio de Paradigma Tecno-económico" [The Challenge of the Techno-Economic Paradigm Shift]. *Revista del Banco Central de Venezuela* 13 (2), 12–29. [J]*

68.   2000. "The Lessons We Have Learned about Technology and Development." Presentation at an UNCTAD High Level Round Table. Bangkok: UNCTAD. [L]

69. 2000. *La Reforma Educativa ante el Nuevo Paradigma* [Educational Reform Facing the New Paradigm]. Caracas: Editorial UCAB-Eureka. [P] *

70. 2000. "Change of Paradigm in Science and Technology Policy." *Cooperation South* 1 (1), 43–48. [J] *

71. 2000. "Cambio de paradigma y Rol de la Tecnología en el Desarrollo" [Paradigm Change and the Role of Technology in Development]. In *Actas Foro de Apertura del Ciclo La Ciencia y la Tecnología en la Construcción del Futuro del País*. Caracas: Ministry of Science and Technology. [CG] *

72.1.1. 2001. "Cambio Tecnológico y Oportunidades de Desarrollo como Blanco Móvil." *Revista de la CEPAL* 75, 115–136. [J] *

72.1.2. Reprinted: 2004. In J. A. Ocampo (ed.). *El Desarrollo Económico en los Albores del Siglo XXI*. Bogotá: Alfaomega, 205–239. [Ch]

72.2.1. English translation: 2001. "Technological Change and Opportunities for Development as a Moving Target." *Cepal Review* 75, 109–130. [J] *

72.2.2. Reprinted: 2003. In J. Toye (ed.). *Trade and Development: Directions for the 21st Century*. Cheltenham: Edward Elgar, 100–130. [Ch]

72.3. French translation: 2005. "Changement Technologique et Opportunités de Développement, une Cible Mouvante." *Revista de la Cepal, Numéro Spécial en Français, Sélection d'articles publiés 1995–2004*, 165–188. [J]

72.4. Chinese translation: 2007. In E. S. Reinert and J. Genliang (eds). *The Other Canon of Economics: A Selection of Essays of Evolutionary Development Economics* 2. Beijing: Higher Education Press, 178–216. [Ch]

73. 2002. "Conocimiento e innovatividad: de la moda a la norma" [Knowledge and Innovativeness: from Fashion to Norm]. In O. Salas et al. (eds). *Gerencia del Conocimiento. Potenciando el capital intelectual para crear valor*. Fondo Editorial del Centro Internacional de Educación y Desarrollo. Caracas: PDVSA-CIED. [CB]

74.1. 2002. *Technological Revolutions and Financial Capital: The Dynamics of Bubbles and Golden Ages*. Cheltenham: Edward Elgar. [B] * (partially)

74.2. Paperback edition: April 2003. Cheltenham: Edward Elgar. [B]

74.3. Spanish translation: 2004. *Revoluciones Tecnológicas y Capital Financiero: La Dinámica de las Grandes Burbujas Financieras y las Épocas de Bonanza*. Mexico: Siglo XXI. [B] * (partially)

74.4. Korean Translation: 2006. Seoul: Korea Economic Daily & Business Publications [for IBM Global Business Services]. [B]

74.5. Chinese translation: 2007. Beijing: Renmin University Press. [B]

75.1. 2004. "Technological Revolutions, Paradigm Shifts and Socio-institutional Change." In E. S. Reinert (ed.). *Globalization, Economic Development and Inequality: An Alternative Perspective*. Cheltenham: Edward Elgar, 217–242. [Ch] *

75.2. Spanish translation: 2003. "Revoluciones Tecnológicas, Cambios de Paradigma y de Marco Socio-institucional." In J. Aboites and G. Dutrénit (eds). *Innovación, Aprendizaje y Creación de Capacidades Tecnológicas*. México: UAM, 13–46. [Ch]

75.3. Chinese translation: 2007. In E. S. Reinert and J. Genliang (eds). *The Other Canon of Economics: A Selection of Essays of Evolutionary Development Economics* 1. Beijing: Higher Education Press, 184–207. [Ch]

76.1. 2004. "Finance and Technical Change: A Long-term View." *CERF Working Paper* 14. Cambridge: CERF (Cambridge Endowment for Research in Finance). [WP] *

76.2. Revised version: 2007. "Finance and Technical Change: A Long-term View." In H. Hanusch and A. Pyka (eds). *The Elgar Companion to Neo-Schumpeterian Economics*. Cheltenham: Edward Elgar, 775–799. [Ch] *

77.1. 2005. "Respecialisation and the Deployment of the ICT Paradigm." Working Paper, FISTERA (Foresight on Information Society Technologies in the European Research Area) Project. Seville: EU/IPTS. [WP]

77.2. 2006. "Respecialisation and the Deployment of the ICT Paradigm: An Essay on the Present Challenges of Globalisation." In R. Compañó et al. (eds). *The Future of the Information Society in Europe.* Technical Report EUR22353EN. Seville: European Commission / IPTS, 27–56. [Ch] *

78.1. 2006. "Great Surges of Development and Alternative Forms of Globalization." *Working Papers in Technology Governance and Economic Dynamics* 15. [WP] *

78.2. Portuguese translation: Forthcoming 2009. "Grandes Ondadas de Desenvolvimento e Formas Alternativas de Globalização." In T. Dos Santos and C. E. Martins (eds). *Longa Duração e Conjuntura no Capitalismo Contemporâneo.* Florianopolis: Universidade Federal de Santa Catarina. [Ch]

79. 2007. "Respecialize to Lift All Boats: A Primer on the Global Redistribution of Market Segments." *Executive Thought Leadership Quarterly* 4 (4), 9–12. [M]

80. 2007. "El CIO de Hoy: Cambio de Contexto, Cambio de Rol" [Today's CIO: Change of Context, Change of Role]. *Tecnología y Negocio* 13 (7), 2–3. [M]

81. 2007. "Two Realities; Two Policies: Policy Notes on Small and Medium Enterprises in the Context of a Dual Strategy for Development in Latin America." Consultancy Report for the Inter-American Development Bank. Washington, DC. [R]

82. 2007. "El Cambio de Paradigma en las Empresas Como Proceso de Cambio Cultural" [Paradigm Shift in Businesses as a Process of Cultural Change]. In R. Casas, C. Fuentes and A. Vera-Cruz (eds). *Acumulación de Capacidades Tecnológicas, Aprendizaje y Cooperación en la Esfera Global y Local.* Mexico: Miguel Angel Porrua. [Ch]

83. 2008. "Sistemas de Innovación para la Competitividad" [Systems of Innovation for Competitiveness]. In A Martinez and P. L. Lopez de Alba (comp.). *Memorias SinncO.* Guanajuato, Mexico: CONCYTEG. [CG]

84.1.1. 2008. "A Vision for Latin America: A Resource-based Strategy for Technological Dynamism and Social Inclusion." Mimeo, ECLAC Program on Technology Policy and Development in Latin America. Santiago: ECLAC. [R] *

84.1.2. Reprint: 2008. *Globelics Working Paper WPG0804* [a]. [WP]

84.2.1. Spanish version: 2008. "Una Visión para América Latina: Dinamismo Tecnológico e Inclusión Social Mediante una Estrategia Basada en los Recursos Naturales." *Globelics Working Paper WPG0804* [b]. [WP]

84.2.2. Revised version: Forthcoming 2009. In M. Cimoli and G. Stiglitz (eds). *Knowledge, Learning and Innovation: Policy Challenges for the 21st Century.* Oxford: Oxford University Press. [Ch]

85. 2009. "La Otra Globalización: los Retos del Colapso Financiero" [The other Globalization: The Challenges of the Financial Collapse]. *Problemas del Desarrollo: Revista Latinoamericana de Economía* 40 (157), 11–37. [J]

86.1. 2009. "Technological Roots and Structural Implications of the Double Bubble at the Turn of the Century." *CERF Working Papers,* 31. [WP] *

86.2. Revised version: 2009. "The Double Bubble at the Turn of the Century: Technological Roots and Structural Implications." *Cambridge Journal of Economics* 33 (4), 779–805. [J]

87.1. 2009. "Technological Revolutions and Techno-Economic Paradigms." *Working Papers in Technology Governance and Economic Dynamics,* The Other Canon Foundation and Tallinn University of Technology, 20. [WP]

87.2. Revised version: Forthcoming 2010. *Cambridge Journal of Economics*, Special Issue on the Nature of Technology. [J]

88. 2009. "After Crisis: Creative Construction." *openDemocracy. free thinking for the world*, 3 May, at http://www.opendemocracy.net/article/economics/email/how-to-make-economic-crisis-creative. [M]

89. Forthcoming 2009. "La Pequeña Empresa Latinoamericana del Futuro: Dinamismo Tecnológico e Inclusión Social" [The future Latin American Small Firm: Technological Dynamism and Social Inclusion]. *Economía: Teoría y Práctica*. [J]

Lightning Source UK Ltd.
Milton Keynes UK
07 October 2010

160886UK00001B/163/P